FA PREMIERSHIP

POCKET ANNUAL 1998-99

Bruce Smith

6th Year of Publication

Virgin

FA Carling Premiership Annual 1998-99

Copyright © Bruce Smith – Author 1998

ISBN: 0-7535-0212-7

First published August 1998 by
Virgin Publishing

Virgin Publishing Limited
Thames Wharf Studios
Rainville Road
London, W6 9HT

Typeset by Bruce Smith

Contact Bruce Smith at:

Bruce Smith,
PO Box 382, St Albans,
Herts, AL2 3JD

email: Bruce-Smith@msn.com

Disclaimer

In a book of this type it is inevitable that some errors will creep in. While every effort has been made to ensure that the details given in this annual are correct at the time of going to press, neither the editor nor the publishers can accept any responsibility for errors within.

We welcome comments, corrections and additions to this annual. Please send them to Bruce Smith at the address opposite or email them direct to him at: Bruce-Smith@msn.com

Printed by: Caledonian International Books, Glasgow, Scotland.

CONTENTS

Introduction 5
'97-'98 Diary 7
Final Tables 1997-98 31
All-Time Tables 35
Promotions and Relegations 37
Results Grids 1997-98 38
Attendance Grids 1997-98 40

FA Premier League Records 1997-98
Top Scorers – All Competitions/Top Scorers by Total 42
Top Scorers by Club/Hat-tricks 43
Attendance Summaries by Club 44
Clubs by Total Number of Players Used 44
Bookings and Dismissals 45
Referees by Number of Bookings 47
Dismissals by Club 47
Referees – Who They Sent Off 48
Highest Aggregate Scores 49
Biggest Home/Biggest Away Wins/Highest Score Draws ...49
Score Frequencies 49

FA Premier League All-Time Records
Premiership Titles by Win/Premiership Runners-up 50
All-Time Biggest Home Wins......................................50
All-Time Biggest Away Wins/Highest Score Draws 51
All-Time General Records – Home and Away 51
Record Attendances by Club 52
Top 10 Attendances 52
Lowest Attendances by Club 53
Lowest 10 Attendances 54
Top Goalscorers by Player 54
All-Time Player: Most Goals in One Game 55
Player: Consecutive Games with Goals 55
Fastest Goals in a Game 56
Fastest Hat-trick in a Game/Player: Most Hat-tricks in Games ...56
Players: Hat-trick Hall of Fame 56
Goalkeepers by Total Apps-Goals Ratio/Total Clean Sheets ...56
Goalkeepers by Consecutive Shut-Outs/Most Clean Sheets/Season ...58
Top Appearances by Player 59
Top Substitute Appearances by Player 60
Managers: Length of Tenure – Current Tenants 61
Managers: Most Games in Charge 61
Managers by Total Points Won 62
Managers by Average Points per Game 62
Crime Count – Year by Year/Last Day Championships 64
Final Tables 93-94, 94-95, 95-96, 96-97 65

Championships, FA Cup, Coca-Cola Cup and Awards

League Champions' Records 67
Championship Wins by Club 70
FA Cup 1997-98 3rd Round to Final 71
FA Cup Final Results 1872-1997 74
FA Cup Wins by Club..78
FA Charity Shield Winners 1908-1997 79
Coca-Cola Cup 1997-98 2nd Round to Final 81
Football League Cup Final Results 1961-1998 83
Football League Cup Wins by Club 84
FWA Footballer of the Year 85
PFA Awards 1997-98 86

Premier League Clubs in Europe 1997-98

UEFA Champions' League 1997-98 87
Cup-Winners' Cup 1997-98/UEFA Cup 1997-98 88

England Internationals

Results 1997-98 91
England Managers' Records/Goalscorers' Summary 1997-98 94
Player Summary 1997-98 95
1997-98 Appearance Chart 97
France '98 98
Euro 2000 Group 5 Fixtures 99

FA Carling Premiership Club Directory 1998-99

Arsenal, Aston Villa, Blackburn Rovers, Charlton Athletic, Chelsea 102
Coventry City, Derby County, Everton, Leeds United, Leicester City....................132
Liverpool, Manchester United, Middlesbrough, Newcastle United 162
Nottingham Forest, Sheffield Wednesday, Southampton 186
Tottenham Hotspur, West Ham United, Wimbledon 204
D1: Barnsley, Bolton Wanderers, Crystal Palace 222

All-Time Stats

Arsenal to Wimbledon 241

Transfers Involving FA Premier League Clubs 1997-98

FA Premier League Transfers 254
Player Loans Involving Premier League Clubs 1997-98 260

A-Z of FA Premier League Players 1997-98

A-Z of FA Premier League Players 263

A-Z of FA Premier League Managers

A-Z of FA Premier League Managers 343

FA Premier League Ground Guide

Maps and directions to all 20 FA Carling Premiership Grounds 347

Form 'n' Encounter Guide

Club v club home records plus all the important game dates along
with full results from previous seasons 369

Introduction...

There were more red cards last season than any other in the six-year history of the Premier League; In fact the number was more than double that of the 1996-97 season. Yellow cards were up as well, but didn't top the all-time season high of 1994-95 – when there were 82 games more played in the last of the 42-game seasons. Of course, it wasn't a particularly 'dirty' season but just another one of those clamp-down years.

FIFA ordered a clamp down in the World Cup on the dangerous 'tackle from behind' and, while eradicating the leg-threatening versions of these, the inconsistency provided the expected number of crazy dismissals. The English leagues have always been at the forefront of carrying through FIFA edicts so can we expect even more sendings off in 1998-99? Probably.

The problem is that this yellow card–red card trend may be seen as increasing fair play for FIFA but it is utterly and totally unfair on the paying fan. The number of games last year – throughout the league – that were reduced to farce because a team was reduced to ten men or less was unacceptable. At a time when open attacking play is edging its way on to our fields of play the reduction of a team to ten players or less converts the contents into negative affairs in which one team become solely intent on preserving the point or three they may have at the time of the dismissal. If you support a particular team and the opposition have a player dismissed then it is often greeted with some pleasure – but only if your team go on and win. If you have to watch an all-hands on-deck performance that ends in stalemate, you are less than happy.

The cost of watching top-flight football is expensive and it is not unreasonable for the lifeblood of the game to expect a fair contest and to see the stars who grace it. So what can be done? Well simply reduce the number of dismissals. Many of the dismissals in the Premiership last season were for the showing of a second yellow card. Why does the brandishing of a second yellow card have to lead to a red? If a player is shown a second yellow card then he could be banned from the next game. This would allow refs to be more consistent with their yellow cards. How many times have we seen yellow card offences go unpunished because it would result in a sending off? A third yellow card in a game would mean a two-match ban and so forth.

Red cards could still mean the dismissal of a player but why not allow a substitute to be used, providing that option still remained open to the team? The player is punished, and so are the team, but the fans are not short-changed. In all cases the game remains what it should always be – evenly contested and an afternoon of fair entertainment for the people who, after all, have paid to watch it.

The use of electronic devices have also been a major debating point throughout the past season. The general call seems to be to have video replays and goal-line cameras introduced. Heaven forbid. Firstly, TV isn't always conclusive. Sky normally have 21 cameras at a live game and while they often resolve a question of doubt in replay there are times when they are inconclusive. What then? Will clubs pay for 21 cameras around the ground for matches that are not live on Sky? Well, if they do it will simply go on the cost of your ticket.

I am one of the few English people who adores American football. This is a one-hour game that takes three hours to play. It has many natural breaks yet the use of video replays was abandoned because it slowed the game down. If this happens in the NFL, what would it do to games in the Premiership? If it was to come into operation perhaps teams could be limited to the number of decisions they could question in a game – say three per game.

The answer is much simpler. And again we can take a leaf out of the book of the NFL and NBA. Introduce more officials. The game desperately needs a referee in each half – it works in many other sports. Each ref could patrol opposite sides of halves with their linesmen (sorry, assistants) doing the line on the other side. Then each goal line could be equipped with a goal-line judge whose sole responsibility it is to judge if the ball goes over the line. Officials will not get so tired and will therefore remain more alert, and they will also be much nearer the action at all times. So simple and surely worthy of experiment.

List of Acknowledgements
Many thanks to everyone who has contributed to this year's annual – not least the following: David Tavener (reviews), Mark Webb, Sarah Smith, Paul Davison and editor Ben Dunn at Virgin.

Deadlines
After a relatively quiet close season on the transfer front things were starting to hot up just as we went to press. The cut-off date for this edition of the annual was July 1st 1998. Although many transfers were pending we have only included those that had actually physically taken place at this point.

The Author
Bruce Smith is an award-winning journalist who has written over 150 books on a variety of topics. He now concentrates on sports titles and also edits a bi-monthly magazine *Stadium & Arena Management*. A former BBC Radio commentator, he appeared on *The Big Breakfast* as their 'World Cup Monitor' throughout France '98. He is an Arsenal season ticket holder and a Green Bay Packers fan.

Back Editions
Limited stocks of the previous editions of the annual are still available at £5.99 each including £1 p&p. Editions available are 92-93, 93-94, 94-95 and 95-96 and the complete set provides a full history of the FA Premier League. Send your requirements along with a cheque/PO payable to 'Words On Sport' to:
Words On Sport, PO Box 382, St Albans, AL2 3DZ

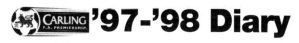

Pre-Season

May: Blackburn midfielder Billy McKinlay receives a £750 fine for possessing the dubious honour of being the first Premiership player to collect 45 disciplinary points in a season. The Premier League confirms that the Sheffield-based Uriah Rennie will be the first black referee to take charge of a game in the top flight.

June: England beat Italy 2-0 and France 1-0 to win the Le Tournoi de France, but Glenn Hoddle's side are brought down to earth by Brazil who claim second place with a 1-0 victory. Martin O'Neill, manager of Coca-Cola Cup winners Leicester City, signs a new three-year contract at Filbert Street. The Premiership announces plans to invest £20m over the next four years in coaching and development initiatives for clubs in the Football League. Middlesbrough's relegation to the Nationwide League is finally settled as the club abandon plans to continue their fight for Premiership survival. Everton's lengthy search for a new manager appears to be nearing its conclusion as former Blues striker and now Sky TV pundit Andy Gray visits Goodison Park for talks. Gray rejects Everton's offer a week later, inciting acrimony on both sides. Everton move swiftly after Gray's rejection and just 24 hours later appoint Howard Kendall into the hot seat for a third spell. Sheffield United, Kendall's previous employers, seek £1m compensation but later drop their claim. Down on the south coast, Southampton finally get their man as Stockport County beat Dave Jones moves to the Dell with a four-year contract. Jones quickly makes his mark by persuading Matt Le Tissier to agree to a new four-year deal.

July: Ian Wright's poor disciplinary record catches up with him as the FA lands the Arsenal and England striker with a £15,000 fine, despite him taking counselling in an attempt to improve his attitude on the pitch. The Gunners are also facing a fine after playing a friendly at non-league St Albans City on 8 July, breaking a little known FA law that no games shall be played during the official close season of 16 June to 15 July. West Ham United lose Julian Dicks for at least four months with a knee injury and later in the month miss out on signing both Stuart Pearce and Paul McGrath.

In the face of growing suspensions year on year, the FA announces a revolutionary policy which will benefit infrequent offenders. The points system is dispensed with and players will instead be suspended after collecting five, eight and 11 cautions. Any player completing five full games without being booked will have one caution wiped from the record.

Southampton are jolted by a major setback with the news that Le Tissier has broken an arm during a friendly in Germany against local side SVP Ansbach. As the pre-season friendlies get into full swing, Manchester United beat the Thailand national team. Following hot on the heels of Le Tissier's injury, fellow England striker Alan Shearer slips on the Goodison Park turf during the final minute of Newcastle's Umbro International Tournament game with Chelsea. Hopes that Shearer had merely twisted an ankle are extinguished in hospital where a catalogue of serious injuries are quickly diagnosed and operated on: fractured fibula and ruptured ligaments on both sides of the ankle on his right foot, a chipped ankle bone and a displaced joint. He is not expected to play again before Christmas and will consequently miss vital England World Cup qualifying matches. The loss of Shearer throws doubt over St. James's Park on the wisdom of selling Les Ferdinand to Tottenham over the same weekend. Chelsea beat Everton 3-1 in the final of the Umbro competition.

Arsenal's dire disciplinary record shows no sign of easing as Patrick Vieira and Matthew Upson are sent off during a 1-0 defeat at PSV Eindhoven. Television evidence suggests that Caucasian Upson is a victim of mistaken identity when the black Luis Boa Morte was the culprit. An irony of the Gunners' ongoing disciplinary problems is that Ian Wright is to star in a publicity campaign on behalf of the FA. Earlier in the day Arsenal conclude a great deal with Nike, which could be worth a staggering £40m over seven years. Peter Beardsley's anticipated departure from Newcastle to Bolton Wanderers is put on hold following the Magpies' sale of Ferdinand and Shearer's long-term injury.

The assistant chief constable of Greater Manchester Police, Malcolm George, asks the FA to help managers and players keep their celebrations in check to avoid inciting crowd disturbances. Robbie Fowler looks set to miss the start of the season after twisting a knee during Liverpool's 3-1 win over a mixed Norwegian side.

August

Manchester United add the Littlewoods Charity Shield to the list of trophies picked up during Alex Ferguson's reign, with a penalty shoot-out victory over Chelsea at Wembley following a drab 1-1 draw. Leeds United are the latest club to lose an international player during a friendly, with Lee Sharpe picking up a knee injury which could sideline him for eight weeks. Barnsley reveal that promotion to the Premiership has resulted in a complete sell-out of their 17,000 season tickets. Back in February 1905, Alf Common became football's first £1,000 player when he moved from Sunderland to Middlesbrough. In the summer of 1997, close on £125m is spent by Premiership clubs alone in the search for success.

Week 1 (Aug 9-15): Coventry City grab the headlines on the opening day of the season as Dion Dublin scores a hat-trick during the Sky Blues 3-2 win over highly fancied Chelsea at Highfield Road. A brace of Asprilla goals, including one in just 100 seconds, gets Newcastle's title bid off to a winning start at the expense of Sheffield Wednesday and Roy Hodgson enjoys a winning return to English football with a Kevin Gallacher goal clinching Blackburn's victory over Derby. Lombardo opens Crystal Palace's account for the season during a surprise win at Everton but honours are even at Elland Road where four overseas Arsenal players, not signed by former Gunners boss George Graham, are booked when facing his latest club. A Michael Owen penalty rescues a point for Liverpool at Wimbledon, for whom Vinnie Jones takes just minutes to collect his first yellow card of the season. Paul Ince makes his debut as Liverpool announce John Barnes can leave. Barnsley's first Premiership match ends in disappointment with John Hartson scoring in West Ham's 2-1 win at Oakwell. Bolton's return to the top flight is more successful with Nathan Blake grabbing the winning goal at Southampton. Champions Manchester United start their campaign 24 hours later and despite Teddy Sheringham missing a penalty on his first return to White Hart Lane, United still win with two late goals.

The irrepressible Ian Wright scores both Arsenal goals in the first Monday match of the season as Coventry's bright start is swiftly extinguished.

Blackburn Rovers' coffers are swelled by another £5m following the sale of Norwegian international Henning Berg to Manchester United. The Reds also extend Ole Gunnar Solskjaer's contract to the year 2004. Arsenal persuade the Dutch FA to look again at a video of Vieira's pre-season sending off against PSV Eindhoven.

The only Tuesday night match sees history created as a Neil Redfearn goal earns Barnsley victory at Crystal Palace and their first Premiership points. Six Premiership games the following night throw up some sensational scores, none more so than at Villa Park where a Chris Sutton hat-trick takes Blackburn – 4-0 winners – to the top of the table and Aston Villa, goalless and pointless after two games, to the foot. David Beckham scores in front of 55,008 to give Manchester United victory over Southampton but there is a shock at Anfield where a late goal from Ince cannot deny Leicester City a 2-1 win and maximum points from two games. Goal-shy Leeds thump Sheffield Wednesday 3-1 at Hillsborough and Hartson is on target again as West Ham defeat Spurs 2-1. Derby's first match at their new £19.5m Pride Park Stadium ends in frustration as floodlight failure calls a premature halt to proceedings with County leading Wimbledon 2-1.

Newcastle create history as the first English team to compete in the qualifying round of the Champions' League; two John Beresford goals give the Magpies a slender 2-1 1st Leg advantage on Tyneside over Croatia Zagreb. United manager Kenny Dalglish snaps up the services of his former Liverpool team mate John Barnes from under the noses of West Ham; the Anfield connection is further strengthened with the signing of Ian Rush from Leeds.

Steve McManaman is offered a new contract at Liverpool after the breakdown of a proposed £12m move to Barcelona.

Week 2 (Aug 16-22): Just eight days into the season and there is no Premiership action on the 16th due to midweek World Cup qualifying ties which do not include England.

Week 3 (Aug 23-29): Leicester lose their winning record to a goalless home draw with Manchester United. Those two clubs are joined on seven points by Arsenal, 3-1 winners at Southampton, and Blackburn who drop two points despite Martin Dahlin's late equaliser at home to Liverpool. Marc Overmars scores his first goal for Arsenal and the outstanding Dennis Bergkamp a pair. Aston Villa's poor start continues with Beresford again on target to give Newcastle victory despite having David Batty dismissed. Derby lose at Tottenham to stay level with Villa and Southampton on no points. Everton are off the mark with victory over West Ham and Sheffield Wednesday, at Wimbledon, also get their first point. Coventry take their tally of goals to five in two home games but surrender a two goal lead to Bolton. Leeds are brought down to earth by Palace for whom Lombardo scores twice during a 2-0 success in Yorkshire; it is United's first home defeat since Boxing Day. The headlines are made on the Sunday at Barnsley where Gianluca Vialli celebrates his return to the Chelsea first team with four goals in a 6-0 drubbing of Danny Wilson's side.

On the Monday night, Blackburn become the first club to hit seven goals in a Premiership match on three separate occasions. Gallacher and Sutton score twice each while Benito Carbone does likewise for the visitors before being sent off. Rovers keeper John Filan suffers a broken arm in a clash with the innocent yet later barracked Wayne Collins. The following night Liverpool record their first win with McManaman and debutant Karlheinz Riedle condemning Leeds to a second successive 2-0 reversal at Elland Road.

Newcastle double England's number of participants in the Champions' League thanks to Temuri Ketsbaia's first goal for the club just 40 seconds from the end of extra time against Croatia Zagreb; United go through 4-3 on aggregate.

Back on the domestic scene, Manchester United, through David Beckham and Sheringham, join Blackburn on ten points with a 2-0 win at Everton. Leicester stage an astonishing comeback to grab a 3-3 draw with two goals in injury time against Arsenal for whom Bergkamp also scores the third of his three goals during added time. At the final whistle referee Graham Barber is surrounded by Arsenal players and officials; Steve Walsh and Ian Wright are hauled before the FA to explain their post-match confrontation. Chelsea continue their rise with a 2-0 victory at still winless Wimbledon but Villa stay bottom despite leading 2-1 at Tottenham before succumbing 3-2 with Les Ferdinand

9

scoring twice for Spurs. After three defeats, Southampton see off Crystal Palace at the Dell and West Ham rise to fifth following a 1-1 draw at Coventry.

September

Week 4 (Aug 3-Sep 5): Manchester United maintain their unbeaten start to the season with a 3-0 win over Coventry at Old Trafford and in so doing set a club record of five consecutive clean sheets plus two from the end of the previous season. Top scorers are Chelsea who put four past Southampton in the first half at Stamford Bridge. They and West Ham, 3-1 winners over now bottom side Wimbledon, leapfrog Arsenal who are frustrated by the Spurs defence and the woodwork during a goalless draw at Highbury; Tottenham defender Justin Edinburgh is dismissed. Leicester's unbeaten start ends at Hillsborough where a Carbone penalty gives Sheffield Wednesday their first win of the season and eases the pressure on manager David Pleat. A twice-taken penalty at Pride Park, converted by Stefano Eranio, earns Derby victory over Barnsley and Aston Villa are also off the mark with Dwight Yorke disposing of Leeds at Villa Park. Liverpool's match with Newcastle, scheduled for Sunday 31 August, is postponed following the death of Diana, Princess of Wales.

The failure of a linesman to spot the spilt-second in which a Nathan Blake effort crosses the line denies Bolton their first success at the new Reebok Stadium. Everton hold out for a goalless draw but fail to sign Fabrizio Ravanelli, who rejects their overtures for a second time.

Rio Ferdinand is dropped from the England squad to face Moldova after being found guilty on a drink-drive charge. Barnsley pay Derby an initial fee of £1.3m for Ashley Ward in an attempt to bolster their attack and Sheffield Wednesday sign Jim Magilton from Southampton.

Week 5 (Sep 6-12): The fifth Saturday of the season is bereft of Premiership action due to midweek international matches but the fixture list would in any case have been rescheduled in any case due to the funeral of Princess Diana. Blackburn sign Norwegian international Tore Pedersen and Southampton take Kevin Richardson from Coventry.

Paul Gascoigne is outstanding on the 10th as England beat Moldova 4-0 at Wembley and climb above Italy who are held 0-0 in Georgia. Blackburn are set to seek compensation to cover Stuart Ripley's wages while he is out of action, having pulled a hamstring during his six-minute appearance against Moldova.

Week 6 (Sep 13-19): Neville Southall becomes the first player to make 200 appearances in the Premiership but has little cause for celebration as Everton have Andy Hinchcliffe dismissed and crash 3-1 at Derby to drop into the bottom three. Defeat for Southampton at Coventry leaves the Saints rooted to the foot of the Premiership. At the opposite end of the table Arsenal and Chelsea maintain their challenge with wins by three clear goals. Ian Wright is the toast of Highbury with a hat-trick in the Gunners' 4-1 victory over Bolton which takes him to 180 goals for the club, two more than previous record Arsenal goalscorer Cliff Bastin. West Ham's hopes of joining Manchester United on 13 points are dashed by Paul Scholes' winner for the champions but Leicester continue their bright start to the campaign with a 3-0 hammering of Spurs. Sheffield Wednesday's goals against record rises to 15 from six games with a 2-1 reversal at Anfield and Barnsley suffer a third home defeat as Aston Villa claim their first away points with a 3-0 success at Oakwell. But the result of the day goes to Wimbledon, who secure their first victory of the season and end Newcastle's winning start with a 3-1 triumph at St James's Park. Free-scoring Blackburn entertain not-so-extravagant Leeds on the Sunday but miss out on an opportunity to regain top spot from Manchester United with an astonishing 4-3 defeat which sees the scoring completed by the 33rd minute; Rod Wallace notches a spectacular brace for the visitors.

Midweek attention is focused on Europe and it's an indifferent night for English clubs. Arsenal surrender their unbeaten record in Greece, going down 1-0 to PAOK Salonika. Leicester lead through an Ian Marshall goal before slipping up 2-1 in Spain to Atletico Madrid, for whom Juninho equalises. Aston Villa gain a creditable goalless draw away to Bordeaux and Liverpool, thanks to a breathtaking last-minute goal by Steve McManaman, rescue a 2-2 draw at Celtic. But the headlines are written on the Wednesday evening in the Champions' League by Newcastle and Manchester United. Denis Irwin sets the Reds on the way to an excellent 3-0 win in Slovakia against Kosice and back home Faustino Asprilla scores a cracking hat-trick, thanks in no small part to Keith Gillespie, as the Magpies overcome Barcelona 3-2. Twenty-four hours later Chelsea defeat Slovan Bratislava 2-0 at Stamford Bridge in the Cup Winners' Cup.

Back on the domestic scene, West Ham sign Ian Pearce from Blackburn for £1.4m as a replacement for Marc Rieper, following his move to Celtic and Southampton agree a fee of £1m for Leeds midfielder Carlton Palmer.

Week 7 (Sep 20-26): Manchester United extend a 19-year unbeaten record at Bolton with a goalless draw to stay three points clear of second-placed Blackburn, who also draw a blank at Tottenham and have Patrick Valery sent off. United defender Gary Pallister and Wanderers striker Nathan Blake are dismissed after squaring up to each other but referee Paul Durkin agrees to look at video evidence which could clear Pallister. Leeds' slump continues with a 1-0 home defeat by Leicester, who climb to fourth. Barnsley are one of just three of the 18 clubs playing on the 20th to score more than one goal but they are on the receiving end of four from a rejuvenated Everton side whose victory spares them the embarrassment of dropping to the foot of the Premiership. Amongst the Blues scorers is 17-year-old Danny Cadamarteri on his debut. The other side notching a brace are Aston Villa who overturn a deficit to see off Derby and clinch a third consecutive league win. Newcastle, playing their first away game of the season, are victorious at Upton Park as West Ham suffer their first home defeat, and bottom dogs Southampton battle back to draw with Liverpool at the Dell. On the Sunday, Nigel Winterburn scores a superb last-minute goal for Arsenal at Chelsea to secure a 3-2 victory and lift Arsène Wenger's side to second place.

The Monday match sees Robbie Fowler in the Liverpool starting line-up for the first time this season; he celebrates his return with the opening goal in a 3-0 win over Aston Villa, his 11th in ten games against the Midlands side. Bruce Grobbelaar, now clear of the bung allegations, returns to the Premiership as cover for the injured Nigel Pressman at Sheffield Wednesday. The FA fines Chelsea defender Frank Sinclair £750 for 'mooning' following his goal against Coventry in August.

On the 23rd, Bolton score their first goal, a penalty, at the new Reebok Stadium through Alan Thompson, but are denied victory by Chris Armstrong's equaliser for Spurs. After taking the lead away to Wimbledon, Barnsley's defence again leaks badly and once teenager Carl Cort has scored his fourth goal in as many games the Dons romp to a 4-1 victory. The attendance of 7,668 is the lowest in the Premiership for two years.

The following night, goals are plentiful and Manchester United are grateful to a late one from Solskjaer which salvages a 2-2 draw from the visit of Chelsea. But it is not sufficient to deny occupancy of pole position switching to the capital on goal difference courtesy of Arsenal's 4-0 thrashing of West Ham at Highbury. The result was, perhaps, of some relief to the Hammers, who trailed by that score at the interval. Leicester and Blackburn stay fifth and fourth respectively with a 1-1 draw at Filbert Street, while Newcastle close the gap with a late 1-0 win over an Everton side which has Slaven Bilic harshly dismissed by Graham Poll. Crystal Palace, still without a home point, collect their

11

tenth from opposition soil with a 1-1 draw at Coventry. Leeds hand Southampton their sixth defeat in eight games with a 2-0 success at the Dell while the outstanding result of the night is at Hillsborough where Derby add to Sheffield Wednesday's problems with a 5-2 rampage; Francesco Baiano scores two for the Rams and all the other five goalscorers are also overseas players. Wednesday have Patrick Blondeau sent off.

October

Week 8 (Sep 27-Oct 3): The final Saturday of the month contains no shortage of shocks, kicking off with Manchester United losing to a David Wetherall strike at Leeds; it is the first away goal conceded by the champions. The Reds have skipper Roy Keane stretchered off with what is thought to be a badly twisted knee but proves to be an horrific injury which brings his season to an early conclusion. Arsenal, despite Ian Wright scoring for the 12th time in nine games against Everton, fail to fully capitalise and haved to settle for a draw on Merseyside after leading by two goals. While all around them are losing their way, Leicester stand firm and condemn Barnsley to a fifth consecutive defeat with a 2-0 win at Oakwell. It is Barnsley's worst run for 11 years. Uruguayan Gustavo Poyet scores Chelsea's winner against Newcastle as the Blues go fourth. West Ham put recent disappointments behind them to beat Liverpool 2-1 at Upton Park while Derby are again amongst the goals as they chalk up a fifth win in six league and cup fixtures with a 4-0 thrashing of Southampton at Pride Park; all the goals come in eight late second-half minutes. Goals inside the opening 20 minutes for Paul Warhurst and Dean Gordon set Palace on course for victory at home to Bolton only for Wanderers to save a point with strikes from Peter Beardsley, his first for the club, and Michael Johansen. There is something of a collector's item at Ewood Park on the Sunday as Blackburn and Coventry fail to muster a single goal but each have a man sent off – Jason Wilcox and Dion Dublin. City have failed to score in any of their four away games this season.

A week of European action kicks off with West Ham defeating Huddersfield Town 3-0, 3-1 on aggregate, in the 2nd Round of the Coca-Cola Cup; John Hartson scores a hat-trick.

Arsenal, at home to PAOK Salonika, wipe out a 1st Leg deficit but concede a decisive goal two minutes from time at Highbury to depart from Europe in the 1st Round for the second consecutive year. Liverpool also draw, 0-0 at Anfield with Celtic, to go through on the away goals. Villa Park has to wait until the 111th minute for Savo Milosevic to score the tie-winning goal against Bordeaux. Juninho is again on target as Leicester go down 2-0 at Filbert Street and 4-1 on aggregate to Atletico Madrid; both sides finish the evening with just ten men.

Premier sides fare reasonably well on aggregate but not so successfully on the night in the Coca-Cola Cup. Barnsley, Spurs and Southampton complete the double over Chesterfield, Carlisle and Brentford respectively. Bolton are held to a remarkable 4-4 home draw by Leyton Orient but pull through 7-5 over two legs. Leeds go down 2-1 at Bristol City but like Blackburn, who lose at Preston, go through on aggregate. Crystal Palace at last win at Selhurst Park, 2-1 against Hull after trailing, but bow out on the away goals rule.

October kicks off with European champions Juventus taking the lead within 25 seconds of their Champions' League match at Old Trafford. Manchester United, though, storm back to take a tight grip on Group B with a fabulous 3-2 victory. Teddy Sheringham, Paul Scholes and Ryan Giggs underline United's supremacy before Zidane reduces the deficit in the closing seconds. Newcastle United look to be heading for defeat in the Ukraine as Dynamo Kiev control proceedings and build up a commanding two-goal lead. John Beresford scores with a soft effort 12 minutes from time and then has a hand in an equaliser with a shot which takes two kind deflections as the Magpies grab a more than useful point.

Despite Sheffield Wednesday being one of five Premiership sides to beat lower league opposition in the Coca-Cola Cup, they are the only one to suffer an aggregate defeat as Grimsby Town pull through 4-3 over the two legs. Earlier in the day, Wednesday completed the signing of Molde midfielder Petter Rudi. Coventry overcome Blackpool 3-2 having been two down on aggregate at one point while Derby, Everton and Wimbledon all go through with emphatic victories.

Week 9 (Oct 4-10): Arsenal bounce back from European elimination to reaffirm their title bid with a 5-0 thrashing of Barnsley which sends Danny Wilson's side to the foot of the table; Dennis Bergkamp continues his exceptional form with the first two goals. Barnsley have not won at Highbury for over 80 years. Manchester United and Blackburn maintain their pursuit of the leaders with respective 2-0 and 1-0 victories over Selhurst Park sides Crystal Palace and Wimbledon. With Matt Le Tissier in the starting line up for only the second time this season, Southampton score three goals in 14 minutes to secure a 3-0 win over West Ham and a leap over Barnsley, while another three late goals at Hillsborough hand Wednesday a welcome 3-1 win over Everton. Coventry draw at home for the fourth occasion, this time with a Leeds side which has not previously drawn away from home. Steve Ogrizovic sets a Coventry club record of 488 League appearances. Bolton suffer their first home defeat at the Reebok Stadium with Milosevic scoring Aston Villa's winner, but the headlines are seized by the feuding and dismissed duo of Andy Todd and Stan Collymore. Liverpool's mixed start to the campaign takes an upturn on the Sunday thanks to a Patrik Berger hat-trick at Anfield, which helps nudge an attack-minded Chelsea side to a 4-2 defeat; the result is of little surprise given that the Reds have lost at home to Chelsea just once since 1935. The Monday match kicks off with the Leicester City boss Martin O'Neill picking up the September Manager of the Month award. The evening ends with a couple of goals by Francesco Baiano ending the Foxes' unbeaten home record and clinching a fifth win in six games for Jim Smith's Derby County.

There is no midweek football as England prepare for Saturday's World Cup qualifying showdown with Italy in Rome. England striker Les Ferdinand adds to Tottenham's injury woes with a stomach operation having suffered discomfort following a summer hernia operation.

Week 10 (Oct 11-17): England are praised by the Italian press in the aftermath of a glorious 0-0 draw which confirms the presence of Glenn Hoddle's side in the 1998 World Cup in France. But English fans are again in the dock following violent clashes with Italian police, who are also blamed for inciting the trouble.

After 16 years at Goodison Park, Everton goalkeeper Neville Southall requests, and is granted, a transfer.

Premiership clubs return to action on the 14th to send sides of varying strength into battle in the 3rd Round of the Coca-Cola Cup. A Manchester United XI is beaten 2-0 at Ipswich Town and Arsenal require three extra-time goals to dispose of Birmingham City 4-1 at Highbury. City have Darren Wassall sent off but his departure after 84 minutes is pretty mundane compared to Jason Crowe, who marks his debut as a 90th-minute substitute, with a dreadful two footed lunge which leads to his expulsion after just 33 seconds. A late Kevin Davies goal earns Southampton a morale-boosting victory at Oakwell over fellow strugglers Barnsley, but with extra-time goals another lowly side, Bolton Wanderers, dispose of Wimbledon. Cup holders Leicester join the list of Premiership clubs to leave early with a surprise 3-1 reversal at Grimsby Town.

Seven Premier sides make progress in the Coca-Cola Cup the following night but Chelsea – on penalties – Coventry, Derby and West Ham do so at the expense of Blackburn, Everton, Spurs and Aston Villa respectively. Chelsea's win is marred by the flaying elbow of Gianluca Vialli, who is promptly dismissed. Also through are Newcastle, with second-half goals against Hull City, Leeds United, who rely on two extra-time Rod Wallace goals to account for Stoke City, and Liverpool, who win with comparative ease away to West Bromwich Albion.

Week 11 (Oct 18-24): Paulo Wanchope follows up his two goals which dumped Spurs out of the Coca-Cola Cup to add to Baiano's early strike and puts Derby in control against Manchester United, but the champions salvage a point at Pride Park through Sheringham, who also misses a penalty, and Andy Cole. Blackburn take full advantage of United's slight blip to move into second place on goal difference courtesy of Tim Sherwood's winning goal against Southampton. Arsenal stay top despite a goalless stalemate at Crystal Palace but have five players booked, including Bergkamp, who faces a three-match ban. Liverpool's brief recovery is halted by neighbours Everton whose 2-0 victory is kick-started by a Neil Ruddock own goal; teenager Danny Cadamarteri claims his first Merseyside derby goal. Top scorers on the day are Leeds who trounce Newcastle 4-1 at Elland Road while West Ham's John Hartson is the only Premiership player to score a brace as the Hammers beat Bolton 3-0 and leave the visitors to reflect on a record of just one victory from ten league outings. Wanderers boss Colin Todd fines the dismissed Gerry Taggart two weeks' wages. Spurs, under fire from their fans, look to be easing their troubles by building up a three-goal lead by half-time on the Sunday against Sheffield Wednesday, but former Tottenham boss David Pleat gains some relief as his side pull back two goals and are only denied a point when a penalty decision goes against them.

On the Monday, Coventry are sucked back into the mire by virtue of a 2-0 defeat at Barnsley, which sees the Yorkshire club end a run of six consecutive defeats. The result lifts Barnsley two places and is the perfect fillip ahead of the following weekend's trip to Old Trafford.

Another week of European club football gets off to an indifferent start for the English clubs. In the UEFA Cup 2nd Round, Aston Villa record a satisfying goalless draw with Athletic Bilbao in Spain but Liverpool are humbled 3-0 in France by Strasbourg. Manchester United show no such inhibitions the following night but are left to reflect on the wasteful finishing of Andy Cole after gaining just a slender 2-1 home win over Feyenoord in the Champions' League. Newcastle's progress past the group stage is in the balance following a defensive display at PSV Eindhoven which ends in a 1-0 defeat. In the face of a second-half blizzard 200 hundred miles above the Arctic circle, Chelsea shiver to a 3-2 defeat to part-timers Tromso in the Cup-Winners' Cup. Two late goals by Vialli keep Chelsea on course for a place in the 3rd Round.

Week 12 (Oct 25-31): Manchester United underline their determination to retain their crown on home soil in addition to placing the European Cup in the Old Trafford trophy cabinet by thrashing Barnsley 7-0. Cole answers his critics with a hat-trick as United move to the summit and Barnsley slump back to the foot of the table. Blackburn come from behind to salvage a point at goal-shy Newcastle with Chris Sutton's tenth league goal of the season. Derby's trip to Anfield looks, on current form, as though it will further weaken Roy Evans' position as 'Pool boss, but the Rams troop off at the final whistle well beaten 4-0, with Robbie Fowler scoring twice. Crystal Palace are also amongst the goals to win 3-2 at Hillsborough against a Wednesday side showing 29 goals conceded in 12 Premiership matches. Two goals for Wednesday old boy David Hirst also see Southampton to a 3-2 home win over Tottenham after twice trailing. Leeds' return to form is halted by a 1-0 defeat away to Wimbledon and on the Sunday one goal is sufficient to ease Bolton's worries and use up one of Chelsea's games in hand on the top three clubs. Arsenal's bid to reclaim top place is frustrated by a goalless encounter at Highbury with Aston Villa. The Gunners have Emmanuel Petit sent off for manhandling referee Paul Durkin but manager Arsène Wenger pledges to appeal against the dismissal.

Leicester reclaim fourth place on the Monday with a late Ian Marshall goal accounting for a spirited West Ham side. John Hartson criticises referee Mike Reed after five of his team mates are booked but later sends a letter of apology.

Southampton reject a reputed £6m bid by Spurs for Le Tissier and Leeds finally say farewell to Tomas Brolin with a £140,000 settlement. The Swede's 19 league appearances cost the club around £6m.

November

Week 13 (Nov 1-7): Sheringham, Cole and Solskjaer score twice each as Manchester United go on another goal spree, this time at the expense of Sheffield Wednesday, who slump to the foot of the table on the back of a 6-1 thrashing. Blackburn drop two points at Barnsley but join Arsenal in second place after the Gunners are blitzed three times in the second half at Pride Park; Paulo Wanchope scores two of the Derby goals. Ian Wright becomes the fourth player out of five this season to miss a penalty against the Rams. Chelsea stay in contention with a 2-0 win at Villa Park, as Villa complete a third game without scoring. But goals are not a problem at Newcastle, for whom John Beresford's injury-time effort ensures equality with Leicester at three apiece. Leicester, though, are short on numbers following Emile Heskey's sending off for striking Philippe Albert. Liverpool also finish a man short when Robbie Fowler, having earlier opened the scoring, is dismissed during a 1-1 draw at the Reebok Stadium. Coventry, at Wimbledon, record their first away success of the season while Leeds chalk up a fourth away-day victory, this time at the expense of an increasingly desperate Tottenham who have Ginola booked for diving. Southampton end the Premiership's sole 100 per cent losing away record with an important 2-0 victory at Goodison Park, which lifts the Saints out of the bottom three.

With more than a touch of irony, during the Monday match the public address system at Upton Park blasts out the song 'Blinded By The Light' as the floodlights fail, shortly after West Ham wipe out Crystal Palace's two-goal first-half lead. Sheffield Wednesday's decline to the foot of the table reaches its expected conclusion with the sacking of manager David Pleat.

Aston Villa revive their season with an excellent 2-1 victory over Athletic Bilbao, which takes the Midlanders through to the 3rd Round of the UEFA Cup for the first time in two decades, and ends the Spaniards' 11-match unbeaten run. Ian Taylor and Dwight Yorke are Villa's goalscoring heroes. Liverpool also score twice, against Strasbourg, but are out of Europe following their tame 3-0 surrender in France in the first meeting. Newcastle are also on the brink of banishment from the Champions' League as an injury-hit side is competently defeated 2-0 at St James's Park by PSV Eindhoven. But while Newcastle falter, Manchester United move within a fingertip of the quarter finals courtesy of a 3-1 victory over an excessively physical Feyenoord in Rotterdam. Defender Denis Irwin is facing a lengthy lay-off after being on the receiving end of a gruesome lunge by Dutchman Paul Bosvelt, which drew criticism from Glenn Hoddle and Ireland manager Mick McCarthy. Cole's remarkable run continues with United's first hat-trick in European football for 19 seasons, which takes his personal tally to eight in three games.

Chelsea overturn their 1st Leg Cup-Winners' Cup deficit against Tromso in some style with Italian Vialli scoring three times in a 7-1 annihilation at Stamford Bridge.

Week 14 (Nov 8-14): Of seven Premiership matches on the 8th only two sides – Bolton and Spurs – fail to score, and both are thrashed. Bolton are the victims of a Peter Shreeves- inspired Sheffield Wednesday who, boosted by the return of several players after injury, cruise to a 5-0 triumph with Andy Booth scoring a hat-trick. Liverpool, after a goalless first half, get four players on the scoresheet as Tottenham are sunk without trace at Anfield. Spurs boss Gerry Francis is rumoured to have offered his resignation.

Blackburn come from behind to add to Everton's woes with a 3-2 win at Ewood Park and, in so doing, move within a point of leaders Manchester United. The comeback of the day, though, is at Elland Road, where visitors Derby build up a three-goal lead by the 33rd minute only for three different players to chip away at that deficit before Lee Bowyer grabs Leeds' last-minute winner. Southampton, two up inside five minutes, also score four times, against Barnsley, to send the Yorkshire side to the foot of the Premiership.

Aston Villa substitute Julian Joachim rescues a point for his side four minutes from time at Selhurst Park to leave Crystal Palace still searching for their first home success after six outings. Palace have Jamie Smith sent off.

Two games on the Sunday provide a further eight goals, with the most decisive one being David Platt's 83rd minute winner for Arsenal at home to Manchester United after the champions had wiped out a two-goal deficit. Arsenal join Blackburn on 27 points, one behind United. An own goal by Rio Ferdinand puts West Ham on the path to a 2-1 defeat at Chelsea as the Blues reclaim fourth place with 25 points.

In the face of mounting speculation, former Sheffield Wednesday boss Ron Atkinson states on the 11th that he will not be the club's next manager. The following day Wednesday offer Atkinson the position. The tale ends on the 13th with Wednesday confirming that Atkinson is back for a second stint in the Hillsborough hot seat after six years away.

Week 15 (Nov 15-21): Paul Scholes and Robbie Fowler are on target as England begin their France '98 preparations with a 2-0 win over Cameroon at Wembley. After a blank weekend, the domestic campaign resumes midweek with 4th Round Coca-Cola Cup ties but it is not a particularly pleasant evening for Premiership sides as four are eliminated. Dennis Bergkamp, currently serving a three-match ban for league games, scores in extra time to put out Coventry at Highbury and a Jon Dahl Tomasson goal is enough to take Newcastle through and hand Derby their first defeat at Pride Park. The biggest shock is in Yorkshire, where Leeds are defeated by lowly Division One side Reading, despite leading 2-1 with more than an hour gone. Bolton, normally the slayers of bigger fish, are the victims of an upset at Middlesbrough, where one of the sides they replaced in the Premiership overturn an Alan Thompson goal to clinch victory in extra time. But there are no surprises at Anfield where Liverpool dispose of Grimsby Town 3-0, with 17-year-old Michael Owen scoring a hat-trick.

Gerry Francis's suffering at White Hart Lane is over as the Spurs boss announces his departure from the club. His replacement is 43-year-old Swiss coach Christian Gross, the present coach of Zurich side Grasshopper. Manchester United announce a profit of £19m and celebrate by agreeing a new five-year contract with the in-form Cole.

Week 16 (Nov 22-29): Manchester United, pegged back to 2-2 against Wimbledon at Selhurst Park after 70 minutes, go on another spree, and substitute David Beckham scores twice during an eventual 5-2 success. Blackburn stay close on United's heels, with an outstanding Gary Croft goal denting Chelsea's challenge. Arsenal lose ground as Sheffield Wednesday, under Atkinson for the first time, stun the Gunners 2-0 at Hillsborough. Everton take an early lead at Aston Villa but leave Villa Park pointless, having lost 2-1. Their Merseyside neighbours Liverpool help to shove them to the bottom of the pile thanks to a staggering 1-0 defeat at home to Barnsley. The Tykes' victory, courtesy of Ashley Ward, takes Danny Wilson's side level with Bolton – held 0-0 at Leicester – and Spurs. Three late goals on the Sunday give Leeds a 3-1 win over West Ham. George Graham's side climb to fourth on the back of their seventh success in ten games. New Spurs boss Christian Gross cannot match Atkinson's winning start as Spurs go down to a Neil Shipperley goal at White Hart Lane. It is Crystal Palace's fifth away win of the season, taking their points tally to 19, 16 of which have come on their travels, the best record in the Premiership.

Aston Villa's continued participation in Europe is under threat as Steaua Bucharest take a two-goal first-half lead in the 1st Leg of their 3rd Round UEFA Cup tie, but Brian Little's third anniversary as Villa manager is brightened by a second-half Dwight Yorke goal. The one midweek league fixture sees Everton come within ten minutes of a valuable point at Stamford Bridge but penalties by Dennis Wise and Zola lift Chelsea to third and condemn Everton to a fourth consecutive defeat. The Toffeemen also have defender Slaven Bilic dismissed for a second time this season. Returning to European action, a depressingly defensive display by Newcastle proves fruitless as an out-of-sorts Barcelona side win 1-0. Both clubs bow out of the Champions League. Manchester United have no such problems in Group B as two late goals, supplemented by another from Cole, complete a 3-0 victory at Old Trafford over Kosice and, with five wins from five outings, United ensure they top the group.

December

Week 17 (Nov 29-Dec 5): Gianfranco Zola is the toast of Stamford Bridge as the long overdue first hat-trick of his career, in front of the Blues' highest league gate for almost nine years, takes Chelsea to joint top and helps condemn Derby to a 4-0 defeat. Coventry's unbeaten home record – two wins and six draws – ends with Leicester's 2-0 victory at Highfield Road. Crystal Palace lose at home again, this time to Newcastle, and it is a good day for several of the lowly sides. Bolton beat Wimbledon through Nathan Blake's late winner. Sheffield Wednesday climb above Southampton with a third successive victory and first away win of the season. Even Spurs enjoy a rare success with a 2-0 win at Everton which, despite the shallow achievements of both clubs this season, attracts the highest attendance of the day. John Hartson scores twice to give West Ham victory over Villa but there are five different scorers at Oakwell as Leeds make light of a two-goal handicap before moving above Arsenal into fourth position.

Two games on the Sunday have a significant bearing on the title race. Blackburn head to Old Trafford knowing that victory will take them to the top but return home smarting from a 4-0 defeat as United, helped by two own goals, reopen a three-point lead from Chelsea. Arsenal's challenge falters with a first home defeat of the season as a spectacular Steve McManaman goal eases some of the pressure on Liverpool boss Roy Evans. The Gunners have scored just once in six Premiership games. The first match of the festive month adds substance to the belief that Newcastle will not be mounting a sustained challenge as Blake, for the second time in three days, strikes to give Bolton maximum points. George Graham accepts an extension to his contract which will tie him to Leeds beyond the millennium. West Ham's near-perfect record at Upton Park is bolstered with an emphatic 4-1 sixth home league win which dents Crystal Palace's fine away record.

Week 18 (Dec 6-12): A morning kick-off at Anfield allows Manchester United to throw down the gauntlet to their challengers and Alex Ferguson's side come up trumps with another Andy Cole double and a stunning David Beckham free kick, giving United a 3-1 victory. Chelsea, Blackburn and Arsenal all respond accordingly with impressive wins. Chelsea give Christian Gross an insight into the problems at Tottenham as Tore Andre Flo grabs a hat-trick during the Blues' 6-1 massacre at White Hart Lane. It is Spurs' heaviest home league defeat for 62 years. Blackburn see off Bolton with ease at Ewood Park 3-1 and the problems mount for the visitors, who have Alan Thompson dismissed for their fifth red card of the season. Arsenal stay in the hunt, with Ian Wright ending his two-month goal drought with the winner at Newcastle, who drop to mid table.

Derby remain unbeaten at Pride Park with a 2-0 victory over West Ham, who have taken just four points from ten away games, and only a last-minute Muzzy Izzett goal at Filbert Street denies Crystal Palace the opportunity of becoming the first Premiership side to record six away wins. Coventry City complete a 34th consecutive trip to Villa Park without a single victory and have Paul Williams and Gary Breen respectively dismissed shortly before the end of either half as Aston Villa fans are treated to a collector's item: a Stan Collymore goal – his first in 18 home games – during a 3-0 win. Another rare feat is achieved at Elland Road as Everton grab an away point with a 0-0 draw and, in the Sunday match, Wimbledon climb four places with a 1-0 home win over Southampton, who stay out of the relegation places on goal difference. The day is blackened by the news of the death of former Scotland and Leeds captain Billy Bremner.

On the Monday night, Barnsley's plight worsens as a late Paolo Di Canio goal gives Sheffield Wednesday a 2-1 victory in the Yorkshire derby. Di Canio frequently flits between genius and sinner before his winning strike in a match involving the Premiership's two leakiest defences. Wimbledon's long search for a new home shows signs of making progress with the Merton Council proposing a site for a 20,000 all-seater stadium.

Aston Villa's indifferent league form is forgotten as goals in the final 19 minutes by Savo Milosevic and Ian Taylor end Steaua Bucharest's stubborn resistance and take Brian Little's side through to the quarter-final of the UEFA Cup. The following night sees Manchester United lose their 100 per cent winning record in the Champions League as Juventus gain a deserved 1-0 victory in Turin to join United in the last eight. Newcastle end Dynamo Kiev's unbeaten record in Group C but the Magpies' 2-0 win is purely academic as the Geordies are already out and Kiev already through.

Week 19 (Dec 13-19): Blackburn move to within a single point of the leaders with a stunning 3-1 victory over Arsenal at Highbury after falling a goal behind. Arsenal are jeered off and Ian Wright, one of eight players booked, is disciplined by the club after getting involved in a slanging match with disgruntled fans after the game. Another impressive away win is chalked up by an erratic Liverpool side who triumph 3-0 at Selhurst Park and leave Crystal Palace still searching for an elusive home win after eight outings. An early Matt Le Tissier goal sets Southampton on the path to an important 2-1 win over Leicester but the loudest cheer is reserved for Francis Benali whose goal is his first after nine years in the Saints first team. Coventry's annual relegation battle is eased by a 4-0 trouncing of a fast-sinking Spurs at Highfield Road. Led by a Darren Huckerby brace, Coventry end a run of four successive defeats with their biggest win over Tottenham since December 1938. Barnsley and Everton stay rooted to the foot of the table after respective home draws with Newcastle and Wimbledon. Leeds and Chelsea are goalless at Stamford Bridge, a remarkable achievement given that George Graham's side have both Alf Inge Haaland and Gary Kelly dismissed within the opening 20 minutes. Sheffield Wednesday become the seventh out of eight visiting sides to lose at Upton Park as Paul Kitson marks his return after four months out through injury with the deciding goal.

The Reebok Stadium, eight goals from the first eight league games staged there, is on course for another shut-out despite a lively first half between Bolton and visitors Derby. But in an astonishing 27-minute flurry, the lead changes hands as the sides battle out an absorbing 3-3 draw. Aston Villa fall to a sixth away defeat on the Monday night as Ryan Giggs rounds off a fine personal display with the goal which takes Manchester United four points clear of the pack. Derby pick up another useful away point midweek despite having winger Stefano Eranio sent off late during a 0-0 draw with fading Newcastle.

Week 20 (Dec 20-26): Blackburn keep up the pressure at the top with a competent 3-0 home victory over West Ham and, such is the ease with which the Hammers are beaten on their travels, even Stuart Ripley is able to score his first goal since April 1994. Rovers' other two goals come from 18-year-old Damien Duff. Other sides to win by three clear goals are Chelsea, who bring Sheffield Wednesday down to earth with a 4-1 drubbing at Hillsborough, and Tottenham, who romp home 3-0 against fellow strugglers Barnsley, with David Ginola scoring twice. Once again Aston Villa follow up a European success with domestic frustration as they are held at home by Southampton. Both Derby's good home record and Crystal Palace's fine away record are maintained as the two sides draw a blank at Pride Park.

It is a good day for Merseyside as a Michael Owen goal gives Liverpool victory over Coventry but, more significantly, a successful 89th minute Gary Speed penalty secures Everton's first away win for a year and four days. Fellow strugglers Bolton lose at Leeds. Newcastle's fleeting hope of making up lost ground on Manchester United with a Sunday showdown at St James's Park is extinguished by old-boy Andy Cole, whose 12th goal in ten games put the Reds 17 points clear of the Magpies.

Selhurst Park becomes the third Premiership venue to suffer floodlight failure this season as the lights go out at the start of the second half of Wimbledon's home match with Arsenal. The game is abandoned after abortive attempts to restart and the following day the Premier League launch an investigation into the spate of floodlight failures. With their position in the Premiership looking increasingly suspect, Tottenham receive a massive boost with the return to White Hart Lane of Jurgen Klinsmann after an unhappy spell with Sampdoria. The German captain signs for the remainder of the season and Spurs also announce that David Pleat is to return to the club in mid-January to orchestrate the youth and scouting structure. Newcastle reveal plans to extend the capacity at St James's Park to 51,000 at a cost of £42m. Coventry bring Romanian international Viorel Moldovan to Highfield Road for a club record fee of £3.75m.

A full programme in the Premiership on Boxing Day ends with five games all square while in the remaining matches Manchester United seize the opportunity to establish a six point lead from second-placed Blackburn. The reigning champions beat Everton 2-0 at Old Trafford without too many problems – Cole elegantly chips in goal number 13 from 11 games – but United's nearest challengers, Blackburn and Chelsea, drop points with draws against Sheffield Wednesday and Wimbledon. Two goals from Robbie Fowler pave the way for Liverpool to move into fourth place, although 12 points behind United, with a 3-1 win over Leeds at Anfield.

Derby beat Newcastle with their 20th home goal of the season which equals the visitors' home and away total for the season. Newcastle's day is made complete with the sending off of David Batty for two yellow card offences. Coventry also finish with ten men at West Ham as Dutchman George Boateng departs following two bookings in only his second game for the club. City stay in trouble as Paul Kitson again scores the winner for the Hammers' eighth home league win of the season, a record only bettered by Manchester United. Bottom dogs Barnsley are the sixth side to draw with Bolton at the Reebok Stadium while fellow strugglers Southampton are the ninth visiting side to avoid defeat at Crystal Palace. With the aid of a truly magnificent Steve Walsh own goal, Arsenal put their poor run behind them to beat Leicester 2-1 at Highbury but the misery continues for neighbours Tottenham who are thrashed 4-1 by Aston Villa, for whom Stan Collymore scores twice.

January

Week 21 (Dec 27-Jan 2): The final Sunday matches of the year offer hope to the chasing pack that Manchester United can be caught as a wonderful late Darren Huckerby goal, three minutes after Dion Dublin equalised against his former club, secures a 3-2 win for

Coventry over the Reds at Highfield Road for the first time in eight years. There are also five goals at Goodison Park where a headed Duncan Ferguson hat-trick gives Everton a 3-2 win over Bolton and takes the Blues to within one point of their visitors. Blackburn fail to capitalise on United's blip and rely on a Chris Sutton goal 12 minutes from time to avoid defeat at home to Palace. Liverpool continue to show signs of a recovery and, with two superb Steve McManaman goals at St James's Park, hand Newcastle their fifth defeat in seven Premiership outings. West Ham move into the top eight with a 2-1 victory over Wimbledon – by the turn of the year the Dons and Palace have mustered just three wins between them from 20 'home' games at Selhurst Park. Wimbledon's task is virtually impossible from the off, with Ben Thatcher dismissed inside two minutes; an Alan Kimble own goal only adds to their troubles. An Ashley Ward strike gives Barnsley victory over Derby. The Yorkshire side are now just two points behind Spurs who – with Klinsmann making his return to the Premiership – are held 1-1 at home by Arsenal. On the transfer front, Karel Poborsky is on the verge of leaving Manchester United to sign for Portuguese side Benfica. Tottenham's problems mount as the Department of Employment refuses an application for a work permit for Christian Gross's fitness coach Fritz Schmid. Gross, who is rumoured to have suggested he may leave if Schmid cannot join him in London, is also thought to be the target as new coach of the Swiss national team. Further gloom for the capital as Chelsea's title bid is dashed by a 1-0 defeat at Southampton on the Monday night.

Teenage West Ham defender Rio Ferdinand signs an extended contract through to 2005. Team-mate Steve Lomas is charged by the FA with misconduct for manhandling referee Gerald Ashby at Blackburn prior to Christmas. Gross denies speculation that he could be leaving Tottenham.

Week 22 (Jan 3-9): All Premiership sides avoid being on the receiving end of a giant killing in the FA Cup on the 3rd although West Ham are thankful for a John Hartson winner just eight minutes from time in their home tie against non-league Emley at Upton Park. Biggest casualties are Liverpool, who take an early lead at Anfield against Coventry before going down 3-1. Fellow Premier sides Bolton and Southampton are beaten at Barnsley and Derby respectively while Sheffield Wednesday hold out for a draw at Aston Villa recover a two-goal deficit at Portsmouth. Arsenal also have to replay after being held at Highbury by Port Vale. Two goals from Neil Emblen give Crystal Palace a rare, and according to manager Steve Coppell, undeserved, home win over Division Three side Scunthorpe. Biggest winners on the day are Leeds and Leicester who see off Oxford United and Northampton, respectively, 4-0. The match of the round takes place at Stamford Bridge 24 hours later and the cup holders trail 5-0 to Manchester United before rallying with three goals in the final 12 minutes. Cole and Sheringham score twice each as United close in on their third league and cup double. Newcastle are also through as Ian Rush's winner at rain-swept Goodison Park ensures that Everton join Merseyside neighbours Liverpool in the departure lounge. A couple of goalkeeping errors help Spurs move through on the Monday night with a 3-1 win over big-spending Division Two side Fulham.

Palace release Israeli Itzik Zohar on a free transfer, having signed him for £1.2m in the summer, but sign controversial Swede Tomas Brolin on a two-week trial.

Cup action continues on the 6th, this time in the Coca-Cola. Ian Wright ends his goal drought with the first Arsenal goal in an absorbing 2-1 win at West Ham, for whom former Gunner Hartson misses a penalty. Chelsea join Arsenal in the semis the following night but are fortunate to do so after holding out for a 2-2 draw at Ipswich Town, despite leading by two goals at one point. Two saves by Ed De Goey help the Blues to a 4-1 penalty shoot-out victory. In the one remaining quarter-final, under-achieving sides Newcastle and Liverpool also go to extra time before the remarkable duo of Michael Owen and Robbie Fowler add to the Magpies' woe. The semi final quartet is completed by Middlesbrough.

Newcastle are also having trouble in the FA Cup. Drawn away to Vauxhall Conference champions Stevenage Borough, Newcastle want the tie switched to St James's, stating that Boro's Broadhall Way ground is 'totally unsuitable'. The FA reject the Magpies' request as the non-league side receive massive public support.

Tottenham abandon hopes of signing Everton defender Andy Hinchcliffe for £3m due to the England international having an on-going Achilles' tendon injury. Spurs do, though, complete the loan signing of Italian Nicola Berti from Inter Milan. Injury-hit Wimbledon sign Charlton striker Carl Leaburn.

Week 23 (Jan 10-16): Two goals from Ryan Giggs ease Manchester United to a 2-0 win over Spurs as Chelsea move into second place with a 3-1 win over Coventry. Substitute Mark Nicholls scores twice for Chelsea and there are also braces for Jamie Redknapp as Liverpool beat Wimbledon, Marc Overmars as George Graham and Leeds return home pointless from Arsenal, and Frenchman Samassi Abou hits two as West Ham bolster the second best home record in the Premiership with a 6-0 thrashing of Barnsley. The Tykes stay one place behind Tottenham at the foot of the table while fellow strugglers Bolton and Southampton are goalless at the Reebok. Francis Benali is dismissed for the tenth time in his career and Saints boss Dave Jones boldly drops the out-of-form Le Tissier. Palace are now ten home winless games into the season following Everton's 3-1 success at Selhurst Park which lifts Howard Kendall's side three places out of the relegation pack. Newcastle's poor run continues as Paolo Di Canio scores after just 50 seconds during Sheffield Wednesday's 2-1 success over the Magpies. Blackburn's title bid fades as Derby retain their unbeaten home record on the Sunday with a 3-1 victory at Pride Park, which includes a double from Dean Sturridge. Derby and Manchester United are the only sides yet to lose at home.

Wimbledon recover from a goal down at the Racecourse Ground to oust Wrexham 3-2 with the aid of two Michael Hughes goals.

Week 24 (Jan 17-23): Blackburn re-establish themselves as the main title challengers outside Old Trafford with a 5-0 hammering of an out-of-form Aston Villa. Kevin Gallacher takes his season's tally to 16 with a hat-trick while Milosevic is placed on the transfer list after spitting at Villa fans. After a thrilling 2-2 draw at Highbury between Coventry and Arsenal, Sky Blues boss Gordon Strachan is heading for more trouble with the FA when he describes referee Steve Lodge as a disgrace. Strachan's fury is sparked by the dismissal of defender Paul Williams for bringing down Dennis Bergkamp with what appeared a faint touch as the striker broke clear. Arsenal also went down to ten men when Patrick Vieira was sent off. The furore surrounding Williams' exit is academic as a hernia operation puts him out of action for up to six weeks. Alan Shearer makes a surprise appearance for Newcastle, as a substitute, well ahead of his planned comeback from injury. Shearer sets up the winning Magpies goal against Bolton for Temuri Ketsbaia, whose bizarre, aggressive celebrations end with him kicking the advertising boards. Jurgen Klinsmann's first goal since rejoining Tottenham condemns West Ham to defeat at White Hart Lane and takes Spurs above Bolton. Hammers have Samassi Abou dismissed amid much sabre rattling after clashing with Ramon Vega. Bolton's position is further weakened by Ashley Ward's winning goal for Barnsley against Palace at Oakwell. Yorkshire pride goes to Sheffield Wednesday with a 2-1 win over Leeds at Elland Road. Everton, on the Sunday, ease their relegation fears and stop Chelsea from moving back into second place with a 3-1 home victory. Manchester United fail to take advantage of Chelsea's defeat as a well taken Kevin Davies goal gives Southampton a third successive victory over the champions at the Dell. The following night, a stunning Michael Owen goal gives

Liverpool victory over Newcastle as 'Pool deny that Barcelona have made a £12m bid for Steve McManaman.

Brian Clough's hopes of a peaceful retirement are shattered by the FA who charge him with misconduct – taking a bung – over two transfers back in 1989. His assistant, Ronnie Fenton, and former Arsenal coach, Steve Burtenshaw, are also charged.

Week 25 (Jan 24-30): FA Cup 4th Round matches go pretty much by the book as no Premiership sides lose to lesser opposition. Arsenal, already in the semi-final of the Coca-Cola Cup, secure a commendable 2-1 victory at Middlesbrough for whom Paul Merson grabs a consolation goal. In goal for the Gunners is the inexperienced Alex Manninger due to David Seaman suffering a chipped finger a week earlier at Coventry. Andy Cole nets another couple as United thrash Walsall 5-1 but the most prolific player on the day is Crystal Palace striker Bruce Dyer who scores a hat-trick as the Eagles grab an unlikely 3-0 win over Leicester at Selhust Park. Coventry continue their good form with Dion Dublin marking his decision to reject a move to Middlesbrough by scoring both goals in seeing off Derby. Also through are Wimbledon, 1-0 winners at Huddersfield, and Leeds who beat Grimsby 2-0. Barnsley fight back to draw at Tottenham and add to the pressure on Christian Gross.

In an astonishing match at Broadhall Way on the Sunday, Newcastle hold out for a fortuitous draw with Vauxhall Conference champions Stevenage Borough after taking a third-minute lead through Shearer. Recent signing Giuliano Grazioli heads home Boro's historic equaliser. West Ham are also on the verge of an embarrassing result at Maine Road but a missed Uwe Rosler penalty allows Steve Lomas to dump his old club out of the competition with a 76th-minute winner. Blackburn's resurgence under Roy Hodgson continues with a 3-0 win at Hillsborough on the Monday which carries them through to the 5th Round.

Merson again scores against Premier opposition for Middlesbrough on the 27th but as before he is on the losing side as Liverpool, thanks to a late goal from Robbie Fowler, take a 2-1 lead into the 2nd Leg of their Coca-Cola Cup semi-final with the Wearsiders. Fowler's goal restores some goodwill amongst the locals after his alleged demand for a weekly wage of £50,000 does not go down well on Merseyside. Tottenham fail in their bid to obtain a work permit for the man Christian Gross favours as his number two, Swede Fritz Schmid.

Chances of last season's FA Cup finalists, Chelsea and Middlesbrough, coming face to face in the Coca-Cola Cup Final recede as Arsenal take a two-goal lead over the Blues at Highbury, but a Mark Hughes goal gives Chelsea hope of turning the tie around.

West Ham sign QPR winger Trevor Sinclair for £3m. Rangers also take two players from Upton Park.

February

Week 26 (Jan 31-Feb 6): Tony Cottee scores his first ever goal at Old Trafford on the final day of January and it proves enough for Leicester to end United's unbeaten home run. Chelsea keep Barnsley rooted to the foot of the table with a 2-0 win at Stamford Bridge and move to within four points of United. Third and fourth placed Liverpool and Blackburn are goalless at Anfield while three goals in eight minutes take Arsenal to a 3-0 victory over Southampton. But while Arsenal complete a tenth game without defeat, neighbours Tottenham lose again, this time 2-1 at Derby who, thanks to Leicester, now have the only unbeaten home record in the Premiership. Coventry double their total of away wins for the season and more than double their away goals with a 5-1 thrashing of Bolton, who had previously lost just once at the Reebok Stadium. Darren Huckerby and

Dion Dublin each score twice as new £3.5m signing Viorel Moldovan has to watch from the bench. Everton and Wimbledon collect a welcome point each at West Ham and Sheffield Wednesday respectively but Palace fail again at home as Leeds win on their travels for the sixth time. On the Sunday, David Batty's first goal for 17 months settles a tedious affair at Villa Park in Newcastle's favour.

Barnsley put their league worries behind them to knock out Spurs 3-1 in a lively encounter at Oakwell. Tottenham also lose Klinsmann with a broken jaw. Newcastle finally remove Stevenage from the FA Cup with a 2-1 victory at St James's. Shearer, as ever, saves United from further embarrassment with both goals. Newcastle end the week by splashing out £5.5m on Everton's Gary Speed.

Week 27 (Feb 7-13): Manchester United fail at home for the second time in a week with only a late Andy Cole goal stopping Bolton from picking up all three points. United though are saved to some degree by poor results for the chasing pack. Liverpool, just as surprisingly, crash 3-2 at home to Southampton and Blackburn succumb 3-0 at home to Spurs, for whom Chris Armstrong scores in his third match back after three months out through injury. Newcastle's recovery is short-lived as Stan Lazaridis scores a magnificent winner for West Ham on Tyneside. Dwight Yorke makes it an exceptionally good day for the claret blues with his last-minute winner which ends Derby's unbeaten record at Pride Park. Garry Parker puts Leicester ahead from the penalty spot against Leeds and when Jimmy Hasselbaink misses from the same spot in injury time the Foxes collect three more points. Dion Dublin's successful penalty also settles Coventry's meeting with Sheffield Wednesday. Everton take another step towards safety with a 2-2 draw at Barnsley. Arsenal re-enter the Championship race the following day with a Steve Hughes brace seeing off Chelsea at Highbury. But the Gunners still trail United by six points.

The Premier League takes a midweek break while England are beaten 2-0 at Wembley by Chile. Salas scores twice, the first being a classic.

The football world is stunned on the 12th as Chelsea dismiss manager Ruud Gullit, citing a breakdown in negotiations over a new contract. Gianluca Vialli is handed the dual role of player/manager at Stamford Bridge.

Week 28 (Feb 14-20): FA Cup 5th Round ties decimate the Premiership programme on the 14th but in one of three games played, Liverpool, at Sheffield Wednesday, concede three goals for a second consecutive week, although a Michael Owen hat-trick salvages a point for the Reds. Leicester record their 11th draw of the season from a trip to Tottenham while Everton end their run of draws with a home defeat by Derby.

In the FA Cup, three Premier sides progress on the Saturday. Leeds, having earlier taken a two-goal lead, see off Birmingham with Hasselbaink's late winner and Moldovan quickly repays some of his fee with the only goal from Coventry's trip to troubled Aston Villa. West Ham and Blackburn share four goals evenly at Upton Park and at Selhurst Park Wimbledon also have to replay after being held by Wolves. Two more ties are played on the Sunday without a clear result achieved. Arsenal and Palace are goalless while Manchester United are not only held by Barnsley at Old Trafford but escape having a blatant penalty given against themselves in the dying moments. Three Barnsley MPs raise the matter of the spot kick that wasn't in the House of Commons.

Aston Villa's problems at Villa Park persist on the 18th as Manchester United, through Beckham and Giggs, get back to winning ways and establish a seven-point lead over second-placed Liverpool. Coventry also win again, this time at Southampton. Vialli is Wembley bound after just one match in charge at Stamford Bridge as Chelsea turf out Arsenal 4-3 on aggregate in the Coca-Cola Cup semi-final. Arsenal have Patrick Vieira sent off. Liverpool fall two behind inside four minutes at the Riverside as promotion-seeking Middlesbrough go through to the final for a second consecutive year.

Week 29 (Feb 21-27): With Liverpool not in action and Chelsea and Blackburn defeated 2-0 and 3-0 respectively at Leicester and Southampton, Arsenal rise to second following Gilles Grimandi's winning goal against Palace at Highbury. Emile Heskey of Leicester and Saints' Egil Ostenstad both score twice. With a 2-0 victory over Derby, Manchester United stay nine points clear of the Gunners but suffer a blow as Giggs pulls a hamstring. Barnsley bow to a late penalty at Coventry and Spurs lose at Sheffield Wednesday. Bolton move a point closer to the Londoners with Nathan Blake's late equaliser against West Ham; the Hammers have John Hartson dismissed. Aston Villa continue to head towards trouble as they go down 2-1 at Wimbledon. On the Sunday, Leeds take a late lead at Newcastle but an embarrassing bloomer by keeper Nigel Martyn allows Newcastle to stave off defeat.

Referee Dermot Gallagher is dropped by the FA for one match in response to his poor handling of the Arsenal v Chelsea match on the 8th. Liverpool battle back to rescue a point from the Merseyside derby on the 23rd but are nine points adrift of the leaders. Robbie Fowler damages medial ligaments and is out for the remainder of the season. Just a week before playing in the UEFA Cup quarter-final, Aston Villa lose the services of manager Brian Little, who resigns.

Four Premier sides are knocked out of the FA Cup on the 25th, the most significant being Manchester United as justice is carried and Barnsley head for the last eight with a 3-2 victory at Oakwell. Selhurst Park will have no representatives in the quarter-finals as Palace go down 2-1 at home to Arsenal and lodgers Wimbledon lose their replay at Wolves, after taking the lead through Vinny Jones's first goal of the season. Blackburn squander several chances during 120 minutes of open play with West Ham and pay the price as the Hammers score all five of their penalties in the shoot-out to go through 5-4.

Wycombe boss John Gregory is appointed manager of Aston Villa. Brian Little's assistant manager, Allan Evans, also moves on.

March

Week 30 (Feb 28-Mar 6): The first goal of Phil Neville's career secures victory for Manchester United at Chelsea and takes the champions 11 points clear at the top. Blackburn claim second place with a remarkable 5-3 win over Leicester at Ewood Park, which includes a hat-trick for England misfit Chris Sutton. Rovers lead 5-0 at one stage. Liverpool, through Michael Owen, take an early lead at Villa Park before former Liverpool bad boy Stan Collymore scores twice to ease Villa's relegation fears. Palace's plight looks hopeless as Coventry win 3-0 at Selhurst Park while Everton and Newcastle slightly aid each other's cause with a draw at Goodison Park. Derby striker Dean Sturridge has a lucky escape from a serious car accident on the Friday night and Sheffield Wednesday boss Ron Atkinson admits his side are fortunate to escape with just a 3-0 defeat against Sturridge's team mates on the Saturday. Carlton Palmer, returning to one of his former clubs, Leeds, sets up Southampton's winner but is later dismissed following two cautions. Barnsley are off the foot of the table as two Jan Aage Fjortoft goals clinch a vital win over Wimbledon. On the Sunday Spurs move five points clear of the bottom three courtesy of Allan Neilsen's winner against Bolton. Despite rising to second with a draw at West Ham 24 hours later, Arsenal's title hopes appear remote as they trail United by 11 points with just two games in hand. The Gunners have Vieira booked but referee Paul Durkin rescinds the caution after watching video evidence.

Aston Villa stay on course for reaching the last four of the UEFA Cup as an inspired performance by goalkeeper Mark Bosnich restricts their deficit against Atletico Madrid to just one goal. Manchester United are in an even more favourable position as they return from Monaco goalless, following an uneventful 90 minutes in the principality. One league game played on the 4th spells more bad news for Tottenham as a Harry Kewell goal gives Leeds three thoroughly deserved points at Elland Road.

Two early goals by Tore Andre Flo give Chelsea an outstanding 2-1 victory over Real Betis in Spain on the 5th in the Cup-Winners' Cup quarter-final.

Week 31 (Mar 7-13): With the Premiership programme depleted by 6th Round FA Cup ties, Liverpool take advantage to move into second place with a 2-1 victory over Bolton at Anfield. Owen's winner makes for a good day for Roy Evans' side, especially as neighbours Everton slip again, this time 2-1 at Southampton, and Manchester United are beaten 2-0 by Sheffield Wednesday. Southampton have Ken Monkou dismissed while Everton lose Slaven Bilic prematurely for the third time this season. Two FA Cup ties on the 7th do not go well for Premiership sides as Coventry are held at home by troubled Sheffield United, and Leeds, despite an amazing finale, are beaten at home by Wolves. The following day sees four top flight sides in Cup action but only Newcastle, 3-1 victors at home to Barnsley, are definitely through. Adie Moses is sent off but the Tykes accuse Alan Shearer of getting his marker dismissed. Arsenal and Palace draw at Highbury. One league match on the Sunday further dents Chelsea's fading hopes of pinching second place as Aston Villa chalk up a 1-0 success in London.

Chelsea put that disappointment behind them midweek to hammer Palace 6-2 with Vialli and Flo each scoring twice. Villa, though, fail to build on their Stamford Bridge success and slither to a home defeat against Barnsley, through an Ashley Ward goal which takes the Tykes within two points of Tottenham. Another London derby at Selhurst Park sees Arsenal move into second place as Christopher Wreh marks his debut with the deciding strike against Wimbledon. Staying in the capital, Manchester United come from behind to take a point from West Ham through Paul Scholes' equaliser. United lead Arsenal by nine points but Wenger's side have three games in hand. Having found their path to Europe via the FA Cup blocked, Leeds get back on course for a place in the UEFA Cup with a 4-0 thrashing of Blackburn, which includes three goals in seven second-half minutes.

Week 32 (Mar 14-20): Manchester United's desire to put the Championship race beyond doubt is destroyed by Arsenal in a morning kick-off showdown at Old Trafford on the 14th. Marc Overmars scores the goal which gives Arsenal the double over the reigning champions, who also lose keeper Peter Schmeichel with a hamstring injury after tackling Bergkamp in the middle of the pitch. Liverpool cling on to third place with a last-minute Steve McManaman goal ensuring an equal share of six goals with Tottenham at White Hart Lane. Everton grab a lifeline with an excellent Michael Madar header seeing off Blackburn who miss the chance to rise above Chelsea following their defeat at West Ham. The loss of two home points for Spurs could prove costly as Barnsley win again with four different scorers in their 4-3 win over Southampton; they join Tottenham on 31 points. Bolton's dirty dozen is over as they win for the first time in 13 games, with Alan Thompson's successful penalty concluding a 3-2 triumph over Sheffield Wednesday. Villa and Wimbledon just about make their positions safe with home wins over Palace and Leicester respectively, but Newcastle still have problems after a dire draw with Coventry at St. James's Park. Derby suffer a second blemish on their record at Pride Park on the Sunday as Leeds storm to an amazing 5-0 win and fifth place in the table; it is Leeds' biggest win under George Graham.

Further turmoil for Newcastle as chairman Freddy Shepherd and vice-chairman Douglas Hall enrage supporters by making disparaging comments about the fans and the womenfolk of the north-east.

Aston Villa's European venture ends on the 17th despite second-half goals from Ian Taylor and Collymore pulling them level on aggregate with visitors Atletico Madrid, who progress on the away goals rule. Two FA Cup 6th Round replays both go to penalties.

Arsenal keep their nerve to put out West Ham after former Gunner John Hartson had equalised to take the game into extra time but Coventry, who lead until the 89th minute, score only once from the spot and are ousted by Sheffield United. Manchester United go the same way as Villa on the Wednesday as Solskjaer's equaliser is only sufficient to save United from defeat at Old Trafford, but Trezeguet's spectacular strike takes Monaco through on the away goals rule. Against a backdrop of anger against their two leading directors, Newcastle suffer a humbling 2-1 home defeat by seemingly doomed Crystal Palace, who end a run of eight consecutive reversals.

Chelsea are left to successfully fly the British flag in Europe as they come from behind at Stamford Bridge to beat Real Betis 3-1 on the night and 5-2 on aggregate to make their way into the last four of the Cup-Winners' Cup.

Week 33 (Mar 21-27): With the home nations involved in international matches during the coming week, the race for domestic honours is put on hold on the 21st. Supporters get their wish on Tyneside as Messrs Shepherd and Hall resign. Sir John Hall returns as chairman at least for the short term. Manchester United announce plans for a new £14m training site alongside the Manchester Ship Canal. England's international with Switzerland ends 1-1 with Paul Merson scoring the visitors' equalising goal.

April

Week 34 (Mar 28-Apr 3): Manchester United leave it late before two goals in the final seven minutes clinch three potentially vital points at home to Wimbledon. An expertly taken goal by Bergkamp gives Arsenal victory over Sheffield Wednesday and puts them just six points behind United with three games in hand. The most remarkable match of the day is at Oakwell where Barnsley, having not seen a single red card all season, have Darren Barnard, Chris Morgan and Darren Sheridan dismissed during a 3-2 home defeat by Liverpool. Referee Gary Willard is locked in his dressing room for two hours after the game for his own safety. Both clubs must appear before the FA to face charges of failing to control supporters following several pitch invasions. Fellow strugglers Bolton are boosted by a brace of Alan Thompson goals which sink Leicester, but the agony continues for Palace as they go down 3-1 at home to Tottenham. That result, coupled with Everton's 4-1 thrashing at home by Aston Villa, leaves the Merseysiders just two points above the bottom three. More misery for Newcastle as Matt Le Tissier scores Southampton's winner after the Magpies had led early in the second half and Coventry climb into the top ten with Darren Huckerby's winning strike against Derby. The Coca-Cola Cup Final goes the same way of the previous season's FA Cup when Chelsea beat Middlesbrough 2-0 at Wembley with extra-time goals from Frank Sinclair and Roberto Di Matteo. In the Monday match, West Ham turn on the style in a 3-0 win over Leeds which takes the Hammers up to seventh. United's problems do not end at the final whistle as their aircraft has to make an emergency landing at Stansted Airport; no one is seriously hurt.

The final day of the month sees Barnsley and Bolton plunge deeper into trouble. Barnsley lose at Blackburn while Bolton are defeated at the Reebok Stadium by Arsenal who close the gap on Manchester United to three points with two games in hand. With the 1-0 win at Bolton, the Gunners set a new Premiership record of eight consecutive clean sheets.

Chelsea's hopes of reaching their second Cup-Winners' Cup Final are dented in Italy as Vincenza take advantage of a poor performance by the Blues to grab a 1-0 1st Leg semi-final lead.

Week 35 (Apr 4-10): Arsenal drastically reduce their odds on a second league and cup double on the 4th with Wreh's early goal removing Wolves from the FA Cup semi-finals.

Looking to deny the Gunners another slice of history are Newcastle, after Alan Shearer's goal takes care of Sheffield United in the other semi. With a goalless draw at Wimbledon, Bolton clamber above Barnsley, who are defeated by a Leeds side showing no ill after effects from their plane crash. Bolton and Barnsley both trail Everton by three points following their 1-1 draw at Tottenham. A Benito Carbone goal just about ensures Sheffield Wednesday's safety as the Owls reach the 40-point barrier with a 1-0 win over Southampton. Honours are even in a Midlands battle between Leicester and Coventry while West Ham's European dreams are damaged by a 2-0 reversal at Aston Villa. Once impregnable, Pride Park is breached again on the Sunday with Mark Hughes scoring Chelsea's winner against Derby.

Manchester United, having been outplayed in the first half, move six points clear of Arsenal, with a stirring second-half display at Ewood Park on the 6th paving the way for a 3-1 victory. Jimmy Hasselbaink takes his season's tally with Leeds to 19 with a brace during a 3-1 win over an off-key Chelsea. A Good Friday meeting with Liverpool at Old Trafford presents United with the opportunity to open a nine-point lead, but after taking an early lead through Ronnie Johnsen the champions are pegged back by Michael Owen, who is sent off before the interval following two hideously late tackles.

Week 36 (Apr 11-17): Warren Barton becomes the first player in 13 hours and 43 minutes to score against Arsenal but he cannot prevent the Gunners from using up one of their four games in hand on Manchester United to reduce the points deficit to just four. Teenager Nicolas Anelka scores twice, with an outstanding goal by Vieira completing Arsenal's 3-1 win. Aston Villa's recovery under John Gregory continues with a sixth win in seven games as Coventry are handed only their second defeat of the season at Highfield Road. Heskey scores twice at Leicester nudge Palace closer to the inevitable and the Eagles' position is further undermined by excellent 2-1 home wins for Barnsley and Bolton against Sheffield Wednesday and Blackburn respectively. With Newcastle's defeat at Highbury and Tottenham going down 2-0 at Chelsea, Barnsley and Bolton may yet escape the drop with just a point keeping Spurs out of the bottom three. Although Everton, with Duncan Ferguson scoring his tenth goal of the season, gain a welcome 2-0 win at home to Leeds they are still just two points better off than Spurs. Leeds have Lucas Radebe carried off and sent off in the same incident. Another heading for an early bath is John Hartson during the Hammers' goalless afternoon with Derby; West Ham's leading scorer will miss the last four games of the season through suspension. An embarrassing blooper by Southampton keeper Paul Jones against Wimbledon hands Carl Leaburn the winning goal at the Dell.

Two goals for Ray Parlour and singles for Bergkamp – back from a three-match ban – and Anelka put Arsenal four up before half-time at Ewood Park on Easter Monday as the destiny of the Championship seems certain to be Highbury for the third time in ten years. Derby also find the target four times before the interval as Bolton's recovery is knocked back at Pride Park. A late David Thompson goal, his first for Liverpool, condemns Palace to an expected defeat at Anfield while, more importantly, Shearer grabs an 86th minute winner for Newcastle at home to Barnsley. Another late goal, this time by Dion Dublin, denies Spurs two extra points at White Hart Lane. The most thankful for that goal are Everton, who grind out a dull draw with Wimbledon. With his first goal since joining Sheffield Wednesday in September, Jim Magilton saves Sheffield Wednesday a point at Hillsborough against West Ham. Leicester's European ambitions are blighted in a six-goal thriller on the Tuesday, despite salvaging a point after trailing Southampton 3-1 at Filbert Street.

Chelsea fall further behind on aggregate at home to Vicenza in the Cup-Winners' Cup on the 16th but, through Uruguayan Gustavo Poyet, Italian Zola and a stunning goal from Welshman Mark Hughes, the Blues ensure that England are represented in one of this season's European finals. Both Chelsea and their opponents in the final, Stuttgart, will receive 12,000 tickets.

Week 37 (Apr 18-24): Reigning champions Manchester United – who have Solskjaer dismissed – come from behind to take a point off Newcastle at Old Trafford, but with another blistering opening burst Arsenal rise to the summit with a 5-0 thrashing of Wimbledon. The Gunners, who go three up inside 19 minutes, lead the table by one point with a further two games in hand. And there is more good news for north London fans as Spurs, despite having Ramon Vega sent off, hold Barnsley to a 1-1 draw at Oakwell and in so doing avoid dropping into the relegation places. Everton also take a point with a draw at home to Leicester. Bolton's position begins to look desperate as Leeds boost their hopes of clinching a UEFA Cup place with a 3-2 win at the Reebok Stadium. Crystal Palace, already certain of chalking up the fewest number of home wins in Premiership history, avoid the humiliation of not winning a home league match all season with a 3-1 victory over fading Derby. Aston Villa and Blackburn continue to head in opposite directions as Villa win at Southampton and Rovers fall to two Hartson goals at Upton Park. On the 19th, Chelsea make seven changes for the fourth consecutive match but still defeat Sheffield Wednesday with a Frank Leboeuf penalty while Liverpool and Coventry finish all square at Highfield Road.

It's another blank midweek on the league front as World Cup warm-up matches take place. Matt Le Tissier makes a late claim for the England squad with a hat trick for the 'B' team in a 4-1 win over Russia. The first team see off Portugal 3-0 at Wembley with Shearer scoring twice.

May

Week 38 (Apr 25-May 1): Irrepressible Arsenal move four points clear and edge Barnsley to the brink of relegation with a convincing 2-0 win at Oakwell courtesy of Dutch masters Denis Bergkamp and Marc Overmars. The race for third place hots up with Chelsea demolishing Liverpool 4-1 at Stamford Bridge. Hasselbaink scores twice for Leeds but the matchball goes to Coventry's Darren Huckerby who notches a hat-trick in a 3-3 draw at Elland Road. Southampton score four times in picking up their fourth away win of the season while West Ham's two goals mirror their second home defeat. There are also plenty of goals at Goodison Park but life is looking uncomfortable for Everton as Sheffield Wednesday, helped by a brace of Mark Pembridge goals, win 3-1. Worse for Everton is the news from Villa Park where Bolton double their away successes for the season with a vital 3-1 win. Newcastle are sucked deep into the relegation mêlée as former Magpie David Ginola sets up both Spurs goals in an invaluable 2-0 success for the Londoners. The only goalless match is at Ewood Park where Blackburn, facing Wimbledon, end a run of four straight defeats. Derby's home record takes another severe beating on the Sunday as Leicester rattle in an amazing four headed goals inside the opening 15 minutes; Emile Heskey strikes twice. Derby manage to draw the remaining 75 minutes.

Manchester United completely overrun Crystal Palace at Selhurst Park in the Monday match to close the gap on Arsenal to one point but the chase looks a forlorn one. For Palace, the 3-0 defeat marks the end of their brief flirtation with life at the top. Italian Attilio Lombardo declares that he is not keen on management after the Eagles' latest defeat and decides to stick to playing. Chairman Ron Noades and coach Ray Lewington take charge of team affairs. Stuttgart, Chelsea's Cup-Winners' Cup Final opponents, return 11,000 unsold tickets of their allocation of 12,000.

The Championship trophy is just one win away from Highbury as Arsenal set a Premiership record of nine consecutive victories as a result of Emmanuel Petit's first-half winner against Derby. Chelsea lose the chance of just about clinching third place by going down 1-0 at home to Blackburn, whose UEFA Cup hopes are revived. Wimbledon block out Coventry to record their fifth goalless game in seven outings and Newcastle get the same result at Leicester to move four points clear of the bottom three. England captain Shearer could be in trouble with the FA after video evidence shows him appearing to kick Leicester's Neil Lennon in the face as the duo tussle on the touchline. Dennis Bergkamp kicks off the final ten days of the league season by adding the Football Writers' Footballer of the Year Award to the players' award he collected in April.

Week 39 (May 2-8): Eight Premiership matches produce 33 goals on the penultimate weekend of the league season. Top scorers are Tottenham, who put six past a Wimbledon side which had recorded six clean sheets in its previous seven games. Jurgen Klinsmann scores four and sets up the others for Les Ferdinand and Moussa Saib as Spurs avoid the drop; Peter Fear strikes two excellent volleys for the Dons. In a match of fluctuating first-half fortunes, Bolton come from behind at the Reebok Stadium to hammer Palace 5-2. In amongst several magnificent goals, Bolton's Jimmy Phillips scores his first goal for four years while Palace have Val Ismail dismissed. Other high scorers are Liverpool, who need only to win on the last day of the season to secure third place following a 5-0 thrashing of West Ham. Jason McAteer scores twice as Liverpool lead 4-0 by the break. Barnsley's defiant stand is over as a 1-0 defeat at Filbert Street sends Danny Wilson's side down and keeps Leicester dreaming of Europe. Newcastle end their anxiety with a 3-1 win over Chelsea and there are also two goal wins for Coventry at home to Blackburn, Villa at Sheffield Wednesday and Derby at Southampton.

With three games in which to wrap up their third Championship in ten years, Arsenal do it in style on the 3rd with a 4-0 destruction of Everton at Highbury. The Blues will probably need to win on the final day to avoid relegation after being completely overrun by Arsenal, who get a helping hand from a Bilic own goal for the initial breakthrough. Marc Overmars confirms the Gunners' supremacy with a pair and Tony Adams slams in a spectacular fourth as Arsène Wenger becomes the first overseas coach to win the Premiership.

Although Manchester United are destined to end the season without a single trophy, over 55,000 turn up to see the Reds trounce Leeds 3-0 on the 4th. Leeds have Gunnar Halle sent off as they fail again to score their first Premiership goal at Old Trafford. Alex Ferguson wastes no time in announcing United's determination to reclaim the title as he unveils record £10.75m signing defender Jaap Stam from PSV Eindhoven. Palace end their Premiership days with a goal glut as they take their total of home goals for the season to 14 with a 3-3 draw with West Ham; the Hammers have David Unsworth sent off.

While the Championship trophy is getting accustomed to Highbury, Arsenal make eight changes for the midweek trip to Liverpool and lose 4-0. Liverpool ensure themselves of third place and participation in the UEFA Cup. Spurs announce that Gary Mabbutt and David Howells, who have played over 950 games for the club between them, are to be given free transfers.

Week 40 (May 9-15): Arsenal suffer what for them is a purely academic last day of the season defeat but for victors Aston Villa, Dwight Yorke's audaciously chipped penalty could mean a place in the UEFA Cup. Their fate depends upon Chelsea winning the Cup-Winners' Cup. Manchester United finish just a point behind Arsenal with Cole and Sheringham taking care of already doomed Barnsley. Blackburn are also in Europe thanks to Chris Sutton's late winner against Newcastle but both West Ham and Leicester miss out at the end of a thrilling contest at Upton Park where the Hammers win 4-3, despite Tony Cottee scoring twice against his former club. Leicester close the season six points better off than the previous year but, strangely, one place lower. Derby round off a successful first year at their new ground with a Paulo Wanchope goal securing the points from

Liverpool. Palace treat their followers to a rare home victory, over Sheffield Wednesday, with a late goal from the debut-making Clinton Morrison. A player at the opposite end of his career, Jurgen Klinsmann says farewell with a spectacular equaliser in his final game for Tottenham; Matt Le Tissier had put Southampton ahead. Leeds – assured of European trips next season – and goal-shy Wimbledon draw 1-1 at Elland Road.

The main focus of attention is divided between Stamford Bridge and Goodison Park. Victory for Bolton would end Everton's long association with the top flight. But after a goalless first half Bolton are defeated at Chelsea by goals from Vialli and Jody Morris. Everton take an early lead through Gareth Farrelly but miss a chance to end the tension when Magnus Hedman saves a Nick Barmby penalty. That leaves sufficient time for Dion Dublin to head Coventry's equaliser but Everton hold out for the point needed to avoid the drop.

After an absence of 27 years, the Cup-Winners' Cup returns to Stamford Bridge as Zola, just seconds after coming on, lashes home a majestic goal on the 13th which ends the resistance of Germans VfB Stuttgart in Stockholm. Three days later, Arsenal fulfil expectations with a 2-0 victory over Newcastle at Wembley in the Littlewoods sponsored FA Cup Final. Goals in either half by Marc Overmars and Nicolas Anelka complete another magnificent chapter in the Gunners' history as they become only the second club to have twice won the league and cup double. ■

FINAL TABLES 1997-98

FA Carling Premiership

		HOME					AWAY					
	P	W	D	L	F	A	W	D	L	F	A	Pts
Arsenal	38	15	2	2	43	10	8	7	4	25	23	78
Manchester United ...	38	13	4	2	42	9	10	4	5	31	17	77
Liverpool	38	13	2	4	42	16	5	9	5	26	26	65
Chelsea	38	13	2	4	37	14	7	1	11	34	29	63
Leeds United	38	9	5	5	31	21	8	3	8	26	25	59
Blackburn Rovers ...	38	11	4	4	40	26	5	6	8	17	26	58
Aston Villa	38	9	3	7	26	24	8	3	8	23	24	57
West Ham United ...	38	13	4	2	40	18	3	4	12	16	39	56
Derby County	38	12	3	4	33	18	4	4	11	19	31	55
Leicester City	38	6	10	3	21	15	7	4	8	30	26	53
Coventry City	38	8	9	2	26	17	4	7	8	20	27	52
Southampton	38	10	1	8	28	23	4	5	10	22	32	48
Newcastle United ...	38	8	5	6	22	20	3	6	10	13	24	44
Tottenham Hotspur ...	38	7	8	4	23	22	4	3	12	21	34	44
Wimbledon	38	5	6	8	18	25	5	8	6	16	21	44
Sheffield Wednesday	38	9	5	5	30	26	3	13	13	22	41	44
Everton	38	7	5	7	25	27	2	8	9	16	29	40
Bolton Wanderers ...	38	7	8	4	25	22	2	5	12	16	39	40
Barnsley	38	7	4	8	25	35	3	1	15	12	47	35
Crystal Palace	38	2	5	12	15	39	6	4	9	22	32	33

Composite Table with Prize Money

Psn		P	W	D	L	F	A	Pts	Prize Money
1	Arsenal	38	23	9	6	68	33	78	£3,250,000
2	Manchester United ...	38	23	8	7	73	26	77	£3,087,500
3	Liverpool	38	18	11	9	68	42	65	£2,945,000
4	Chelsea	38	20	3	15	71	43	63	£2,762,500
5	Leeds United	38	17	8	13	57	46	59	£2,600,000
6	Blackburn Rovers	38	16	10	12	57	52	58	£2,437,000
7	Aston Villa	38	17	6	15	49	48	57	£2,750,000
8	West Ham United	38	16	8	14	56	57	56	£2,112,500
9	Derby County	38	16	7	15	52	49	55	£1,950,000
10	Leicester City	38	13	14	11	51	41	53	£1,787,500
11	Coventry City	38	12	16	10	46	44	52	£1,625,000
12	Southampton	38	14	6	18	50	55	48	£1,462,500
13	Newcastle United	38	11	11	16	35	44	44	£1,300,000
14	Tottenham Hotspur ...	38	11	11	16	44	56	44	£1,137,500
15	Wimbledon	38	10	14	14	34	46	44	£975,000
16	Sheffield Wednesday ...	38	12	8	18	52	67	44	£812,500
17	Everton	38	9	13	16	41	56	40	£650,000
18	Bolton Wanderers	38	9	13	16	41	61	40	£487,500
19	Barnsley	38	10	5	23	37	82	35	£325,000
20	Crystal Palace	38	8	9	21	37	71	33	£162,600

Nationwide League Division 1

Psn		P	W	D	L	F	A	Pts	
1	Nottingham Forest... ...	46	28	10	8	82	42	94	P
2	Middlesbrough	46	27	10	9	77	41	91	P
3	Sunderland	46	26	12	8	86	50	90	
4	Charlton Athletic	46	26	10	10	80	49	88	P
5	Ipswich Town	46	23	14	9	77	43	83	
6	Sheffield United	46	19	17	10	69	54	74	
7	Birmingham City	46	19	17	10	60	35	74	
8	Stockport County	46	19	8	19	71	69	65	
9	Wolverhampton W. ...	46	18	11	17	57	53	65	
10	WBA	46	16	13	17	50	56	61	
11	Crewe Alexandra	46	18	5	23	58	65	59	
12	Oxford United	46	16	10	20	60	64	58	
13	Bradford City	46	14	15	17	46	59	57	
14	Tranmere Rovers	46	14	14	18	54	57	56	
15	Norwich City	46	14	13	19	52	69	55	
16	Huddersfield Town ...	46	14	11	21	50	72	53	

Psn		P	W	D	L	F	A	Pts	
17	Bury	46	11	19	16	42	58	52	
18	Swindon Town	46	14	10	22	42	73	52	
19	Port Vale...	46	13	10	23	56	66	49	
20	Portsmouth	46	13	10	23	51	63	49	
21	QPR	46	10	19	17	51	63	49	
22	Manchester City	46	12	12	22	56	57	48	R
23	Stoke City	46	11	13	22	44	74	46	R
24	Reading	46	11	9	26	39	78	42	R

Nationwide League Division 2

Psn		P	W	D	L	F	A	Pts	
1	Watford	46	24	16	6	67	41	88	P
2	Bristol City	46	25	10	11	69	39	85	P
3	Grimsby Town	46	19	15	12	55	37	72	P
4	Northampton Town ...	46	18	17	11	52	37	71	
5	Bristol Rovers	46	20	10	16	70	64	70	
6	Fulham	46	20	10	16	60	43	70	
7	Wrexham	46	18	16	12	55	51	70	
8	Gillingham	46	19	13	14	52	47	70	
9	Bournemouth	46	18	12	16	57	52	66	
10	Chesterfield	46	16	17	13	46	44	65	
11	Wigan	46	17	11	18	64	66	62	
12	Blackpool	46	17	11	18	59	67	62	
13	Oldham Athletic	46	15	16	15	62	54	61	
14	Wycombe Wanderers ...	46	14	18	14	51	53	60	
15	Preston NE	46	15	14	17	56	56	59	
16	York City	46	14	17	15	52	58	59	
17	Luton Town	46	14	15	17	60	64	57	
18	Millwall	46	14	13	19	43	54	55	
19	Walsall	46	14	12	20	43	52	54	
20	Burnley	46	13	13	20	55	65	52	
21	Brentford	46	11	17	18	50	71	50	R
22	Plymouth Argyll	46	12	13	21	55	70	49	R
23	Carlisle United	46	12	8	26	57	73	44	R
24	Southend United	46	11	10	25	47	79	43	R

Nationwide League Division 3

Psn		P	W	D	L	F	A	Pts	
1	Notts County	46	29	12	5	82	43	99	P
2	Macclesfield Town ...	46	23	13	10	63	44	82	P
3	Lincoln City...	46	20	15	11	60	51	75	P
4	Colchester United	46	21	11	14	72	60	74	P
5	Torquay United	46	21	11	14	68	59	74	
6	Scarborough	46	19	15	12	67	58	72	
7	Barnet	46	19	13	14	61	51	70	
8	Scunthorpe United... ...	46	19	12	15	56	52	69	
9	Rotherham	46	16	19	11	67	61	67	
10	Peterborough United ...	46	18	13	15	63	51	67	
11	Leyton Orient *	46	19	12	15	62	47	66	
12	Mansfield Town	46	16	17	13	64	55	65	
13	Shrewsbury	46	16	13	17	61	62	61	
14	Chester City...	46	17	10	19	60	61	61	
15	Exeter City	46	15	15	16	68	63	60	
16	Cambridge United	46	14	18	14	63	57	60	
17	Hartlepool United	46	12	23	11	61	53	59	
18	Rochdale...	46	17	7	22	56	55	58	
19	Darlington	46	14	12	20	56	72	54	
20	Swansea	46	13	11	22	49	62	50	
21	Cardiff City	46	9	23	14	48	52	50	
22	Hull City...	46	11	8	27	56	83	41	
23	Brighton & HA...	46	6	17	23	38	66	35	
24	Doncaster Rovers	46	4	8	34	30	113	20	R

* Leyton Orient deducted three points for fielding ineligible players.

ALL-TIME TABLES
1992/93-97/98

Positions Based on Points

Psn		P	W	D	L	F	A	Pts	Yrs	H	L
1	Manchester United	240	146	60	34	446	202	498	6	1	2
2	Blackburn Rovers	240	115	60	65	371	263	405	6	1	13
3	Liverpool	240	111	64	65	386	260	397	6	3	8
4	Arsenal	240	105	72	63	324	212	387	6	1	12
5	Aston Villa	240	99	63	78	302	263	360	6	2	18
6	Leeds United	240	90	72	78	306	280	342	6	5	17
7	Newcastle United	198	97	48	53	323	209	339	5	2	13
8	Chelsea	240	88	69	83	325	304	333	6	4	14
9	Tottenham Hotspur	240	83	68	89	318	328	317	6	7	15
10	Wimbledon	240	82	70	88	298	335	316	6	6	15
11	Sheffield Wednesday	240	80	75	85	330	341	315	6	7	16
12	Everton	240	74	68	98	288	326	290	6	6	17
13	Coventry City	240	68	85	87	265	322	289	6	11	17
14	Southampton	240	70	64	106	298	353	274	6	10	18
15	West Ham United	198	66	53	79	229	263	251	5	8	14
16	QPR	164	59	39	66	224	232	216	4	5	19
17	Nottingham Forest	160	53	50	57	194	218	209	4	3	22
18	Manchester City	164	45	54	65	180	222	189	4	9	18
19	Norwich City	126	43	39	44	163	180	168	3	3	20
20	Leicester City	118	31	36	51	142	175	129	3	9	21
21	Crystal Palace	122	30	37	55	119	181	127	3	19	20
22	Middlesbrough *	118	32	33	53	140	185	126	3	12	21
23	Ipswich Town	126	28	38	60	121	206	122	3	16	22
24	Derby County	76	27	20	29	97	107	101	2	9	12
25	Sheffield United	84	22	28	34	96	113	94	2	14	20
26	Oldham Athletic	84	22	23	39	105	142	89	2	19	21
27	Bolton Wanderers	76	17	18	41	80	132	69	2	18	20
28	Sunderland	38	10	10	18	35	53	40	1	18	18
29	Barnsley	38	10	5	23	37	82	35	1	19	19
30	Swindon Town	42	5	15	22	47	100	30	1	22	22

Yrs=Number of Years (seasons) competed in Premiership.
H=Highest Premiership Position. L=Lowest Premiership Position.
* Middlesbrough 3 points deducted 1996/97 season.

Positions Based on Points-Games Average

Psn		P	W	D	L	F	A	Pts	Yrs	%
1	Manchester United	240	146	60	34	446	202	498	6	69.17
2	Newcastle United	198	97	48	53	323	209	339	5	57.07
3	Blackburn Rovers	240	115	60	65	371	263	405	6	56.25
4	Liverpool	240	111	64	65	386	260	397	6	55.14
5	Arsenal	240	105	72	63	324	212	387	6	53.75
6	Aston Villa	240	99	63	78	302	263	360	6	50.00
7	Leeds United	240	90	72	78	306	280	342	6	47.50
8	Chelsea	240	88	69	83	325	304	333	6	46.25
9	Norwich City	126	43	39	44	163	180	168	3	44.44
10	Derby County	76	27	20	29	97	107	101	2	44.30
11	Tottenham Hotspur	240	83	68	89	318	328	317	6	44.03
12	QPR	164	59	39	66	224	232	216	4	43.90
13	Wimbledon	240	82	70	88	298	335	316	6	43.89
14	Sheffield Wednesday	240	80	75	85	330	341	315	6	43.75
15	Nottingham Forest	160	53	50	57	194	218	209	4	43.54
16	West Ham United	198	66	53	79	229	263	251	5	42.26
17	Everton	240	74	68	98	288	326	290	6	40.28
18	Coventry City	240	68	85	87	265	322	289	6	40.14
19	Manchester City	164	45	54	65	180	222	189	4	38.41
20	Southampton	240	70	64	106	298	353	274	6	38.06
21	Sheffield United	84	22	28	34	96	113	94	2	37.30
22	Leicester City	118	31	36	51	142	175	129	3	36.44
23	Middlesbrough *	118	32	33	53	140	185	126	3	35.59
24	Oldham Athletic	84	22	23	39	105	142	89	2	35.32
25	Sunderland	38	10	10	18	35	53	40	1	35.09
26	Crystal Palace	122	30	37	55	119	181	127	3	34.70
27	Ipswich Town	126	28	38	60	121	206	122	3	32.28
28	Barnsley	38	10	5	23	37	82	35	1	30.70
29	Bolton Wanderers	76	17	18	41	80	132	69	2	30.26
30	Swindon Town	42	5	15	22	47	100	30	1	23.81

Middlesbrough 3 points deducted 1996/97 season.

PROMOTIONS and RELEGATIONS

1997-98	Promoted	Nottingham Forest	Champions
		Middlesbrough	Runners-up
		Charlton Athletic	Play-off winners (4th)
	Relegated	Bolton Wanderers	20th
		Barnsley	21st
		Crystal Palace	22nd
1996-97	Promoted	Bolton Wanderers	Champions
		Barnsley	Runners-up
		Crystal Palace	Play-off winners (6th)
	Relegated	Sunderland	20th
		Middlesbrough	21st
		Nottingham Forest	22nd
1995-96	Promoted	Sunderland	Champions
		Derby County	Runners-up
		Leicester City	Play-off winners (5th)
	Relegated	Manchester City	20th
		QPR	21st
		Bolton Wanderers	22nd
1994-95*	Promoted	Middlesbrough	Champions
		Bolton Wanderers	Play-off winners (3rd)
	Relegated	Crystal Palace	19th
		Norwich City	20th
		Leicester City	21st
		Ipswich Town	22nd
1993-94	Promoted	Crystal Palace	Champions
		Nottingham Forest	Runners-up
		Leicester City	Play-off winners (4th)
	Relegated	Sheffield United	20th
		Oldham Athletic	21st
		Swindon Town	22nd
1992-93	Promoted	Newcastle United	Champions
		West Ham United	Runners-up
		Swindon Town	Play-off winners (5th)
	Relegated	Crystal Palace	20th
		Middlesbrough	21st
		Nottingham Forest	22nd
1991-92†	Promoted	Ipswich Town	Champions
		Middlesbrough	Runners-up
		Blackburn Rovers	Play-off winners (6th)

* FA Premier League reduced to 20 clubs.
† Promoted from Division 2 to newly formed FA Premier League.

FA PREMIER LEAGUE

	Arsenal	Aston Villa	Barnsley	Blackburn R.	Bolton W.	C. Palace	Chelsea	Coventry C.	Derby Co.	Everton
Arsenal	—	0-0	5-0	1-3	4-1	1-0	2-0	2-0	1-0	4-0
Aston Villa	1-0	—	0-1	0-4	1-3	3-1	0-2	3-0	2-1	2-1
Barnsley	0-2	0-3	—	1-1	2-1	1-0	0-6	2-0	1-0	2-2
Blackburn R.	1-4	5-0	2-1	—	3-1	2-2	1-0	0-0	1-0	3-2
Bolton W.	0-1	0-1	1-1	2-1	—	5-2	0-3	1-5	3-3	0-0
C. Palace	0-0	1-1	0-1	1-2	2-2	—	3-2	0-3	3-1	1-3
Chelsea	2-3	0-1	2-0	0-1	2-2	6-2	—	3-1	4-0	2-0
Coventry C.	2-2	1-2	1-0	2-0	4-0	1-1	0-1	—	1-0	3-1
Derby Co.	3-0	0-1	1-0	3-1	3-2	0-0	3-1	3-1	—	0-0
Everton	2-2	1-4	4-2	1-0	2-0	1-2	3-1	1-1	1-2	—
Leeds Utd	1-1	1-1	2-1	4-0	2-1	0-2	2-0	3-3	4-3	0-1
Leicester C.	3-3	1-0	1-0	1-1	1-1	1-1	4-2	1-1	1-2	1-1
Liverpool	4-0	3-0	0-1	0-0	5-0	2-1	2-2	1-0	4-0	2-0
Man Utd	0-1	1-0	7-0	4-0	0-1	2-0	3-1	3-0	2-0	1-0
Newcastle U.	0-1	1-3	2-1	1-1	1-0	1-2	1-4	0-0	0-0	3-1
Sheffield W.	2-0	1-2	2-1	0-0	1-0	1-3	1-0	1-2	2-5	3-1
Southampton	1-3	4-1	4-1	3-0	3-0	1-0	1-6	1-1	0-2	1-1
Tottenham H.	1-1	3-2	3-0	0-0	0-0	0-1	2-1	1-0	1-0	1-1
West Ham U.	0-0	2-1	6-0	2-1	3-0	4-1	0-2	0-0	0-0	2-2
Wimbledon	0-1	2-1	4-1	0-1	0-0	0-1	0-1	1-2	0-0	0-0

	Leeds U.	Leicester C.	Liverpool	Manchester U.	Newcastle Utd	Sheffield W.	Southampton	Tottenham H.	West Ham U.	Wimbledon
Arsenal	2-1	2-1	0-1	3-2	3-1	1-0	3-0	0-0	4-0	5-0
Aston Villa	1-0	1-1	2-1	0-2	0-1	2-2	1-1	4-1	2-0	1-2
Barnsley	2-3	0-2	2-3	0-2	2-2	2-1	4-3	1-1	1-2	2-1
Blackburn R.	3-4	5-3	1-1	1-3	1-0	7-2	1-0	0-3	3-0	0-0
Bolton W.	2-3	2-0	1-1	0-0	1-0	3-2	0-0	1-1	3-3	1-0
C. Palace	0-2	0-3	0-3	0-3	1-2	1-0	1-1	1-3	3-3	0-3
Chelsea	0-0	1-0	4-1	0-1	0-1	1-0	4-2	2-0	2-1	1-1
Coventry C.	0-0	0-2	1-1	3-2	2-2	1-0	1-0	4-0	1-1	0-0
Derby Co.	0-5	0-4	1-0	2-2	1-0	3-0	4-0	2-1	2-1	1-1
Everton	2-0	1-1	2-0	0-2	0-0	1-3	0-2	0-2	2-1	0-0
Leeds Utd	—	0-1	0-2	1-0	4-1	1-2	0-1	1-0	3-1	1-1
Leicester C.	1-0	—	0-0	0-0	0-0	1-1	3-3	1-0	2-1	0-1
Liverpool	3-1	1-2	—	1-3	1-0	2-1	2-3	4-0	5-0	2-0
Man Utd	3-0	0-1	1-1	—	1-1	6-1	1-0	2-0	2-1	2-0
Newcastle U.	1-1	3-3	1-2	0-1	—	2-1	2-1	1-0	0-1	1-3
Sheffield W.	1-3	1-0	3-3	2-0	2-1	—	1-0	1-0	1-1	1-1
Southampton	0-2	2-1	1-1	1-0	2-1	2-3	—	3-2	3-0	0-1
Tottenham H.	0-1	1-1	3-3	0-2	2-0	3-2	1-1	—	1-0	0-0
West Ham U.	3-0	4-3	2-1	1-1	0-1	1-0	2-1	2-1	—	3-1
Wimbledon	1-0	2-1	1-1	2-5	0-0	1-1	1-0	2-6	1-2	—

FA PREMIER LEAGUE

	Arsenal	Aston Villa	Barnsley	Blackburn R.	Bolton W.	C. Palace	Chelsea	Coventry C.	Derby Co.	Everton
Arsenal	–	38,081	38,049	38,147	38,138	38,094	38,083	37,324	38,121	38,269
Aston Villa	39,372	–	29,519	37,112	38,392	33,781	39,372	33,250	35,444	36,389
Barnsley	18,691	18,649	–	18,665	18,661	17,819	18,170	17,463	18,686	18,672
Blackburn R.	28,212	24,834	24,179	–	29,503	24,449	27,683	19,086	23,557	25,397
Bolton W.	25,000	24,196	25,000	25,000	–		24,080	25,000	23,037	23,131
C. Palace	26,180	21,097	21,547	20,849	17,134	–	26,186	21,810	18,101	23,311
Chelsea	33,012	33,018	34,442	33,311	34,845	31,917	–	34,647	36,544	34,148
Coventry C.	22,864	22,792	20,265	18,794	16,633	15,900	22,686	–	18,705	18,760
Derby Co.	30,004	30,251	27,232	27,823	29,126	26,950	30,062	29,351	–	27,828
Everton	35,457	36,471	32,659	33,423	37,149	35,716	32,355	40,109	34,876	–
Leeds Utd	37,993	36,287	37,749	32,933	31,163	29,076	37,276	36,522	33,572	34,986
Leicester C.	21,089	20,304	21,293	19,921	20,564	19,191	21,335	21,137		20,628
Liverpool	44,417	34,843	41,001	43,890	44,532		36,647	39,707	38,017	44,501
Man Utd	55,174	55,151	55,142	55,175	55,156	55,143	55,163	55,074	55,170	55,167
Newcastle U.	36,571	36,783	36,534	36,716	36,767	36,565	36,710	36,767	36,289	36,705
Sheffield W.	34,373	34,177	29,086	33,502	25,067	22,072	28,334	21,087	22,391	24,486
Southampton	15,246	15,238	15,018	15,206	15,206	15,032	15,231	15,091	15,202	15,102
Tottenham H.	29,610	26,317	28,232	26,573	29,032	25,634	28,476	33,463	25,886	35,624
West Ham U.	25,717	24,976	23,714	24,733	24,867	23,335	25,829	22,477	25,155	25,905
Wimbledon	22,291	13,131	7,976	15,600	11,356	16,747	22,237	11,210	13,031	15,131

	Leeds U.	Leicester C.	Liverpool	Manchester U.	Newcastle Utd	Sheffield W.	Southampton	Tottenham H.	West Ham U.	Wimbledon
Arsenal	38,018	38,023	38,094	38,083	38,102	38,087	38,056	38,102	38,012	38,024
Aston Villa	39,027	36,429	39,377	39,372	38,266	32,044	29,343	38,644	39,372	32,087
Barnsley	18,690	18,660	18,684	18,694	18,687	18,692	18,368	18,692	18,667	17,102
Blackburn R.	21,956	24,854	30,187	30,547	29,300	19,618	24,130	30,388	21,653	24,848
Bolton W.	25,000	25,000	25,000	25,000	24,494	24,847	23,333	23,433	25,000	22,703
C. Palace	25,248	18,771	25,790	26,180	26,085	16,876	22,853	26,116	19,129	14,410
Chelsea	34,690	33,356	34,639	34,511	31,563	29,075	30,008	34,149	34,382	34,100
Coventry C.	17,770	18,309	22,721	23,054	22,679	18,375	18,659	19,499	18,289	17,968
Derby Co.	30,217	29,855	30,492	30,014	30,302	30,203	25,625	30,187	29,300	28,595
Everton	37,099	33,642	41,112	40,079	37,972	35,497	29,958	36,670	34,356	28,533
Leeds Utd	—	29,620	39,775	39,952	39,834	20,800	28,791	31,394	30,031	38,172
Leicester C.	21,244	—	21,633	21,221	21,699	20,680	20,708	20,683	20,021	18,553
Liverpool	43,854	35,007	—	41,027	42,791	34,705	43,550	38,005	44,414	55,306
Man Utd	55,167	55,156	55,171	—	55,194	55,259	55,008	55,281	55,068	36,256
Newcastle U.	36,511	36,574	36,718	36,767	—	36,771	37,759	36,709	36,736	22,655
Sheffield W.	31,520	24,851	35,405	39,427	29,446	—	29,677	29,871	28,036	14,815
Southampton	15,102	15,121	15,252	15,241	15,251	15,442	—	15,225	15,212	26,261
Tottenham H.	26,441	28,355	30,245	26,359	35,847	25,097	35,995	—	30,284	24,516
West Ham U.	24,107	25,781	25,908	25,892	25,884	24,344	25,908	25,354	—	—
Wimbledon	15,718	13,229	26,106	26,309	15,478	11,503	12,009	25,820	22,087	—

FA PREMIER LEAGUE RECORDS 1997-98

SCORERS

Top Scorers – All Competitions

Player	Club	L	F	C	E	Total
Andy COLE	Manchester United	15	5	0	5	25
John HARTSON	West Ham United	15	3	6	0	24
Dion DUBLIN	Coventry City	18	4	1	0	23
Michael OWEN	Liverpool	18	0	4	1	23
Jimmy HASSELBAINK	Leeds United	16	4	2	0	22
Dennis BERGKAMP	Arsenal	16	3	2	1	22
Chris SUTTON	Blackburn Rovers	18	2	1	0	21
Kevin GALLACHER	Blackburn Rovers	16	3	1	0	20
Gianluca VIALLI	Chelsea	11	2	0	6	19
Paulo WANCHOPE	Derby County	13	0	4	0	17

L=League, F=FA Cup, C=Coca-Cola Cup, E=Europe

FA Carling Premiership Top Scorers

Player	Club	Goals	All-time Total
Dion DUBLIN	Coventry City	18	61
Michael OWEN	Liverpool	18	19
Chris SUTTON	Blackburn Rovers	18	77
Dennis BERGKAMP	Arsenal	16	39
Kevin GALLACHER	Blackburn Rovers	16	47
Jimmy HASSELBAINK	Leeds United	16	16
Andy COLE	Manchester United	15	88
John HARTSON	West Ham United	15	34
Darren HUCKERBY	Coventry City	14	19
Paulo WANCHOPE	Derby County	13	14
Francesco BAIANO	Derby County	12	12
Nathan BLAKE	Bolton Wanderers	12	13
Paolo DI CANIO	Sheffield Wednesday	12	12
Marc OVERMARS	Arsenal	12	12
Dwight YORKE	Aston Villa	12	60

FA Carling Premiership Club Top Scorers

Club	Scorers
Arsenal	16 – Bergkamp; 12 – Overmars; 10 – Wright
Aston Villa	12 – Yorke; 8 – Joachim; 7 – Milosevic
Barnsley	10 – Redfearn; 8 – Ward; 6 – Fjortoft
Blackburn Rovers	18 – Sutton; 16 Gallacher; 5 – Sherwood
Bolton Wanderers	12 – Blake; 9 – Thompson
Chelsea	11 – Flo, Vialli; 9 – M. Hughes; 8 – Zola
Coventry City	18 – Dublin; 14 – Huckerby; 6 – Whelan
Crystal Palace	7 – Shipperley; 5 – Bent, Lombardo
Derby County	13– Wanchope; 12 – Baiano, 9 – Sturridge
Everton	11 – Ferguson; 7 – Speed; 6 – Madar
Leeds United	16 – Hasselbaink; 10 – Radebe
Leicester City	10 – Heskey; 7 – Elliott
Liverpool	18 – Owen; 11 – McManaman; 9 – Fowler
Manchester United	16 – Cole; 9 – Sheringham; 8 – Giggs, Scholes
Newcastle United	6 – Barnes; 4 – Lee, Gillespie
Sheffield Wednesday	12 – Di Canio; 9 – Carbone
Southampton	11 – Le Tissier, Ostenstad; 9 – Davies, Hirst
Tottenham Hotspur	9 – Klinsmann; 5 – Ferdinand, Armstrong
West Ham United	15 – Hartson; 7 – Berkovic, Sinclair
Wimbledon	4 – Cort, Ekoku, Euell, M. Hughes, Leaburn

FA Carling Premiership Hat-tricks

Player	Goals	Match (result)	Date
D. Dublin	3	COVENTRY C. v Chelsea	9 -Aug-97
G. Vialli	4	Barnsley v CHELSEA	24-Aug-97
D. Bergkamp	3	Leicester City v ARSENAL	27-Aug-97
I. Wright	3	ARSENAL v Bolton W.	13-Sep-97
P. Berger	3	LIVERPOOL v Chelsea	6-Oct-98
A. Cole	3	MANCHESTER U. v Barnsley	25-Oct-97
A. Booth	3	SHEFFIELD W. v Bolton W.	8-Nov-97
G. Zola	3	CHELSEA v Derby Co.	29-Nov-97
T. A. Flo	3	Tottenham H. v CHELSEA	6-Dec-97
D. Ferguson	3	EVERTON v Bolton W.	28-Dec-97
K. Gallacher	3	BLACKBURN R. v Aston Villa	17-Jan-98
M. Owen	3	Sheffield W. v LIVERPOOL	14-Feb-98
C. Sutton	3	BLACKBURN R. v Leicester C.	28-Feb-98
D. Huckerby	3	Leeds U. v COVENTRY C.	25-Apr-98
J. Klinsmann	4	Wimbledon v TOTTENHAM H.	2-May-98

ATTENDANCES

Top Attendances by Club and Number

Club	Posn	Total	Ave
Manchester United 1		1,048,125	55,164
Liverpool 3		771,926	40,628
Arsenal 2		722,907	38,048
Newcastle United 13		697,208	36,695
Aston Villa 7		686,592	36,136
Everton 17		673,133	35,428
Leeds United 5		658,292	34,647
Chelsea 4		636,357	33,492
Tottenham Hotspur 14		553,731	29,144
Derby County 9		553,417	29,127
Sheffield Wednesday 16		545,463	28,709
Blackburn Rovers 6		483,804	25,463
West Ham United 8		474,402	24,969
Bolton Wanderers 18		462,703	24,353
Crystal Palace 20		417,673	21,983
Leicester City 10		391,409	20,600
Coventry City 11		374,722	19,722
Barnsley 19		350,412	18,443
Wimbledon 15		316,969	16,683
Southampton 12		288,189	15,168
Totals		*11,107,434*	*29,230*

CLUBS BY TOTAL NUMBER OF PLAYERS USED

		Total	Start	Sub	Snu	Ps
1	West Ham U.	469	418	51	139	51
2	Aston Villa	472	418	55	135	55
3	Coventry C.	473	418	55	135	55
4	Leeds United	473	418	55	135	55
5	Liverpool	477	418	59	131	59
6	Bolton W.	480	418	62	128	62
7	Newcastle U.	480	418	62	128	62
8	Wimbledon	487	418	69	121	69

9	Blackburn R.	 492	418	74	116	74
10	Manchester U.	 494	418	76	114	76
11	Leicester C.	 497	418	79	111	79
12	Crystal Palace	 499	418	81	109	81
13	Chelsea	 500	418	82	108	82
14	Everton	 503	418	85	105	85
15	Arsenal	 504	418	86	104	86
16	Sheffield W.	 505	418	87	103	87
17	Southampton	 505	418	87	103	87
18	Derby County	 507	418	89	101	89
19	Tottenham H.	 507	418	89	100	89
20	Barnsley	 511	418	93	97	93

BOOKINGS & DISMISSALS

Players Sent Off

Player	Match	Date	Official
David Batty	NEWCASTLE U. v Aston Villa	23/08/97	GS Willard
Benito Carbone	Blackburn R. v SHEFFIELD W.	25/08/97	JT Winter
Frank Sinclair	CHELSEA v Southampton	30/08/97	AB Wilkie
Justin Edinburgh	Arsenal v TOTTENHAM H.	30/08/97	GS Willard
Andy Hinchcliffe	Derby Co. v EVERTON	13/09/97	MA Riley
Harry Kewell	Blackburn R. v LEEDS U.	14/09/97	SW Dunn
Patrick Valery	Tottenham H. v BLACKBURN R.	20/09/97	GP Barber
Nathan Blake	BOLTON W. v Manchester U.	20/09/97	PA Durkin
Gary Pallister	Bolton W. v MANCHESTER U.	20/09/97	PA Durkin
Frank Leboeuf	CHELSEA v Arsenal	21/09/97	DJ Gallagher
Slaven Bilic	Newcastle U. v EVERTON	24/09/97	G Poll
Patrick Blondeau	SHEFFIELD W. v Derby Co.	24/09/97	MD Reed
Jason Wilcox	BLACKBURN R. v Coventry C.	28/09/97	P Jones
Dion Dublin	Blackburn R. v COVENTRY C.	28/09/97	P Jones
Stan Collymore	Bolton W. v ASTON VILLA	04/10/97	G Poll
Andy Todd	BOLTON W. v Aston Villa	04/10/97	G Poll
Bernard Lambourde	Liverpool v CHELSEA	05/10/97	DR Elleray
Gerry Taggart	West Ham v BOLTON W.	18/10/97	GR Ashby
Emmanuel Petit	ARSENAL v Aston Villa	26/10/97	PA Durkin
Emile Heskey	Newcastle U. v LEICESTER C.	01/11/97	GS Willard
Robbie Fowler	Bolton W. v LIVERPOOL	01/11/97	DJ Gallagher
Jamie Smith	C. PALACE v Aston Villa	08/11/97	JT Winter
Slaven Bilic	Chelsea v EVERTON	26/11/97	NS Barry
Chris Sutton	Manchester U. v BLACKBURN R.	30/11/97	AB Wilkie
Alan Thompson	Blackburn R. v BOLTON W.	06/12/97	MA Riley

Paul Williams	Aston Villa v COVENTRY C.	06/12/97	GP Barber
Gary Breen	Aston Villa v COVENTRY C.	06/12/97	GP Barber
Marc Edworthy	Leicester C. v C. PALACE	06/12/97	UD Rennie
Alf Inge Haaland	Chelsea v LEEDS U.	13/12/97	G Poll
Gary Kelly	Chelsea v LEEDS U.	13/12/97	G Poll
Stefano Eranio	Newcastle U. v DERBY CO.	17/12/97	KW Burge
Steve Lomas	Blackburn R. v WEST HAM U.	20/12/97	GR Ashby
George Boateng	West Ham U. v COVENTRY C.	26/12/97	G Poll
David Batty	Derby Co. v NEWCASTLE U.	26/12/97	MD Reed
Dejan Stefanovic	Leicester C. v SHEFFIELD W.	28/12/97	G Poll
Ben Thatcher	WIMBLEDON v West Ham U.	28/12/97	PA Durkin
Francis Benali	Bolton W. v SOUTHAMPTON	10/01/98	GS Willard
Patrick Vieira	Coventry C. v ARSENAL	17/01/98	SJ Lodge
Paul Williams	COVENTRY C. v Arsenal	17/01/98	SJ Lodge
Samassi Abou	Tottenham H. v WEST HAM U.	17/01/98	DR Elleray
Duncan Ferguson	EVERTON v Derby Co.	14/02/98	SW Dunn
John Hartson	Bolton W. v WEST HAM U.	21/02/98	PE Alcock
Carlton Palmer	Leeds U. v SOUTHAMPTON	28/02/98	KW Burge
Slaven Bilic	Southampton v EVERTON	07/03/98	DR Elleray
Ken Monkou	SOUTHAMPTON v Everton	07/03/98	DR Elleray
Darren Barnard	BARNSLEY v Liverpool	28/03/98	GS Willard
Chris Morgan	BARNSLEY v Liverpool	28/03/98	GS Willard
Darren Sheridan	BARNSLEY v Liverpool	28/03/98	GS Willard
Gudni Bergsson	BOLTON W. v Leicester C.	28/03/98	UD Rennie
Robert Ullathorne	Bolton W. v LEICESTER C.	28/03/98	UD Rennie
Martin Keown	Bolton W. v ARSENAL	31/03/98	KW Burge
Georgi Hristov	Leeds U. v BARNSLEY	04/04/98	KW Burge
Michael Owen	Manchester U. v LIVERPOOL	10/04/98	G Poll
Jason Wilcox	Bolton W. v BLACKBURN R.	11/04/98	MA Riley
Lucas Radebe	Everton v LEEDS U.	11/04/98	UD Rennie
John Hartson	WEST HAM U. v Derby Co.	11/04/98	GP Barber
David Unsworth	WEST HAM U. v C. Palace	12/04/98	G.Poll
Ole Gunnar Solskjaer	MANCHESTER U. v Newcastle U.	18/04/98	UD Rennie
Ramon Vega	Barnsley v TOTTENHAM H.	18/04/98	MJ Bodenham
Andy Booth	Everton v SHEFFIELD W.	25/04/98	GP Barber
Tim Flowers	Coventry C. v BLACKBURN R.	02/05/98	SJ Lodge
Valerien Ismael	Bolton W. v C. PALACE	02/05/98	NS Barry
Francis Benali	SOUTHAMPTON v Derby Co.	02/05/98	MA Riley
Ben Thatcher	WIMBLEDON v Tottenham H.	02/05/98	GP Barber
Jovo Bosancic	Leicester C. v BARNSLEY	02/05/98	DJ Gallagher
Gunnar Halle	Manchester U. v LEEDS U.	04/05/98	GS Willard
David Unsworth	Crystal Palace v WEST HAM U.	05/05/98	G Poll
David Batty	NEWCASTLE U. v Blackburn R.	10/05/98	DR Elleray
Ugo Ehiogu	ASTON VILLA v Arsenal	10/05/98	G Poll

The number of yellows and reds shown by card sharks increased last season. While there was only a small increase on the yellow front, there was a staggering 100% increase in dismissals. Up from 31 reds to 69, and this after the number had fallen during the 1996-97 season. Gary Willard topped the yellow chart by increasing his brandishing by 20 over 1997-98. Graham Poll swept away all-comers in the red card league with a massive 11 *cartes rouges*. He showed just one red in 1996-97! General consensus though was that newly promoted Uriah Rennie was the best Man in Black for 1997-98. The average listed below is for yellow cards per game.

	Referee	*Matches*	*Yellow*	*Red*	*Average*
1	WILLARD, Gary … … … … … 20		87	8	4.35
2	REED, Mike … … … … … 18		*16*	2	4.22
3	POLL, Graham … … … … … 21		83	11	3.95
4	WINTER, Jeff … … … … … 20		79	2	3.95
5	RENNIE, Uriah … … … … … 19		75	5	3.95
6	BARBER, Graham … … … … … 23		90	6	3.91
7	ELLERAY, David … … … … … 17		62	5	3.65
8	BARRY, Neale … … … … … 19		69	2	3.63
9	WILKIE, Alan … … … … … 19		67	2	3.53
10	DURKIN, Paul … … … … … 17		59	4	3.47
11	DUNN, Steve … … … … … 16		54	2	3.38
12	RILEY, Mike … … … … … 20		65	4	3.25
13	BODENHAM, Martin … … … 21		63	1	3.00
14	JONES, Peter … … … … … 18		53	2	2.94
15	ASHBY, Gerald … … … … … 19		55	2	2.89
16	ALCOCK, Paul … … … … … 19		54	1	2.84
17	GALLAGHER, Dermot … … … 19		51	3	2.68
18	BURGE, Keith … … … … … 19		49	4	2.58
19	LODGE, Steve … … … … … 19		47	3	2.47
			1238	*69*	

Club	*No.*	*Player(s)*
Arsenal	3	Keown, Petit, Vieira
Aston Villa	2	Collymore, Ehiogu
Barnsley	5	Barnard, Bosancic, Hristov, Morgan, Sheridan
Blackburn Rovers	5	Flowers, Sutton, Wilcox (2), Valery
Bolton Wanderers	5	Bergsson, Blake, Taggart, Thompson, Todd
Chelsea	3	Lambourde, Leboeuf, Sinclair
Coventry City	5	Dublin, Boateng, Breen, Williams (2)
Crystal Palace	3	Edworthy, Ismael, Smith

Derby County	1	Eranio
Everton	5	Bilic (3), Hinchcliffe, Ferguson
Leeds	5	Haaland, Halle, Kelly, Kewell, Radebe
Leicester City	2	Heskey, Ullathorne
Liverpool	2	Fowler, Owen
Manchester United	2	Pallister, Solskjaer
Newcastle United	3	Batty (3)
Sheffield Wednesday	4	Blondeau, Booth, Carbone, Stefanovic
Southampton	4	Benali (2), Monkou, Palmer
Tottenham Hotspur	2	Edinburgh, Vega
West Ham United	6	Abou, Hartson (2), Lomas, Unsworth (2)
Wimbledon	2	Thatcher (2)

Referees – Who They Sent Off

Referee	No.	Players
POLL	11	Bilic, Boateng, Collymore, Ehiogu, Haaland, Kelly, Owen, Stefanovic, Todd, Unsworth (2)
WILLARD	8	Barnard, Batty, Benali, Edinburgh, Halle, Heskey, Morgan, Sheridan
BARBER	6	Ferguson, Kewell
ELLERAY	5	Abou, Batty, Bilic, Lambourde, Monkou
RENNIE	5	Bergsson, Edworthy, Radebe, Solskjaer, Ullathorne
BURGE	4	Eranio, Hristov, Keown, Palmer
DURKIN	4	Blake, Pallister, Petit, Thatcher
RILEY	4	Benali, Hinchcliffe, Thompson, Wilcox
GALLAGHER	3	Bosancic, Fowler, Leboeuf
LODGE	3	Flowers, Vieira, Williams
ASHBY	2	Lomas, Taggart
BARRY	2	Bilic, Ismael
DUNN	2	Ferguson, Kewell
JONES	2	Dublin, Wilcox
REED	2	Batty, Blondeau
WILKIE	2	Sinclair, Sutton
WINTER	2	Carbone, Smith
ALCOCK	1	Hartson
BODENHAM	1	Vega

SCORES

Highest Aggregate Scorers

9   7-2   Blackburn Rovers v Sheffield Wednesday

Biggest Home Wins

7-0   Manchester United v Barnsley
7-2   Blackburn Rovers v Sheffield Wednesday
6-0   West Ham United v Barnsley
6-1   Manchester United v Sheffield Wednesday
6-2   Chelsea v Crystal Palace

Biggest Away Wins

0-6   Barnsley v Chelsea
1-6   Tottenham Hotspur v Chelsea
2-6   Wimbledon v Tottenham Hotspur

Highest Score Draw

3-3   Newcastle United v Leicester City
        Bolton Wanderers v Derby County
        Leicester City v Arsenal

FA PREMIER LEAGUE ALL-TIME RECORDS

Premiership Titles by Number

4	Manchester United	1992-93, 1993-94, 1995-96, 1996-97
1	Arsenal	1997-98
1	Blackburn Rovers	1994-95

Premiership Runners-up by Number

2	Manchester United	1994-95, 1997-98
2	Newcastle United	1995-96, 1996-97
1	Aston Villa	1992-93
1	Blackburn Rovers	1993-94

Championship Records

	Season	Champions	P	W	D	L	F	A	Pts	%
1	1992-93	Manchester United	42	24	12	6	67	31	84	66.67
2	1993-94	Manchester United	42	27	11	4	80	38	92	73.02
3	1994-95	Blackburn Rovers	42	27	8	7	80	39	89	70.63
4	1995-96	Manchester United	38	25	7	6	73	35	82	71.93
5	1996-97	Manchester United	38	21	12	5	76	44	75	65.79
6	1997-98	Arsenal	38	23	9	6	68	33	78	68.42

All-Time Biggest Home Wins

9-0	Manchester United v Ipswich Town	04/03/95
7-0	Blackburn Rovers v Nottingham Forest	18/11/95
7-0	Manchester United v Barnsley	25/10/97
7-1	Aston Villa v Wimbledon	11/02/93
7-1	Blackburn Rovers v Norwich City	02/10/92
7-1	Newcastle United v Swindon Town	12/03/94
7-1	Everton v Southampton	28/12/96
7-1	Newcastle United v Tottenham Hotspur	05/03/97
7-2	Blackburn Rovers v Sheffield Wednesday	28/08/97

All-Time Biggest Away Wins

1-7	Sheffield Wednesday v Nottingham Forest	01/04/95
0-6	Bolton Wanderers v Manchester United	25/02/96
1-6	Crystal Palace v Liverpool	20/08/94
1-6	Tottenham Hotspur v Chelsea	02/05/98
2-6	Wimbledon v Tottenham Hotspur	06/12/97
0-5	Swindon Town v Liverpool	22/08/93
0-5	Swindon Town v Leeds United	07/05/94

All-Time Highest Aggregate Scores

9	9-0	Manchester United v Ipswich Town	04/03/95
	7-2	Blackburn Rovers v Sheffield United	11/03/98
	6-3	Southampton v Manchester United	26/10/96

All-Time Highest Score Draw

4-4	Aston Villa v Leicester City	22/02/95

All-Time General Records

Most Goals Scored in a Season	Newcastle United	84	1993-94	42
	Manchester United	76	1996-97	38
Fewest Goals Scored in a Season	Crystal Palace	34	1994-95	42
	Manchester City	31	1996-97	38
Most Goals Conceded in a Season	Swindon Town	100	1993-94	42
	Barnsley	82	1997-98	38
Fewest Goals Conceded in a Season	Arsenal	28	1993-94	42
	Manchester United	28	1994-95	42
	Manchester United	26	1997-87	38
Most Points in a Season	Manchester United	92	1993-94	42
	Manchester United	82	1995-96	38
Fewest Points in a Season	Ipswich Town	27	1994-95	42
Most Wins in a Season	Manchester United	27	1993-94	42
	Blackburn Rovers	27	1994-95	42
Fewest Wins in a Season	Swindon Town	5	1993-94	42
Fewest Defeats in a Season	Manchester United	4	1993-94	42
Most Defeats in a Season	Ipswich Town	29	1994-95	42
	Bolton Wanderers	25	1995-96	38

Most Draws in a Season	Manchester City	18	1993-94	42
	Sheffield United	18	1993-94	42
	Southampton	18	1994-95	42
	Nottingham Forest	16	1996-97	38
	Coventry City	16	1997-98	38

NB: 38 or 42 refers to the number of games played in that season.

Record Attendances by Club

Club	Att	Opponents	Date
Arsenal	38,377	Tottenham Hotspur	29/04/95
Aston Villa	45,347	Liverpool	07/05/94
Blackburn Rovers	30,895	Liverpool	24/02/95
Bolton Wanderers	25,000	multiple occasions	1997-98
Chelsea	37,064	Manchester United	11/09/93
Coventry City	24,410	Manchester United	12/04/94
Crystal Palace	30,115	Manchester United	21/04/93
Derby County	30,492	Liverpool	10/05/98
Everton	40,177	Liverpool	16/04/97
Ipswich Town	22,559	Manchester United	01/05/94
Leeds United	41,125	Manchester United	27/04/94
Leicester City	21,699	Newcastle United	29/04/97
Liverpool	44,619	Everton	20/03/93
Manchester City	37,136	Manchester United	20/03/93
Manchester United	55,314	Wimbledon	29/01/97
Middlesbrough	30,215	Tottenham Hotspur	19/10/96
Newcastle United	36,783	Aston Villa	23/08/97
Norwich City	21,843	Liverpool	29/04/95
Nottingham Forest	29,263	Manchester United	27/11/95
Queens Park Rangers	21,267	Manchester United	05/02/94
Sheffield United	30,044	Sheffield Wednesday	23/10/93
Sheffield Wednesday	38,943	Liverpool	11/05/97
Southampton	19,654	Tottenham Hotspur	15/08/92
Sunderland	22,512	Derby County	26/12/96
Swindon Town	18,108	Manchester United	19/03/94
Tottenham Hotspur	35,624	Everton	04/04/98
West Ham United	28,832	Manchester United	25/02/94
Wimbledon	30,115	Manchester United	08/05/93

Top 10 Attendances

Psn	Att	Match	Date
1	55,314	Manchester United v Wimbledon	29/01/97
2	55,306	Manchester United v Wimbledon	28/03/98

3	55,281	Manchester United v Tottenham Hotspur	10/01/98
4	55,269	Manchester United v Southampton	01/02/97
5	55,267	Manchester United v Sheffield Wednesday	15/03/97
6	55,259	Manchester United v Sheffield Wednesday	01/11/97
7	55,256	Manchester United v Leeds United	28/12/96
8	55,249	Manchester United v West Ham United	12/05/97
9	55,243	Manchester United v Derby County	05/04/97
10	55,236	Manchester United v Newcastle United	08/05/97

Biggest attendance not at Old Trafford

| | 45,347 | Aston Villa v Liverpool | 07/05/94 |

Lowest Attendances by Club

Club	Att	Opponents	Date
Arsenal	18,253	Wimbledon	10/02/92
Aston Villa	16,180	Southampton	24/11/93
Barnsley	17,102	Wimbledon	28/02/98
Blackburn Rovers	13,505	Sheffield United	18/10/93
Bolton Wanderers	16,216	Wimbledon	13/01/96
Chelsea	8,923	Coventry City	04/05/94
Coventry City	9,526	Ipswich Town	10/10/94
Crystal Palace	10,422	Sheffield Wednesday	14/03/95
Derby County	17,022	Wimbledon	28/09/96
Everton	13,660	Southampton	04/12/93
Ipswich Town	10,747	Sheffield United	21/08/93
Leeds United	25,774	Wimbledon	15/08/92
Leicester City	15,489	Wimbledon	01/04/95
Liverpool	24,561	QPR	08/12/93
Manchester City	19,150	West Ham United	24/08/85
Manchester United	29,736	Crystal Palace	02/09/92
Middlesbrough	12,290	Oldham Athletic	22/03/93
Newcastle United	32,067	Southampton	22/01/94
Norwich City	12,452	Southampton	05/09/92
Nottingham Forest	17,525	Blackburn Rovers	25/11/96
Oldham Athletic	9,633	Wimbledon	28/08/93
Queens Park Rangers	9,875	Swindon Town	30/04/94
Sheffield United	13,646	West Ham United	28/03/94
Sheffield Wednesday	16,390	Nottingham Forest	18/11/96
Southampton	9,028	Ipswich Town	08/12/93
Sunderland	18,642	West Ham United	08/09/96
Swindon Town	11,970	Oldham Athletic	18/08/93
Tottenham Hotspur	17,452	Aston Villa	02/03/94
West Ham United	15,777	Swindon Town	11/09/93
Wimbledon	3,039	Everton	26/01/93

Lowest 10 Attendances

Psn	Att	Match	Date
1	3,039	Wimbledon v Everton	26/01/93
2	3,386	Wimbledon v Oldham Athletic	12/12/92
3	3,759	Wimbledon v Coventry City	22/08/92
4	3,979	Wimbledon v Sheffield United	20/02/93
5	4,534	Wimbledon v Southampton	06/03/93
6	4,714	Wimbledon v Manchester City	01/09/92
7	4,739	Wimbledon v Coventry City	26/12/93
8	4,954	Wimbledon v Ipswich Town	18/08/92
9	5,268	Wimbledon v Manchester City	21/03/95
10	5,536	Wimbledon v Sheffield Wednesday	15/01/94

Despite taking a clean sweep in the lowest ever attendances in the Premiership, Wimbledon have been involved in the fixtures that provided the two biggest Premiership attendances ever – Manchester United v Wimbledon!

THE GOALSCORERS

Top Goalscorers by Player

S/R=Strike rate – number of games per goal, ie Alan Shearer has a S/R of 1.34 – he scores a goal every 1.34 games on average. Club is the club where player made his last Premiership appearance as of the end of the 1997-98 season.

Player	Club	Goals	Tot	S/R	St	Sub
SHEARER Alan	Newcastle United	139	186	1.34	178	8
FERDINAND Les	Tottenham Hotspur	106	199	1.88	195	4
WRIGHT Ian	Arsenal	104	191	1.84	182	9
FOWLER Robbie	Liverpool	92	160	1.74	156	4
LE TISSIER Matthew	Southampton	91	210	2.31	203	7
COLE Andy	Manchester United	88	163	1.85	148	15
SHERINGHAM Teddy	Manchester United	85	199	2.34	193	6
SUTTON Chris	Blackburn Rovers	77	192	2.49	181	11
CANTONA Eric	Manchester United	70	156	2.23	154	2
HOLDSWORTH Dean	Bolton Wanderers	61	189	3.10	165	24
DUBLIN Dion	Coventry City	61	147	2.41	138	9
HUGHES Mark	Chelsea	60	206	3.43	198	8
BEARDSLEY Peter	Bolton Wanderers	60	185	3.08	179	6
YORKE Dwight	Aston Villa	60	178	2.97	159	19

COTTEE Tony	Leicester City	55	154	2.80	134	20
COLLYMORE Stan	Aston Villa	55	124	2.25	114	10
RUSH Ian	Newcastle United	48	176	3.67	158	18
ARMSTRONG Chris	Tottenham Hotspur	48	142	2.96	136	6
BRIGHT Mark	Sion	48	138	2.88	117	21
DEANE Brian	Leeds United	47	179	3.81	172	7
GALLACHER Kevin	Blackburn Rovers	47	143	3.04	135	8
EKOKU Efan	Wimbledon	46	138	3.00	117	21
GIGGS Ryan	Manchester United	45	196	4.36	184	12

All-Time Player: Most Goals in One Game

Gls	Player	Match	Date	Res
5	Andy COLE	MANCHESTER U. v Ipswich T.	04/03/95	9-0
4	Efan EKOKU	Everton v NORWICH C.	25/09/93	1-5
	Robbie FOWLER	LIVERPOOL v Middlesbrough	14/12/96	5-1
	Gianluca VIALLI	Barnsley v CHELSEA	24/08/97	6-0
	Jurgen KLINSMANN	Wimbledon v TOTTENHAM H.	02/05/98	6-2

Player: Consecutive Games with Goals

7   Mark Stein, Chelsea   1993-94

Dec 27	Southampton	Away	1-3	Stein
Dec 28	Newcastle United	Home	1-0	Stein
Jan 1	Swindon Town	Away	3-0	Stein
Jan 3	Everton	Home	4-2	Stein x 2 (1 penalty)
Jan 15	Norwich City	Away	1-1	Stein
Jan 22	Aston Villa	Home	1-1	Stein
Feb 5	Everton	Away	2-4	Stein x 2 (1 penalty)

*(Stein actually scored 9 goals – inc. two penalties – in this sequence.
These goals were scored in consecutive Chelsea matches as well.)*

7   Alan Shearer, Newcastle United   1996-97

Sep 14	Blackburn Rovers	Home	2-1	Shearer (penalty)
Sep 21	Leeds United	Away	1-0	Shearer
Sep 30	Aston Villa	Home	4-3	Shearer
Oct 12	Derby Co.	Away	1-0	Shearer
Oct 20	Manchester United	Home	5-0	Shearer
Nov 23	Chelsea	Away	1-1	Shearer
Nov 30	Arsenal	Home	1-2	Shearer

(Newcastle played Leicester City, Middlesbrough and West Ham after playing Man. United and before Chelsea but Shearer was injured for these matches.)

Fastest Goals in a Game

13 seconds	Chris Sutton	BLACKBURN ROVERS v Everton	01/04/94
17 seconds	John Spencer	CHELSEA v Leicester City	08/10/94

Fastest Hat-trick in a Game

4 min 33 secs	Robbie Fowler LIVERPOOL v Arsenal	28/08/94

Player: Most Hat-tricks in a Season

5   Alan Shearer, Blackburn Rovers   1995-96
     v Coventry City, Nottingham Forest, West Ham United, Bolton Wanderers
       and Tottenham Hotspur

Player: Hat-trick Hall of Fame

No.	Player	Team(s)
9	Alan Shearer	Blackburn Rovers and Newcastle United
5	Robbie Fowler	Liverpool
	Ian Wright	Arsenal
4	Matt Le Tissier	Southampton
	Andy Cole	Newcastle United

THE GOALKEEPERS

Goalkeepers by Total App-Goals Ratio

Surname	Club	App	Sub	GA	GkA	CS	GaR
SEAMAN	Arsenal	200	0	212	169	86	0.85
SCHMEICHEL	Manchester United	220	0	202	187	105	0.85
SPINK	Aston Villa	51	4	181	50	15	0.91
JAMES	Liverpool	187	1	260	184	66	0.98
SRNICEK	Newcastle United	96	1	209	95	33	0.98
DE GOEY	Chelsea	32	0	43	32	12	1.00
HISLOP	Newcastle United	53	0	121	54	13	1.02
HOOPER	Newcastle United	31	3	143	35	10	1.03
MIMMS	Blackburn Rovers	59	2	168	66	22	1.08
FLOWERS	Blackburn Rovers	219	1	344	243	67	1.10
BOSNICH	Aston Villa	163	0	263	183	54	1.12
COTON	Sunderland	103	1	217	117	27	1.13
BEENEY	Leeds United	35	0	242	40	13	1.14

LUKIC	Arsenal	144	0	228	169	49	1.17
MARTYN	Leeds United	153	0	194	184	56	1.20
HITCHCOCK	Chelsea	55	3	261	70	9	1.21
KELLER	Leicester City	64	0	95	78	23	1.22
THORSTVEDT	Tottenham Hotspur	60	0	183	76	14	1.27
WOODS	Southampton	69	1	279	89	17	1.27
KHARINE	Chelsea	113	0	304	146	38	1.29
STEJSKAL	QPR	41	0	116	53	11	1.29
SEGERS	Wimbledon	116	2	243	153	30	1.30

Key: GA=Goals conceded by team overall; GkA=Goals conceded by goalkeeper; CS =number of Clean Sheets; GaR=GkA divided by total appearances (App+Sub) to give number of goals conceded per game on average. Only players with a ration of 1.30 or less are listed. A minimum of 30 games are required to qualify for the rating. Club list is the last club played for in the Premiership.

Goalkeepers by Total Most Clean Sheets

Surname	Club	CS	Apps	Sub	%
SCHMEICHEL	Manchester United	105	220	0	47.73
SEAMAN	Arsenal	86	200	0	43.00
FLOWERS	Blackburn Rovers	67	219	1	30.45
JAMES	Liverpool	66	187	1	35.11
SOUTHALL	Everton	62	207	0	29.95
MARTYN	Leeds United	56	153	0	36.60
BOSNICH	Aston Villa	54	163	0	33.13
LUKIC	Arsenal	49	144	0	34.03
OGRIZOVIC	Coventry City	47	186	0	25.27
MIKLOSKO	West Ham United	47	170	0	27.65
WALKER	Tottenham Hotspur	45	172	1	26.01
PRESSMAN	Sheffield Wednesday	41	173	0	23.70
KHARINE	Chelsea	38	113	0	33.63
CROSSLEY	Nottingham Forest	36	150	0	24.00
SULLIVAN	Wimbledon	34	103	1	32.69

Goalkeepers by Consecutive Shut-outs

Surname	Club	CSO	Rp	CS	Season
SOUTHALL	Everton	7	0	14	1994-95
MANINGER	Arsenal	6	0	6	1997-98
SEAMAN	Arsenal	5	0	10	1996-97
SCHMEICHEL	Manchester United	5	0	17	1997-98
WALKER	Tottenham Hotspur	5	0	11	1995-96

JAMES	Liverpool	5	0	12	1996-97
SEAMAN	Arsenal	5	2	20	1993-94
WALKER	Tottenham Hotspur	5	0	11	1994-95
SCHMEICHEL	Manchester United	5	0	18	1992-93

CSO=Consecutive shut-outs (number of full games without conceding a goal); Rp=No. of times repeated; CS=Clean Sheets.

Goalkeepers by Most Clean Sheets/Season

Surname	Club	CS	Apps	%	GkA	Season
SCHMEICHEL	Manchester United	24	32	75.00	22	1994-95
SEAMAN	Arsenal	20	39	51.28	24	1993-94
MARTYN	Leeds United	20	37	54.05	38	1996-97
SCHMEICHEL	Manchester United	18	36	50.00	38	1995-96
SCHMEICHEL	Manchester United	18	42	42.86	31	1992-93
MIMMS	Blackburn Rovers	18	42	42.86	46	1992-93
SCHMEICHEL	Manchester United	17	34	50.00	24	1997-98
LUKIC	Leeds United	17	42	40.48	38	1994-95
JAMES	Liverpool	17	42	40.48	37	1994-95
SEAMAN	Arsenal	16	38	42.11	32	1995-96
SEAMAN	Arsenal	16	39	41.03	34	1992-93
JAMES	Liverpool	16	38	42.11	34	1995-96
FLOWERS	Blackburn Rovers	16	39	41.03	30	1994-95
SOUTHALL	Everton	15	38	39.47	44	1995-96
SCHMEICHEL	Manchester United	15	40	37.50	38	1993-94
SOUTHALL	Everton	14	41	34.15	51	1994-95
MIKLOSKO	West Ham United	14	42	33.33	58	1993-94
MARTYN	Crystal Palace	14	37	37.84	41	1994-95
WALKER	Tottenham Hotspur	13	37	35.14	49	1996-97
SULLIVAN	Wimbledon	13	38	34.21	46	1997-98
SRNICEK	Newcastle United	13	38	34.21	43	1994-95
SEGERS	Wimbledon	13	41	31.71	53	1992-93
SEAMAN	Arsenal	13	31	41.94	33	1997-98
SCHMEICHEL	Manchester United	13	36	36.11	42	1996-97
POOM	Derby County	13	36	36.11	47	1997-98
MIKLOSKO	West Ham United	13	42	30.95	48	1994-95
KHARINE	Chelsea	13	31	41.94	46	1994-95
FLOWERS	Blackburn Rovers	13	29	44.83	23	1993-94
CROSSLEY	Nottingham Forest	13	42	30.95	43	1994-95
BOSNICH	Aston Villa	13	38	34.21	34	1995-96
JAMES	Liverpool	12	38	31.58	37	1996-97
DE GOEY	Chelsea	12	32	37.50	32	1997-98

THE PLAYERS

Top Appearances by Player

Maximum number of games possible is 240.
NB: Clubs listed are those that player played last Premiership match with.

Player	Club	Tot	Start	Sub	Gls
FLOWERS Tim	Blackburn Rovers	220	219	1	0
SCHMEICHEL Peter	Manchester United	219	219	0	0
ATHERTON Peter	Sheffield Wednesday	219	218	1	6
SHERWOOD Tim	Blackburn Rovers	217	214	3	22
SPEED Gary	Newcastle United	214	213	1	39
KENNA Jeff	Blackburn Rovers	213	210	3	5
WINTERBURN Nigel	Arsenal	212	211	1	4
McMANAMAN Steve	Liverpool	212	207	5	37
LE TISSIER Matthew	Southampton	210	203	7	91
IRWIN Denis	Manchester United	209	205	4	13
SOUTHALL Neville	Everton	207	207	0	0
RICHARDSON Kevin	Southampton	207	200	7	8
PALLISTER Gary	Manchester United	206	206	0	8
HUGHES Mark	Chelsea	206	198	8	60
HENDRY Colin	Blackburn Rovers	204	203	1	8
McALLISTER Gary	Coventry City	203	203	0	31
PEACOCK Darren	Blackburn Rovers	201	196	5	7
SEAMAN David	Arsenal	200	200	0	0
FOX Ruel	Tottenham Hotspur	200	190	10	33
PALMER Carlton	Southampton	199	196	3	14
DIXON Lee	Arsenal	199	195	4	5
FERDINAND Les	Tottenham Hotspur	199	195	4	106
SHERINGHAM Teddy	Manchester United	199	193	6	85
GIGGS Ryan	Manchester United	196	184	12	45
WATSON Dave	Everton	195	193	2	6
SUTTON Chris	Blackburn Rovers	192	181	11	77
WRIGHT Ian	Arsenal	191	182	9	104
WALKER Des	Sheffield Wednesday	190	190	0	0

Top Substitute Appearances by Player

NB: Clubs listed are those that player played last Premiership match with.

Player	Club	Sub	Tot	Start	Gls
CLARKE Andy	Wimbledon	70	124	54	11
McCLAIR Brian	Manchester United	56	162	106	18
FENTON Graham	Leicester City	48	82	34	13
ROSENTHAL Ronny	Tottenham Hotspur	47	118	71	10
BARLOW Stuart	Everton	41	62	21	10
WATSON Gordon	Bradford City	40	94	54	21
HYDE Graham	Sheffield Wednesday	36	138	102	9
JOACHIM Julian	Aston Villa	33	67	34	15
CLARK Lee	Sunderland	32	101	69	7
SCHOLES Paul	Manchester United	32	98	66	26
LEE Jason	Nottingham Forest	32	63	31	12
PARLOUR Ray	Arsenal	31	164	133	10
WARHURST Paul	Crystal Palace	31	112	81	13
SPENCER John	Everton	31	109	78	36
GOODMAN Jon	Wimbledon	31	59	28	11
WHITTINGHAM Guy	Sheffield Wednesday	30	136	106	27
SLATER Robbie	Southampton	29	84	55	4
HUGHES David	Southampton	29	44	15	3
STUART Graham	Everton	28	175	147	31
WALTERS Mark	Southampton	28	72	44	11
CORK Alan	Wimbledon	28	46	18	5
THOMAS Michael	Liverpool	27	106	79	6
LIMPAR Anders	Birmingham City	27	99	72	16
BART-WILLIAMS Chris	Nottingham Forest	26	158	132	18
HARFORD Mick	Wimbledon	26	90	64	19
BERGER Patrik	Liverpool	26	45	19	9
BANGER Nicky	Oldham Athletic	26	34	8	8

THE MANAGERS

Length of Tenure – Current Tenants

	Club	Manager	Arrived
1	Manchester United	Alex Ferguson	November '86
2	Wimbledon	Joe Kinnear	January '91
3	Liverpool	Roy Evans	January '94
4	Middlesbrough	Bryan Robson	May '94
5	West Ham United	Harry Redknapp	August '94
6	Charlton Athletic	Alan Curbishley	June '95
7	Derby County	Jim Smith	June '95
8	Leicester City	Martin O'Neill	December '95
9	Leeds United	George Graham	September '96
10	Arsenal	Arsène Wenger	August '96
11	Coventry City	Gordon Strachan	November '96
12	Newcastle United	Kenny Dalglish	January '97
13	Blackburn Rovers	Roy Hodgson	June '97
14	Southampton	Dave Jones	June '97
15	Nottingham Forest	Dave Bassett	June '97
16	Tottenham Hotspur	Christian Gross	November '97
17	Chelsea	Gianluca Vialli	February '98
18	Aston Villa	John Gregory	February '98
19	Everton	Walter Smith	July '98
20	Sheffield Wednesday	tba	

See later in this annual for full records of all Premiership managers

Managers: Most Games in Charge

Manager	Clubs	P	W	D	L	F	A	PTS	PPG
FERGUSON Alex	1	240	146	60	34	446	202	498	2.08
KINNEAR Joe	1	240	82	70	88	298	335	316	1.32
ATKINSON Ron	3	184	64	49	71	203	227	241	1.31
GRAHAM George	2	183	67	58	58	212	173	259	1.42
ROYLE Joe	2	181	58	54	69	241	258	228	1.26
DALGLISH Kenny	2	180	91	45	44	279	181	318	1.77
FRANCIS Gerry	2	175	67	50	58	244	227	251	1.43
WILKINSON Howard	1	174	66	53	55	231	214	250	1.44
EVANS Roy	1	172	83	46	43	280	173	295	1.72
REDKNAPP Harry	1	156	53	40	63	182	205	199	1.28
LITTLE Brian	2	144	53	39	52	173	162	198	1.38
KEEGAN Kevin	1	143	78	30	35	253	147	264	1.85

61

FRANCIS Trevor	1	126	44	42	40	180	162	174	1.38
HODDLE Glenn	1	122	38	41	43	145	152	155	1.27
WILKINS Ray	1	108	35	25	48	136	156	130	1.20
SOUNESS Graeme	2	106	38	29	39	156	143	143	1.35
LYALL John	1	101	24	34	43	101	146	106	1.05

Managers by Total Points Won

Manager	Clubs	P	W	D	L	F	A	Pts	PPG
FERGUSON Alex	1	240	146	60	34	446	202	498	2.08
DALGLISH Kenny	2	180	91	45	44	279	181	318	1.77
KINNEAR Joe	1	240	82	70	88	298	335	316	1.32
EVANS Roy	1	172	83	46	43	280	173	295	1.72
KEEGAN Kevin	1	143	78	30	35	253	147	264	1.85
GRAHAM George	2	183	67	58	58	212	173	259	1.42
FRANCIS Gerry	2	175	67	50	58	244	227	251	1.43
WILKINSON Howard	1	174	66	53	55	231	214	250	1.44
ATKINSON Ron	3	184	64	49	71	203	227	241	1.31
ROYLE Joe	2	181	58	54	69	241	258	228	1.26
REDKNAPP Harry	1	156	53	40	63	182	205	199	1.28
LITTLE Brian	2	144	53	39	52	173	162	198	1.38
FRANCIS Trevor	1	126	44	42	40	180	162	174	1.38
HODDLE Glenn	1	122	38	41	43	145	152	155	1.27
CLARK Frank	1	97	38	31	28	136	126	145	1.49
SOUNESS Graeme	2	106	38	29	39	156	143	143	1.35
WALKER Mike	2	96	37	25	34	126	143	136	1.42
WILKINS Ray	1	108	35	25	48	136	156	130	1.20
WENGER Arsène	1	68	37	18	13	113	57	129	1.90
BALL Alan	2	98	28	33	37	120	151	117	1.19
KENDALL Howard	2	98	31	24	43	114	134	117	1.19
LYALL John	1	101	24	34	43	101	146	106	1.05
PLEAT David	1	89	26	28	35	116	147	106	1.19
GULLITT Ruud	1	64	30	14	19	110	82	104	1.63
SMITH Jim	1	76	27	20	29	97	107	101	1.33
O'NEILL Martin	1	76	25	25	26	97	105	100	1.32

Managers by Average Points/Game

Manager	Clubs	P	W	D	L	F	A	Pts	PPG
FERGUSON Alex	1	240	146	60	34	446	202	498	2.08
WENGER Arsène	1	68	37	18	13	113	57	129	1.90
KEEGAN Kevin	1	143	78	30	35	253	147	264	1.85
DALGLISH Kenny	2	180	91	45	44	279	181	318	1.77
EVANS Roy	1	172	83	46	43	280	173	295	1.72
RIOCH Bruce	1	38	17	12	9	49	32	63	1.66

GULLITT Ruud	1	64	30	14	19	110	82	104	1.63
HODGSON Ray	1	38	16	10	12	57	52	58	1.53
CLARK Frank	1	97	38	31	28	136	126	145	1.49
WILKINSON Howard	1	174	66	53	55	231	214	250	1.44
FRANCIS Gerry	2	175	67	50	58	244	227	251	1.43
GRAHAM George	2	183	67	58	58	212	173	259	1.42
WALKER Mike	2	96	37	25	34	126	143	136	1.42
LIVERMORE/CLEMENCE									
Doug/Ray	1	42	16	11	15	60	66	59	1.40
FRANCIS Trevor	1	126	44	42	40	180	162	174	1.38
LITTLE Brian	2	144	53	39	52	173	162	198	1.38
SOUNESS Graeme	2	106	38	29	39	156	143	143	1.35
SMITH Jim	1	76	27	20	29	97	107	101	1.33
KINNEAR Joe	1	240	82	70	88	298	335	316	1.32
O'NEILL Martin	1	76	25	25	26	97	105	100	1.32
STRACHAN Gordon	1	66	20	27	19	80	84	87	1.32
ATKINSON Ron	3	184	64	49	71	203	227	241	1.31

Managers must have been in charge for a minimum of 38 games to qualify for classification.

SEASON BY SEASON

Crime Count – Year-by-Year

Season	Games	Red Cards	Ave	Yellow Cards	Ave
1992-93	462	34	0.077	760	1.65
1993-94	462	25	0.054	599	1.30
1994-95	462	65	0.140	1294	2.80
1995-96	380	57	0.150	1180	3.11
1996-97	380	31	0.082	1211	3.18
1997-98	380	69	0.182	1238	3.26
Total	*2526*	*281*	*0.111*	*6282*	*2.93*

Last Day Championships

The FA Premier League Championship has twice gone to the last day of the season to be decided.

1994-95

	P	W	D	L	F	A	Pts	GD
Blackburn Rovers	41	27	8	6	79	37	89	+42
Manchester United	41	26	9	6	76	27	87	+48

On the last day of the season Blackburn travelled to Liverpool needing a win to secure the title. Manchester United went to Upton Park needing three points from West Ham and hoping that Rovers would fail to win. A last minute goal gave Liverpool a 2-1 win over Blackburn, but despite a succession of missed chances Manchester United could only draw and the title went to Blackburn Rovers.

1995-96

	P	W	D	L	F	A	Pts	GD
Manchester United	41	24	7	6	70	35	79	+35
Newcastle United	41	24	5	8	65	36	77	+29

At one point Newcastle led the table by 12 points but a string of last-minute reversals and a relentless attack by the Red Devils allowed them to peg the Magpies back. On the final day of the season the United of Manchester travelled to the north-east to play Middlesbrough, needing a point to take the title. Newcastle entertained Spurs at home and needed to win and look a few miles south for a result. The United of Manchester prevailed, winning 3-0 at the Riverside as Newcastle drew 1-1 with Spurs.

Final Table 1993-94 Season

		P	W	D	L	F	A	Pts	
1	Manchester United	42	27	11	4	80	38	92	
2	Blackburn Rovers	42	25	9	8	63	36	84	
3	Newcastle United	42	23	8	11	82	41	77	
4	Arsenal	42	18	17	7	53	28	71	
5	Leeds United	42	18	16	8	65	39	70	
6	Wimbledon	42	18	11	13	56	53	65	
7	Sheffield Wednesday	42	16	16	10	76	54	64	
8	Liverpool	42	17	9	16	59	55	60	
9	QPR	42	16	12	14	62	61	60	
10	Aston Villa	42	15	12	15	46	50	57	
11	Coventry City	42	14	14	14	43	45	56	
12	Norwich City	42	12	17	13	65	61	53	
13	West Ham United	42	13	13	16	47	58	52	
14	Chelsea	42	13	12	17	49	53	51	
15	Tottenham Hotspur	42	11	12	19	54	59	45	
16	Manchester City	42	9	18	15	38	49	45	
17	Everton	42	12	8	22	42	63	44	
18	Southampton	42	12	7	23	49	66	43	
19	Ipswich Town	42	9	16	17	35	58	43	
20	Sheffield United	42	8	18	16	42	60	42	
21	Oldham Athletic	42	9	13	20	42	68	40	R
22	Swindon Town	42	5	15	22	47	100	30	R

Promoted:
Crystal Palace – Champions
Nottingham Forest – Runners-up
Leicester City – Play-off Winners

Final Table 1994-95 Season

		P	W	D	L	F	A	Pts	
1	Blackburn Rovers	42	27	8	7	80	39	89	
2	Manchester United	42	26	10	6	77	28	88	
3	Nottingham Forest	42	22	11	9	72	43	77	
4	Liverpool	42	21	11	10	65	37	74	
5	Leeds United	42	20	13	9	59	38	73	
6	Newcastle United	42	20	12	10	67	47	72	
7	Tottenham Hotspur	42	16	14	12	66	58	62	
8	Queens Park Rangers	42	17	9	16	61	59	60	
9	Wimbledon	42	15	11	16	48	65	56	
10	Southampton	42	12	18	12	61	63	54	
11	Chelsea	42	13	15	14	50	55	54	
12	Arsenal	42	13	12	17	52	49	51	
13	Sheffield Wednesday	42	13	12	17	49	57	51	
14	West Ham United	42	13	11	18	44	48	50	
15	Everton	42	11	17	14	44	51	50	
16	Coventry City	42	12	14	16	44	62	50	
17	Manchester City	42	12	13	17	53	64	49	
18	Aston Villa	42	11	15	16	51	56	48	
19	Crystal Palace	42	11	12	19	34	49	45	R
20	Norwich City	42	10	13	19	37	54	43	R
21	Leicester City	42	6	11	25	45	80	29	R
22	Ipswich Town	42	7	6	29	36	93	27	R

Promoted:
Middlesbrough – Champions
Bolton Wanderers – Play-off Winners

Final Table 1995-96 Season

		P	W	D	L	F	A	Pts	
1	Manchester United	38	25	7	6	73	35	82	
2	Newcastle United	38	24	6	8	66	37	78	
3	Liverpool	38	20	11	7	70	34	71	
4	Aston Villa	38	18	9	11	52	35	63	
5	Arsenal	38	17	12	9	49	32	63	
6	Everton	38	17	10	11	64	44	61	
7	Blackburn Rovers	38	18	7	13	61	47	61	
8	Tottenham Hotspur	38	16	13	9	50	38	61	
9	Nottingham Forest	38	15	13	10	50	54	58	
10	West Ham United	38	14	9	15	43	52	51	
11	Chelsea	38	12	14	12	46	44	50	
12	Middlesbrough	38	11	10	17	35	50	43	
13	Leeds United	38	12	7	19	40	57	43	
14	Wimbledon	38	10	11	17	55	70	41	
15	Sheffield Wednesday	38	10	10	18	48	61	40	
16	Coventry City	38	8	14	16	42	60	38	
17	Southampton	38	9	11	18	34	52	38	
18	Manchester City	38	9	11	18	33	58	38	R
19	QPR	38	9	6	23	38	57	33	R
20	Bolton Wanderers	38	8	5	25	39	71	29	R

Promoted:
Sunderland – Champions
Derby County – Runners-up
Leicester City – Play-off Winners

Final Table 1996-97 Season

		P	W	D	L	F	A	Pts	
1	Manchester United	38	21	12	5	76	44	75	
2	Newcastle United	38	19	11	8	73	40	68	
3	Arsenal	38	19	11	8	62	32	68	
4	Liverpool	38	19	11	8	62	37	68	
5	Aston Villa	38	17	10	11	47	34	61	
6	Chelsea	38	16	11	11	58	55	59	
7	Sheffield Wednesday	38	14	15	9	50	51	57	
8	Wimbledon	38	15	11	12	49	46	56	
9	Leicester City	38	12	11	15	46	54	47	
10	Tottenham Hotspur	38	13	7	18	44	51	46	
11	Leeds United	38	11	13	14	28	38	46	
12	Derby County	38	11	13	14	45	58	46	
13	Blackburn Rovers	38	9	15	14	42	43	42	
14	West Ham United	38	10	12	16	39	48	42	
15	Everton	38	10	11	17	44	57	42	
16	Southampton	38	10	11	17	50	56	41	
17	Coventry City	38	9	14	15	38	54	41	
18	Sunderland	38	10	10	18	35	53	40	R
19	Middlesbrough	38	10	12	16	51	60	39	R
20	Nottingham Forest	38	6	16	16	31	59	34	R

Middlesbrough deducted 3 points for failing to fulfil fixture.

Promoted:
Bolton Wanderers – Champions
Barnsley – Runners-up
Crystal Palace – Play-off Winners

LEAGUE CHAMPIONS' RECORDS

FOOTBALL LEAGUE

Season	Champions	P	W	D	L	F	A	Pts
1888-89	Preston North End	22	18	4	0	74	15	40
1889-90	Preston North End	22	15	3	4	71	30	33
1890-91	Everton	22	14	1	7	63	29	29
1891-92	Sunderland	26	21	0	5	93	36	42

FOOTBALL LEAGUE DIVISION 1

Season	Champions	P	W	D	L	F	A	Pts
1892-93	Sunderland	30	22	4	4	100	36	48
1893-94	Aston Villa	30	19	6	5	84	42	44
1894-95	Sunderland	30	21	5	4	80	37	47
1895-96	Aston Villa	30	20	5	5	78	45	45
1896-97	Aston Villa	30	21	5	4	73	38	47
1897-98	Sheffield United	30	17	8	5	56	31	42
1898-99	Aston Villa	34	19	7	8	76	40	45
1899-00	Aston Villa	34	22	6	6	77	35	50
1900-01	Liverpool	34	19	7	8	59	35	45
1901-02	Sunderland	34	19	6	9	50	35	44
1902-03	Sheffield Wednesday	34	19	4	11	54	36	42
1903-04	Sheffield Wednesday	34	20	7	7	48	28	47
1904-05	Newcastle United	34	23	2	9	72	33	48
1905-06	Liverpool	38	23	5	10	79	46	51
1906-07	Newcastle United	38	22	7	9	74	46	51
1907-08	Manchester United	38	23	6	9	81	48	52
1908-09	Newcastle United	38	24	5	9	65	41	53
1909-10	Aston Villa	38	23	7	8	84	42	53
1910-11	Manchester United	38	22	8	8	72	40	52
1911-12	Blackburn Rovers	38	20	9	9	60	43	49
1912-13	Sunderland	38	25	4	9	86	43	54
1913-14	Blackburn Rovers	38	20	11	7	78	42	51
1914-15	Everton	38	19	8	11	76	47	46
	World War I							
1919-20	West Bromwich Albion	42	28	4	10	104	47	60
1920-21	Burnley	42	23	13	6	79	36	59
1921-22	Liverpool	42	22	13	7	63	36	57
1922-23	Liverpool	42	26	8	8	70	31	60

Season	Champions	P	W	D	L	F	A	Pts
1923-24	Huddersfield Town *	42	23	11	8	60	33	57
1924-25	Huddersfield Town	42	21	16	5	69	28	58
1925-26	Huddersfield Town	42	23	11	8	92	60	57
1926-27	Newcastle United	42	25	6	11	96	58	56
1927-28	Everton	42	20	13	9	102	66	53
1928-29	Sheffield Wednesday	42	21	10	11	86	62	52
1929-30	Sheffield Wednesday	42	26	8	8	105	57	60
1930-31	Arsenal	42	28	10	4	127	59	66
1931-32	Everton	42	26	4	12	116	64	56
1932-33	Arsenal	42	25	8	9	118	61	58
1933-34	Arsenal	42	25	9	8	75	47	59
1934-35	Arsenal	42	23	12	7	115	46	58
1935-36	Sunderland	42	25	6	11	109	74	56
1936-37	Manchester City	42	22	13	7	107	61	57
1937-38	Arsenal	42	21	10	11	77	44	52
1938-39	Everton	42	27	5	10	88	52	59
	World War II							
1946-47	Liverpool	42	25	7	10	84	52	57
1947-48	Arsenal	42	23	13	6	81	32	59
1948-49	Portsmouth	42	25	8	9	84	42	58
1949-50	Portsmouth *	42	22	9	11	74	38	53
1950-51	Tottenham Hotspur	42	25	10	7	82	44	60
1951-52	Manchester United	42	23	11	8	95	52	57
1952-53	Arsenal *	42	21	12	9	97	64	54
1953-54	Wolverhampton W.	42	25	7	10	96	56	57
1954-55	Chelsea	42	20	12	10	81	57	52
1955-56	Manchester United	42	25	10	7	83	51	60
1956-57	Manchester United	42	28	8	6	103	54	64
1957-58	Wolverhampton W.	42	28	8	6	103	47	64
1958-59	Wolverhampton W.	42	28	5	9	110	49	61
1959-60	Burnley	42	24	7	11	85	61	55
1960-61	Tottenham Hotspur	42	31	4	7	115	55	66
1961-62	Ipswich Town	42	24	8	10	93	67	56
1962-63	Everton	42	25	11	6	84	42	61
1963-64	Liverpool	42	26	5	11	92	45	57
1964-65	Manchester United *	42	26	9	7	89	39	61
1965-66	Liverpool	42	26	9	7	79	34	61
1966-67	Manchester United	42	24	12	6	84	45	60
1967-68	Manchester City	42	26	6	10	86	43	58
1968-69	Leeds United	42	27	13	2	66	26	67
1969-70	Everton	42	29	8	5	72	34	66
1970-71	Arsenal	42	29	7	6	71	29	65
1971-72	Derby County	42	24	10	8	69	33	58

Season	Champions	P	W	D	L	F	A	Pts
1972-73	Liverpool	42	25	10	7	72	42	60
1973-74	Leeds United	42	24	14	4	66	31	62
1974-75	Derby County	42	21	11	10	67	49	53
1975-76	Liverpool	42	23	14	5	66	31	60
1976-77	Liverpool	42	23	11	8	62	33	57
1977-78	Nottingham Forest	42	25	14	3	69	24	64
1978-79	Liverpool	42	30	8	4	85	16	68
1979-80	Liverpool	42	25	10	7	81	30	60
1980-81	Aston Villa	42	26	8	8	72	40	60
1981-82	Liverpool	42	26	9	7	80	32	87
1982-83	Liverpool	42	24	10	8	87	37	82
1983-84	Liverpool	42	22	14	6	73	32	80
1984-85	Everton	42	28	6	8	88	43	90
1985-86	Liverpool	42	26	10	6	89	37	88
1986-87	Everton	42	26	8	8	76	31	86
1987-88	Liverpool	40	26	12	2	87	24	90
1988-89	Arsenal †	38	22	10	6	73	36	76
1989-90	Liverpool	38	23	10	5	78	37	79
1990-91	Arsenal +	38	24	13	1	74	18	83
1991-92	Leeds United	42	22	16	4	74	37	82

FA PREMIER LEAGUE

Season	Champions	P	W	D	L	F	A	Pts
1992-93	Manchester United	42	24	12	6	67	31	84
1993-94	Manchester United	42	27	11	4	80	38	92
1994-95	Blackburn Rovers	42	27	8	7	80	39	89
1995-96	Manchester United	38	25	7	6	73	35	82
1996-97	Manchester United	38	21	12	5	76	44	75
1997-98	Arsenal	38	23	9	6	68	33	78

* Won on goal average/goal difference.
† Won on goals scored.
+ 2 points deducted.

CHAMPIONSHIP WINS BY CLUB

FA Premier League and Football League Combined

Club	Years
Liverpool (18)	1901, 1906, 1922, 1923, 1947, 1964, 1966, 1973, 1976, 1977, 1979, 1980, 1982, 1983, 1984, 1986, 1988, 1990
Arsenal (11)	1931, 1933, 1934, 1935, 1938, 1948, 1953, 1971, 1989, 1991, 1998
Manchester United (11)	1908, 1911, 1952, 1956, 1957, 1965, 1967, 1993, 1994, 1996, 1997
Everton (9)	1891, 1915, 1928, 1932, 1939, 1963, 1970, 1985, 1987
Aston Villa (7)	1894, 1896, 1897, 1899, 1900, 1910, 1981
Sunderland (6)	1892, 1893, 1895, 1902, 1913, 1936
Newcastle United (4)	1905, 1907, 1909, 1927
Sheffield Wednesday (4)	1903, 1904, 1929, 1930
Huddersfield Town (3)	1924, 1925, 1926
Leeds United (3)	1969, 1974, 1992
Wolverhampton W. (3)	1954, 1958, 1959
Blackburn Rovers (3)	1912, 1914, 1995
Portsmouth (2)	1949, 1950
Preston NE (2)	1889, 1890
Burnley (2)	1921, 1960
Manchester City (2)	1937, 1968
Tottenham Hotspur (2)	1951, 1961
Derby County (2)	1972, 1975
Chelsea (1)	1955
Sheffield United (1)	1898
WBA (1)	1920
Ipswich Town (1)	1962
Nottingham Forest (1)	1978

FA CHALLENGE CUP
1997-98 Sponsored by Littlewoods

Note: Dates given are for official date of round – games may have taken place on different dates.

Third Round

AFC Bournemouth	v	Huddersfield Town	0-1	7,385
Arsenal	v	Port Vale	0-0	37,471
Barnsley	v	Bolton Wanderers	1-0	15,042
Blackburn Rovers	v	Wigan Athletic	4-2	22,402
Bristol Rovers	v	Ipswich Town	1-1	8,610
Crystal Palace	v	Scunthorpe United	2-0	11,624
Cardiff City	v	Oldham Athletic	1-0	6,635
Charlton Athletic	v	Nottingham Forest	4-1	13,827
Chelsea	v	Man. United	3-5	34,792
Cheltenham	v	Reading	1-1	6,000
Crewe Alexandra	v	Birmingham City	1-2	4,607
Darlington	v	Wolverhampton W.	0-4	5,018
Derby County	v	Southampton	2-0	27,992
Everton	v	Newcastle United	0-1	20,885
Grimsby Town	v	Norwich City	3-0	8,161
Hereford United	v	Tranmere Rovers	0-3	7,473
Leeds United	v	Oxford United	4-0	20,568
Leicester City	v	Northampton Town	4-0	20,608
Liverpool	v	Coventry City	1-3	33,888
Manchester City	v	Bradford City	2-0	23,686
Peterborough United	v	Walsall	0-2	12,809
Portsmouth	v	Aston Villa	2-2	16,013
Preston North End	v	Stockport County	1-2	12,180
QPR	v	Middlesbrough	2-2	13,379
Rotherham United	v	Sunderland	1-5	11,500
Sheffield United	v	Bury	1-1	14,009
Swindon Town	v	Stevenage Borough	1-2	9,422
Tottenham Hotspur	v	Fulham	3-1	27,909
Watford	v	Sheffield Wednesday	1-1	18,306
WBA	v	Stoke City	3-1	17,598
West Ham United	v	Emley	2-1	18,629
Wimbledon	v	Wrexham	0-0	6,349

Third Round Replays

Aston Villa	v	Portsmouth	1-0	23,365
Bury	v	Sheffield United	1-2	4,920
Ipswich Town	v	Bristol Rovers	1-0	11,362
Middlesbrough	v	QPR	2-0	21,817
Port Vale	v	Arsenal	1-1	14,964

aet. Arsenal win 4-3 on penalties

Reading	v	Cheltenham	2-1	9,686
Sheffield Wednesday	v	Watford	0-0	18,707

aet. Sheffield Wednesday win 5-3 on penalties

Wrexham	v	Wimbledon	2-3	9,539

Fourth Round

Aston Villa	v	WBA	4-0	39,372
Birmingham City	v	Stockport County	2-1	15,882
Crystal Palace	v	Leicester City	3-0	15,489
Cardiff City	v	Reading	1-1	10,174
Charlton Athletic	v	Wolverhampton W.	1-1	15,540
Coventry City	v	Derby County	2-0	22,864
Huddersfield Town	v	Wimbledon	0-1	14,533
Ipswich Town	v	Sheffield United	1-1	14,654
Leeds United	v	Grimsby Town	2-0	29,598
Manchester City	v	West Ham United	1-2	26,495
Manchester United	v	Walsall	5-1	54,669
Middlesbrough	v	Arsenal	1-2	28,264
Sheffield Wednesday	v	Blackburn Rovers	0-3	15,940
Stevenage Borough	v	Newcastle United	1-1	8,040
Tottenham Hotspur	v	Barnsley	1-1	28,722
Tranmere Rovers	v	Sunderland	1-0	14,055

Fourth Round Replays

Barnsley	v	Tottenham Hotspur	3-1	18,705
Newcastle United	v	Stevenage Borough	2-1	36,705
Reading	v	Cardiff City	1-1	11,808

aet. Reading win 4-3 on penalties

Sheffield United	v	Ipswich Town	1-0	14,144
Wolverhampton W.	v	Charlton Athletic	3-0	20,429

Fifth Round

Arsenal	v	Crystal Palace	0-0	37,164
Aston Villa	v	Coventry City	0-1	26,979

Leeds United	v	Birmingham City	3-2	35,463
Manchester United	v	Barnsley	1-1	54,700
Newcastle United	v	Tranmere Rovers	1-0	36,675
Sheffield United	v	Reading	1-0	17,845
West Ham United	v	Blackburn Rovers	2-2	25,729
Wimbledon	v	Wolverhampton W.	1-1	15,608

Fifth Round Replays

Barnsley	v	Man. United	3-2	18,655
Blackburn Rovers	v	West Ham United	1-1	21,972
		aet. West Ham United win 5-4 on pens		
Crystal Palace	v	Arsenal	1-2	15,674
Wolverhampton W.	v	Wimbledon	2-1	25,112

Sixth Round

Arsenal	v	West Ham United	1-1	38,077
Coventry City	v	Sheffield United	1-1	23,084
Leeds United	v	Wolverhampton W.	0-1	39,902
Newcastle United	v	Barnsley	3-1	36,695

Sixth Round Replays

Sheffield United	v	Coventry City	1-1	29,034
		aet. Sheffield United win 3-1 on pens		
West Ham United	v	Arsenal	1-1	25,859
		aet. Arsenal win 4-3 on pens		

Semi Finals

Sheffield United	v	Newcastle United	0-1	53,452
		at Old Trafford, Manchester		
Wolverhampton W.	v	Arsenal	0-1	39,372
		at Villa Park, Birmingham		

Final – 16 May 1998 at Wembley Stadium

| Arsenal | v | Newcastle United | 2-0 | 79,183 |

Overmars (23); Anelka (69)

Arsenal: Seaman, Dixon, Keown, Adams, Winterburn, Parlour, Vieira, Petit, Overmars, Wreh (Platt 63), Anelka. *Subs not used:* Bould, Wright, Manninger, Grimandi.

Newcastle United: Given, Pistone, Dabizas, Howey, Pearce (Andersson 72), Barton (Watson 77), Lee, Batty, Speed, Ketsbaia (Barnes 85), Shearer. *Subs not used:* Hislop, Albert.

Referee: Mr Paul Durkin (Portland)

FA CHALLENGE CUP FINALS 1872-1997

Year	Winners	Runners-up	Score
1872	The Wanderers	Royal Engineers	1-0
1873	The Wanderers	Oxford University	2-0
1874	Oxford University	Royal Engineers	2-0
1875	Royal Engineers	Old Etonians	1-1
	Royal Engineers	Old Etonians	2-0
1876	The Wanderers	Old Etonians	1-1 †
	The Wanderers	Old Etonians	3-0
1877	The Wanderers	Oxford University	2-1 †
1878	The Wanderers*	Royal Engineers	3-1
1879	Old Etonians	Clapham Rovers	1-0
1880	Clapham Rovers	Oxford University	1-0
1881	Old Carthusians	Old Etonians	3-0
1882	Old Etonians	Blackburn Rovers	1-0
1883	Blackburn Olympic	Old Etonians	2-1 †
1884	Blackburn Rovers	Queen's Park, Glasgow	2-1
1885	Blackburn Rovers	Queen's Park, Glasgow	2-0
1886	Blackburn Rovers**	West Bromwich Albion	0-0
	Blackburn Rovers**	West Bromwich Albion	2-0
1887	Aston Villa	West Bromwich Albion	2-0
1888	West Bromwich Albion	Preston North End	2-1
1889	Preston North End	Wolverhampton Wanderers	3-0
1890	Blackburn Rovers	Sheffield Wednesday	6-1
1891	Blackburn Rovers	Notts County	3-1
1892	West Bromwich Albion	Aston Villa	3-0
1893	Wolverhampton Wanderers	Everton	1-0
1894	Notts County	Bolton Wanderers	4-1
1895	Aston Villa	West Bromwich Albion	1-0
1896	Sheffield Wednesday	Wolverhampton Wanderers	2-1
1897	Aston Villa	Everton	3-2
1898	Nottingham Forest	Derby County	3-1
1899	Sheffield United	Derby County	4-1
1900	Bury	Southampton	4-0
1901	Tottenham Hotspur	Sheffield United	2-2
	Tottenham Hotspur	Sheffield United	3-1
1902	Sheffield United	Southampton	1-1
	Sheffield United	Southampton	2-1
1903	Bury	Derby County	6-0

Year	Winners	Runners-up	Score
1904	Manchester City	Bolton Wanderers	1-0
1905	Aston Villa	Newcastle United	2-0
1906	Everton	Newcastle United	1-0
1907	Sheffield Wednesday	Everton	2-1
1908	Wolverhampton Wanderers	Newcastle United	3-1
1909	Manchester United	Bristol City	1-0
1910	Newcastle United	Barnsley	1-1
	Newcastle United	Barnsley	2-0
1911	Bradford City	Newcastle United	0-0
	Bradford City	Newcastle United	1-0
1912	Barnsley	West Bromwich Albion	0-0 †
	Barnsley	West Bromwich Albion	1-0
1913	Aston Villa	Sunderland	1-0
1914	Burnley	Liverpool	1- 0
1915	Sheffield United	Chelsea	3-0
1920	Aston Villa	Huddersfield Town	1-0 †
1921	Tottenham Hotspur	Wolverhampton Wanderers	1-0
1922	Huddersfield Town	Preston North End	1-0
1923	Bolton Wanderers	West Ham United	2-0
1924	Newcastle United	Aston Villa	2-0
1925	Sheffield United	Cardiff City	1-0
1926	Bolton Wanderers	Manchester City	1-0
1927	Cardiff City	Arsenal	1-0
1928	Blackburn Rovers	Huddersfield Town	3-1
1929	Bolton Wanderers	Portsmouth	2-0
1930	Arsenal	Huddersfield Town	2-0
1931	West Bromwich Albion	Birmingham	2-1
1932	Newcastle United	Arsenal	2-1
1933	Everton	Manchester City	3-0
1934	Manchester City	Portsmouth	2-1
1935	Sheffield Wednesday	West Bromwich Albion	4-2
1936	Arsenal	Sheffield United	1-0
1937	Sunderland	Preston North End	3-1
1938	Preston North End	Huddersfield Town	1-0 †
1939	Portsmouth	Wolverhampton Wanderers	4-1
1946	Derby County	Charlton Athletic	4-1 †
1947	Charlton Athletic	Burnley	1-0 †
1948	Manchester United	Blackpool	4-2
1949	Wolverhampton Wanderers	Leicester City	3-1
1950	Arsenal	Liverpool	2-0
1951	Newcastle United	Blackpool	2-0
1952	Newcastle United	Arsenal	1-0
1953	Blackpool	Bolton Wanderers	4-3

Year	Winners	Runners-up	Score	
1954	West Bromwich Albion	Preston North End	3-2	
1955	Newcastle United	Manchester City	3-1	
1956	Manchester City	Birmingham City	3-1	
1957	Aston Villa	Manchester United	2-1	
1958	Bolton Wanderers	Manchester United	2-0	
1959	Nottingham Forest	Luton Town	2-1	
1960	Wolverhampton Wanderers	Blackburn Rovers	3-0	
1961	Tottenham Hotspur	Leicester City	2-0	
1962	Tottenham Hotspur	Burnley	3-1	
1963	Manchester United	Leicester City	3-1	
1964	West Ham United	Preston North End	3-2	
1965	Liverpool	Leeds United	2-1	†
1966	Everton	Sheffield Wednesday	3-2	
1967	Tottenham Hotspur	Chelsea	2-1	
1968	West Bromwich Albion	Everton	1-0	†
1969	Manchester City	Leicester City	1-0	
1970	Chelsea	Leeds United	2-2	†
	Chelsea	Leeds United	2-1	†
1971	Arsenal	Liverpool	2-1	†
1972	Leeds United	Arsenal	1-0	
1973	Sunderland	Leeds United	1-0	
1974	Liverpool	Newcastle United	3-0	
1975	West Ham United	Fulham	2-0	
1976	Southampton	Manchester United	1-0	
1977	Manchester United	Liverpool	2-1	
1978	Ipswich Town	Arsenal	1-0	
1979	Arsenal	Manchester United	3-2	
1980	West Ham United	Arsenal	1-0	
1981	Tottenham Hotspur	Manchester City	1-1	†
	Tottenham Hotspur	Manchester City	3-2	
1982	Tottenham Hotspur	Queens Park Rangers	1-1	†
	Tottenham Hotspur	Queens Park Rangers	1-0	
1983	Manchester United	Brighton & Hove Albion	2-2	
	Manchester United	Brighton & Hove Albion	4-0	
1984	Everton	Watford	2-0	
1985	Manchester United	Everton	1-0	†
1986	Liverpool	Everton	3-1	
1987	Coventry City	Tottenham Hotspur	3-2	†
1988	Wimbledon	Liverpool	1-0	
1989	Liverpool	Everton	3-2	†
1990	Manchester United	Crystal Palace	3-3	†
	Manchester United	Crystal Palace	1-0	
1991	Tottenham Hotspur	Nottingham Forest	2-1	†

Year	Winners	Runners-up	Score
1992	Liverpool	Sunderland	2-0
1993	Arsenal	Sheffield Wednesday	1-1 †
	Arsenal	Sheffield Wednesday	2-1 †
1994	Manchester United	Chelsea	4-0
1995	Everton	Manchester United	1-0
1996	Manchester United	Liverpool	1-0
1997	Chelsea	Middlesbrough	2-0
1998	Arsenal	Newcastle United	2-0

Final Venues

1872	Kennington Oval
1873	Lillie Bridge
1874-92	Kennington Oval
1893	Fallowfield, Manchester
1894	Everton
1895-1914	Crystal Palace
1915	Old Trafford
1920-22	Stamford Bridge
1923-1998	Wembley

Replay Venues

1886	Derby
1901	Bolton
1910	Everton
1911	Old Trafford
1912	Bramall Lane
1970	Old Trafford
1981	Wembley
1982	Wembley
1983	Wembley
1990	Wembley
1993	Wembley

Trophy won outright by The Wanderers, but restored to the FA.
** Special trophy awarded for a third consecutive win.
† After extra time.

FA CHALLENGE CUP WINS BY CLUB

Manchester United (9)	1909, 1948, 1963, 1977, 1983, 1985, 1990, 1994, 1996
Tottenham Hotspur (8)	1901, 1921, 1961, 1962, 1967, 1981, 1982, 1991
Arsenal (7)	1930, 1936, 1950, 1971, 1979, 1993, 1998
Aston Villa (7)	1887, 1895, 1897, 1905, 1913, 1920, 1957
Blackburn Rovers (6)	1884, 1885, 1886, 1890, 1891, 1928
Newcastle United (6)	1910, 1924, 1932, 1951, 1952, 1955
Everton (5)	1894, 1906, 1933, 1966, 1995
Liverpool (5)	1965, 1974, 1986, 1989, 1992
The Wanderers (5)	1872, 1873, 1876, 1877, 1878
West Bromwich Albion (5)	1888, 1892, 1931, 1954, 1968
Bolton Wanderers (4)	1923, 1926, 1929, 1958
Manchester City (4)	1904, 1934, 1956, 1969
Sheffield United (4)	1899, 1902, 1915, 1925
Wolverhampton Wdrs (4)	1893, 1908, 1949, 1960
Sheffield Wednesday (3)	1896, 1907, 1935
West Ham United (3)	1964, 1975, 1980
Bury (2)	1900, 1903
Chelsea (2)	1970, 1997
Nottingham Forest (2)	1898, 1959
Old Etonians (2)	1879, 1882
Preston North End (2)	1889, 1938
Sunderland (2)	1937, 1973

Barnsley	1912	Notts County	1894
Blackburn Olympic	1883	Old Carthusians	1881
Blackpool	1953	Oxford University	1874
Bradford City	1911	Portsmouth	1939
Burnley	1914	Royal Engineers	1875
Cardiff City	1927	Southampton	1976
Charlton Athletic	1947	Wimbledon	1988
Clapham Rovers	1880		
Coventry City	1987		
Derby County	1946		
Huddersfield Town	1922		
Ipswich Town	1978		
Leeds United	1972		

FA CHARITY SHIELD
WINNERS 1908-96

1908	Manchester United v Queens Park Rangers 4-0	
	after 1-1 draw	
1909	Newcastle United v Northampton Town 2-0	
1910	Brighton & Hove Albion v Aston Villa 1-0	
1911	Manchester United v Swindon Town 8-4	
1912	Blackburn Rovers v Queens Park Rangers 2-1	
1913	Professionals v Amateurs... 7-2	
1919	West Bromwich Albion v Tottenham Hotspur 2-0	
1920	Tottenham Hotspur v Burnley 2-0	
1921	Huddersfield Town v Liverpool... 1-0	
1922	*Not Played*	
1923	Professionals v Amateurs... 2-0	
1924	Professionals v Amateurs... 3-1	
1925	Amateurs v Professionals... 6-1	
1926	Amateurs v Professionals... 6-3	
1927	Cardiff City v Corinthians 2-1	
1928	Everton v Blackburn Rovers 2-1	
1929	Professionals v Amateurs... 3-0	
1930	Arsenal v Sheffield Wednesday 2-1	
1931	Arsenal v West Bromwich Albion 1-0	
1932	Everton v Newcastle United 5-3	
1933	Arsenal v Everton 3-0	
1934	Arsenal v Manchester City 4-0	
1935	Sheffield Wednesday v Arsenal... 1-0	
1936	Sunderland v Arsenal 2-1	
1937	Manchester City v Sunderland 2-0	
1938	Arsenal v Preston North End 2-1	
1948	Arsenal v Manchester United 4-3	
1949	Portsmouth v Wolverhampton Wanderers 1-1	*
1950	World Cup Team v Canadian Touring Team 4-2	
1951	Tottenham Hotspur v Newcastle United 2-1	
1952	Manchester United v Newcastle United 4-2	
1953	Arsenal v Blackpool 3-1	*
1954	Wolverhampton Wanderers v West Bromwich Albion	4-4	*
1955	Chelsea v Newcastle United 3-0	
1956	Manchester United v Manchester City 1-0	
1957	Manchester United v Aston Villa 4-0	

1958	Bolton Wanderers v Wolverhampton Wanderers	......	4-1	
1959	Wolverhampton Wanderers v Nottingham Forest	...	3-1	
1960	Burnley v Wolverhampton Wanderers	... ...	2-2	*
1961	Tottenham Hotspur v FA XI		3-2	
1962	Tottenham Hotspur v Ipswich Town	... ...	5-1	
1963	Everton v Manchester United	... ...	4-0	
1964	Liverpool v West Ham United	... ...	2-2	*
1965	Manchester United v Liverpool		2-2	*
1966	Liverpool v Everton	... ...	1-0	
1967	Manchester United v Tottenham Hotspur...		3-3	*
1968	Manchester City v West Bromwich Albion	... ...	6-1	
1969	Leeds United v Manchester City	... ...	2-1	
1970	Everton v Chelsea	... ...	2-1	
1971	Leicester City v Liverpool	... ...	1-0	
1972	Manchester City v Aston Villa	... ...	1-0	
1973	Burnley v Manchester City	... ...	1-0	
1974	Liverpool v Leeds United	... ...	1-1	

Liverpool won on penalties

1975	Derby County v West Ham United		2-0	
1976	Liverpool v Southampton	... ...	1-0	
1977	Liverpool v Manchester United		0-0	*
1978	Nottingham Forest v Ipswich Town	... ...	5-0	
1979	Liverpool v Arsenal	... ...	3-1	
1980	Liverpool v West Ham United	... ...	1-0	
1981	Aston Villa v Tottenham Hotspur	... ...	2-2	*
1982	Liverpool v Tottenham Hotspur		1-0	
1983	Manchester United v Liverpool		2-0	
1984	Everton v Liverpool	... ...	1-0	
1985	Everton v Manchester United	... ...	2-0	
1986	Everton v Liverpool	... ...	1-1	*
1987	Everton v Coventry City	... ...	1-0	
1988	Liverpool v Wimbledon	... ...	2-1	
1989	Liverpool v Arsenal	... ...	1-0	
1990	Liverpool v Manchester United		1-1	*
1991	Arsenal v Tottenham Hotspur	... ...	0-0	*
1992	Leeds United v Liverpool	... ...	4-3	
1993	Manchester United v Arsenal	... ...	1-1	

Manchester United won on penalties

1994	Manchester United v Blackburn Rovers	... ...	2-0	
1995	Everton v Blackburn Rovers		1-0	
1996	Manchester United v Newcastle United	... ...	4-0	
1997	Manchester United v Chelsea	... ...	1-1	

* Each club retained shield for six months.

COCA-COLA FOOTBALL LEAGUE CUP 97-98

Second Round

			1st	2nd	Agg
Birmingham City	v	Stockport County	4-1	1-2	5-3
Blackburn Rovers	v	Preston NE	6-0	0-1	6-1
Blackpool	v	Coventry City	1-0	1-3	2-3
Burnley	v	Stoke City	0-4	0-2	0-6
Chesterfield	v	Barnsley	1-2	1-4	2-6
Fulham	v	Wolverhampton W.	0-1	0-1	0-2
Grimsby Town	v	Sheffield Wednesday	2-0	2-3	4-3
Huddersfield Town	v	West Ham United	1-0	0-3	1-3
Hull City	v	Crystal Palace	1-0	1-2 †	2-2
		Hull City win on away goals rule			
Ipswich Town	v	Torquay United	1-1	3-0	4-1
Leeds United	v	Bristol City	3-1	1-2	4-3
Leyton Orient	v	Bolton Wanderers	1-3	4-4	5-7
Luton Town	v	WBA	1-1	2-4	3-5
Middlesbrough	v	Barnet	1-0	2-0	3-0
Nottingham Forest	v	Walsall	0-1	2-2 †	2-3
Notts County	v	Tranmere Rovers	0-2	1-0	1-2
Oxford United	v	York City	4-1	2-1	6-2
Scunthorpe United	v	Everton	0-1	0-5	0-6
Southampton	v	Brentford	3-1	2-0	5-1
Southend United	v	Derby County	0-1	0-5	0-6
Sunderland	v	Bury	2-1	2-1	4-2
Tottenham Hotspur	v	Carlisle United	3-2	2-0	5-2
Watford	v	Sheffield United	1-1	0-4	1-5
Wimbledon	v	Millwall	5-1	4-1	9-2

Byes: Arsenal, Aston Villa, Leicester City, Liverpool, Manchester United, Newcastle United.

Third Round

Arsenal	v	Birmingham City	4-1	27,097
Barnsley	v	Southampton	1-2	9,019
Bolton Wanderers	v	Wimbledon	2-0 †	9,875
Chelsea	v	Blackburn Rovers	1-1 †	18,671
		Chelsea win 4-1 on penalties		
Coventry City	v	Everton	4-1	10,087
Grimsby Town	v	Leicester City	3-1	7,738
Ipswich Town	v	Manchester United	2-0	22,173
Middlesbrough	v	Sunderland	2-0	26,451
Newcastle United	v	Hull City	2-0	35,856

| Oxford United | v | Tranmere Rovers | 1-1 † | 3,878 |

Oxford United win 6-5 on penalties

Reading	v	Wolverhampton W.	4-2	11,080
Stoke City	v	Leeds United	1-3 †	16,203
Tottenham Hotspur	v	Derby County	1-2	20,390
Walsall	v	Sheffield United	2-1	8,239
WBA	v	Liverpool	0-2	21,986
West Ham United	v	Aston Villa	3-0	20,360

Fourth Round

Arsenal	v	Coventry City	1-0 †	30,199
Chelsea	v	Southampton	2-1 †	20,968
Derby County	v	Newcastle United	0-1	27,364
Leeds United	v	Reading	2-3	15,069
Liverpool	v	Grimsby Town	3-0	28,515
Middlesbrough	v	Bolton Wanderers	2-1	22,801
Oxford United	v	Ipswich Town	1-2 †	5,723
West Ham United	v	Wallsall	4-1	17,463

Fifth Round

| Ipswich Town | v | Chelsea | 2-2 | 22,088 |

aet. Chelsea win 4-1 on penalties

Reading	v	Middlesbrough	0-1	13,072
Newcastle United	v	Liverpool	0-2 †	33,207
West Ham United	v	Arsenal	1-2	24,770

Semi-Finals First Leg

| Arsenal | v | Chelsea | 2-1 | 38,114 |
| Liverpool | v | Middlesbrough | 2-1 | 33,438 |

Semi-Finals Second Leg

| Chelsea | v | Arsenal | 3-1 | 34,330 |

Chelsea win 4-3 on aggregate

| Middlesbrough | v | Liverpool | 2-0 | 29,824 |

Middlesbrough win 3-2 on aggregate

Final – 29th March 1998 at Wembley Stadium

| Chelsea | v | Middlesbrough | 2-0 | 77,698 |

Sinclair (95); di Matteo (107)   *aet*

Chelsea: de Goey, Sinclair, Leboeuf, Dubbery, Le Saux, Petrescu (Clarke, 74), Wise, Newton, di Matteo, Zola, M.Hughes (Flo, 81). Sub not used: Hitchcock.
Booked: M.Hughes (34 foul), Le Saux (40 dissent), Wise (75 foul), Leboeuf (87 foul).
Middlesbrough: Schwarzer, Festa, Kinder, Vickers, Pearson, Mustoe, Maddison (Beck, 101), Ricard (Gascoigne, 63), Branca, Merson, Townsend. Sub not used: Fleming.
Booked: Townsend (52 foul), Gascoigne (69 foul).
Ref: Mr P. Jones (Loughborough)
† = *after extra time*

FOOTBALL LEAGUE CUP FINALS 1961-1998

Year	Winners	Runners-up	1st	2nd	Agg
1961	Aston Villa	Rotherham United	0-2	†3-0	3-2
1962	Norwich City	Rochdale	3-0	1-0	4-0
1963	Birmingham City	Aston Villa	3-1	0-0	3-1
1964	Leicester City	Stoke City	1-1	3-2	4-3
1965	Chelsea	Leicester City	3-2	0-0	3 2
1966	West Bromwich Albion	West Ham United	1-2	4-1	5-3
1967	Queens Park Rangers	West Bromwich Albion	3-2		
1968	Leeds United	Arsenal	1-0		
1969	Swindon Town	Arsenal	† 3-1		
1970	Manchester City	West Bromwich Albion	2-1		
1971	Tottenham Hotspur	Aston Villa	† 2-0		
1972	Stoke City	Chelsea	2-1		
1973	Tottenham Hotspur	Norwich City	1-0		
1974	Wolverhampton W.	Manchester City	2-1		
1975	Aston Villa	Norwich City	1-0		
1976	Manchester City	Newcastle United	2-1		
1977	Aston Villa	Everton	† 3-2		
	after 0-0 draw and 1-1 draw aet				
1978	Nottingham Forest	Liverpool	1-0		
	after 0-0 draw aet				
1979	Nottingham Forest	Southampton	3-2		
1980	Wolverhampton W.	Nottingham Forest	1-0		
1981	Liverpool	West Ham United	2-1		
	after 1-1 draw aet				

Milk Cup

Year	Winners	Runners-up	1st	2nd	Agg
1982	Liverpool	Tottenham Hotspur	† 3-1		
1983	Liverpool	Manchester United	† 2-1		
1984	Liverpool	Everton	1-0		
	after 0-0 draw aet				
1985	Norwich City	Sunderland	1-0		
1986	Oxford United	Queens Park Rangers	3-0		

Littlewoods Cup

Year	Winners	Runners-up	1st	2nd	Agg
1987	Arsenal	Liverpool	2-1		
1988	Luton Town	Arsenal	3-2		

| 1989 | Nottingham Forest | Luton Town | 3-1 |
| 1990 | Nottingham Forest | Oldham Athletic | 1-0 |

Rumbelows League Cup

| 1991 | Sheffield Wednesday | Manchester United | 1-0 |
| 1992 | Manchester United | Nottingham Forest | 1-0 |

Coca-Cola Cup

1993	Arsenal	Sheffield Wednesday	2-1
1994	Aston Villa	Manchester United	3-1
1995	Liverpool	Bolton Wanderers	2-1
1996	Aston Villa	Leeds United	3-0
1997	Leicester City	Middlesbrough	† 1-0
	after 1-1 aet draw at Wembley		
1998	Chelsea	Middlesbrough	† 2-0

† *after extra time*

FOOTBALL LEAGUE CUP WINS BY CLUB

Aston Villa (5) 1961, 1975, 1977, 1994, 1996
Liverpool (5) 1981, 1982, 1983, 1984, 1995
Nottingham Forest (4) 1978, 1979, 1989, 1990
Arsenal (2) 1987, 1993
Manchester City (2) 1970, 1976
Tottenham Hotspur (2) ... 1971, 1973
Norwich City (2) 1962, 1985
Wolverhampton Wders (2) 1974, 1980
Leicester City (2) 1964, 1997
Chelsea (2) 1965, 1998
Birmingham City 1963
WBA 1966
QPR 1967
Leeds United 1968
Swindon Town 1969
Stoke City 1972
Oxford United 1986
Luton Town 1988
Sheffield Wednesday 1991
Manchester United 1992

FWA FOOTBALLER OF THE YEAR WINNERS

Season	Winner	Club
1947-48	Stanley Matthews	Blackpool & England
1948-49	Johnny Carey	Manchester United & Rep of Ireland
1949-50	Joe Mercer	Arsenal & England
1950-51	Harry Johnston	Blackpool & England
1951-52	Billy Wright	Wolverhampton Wanderers & England
1952-53	Nat Lofthouse	Bolton Wanderers & England
1953-54	Tom Finney	Preston North End & England
1954-55	Don Revie	Manchester City & England
1955-56	Bert Trautmann	Manchester City
1956-57	Tom Finney	Preston North End & England
1957-58	Danny Blanchflower	Tottenham Hotspur & Northern Ireland
1958-59	Syd Owen	Luton Town & England
1959-60	Bill Slater	Wolverhampton Wanderers & England
1960-61	Danny Blanchflower	Tottenham Hotspur & Northern Ireland
1961-62	Jimmy Adamson	Burnley
1962-63	Stanley Matthews	Stoke City & England
1963-64	Bobby Moore	West Ham United & England
1964-65	Bobby Collins	Leeds United & Scotland
1965-66	Bobby Charlton	Manchester United & England
1966-67	Jack Charlton	Leeds United & England
1967-68	George Best	Manchester United & Northern Ireland
1968-69	Dave Mackay	Derby County & Scotland
	Tony Book	Manchester City
1969-70	Billy Bremner	Leeds United & Scotland
1970-71	Frank McLintock	Arsenal & Scotland
1971-72	Gordon Banks	Stoke City & England
1972-73	Pat Jennings	Tottenham Hotspur & Northern Ireland
1973-74	Ian Callaghan	Liverpool & England
1974-75	Alan Mullery	Fulham & England
1975-76	Kevin Keegan	Liverpool & England
1976-77	Emlyn Hughes	Liverpool & England
1977-78	Kenny Burns	Nottingham Forest & Scotland
1978-79	Kenny Dalglish	Liverpool & Scotland
1979-80	Terry McDermott	Liverpool & England
1980-81	Frans Thijssen	Ipswich Town & Holland
1981-82	Steve Perryman	Tottenham Hotspur & England
1982-83	Kenny Dalglish	Liverpool & Scotland
1983-84	Ian Rush	Liverpool & Wales
1984-85	Neville Southall	Everton & Wales

1985-86	Gary Lineker	Everton & England
1986-87	Clive Allen	Tottenham Hotspur & England
1987-88	John Barnes	Liverpool & England
1988-89	Steve Nicol	Liverpool & England
1989-90	John Barnes	Liverpool & England
1990-91	Gordon Strachan	Leeds United & Scotland
1991-92	Gary Lineker	Tottenham Hotspur & England
1992-93	Chris Waddle	Sheffield Wednesday & England
1993-94	Alan Shearer	Blackburn Rovers & England
1994-95	Jurgen Klinsmann	Tottenham Hotspur & Germany
1995-96	Eric Cantona	Manchester United & France
1996-97	Gianfranco Zola	Chelsea & Italy
1997-98	Dennis Bergkamp	Arsenal & Holland

PFA AWARDS 1997-98

Player of the Year
1.	Dennis Bergkamp	Arsenal
2.	Andy Cole	Manchester United
3.	Michael Owen	Liverpool

Young Player of the Year
1.	Michael Owen	Liverpool
2.	Kevin Davies	Southampton
3.	Rio Ferdinand	West Ham United

Premiership Team
Goalkeeper	Nigel Martin	Leeds United
Defenders	Gary Neville	Manchester United
	Colin Hendry	Blackburn Rovers
	Gary Pallister	Manchester United
	Graeme Le Saux	Chelsea
Midfield	David Beckham	Manchester United
	David Batty	Newcastle United
	Nicky Butt	Manchester United
Forwards	Ryan Giggs	Manchester United
	Michael Owen	Liverpool
	Dennis Bergkamp	Arsenal

Merit Award
Steve Ogrizovic   Coventry City

CLUBS IN EUROPE 97-98

UEFA Champions' League – Manchester United

Group B Matches

Kosice	**Manchester United**	**0-3**	9,950
	Irwin (31); Berg (61); Cole (88)		
Manchester United	**Juventus**	**3-2**	53,429
Sheringham (28); Scholes (69); Giggs (90)	Del Piero (91); Zidane (90)		
Manchester United	**Fcycnoord**	**2-1**	53,118
Scholes (31); Irwin (72 pen)	Vos (83)		
Feyenoord	**Manchester United**	**1-3**	45,000
Korneev (87)	Cole (31, 44, 74)		
Manchester United	**Kosice**	**3-0**	53,535
Cole (39); Own Goal (85); Sheringham (90)			
Juventus	**Manchester United**	**1-0**	47,786
Inzaghi (84)			

Final Group Table	P	W	D	L	F	A	Pts
Manchester United	6	5	0	1	14	5	15
Juventus	6	4	0	2	12	8	12
Feyenoord	6	3	0	3	8	10	9
Kosice	6	0	0	6	2	13	0

Quarter-Final

Monaco	**Manchester United**	**0-0**	15,000
Manchester United	**Monaco**	**1-1**	53,683
Solskjaer (53)	Trezeguet (5)		

1-1 on aggregate. Monaco win on away goals rule.

UEFA Champions' League – Newcastle United

Qualifying Round

Newcastle United	**Croatia Zagreb**	**2-1**	34,465
Beresford (21, 71)	Cvitanovic (51)		
Croatia Zagreb	**Newcastle United**	**2-2**	34,000
Simic (59); Cvitanovic (90)	Asprilla (44 pen); Ketsbaia (119)		

After extra time. Newcastle United win 4-3 on aggregate.

Group C Matches

Newcastle United   **Barcelona**   3-2 35,274
Asprilla (21 pen, 30, 49)   Luis Enrique (73); Figo (88)

Dynamo Kiev   **Newcastle United**   2-2 100,000
Rebrov (4); Shevchenko (28)   Beresford (78); Own Goal (84)

PSV Eindhoven   **Newcastle United**   1-0 29,200
Jonk (38)

Newcastle United   **PSV Eindhoven**   0-2 35,214
Nilis (32); de Bilde (90)

Barcelona   **Newcastle United**   1-0
Giovanni (17)

Newcastle United   **Dynamo Kiev**   2-0 33,694
Barnes (10); Pearce (21)

Final Group Table	P	W	D	L	F	A	Pts
Dynamo Kiev	6	3	2	1	13	6	11
PSV Eindhoven	6	2	3	1	9	8	9
Newcastle United	6	2	1	3	7	8	7
Barcelona	6	1	2	3	7	14	5

Cup-Winners' Cup – Chelsea

1st Round

Chelsea   **Slovan Bratislava**   2-0 23,067
Di Matteo (51); Granville (80)

Slovan Bratislava   **Chelsea**   0-2 13,850
Vialli (27); Di Matteo (60)

Chelsea win 4-0 on aggregate.

2nd Round

Tromso   **Chelsea**   3-2 6,438
Nilsen (6); Fermann (19); Aarst (87)   Vialli (86, 90)

Chelsea   **Tromso**   7-1 29,363
Petrescu (13, 86); Vialli (24, 60, 75);   B.Johansen (39)
Zola (43); Leboeuf (55 pen)

Chelsea win 10-3 on aggregate.

Quarter-Final

Real Betis   **Chelsea**   1-2 31,000
Alfonso (46)   Flo (8, 12)

Chelsea	**Real Betis**	**3-1**	32,300
Sinclair (29); Di Matteo (49); Zola (90)	George (20)		

Chelsea win 5-2 on aggregate.

Semi Final

Vicenza	**Chelsea**	**1-0**	19,319
Zauli (16)			
Chelsea	**Vicenza**	**3-1**	33,810
Poyet (35); Zola (51); M.Hughes (76)	Luiso (32)		

Chelsea win 3-2 on aggregate.

Final in Stockholm

Chelsea	**VfB Stuttgart**	**1-0**	30,216
Zola (71)			

UEFA Cup – Arsenal, Villa, Liverpool, Leicester

1st Round

PAOK Salonika	**Arsenal**	**1-0**	33,117
Fratzeskos (61)			
Arsenal	**PAOK Salonika**	**1-1**	37,982
Bergkamp (22)	Virzas (86)		

PAOK win 2-1 on aggregate.

Bordeaux	**Aston Villa**	**0-0**	16,000
Aston Villa	**Bordeaux**	**1-0**	33,072
Milosevic (111)			

After extra time. Aston Villa win 1-0 on aggregate.

Atletico Madrid	**Leicester City**	**2-1**	23,000
Juninho (69); Vieri (71 pen)	Marshall (12)		
Leicester City	**Atletico Madrid**	**0-2**	20,776
	Juninho (72); Kiko (82)		

Atletico Madrid win 4-1 on aggregate.

Celtic	**Liverpool**	**2-2**	50,000
McNamara (52); Donnelly (73 pen)	Owen (6); McManaman (89)		
Liverpool	**Celtic**	**0-0**	38,205

2-2 on aggregate. Liverpool win on away goals.

2nd Round

Athletic Bilbao	**Aston Villa**	**0-0**	46,000

Aston Villa   **Athletic Bilbao**   **2-1** 35,915
Taylor (28); Yorke (50)   Gonzalez (70)

Aston Villa win 2-1 on aggregate.

Strasbourg   **Liverpool**   **3-0** 18,813
Zitelli (20, 62); Conteh (70)

Liverpool   **Strasbourg**   **2-0** 32,426
Fowler (63 pen); Riedle (84)

Strasbourg win 3-2 on aggregate.

3rd Round

Steaua Bucharest   **Aston Villa**   **2-1** 25,000
Own Goal (29); Ciocoiu (32)   Yorke (54)

Aston Villa   **Steaua Bucharest**   **2-0** 35,102
Milosevic (71); Taylor (85)

Aston Villa win 3-2 on aggregate.

Quarter-Final

Atletico Madrid   **Aston Villa**   **1-0** 47,000
Vieri (42 pen)

Aston Villa   **Atletico Madrid**   **2-1** 39,163
Taylor (72); Collymore (74)   Caminero (30)

2-2 on aggregate. Atletico Madrid win on away goals rule.

ENGLAND

Wembley, September 10th 1997 – World Cup Qualifying Group Two
ENGLAND   MOLDOVA   4-0 74,102
Scholes (28), Wright (46, 90),
Gascoigne (81)
England: Seaman, G. Neville, Southgate, Campbell, Beckham (Ripley 67) (Butt 75), Batty, Gascoigne, P. Neville, Scholes, L. Ferdinand (Collymore 82), Wright. Subs not used: Pallister, Walker, Le Saux, Lee.
Moldova: Roumanenco, Stroenco, Fistican, Tistimitstanu, Spinu, Shishkin (Popovici 60), Curtean, Culibaba (Suharev 52), Rebetadj, Miterev, Rogaciov (Cibotari 74).

Rome, October 11th 1997 – World Cup Qualifying Group Two
ITALY   ENGLAND   0-0 81,200
Italy: Peruzzi, Nesta, Costacurta, Cannavaro, Maldini (Benarrivo 31), Di Livio (sent off), Dino Baggio, Albertini, Zola (Del Piero 64), Inzaghi (Cheisa 46), Vieri.
England: Seaman, Beckham, Campbell, Adams, Southgate, Le Saux, Ince, Gascoigne (Butt 88), Batty, Sheringham, Wright. Subs not used: G. Neville, Walker, P. Neville, Scholes, McManaman, Fowler.

Wembley, November 15th 1997 – International
ENGLAND   CAMEROON   2-0 46,176
Scholes (45), Fowler (45)
England: Martyn, Campbell, P. Neville, Ince, Southgate (R. Ferdinand 38), Hinchcliffe, Beckham, Gascoigne (R. Lee 73), Fowler, Scholes (Sutton 79), McManaman. Subs not used: Seaman, Batty, Butt, Cole.
Cameroon: Ongandzi, Song, Wome, Mimboe, Kalla, Job, Mboma (Njitap 75), Etchi, Etame (Olembe 73), Foe, Ipoua (Billong 46). Subs not used: Mangan, Mettomo, Njeukam, Zoalang.

Wembley, February 2nd 1998 – International
ENGLAND   CHILE   0-2 65,228
Salas (45, 79)
England: Martyn, G. Neville, Campbell, Batty (Ince 62), Adams, P. Neville (Le Saux 46), Lee, Butt, Dublin, Sheringham (Shearer 62), Owen. Subs not used: Southgate, Hislop, McManaman, Gascoigne.
Chile: Tapia, Villarroel, Reyes, Fuentes, Margas, Rojas, Parraguez, Acuna, Sierra (Valenzuela 88), Barrera (Carreno 77), Salas. Subs not used: Ramirez, Cornejo, Vega, Galdames, Rozental.

Berne, March 25th 1998 – International

SWITZERLAND   ENGLAND   1-1   17,000
Vega (37)   Merson (70)

England: Flowers, Keown, Hinchcliffe, Ince, Southgate, R. Ferdinand, McManaman, Merson (Batty 81), Shearer, Owen (Sheringham 69), Lee. Subs not used: Campbell, Redknapp, Dublin, Matteo, Martyn.

Switzerland: Corminboeuf, Vogel, Fornier, Henchoz, Vega, Yakin, Sesa (Kunz 88), Wicky (Lonfat 81), Grassi, Sforza, Chapuisat. Subs not used: Jeanneret, Wolf, Muller, Zuberbuhler.

Wembley, April 22nd 1998 – International

ENGLAND   PORTUGAL   3-0   63,463
Shearer (5, 65),
Sheringham (46)

England: Seaman, G. Neville, (P. Neville 82), Le Saux, Adams, Campbell, Ince, Batty, Scholes, Beckham, (Merson 46), Sheringham (Owen 76), Shearer. Subs not used: Martyn, Southgate, Parlour, Dublin.

Portugal: Baia, Xavier, Dimas, (Pedro Barbosa 53), Beto, Fernando Couto, Paulo Sousa (Oceano 75 mins), Figo, Joao Pinto (Capucho 68 – sent off), Calado, Paulinho Santos, Cadete. Subs not used: Silvino, Joao Manuel Pinto, Sergio Conceicao, Gomes.

Wembley, May 24th 1998 – International

ENGLAND   SAUDI ARABIA   0-0   63,733
England: Seaman, G. Neville, Hinchcliffe (P. Neville 74), Batty, Adams, Southgate, Beckham (Gascoigne 60), Anderton, Shearer (L. Ferdinand 74), Sheringham (Wright 60), Scholes. Subs not used: Campbell, Flowers, Merson.

Saudi Arabia: Al-Daye, Al-Jahni, Al-Khlaiwi, Zebramawi, Amin (Al-Dosary 78), Al-Shahrani, Al-Jaber, S Al-Owairan (Al-Temiyat 75), Solaimani, Al-Muwalid, K Al-Owairan, Subs not used: Madani, Al-Thyniyan, Saleh, Al-Sadiq, Al-Dossary.

Wembley, May 27th 1998 – International

MOROCCO   ENGLAND   0-1   80,000
                    Owen (59)

Morocco: Benzekri, Saber, Rossi, Negrouz, Hadrioui, Chiba (Amzine 63), Taher, Chippo (Sellami 79), Bassir, Ouakili (Reda 73), Robbi (El Khattabi 63). Subs not used: Triki, Abrami, Azzouzi, Laroussi, Abdeiaoui, Chadi, Chadili.

England: Flowers, Keown, Le Saux, Ince, Campbell, Southgate, Anderton, Gascoigne, Dublin (L. Ferdinand 79), Wright (Owen 26), McManaman. Subs not used: R. Ferdinand, Walker, Neville, Butt, Lee.

Wembley, May 29th 1998 – International

BELGIUM   ENGLAND   0-0   25,000

Belgium: Van de Walle, Deflandre, Van Meir, Verstraeten, Borkelmans, De Boeck, Verheyen (Claessens 62), L. M'Penza, Goossens (M. M'Penza 45), Scifo, Boffin. Subs not used: De Wilde, Staerens, Crasson, Leonard.
England: Martyn, G. Neville (R. Ferdinand 45). P. Neville (Owen 45), Butt, Campbell (Dublin 76), Keown, Lee, Gascoigne (Beckham 50), L. Ferdinand, Merson, Le Saux. Subs not used: Walker, Batty, Sheringham, Shearer, McManaman, Scholes, Anderton.

Marseille, June 15th 1998 – World Cup Finals, Group G

ENGLAND   TUNISIA   2-0   54,587

Shearer (42), Scholes (90)
England: Seaman, Campbell, Adams, Southgate, Le Saux, Anderton, Ince, Batty, Scholes, Sheringham (Owen 85), Shearer. Subs not used: Flowers, Martyn, Keown, R. Ferdinand, G. Neville, Beckham, Lee, McManaman, Merson, L. Ferdinand.
Tunisia: El Ouaer, H Trabelsi (Thabet 79 mins), S Trabelsi, Badra, Boukadida, Clayton, Ghadhbane, Chihi, Souayah (Beya 45 mins), Ben Slimane (Ben Younes 65 mins), Sellimi. Subs not used: Boumnijel, Salhi, Chouchane, Jabaliah, Bouazizi, Ben Ahmen, Jelassi, Melki.

Toulouse, June 22nd 1998 – World Cup Finals, Group G

ENGLAND   ROMANIA   1-2   37,500

Owen (83)   Moldovan (47); Petrescu (90)
England: Seaman, G. Neville, Campbell, Adams, Le Saux, Anderton, Ince (Beckham 33), Batty, Scholes, Sheringham (Owen 73), Shearer. Subs not used: Flowers, Martyn, Keown, R. Ferdinand, Lee, McManaman, Merson, L. Ferdinand.
Romania: Stelea, Petrescu, Ciobotariu, Gheorghe Popescu, Filipescu, Munteanu, Hagi (Stanga 73, Marinescu 84), Galca, Gabriel Popescu, Moldovan (Lacatus 86), Ilie.

Lens, June 26th 1998 – World Cup Finals, Group G

ENGLAND   COLOMBIA   2-0   41,275

Anderton (20); Beckham (30)
England: Seaman, G. Neville, Campbell, Adams, Le Saux, Anderton (Lee 79), Ince (Batty 82), Beckham, Scholes (McManaman 73), Owen, Shearer. Subs not used: Flowers, Martyn, Keown, R. Ferdinand, Merson, L. Ferdinand.
Colombia: Mondragon, Cabrera, Bermudez, Palacios, Moreno, Ricon, Serna (Aristazabal 46), Lozano, Valderrama, Preciado (Valencia 46), De Avila (Ricard 56).

St Etienne, June 30th 1998 – World Cup Finals, Second Round

ARGENTINA   ENGLAND   2-2 30,600

Batistuta (6 pen); Zanetti (45)   Shearer (10 pen); Owen (16)

aet Argentina win 4-3 on penalties.

Argentina: Roa, Vivas, Ayala, Charmot, Zanetti, Almeyda, Simone (Berti 91), Ortega, Veron, Batistuta (Balbo 68), Lopez (Gallardo 68).

England: Seaman, G. Neville, Campbell, Adams, Le Saux (Southgate 70), Anderton (Batty 96), Ince, Beckham (sent off), Scholes (Merson 78), Owen, Shearer. Subs not used: Flowers, Martyn, Keown, R. Ferdinand, Sheringham, L. Ferdinand.

Post-War England Manager Records

Manager	Tenure	P	W	D	L	F	A
Glenn Hoddle	7/96-	24	15	4	5	36	10
Terry Venables	01/94-06/96	23	11	11	1	35	13
Graham Taylor	08/90-11/93	38	18	12	8	62	32
Bobby Robson	08/82-07/90	95	47	30	18	158	60
Ron Greenwood	08/77-07/82	56	33	13	10	93	40
Don Revie	10/74-07/77	29	14	8	7	49	25
Joe Mercer	04/74-10/74	7	3	3	1	9	7
Sir Alf Ramsey	01/63-03/74	110	67	26	17	224	98
Sir Walter Winterbottom	08/46-12/62	139	78	33	28	383	196

Goalscorer Summary 1997-98

	Player	Goals	
Alan	SHEARER	4	Portugal (2), Tunisia, Argentina (pen)
Michael	OWEN	3	Morocco, Romania, Argentina
Paul	SCHOLES	3	Moldova, Cameroon, Tunisia
Ian	WRIGHT	2	Moldova (2),
Paul	GASCOIGNE	1	Moldova
Robbie	FOWLER	1	Cameroon
Paul	MERSON	1	Switzerland
Teddy	SHERINGHAM	1	Portugal
Darren	ANDERTON	1	Colombia
David	BECKHAM	1	Colombia

Appearance Summary 1997-98

	Player	Club	Tot	St	Sub	SNU	PS
Tony	ADAMS	Arsenal	8	8	0	0	0
Darren	ANDERTON	Tottenham Hotspur	6	6	0	1	2
David	BATTY	Newcastle United	10	7	3	2	1
David	BECKHAM	Manchester United	9	7	2	1	3
Nicky	BUTT	Manchester United	4	2	2	2	0
Sol	CAMPBELL	Tottenham Hotspur	11	11	0	2	1
Andy	COLE	Manchester United	0	0	0	1	0
Stan	COLLYMORE	Liverpool	1	0	1	0	0
Dion	DUBLIN	Coventry City	3	2	1	2	1
Les	FERDINAND	Tottenham Hotspur	4	1	2	4	1
Rio	FERDINAND	West Ham United	3	1	2	5	0
Tim	FLOWERS	Blackburn Rovers	2	2	0	5	0
Robbie	FOWLER	Liverpool	1	1	0	1	0
Paul	GASCOIGNE	Rangers/Middlesbro'	6	5	1	1	3
Andy	HINCHCLIFFE	Everton	3	3	0	0	1
Shaka	HISLOP	Newcastle United	0	0	0	1	0
Paul	INCE	Liverpool	10	9	1	0	2
Martin	KEOWN	Arsenal	3	3	0	0	4
Graeme	LE SAUX	Chelsea	9	8	1	0	1
Robert	LEE	Newcastle United	5	3	2	6	0
Nigel	MARTYN	Leeds United	3	0	0	6	0
Steve	McMANAMAN	Liverpool	4	3	1	6	0
Paul	MERSON	Middlesbrough	4	2	2	4	1
Gary	NEVILLE	Manchester United	8	8	0	3	2
Phil	NEVILLE	Manchester United	6	4	2	1	2
Michael	OWEN	Liverpool	9	4	5	0	1
Gary	PALLISTER	Manchester United	0	0	0	1	0
Ray	PARLOUR	Arsenal	0	0	0	1	0
Jamie	REDKNAPP	Liverpool	0	0	0	1	0
Stuart	RIPLEY	Blackburn Rovers	1	0	1	0	1
Paul	SCHOLES	Manchester United	8	8	0	2	3
David	SEAMAN	Arsenal	8	8	0	1	0
Alan	SHEARER	Newcastle United	8	7	1	1	1
Teddy	SHERINGHAM	Manchester United	7	6	1	3	5
Gareth	SOUTHGATE	Aston Villa	8	7	1	2	1
Chris	SUTTON	Blackburn Rovers	1	0	1	0	0
Ian	WALKER	Tottenham	0	0	0	3	0
Ian	WRIGHT	Arsenal	4	3	1	0	1

1997-98 APPEARANCE CHART

	Moldova	Italy	Cameroon	Chile	Switzerland	Portugal	Saudi Arabia	Morocco	Belgium	Tunisia	Romania	Colombia	Argentina
ADAMS	–	•	–	–	–	–	–	–	•	•	–	•	•
ANDERTON	–	–	–	–	–	•	•	•	*	•	•	•(79)	•(96)
BATTY	•	•	*	•(62)	*(81)	–	–	–	*	•	•	*(82)	*(96)
BECKHAM	•(67)	–	–	–	–	•(46)	•(60)	–	•(50)	*	*(33)	•	•
BUTT	*(75)	*(88)	*	–	–	–	–	*	•	–	–	–	–
CAMPBELL	•	•	•	•	*	•	*	•	•(76)	•	•	•	•
COLE	–	–	*	–	–	–	–	–	–	–	–	–	–
COLLYMORE	*(82)	–	–	–	–	–	–	–	–	–	–	–	–
DUBLIN	–	–	–	*	*	–	–	•(79)	*(76)	•	•	•	–
FERDINAND, L.	•(82)	–	–	–	–	–	*(74)	*(79)	•	*	*	*	*
FERDINAND, R.	–	–	*(38)	–	•	–	–	*	*(46)	–	*	*	*
FLOWERS	–	–	–	–	–	–	*	•	–	*	•	•	•
FOWLER	–	*	–	–	–	–	–	–	–	–	–	–	–
GASCOIGNE	•	•(88)	•(73)	*	–	–	*(60)	•	•(50)	–	–	–	–
HINCHCLIFFE	–	–	–	–	–	–	•(74)	–	–	–	–	–	–
HISLOP	–	–	–	–	–	–	–	–	–	–	–	–	–
INCE	–	•	–	*(62)	–	–	–	–	–	•	•(33)	•(82)	–
KEOWN	–	–	–	–	•	–	–	•	*	*	*	*	–
LE SAUX	*	–	•	–	*(46)	–	–	–	–	–	–	–	•(70)
LE TISSIER	–	–	–	–	–	–	–	–	–	–	–	–	–
LEE	*	–	–	*(73)	•	•	–	•	*	•	*(79)	•	*
MARTYN	–	–	–	–	*	*	–	–	–	–	–	–	–
MATTEO	–	–	–	–	*	–	–	–	–	–	–	–	–
McMANAMAN	–	*	*	*	–	•	–	*	*	*	•	*(73)	•
MERSON	–	–	–	•(81)	*(46)	–	–	•	*	*	*	–	*(78)
NEVILLE, G.	•	*	–	–	•	•(82)	•	*	•(46)	•	•	•	•
NEVILLE, P.	•	*	–	•	•(46)	–	*(82)	*(74)	–	•(46)	•	•	•
OWEN	–	–	–	•	•(69)	•(76)	–	*(26)	•(46)	•(85)	•(73)	–	•
PALLISTER	*	–	–	–	–	–	–	–	–	–	–	–	–
PARLOUR	–	–	–	–	–	*	–	–	–	–	–	–	–

• Started match. * Substitute - No appearance. A number next to an * indicates an appearance as substitute, the number giving the minute the player entered the match.

	Moldova	Italy	Cameroon	Chile	Switzerland	Portugal	Saudi Arabia	Morocco	Belgium	Tunisia	Romania	Colombia	Argentina
REDKNAPP	–	–	–	–	*	–	–	–	–	–	–	–	–
RIPLEY	*(67)	(75)	–	–	–	–	–	–	–	–	–	–	–
SCHOLES	•	*	•(79)	–	–	•	•	–	*	•	•	•(73)	•(78)
SEAMAN	•	•	*	–	–	•	•	–	–	•	•	•	•
SHEARER	–	–	–	*(62)	–	•	•	•(74)	–	*	•	•	•
SHERINGHAM	–	•	–	•(62)	*(69)	•(76)	•(60)	–	*	•(85)	•(73)	*	*
SOUTHGATE	•	•	•(38)	*	*	•	•	•	–	•	–	–	*(70)
SUTTON	–	–	*(79)										
WALKER	*	*	–	–	–	–	–	–	*	*	–	–	–
WRIGHT	•	•	–	–	–	–	*(60)	•(26)	–	–	–	–	–

England Red Cards

Player	Opponents	Venue	Year	Score
Alan Mullery	Yugoslavia	Florence	1968	0-1
Alan Ball	Poland	Chorzow	1973	0-2
Trevor Cherry	Argentina	Buenos Aires	1977	1-1
Ray Wilkins	Morocco	Monterrey	1986	0-0
David Beckham	Argentina	Saint-Etienne	1998	2-2 aet

England have never won a game in which they have had a player sent off.

FRANCE '98

GROUP A

Brazil v Scotland	... ...	2-1
Morocco v Norway	... ...	2-2
Scotland v Norway	... ...	1-1
Brazil v Morocco	... ...	3-0
Scotland v Morocco	... ...	0-3
Brazil v Norway	... ...	1-2

	P	W	D	L	F	A	Pt
Brazil *	3	2	0	1	6	3	6
Norway *	3	1	2	0	5	4	5
Morocco	3	1	1	1	5	5	4
Scotland	3	0	1	2	2	6	1

GROUP B

Italy v Chile	... ...	2-2
Cameroon v Austria	... ...	1-1
Chile v Austria	... ...	1-1
Italy v Cameroon	... ...	3-0
Chile v Cameroon	... ...	1-1
Italy v Austria	... ...	2-1

	P	W	D	L	F	A	Pt
Italy *	3	2	1	0	7	3	7
Chile *	3	0	3	0	4	4	3
Austria	3	0	2	1	3	4	2
Cameroon	3	0	2	1	2	5	2

GROUP C

Saudi Arabia v Denmark	... ...	0-1
France v South Africa	... ...	3-0
South Africa v Denmark	... ...	1-1
France v Saudi Arabia	... ...	4-0
France v Denmark	... ...	2-1
South Africa v Saudi Arabia	...	2-2

	P	W	D	L	F	A	Pt
France *	3	3	0	0	9	1	9
Denmark *	3	1	1	1	3	3	4
S. Africa	3	0	2	1	3	6	2
S. Arabia	3	0	1	2	1	7	1

GROUP D

Paraguay v Bulgaria	... ...	0-0
Spain v Nigeria	... ...	2-3
Nigeria v Bulgaria	... ...	1-0
Spain v Paraguay	... ...	0-0
Spain v Bulgaria	... ...	6-1
Nigeria v Paraguay	... ...	1-3

	P	W	D	L	F	A	Pt
Nigeria *	3	2	0	1	5	5	6
Paraguay *	3	1	2	0	3	1	5
Spain	3	1	1	1	8	4	4
Bulgaria	3	0	1	2	1	7	1

GROUP E

S. Korea v Mexico	... ...	1-3
Holland v Belgium	... ...	0-0
Belgium v Mexico	... ...	2-2
Holland v S. Korea	... ...	5-0
Belgium v S. Korea	... ...	1-1
Holland v Mexico	... ...	2-2

	P	W	D	L	F	A	Pt
Holland *	3	1	2	0	7	2	5
Mexico *	3	1	2	0	7	5	5
Belgium	3	0	3	0	3	3	3
S. Korea	3	0	1	2	2	9	1

GROUP F

Yugoslavia v Iran	... ...	1-0
Germany v USA	... ...	2-0
Germany v Yugoslavia	... ...	2-2
USA v Iran	... ...	1-2
Germany v Iran	... ...	2-0
USA v Yugoslavia	... ...	0-1

	P	W	D	L	F	A	Pt
Germany *	3	2	1	0	6	2	7
Yugoslavia *	3	2	1	0	4	2	7
Iran	3	1	0	2	2	4	3
USA	3	0	0	3	1	5	0

GROUP G

England v Tunisia … … … … 2-0
Romania v Colombia … … … 1-0
Colombia v Tunisia… … … … 1-0
Romania v England… … … … 2-1
Colombia v England … … … 2-0
Romania v Tunisia … … … … 1-1

	P	W	D	L	F	A	Pt
Romania *	3	2	1	0	4	2	7
England *	3	2	0	1	5	2	6
Colombia	3	1	0	2	1	3	3
Tunisia	3	0	1	2	1	4	1

GROUP H

Argentina v Japan … … … … 1-0
Jamaica v Croatia … … … … 1-3
Japan v Croatia … … … … 0-1
Argentina v Jamaica … … … 5-0
Argentina v Croatia… … … … 1-0
Japan v Jamaica … … … … … 1-2

	P	W	D	L	F	A	Pt
Argentina *	3	3	0	0	7	0	9
Croatia *	3	2	0	1	4	2	6
Jamaica	3	1	0	2	3	9	3
Japan	3	0	0	3	1	4	0

* qualify for Second Round

SECOND ROUND

Saturday, June 27th

Italy v Norway … … … … … 1-0
Brazil v Chile   … … … … … 4-1

Sunday, June 28th

France v Paraguay †* … … … 1-0
Nigeria v Denmark … … … … 1-4

Monday, June 29th

Germany v Mexico … … … … 2-1
Holland v Yugoslavia … … … 2-1

Tuesday, June 30th

Romania v Croatia … … … … 0-1
Argentina v England † … … … 2-2
Argentina win 4-3 on pens
*† aet. * golden goal*

Euro 2000 Group 5 Fixtures

05/09/98	Sweden	v	England
10/10/98	England	v	Bulgaria
14/10/98	Luxembourg	v	England
27/03/99	England	v	Poland
05/06/99	England	v	Sweden
09/06/99	Bulgaria	v	England
04/09/99	England	v	Luxembourg
08/09/99	Poland	v	England

Sixteen countries will make the Finals: the co-hosts, Belgium and Holland; the nine group winners; the best runner-up; and four teams from a play-off system, which will take place in November 1999.

England v Sweden – The Record

Date	Result	Venue	Competiton
20/10/08	12-1	London	OGr1
21/05/23	4-2	Stockholm	Friendly
17/05/37	4-0	Stockholm	Friendly
19/11/47	4-2	London	Friendly
13/05/49	1-3	Stockholm	Friendly
16/05/56	0-0	Stockholm	Friendly
28/10/59	2-3	London	Friendly
16/05/65	2-1	Gothenburg	Friendly
22/05/68	3-1	London	Friendly
10/06/79	0-0	Stockholm	Friendly
10/09/86	0-1	Stockholm	Friendly
19/10/88	0-0	London	World Cup Qualifier
06/09/89	0-0	Stockholm	World Cup Qualifier
17/06/92	1-2		Euro Championship Finals
08/06/95	3-3	Leeds	Umbro Cup

England v Poland – The Record

Date	Result	Venue	Competiton
05/01/66	1-1	Liverpool	Friendly
05/07/66	1-0	Chorzow	Friendly
06/06/73	0-2	Chorzow	World Cup Qualifier
17/10/73	1-1	London	World Cup Qualifier
11/06/86	3-0	Monterrey	World Cup Group
03/06/89	3-0	London	World Cup Qualifier
11/10/89	0-0	Chorzow	World Cup Qualifier
17/10/90	2-0	London	European Cup Qualifier
13/11/91	1-1	Poznan	European Cup Qualifier
29/05/93	1-1	Katowice	World Cup Qualifier
08/09/93	3-0	Wembley	World Cup Qualifier
09/10/96	2-0	Wembley	World Cup Qualifier
31/05/96	2-0	Katowice	World Cup Qualifier

England v Bulgaria – The Record

Date	Result	Venue	Competiton
07/06/62	0-0	Rancagua	World Cup Group Four
11/12/68	1-1	London	Friendly
01/06/74	1-0	Sofia	Friendly
06/06/79	3-0	Sofia	European Cup Qualifier
22/11/79	2-0	London	European Cup Qualifier
02/03/96	1-0	Wembley	Friendly

England v Luxembourg – The Record

Date	Result	Venue	Competiton
21/05/27	5-2	Luxembourg	Friendly
19/10/60	9-0	Luxembourg	World Cup Qualifier
28/09/61	4-1	London	World Cup Qualifier
30/03/77	5-0	London	World Cup Qualifier
12/10/77	2-0	Luxembourg	World Cup Qualifier
15/12/82	9-0	London	European Cup Qualifier
16/11/83	4-0	Luxembourg	European Cup Qualifier

CLUB DIRECTORY
1998-99

Arsenal
Aston Villa
Blackburn Rovers
Charlton Athletic
Chelsea
Coventry City
Derby County
Everton
Leeds United
Leicester City
Liverpool
Manchester United
Middlesbrough
Newcastle United
Nottingham Forest
Sheffield Wednesday
Southampton
Tottenham Hotspur
West Ham United
Wimbledon

Arsenal

Formed as Dial Square, a workshop in Woolwich Arsenal with a sundial over the entrance, in October 1886, becoming Royal Arsenal, the 'Royal' possibly from a local public house, later the same year. Turned professional and became Woolwich Arsenal in 1891. Selected for an expanded Football League Division Two in 1893, the first southern team to join.

   Moved from the Manor Ground, Plumstead, south-east London, to Highbury, north London, in 1913, changing name again at the same time. Elected from fifth in Division Two to the expanded First Division for the 1919-20 season and never relegated. Premier League founder members 1992. Last season became only second team to do the Double twice.

Ground:	Arsenal Stadium, Avenell Road, Highbury, London N5 1BU
Club No.:	0171-704-4000 **Information:** 0171-704-4242
Box Office:	0171-704-4040 **CC Bookings:** 0171-413-3370
News:	0891 20 20 21
Capacity:	39,497 **Pitch size:** 110 yds x 71 yds
Colours:	Red/White sleeves, White, Red **Nickname:** Gunners
Radio:	1548AM Capital Radio
Internet:	http://www.arsenal.co.uk

Chairman: P.D. Hill-Wood   **Vice-Chairman:** David Dein
MD: Ken Friar   **Manager:** Arsène Wenger
Assistant/Coach: Pat Rice   **Physio:** Gary Lewin MCSP SRP

League History: 1893 Elected to Division 2; 1904-13 Division 1; 1913-19 Division 2; 1919-92 Division 1; 1992- FA Premier League.

Honours: *FA Premier League: Champions* 1997-98; *Football League: Division 1 Champions* 1930-31, 1932-33, 1933-34, 1934-35, 1937-38, 1947-48, 1952-53, 1970-71, 1988-89, 1990-91; *Runners-up* 1925-26, 1931-32, 1972-73; *Division 1 Runners-up* 1903-04. *FA Cup: Winners* 1929-30, 1935-36, 1949-50, 1970-71, 1978-79, 1992-93, 1997-98; *Runners-up* 1926-27, 1931-32, 1951-52, 1971-72, 1977-78, 1979-80. *Football League Cup: Winners* 1986-87, 1992-93; *Runners-up* 1967-68, 1968-69, 1987-88. *League-Cup Double Performed:* 1970-71, 1997-98. *Cup-Cup Double Performed:* 1992-93. *Cup-Winners' Cup Winners* 1993-94; *Runners-up* 1979-80, 1994-95. *Fairs Cup: Winners* 1969-70. *European Super Cup: Runners-up* 1994-95.

European Record: Champions' Cup (2): 71-72 (QF), 91-92 (2); Cup-Winners' Cup (3): 79-80 (F), 93-94 (W), 94-95 (F); UEFA Cup (8): 63-64

(2), 69-70 (W), 71-70 (Q), 78-79 (3), 81-82 (2), 82-83 (1), 96-97 (1), 97-98 (1).

Managers: Sam Hollis 1894-97; Tom Mitchell 1897-98; George Elcoat 1898-99; Harry Bradshaw 1899-1904; Phil Kelso 1904-08; George Morrell 1908-15; Leslie Knighton 1919-25; Herbert Chapman 1925-34; George Allison 1934-47; Tom Whittaker 1947-56; Jack Crayston 1956-58; George Swindin 1958-62; Billy Wright 1962-66; Bertie Mee 1966-76; Terry Neill 1976-83; Don Howe 1984-86; *(FAPL)* George Graham May 1986-Feb 1995; Stewart Houston (caretaker) Feb 1995-May 1995; Bruce Rioch May 1995-Aug 1996; Stewart Houston (caretaker) Aug 1996; Pat Rice (caretaker) Sept 1996; Arsène Wenger Sept 1996-.

Season 1997-98

Biggest Home Win:	5-0 v Barnsley and Wimbledon
Biggest Home Defeat:	1-3 v Blackburn Rovers
Biggest Away Win:	4-1 v Blackburn Rovers
Biggest Away Defeat:	0-4 v Liverpool
Biggest Home Att:	38,269 v Everton
Smallest Home Att:	37,324 v Coventry City
Average Attendance:	38,048
Leading Scorer:	Dennis Bergkamp – 16

All-Time Records

Record FAPL Win:	5-0 v Barnsley and Wimbledon, 1997-98
Record FAPL Defeat:	0-4 v Liverpool, 1997-98
Record FL Win:	12-0 v Loughborough Town, Division 2, 12/3/1900
Record FL Defeat:	0-8 v Loughborough Town, Division 2, 12/12/1896
Record Cup Win:	11-1 v Darwen, FA Cup R3, 9/1/32
Record Fee Received:	£3.2m rising to £5m, John Hartson, West Ham United, 3/97
Record Fee Paid:	£7.5m Dennis Bergkamp, Internazionale, 6/95
Most FL Apps:	547 – David O'Leary, 1975-92
Most FAPL Apps:	212 – Nigel Winterburn, 1992-98
Most FAPL Goals:	104 – Ian Wright, 1992-98

Highest Scorer in FAPL Season: Ian Wright, 30, 1992-93
Record Attendance (all-time): 73,295 v Sunderland, Division 1, 9/3/35
Record Attendance (FAPL): 38,377 v Tottenham Hotspur 29/4/95
Most FAPL Goals in Season: 68, 1997-98 – 38 games
Most FAPL Points in Season: 78, 1997-98 – 38 games

Player	Tot	St	Sb	Snu	PS	Gls	Y	R	Fa	La	Fg	Lg
ADAMS	26	26	0	0	0	3	6	0	6	2	0	0
ANELKA	26	16	10	8	13	6	3	0	9	4	3	0
BERGKAMP	28	28	0	0	2	16	6	0	7	4	3	2
BOA MORTE ...	15	4	11	8	2	0	2	0	4	1	0	2
BOULD	24	21	3	4	0	0	8	0	5	3	0	0
CROWE	0	0	0	2	0	0	0	0	1	1	0	0
DAY	0	0	0	1	0	0	0	0	0	0	0	0
DIXON	28	26	2	0	3	0	3	0	7	3	0	0
GARDE	10	6	4	3	1	0	3	0	1	0	0	0
GRIMANDI	22	16	6	8	3	1	5	0	5	3	0	0
HUGHES	17	7	10	10	2	2	0	0	6	4	0	1
KEOWN	18	18	0	0	1	0	2	1	7	2	0	0
LUKIC	0	0	0	14	0	0	0	0	0	0	0	0
MANNINGER	7	7	0	24	0	0	0	0	5	5	0	0
MARSHALL	3	1	2	9	0	0	0	0	0	2	0	0
McGOWAN	1	0	1	0	0	0	0	0	0	0	0	0
MENDEZ	3	1	2	1	1	0	0	0	0	2	0	1
MUNTASSER	0	0	0	0	0	0	0	0	0	1	0	0
OVERMARS	32	32	0	0	13	12	0	0	9	3	2	2
PARLOUR	34	34	0	0	15	5	6	0	7	4	1	0
PETIT	32	32	0	0	5	2	4	1	7	3	0	0
PLATT	31	11	20	1	3	3	4	0	4	4	0	1
RANKIN	1	0	1	2	0	0	0	0	0	0	0	0
ROSE	0	0	0	0	0	0	0	0	0	0	0	0
SEAMAN	31	31	0	0	0	0	1	0	4	1	0	0
UPSON	5	5	0	6	1	0	0	0	1	2	0	0
VERNAZZA	1	1	0	0	1	0	0	0	0	1	0	0
VIEIRA	33	31	2	0	4	2	8	1	9	2	0	0
WINTERBURN ...	36	35	1	0	2	1	3	0	8	3	0	0
WREH	16	7	9	3	7	3	0	0	6	3	1	0
WRIGHT	24	22	2	0	7	10	7	0	1	1	0	1
Own Goals						2						

5-Year Record

	Div.	P	W	D	L	F	A	Pts	Pos	FAC	FLC
93-94	PL	42	18	17	7	53	28	71	4	4	4
94-95	PL	42	13	12	17	52	49	51	12	3	5
95-96	PL	38	17	12	9	49	32	63	5	3	SF
96-97	PL	38	19	11	8	62	32	68	3	4	4
97-98	PL	38	23	9	6	68	33	78	1	W	SF

NB: A key to the abbreviations used in this Club Directory section can be found at the end of this section after the entry for Crystal Palace.

Gunners Blazing Double

Approaching his first full season as manager of a Premiership club, Arsenal manager Arsène Wenger invested heavily in overseas players. In came Marc Overmars for £7m, and Emmanuel Petit, Luis Boa Morte, Gilles Grimandi and Matthew Upson for a combined fee of close on £8m; £5m was recouped from the sale of Paul Merson. Petit forged an almost perfect partnership with Patrick Vieira in midfield while Ray Parlour flourished to become a player of genuine international quality despite being constantly overlooked by Glenn Hoddle. Down the flank Dutchman Overmars more than made up for the loss of Merson.

Arsenal were quickly into their stride, finding the target nine times in their opening four league games. Ian Wright struck three times in the first two games before Dennis Bergkamp, the eventual PFA and Sports Writers' Player of the Year, hit five goals in two games including a hat trick in a stormy 3-3 draw at Leicester. That hat-trick earned him the first ever 1-2-3 in Goal of the Month. Two games later Wright scored three times during a 4-1 destruction of Bolton at Highbury which took him past Cliff Bastin's club record of 178 goals. Arsenal headed into November on the back of an unbeaten 12-match run in the Premiership.

The bubble burst at Derby before Manchester United were defeated 3-2 at Highbury in an absorbing contest but it was the only game in a six-match spell in which the Gunners scored. Arsenal's hopes looked to be shattered following a home defeat by Blackburn in December and despite taking 17 points from the next seven games, when Arsenal took to the pitch prior to a goalless draw at West Ham on 2 March they trailed United by an almighty twelve points, but did have three games in hand.

In Arsenal's favour, though, was a magnificent defence which has served the club so well for a decade. The draw at West Ham was the last time Arsenal were to drop points in a match of any significance. With young Christopher Wreh, a bargain buy at £300,000, blossoming without playing a full league game all season, Arsenal became an unstoppable force as a Premiership record of ten consecutive victories was achieved. The match which turned the Championship race in their favour was played in the morning of 14 March when Overmars' second-half goal gave Arsenal the double over Manchester United. The champions were now just six points ahead but Arsenal had three games in hand. After four successive 1-0 wins and eight consecutive clean sheets, the Gunners went into overdrive with 19 goals in six games as United's lead was wiped out. With an awesome performance on 2 May Arsenal destroyed Everton 4-0 at Highbury to clinch their third title in ten years. Few who saw it will ever forget skipper Tony Adams' goal minutes from time which more than anything summed up the Arsenal of 1998.

The one disappointment in Arsenal's season was in the UEFA Cup where an early exit was endured. But in the FA Cup there was no stopping the Gunners although they did need penalty shoot-outs to account for Port Vale and West Ham. Two games were also required to repel Palace but Middlesbrough and Wolves, in the semi final, were seen off at the first attempt. Goals by Overmars and Anelka in the Final against Newcastle ensured Wenger's place in folklore as the first overseas manager to win not only the league title but the historic Double. Hopes of lifting the Coca-Cola Cup for a third time were dashed at the penultimate stage as Chelsea blocked that path to Wembley. ■

Results 1997-98

FA Carling Premiership

Date	Opponents	Ven	Res	Atten	Scorers
08-Aug	Leeds U.	A	1-1	37,993	Wright (35)
10-Aug	Coventry C.	H	2-0	37,324	Wright (29, 47)
22-Aug	Southampton	A	3-1	15,246	Overmars (19); Bergkamp (57, 78)
26-Aug	Leicester C.	A	3-3	21,089	Bergkamp (9, 22, 90)
29-Aug	Tottenham H.	H	0-0	38,102	
12-Sep	Bolton W.	H	4-1	38,138	Wright (20, 25, 81); Parlour (44)
20-Sep	Chelsea	A	3-2	33,012	Bergkamp (45, 59); Winterburn (89)
22-Sep	West Ham U.	H	4-0	38,012	Bergkamp (12); Wright (12 pen); Overmars (39, 45)
26-Sep	Everton	A	2-2	32,044	Wright (32); Overmars (41)
03-Oct	Barnsley	H	5-0	38,049	Bergkamp (25, 31); Wright (26); Parlour (44); Platt (63)
17-Oct	C. Palace	A	0-0	26,918	
25-Oct	Aston Villa	H	0-0	38,081	
31-Oct	Derby Co.	A	0-3	30,004	
08-Nov	Man Utd	H	3-2	38,083	Anelka (9); Vieira (26); Platt (83)
21-Nov	Sheffield W.	A	0-2	34,373	
29-Nov	Liverpool	H	0-1	38,094	
05-Dec	Newcastle U.	A	1-0	36,751	Wright (36)
12-Dec	Blackburn R.	H	1-3	38,147	Overmars (18)
25-Dec	Leicester C.	H	2-1	38,023	Platt (36); OG (56, Walsh)
27-Dec	Tottenham H.	A	1-1	29,610	Parlour (62)
09-Jan	Leeds U.	H	2-1	38,018	Overmars (60, 72)
16-Jan	Coventry C.	A	2-2	22,864	Bergkamp (50); Anelka (57)
30-Jan	Southampton	H	3-0	38,056	Bergkamp (62); Adams (67); Anelka (68)
07-Feb	Chelsea	H	2-0	38,083	Hughes (4, 42)
20-Feb	C. Palace	H	1-0	38,094	Grimandi (49)
01-Mar	West Ham U.	H	0-0	25,717	
10-Mar	Wimbledon	A	1-0	22,291	Wreh (21)
13-Mar	Man Utd	A	1-0	55,175	Overmars (79)
27-Mar	Sheffield W.	H	1-0	38,087	Bergkamp (35)
30-Mar	Bolton W.	A	1-0	25,000	Wreh (47)
10-Apr	Newcastle U.	H	3-1	38,102	Anelka (41, 64); Vieira (72)
12-Apr	Blackburn R.	A	4-1	28,212	Bergkamp (2); Parlour (7, 14); Anelka (42)
17-Apr	Wimbledon	H	5-0	38,024	Adams (11); Overmars (17); Bergkamp (19); Petit (54); Wreh (88)

24-Apr	Barnsley	A	2-0	18,691	Bergkamp (23); Overmars (76)
27-Apr	Derby Co.	H	1-0	38,121	Petit (34)
02-May	Everton	H	4-0	38,269	OG (6, Bilic); Overmars (28, 57); Adams (89)
05-May	Liverpool	A	0-4	44,417	
09-May	Aston Villa	A	0-1	39,373	

FA Challenge Cup

Sponsored by Littlewoods Pools

Date	Opponents	Vn	Rnd	Res	Atten	Scorers
03-Jan	Port Vale	H	3R	0-0	37,471	
14-Jan	Port Vale	A	3RR	1-1	14,964	Bergkamp (100)
	aet. Arsenal win 4-3 on penalties					
24-Jan	Middlesbrough	A	4R	2-1	28,264	Overmars (1); Parlour (19)
15-Feb	C. Palace	H	5R	0-0	37,164	
25-Feb	C. Palace	A	5RR	2-1	15,674	Anelka (2); Bergkamp (28)
08-Mar	West Ham Utd	H	6R	1-1	38,077	Bergkamp (26 pen)
17-Mar	West Ham Utd	A	6RR	1-1	25,859	Anelka (45)
	aet. Arsenal win 4-3 on penalties					
05-Apr	Wolverham'n	A	SF	1-0	39,372	Wreh (12)
16-May	Newcastle U.	H	F	2-0		Overmars (23); Anelka (69)

Coca-Cola League Cup

Date	Opponents	Vn	Rnd	Res	Atten	Scorers
14-Oct	Birmingham C.	H	3R	4-1	27,097	Boa Morte (62, 108); Platt (99 pen); Mendez (113) *aet*
18-Nov	Coventry C.	H	4R	1-0	30,199	Bergkamp (99) *aet*
06-Jan	West Ham U.	A	QF	2-1	24,770	Wright (25); Overmars (52)
28-Jan	Chelsea	H	SF1L	2-1	38,114	Overmars (23); S.Hughes (47)
18-Feb	Chelsea	A	SF2L	1-3	34,330	Bergkamp (81 pen)
	Chelsea win 4-3 on aggregate					

UEFA Cup

Date	Opponents	Vn	Rnd	Res	Atten	Scorers
16-Sep	PAOK	A	1R1L	0-1	33,117	
30-Sep	PAOK	H	1R2L	1-1	37,982	Bergkamp (22)
	PAOK win 2-1 on aggregate					

Aston Villa

Founded in 1874 by cricketers from the Aston Wesleyan Chapel, Lozells, who played on Aston Park, moving to a field in Wellington Road, Perry Barr in 1876. Prominent nationally, the club was a founder member of the Football League in 1888.

The landlord at Perry Barr made such demands that the club sought its own ground and eventually moved back to Aston occupying the Aston Lower Grounds, which had already been used for some big games. Not known as Villa Park until some time later, the ground first saw league football in 1897. Premier League founder members 1992.

Ground: Villa Park, Trinity Rd, Birmingham, B6 6HE
Club No.: 0121-327 2299 **Fax:** 0121-322 2107
Box Office: 0121-327 5353 **CC Bookings:** 0121-607 8000
News: 0891 12 11 48 **Ticket:** 0891 12 18 48
Capacity: 40,530 **Pitch:** 115 yds x 75 yds
Colours: Claret/Blue, White, Blue/Claret **Nickname:** The Villains
Radio: 1152AM Sport Extra
Internet: –

President: J.A. Alderson **Chairman:** Doug Ellis
Secretary: Steven Stride
Manager: John Gregory **Assistant:** Allan Evans
First Team Coach: Steve Harrison **Physio:** Jim Walker

League History: 1888 Founder Member of the League; 1936-38 Division 2; 1938-59 Division 1; 1959-60 Division 2; 1960-67 Division 1; 1967-70 Division 2; 1970-72 Division 3; 1972-75 Division 2; 1975-87 Division 1; 1987-88 Division 2; 1988-92 Division 1; 1992- FA Premier League.

Honours: *FA Premier League: Runners-up 1992-93; Football League: Division 1 Champions 1893-94, 1895-96, 1896-97, 1898-99, 1899-1900, 1909-10, 1980-81; Runners-up 1888-89, 1902-03, 1907-08, 1910-11, 1912-13, 1913-14, 1930-31, 1932-33, 1989-90; Division 1 Champions 1937-38, 1959-60; Runners-up 1974-75, 1987-88; Division 3 Champions 1971-72. FA Cup: Winners 1887, 1895, 1897, 1905, 1913, 1920, 1957; Runners-up 1892, 1924. League-Cup Double Performed: 1896-97. Football League Cup: Winners 1961, 1975, 1977, 1994, 1996; Runners-up 1963, 1971. Champions' Cup: Winners 1981-82. European Super Cup: Winners 1982-83. World Club Championship: Runners-up 1982-83.*

European Record: CC (2): 81 82 (W), 82-83 (QF); CWC (0); UEFA (7): 75-76 (1), 77-78 (Q), 83-84 (2), 90-91 (2), 93-94 (2), 94-95 (2), 96-97 (1), 97-98 (QF).

Managers: George Ramsay 1884-1926; W.J. Smith 1926-34; Jimmy McMullan 1934-35; Jimmy Hogan 1936-44; Alex Massie 1945-50; George Martin 1950-53; Eric Houghton 1953-58; Joe Mercer 1958-64; Dick Taylor 1965-67; Tommy Cummings 1967-68; Tommy Docherty 1968-70; Vic Crowe 1970-74; Ron Saunders 1974-82; Tony Barton 1982-84; Graham Turner 1984-86; Billy McNeill 1986-87; Graham Taylor 1987-91; Dr Jozef Venglos 1990-91; *(FAPL)* Ron Atkinson June 1991-Nov 1994; Brian Little Nov 94-Feb 98; John Gregory Feb 1998-.

Season 1997-98

Biggest Home Win:	4-1 v Tottenham Hotspur
Biggest Home Defeat:	0-4 v Blackburn Rovers
Biggest Away Win:	4-1 v Everton
Biggest Away Defeat:	0-5 v Blackburn Rovers
Biggest Home Att:	39,377 v Liverpool
Smallest Home Att:	29,343 v Southampton
Average Attendance:	36,136
Leading Scorer:	Dwight Yorke – 12

All-Time Records

Record FAPL Win:	7-1 v Wimbledon, 11/2/95
Record FAPL Defeat:	1-5 v Newcastle United, 27/4/94
Record FL Win:	12-2 v Accrington S, Division 1, 12/3/1892
Record FL Defeat:	1-8 v Blackburn R, FA Cup R3, 16/2/1889
Record Cup Win:	13-0 v Wednesbury Old Ath, FA Cup R1, 30/10/1886
Record Fee Received:	£5.5m from Bari for David Platt, 8/1991
Record Fee Paid:	£7m to Liverpool for Stan Collymore, 5/97
Most FL Apps:	Charlie Aitken, 561, 1961-76
Most FAPL Apps:	178 – Dwight Yorke, 1992-98
Most FAPL Goals:	60 – Dwight Yorke, 1992-98

Highest Scorer in FAPL Season: Dean Saunders, 17, 1992-93; Dwight Yorke, 17, 1995-96 and 1996-97

Record Attendance (all-time): 76,588 v Derby Co., FA Cup R6, 2/2/1946

Record Attendance (FAPL): 45,347 v Liverpool, 7/5/94

Most FAPL Goals in Season: 57, 1992-93 – 42 games

Most FAPL Points in Season: 74, 1992-93 – 42 games

Player	Tot	St	Sb	Snu	PS	Gls	Y	R	Fa	La	Fg	Lg
BARRY	2	1	1	1	0	0	0	0	0	0	0	0
BOSNICH	30	30	0	0	0	0	1	0	4	1	0	0
BYFIELD	7	1	6	6	1	0	1	0	1	0	0	0
CHARLES	18	14	4	11	3	1	1	0	1	1	0	0
COLLINS	0	0	0	10	0	0	0	0	0	0	0	0
COLLYMORE	25	23	2	1	3	6	4	1	4	1	1	0
CRICHTON	0	0	0	3	0	0	0	0	0	0	0	0
CURCIC	7	3	4	6	3	0	0	0	0	1	0	0
DRAPER	31	31	0	3	2	3	4	0	4	1	0	0
EHIOGU	37	37	0	1	2	2	7	1	4	1	0	0
GHENT	0	0	0	2	0	0	0	0	0	0	0	0
GRAYSON	33	28	5	4	5	0	2	0	4	1	2	0
HENDRIE	17	13	4	9	2	3	1	0	4	0	0	0
HUGHES	0	0	0	5	0	0	0	0	0	0	0	0
JOACHIM	26	16	10	7	3	8	0	0	2	0	0	0
MILOSEVIC	23	19	4	8	7	7	5	0	2	1	1	0
MURRAY	0	0	0	2	0	0	0	0	0	0	0	0
NELSON	25	21	4	11	6	0	1	0	1	1	0	0
OAKES	8	8	0	29	0	0	0	0	0	0	0	0
RACHEL	0	0	0	3	0	0	0	0	0	0	0	0
SCIMECA	21	16	5	7	3	0	0	0	3	1	0	0
SOUTHGATE	32	32	0	0	1	0	2	0	3	1	0	0
STAUNTON	27	27	0	1	5	1	5	0	4	0	1	0
TAYLOR	32	30	2	0	3	6	6	0	3	1	0	0
TOWNSEND	3	3	0	0	0	0	0	0	0	0	0	0
VASSELL	0	0	0	2	0	0	0	0	0	0	0	0
WALKER	1	0	1	2	0	0	0	0	0	0	0	0
WRIGHT	37	35	2	1	3	0	1	0	4	1	0	0
YORKE	30	30	0	0	2	12	5	0	2	1	2	0

5-Year Record

	Div.	P	W	D	L	F	A	Pts	Pos	FAC	FLC
93-94	PL	42	15	12	15	46	50	57	10	5	W
94-95	PL	42	11	15	16	51	56	48	18	4	4
95-96	PL	38	18	9	11	52	35	63	4	SF	W
96-97	PL	38	17	10	11	47	34	61	5	4	4
97-98	PL	38	17	6	15	49	48	57	7	5	3

Gregory Rekindles Spark

Following a season in which Aston Villa performed disappointingly in the various cup competitions but claimed fifth place in the Premiership, manager Brian Little sought to boost the club's firepower with record signing Stan Collymore from Liverpool. But Villa fan Collymore gave a poor return on the £7m invested in him and took 18 games to record his first goal on home soil. Once again it was Dwight Yorke who Villa turned to for most of their goals as he became top scorer for a third consecutive season. In addition to Collymore, Little made just one other signing with Phil Grayson switching from Leicester for a modest £1.35m.

Villa took four games to get their first goals, by Yorke and Collymore at Tottenham, but it was in their fifth match, at home to Leeds, that they picked up their first points of the season when Yorke scored the winner. Just one of the next six league games were lost as Villa rose up the table but it was to be one of the few times prior to the spring when there was any consistency to their results. Stories of unrest seeped from Villa Park as their league performances varied wildly from three-goal victories over Coventry and Tottenham to a run of one win in seven and a 5-0 defeat at Blackburn Rovers which ended with Sava Milosevic being severely reprimanded after spitting at Villa fans. Three of the next four games were lost, Yorke's last-minute winner against Derby bucking the trend, and on 24 February Little decided to terminate his three-year spell as Aston Villa manager. During his time as Villa boss, Little spent close on £30m on players and recouped around £18m. Assistant manager Allan Evans also departed.

Doug Ellis turned to former Villa player John Gregory, then at Wycombe, to replace Little. Under Gregory Villa produced a remarkable transformation and were to win nine of their final 11 Premiership matches of the season. Gregory opened with a 2-1 win over Liverpool which was particularly satisfying for Collymore, who scored both goals. Chelsea were defeated at Stamford Bridge, Coventry's good home record was also damaged through a Yorke double, Everton were hammered 4-1 at Goodison Park and the league campaign was rounded off by good wins over Sheffield Wednesday and Arsenal, which proved just sufficient to take the club back into Europe for another season.

The main highlights to Villa's season came in the UEFA Cup where a good home record, after being away in the 1st Leg each round, made amends for not winning on the continent. Bordeaux and Athletic Bilbao were both despatched at Villa Park following away draws before Steaua Bucharest handed Little's side their first defeat. A 2-0 victory for Villa in the return match set up a 4th Round meeting with Atletico Madrid and this time a 1-0 away defeat was too much for Villa as goals in Birmingham by Ian Taylor and Collymore could not prevent an away goals exit.

Looking to win the FA Cup for an eighth time, a good start was made with wins over Portsmouth, after a replay, and West Bromwich Albion. Coventry ended the run with the second of three successive home defeats which paved the way for Little's resignation. Villa's Coca-Cola Cup run consisted solely of a 3-0 3rd Round defeat at West Ham. ■

Results 1997-98

Date	Opponents	Ven	Res	Atten	Scorers
08-Aug	Leicester C.	A	0-1	20,304	
12-Aug	Blackburn R.	H	0-4	37,112	
22-Aug	Newcastle U.	A	0-1	36,783	
26-Aug	Tottenham H.	A	2-3	26,317	Yorke (27); Collymore (87)
29-Aug	Leeds U.	H	1-0	39,027	Yorke (67)
12-Sep	Barnsley	A	3-0	18,649	Ehiogu (25); Draper (50); Taylor (72)
19-Sep	Derby Co.	H	2-1	35,444	Yorke (73); Joachim (75)
21-Sep	Liverpool	A	0-3	34,843	
26-Sep	Sheffield W.	H	2-2	32,044	Staunton (32); Taylor (49)
03-Oct	Bolton W.	A	1-0	24,196	Milosevic (12)
17-Oct	Wimbledon	H	1-2	32,087	Taylor (44)
25-Oct	Arsenal	A	0-0	38,081	
01-Nov	Chelsea	H	0-2	39,372	
08-Nov	C. Palace	A	1-1	21,097	Joachim (86)
21-Nov	Everton	H	2-1	36,389	Milosevic (38); Ehiogu (56)
28-Nov	West Ham U.	A	1-2	24,976	Yorke (46)
05-Dec	Coventry C.	H	3-0	33,250	Collymore (21); Hendrie (71); Joachim (84)
14-Dec	Man Utd	A	0-1	55,151	
19-Dec	Southampton	H	1-1	29,343	Taylor (64)
25-Dec	Tottenham H.	H	4-1	38,644	Draper (38, 68); Collymore (81, 88)
27-Dec	Leeds U.	A	1-1	36,287	Milosevic (85)
09-Jan	Leicester C.	H	1-1	36,429	Joachim (87)
16-Jan	Blackburn R.	A	0-5	24,834	
31-Jan	Newcastle U.	H	0-1	38,266	
06-Feb	Derby Co.	H	1-0	30,251	Yorke (90)
17-Feb	Man.Utd	H	0-2	39,372	
20-Feb	Wimbledon	A	1-2	13,131	Milosevic (41)
27-Feb	Liverpool	H	2-1	39,377	Collymore (10, 64)
07-Mar	Chelsea	A	1-0	33,018	Joachim (50)
10-Mar	Barnsley	H	0-1	29,519	
13-Mar	C. Palace	H	3-1	33,781	Taylor (1); Milosevic (14 pen, 36)
27-Mar	Everton	A	4-1	36,471	Joachim (11); Charles (62); Yorke (72 pen, 81)
03-Apr	West Ham U.	H	2-0	39,372	Joachim (75); Milosevic (83)
10-Apr	Coventry C.	A	2-1	22,792	Yorke (5, 48)
17-Apr	Southampton	A	2-1	15,238	Hendrie (6); Yorke (60)

24-Apr	Bolton W.	H	1 3	38,392	Taylor (57)
01-May	Sheffield W.	A	3 1	34,177	Yorke (21); Hendrie (25); Joachim (50)
09-May	Arsenal	H	1-0	39,372	Yorke (37 pen)

FA Challenge Cup

Date	Opponents	Vn	Rnd	Res	Atten	Scorers
03-Jan	Portsmouth	A	3R	2-2	16,013	Staunton (41); Grayson (88)
14-Jan	Portsmouth	H	3RR	1-0	23,365	Milosevic (21)
24-Jan	WBA	H	4R	4-0	39,372	Grayson (4); Yorke (62, 64); Collymore (72)
14-Feb	Coventry C.	H	5R	0-1	26,979	

Coca-Cola League Cup

Date	Opponents	Vn	Rnd	Res	Atten	Scorers
15-Oct	West Ham Utd	A	3R	0-3	20,360	

UEFA Cup

Date	Opponents	Vn	Rnd	Res	Atten	Scorers
16-Sep	Bordeaux	A	1R1L	0-0	16,000	
30-Sep	Bordeaux	H	1R2L	1-0	33,072	Milosevic (111)
			aet. Aston Villa win 1-0 on aggregate.			
21-Oct	A.Bilbao	A	2R1L	0-0	46,000	
04-Nov	A.Bilbao	H	2R2L	2-1	35,915	Taylor (28); Yorke (50)
			Aston Villa win 2-1 on aggregate.			
04-Nov	S.Bucharest	A	3R1L	1-2	25,000	Yorke (54)
25-Nov	S.Bucharest	H	3R2L	2-0	35,102	Milosevic (71); Taylor (85)
			Aston Villa win 3-2 on aggregate.			
03-Mar	A.Madrid	A	QF1L	0-1	47,000	
17-Mar	A.Madrid	H	QF2L	2-1	39,163	Taylor (72); Collymore (74)
			2-2 on aggregate. Atletico Madrid win on away goals rule.			

Blackburn Rovers

Founded in 1875 by local school-leavers. Used several pitches, including Alexander Meadows, the East Lancashire Cricket Club ground, and became known nationally for their FA Cup exploits, eclipsing the record of Blackburn Olympic, the first club to take the trophy away from London. Three consecutive wins in the 1880s, when in the finals Queen's Park (twice) and West Bromwich Albion were beaten, brought recognition by way of a special shield awarded by the FA to commemorate the achievement.

Founder members of the Football League in 1888, the club settled at Ewood Park in 1890, purchasing the ground outright in 1893-94. Premier League founder members 1992 and champions in 1994-95.

Ground:	Ewood Park, Blackburn, BB2 4JF		
Phone:	01254-698888	**Fax:** 01254-671042	
Box Office:	01254-671666	**CC Bookings:** 01254 671666	
News:	0891 12 10 14		
Capacity:	30,591	**Pitch:** 115 yds x 76 yds	
Colours:	Blue/White, White, Blue	**Nickname:** Blue and Whites	
Radio:	999AM Red Rose Gold		
Internet:	http://www.rovers.co.uk		

Club President: W.H. Bancroft   **Snr-Vice President:** J. Walker
Chairman: R.D. Coar BSC   **Vice-Chairman:** R. L. Matthewman
Secretary: Tom Finn
Manager: Roy Hodgson   **Assistant:** Tony Parkes
Physio: Steve Foster

League History: 1888 Founder member of the League; 1936-39 Division 2; 1946-48 Division 1; 1948-58 Division 2; 1958-66 Division 1; 1966-71 Division 2; 1971-75 Division 3; 1975-79 Division 2; 1979-80 Division 3; 1980-92 Division 2; 1992- FA Premier League.

Honours: *FA Premier League: Champions* 1994-95; *Runners-up* 1993-94. *Football League: Division 1 Champions* 1911-12, 1913-14; *Division 1 Champions* 1938-39; *Runners-up* 1957-58; *Division 3 Champions* 1974-75; *Runners-up* 1979-1980. *FA Cup: Winners* 1884, 1885, 1886, 1890, 1891, 1928; *Runners-up* 1882, 1960. *Full Members' Cup: Winners* 1986-87.

European Record: CC (1): 95-96; CWC (0): UEFA (1): 94-95 (1).

Managers: Thomas Mitchell 1884 96; J. Walmsley 1896-1903; R.B. Middleton 1903-25; Jack Carr 1922-26 (TM under Middleton to 1925); Bob Crompton 1926-31 (Hon. TM); Arthur Barritt 1931-36 (had been Secretary from 1927); Reg Taylor 1936-38; Bob Crompton 1938-41; Eddie Hapgood 1944-47; Will Scott 1947; Jack Burton 1947-49; Jackie Bestall 1949-53; Johnny Carey 1953-58; Dally Duncan 1958-60; Jack Marshall 1960-67; Eddie Quigley 1967-70; Johnny Carey 1970-71; Ken Furphy 1971-73; Gordon Lee 1974-75; Jim Smith 1975-78; Jim Iley 1978; John Pickering 1978-79; Howard Kendall 1979-81; Bobby Saxton 1981-86; Don Mackay 1987-91; *(FAPL)* Kenny Dalglish October 1991-May 1995; Ray Harford May 1995-Oct 1996; Tony Parkes (caretaker) Oct 1996-June 97; Roy Hodgson July 97-.

Season 1997-98

Biggest Home Win:	7-2 v Sheffield Wednesday
Biggest Home Defeat:	1-4 v Arsenal
Biggest Away Win:	4-0 v Aston Villa
Biggest Away Defeat:	4-0 v Leeds United and Manchester United
Biggest Home Att:	30,547 v Manchester United
Smallest Home Att:	19,086 v Coventry City
Average Attendance:	25,463
Leading Scorer:	Chris Sutton – 18

All-Time Records

Record FAPL Win:	7-0 v Nottingham Forest, 18/11/95
	7-1 v Norwich City, 3/10/92
	7-2 v Sheffield Wednesday, 25/8/97
Record FAPL Defeat:	0-5 v Coventry City, 9/1/95
Record FL Win:	9-0 v Middlesbrough, Division 2, 6/11/54
Record FL Defeat:	0-8 v Arsenal, Division 1, 25/2/33
Record Cup Win:	11-0 v Rossendale, FA Cup R1, 13/10/1884
Record Fee Received:	£15m from Newcastle Utd for Alan Shearer, 7/96
Record Fee Paid:	£7.5m to Southampton for Kevin Davies, 7/98
Most FL Apps:	Derek Fazackerley, 596, 1970-86
Most FAPL Apps:	204 – Colin Hendry, 1992-98
Most FAPL Goals:	112 – Alan Shearer, 1992-96
Highest Scorer in FAPL Season:	Alan Shearer, 34, 1994-95
Record Attendance (all-time):	61,783 v Bolton W, FA Cup R6, 2/3/29
Record Attendance (FAPL):	30,895 v Liverpool, 24/2/96
Most FAPL Goals in Season:	80, 1994-95 – 42 games
Most FAPL Points in Season:	89, 1994-95 – 42 games

Player	Tot	St	Sb	Snu	PS	Gls	Y	R	Fa	La	Fg	Lg
ANDERSSON	4	1	3	8	1	0	0	0	1	3	0	1
BEATTIE	3	0	3	5	0	0	0	0	1	1	0	0
BOHINEN	16	6	10	7	2	1	0	0	1	2	0	1
BROOMES	4	2	2	14	0	0	1	0	0	1	0	0
COLEMAN	0	0	0	0	0	0	0	0	0	0	1	0
CROFT	23	19	4	5	5	1	0	0	2	3	0	0
DAHLIN	21	11	10	5	7	4	2	0	1	2	0	2
DAVIDSON	1	1	0	3	1	0	0	0	0	0	0	0
DUFF	26	17	9	4	5	4	0	0	0	3	1	0
FETTIS	8	7	1	20	0	0	0	0	3	0	0	0
FILAN	7	7	0	3	1	0	0	0	1	0	0	0
FLITCROFT	33	28	5	3	3	0	6	0	3	2	0	0
FLOWERS	25	24	1	3	1	0	0	1	3	3	0	0
GALLACHER	33	31	2	0	5	16	2	0	4	1	3	1
HENCHOZ	36	36	0	0	4	0	6	0	4	1	0	0
HENDRY	34	34	0	0	4	1	6	0	4	1	0	0
JOHNSON	0	0	0	0	0	0	0	0	0	0	1	0
KENNA	37	37	0	0	0	0	0	0	3	1	0	0
McKINLAY	30	26	4	3	6	0	7	0	4	2	0	1
PEARCE	5	1	4	1	0	0	1	0	0	0	0	0
PEDERSEN, T	5	3	2	12	0	0	0	0	0	3	0	0
PEDERSEN, P	0	0	0	1	0	0	0	0	0	2	0	0
RIPLEY	29	25	4	2	14	2	0	0	3	0	1	0
SHERWOOD	31	29	2	0	3	5	5	0	4	2	2	0
SUTTON	35	35	0	0	1	18	10	1	4	2	2	1
VALERY	15	14	1	5	5	0	2	1	2	2	0	0
WATT	0	0	0	2	0	0	0	0	0	0	0	0
WILCOX	31	24	7	2	6	3	4	2	4	1	0	0
WILLAMS	0	0	0	8	0	0	0	0	0	0	0	0
Own Goals						1						

5-Year Record

	Div.	P	W	D	L	F	A	Pts	Pos	FAC	FLC
93-94	PL	42	25	9	8	63	36	84	2	4	4
94-95	PL	42	27	8	7	80	39	89	1	3	4
95-96	PL	38	18	7	13	61	47	61	7	3	4
96-97	PL	38	9	15	14	42	43	42	13	4	3
97-98	PL	38	16	10	12	57	52	58	6	4	3

Flying Start Ultimately Dives

After the struggle of the previous campaign, Blackburn Rovers banked on the experience of new manager Roy Hodgson gained during his time on the continent to bring a return to the glory days. Hodgson was very active in the transfer market with six players being sold for a combined fee of £3.65m and two days either side of the start of the season a further £10m was collected from the sale of Graeme Le Saux and Henning Berg. Blackburn used £6.7m of Jack Walker's funds to bring in Stephane Henchoz, Martin Dahlin, John Filan and Anders Andersson. Despite the arrival of Dahlin, Chris Sutton and Kevin Gallacher were Blackburn's leading scorers for a second successive year.

The new-look Rovers made a flying start to the season with 13 points from the opening five games. Aston Villa were thrashed 4-0 at Villa Park with Sutton scoring a hat-trick and Sheffield Wednesday were annihilated 7-2 at Ewood Park; Sutton and Gallacher both scored twice with Wednesday 4-1 down inside ten minutes. The only defeat suffered in the first 15 Premiership matches was another goal feast with Leeds winning 4-3 at Ewood Park. Sutton's early season goalscoring form had the media calling for his return to the England set-up but Sutton probably ruled himself out of the World Cup after rejecting Glenn Hoddle's invitation to play for the B team.

After scoring 18 times in their first six games Rovers suddenly found goals hard to come by with just five being scored in the next seven games, but on the plus side the defence tightened up and just three goals were conceded during the same period. Wins over Everton and Chelsea saw Rovers installed as the main threat to Manchester United's title challenge but Blackburn were put in their place on 30 November with a 4-0 drubbing at Old Trafford. Rovers bounced back to be unbeaten throughout December, a run which included a memorable 3-1 victory at Arsenal. By the end of the year Blackburn trailed United by just five points but with just two victories over the next ten weeks the title hope vanished. A defeat at Derby was nothing more than a blip, and it was followed by a 5-0 win over Villa, with Gallacher scoring a hat-trick. However, a shock 3-0 home reverse by Tottenham sparked a run of four successive games when three or more goals were conceded. A run of four straight defeats in April – including a 4-1 home trouncing by Arsenal – threatened Rovers' prospects of qualifying for Europe but two wins in the last three games secured seventh place and only the club's third appearance in European football.

Rovers' loss of form in the league after the turn of the year was offset to some degree in the FA Cup as Wigan Athletic were comfortably beaten before Sheffield Wednesday were brushed aside 3-0 at Hillsborough barely a month since the two sides had been goalless at Hillsborough. But following a good draw at West Ham in the 5th Round, Rovers endured the anguish of defeat in a penalty shoot-out and hopes of bringing the cup to Ewood Park after a 70-year absence were scuppered.

The script changed very little in the Coca-Cola Cup for, after hammering Preston 6-1 on aggregate, Rovers drew at Chelsea but could only locate the target once in the penalty shoot-out. Looking to rebuild for 1998-99, Roy Hodgson broke the Blackburn bank to take Kevin Davies to Ewood Park, paying Southampton £7.5m for his services. ∎

Results 1997-98

Date	Opponents	Ven	Res	Atten	Scorers
08-Aug	Derby Co.	H	1-0	23,557	Gallacher (21)
12-Aug	Aston Villa	A	4-0	37,112	Sutton (21, 25, 41); Gallacher (71)
22-Aug	Liverpool	H	1-1	30,187	Dahlin (84)
24-Aug	Sheffield W.	H	7-2	19,618	Gallacher (2, 6); OG (10, Hyde); Wilcox (19); Sutton (23, 74); Bohinen (53)
29-Aug	C. Palace	A	2-1	20,849	Sutton (23); Gallacher (32)
13-Sep	Leeds U.	H	3-4	21,956	Gallacher (8); Sutton (16 pen); Dahlin (33)
19-Sep	Tottenham H.	A	0-0	26,573	
23-Sep	Leicester C.	A	1-1	19,921	Sutton (36)
27-Sep	Coventry C.	H	0-0	19,086	
03-Oct	Wimbledon	A	1-0	15,600	Sutton (6)
17-Oct	Southampton	H	1-0	24,130	Sherwood (26)
24-Oct	Newcastle U.	A	1-1	36,716	Sutton (57)
31-Oct	Barnsley	A	1-1	18,665	Sherwood (30)
07-Nov	Everton	H	3-2	25,397	Gallacher (37); Duff (81); Sherwood (85)
21-Nov	Chelsea	H	1-0	27,683	Croft (11)
29-Nov	Manchester U.	A	0-4	56,165	
05-Dec	Bolton W.	H	3-1	29,503	Gallacher (3); Sutton (20); Wilcox (90)
12-Dec	Arsenal	A	3-1	38,147	Wilcox (57); Gallacher (65): Sherwood (89)
19-Dec	West Ham	H	3-0	21,653	Ripley (22); Duff (50, 72)
25-Dec	Sheffield W.	A	0-0	33,502	
27-Dec	C. Palace	H	2-2	23,872	Gallacher (26); Sutton (77)
10-Jan	Derby	A	1-3	27,823	Sutton (87)
16-Jan	Aston Villa	H	5-0	24,834	Sherwood (22); Gallacher (30, 54, 69); Ripley (81)
30-Jan	Liverpool	A	0-0	43,890	
06-Feb	Tottenham H.	H	0-3	30,388	
20-Feb	Southampton	A	0-3	15,152	
27-Feb	Leicester C.	H	5-3	24,854	Dahlin (11); Sutton (25, 45, 47); Hendry (63)
10-Mar	Leeds U.	A	0-4	32,933	
13-Mar	Everton	A	0-1	33,423	
30-Mar	Barnsley	H	2-1	24,179	Dahlin (9); Gallacher (87)

05-Apr	Manchester U.	H	1-3	30,547	Sutton (32 pen)
10-Apr	Bolton W.	A	1-2	25,000	Duff (51)
12-Apr	Arsenal	H	1-4	28,212	Gallacher (51)
17-Apr	West Ham U.	A	1-2	24,733	Wilcox (44)
24-Apr	Wimbledon	H	0-0	24,848	
28-Apr	Chelsea	A	1-0	33,311	Gallacher (48)
01-May	Coventry C.	A	0-2	18,794	
09-May	Newcastle U.	H	1-0	29,300	Sutton (88)

FA Challenge Cup

Date	Opponents	Vn	Rnd	Res	Atten	Scorers
03-Jan	Wigan Ath	H	3R	4-2	22,402	OG (20 McGibbon); Gallacher (37, 60); Sherwood (48)
26-Jan	Sheffield W.	A	4R	3-0	15,940	Sutton (6); Sherwood (37); Duff (87)
14-Feb	West Ham U.	A	5R	2-2	25,729	Gallacher (3); Sutton (62)
25-Feb	West Ham U.	H	5RR	1-1	21,972	Ripley (114)
	aet. West Ham win 5-4 on penalties.					

Coca-Cola League Cup

Date	Opponents	Vn	Rnd	Res	Atten	Scorers
14-Sep	Preston NE	H	2R1L	6-0	22,564	Dahlin (26, 54); Sutton (24); Gallacher (78); Andersson (84); Bohinen (89)
30-Sep	Preston NE	A	2R2L	0-1	11,472	
	Blackburn win 6-1 on aggregate.					
15-Oct	Chelsea	A	3R	1-1	18,671	McKinlay
	aet. Chelsea win 4-1 on penalties.					

Charlton Athletic

Reformed in 1984 after a traumatic period in their history that saw them move away from The Valley and played for a while at West Ham. Revitalised and regenerated the club achieved Premiership status for the first time in 1998 having won through the play-offs. Originally formed in 1905 by a number of youths, they joined the Football League in 1921 as members of Division 3 South. Played largely in Division 2 and 3 throughout their years. The Addicks flirted briefly with the old Division 1 at the end of the 1980s, having been runners-up in their first season in the top flight (1936-37).

Their success in recent years and return to their original roots have been one of the more romantic footballing stories of modern times.

Ground:	The Valley, Floyd Road, Charlton, London SE7 8BL

Phone:	0181-333 4000	**Fax:**	0181-333 4001
Box Office:	0181-334 4010	**News:**	0891 12 11 40
Capacity:	21,500	**Pitch:**	111yds x 73 yds
Colours:	Red with White trim, White with Red trim, Red with White.		
Nickname:	Addicks		
Radio:	1548AM Capital Radio		
Internet:	http://www.charlton-athletic.co.uk		

Chairman:	Martin Simons	**MD:**	Peter Varney
Secretary:	Chris Parkes		
Manager:	Alan Curbishley	**Coach:**	Les Reed
Physio:	Jimmy Hendry		

League History: 1921 Elected to Division 3(S); 1929-33 Division 2; 1933-35 Division 3(S); 1935-36 Division 2; 1936-57 Division 1; 1957-72 Division 2; 1972-75 Division 3; 1975-80 Division 2; 1980-81 Division 3; 1981-86 Division 2; 1986-90 Division 1; 1990-92 Division 2; 1992-98 Division 1; 1998 – FA Premier League.

Honours: *Football League: Division 1 Runners-up 1936-37; Play-Off winners 1997-98; Division 1 Runners-up 1935-36, 1985-86; Division 3 South Champions 1928-29, 1934-35. FA Cup: Winners 1946-47. Full Members' Cup: Runners-up 1986-87.*

European Record: Never qualified.

Managers: Walter Rayner 1920-25; Alex McFarlane 1925-28; Albert Lindon 1928; Alex McFarlane 1928-32; Albert Lindon 1932-33; Jimmy Seed 1935-

56; Jimmy Trotter 1956-61; Frank Hill 1961-65; Bob Stokoe 1965-67; Eddie Firmani 1967-70; Theo Foley 1970-74; Andy Nelson 1974-80; Mike Bailey 1980-81; Alan Mullery 1981-82; Ken Craggs 1982; Lennie Lawrence 1982-91; Alan Curbishley and Steve Gritt 1991-95; Alan Curbishley 1995-.

Season 1997-98

Biggest Home Win:	5-0 v WBA
Biggest Home Defeat:	1-3 v Stockport County
Biggest Away Win:	4-0 v Norwich City
Biggest Away Defeat:	2-5 v Nottingham Forest
Biggest Home Att:	15,815 v Nottingham Forest
Smallest Home Att:	9,580 v Sheffield United
Leading Scorer:	Clive Mendonca – 23

All-Time Records

Record FAPL Win:	–
Record FAPL Defeat:	–
Record FL Win:	8-1 v Middlesbrough, Division 1, 12/9/53
Record FL Defeat:	1-11 v Aston Villa, Division 2, 14/11/59
Record Cup Win:	7-0 v Burton Albion, FA Cup R3, 1/1/56
Record Fee Received:	£2.8m from Leeds United for Lee Bowyer, 7/96
Record Fee Paid:	£700,000 for Clive Mendonca from Grimsby, 5/97
Most FL Apps:	Sam Bartram, 583, 1934-56
Most FAPL Apps:	
Most FAPL Goals:	
Highest Scorer in FAPL Season:	–
Record Attendance (all-time):	75,031 v Aston Villa, FA Cup R5 12/2/38
Record Attendance (FAPL):	–
Most FAPL Goals in Season:	–
Most FAPL Points in Season:	–

Player	Tot	St	Sb	Snu	PS	Gls	Fa	La	Fg	Lg
ALLEN	12	7	5	9	2	2	1	0	0	0
BALMER	16	13	3	4	1	0	1	2	0	0
BARNESS	30	21	9	9	4	1	1	1	0	0
BOWEN	37	35	2	1	5	0	3	0	0	0
BRIGHT	17	14	3	1	3	7	2	2	0	0
BROWN	35	27	8	2	6	2	3	2	1	0
CHAPPLE	35	29	6	3	1	4	3	1	0	0
EMBLEN	4	0	4	1	0	0	0	0	0	0
HEANEY	7	5	2	1	3	0	0	0	0	0
HOLMES	16	10	6	1	2	1	1	0	0	0
ILIC	15	15	0	1	0	0	0	0	0	0
JONES, K	45	45	0	0	8	3	2	1	1	0
JONES, S	24	18	6	1	7	7	1	2	0	0
KERSLAKE	0	0	0	1	0	0	0	0	0	0
KINSELLA	46	46	0	0	3	5	3	2	0	0
KONCHESKY	3	2	1	0	2	0	0	1	0	0
LEABURN	14	13	1	0	2	3	1	0	1	0
LISBIE	17	1	16	3	1	1	0	1	0	0
MENDONCA	41	41	0	0	2	23	2	2	1	1
MILLS	10	10	0	0	1	1	0	0	0	0
MORTIMER	13	8	5	0	4	4	0	0	0	0
NEWTON	42	34	8	2	9	5	3	2	0	0
NICHOLLS	6	1	5	1	0	0	0	2	0	0
PARKER	3	0	3	1	0	0	0	0	0	0
PETTERSON	23	23	0	0	0	0	1	2	0	0
ROBINSON	38	37	1	0	8	5	3	2	1	0
RUFUS	43	43	0	0	7	0	3	1	0	0
SALMON	9	9	0	0	1	0	2	0	0	0
STUART	1	0	1	1	0	0	0	1	0	0
YOUDS	9	9	0	0	0	0	0	0	0	0

5-Year Record

	Div.	P	W	D	L	F	A	Pts	Pos	FAC	FLC
93-94	1	46	19	8	19	61	58	65	11	6	2
94-95	1	46	16	11	19	58	66	59	15	3	2
95-96	1	46	17	20	9	57	45	71	6	5	3
96-97	1	46	16	11	19	52	66	59	15	3	3
97-98	1	46	26	10	10	80	49	88	4	11	3

Exciting Athletic

The return of top-flight football to the Valley after a gap of 41 years is a magnificent tribute to the managerial skills of Charlton Athletic boss Alan Curbishley, who fashioned an exciting promotion-winning side without spending a seven figure sum on a single player. Curbishley, in charge of Charlton since July 1991, proved that he knows his way round the transfer market in the Nationwide League with the £700,000 summer signing of experienced Grimsby striker Clive Mendonca. Curbishley made just one other signing during the season for a relatively sizeable fee when he took on board Eddie Youds from Bradford in March for £550,000. But the man who seized the headlines was a free transfer from non-league St Leonards – goalkeeper Sasa Ilic, whose form was priceless.

Charlton, rated no higher than 16th for promotion by the bookies, made a mediocre start with defeats by Middlesbrough, Wolves and Stockport within the opening eight games, but also showed their credentials in that time with 4-0 and 4-1 wins over Norwich and Bradford. The Norwich match featured Mendonca's first hat-trick The defeat by Stockport was Charlton's only home reversal of the season – a record only bettered by Macclesfield – and they bounced back with a seven match unbeaten run. That spell of success was ended by a crushing 5-2 defeat at Nottingham Forest. Again Charlton hit back well with five wins in six games and by the turn of the year they had taken up residency in a play-off position. An important showdown with Middlesbrough at the Valley ended in an emphatic 3-0 success for Curbishley's side with Shaun Newton scoring twice. Charlton's hopes of gaining an automatic promotion place were boosted at the start of March when Forest and Middlesbrough both lost heavily while the Londoners beat Huddersfield and West Brom, the latter 5-0. But one point from two games against Ipswich and Sunderland reduced their sights to a top six finish. Even though Charlton embarked on a breathtaking run of eight consecutive wins they still required, and achieved, a draw at Birmingham on the last day to clinch a shot at the play-offs.

Having lost three times to Ipswich in the league and Coca-Cola Cup, Charlton completed a 1-0 double over the East Anglian club in the play-off semi-final, with Ilic setting a remarkable new club record of ten consecutive clean sheets. The final with Sunderland at a packed Wembley was one of the most gripping matches ever played at the stadium. Mendonca scored another hat-trick as the Addicks came back from behind three times to force a 4-4 draw and a penalty shoot-out for the multi million pound prize of a Premiership place. With both sides netting their first six spot kicks, Ilic became the toast of the Valley when he saved Michael Gray's shot to secure Charlton's return to the top flight after an eight-year absence.

Charlton made two appearances in the FA Cup Final over 50 years ago but never threatened to break that run as they went out in the 4th Round in a replay at Wolves, after handing Forest a hefty 4-1 defeat in the 3rd Round. The Addicks' Coca-Cola Cup record run to the 4th Round was also untouched as Ipswich won both 2nd Round ties between the two clubs. ■

Results 1997-98

Date	Opponents	Ven	Res	Atten	Scorers
09-Aug	Middlesbrough	A	1-2	29,414	S.Jones (8)
16-Aug	Oxford U.	H	3-2	10,145	S.Jones (20); Mendonca (57); Lisbie (90)
23-Aug	Bury	A	0-0	4,657	
30-Aug	Manchester C.	H	2-1	14,014	OG (Van Blerk 67); K.Jones (69)
13-Sep	Wolverh'n W.	A	1-3	22,683	Chapple (72)
17-Sep	Norwich C.	A	4-0	10,157	Mendonca (7, 22, 28); Chapple (84)
21-Sep	Bradford C.	H	4-1	11,640	Mendonca (8, 69); Mortimer (18); Brown (23)
27-Sep	Stockport Co.	H	1-3	12,074	Mortimer (40)
04-Oct	QPR	A	4-2	14,825	Robinson (16, 58); S.Jones (42); Chapple (62)
14-Oct	Huddersfield T.	A	3-0	9,596	Mendonca (15); Brown (69); Robinson (75)
19-Oct	Stoke C.	H	1-1	12,366	Kinsella (79)
22-Oct	Birmingham C.	H	1-1	10,070	Mendonca (62)
25-Oct	Tranmere R.	A	2-2	5,911	Kinsella (57); Leaburn (59)
01-Nov	Ipswich T.	H	3-0	12,606	Mendonca (10); Chapple (34); Leaburn (90)
04-Nov	Sunderland	A	0-0	25,455	
08-Nov	WBA	A	0-1	16,124	
15-Nov	Crewe Alex.	H	3-2	14,137	K.Jones (6); Allen (27); Holmes (76)
22-Nov	N. Forest	A	2-5	18,532	Allen (58); OG (Woan, 79)
28-Nov	Swindon T.	H	3-0	13,789	K.Jones (9); Mendonca (42 pen, 57)
06-Dec	Reading	A	0-2	8,076	
09-Dec	Sheffield U.	H	2-1	9,850	Mendonca (44 pen, 75)
13-Dec	Port Vale	H	1-0	11,066	Newton (84)
20-Dec	Portsmouth	A	2-0	8,581	Robinson (44); Leaburn (52)
26-Dec	Norwich C.	H	2-1	14,475	Kinsella (59); Robinson (62)
28-Dec	Sheffield U.	A	1-4	18,677	Bright (89)
10-Jan	Middlesbrough	H	3-0	15,729	Newton (20, 59); Bright (36)
17-Jan	Oxford U.	A	2-1	7,234	Mendonca (81); Robinson (87)
28-Jan	Manchester C.	A	2-2	24,058	S. Jones (74, 90)
31-Jan	Bury	H	0-0	15,288	
07-Feb	Bradford C.	A	0-1	14,851	
17-Feb	QPR	H	1-1	15,479	Robinson (42)
21-Feb	Stockport Co.	A	0-3	7,705	
25-Feb	Stoke C.	A	2-1	10,027	Robinson (17); Barness (73)

124

28-Feb	Huddersfield T.	H	1-0	12,891	Bright (79)
03-Mar	WBA	H	5-0	10,923	Bright (43); Newton (53) Mendonca (70, 79 pen); Kinsella (73)
07-Mar	Ipswich T.	A	1-3	19,841	Mendonca (22)
15-Mar	Sunderland	H	1-1	15,385	Bright (55)
21-Mar	Crewe Alex.	A	3-0	5,252	Mills (3); Newton (44); Kinsella (77)
28-Mar	N. Forest	H	4-2	15,815	Bright (4); Mortimer (60); Mendonca (89); Kinsella (90)
04-Apr	Swindon Town	A	1-0	7,845	S. Jones (80)
07-Apr	Wolvh'n W.	H	1-1	13,731	Mendonca (8)
10-Apr	Reading	H	3-0	14,346	Mendonca (6); Mortimer (43); Bright (79)
13-Apr	Port Vale	A	1-0	9,973	Mendonca (73)
18-Apr	Portsmouth	H	1-0	14,092	S. Jones (57)
25-Apr	Tranmere R.	H	2-0	15,409	Mendonca (10, 63)
03-May	Birmingham C.	A	0-0	25,877	

Division 1 Play-Offs

Date	Opponents	Vn	Rnd	Res	Atten	Scorers
09-May	Ipswich T.	A	SF1L	1-0	21,681	OG (Clapham, 12)
13-May	Ipswich T.	H	SF2L	1-0	15,585	Newton (36)

Charlton Athletic win 2-0 on aggregate

| 25-May | Sunderland | W | Final | 4-4 | 77,739 | Mendonca (23, 71, 103); Rufus (85) |

aet. Charlton Athletic win 7-6 on penalties

FA Challenge Cup

Date	Opponents	Vn	Rnd	Res	Atten	Scorers
03-Jan	N. Forest	H	3R	4-1	13,827	Robinson (38); Brown (42); Leaburn (64); Mendonca (75)
24-Jan	Wolvh'n W.	H	4R	1-1	15,540	Jones (64)
03-Feb	Wolvh'n W.	A	4RR	0-3	20,429	

Coca-Cola League Cup

Date	Opponents	Vn	Rnd	Res	Atten	Scorers
13-Aug	Ipswich T.	H	1R1L	0-1	6,598	
26-Aug	Ipswich T	A	1R2L	1-3	10,989	Mendonca (88)

Ipswich win 4-1 on aggregate

Chelsea

Founded in 1905. The Mears brothers developed Stamford Bridge Athletic Ground, which they owned, into a football stadium for prestigious matches and, prospectively, nearby Fulham FC. But Fulham did not take up the chance so the Mears brothers established their own club, rejecting possible names such as 'London' and 'Kensington' in favour, eventually, of Chelsea.

Judging that the club would not be accepted into the Southern League, it sought membership of the Football League. This was gained at the first attempt and it started the 1906-07 season in Division Two. Premier League founder members 1992. Completed League Cup–Cup-Winners' Cup double in 1997-98.

Ground:	Stamford Bridge, London SW6 1HS		
Phone:	0171-385 5545		
Box Office:	0171-386 7799	**CC Booking:**	0171-386 7799
News:	0891 12 11 59	**Tickets:**	0891 12 10 11
Capacity:	37,000 +	**Pitch:**	110 yds x 72 yds
Colours:	Royal Blue, Royal Blue, White	**Nickname:**	The Blues
Radio:	1548AM Capital Gold		
Internet:	http://www.chelseafc.co.uk		

Patron:	Ruth Harding	**Chairman:**	Ken W. Bates
MD:	Colin Hutchinson		
Match Secretary:	Keith Lacy	**Company Secretary:**	Alan Shaw
Manager:	Gianluca Vialli	**Coach:**	Graham Rix
Physio:	Micheal Banks		

League History: 1905 Elected to Division 2; 1907-10 Division 1; 1910-12 Division 2; 1912-24 Division 1; 1924-30 Division 2; 1930-62 Division 1; 1962-63 Division 2; 1963-75 Division 1; 1975-77 Division 2; 1977-79 Division 1; 1979-84 Division 2; 1984-88 Division 1; 1988-89 Division 2; 1989-92 Division 1; 1992- FA Premier League.

Honours: *Football League: Division 1 Champions* 1954-55; *Division 2 Champions* 1983-84, 1988-89; *Runners-up* 1906-07, 1911-12, 1929-30,1962-63, 1976-77. *FA Cup: Winners* 1969-70, 1996-97; *Runners-up* 1914-15, 1966-67, 1993-94. *Football League Cup: Winners* 1964-65, 1997-98; *Runners-up* 1971-72. *Cup-Winners' Cup: Winners* 1970-71, 1997-98. *Full Members' Cup: Winners* 1985-86. *Zenith Data Systems Cup: Winners* 1989-90.

European Record: CC (0) – ; CWC (4): 70-71 (W), 71-72 (2), 94-95 (SF), 97-98 (W); UEFA (3): 58-60(QF), 65-66 (SF), 68-69 (2).

Managers: John Tait Robertson 1905-07; David Calderhead 1907-33; A. Leslie Knighton 1933-39; Billy Birrell 1939-52; Ted Drake 1952-61; Tommy Docherty 1962-67; Dave Sexton 1967-74; Ron Stuart 1974-75; Eddie McCreadie 1975-77; Ken Shellito 1977-78; Danny Blanchflower 1978-79; Geoff Hurst 1979-81; John Neal 1981-85 (Director to 1986); John Hollins 1985-88; Bobby Campbell 1988-91; *(FAPL)* Ian Porterfield June 1991-1993; Dave Webb 1993; Glenn Hoddle July 1993-June 1996; Ruud Gullit June 96-Feb 98; Gianluca Vialli Feb 1998-.

Season 1997-98

Biggest Home Win:	6-2 v Crystal Palace
Biggest Home Defeat:	2-3 v Arsenal
Biggest Away Win:	6-0 v Barnsley
Biggest Away Defeat:	2-4 v Liverpool
Biggest Home Att:	34,690 v Leeds United
Smallest Home Att:	29,075 v Sheffield Wednesday
Average Attendance:	33,492
Leading Scorer:	Tore Andre Flo, Gianluca Vialli – 11

All-Time Records

Record FAPL Win:	6-0 v Barnsley (away) 1997-98
Record FAPL Defeat:	1-4 v Leeds United, 6/11/93,
	1-4 v Manchester United, 21/10/95
Record FL Win:	9-2 v Glossop NE, Division 2, 1/9/1906
Record FL Defeat:	1-8 v Wolverhampton W., Division 1, 26/9/53
Record Cup Win:	13-0 v Jeunesse Hautcharage, CWC, 1R2L, 29/9/1971
Record Fee Received:	£2.5m from QPR for John Spencer, 11/96
Record Fee Paid:	£5.5m to Milan for Marcel Desailly, 7/98
Most FL Apps:	Ron Harris, 655, 1962-80
Most FAPL Apps:	173 – Dennis Wise, 1992-98
Most FAPL Goals:	36 – John Spencer, 1992-97
Highest Scorer in FAPL Season:	13:Mark Stein, 1993-94
	John Spencer (1995-96)
Record Attendance (all-time):	82,905 v Arsenal, Div 1, 12/10/35
Record Attendance (FAPL):	37,064 v Manchester United, 11/9/93
Most FAPL Goals in Season:	71, 1997-98 – 38 games
Most FAPL Points in Season:	63, 1997-98 – 38 games

Summary 1997-98

Player	Tot	St	Sb	Snu	PS	Gls	Y	R	Fa	La	Fg	Lg
BABAYARO	8	8	0	1	1	0	0	0	0	2	0	0
CHARVET	11	7	4	1	0	2	3	0	0	1	0	0
CLARKE	26	22	4	2	2	1	2	0	1	6	0	0
COLGAN	0	0	0	1	0	0	0	0	0	0	0	0
CRITTENDEN	2	0	2	1	0	0	0	0	0	1	0	0
DE GOEY	28	28	0	0	0	0	0	0	1	4	0	0
DI MATTEO	30	28	2	1	6	4	6	0	1	4	0	3
DUBERRY	23	23	0	0	0	0	2	0	1	3	0	0
FLO	34	16	18	4	6	11	0	0	1	4	0	2
GRANVILLE	13	9	4	6	2	0	2	0	0	3	0	0
GULLIT	6	0	6	1	0	0	0	0	0	4	0	0
HAMPSHIRE	0	0	0	0	0	0	0	0	0	1	0	0
HARLEY	3	3	0	0	3	0	0	0	0	0	0	0
HITCHCOCK	0	0	0	36	0	0	0	0	0	2	0	0
HUGHES, M.	29	25	4	4	4	9	9	0	1	6	0	2
HUGHES, P.	9	5	4	4	2	0	1	0	0	0	0	0
KHARINE	10	10	0	1	0	0	0	0	0	0	0	0
LAMBOURDE	7	5	2	8	0	0	3	1	0	3	0	0
LE SAUX	26	26	0	0	1	1	3	0	1	4	1	1
LEBOEUF	32	32	0	0	4	5	8	1	1	4	0	0
LEE	1	1	0	2	0	0	0	0	0	2	0	0
MORRIS	12	9	3	2	5	0	0	0	0	1	0	1
MYERS	12	11	1	5	1	0	0	0	1	1	0	0
NEWTON	18	17	1	2	5	0	0	0	0	4	0	0
NICHOLLS	19	8	11	10	3	3	2	0	1	2	0	0
PETRESCU	31	31	0	1	13	5	3	0	1	3	0	1
POYET	14	11	3	0	1	4	2	0	0	0	0	0
SHEERIN	0	0	0	1	0	0	0	0	0	0	0	0
SINCLAIR	22	20	2	0	4	1	3	1	0	5	0	1
VIALLI	21	14	7	10	6	11	4	0	1	3	2	0
WISE	26	26	0	0	2	3	10	0	0	4	0	0
ZOLA	27	23	4	4	11	8	2	0	1	4	0	0
Own Goals						2						

5-Year Record

	Div.	P	W	D	L	F	A	Pts	Pos	FAC	FLC
93-94	PL	42	13	12	17	49	53	51	14	F	3
94-95	PL	42	13	15	14	50	55	54	11	4	3
95-96	PL	38	12	14	12	46	44	50	11	SF	2
96-97	PL	38	16	11	11	58	55	59	6	W	3
97-98	PL	38	20	3	15	71	43	63	4	3	W

Cups Galore as Bridge Revolution Continues

With the FA Cup locked away in the trophy cabinet, Chelsea, under Ruud Gullit, appeared to be on the verge of greater glory as he led them through the early rounds of the Cup-Winners' Cup, to the semi-final of the Coca-Cola Cup and a healthy position in the Premiership. Gullit's position should have been just about the safest in the Premiership but completely out of the blue he was dismissed on 12 February after, apparently, making excessive wage demands. The Dutchman was replaced by a man he frequently kept on the sidelines, Italian Gianluca Vialli, who did well to keep Chelsea sailing along to success in two major tournaments.

Gullit made several new signings during the close season, the most successful being goalkeeper Ed de Goey for £2.3m, Tore Andre Flo and Gustav Poyet. On the eve of the season he brought Graeme Le Saux back to the Bridge for £5m.

Goals were aplenty for Chelsea early on, with 21 being scored in the first seven games. Six came at Barnsley with Vialli netting four. After a run of four straight wins, Chelsea's first real test was at home to Arsenal, who battled well for a 3-2 victory. Within the next fortnight a win over Newcastle was offset by just one point being gathered from away games with Manchester United and Liverpool. Consistency was proving to be beyond Chelsea's capabilities, until November when five of six games were won. Tottenham were slaughtered 6-1 at White Hart Lane with Flo notching a hat-trick. Chelsea were now just three points behind Manchester United and maintained the challenge when dishing out a 4-1 defeat for Sheffield Wednesday. But thereafter Chelsea's form was again inconsistent. Gullit's final league match was a 2-0 defeat at Arsenal and when the next three games were also lost without scoring, the Blues were eyeing the cups for silverware. There were still some high points to be enjoyed, chiefly a 4-1 thrashing of Liverpool, a 6-2 drubbing of Palace and the completion of the double over Spurs. The season was concluded by a home win over Bolton which relegated the visitors.

Chelsea were almost imperious in the Cup-Winners' Cup with Slovan Bratislava and Real Betis beaten in both legs of their 1st and 3rd Round ties while Tromso, having won the first meeting of their 2nd Round encounter, were duly thrashed 7-1 in the return with Vialli scoring a hat-trick. Vicenza brought a single goal advantage with them to London in the semi-final and increased that lead before Poyet, Zola and Mark Hughes took the Blues through to the final. As they did 27 years earlier, Chelsea followed up their FA Cup success by lifting the Cup-Winners' Cup, courtesy of Zola's majestic strike against Stuttgart.

Chelsea's grip on the FA Cup, though, was brief with Manchester United winning 5-3 at Stamford Bridge in the 3rd Round. Coming in at the 3rd Round stage of the Coca-Cola Cup, Chelsea put out Blackburn in a penalty shoot-out, were taken to extra time by Southampton and needed another penalty showdown to remove Ipswich. In the semi-final, Chelsea, 2-1 down from the 1st Leg, celebrated Vialli's first match as manager by beating Arsenal 3-1 – to go through to the final for the first time in 26 years where for the second time in a year they had the pleasure of beating Middlesbrough 2-0 at Wembley. ∎

Results 1997-98

FA Carling Premiership

Date	Opponents	Ven	Res	Atten	Scorers
08-Aug	Coventry C.	A	2-3	22,686	Sinclair (39); Flo (71)
23-Aug	Barnsley	A	6-0	18,170	Petrescu (25); Poyet (37); Vialli (43, 57, 64, 81)
25-Aug	Wimbledon	A	2-0	22,237	Di Matteo (60); Petrescu (62)
29-Aug	Southampton	H	4-2	30,008	Petrescu (7); Leboeuf (30); M.Hughes (31); Wise (34)
12-Sep	C. Palace	A	3-0	26,186	M.Hughes (20); Leboeuf (26 pen); Le Saux (89)
20-Sep	Arsenal	H	2-3	33,012	Poyet (40); Zola (60)
23-Sep	Manchester U.	A	2-2	55,183	OG (25, Berg); M.Hughes (68)
26-Sep	Newcastle U.	H	1-0	31,563	Poyet (75)
04-Oct	Liverpool	A	2-4	36,647	Zola (22); Poyet (85 pen)
17-Oct	Leicester C.	H	1-0	33,356	Leboeuf (86)
25-Oct	Bolton W.	A	0-1	24,080	
31-Oct	Aston Villa	A	2-0	39,372	M.Hughes (38); Flo (82)
08-Nov	West Ham U.	H	2-1	34,382	OG (56, Ferdinand); Zola (81)
21-Nov	Blackburn R.	A	0-1	27,863	
25-Nov	Everton	H	2-0	34,148	Wise (80 pen); Zola (90 pen)
28-Nov	Derby Co.	H	4-0	36,544	Zola (11, 62, 76); M.Hughes (34)
05-Dec	Tottenham H.	A	6-1	26,465	Flo (39, 62, 89); Di Matteo (47); Petrescu (59); Nicholls (77)
12-Dec	Leeds Utd	H	0-0	34,690	
19-Dec	Sheffield W.	A	4-1	28,334	Petrescu (30); Vialli (56); Leboeuf (65 pen); Flo (84)
25-Dec	Wimbledon	H	1-1	34,100	Vialli (8)
28-Dec	Southampton	A	0-1	15,231	
09-Jan	Coventry C.	H	3-1	34,647	Nicholls (65, 70); Di Matteo (77)
17-Jan	Everton	A	1-3	32,355	Flo (37)
30-Jan	Barnsley	H	2-0	34,442	Vialli (22); M.Hughes (47)
07-Feb	Arsenal	A	0-2	38,083	
20-Feb	Leicester C.	A	0-2	21,335	
27-Feb	Manchester U.	H	0-1	34,511	
07-Mar	Aston Villa	H	0-1	33,018	
10-Mar	C. Palace	H	6-2	31,917	Vialli (14, 43); Zola (16); Wise (85); Flo (88, 90)
13-Mar	West Ham U.	A	1-2	25,829	Charvet (52)
04-Apr	Derby Co.	A	1-0	30,062	M.Hughes (37)
07-Apr	Leeds U.	A	1-3	37,276	Charvet (11)
10-Apr	Tottenham H.	H	2-0	34,149	Flo (75); Vialli (88)

130

18-Apr	Sheffield W.	H	1-0	29,075	Leboeuf (22 pen)
24-Apr	Liverpool	H	4-1	34,639	M.Hughes (10, 75); Clarke (69); Flo (70)
28-Apr	Blackburn R.	H	0-1	33,311	
01-May	Newcastle U.	A	1-3	36,710	Di Matteo (78)
09-May	Bolton W.	H	2-0	34,845	Vialli (73); Morris (90)

FA Challenge Cup

Date	Opponents	Vn	Rnd	Res	Atten	Scorers
04-Jan	Man. Utd	H	3R	3-5	34,792	Le Saux (78); Vialli (83, 88)

Coca-Cola League Cup

Date	Opponents	Vn	Rnd	Res	Atten	Scorers
15-Oct	Blackburn R.	H	3R	1-1	18,671	Di Matteo (61)
	aet. Chelsea win 4-1 on penalties					
19-Nov	Southampton	H	4R	2-1	20,968	Flo (61); Morris (118)
	aet					
07-Jan	Ipswich T	A	QF	2-2	22,088	Flo (32); Le Saux (45)
	aet. Chelsea win 4-1 on penalties					
28-Jan	Arsenal	A	SF1L	1-2	38,114	M.Hughes (68)
18-Feb	Arsenal	H	SF2L	3-1	34,330	M.Hughes (11); Di Matteo (50); Petrescu (53)
	Chelsea win 4-3 on aggregate					
29-Mar	Middlesbrough	H	F	2-0	77,698	Sinclair (95); Di Matteo (107)
	aet. Played at Wembley					

Cup-Winners' Cup

Date	Opponents	Vn	Rnd	Res	Atten	Scorers
18-Sep	S. Bratislava	H	1R1L	2-0	23,067	Di Matteo (51); Granville (80)
02-Oct	S. Bratislava	A	1R2L	2-0	13,850	Vialli (27); Di Matteo (60)
23-Oct	Tromso	A	2R1L	2-3	6,438	Vialli (86, 90)
06-Nov	Tromso	H	2R2L	7-1	29,363	Petrescu (13, 86); Vialli (24, 60, 75); Zola (43); Leboeuf (55 pen)
05-Mar	Real Betis	A	QF1L	2-1	31,000	Flo (8, 12)
19-Mar	Real Betis	H	QF2L	3-1	32,300	Sinclair (29); Di Matteo (49); Zola (90)
02-Apr	Vicenza	A	SF1L	0-1	19,319	
16-Apr	Vicenza	H	SF2L	3-1	33,810	Poyet (35); Zola (51); M.Hughes (76)
13-May	VfB Stuttgart	S	F	1-0	30,216	Zola (71)

Coventry City

Founded as Singer's FC, cycle manufacturers, in 1883. Joined the Birmingham and District League in 1894; in 1898 changed name to Coventry City; and in 1905 moved to the Athletic Ground, Highfield Road. Elected to Division One of the Southern League in 1908, but relegated to the Second in 1914.

Joined the Wartime Midland Section of the Football League in 1918 and elected to an expanded Second Division of the Football League for 1919-20. Founder members of the Fourth Division in 1958. Promoted to Division One for the first time in 1967 and never relegated. Premier League founder members 1992.

Ground:	Highfield Road Stadium, King Richard St, Coventry, CV2 4FW
Phone: 01203-234000	**Fax:** 01203-234099
Box Office: 01203-234020	**CC Booking:** 01203-578000
News: 0891 12 11 66	
Capacity: 24,021	**Pitch:** 110 yds x 75 yds
Colours: All Sky Blue	**Nickname:** Sky Blues
Radio: 95.6FM BBC Radio West Midlands	
Internet: http://www.ccfc.co.uk	

President: Eric Grove	**Chairman:** Bryan Richardson
Deputy-Chairman: Mike McGinnity	**Secretary:** Graham Hover
Manager: Gordon Strachan OBE	**Assistant:** Alec Miller
Physio: George Dalton	

League History: 1919 Elected to Division 2; 1925-26 Division 3 (N); 1926-36 Division 3 (S); 1936-52 Division 2; 1952-58 Division 3 (S); 1958-59 Division 4; 1959-64 Division 3; 1964-67 Division 2; 1967-92 Division 1; 1992- FA Premier League.

Honours: *Football League: Division 2 Champions* 1966-67; *Division 3 Champions* 1963-64; *Division 3 (S) Champions* 1935-36; *Runners-up* 1933-34; *Division 4 Runners-up* 1958-59. *FA Cup: Winners* 1986-87.

European Record: CC (0): – ; CWC (0) – ; UEFA (1): 70-71 (2)

Managers: H.R. Buckle 1909-10; Robert Wallace 1910-13; Frank Scott-Walford 1913-15; William Clayton 1917-19; H. Pollitt 1919-20; Albert Evans 1920-24; Jimmy Ker 1924-28; James McIntyre 1928-31; Harry Storer 1931-45; Dick Bayliss 1945-47; Billy Frith 1947-48; Harry Storer 1948-53; Jack

Fairbrother 1953-54; Charlie Elliott 1954-55; Jesse Carver 1955-56; Harry Warren 1956-57; Billy Firth 1957-61; Jimmy Hill 1961-67; Noel Cantwell 1967-72; Bob Dennison 1972; Joe Mercer 1972-75; Gordon Milne 1972-81; Dave Sexton 1981-83; Bobby Gould 1983-84; Don Mackay 1985-86; George Curtis 1986-87 (became MD); John Sillett 1987-90; Terry Butcher 1990-92; Don Howe 1992; *(FAPL)* Bobby Gould July 1992-93; Phil Neal Nov 1993-Feb 1995; Ron Atkinson Feb 1995-Nov 1996; Gordon Strachan Nov 1996-.

Season 1997-98

Biggest Home Win:	4-0 v Tottenham Hotspur
Biggest Home Defeat:	0-2 v Leicester City
Biggest Away Win:	5-1 v Bolton Wanderers
Biggest Away Defeat:	0-3 v Aston Villa and Manchester United
Biggest Home Att:	23,054 v Manchester United
Smallest Home Att:	15,900 v Crystal Palace
Average Attendance:	19,722
Leading Scorer:	Dion Dublin – 18

All-Time Records

Record FAPL Win:	5-0 v Blackburn Rovers, 9/12/95
	5-1 v Liverpool, 19/12/92
	5-1 v Bolton Wanderers 97-98, 31/1/98
Record FAPL Defeat:	0-5 v Manchester United, 28/12/92
Record FL Win:	9-0 v Bristol C, Division 3 (S), 28/4/34
Record FL Defeat:	2-10 v Norwich C, Division 3 (S), 15/3/30
Record Cup Win:	7-0 v Scunthorpe U, FA Cup R1, 24/11/34
Record Fee Received:	£3.6m from Liverpool for Phil Babb, 9/94
Record Fee Paid:	£3.25m to Grasshopper for Viorel Moldovan, 12/97
Most FL Apps:	George Curtis, 486, 1956-70
Most FAPL Apps:	186 – Steve Ogrizovic, 1992-98
Most FAPL Goals:	59 – Dion Dublin, 1992-98

Highest Scorer in FAPL Season: Dion Dublin, 18, 1997-98
Record Attendance (all-time): 51,455 v Wolves, Division 2, 29/4/67
Record Attendance (FAPL): 24,410 v Manchester United 12/04/93
Most FAPL Goals in Season: 62, 1992-93 – 42 games
Most FAPL Points in Season: 56, 1993-94 – 42 games

Player	Tot	St	Sb	Snu	PS	Gls	Y	R	Fa	La	Fg	Lg
BOATENG …… …	14	14	0	0	4	1	4	1	5	0	0	0
BOLAND ……	19	8	11	10	2	0	4	0	1	2	0	0
BORROWS …… …	1	1	0	1	0	0	0	0	4	0	0	0
BREEN …… …	30	30	0	2	2	1	1	1	5	4	0	0
BURROWS ……	32	32	0	0	0	0	8	0	1	4	0	0
DUBLIN …… …	36	36	0	0	0	18	4	1	5	2	4	1
DUCROS …… …	3	1	2	1	2	0	0	0	0	1	0	0
EUSTACE…… …	0	0	0	1	0	0	0	0	0	0	0	0
HALL ……	25	20	5	6	3	1	7	0	4	4	0	1
HAWORTH ……	10	4	6	8	2	0	1	0	1	2	0	1
HEDMAN ……	14	14	0	23	0	0	0	0	3	0	0	0
HOWIE …… …	0	0	0	2	0	0	0	0	0	0	0	0
HUCKERBY ……	34	32	2	0	9	14	9	0	5	1	1	0
JOHANSEN ……	2	0	2	8	0	0	0	0	0	1	0	0
LIGHTBOURNE…	7	1	6	8	1	0	1	0	0	3	0	0
McALLISTER ……	14	14	0	0	2	0	1	0	0	4	0	2
MOLDOVAN ……	10	5	5	6	3	1	0	0	4	0	1	0
NILSSON ……	32	32	0	1	0	0	3	0	4	3	0	0
OGRIZOVIC ……	24	24	0	13	0	0	0	0	2	4	0	0
O'NEILL ……	4	2	2	4	2	0	0	0	0	1	0	0
PRENDERVILLE …	0	0	0	2	0	0	0	0	0	0	0	0
RICHARDSON ……	3	3	0	2	0	0	0	0	0	0	0	0
SALAKO…… …	11	11	0	2	2	0	0	0	4	0	2	2
SHAW ……	33	33	0	2	1	0	2	0	3	4	0	0
SHILTON …… …	2	2	0	5	1	0	0	0	0	0	0	0
SOLTVEDT ……	30	26	4	8	10	1	1	0	4	2	0	0
STRACHAN,Gavin	9	2	7	11	2	0	0	0	4	0	0	0
TELFER ……	33	33	0	0	4	3	9	0	4	2	2	0
WHELAN …… …	21	21	0	0	2	6	4	0	4	0	0	0
WILLIAMS, P ……	20	17	3	8	1	0	10	2	1	4	0	0
WILLIS …… …	0	0	0	1	0	0	0	0	0	0	0	0

5-Year Record

	Div.	P	W	D	L	F	A	Pts	Pos	FAC	FLC
93-94	PL	42	14	14	14	43	45	56	11	3	3
94-95	PL	42	12	14	16	44	62	50	16	4	3
95-96	PL	38	8	14	16	42	60	38	16	4	4
96-97	PL	38	9	14	15	38	54	41	17	5	3
97-98	PL	38	12	16	10	46	44	52	11	6	4

Blues Climb towards the Sky

Having successfully battled against relegation on the final day of the season for three consecutive years, Coventry City, under Gordon Strachan, attained their joint highest Premiership position and their second highest Premiership points total.

Strachan was cautious in the transfer market during the close season with just £2.2m being used to bring in Simon Haworth, Markus Hedman, Trong Egil Soltvedt, Kyle Lightbourne, Roland Nilsson and Martin Johansen. The £500,000 invested in Lightbourne was recouped later in the season when he left the club. Amongst those also departing were John Filan, Eoin Jess and Peter Ndlovu.

Coventry made a sensational start with club captain Dion Dublin scoring a match-winning hat-trick. Such was Dublin's form throughout the season that he won a deserved England call up. The win over Chelsea, though, was one of only two successes in 12 games and by the end of October a run of five draws and a defeat in six games left them just three points clear of the bottom three. The Sky Blues had yet to lose at Highfield Road but somewhat embarrassingly they were the only club in the Premiership and the Nationwide League still to score on their travels. Coventry put that record straight on 1 November with a 2-1 win at Selhurst Park over Wimbledon which also ended a goal drought lasting 458 minutes. Unfortunately, Coventry again failed to build on a good result and lost their unbeaten record at Highfield Road when Leicester won 2-0. That defeat was sandwiched between 3-1 and 3-0 defeats at Derby and Aston Villa.

Strachan broke the club transfer record to sign Viorel Moldovan in December and the month started well on the pitch for the Sky Blues with Spurs being hammered 4-0; the exciting Darren Huckerby scored twice. Two more away games were lost before Coventry helped to prise open the title race with two late goals from the deadly duo of Huckerby and Dublin clinching a 3-2 win over league leaders Manchester United just after Christmas. The new year kicked off with defeat at Chelsea but Coventry were not to lose another league match until April. Arsenal drew at Highfield Road before Bolton were thrashed 5-1 at the Reebok Stadium while other lower mid-table sides Sheffield Wednesday, Southampton, Barnsley and Palace were also beaten, along with a couple of cup victories to help Coventry equal the club record of seven straight wins.

Although only two of the last ten league games were won, a good number of draws left Coventry reflecting on an outstanding record of one defeat from their final 15 outings.

Coventry's problems away from home in the league were not repeated in the FA Cup where exceptional wins were recorded at Liverpool with Huckerby, Dublin and Paul Telfer scoring, and at Aston Villa, 1-0, where Moldovan notched the winner. These wins came either side of a brace of Dublin goals putting out Derby at Highfield Road in the 4th Round. But hopes of reaching the last four were blown away in a penalty shoot-out defeat by Sheffield United at Bramall Lane.

Good progress was also made in the Coca-Cola Cup with a 2nd Round 1st Leg deficit against Blackpool being successfully overturned and followed by a thumping 4-1 victory over Everton. Arsenal brought the run to a close in the 4th Round with an extra-time win at Highbury. ■

Results 1997-98

FA Carling Premiership

Date	Opponents	Ven	Res	Atten	Scorers
08-Aug	Chelsea	H	3-2	22,686	Dublin (41, 82, 88)
10-Aug	Arsenal	A	0-2	37,324	
22-Aug	Bolton W.	H	2-2	16,633	Telfer (8); Huckerby (20)
26-Aug	West Ham U.	H	1-1	18,289	Huckerby (38)
29-Aug	Manchester U.	A	0-3	55,074	
12-Sep	Southampton	H	1-0	18,659	Soltvedt (65)
19-Sep	Sheffield W.	A	0-0	21,087	
23-Sep	C. Palace	H	1-1	15,900	Dublin (8)
27-Sep	Blackburn R.	A	0-0	19,086	
03-Oct	Leeds U.	H	0-0	17,770	
19-Oct	Barnsley	A	0-2	17,463	
24-Oct	Everton	H	0-0	18,760	
31-Oct	Wimbledon	A	2-1	11,201	Huckerby (16); Dublin (22)
07-Nov	Newcastle U.	H	2-2	22,679	Dublin (4, 82)
21-Nov	Derby Co.	A	1-3	29,351	Huckerby (71)
28-Nov	Leicester C.	H	0-2	18,309	
05-Dec	Aston Villa	A	0-3	33,250	
12-Dec	Tottenham H.	H	4-0	19,499	Huckerby (42, 84); Breen (63); Hall (87)
19-Dec	Liverpool	A	0-1	39,707	
25-Dec	West Ham U.	A	0-1	22,477	
27-Dec	Manchester U.	H	3-2	23,054	Whelan (12); Dublin (86 pen); Huckerby (87)
09-Jan	Chelsea	A	1-3	34,647	Telfer (30)
16-Jan	Arsenal	H	2-2	22,864	Whelan (21); Dublin (66 pen)
30-Jan	Bolton W.	A	5-1	25,000	Whelan (25); Huckerby (57, 65); Dublin (73, 79)
06-Feb	Sheffield W.	H	1-0	18,375	Dublin (74 pen)
17-Feb	Southampton	A	2-1	15,091	Whelan (14); Huckerby (29)
20-Feb	Barnsley	H	1-0	20,265	Dublin (89 pen)
27-Feb	C. Palace	H	3-0	21,810	Telfer (1); Moldovan (40); Dublin (77)
13-Mar	Newcastle U.	A	0-0	36,767	
27-Mar	Derby Co.	H	1-0	18,705	Huckerby (44)
03-Apr	Leicester C.	A	1-1	21,137	Whelan (80)
10-Apr	Aston Villa	H	1-2	22,792	Whelan (59)
12-Apr	Tottenham H.	A	1-1	33,463	Dublin (86)
17-Apr	Liverpool	H	1-1	22,721	Dublin (47 pen)

24-Apr	Leeds U.	A	3-3	36,522	Huckerby (20, 34, 62)
28-Apr	Wimbledon	H	0-0	17,968	
01-May	Blackburn R.	H	2-0	18,794	Dublin (19 pen); Boateng (34)
09-May	Everton	A	1-1	40,109	Dublin (89)

FA Challenge Cup

Date	*Opponents*	*Vn*	*Rnd*	*Res*	*Atten*	*Scorers*
03-Jan	Liverpool	A	3R	3-1	33,888	Huckerby (45); Dublin (62); Telfer (87)
24-Jan	Derby Co.	H	4R	2-0	22,864	Dublin (38, 45)
14-Feb	Aston Villa	H	5R	1-0	26,979	Moldovan (72)
07-Mar	Sheffield U.	H	6R	1-1		Dublin (32 pen)
17-Mar	Sheffield U.	A	6RR	1 1	29,034	Telfer (10)
	aet. Sheffield U. win 3-1 on pens					

Coca-Cola League Cup

Date	*Opponents*	*Vn*	*Rnd*	*Res*	*Atten*	*Scorers*
16-Sep	Blackpool	A	2R1L	0-1	5,884	
01-Oct	Blackpool	H	2R2L	3-1	9,565	McAllister (61 pen, 89 pen); Dublin (70)
	Coventry C. win 3-2 on aggregate					
15-Oct	Everton	H	3R	4-1	10,087	Hall (6); Salako (33, 59); Haworth (62)
18-Nov	Arsenal	A	4R	0-1	30,199	
	aet					

Derby County

In 1884 members of the Derbyshire County Cricket team formed the football club as a way of boosting finances in the cricket close season. They played their first season at the Racecourse Ground and entered the FA Cup. A year later the club moved to the Baseball Ground where they remained until a move to Pride Park Stadium for the 1997-98 season. In 1888 they became founder members of the Football League. Since their formation they have fluctuated through the top divisions, but enjoyed a sparkling spell during the 1970s.

Ground: Pride Park Stadium, Derby, DE24 8XL
Phone: 01332-202202   **Fax:** 01332-667540
News: 0891 12 11 87   **Tickets:** 0891 33 22 12
Capacity: 30,500 > 33,000   **Pitch:** 110 yds x 74 yds
Colours: White & Black, Black, White & Black
Nickname: The Rams
Radio: BBC Radio Derby 1116AM/104.5FM
Internet: www.dcfc.co.uk
E-mail: press.office@dcfc.co.uk

Chairman: Lionel Pickering   **Vice-Chairman:** Peter Gadsby
CEO: Keith Loring   **Secretary:** Keith Pearson
Manager: Jim Smith   **Coach:** Steve McClaren
Physio: Peter Melville

League History: 1888 Founder members of Football League; 107-12 Division 1; 1912-14 Division 2; 1914-15 Division 1; 1915-21 Division 1; 1921-26 Division 2; 1926-53 Division 1; 1953-55 Division 2; 1955-57 Division 3N; 1957-69 Division 2; 1969-80 Division 1; 1980-84 Division 2; 1984-86 Division 3; 1986-87 Division 2; 1987-91 Division 1; 1991-92 Division 2; 1992-96 Division 1; 1996- FA Premier League.

Honours: *Football League: Division 1 Champions 1971-72, 1974-75; Runners-up 1895-96, 1929-30, 1935-36, 1995-96; Division 2 Champions 1911-12, 1914-15, 1968-69, 1986-87; Runners-up 1925-26; Division 3N Champions 1956-57; Runners-up 1955-56. FA Cup: Winners 1945-46; Runners-up 1897-98, 1888-89, 1902-03. Anglo Italian Cup: Runners-up 1992-93.*

European Record: CC (2): 1972-73 (SF), 1975-76 (2); CWC (0) – ; UEFA (2): 1974-75 (3), 1976-77 (2).

Managers: Harry Bradshaw 1904-09; Jimmy Methven 1906-22; Cecil Potter 1922-25; George Jobey 1925-41; Ted Manger 1944-46; Stuart McMillan 1946-53; Jack Barker 1953-55; Harry Storer 1955-62; Tim Ward 1962-67; Brian Clough 1967-73; Dave Mackay 1973-76; Colin Murphy 1977; Tommy Docherty 1977-79; Colin Addison 1979-82; Johnny Newman 1982; Peter Taylor 1982-84; Roy McFarland 1984, Arthur Cox 1984-93; Roy McFarland 1993-95; *(FAPL)* Jim Smith June 1995-.

Season 1997-98

Biggest Home Win:	4-0 v Bolton W. and Southampton
Biggest Home Defeat:	0-5 v Leeds United
Biggest Away Win:	5-2 v Sheffield Wednesday
Biggest Away Defeat:	0-4 v Chelsea
Biggest Home Att:	30,492 v Liverpool
Smallest Home Att:	25,625 v Southampton
Average Attendance:	29,127
Leading Scorer:	Paulo Wanchope – 13

All-Time Records

Record FAPL Win:	4-0 v Southampton, 28/9/97 and Bolton W. 13/4/98
Record FAPL Defeat:	1-6 v Middlesbrough, 5/3/97
Record FL Win:	9-0 v Wolverhampton Wanderers, Div. 1 10/1/1891
Record Cup Win:	12-0 v Finn Harps, UEFA Cup 1R1L, 15/9/76
Record Fee Received:	£2.9m from Liverpool for Dean Saunders, 7/91
Record Fee Paid:	£2.5m to Notts County for Craig Short, 9/92
Most FL Apps:	Kevin Hector, 486, 1966-78, 1980-82
Most FAPL Apps:	71 – Chris Powell, 1996-98
Most FAPL Goals:	20 – Dean Sturridge, 1996-98

Highest Scorer in FAPL Season: Paulo Wanchope, 13, 1997-98
Record Attendance (all-time): 41,826 v Tottenham H., Division 1, 20/9/69
Record Attendance (FAPL): 30,492 v Liverpool 97-98
Most FAPL Goals in Season: 52, 1997-98 – 38 games
Most FAPL Points in Season: 55, 1997-98 – 38 games

Summary 1997-98

Player	Tot	St	Sb	Snu	PS	Gls	Y	R	Fa	La	Fg	Lg
ASANOVIC	4	3	1	1	3	1	1	0	0	1	0	0
BAIANO	33	30	3	0	16	12	2	0	0	1	1	0
BOHINEN	9	9	0	0	3	1	1	0	2	0	0	0
BRIDGE-WILKINSON	0	0	0	3	0	0	0	0	0	0	0	0
BURTON	29	12	17	3	8	3	0	0	2	1	0	0
CARBON	4	3	1	2	2	0	1	0	0	0	0	0
CARSLEY	34	34	0	0	1	1	11	0	2	2	0	0
DAILLY	30	30	0	1	0	1	7	0	1	4	0	0
DELAP	13	10	3	1	3	0	2	0	0	0	0	0
ELLIOTT	3	3	0	5	2	0	0	0	1	2	0	0
ERANIO	23	23	0	0	6	5	9	2	1	1	0	0
HOULT	2	2	0	34	0	0	0	0	0	1	0	0
HUNT	19	7	12	7	3	1	1	0	0	4	0	0
KNIGHT	0	0	0	3	0	0	0	0	0	0	0	0
KOZIUK	9	6	3	11	2	0	1	0	1	2	0	0
LAURSEN	28	27	1	0	5	1	5	0	1	2	0	0
POOM	36	36	0	1	0	0	2	0	2	3	0	0
POWELL, C	36	34	2	1	2	1	3	0	2	4	1	0
POWELL, D	24	13	11	1	4	0	4	0	2	1	0	0
ROWETT	35	32	3	3	2	1	3	0	2	4	0	2
SIMPSON	1	1	0	4	1	0	0	0	0	2	0	0
SMITH	0	0	0	1	0	0	0	0	0	0	0	0
SOLIS	9	3	6	6	3	0	0	0	0	3	0	0
STIMAC	22	22	0	0	2	1	6	0	2	0	0	0
STURRIDGE	30	24	6	0	7	9	8	0	0	4	0	1
TROLLOPE	10	4	6	1	0	0	3	0	0	3	0	1
VAN DER LAAN	10	7	3	6	5	0	2	0	0	3	0	0
WANCHOPE	32	30	2	0	6	13	7	0	2	4	0	4
WARD	3	2	1	0	0	0	0	0	0	0	0	0
WILLEMS	10	3	7	4	1	0	0	0	2	0	0	0
YATES	9	8	1	2	2	0	2	0	2	0	0	0
Own Goals						1						

5-Year Record

	Div.	P	W	D	L	F	A	Pts	Pos	FAC	FLC
93-94	1	46	20	11	15	73	68	71	6	3	3
94-95	1	46	18	12	16	66	51	66	9	3	4
95-96	1	46	21	16	9	71	51	79	2	3	3
96-97	PL	38	11	13	14	45	58	46	12	6	2

UEFA Spot Missed

Having secured a safe mid-table position in their first season of Premiership football, Derby County looked forward to the second campaign with increased expectations as the club moved to its new Pride Park Stadium. Manager Jim Smith kept faith in those who cemented the club's position in the Premiership with Sean Flynn and veteran Paul McGrath being the only departures from the previous campaign's regulars. Smith invested £1m in Portsmouth striker Deon Burton, and just over that figure to acquire the services of Francesco Baiano from Fiorentina and Jonathan Hunt from Birmingham. Later in the season he added Blackburn's Norwegian international midfielder Lars Bohinen to the squad.

The season began disappointingly for Derby with 1-0 defeats at Blackburn and Tottenham, but once installed in their new stadium the Rams went on the rampage. Stefano Eranio, from the penalty spot, clinched Derby's first points at Pride Park, against Barnsley, and Everton were then seen off 3-1 with Hunt scoring his first, and last, Premiership goal of the season. After a defeat at Aston Villa, Derby ended a wait of more than six decades for a win at Hillsborough with Baiano scoring twice in a 5-2 romp. The Italian had also scored at Villa and went on a marvellous run of scoring in six consecutive Premiership games, including a brace in successive matches against Wednesday, Southampton and Leicester. Baiano's run coincided with a five-match unbeaten run for the Rams, which was their best spell of the season. Liverpool brought the sequence to its conclusion with a 4-0 reversal at Anfield but Derby stayed in excellent touch at Pride Park and only fell at the 13th attempt when Aston Villa completed the double. Indeed, their outstanding home form was in stark contrast to that of their away performances which were inconsistent in the extreme. After losing their first three away games, the next two were won. Fifteen goals were then leaked in four ventures away from Pride Park which was followed by conceding just two goals in four away games.

But once the Pride Park fortress had been breached Derby fell to a couple of spectacular defeats, with Leeds and Leicester winning 5-0 and 4-0 respectively at the new ground. The defeat by Leeds sparked a run of four games – 410 minutes in total – without a goal, which ended with a 4-0 drubbing of Bolton. Another four successive defeats, including being Crystal Palace's first victims at Selhurst Park, ensured that the Rams would not claim a UEFA Cup place.

Derby made a good start in the 3rd Round of the FA Cup with a 2-0 home victory over Southampton. Derby beat the Saints three times during the season without conceding a goal. But dreams of bringing to an end a wait of more than 50 years for a place in the final were quickly extinguished by a 2-0 defeat at Coventry in Round 4.

Other than reaching the semi-final in 1968, Derby have enjoyed little success in the Coca-Cola (League) Cup but made a positive start this year with wins in both legs of their 2nd Round meeting with Southend United. After falling behind at Tottenham in the 3rd Round, two goals from top scorer Paulo Wanchope carried the Rams through to a 5th Round showdown with Newcastle, which ended in a 1-0 home defeat for the Midlands club. ■

Results 1996-97

FA Carling Premiership

Date	Opponents	Ven	Res	Atten	Scorers
08-Aug	Blackburn R.	A	0-1	23,557	
22-Aug	Tottenham H.	A	0-1	25,886	
29-Aug	Barnsley	H	1-0	27,232	Eranio (43 pen)
12-Sep	Everton	H	3-1	27,828	Hunt (23); C.Powell (33); Sturridge (66)
19-Sep	Aston Villa	A	1-2	35,444	Baiano (15)
23-Sep	Sheffield W.	A	5-2	22,391	Baiano (8, 48); Burton (74); Wanchope (33); Laursen (79)
27-Sep	Southampton	H	4-0	25,625	Baiano (82); Carsley (83); Wanchope (79); Eranio (75 pen)
05-Oct	Leicester C.	A	2-1	19,585	Baiano (21, 62)
17-Oct	Manchester U.	H	2-2	30,014	Baiano (23); Wanchope (38)
21-Oct	Wimbledon	H	1-1	28,595	Baiano (53)
24-Oct	Liverpool	A	0-4	38,072	
31-Oct	Arsenal	H	3-0	30,004	Wanchope (46, 65); Sturridge (82)
07-Nov	Leeds U.	A	3-4	33,572	Sturridge (4, 11); Asanovic (33 pen)
21-Nov	Coventry C.	H	3-1	29,351	Baiano (3); Eranio (30 pen); Wanchope (39)
28-Nov	Chelsea	A	0-4	34,544	
05-Dec	West Ham U.	H	2-0	29,300	OG (10, Miklosko); Sturridge (49)
13-Dec	Bolton W.	A	3-3	23,037	Eranio (54); Baiano (64, 68)
16-Dec	Newcastle U.	A	0-0	36,289	
19-Dec	C. Palace	H	0-0	26,950	
25-Dec	Newcastle U.	H	1-0	30,302	Eranio (4 pen)
27-Dec	Barnsley	A	0-1	18,866	
10-Jan	Blackburn R.	H	3-1	27,823	Sturridge (15, 41); Wanchope (88)
16-Jan	Wimbledon	A	0-0	13,031	
30-Jan	Tottenham H.	H	2-1	30,187	Sturridge (25); Wanchope (76)
06-Feb	Aston Villa	H	0-1	30,251	
13-Feb	Everton	A	2-1	34,876	Stimac (21); Wanchope (50)
20-Feb	Manchester U.	A	0-2	55,170	
27-Feb	Sheffield W.	H	3-0	30,203	Wanchope (3, 49); Rowett (67)
14-Mar	Leeds U.	H	0-5	30,217	
27-Mar	Coventry C.	A	0-1	18,705	
04-Apr	Chelsea	H	0-1	30,062	
10-Apr	West Ham U.	A	0-0	25,155	

12-Apr	Bolton W.	H	4-0	29,126	Wanchope (27);
					Burton (37, 40); Baiano (45)
17-Apr	C. Palace	A	1-3	18,101	Bohinen (85)
25-Apr	Leicester C.	H	0-4	29,855	
28-Apr	Arsenal	A	0-1	38,121	
01-May	Southampton	A	2-0	15,202	Dailly (50); Sturridge (88)
09-May	Liverpool	H	1-0	30,492	Wanchope (63)

FA Challenge Cup

Date	Opponents	Vn	Rnd	Res	Atten	Scorers
03-Jan	Southampton	H	3R	2-0	27,992	Baiano (68 pen);
						C.Powell (73)
24-Jan	Coventry C.	A	4R	0-2	22,864	

Coca-Cola League Cup

Date	Opponents	Vn	Rnd	Res	Atten	Scorers
16-Sep	Southend Utd	A	2R1L	1-0	4,011	Wanchope (43)
01-Oct	Southend Utd	H	2R2L	5-0	18,490	Rowett (43, 57);
						Wanchope (60);
						Sturridge (64); Trollope (83)
	Derby Co. win 6-0 on aggregate					
15-Oct	Tottenham H.	A	3R	2-1	20,390	Wanchope (27, 71)
18-Nov	Newcastle Utd	H	4R	0-1	27,364	

5-Year Record

	Div.	P	W	D	L	F	A	Pts	Pos	FAC	FLC
93-94	1	46	20	11	15	73	68	71	6	3	3
94-95	1	46	18	12	16	66	51	66	9	3	4
95-96	1	46	21	16	9	71	54	79	2	3	3
96-97	PL	38	11	13	14	45	58	46	12	6	2
97-98	PL	38	16	7	15	52	49	55	9	4	4

Everton

The cricket team of St Domingo's Church turned to football around 1878. Playing in Stanley Park, in late 1879 changed name to Everton FC, the name of the district to the west of the park.

Moved to a field at Priory Road in 1882 and then, in 1884, moved to a site in Anfield Road. As one of the country's leading teams, became founder members of the Football League in 1888. Moved to Goodison Park, a field on the north side of Stanley Park, in 1892 following a dispute with the ground's landlord. Premier League founder members 1992.

Ground: Goodison Park, Liverpool, L4 4EL
Phone: 0151 330 2200
Box Office: 0151 330 2300   **CC Bookings:** 0151 471 8000
Info: 0891 12 11 99
Colours: Royal Blue, White, Blue   **Nickname:** The Toffees
Capacity: 40,160   **Pitch:** 112 yds x 78 yds
Radio: Radio Everton 1602AM
Internet: http://evertonfc.com

Chairman: Peter Johnson   **Secretary:** Michael Dunford
Manager: Walter Smith   **Assistant:** Archie Knox
Physio: Les Helm

League History: 1888 Founder Member of the Football League; 1930-31 Division 2; 1931-51 Division 1; 1951-54 Division 2; 1954-92 Division 1; 1992- FA Premier League.

Honours: *Football League: Division 1 Champions* 1890-91, 1914-15, 1927-28, 1931-32, 1938-39, 1962-63, 1969-70, 1984-85, 1986-87; *Runners-up* 1889-90, 1894-95, 1901-02, 1904-05, 1908-09, 1911-12, 1985-86; *Division 2 Champions* 1930-31; *Runners-up* 1953-54. *FA Cup: Winners* 1906, 1933, 1966, 1984, 1995; *Runners-up* 1893, 1897, 1907, 1968, 1985, 1986, 1989. *Football League Cup: Runners-up* 1976-77, 1983-84. *League Super Cup: Runners-up* 1986. *Cup-Winners' Cup: Winners* 1984-85. *Simod Cup: Runners-up* 1989. *Zenith Data Systems Cup: Runners-up* 1991.

European Record: CC (2): 63-64 (1), 70-71 (QF); CWC (3): 66-67 (2), 84-85 (W), 95-96 (2). UEFA (6): 62-63 (1), 64-65 (3), 65-66 (2), 75-76 (1), 78-79 (2), 79-80 (1).

Managers: W.E. Barclay 1888-89; Dick Molyneux 1889-1901; William C. Cuff 1901-18; W.J. Sawyer 1918-19; Thomas H. McIntosh 1919-35; Theo Kelly 1936-48; Cliff Britton 1948-56; Ian Buchan 1956-58; Johnny Carey 1958-61; Harry Catterick 1961-73; Billy Bingham 1973-77; Gordon Lee 1977-81; Howard Kendall 1981-87; Colin Harvey 1987-90; *(FAPL)* Howard Kendall Nov 1990-93; Mike Walker Jan 1993-Nov 1994; Joe Royle Nov 1994-Mar 1997; Dave Watson (Caretaker) Apr 1997-July 1997; Howard Kendall July 1997-July 1998; Walter Smith Jul 1998-.

Season 1997-98

Biggest Home Win:	4-2 v Barnsley
Biggest Home Defeat:	1-4 v Aston Villa
Biggest Away Win:	3-1 v Crystal Palace
Biggest Away Defeat:	0-4 v Arsenal
Biggest Home Att:	40,109 v Coventry City
Smallest Home Att:	28,533 v Wimbledon
Average Attendance:	35,428
Leading Scorer:	Duncan Ferguson – 11

All-Time Records

Record FAPL Win:	7-1 v Southampton, 16/11/96
Record FAPL Defeat:	1-5 v Norwich City 25/9/93; Sheffield W. 2/4/94
Record FL Win:	9-1 v Manchester City, Division 1, 3/9/06; Plymouth Argyle, Division 2, 27/12/30
Record FL Defeat:	4-10 v Tottenham H, Division 1, 11/10/58
Record Cup Win:	11-2 v Derby County, FA Cup R1, 18/1/90
Record Fee Received:	£8m from Fiorentina for Andrei Kanchelskis, 1/97
Record Fee Paid:	£5.75m to Middlesbrough for Nick Barmby, 10/96
Most FL Apps:	Ted Sagar, 465, 1929-53
Most FAPL Apps:	207 – Neville Southall, 1992-98
Most FAPL Goals:	33 – Duncan Ferguson, 1994-98
Highest Scorer in FAPL Season:	Tony Cottee, 16, 93-94 and Andrei Kanchelskis, 16, 95-96
Record Attendance (all-time):	78,299 v Liverpool, Division 1, 18/9/48
Record Attendance (FAPL):	40,177 v Liverpool, 16/04/97
Most FAPL Goals in Season:	64, 1995-96 – 38 games
Most FAPL Points in Season:	61, 1995-96 – 38 games

Player	Tot	St	Sb	Snu	PS	Gls	Y	R	Fa	La	Fg	Lg
ALLEN	5	2	3	6	1	0	1	0	0	0	0	0
BALL	25	21	4	6	2	1	2	0	1	2	0	0
BARMBY	30	26	4	1	7	2	7	0	1	2	0	2
BARRETT	13	12	1	4	5	0	3	0	0	0	0	0
BEAGRIE	6	4	2	2	3	0	1	0	0	0	0	0
BILIC	24	22	2	3	1	0	4	3	0	3	0	0
BRANCH	6	1	5	1	1	0	0	0	0	0	0	0
CADAMARTERI	26	15	11	3	9	4	4	0	1	3	0	1
DUNNE	3	2	1	4	0	0	0	0	1	0	0	0
FARRELLY	26	18	8	5	6	1	3	0	1	1	0	1
FERGUSON	29	28	1	0	1	11	6	1	1	2	0	0
GERRARD	4	4	0	28	0	0	1	0	0	2	0	0
GRANT	7	7	0	1	4	1	0	0	1	1	0	0
HINCHCLIFFE	17	15	2	0	1	0	3	1	0	3	0	0
HUTCHISON	11	11	0	0	0	1	2	0	0	0	0	0
JEFFERS	1	0	1	3	0	0	0	0	0	0	0	0
JEVONS	0	0	0	4	0	0	0	0	0	0	0	0
MADAR	17	15	2	0	11	6	2	0	0	0	0	0
McCANN	11	5	6	3	1	0	2	0	0	0	0	0
MYRHE	22	22	0	1	0	0	1	0	1	0	0	0
O'CONNOR	1	0	1	4	0	0	0	0	0	0	0	0
O'KANE	12	12	0	0	4	0	5	0	0	0	0	0
OSTER	31	16	15	5	5	1	2	0	1	3	0	2
O'TOOLE	0	0	0	4	0	0	0	0	0	0	0	0
PHELAN	9	8	1	2	2	0	2	0	0	1	0	0
SHORT	31	27	4	1	6	0	3	0	0	2	0	0
SOUTHALL	12	12	0	5	0	0	0	0	0	1	0	0
SPEED	21	21	0	0	0	7	4	0	0	3	0	0
SPENCER	6	3	3	0	0	0	1	0	0	0	0	0
STUART	14	14	0	0	1	2	6	0	0	3	0	1
THOMAS	7	6	1	6	3	0	1	0	1	1	0	0
THOMSEN	8	2	6	1	1	1	0	0	1	0	0	0
TILER	19	19	0	0	1	1	5	0	1	0	0	0
WARD	8	8	0	0	2	0	0	0	0	0	0	0
WATSON	26	25	1	2	0	0	2	0	0	3	0	0
WILLIAMSON	15	15	0	0	5	0	1	0	0	2	0	0
Own Goals						2						

Matt Under the Gloss

After battling against relegation for three of the previous four seasons, Everton looked to turn back time in the summer of 1997 with the appointment of Howard Kendall as manager. Kendall enjoyed great success as Everton boss during the previous decade, but a second spell in the early '90s was less profitable and the first season of his third stint almost ended in complete disaster with the drop only being avoided on the final day of the campaign.

Kendall spent almost £7.5m in the close season in attracting to Goodison Park Slaven Bilic, John Oster, Gareth Farrelly and Tony Thomas. Departures included Paul Rideout, Marc Hottiger and David Unsworth. Bilic was seen as a more than useful acquisition but the Croatian defender spent a good part of the season on the sidelines following three dismissals. The midfield was strengthened later in the season with the signing of Don Hutchison from West Ham while £8.5m was collected from the sale of Gary Speed and Andy Hinchcliffe.

Everton kicked off the season with three successive home games but despite Duncan Ferguson scoring in the opening game against Crystal Palace, the Toffeemen went down to a 2-1 defeat. Goals by the soon departing Speed and Graham Stuart saw off West Ham but when Manchester United won at Goodison the writing was on the wall for another season of struggle. Everton were unbeaten for the next three home games but it was only a temporary reprieve before slipping into serious relegation problems. Away from home Everton had a disastrous time with only two successes all season, the first of which didn't arrive until just before Christmas when Speed's last-minute penalty at Leicester ended an inglorious run of one year and four days without a victory on opposition turf.

A sequence of five consecutive defeats, begun at Goodison Park by Southampton on 2 November and ended 27 days later by Tottenham in Neville Southall's 750th match between the sticks, saw Everton plummet from 16th to bottom. With just one defeat from the next nine games – including wins over fellow strugglers Bolton and Palace – Everton rose to 15th, some five points clear of the bottom three.

But it was a false dawn and Kendall's side could muster just two wins from the last 15 outings. One win from the final three games would probably guarantee safety but their survival went to the wire after defeats by Sheffield Wednesday and Arsenal when they were totally outclassed by the new champions. With an early strike against Coventry, Farrelly repaid his £900,000 transfer fee in one swoop but when the visitors grabbed a late equaliser Everton still had to rely on Bolton losing at Chelsea for their own safety to be secured.

Everton's cup form was no less unspectacular than their league performances. The club said farewell to the FA Cup in the 3rd Round for the first time in four years with a home defeat by Newcastle while a 2nd Round Coca-Cola Cup triumph over Scunthorpe was followed by a 4-1 exit at Coventry.

The Blues can possibly look to mitigating circumstances – like a lengthy injury list and numerous suspensions – for their troubles and can also find encouragement in young Danny Cadamarteri and the inspired signing of Spaniard Mickael Madar, but that may well be a case of glossing over the facts. ■

Results 1996-97

FA Carling Premiership

Date	Opponents	Ven	Res	Atten	Scorers
08-Aug	C. Palace	H	1-2	35,716	Ferguson (85)
22-Aug	West Ham U.	H	2-1	34,356	Speed (67); Stuart (83)
26-Aug	Manchester U.	H	0-2	40,079	
31-Aug	Bolton W.	A	0-0	23,131	
12-Sep	Derby Co.	A	1-3	27,828	Stuart (28)
19-Sep	Barnsley	H	4-2	32,659	Speed (12, 72 pen); Oster (84); Cadamarteri (42)
23-Sep	Newcastle U.	A	0-1	36,705	
26-Sep	Arsenal	H	2-2	35,457	Ball (49); Cadamarteri (56)
03-Oct	Sheffield W.	A	1-3	24,486	Cadamarteri (84)
17-Oct	Liverpool	H	2-0	41,112	OG (45, Ruddock); Cadamarteri (75)
24-Oct	Coventry C.	A	0-0	18,760	
01-Nov	Southampton	H	0-2	29,958	
07-Nov	Blackburn R.	A	2-3	25,397	Speed (7); Ferguson (55)
21-Nov	Aston Villa	A	1-2	36,389	Speed (11 pen)
25-Nov	Chelsea	A	0-2	34,148	
28-Nov	Tottenham H.	H	0-2	36,670	
05-Dec	Leeds Utd	A	0-0	34,986	
12-Dec	Wimbledon	H	0-0	28,533	
19-Dec	Leicester C.	A	1-0	20,628	Speed (89 pen)
25-Dec	Manchester U.	A	0-2	55,167	
27-Dec	Bolton W.	H	3-2	37,149	Ferguson (17, 41, 67)
09-Jan	C. Palace	A	3-1	23,311	Barmby (3); Ferguson (12); Madar (34)
17-Jan	Chelsea	H	3-1	32,355	Speed (39); Ferguson (62); OG (82, Duberry)
30-Jan	West Ham U.	A	2-2	25,905	Barmby (25); Madar (58)
06-Feb	Barnsley	A	2-2	18,672	Ferguson (40); Grant (50)
13-Feb	Derby	H	1-2	34,876	Thomsen (85)
22-Feb	Liverpool	A	1-1	44,501	Ferguson (58)
27-Feb	Newcastle U.	H	0-0	37,972	
06-Mar	Southampton	A	1-2	15,102	Tiler (89)
13-Mar	Blackburn R.	H	1-0	33,423	Madar (62)
27-Mar	Aston Villa	H	1-4	36,471	Madar (38)
03-Apr	Tottenham H.	A	1-1	35,624	Madar (24)
10-Apr	Leeds U.	H	2-0	37,099	Hutchison (10); Ferguson (38)
12-Apr	Wimbledon	A	0-0	15,131	
17-Apr	Leicester C.	H	1-1	33,642	Madar (2)
24-Apr	Sheffield W.	H	1-3	35,497	Ferguson (72)

| 02-May | Arsenal | A | 0-4 | 38,269 | |
| 09-May | Coventry C. | H | 1-1 | 40,109 | Farrelly (7) |

FA Challenge Cup

Date	Opponents	Vn	Rnd	Res	Atten	Scorers
04-Jan	Newcastle Utd	H	3R	0-1	20,885	

Coca-Cola League Cup

Date	Opponents	Vn	Rnd	Res	Atten	Scorers
16-Sep	Scunthorpe Utd	A	2R1L	1-0	7,145	Farrelly (36)
01-Oct	Scunthorpe Utd	H	2R2L	5-0	11,562	Stuart (11); Oster (23, 67); Barmby (66); Cadamarteri (69)
	Everton won 6-0 on aggregate					
15-Oct	Coventry C.	A	3R	1-4	10,087	Barmby (16)

5-Year Record

	Div.	P	W	D	L	F	A	Pts	Pos	FAC	FLC
93-94	PL	42	12	8	22	42	63	44	17	3	4
94-95	PL	42	11	17	14	44	51	50	15	W	2
95-96	PL	38	17	10	11	64	44	61	6	4	2
96-97	PL	38	10	12	16	44	57	42	15	4	2
97-98	PL	38	9	13	16	41	56	40	17	3	3

Leeds United

Leeds City, founded in 1904, took over the Elland Road ground of the defunct Holbeck Club and in 1905 gained a Football League Division Two place. The club was, however, expelled in 1919 for disciplinary reasons associated with payments to players during the War. The club closed down.

Leeds United FC, a new professional club, emerged the same year and competed in the Midland League. The club was elected to Football League Division Two for season 1920-21. The club has subsequently never been out of the top two divisions. Premier League founder members 1992.

Ground:	Elland Road, Leeds, LS11 0ES		
Phone:	0113-226 6000		
Box Office:	0113-226 1000	**CC Bookings**: 0113-271 0710	
Info:	0891 12 11 80		
Colours:	All White	**Nickname:** United	
Capacity:	39,704	**Pitch:** 117 yds x 76 yds	
Radio:	Radio Leeds United 1323AM		
Internet:	http://www.lufc.co.uk		

President: Rt Hn The Earl of Harewood
Chairman: Peter Ridsdale   **MD:** Jeremy Fenn
Secretary: Nigel Pleasants
Manager: George Graham   **Assistant:** David O'Leary
Coaches: Eddie Gray and John Dungworth
Physios: David Swift and Alan Sutton

League History: 1920 Elected to Division 2; 1924-27 Division 1; 1927-28 Division 2; 1928-31 Division 1; 1931-32 Division 2; 1932-47 Division 1; 1947-56 Division 2; 1956-60 Division 1; 1960-64 Division 2; 1964-82 Division 1; 1982-90 Division 2; 1990-92 Division 1; 1992- FA Premier League.

Honours: *Football League: Division 1 Champions* 1968-69, 1973-74, 1991-92; *Runners-up* 1964-65, 1965-66, 1969-70, 1970-71, 1971-72; *Division 2 Champions* 1923-24, 1963-64, 1989-90; *Runners-up* 1927-28, 1931-32, 1955-56. *FA Cup: Winners* 1971-72; *Runners-up* 1964-65, 1969-70, 1972-73. *Football League Cup: Winners* 1967-68. *Runners-up* 1995-96 *Champions' Cup: Runners-up* 1974-75. *Cup-Winners' Cup: Runners-up* 1972-73. *UEFA Cup: Winners* 1967-68, 1970-71; *Runners-up* 1966-67.

European Record: CC (3): 69-70 (SF), 74-75 (F), 92-93 (2). CWC (1): 72-73 (F); UEFA (9): 65-66 (SF), 66-67 (F), 67 68 (W), 68-69 (QF), 70-71 (W), 71-72 (1), 73-74 (3), 79-80 (2), 95-96 (2).

Managers: Dick Ray 1919-20; Arthur Fairclough 1920-27; Dick Ray 1927-35; Bill Hampson 1935-47; Willis Edwards 1947-48; Major Frank Buckley 1948-53; Raich Carter 1953-58; Bill Lambton 1958-59; Jack Taylor 1959-61; Don Revie 1961-74; Brian Clough 1974; Jimmy Armfield 1974-78; Jock Stein 1978; Jimmy Adamson 1978-80; Allan Clarke 1980-82; Eddie Gray 1982-85; Billy Bremner 1985-88; *(FAPL)* Howard Wilkinson October 1988-Sept 1996; George Graham Sept 1996-.

Season 1997-98

Biggest Home Win:	4-0 v Blackburn Rovers
Biggest Home Defeat:	1-2 v Sheffield Wednesday
Biggest Away Win:	5-0 v Derby County
Biggest Away Defeat:	0-3 v Manchester United
Biggest Home Att:	39,952 v Manchester United
Smallest Home Att:	29,076 v Crystal Palace
Average Attendance:	34,647
Leading Scorer:	Jimmy Floyd Hasselbaink – 16

All-Time Records

Record FAPL Win:	5-0 v Tottenham H, 25/8/92*;* Swindon Tn, 7/5/94 Derby County 15/3/98
Record FAPL Defeat:	2-6 v Sheffield Wednesday (A), 16/12/95
Record FL Win:	8-0 v Leicester City, Division 1, 7/4/1934
Record FL Defeat:	1-8 v Stoke City, Division 1, 27/8/1934
Record Cup Win:	10-0 v Lyn (Oslo), European Cup, 1R1L, 17/9/69
Record Fee Received:	£2.75 from Blackburn R. for David Batty, 10/93
Record Fee Paid:	£4.5m to Parma for Tomas Brolin, 11/95
Most FL Apps:	Jack Charlton, 629, 1953-73
Most FAPL Apps:	186 – Gary Kelly, 1993-98
Most FAPL Goals:	42 – Rod Wallace, 1992-98

Highest Scorer in FAPL Season: Rod Wallace, 17, 1993-94
Record Attendance (all-time): 57,892 v Sunderland, FA Cup 5R replay, 15/3/67
Record Attendance (FAPL): 41,125 v Manchester United, 27/4/94
Most FAPL Goals in Season: 65, 1993-94 – 42 games
Most FAPL Points in Season: 73, 1994-95 – 42 games

Player	Tot	St	Sb	Snu	PS	Gls	Y	R	Fa	La	Fg	Lg
BEENEY	1	1	0	35	0	0	0	0	1	0	0	0
BOWYER	25	21	4	11	6	3	4	0	3	3	0	1
GRAY	0	0	0	1	0	0	0	0	0	0	0	0
HAALAND	32	26	6	1	2	7	6	1	2	3	0	0
HALLE	33	31	2	3	3	2	5	1	3	3	0	0
HARTE	12	12	0	9	2	0	3	0	0	0	0	0
HASSELBAINK	33	30	3	3	7	16	5	0	4	3	4	2
HIDEN	11	11	0	0	1	0	2	0	1	0	0	0
HOPKIN	25	22	3	6	8	1	5	0	1	4	0	0
JACKSON	1	0	1	8	0	0	4	0	0	0	0	0
JONES	0	0	0	3	0	0	0	0	0	0	0	0
KELLY	34	34	0	0	0	0	6	1	4	3	0	0
KEWELL	29	26	3	3	3	5	2	1	4	2	2	1
LAURENT	0	0	0	3	0	0	0	0	0	0	0	0
LILLEY	12	0	12	13	0	1	1	0	1	3	0	0
MARTYN	37	37	0	0	0	0	0	0	4	4	0	0
MATTHEWS	3	0	3	5	0	0	0	0	0	0	0	0
MAYBURY	12	9	3	5	4	0	0	0	0	1	0	0
McPHAIL	4	0	4	6	0	0	0	0	2	0	0	0
MOLENAAR	22	18	4	12	5	2	4	0	3	3	1	0
RADEBE	27	26	1	0	2	0	10	1	2	4	1	0
RIBEIRO	29	28	1	0	6	3	1	0	3	3	0	1
ROBERTSON	26	24	2	0	0	0	0	0	1	4	0	0
ROBINSON	0	0	0	4	0	0	0	0	0	0	0	0
WALLACE	31	29	2	2	6	10	1	0	4	4	1	2
WETHERALL	34	33	1	2	0	3	6	0	3	4	0	2
Own Goals						4						

62/5

5-Year Record

	Div.	P	W	D	L	F	A	Pts	Pos	FAC	FLC
93-94	PL	42	18	16	8	65	39	70	5	4	2
94-95	PL	42	20	13	9	59	38	73	5	5	2
95-96	PL	38	12	7	19	40	57	43	13	QF	F
96-97	PL	38	11	13	14	28	38	46	11	5	3
97-98	PL	38	17	8	13	57	46	59	5	6	4

Constancy Nearly There

Understanding the need to improve an attack which scored just 28 times in the Premiership during 1996/97, Leeds United manager George Graham parted company with striker Brian Deane for £1.5m and brought in Dutchman Jimmy Floyd Hasselbaink for £2m. The investment was quickly justified with Hasselbaink going on to be Leeds' top scorer with 22 league and cup goals, 14 more than the previous season's top scorer.

In total, Graham released five players during the summer and made several significant signings, including David Hopkin for £3.25m, Alf-Inge Haaland for £1.6m and Bruno Ribeiro and David Robertson for a combined fee of £1m. Early in the new season Graham helped balance the books when collecting £2m from the sale of Tony Yeboah and Carlton Palmer. One transfer which didn't work out was that of Tomas Brolin, whose 19 games for the club cost somewhere in the region of £6m. Another out of favour player was Rod Wallace who, nevertheless, chipped in with 13 goals, of which just two were at Elland Road.

On the pitch, Leeds achieved their highest points total and scored their most goals from a 38-match programme, as the club reclaimed fifth position after two seasons in the lower half of the table, although the number of clean sheets dropped from 20 to 11.

Although Leeds secured a place in the UEFA Cup, their start to the season was indifferent. An opening day draw with Arsenal was followed by victory at Sheffield Wednesday but Leeds failed to score in the next three games, all of which were lost including a 2-0 reversal by Hopkin's old club Crystal Palace. United's season stepped up a gear in mid September with a pulsating 4-3 win at Ewood Park over the previously all-conquering Blackburn; Wallace scored twice, having done likewise at Hillsborough. But Leicester handed Leeds a third successive defeat at Elland Road before United started to climb the table with victory at Southampton and a 1-0 home success over Manchester United in front of their best home gate of the season.

The win over Southampton ignited an impressive run of just one defeat in 12 games which took Leeds to fourth, although Manchester United were still a healthy nine points away. Along the way Newcastle were rolled over 4-1 and Derby, having led 3-0 after just 33 minutes, were defeated 4-3 with Lee Bowyer grabbing a last-minute winner. Leeds won the return 5-0, having beaten Blackburn 4-0 four days earlier. Both of those results came in the wake of a disappointing FA Cup exit at the hands of Wolves. A remarkable point was taken off Chelsea in spite of having Speed and Haaland sent off inside 20 minutes. A trip to West Ham brought that flurry of success to a close but it was overshadowed by events later in the night as the aircraft in which the team travelled was forced to abort its take-off. Fortunately, there were no serious casualties.

In the FA Cup, Nationwide League sides Oxford United and Grimsby were beaten without a goal being conceded before a late Hasselbaink goal clinched a 3-2 win over Birmingham. A fourth consecutive home tie ended in a surprise defeat by Wolves. It was also a shock home defeat which cut short their Coca-Cola Cup dreams, with Reading recording a 3-2 victory after Leeds had already put out Bristol City and Stoke. ∎

Results 1997-98

Date	Opponents	Ven	Res	Atten	Scorers
8-Aug	Arsenal	H	1-1	37,993	Hasselbaink (42)
12-Aug	Sheffield W.	A	3-1	31,520	Wallace (7, 62); Ribeiro (36)
22-Aug	C. Palace	H	0-2	29,076	
25-Aug	Liverpool	H	0-2	39,775	
29-Aug	Aston Villa	A	0-1	39,027	
13-Sep	Blackburn R.	A	4-3	21,956	Wallace (3,17); Molenaar (6); Hopkin (23)
19-Sep	Leicester C.	H	0-1	29,620	
23-Sep	Southampton	A	2-0	15,102	Molenaar (36); Wallace (55)
26-Sep	Manchester U.	H	1-0	39,952	Wetherall (34)
03-Oct	Coventry C.	A	0-0	17,770	
17-Oct	Newcastle U.	H	4-1	39,834	Ribeiro (30); Kewell (38) ; OG (43, Beresford); Wetherall (47)
24-Oct	Wimbledon	A	0-1	15,718	
31-Oct	Tottenham H.	A	1-0	26,411	Wallace (19)
07-Nov	Derby Co.	H	4-3	33,572	Wallace (37); Kewell (40); Hasselbaink (82 pen); Bowyer (90)
22-Nov	West Ham U.	H	3-1	30,031	Hasselbaink (76, 90); Haaland (88)
28-Nov	Barnsley	A	3-2	18,690	Haaland (35); Wallace (72); Lilley (82)
05-Dec	Everton	H	0-0	34,986	
12-Dec	Chelsea	A	0-0	34,690	
19-Dec	Bolton W.	H	2-0	31,163	Ribeiro (68); Hasselbaink (81)
25-Dec	Liverpool	A	1-3	43,854	Haaland (85)
27-Dec	Aston Villa	H	1-1	36,287	Hasselbaink (79)
09-Jan	Arsenal	A	1-2	38,018	Hasselbaink (69)
16-Jan	Sheffield W.	H	1-2	33,166	OG (Pembridge 63)
30-Jan	C. Palace	A	2-0	25,248	Wallace (7); Hasselbaink (13)
06-Feb	Leicester C.	A	0-1	21,244	
21-Feb	Newcastle U.	A	1-1	36,511	Wallace (83)
27-Feb	Southampton	H	0-1	28,791	
03-Mar	Tottenham H.	H	1-0	31,394	Kewell (45)
10-Mar	Blackburn R.	H	4-0	32,933	Bowyer (48); Hasselbaink (53); Haaland (56, 89)
14-Mar	Derby Co.	A	5-0	30,217	OG (8 Laurensen); Halle (32); Bowyer (42); Kewell (60); Hasselbaink (72)

29-Mar	West Ham U.	A	0-3	24,107	
03-Apr	Barnsley	H	2-1	37,749	Hasselbaink (20); OG (80, Moses)
07-Apr	Chelsea	H	3-1	37,276	Hasselbaink (7, 47); Wetherall (22)
10-Apr	Everton	A	0-2	37,099	
17-Apr	Bolton W.	A	3-2	25,000	Haaland (17); Halle (34); Hasselbaink (86)
24-Apr	Coventry C.	H	3-3	36,522	Hasselbaink (16, 28); Kewell (75)
03-May	Manchester U.	A	0-3	55,167	
09-May	Wimbledon	H	1-1	38,172	Haaland (81)

FA Challenge Cup

Date	Opponents	Vn	Rnd	Res	Atten	Scorers
03-Jan	Oxford Utd	H	3R	4-0	20,568	Radebe (17); Hasselbaink (45 pen); Kewell (71, 72)
24-Jan	Grimsby T.	H	4R	2-0	29,598	Molenaar (45); Hasselbaink (79)
14-Feb	Birmingham C.	H	5R	3-2	35,463	Wallace (5); Hasselbaink (27, 87)
07-Mar	Wolverh'n W.	H	6R	0-1		

Coca-Cola League Cup

Date	Opponents	Vn	Rnd	Res	Atten	Scorers
17-Sep	Bristol C.	H	2R1L	3-1	8,806	Wetherall (20); Hasselbaink (70 pen); Ribeiro (90)
30-Sep	Bristol C.	A	2R2L	1-2	10,857	Hasselbaink (8)
	Leeds Utd win 4-3 on aggregate					
15-Oct	Stoke C.	A	3R	3-1	16,203	Kewell (69); Wallace (93, 105)
	aet					
18-Nov	Reading	H	4R	2-3	15,069	Wetherall (16); Bowyer (54)

Leicester City

Founded in 1884 as Leicester Fosse by former pupils of the Wyggeston School from the western part of the city near the old Roman Fosse Way. Moved to their present ground in 1891 and from the Midland League joined Division Two of the Football League in 1894. Promoted for the first time in 1908, they have been relegated seven times from the top flight.

FA Cup runners-up four times, they gained European Cup-Winners' Cup experience in 1961-62. Members of the new Division One in its first season, 1992-93, and promoted to the Premier League following play-off success in 1994. Relegated straight back but repromoted, again via the play-offs at the end of the 1995-96 season. Won the League Cup in 1997.

Ground:	City Stadium, Filbert Street, Leicester LE2 7FL		
Phone:	0116-255 5000	**Fax:**	0116-247 0585
Box Office:	0116- 291 5232	**CC Bookings:**	0116-291 5232
Info:	0891-12 11 85		
Colours:	All Blue	**Club Nickname:**	Filberts or Foxes
Capacity:	22,517	**Pitch:**	112 x 75 yds

President:	tba	**Chairman:**	tba
CEO:	Barrie Pierpoint	**Secretary:**	Ian Silvester
Manager:	Martin O'Neill	**Assistant:**	John Robertson
Coaches:	Paul Franklin, Steve Walford		
Physios:	Alan Smith, Mick Yeomans		
Radio:	104.9FM BBC Radio Leicester		
Internet:	http://www.lcfc.co.uk		

League History: 1894 Elected to Division 2; 1908-09 Division 1; 1909-25 Division 2; 1925-35 Division 1; 1935-37 Division 2; 1937-39 Division 1; 1946-54 Division 2; 1954-55 Division 1; 1955-57 Division 2; 1957-69 Division 1; 1969-71 Division 2; 1971-78 Division 1; 1978-80 Division 2; 1980-81 Division 1; 1981-83 Division 2; 1983-87 Division 1; 1987-92 Division 2; 1992-94 Division 1; 1994-95 FA Premier League; 1995-96 Division 1; 1996- FA Premier League.

Honours: *Football League: Division 1 Runners-up* 1928-29; *Division 2 Champions* 1924-25, 1936-37, 1953-54, 1956-57, 1970-71, 1979-80; *Runners-up* 1907-08. *FA Cup: Runners-up* 1949, 1961, 1963, 1969. *Football League Cup: Winners* 1964, 1997; *Runners-up* 1965.

European Competitions: CC (0) – ; CWC (1): 61-62 (2); UEFA (1) 97-98 (1).

Managers (and secretary-managers): William Clarke 1896-97, George Johnson 1898-1907, James Blessington 1907-09, Andy Aitkin 1909-11, J.W. Bartlett 1912-14, Peter Hodge 1919-26, William Orr 1926-32, Peter Hodge 1932-34, Andy Lochead 1934-36, Frank Womack 1936-39, Tom Bromilow 1939-45, Tom Mather 1945-46, Johnny Duncan 1946-49, Norman Bullock 1949-55, David Halliday 1955-58, Matt Gillies 1959-68, Frank O'Farrell 1968-71, Jimmy Bloomfield 1971-77, Frank McLintock 1977-78, Jock Wallace 1978-82, Gordon Milne 1982-86, Bryan Hamilton 1986-87, David Pleat 1987-91, Brian Little May 1991-Nov 94; Mark McGhee Dec 94-Dec 95; *(FAPL)*: Martin O'Neill Dec 95 -.

Season 1997-98

Biggest Home Win:	3-0 v Tottenham Hotspur
Biggest Home Defeat:	0-1 v Everton and Wimbledon
Biggest Away Win:	4-0 v Derby County
Biggest Away Defeat:	3-5 v Blackburn Rovers
Biggest Home Att:	21,699 v Newcastle United
Smallest Home Att:	18,553 v Wimbledon
Average Attendance:	20,600
Leading Scorer:	Emile Heskey – 10

All-Time Records

Record FAPL Win:	4-0 v Derby County 97-98, 4-2 v Derby County 22/2/97, 4-2 v Blackburn Rovers 11/5/97
Record FAPL Defeat:	3-5 v Blackburn Rovers, 28/2/98 0-4 v Manchester United, 15/4/95
Record FL Win:	10-0 v Portsmouth, Division 1, 20/10/28
Record FL Defeat:	0-12 v Nottingham Forest, Division 1, 21/4/09
Record Cup Win:	8-1 v Coventry City (A), LC R5, 1/12/64
Record Fee Received:	£3.5m from Aston Villa for Mark Draper, 7/95
Record Fee Paid:	£1.25m to Notts County for Mark Draper, 8/94
Most FL Apps:	Adam Black, 528, 1920-35
Most FAPL Apps:	72 – Neil Lennon, 1996-98
Most FAPL Goals:	20 – Emile Heskey , 1997-98

Highest Scorer in FAPL Season: Steve Claridge, 12, 1996-97
Record Attendance (all-time): 47,298 v Tottenham H., FAC Rd5, 18/2/28
Record Attendance (FAPL): 21,393 v Liverpool, 26/12/94
Most FAPL Goals in Season: 51, 1997-98 – 38 games
Most FAPL Points in Season: 47, 1996-97 – 38 games

Summary 1997-98

Player	Tot	St	Sb	Snu	PS	Gls	Y	R	Fa	La	Fg	Lg
ANDREWS	0	0	0	14	0	0	0	0	0	0	0	0
ARPHEXAD	5	5	0	23	0	0	0	0	0	0	0	0
CAMPBELL	11	6	5	13	5	0	1	0	0	1	0	0
CARLSTRAND	0	0	0	1	0	0	0	0	0	0	0	0
CLARIDGE	17	10	7	3	8	0	0	0	0	0	0	0
COTTEE	19	7	12	6	4	4	0	0	2	1	1	0
ELLIOTT	37	37	0	0	0	7	6	0	2	1	0	0
FENTON	23	9	14	14	7	3	1	0	1	1	0	0
GUPPY	37	37	0	0	2	2	3	0	2	1	0	0
HESKEY	35	35	0	2	10	10	5	1	2	0	0	0
IZZETT	36	36	0	0	3	4	5	0	2	0	0	0
KAAMARK	35	35	0	1	4	0	2	0	2	0	0	0
KELLER	33	33	0	1	0	0	2	0	2	0	0	0
LENNON	37	37	0	0	1	2	6	0	2	1	0	0
MARSHALL	24	22	2	0	10	7	2	0	2	1	1	1
McMAHON	1	0	1	0	0	0	0	0	0	1	0	0
OAKES	0	0	0	1	0	0	0	0	0	0	0	0
PARKER	22	15	7	6	8	3	1	0	2	0	1	0
PRIOR	30	28	2	2	5	0	2	0	1	0	0	0
SAVAGE	35	28	7	2	6	2	4	0	2	1	1	0
ULLATHORNE	6	3	3	1	1	1	0	1	0	0	0	0
WALSH	26	23	3	1	6	3	4	0	1	1	0	0
WATTS	2	0	2	5	0	0	0	0	0	1	0	0
WHITLOW	1	0	1	2	0	0	0	0	0	0	0	0
WILLIS	0	0	0	0	0	0	0	0	0	0	0	0
WILSON	11	0	11	15	0	2	0	0	2	1	0	0
ZAGORAKIS	14	12	2	0	7	1	1	0	0	0	0	0

5-Year Record

	Div.	P	W	D	L	F	A	Pts	Pos	FAC	FLC
93-94	1	46	19	16	11	72	59	73	4	3	3
94-95	PL	42	6	11	25	45	80	29	21	5	2
95-96	1	46	19	14	13	66	60	71	5	3	3
96-97	PL	38	12	11	15	46	54	47	9	5	W
97-98	PL	38	13	14	11	51	41	53	10	4	3

Back to Reality

Following a season in which Leicester City won their first silverware for 33 years and claimed a position inside the top ten of the Premiership for the first time was always going to be a tall order for Foxes manager Martin O'Neill. By slipping one place in the table and making early exits in the cups it could be said that Leicester failed to match the achievements of the previous campaign. Certainly they did not threaten to repeat their Coca-Cola Cup success but Leicester established themselves firmly amongst the middle group and, despite finishing a place lower than in 1996/97, the Foxes did actually improve their points total by six to 53.

O'Neill made just two signings during the close season: Graham Fenton and Robbie Savage for a combined total of just £1.4m. Before August was out the experienced Tony Cottee moved to Filbert Street for £500,000. Six players were released, the most significant being Simon Grayson to Aston Villa for £1.3m.

With an Ian Marshall goal seeing off Villa on the first day of the season and efforts from Matt Elliott and Fenton clinching an excellent victory at Liverpool, Leicester made their best start since 1956 and it took champions Manchester United (0-0) to deny the Foxes from completing a winning hat-trick which would have equalled their best start for 75 years. Leicester scored three times in the closing minutes of a fiery clash with Arsenal to preserve their unbeaten start with a 3-3 draw before the first reversal was suffered at Sheffield Wednesday. But Leicester bounced back well with three wins and a draw lifting them to third, just a point behind leaders Arsenal.

The bubble burst with a home defeat by Derby and with just one win from six games Leicester gradually slid out of the frame. Hopes of retaining a place in Europe through their league position faded under the strain of ten home draws. Only Coventry drew more games in total while only two sides scored less at home. The Foxes got their season back on course with Tony Cottee's first goal at Old Trafford securing an unlikely victory and it was followed with home wins over Leeds and Chelsea and a draw at Tottenham. As with earlier in the season Leicester failed to maintain the momentum though and went down to three successive defeats. Lingering European dreams were extinguished on the final day of the season with a fluctuating 4-3 defeat at West Ham. Top scorer for the second consecutive season was Emile Heskey who remains one of the brightest English-born prospects in the Premiership.

After a break of 36 years Leicester ventured back into Europe but the UEFA Cup run was brief with Marshall's early lead against Atletico Madrid not being enough to stave off defeats of 2-1 at home and 2-0 in Spain.

Leicester's FA Cup campaign began confidently enough with a comfortable 4-0 win over Northampton at Filbert Street but the Foxes then had the dubious honour of being the first Premiership side this season to lose to Crystal Palace at Selhurst Park when going down 4-0 in the 4th Round. Playing away to Grimsby Town, Leicester's bid to retain the Coca-Cola Cup got off to a decent start with Marshall scoring, but the night ended in disaster with the Division Two side running out 3-1 winners. ∎

Results 1997-98

FA Carling Premiership

Date	Opponents	Ven	Res	Atten	Scorers
08-Aug	Aston Villa	H	1-0	20,304	Marshall (37)
12-Aug	Liverpool	A	2-1	35,007	Elliott (2); Fenton (83)
22-Aug	Manchester U.	H	0-0	21,221	
26-Aug	Arsenal	H	3-3	21,089	Heskey (84); Elliott (89); Walsh (90)
29-Aug	Sheffield W.	A	0-1	24,851	
12-Sep	Tottenham H.	H	3-0	20,683	Walsh (55); Guppy (68); Heskey (77)
19-Sep	Leeds U.	A	1-0	29,620	Walsh (32)
23-Sep	Blackburn R.	H	1-1	19,921	Izzett (43)
26-Sep	Barnsley	A	2-0	18,660	Marshall (55); Fenton (63)
05-Oct	Derby Co.	H	1-2	19,385	Elliott (67)
17-Oct	Chelsea	A	0-1	35,356	
26-Oct	West Ham U.	H	2-1	20,021	Heskey (16); Marshall (82)
31-Oct	Newcastle U.	A	3-3	36,547	Marshall (12, 31); Elliott (54)
09-Nov	Wimbledon	H	0-1	18,553	
21-Nov	Bolton W.	H	0-0	20,564	
28-Nov	Coventry C.	A	2-0	18,409	Fenton (32); Elliott (74 pen)
05-Dec	C. Palace	H	1-1	19,191	Izzett (90)
12-Dec	Southampton	A	1-2	15,121	Savage (84)
19-Dec	Everton	H	0-1	20,628	
25-Dec	Arsenal	A	1-2	30,023	Lennon (77)
27-Dec	Sheffield W.	H	1-1	20,800	Guppy (28)
09-Jan	Aston Villa	A	1-1	36,429	Parker (53 pen)
16-Jan	Liverpool	H	0-0	21,633	
30-Jan	Manchester U.	A	1-0	55,156	Cottee (28)
06-Feb	Leeds U.	H	1-0	21,244	Parker (44 pen)
13-Feb	Tottenham H.	A	1-1	28,355	Cottee (34)
20-Feb	Chelsea	H	2-0	21,335	Heskey (2, 89)
27-Feb	Blackburn R.	A	3-5	24,854	Wilson (72); Izzett (79); Ullathorne (81)
13-Mar	Wimbledon	A	1-2	13,229	Savage (57)
27-Mar	Bolton W.	A	0-2	25,000	
03-Apr	Coventry C.	H	1-1	21,137	Wilson (78)
10-Apr	C. Palace	A	3-0	18,771	Heskey (44, 60); Elliott (74)
13-Apr	Southampton	H	3-3	20,708	Lennon (18); Elliott (52); Parker (90 pen)
17-Apr	Everton	A	1-1	33,642	Marshall (38)
25-Apr	Derby Co.	A	4-0	29,855	Heskey (2, 9); Izzett (3); Marshall (15)

28-Apr	Newcastle U.	H	0-0	21,699	
01-May	Barnsley	H	1-0	21,293	Zagorakis (57)
09-May	West Ham U.	A	3-4	25,781	Cottee (59, 83); Heskey (66)

FA Challenge Cup

Date	Opponents	Vn	Rnd	Res	Atten	Scorers
03-Jan	Northampton T.H		3R	4-0	20,608	Marshall (17); Parker (26 pen); Savage (53); Cottee (58)
24-Jan	C. Palace	A	4R	0-3	15,489	

Coca-Cola League Cup

Date	Opponents	Vn	Rnd	Res	Atten	Scorers
14-Oct	Grimsby T.	A	3R	1-3	7,738	Marshall (18)

UEFA Cup

Date	Opponents	Vn	Rnd	Res	Atten	Scorers
16-Sep	A. Madrid	A	1R1L	1-2	23,000	Marshall (12)
30-Sep	A. Madrid	H	1R2L	0-2	20,776	

Atletico Madrid win 4-1 on aggregate.

Liverpool

Following a dispute between Everton and its Anfield landlord a new club, Liverpool AFC, was formed in 1892 by the landlord, former Everton committee-man John Houlding, with its headquarters at Anfield. An application for Football League membership was rejected without being put to the vote. Instead the team joined the Lancashire League and immediately won the Championship.

After that one campaign, when the Liverpool Cup was won but there was early FA Cup elimination, Liverpool was selected to fill one of two vacancies in an expanded Football League Second Division in 1893. Premier League founder members 1992.

Ground: Anfield Road, Liverpool L4 0TH
Phone: 0151-263 2361   **Match Info:** 0151-260 9999 (24 hrs)
Box Office: 0151-260 8680   **CC Bookings:** 0151-263 5727
News: 0891 12 11 84   **Ticket Info:** 0891 12 15 85
Capacity: 41,000   **Pitch:** 110 yds x 75 yds
Colours: All Red/White Trim   **Nickname:** Reds or Pool
Radio: 1485AM/95.8FM BBC Radio Merseyside
Internet: –

Chairman: D.R. Moores   **Vice-Chairman:** P.B.Robinson
CEO: Rick Parry   **Secretary:** Bryce Morrison
Manager: Roy Evans   **Coach:** Ronnie Moran

League History: 1893 Elected to Division 2; 1894-95 Division 1; 1895-96 Division 2; 1896-1904 Division 1; 1904-05 Division 2; 1905-54 Division 1; 1954-62 Division 2; 1962-92 Division 1; 1992- FA Premier League.

Honours: *Football League: Division 1 Champions* 1900-01, 1905-06, 1921-22, 1922-23, 1946-47, 1963-64, 1965-66, 1972-73, 1975-76, 1976-77, 1978-79, 1979-80, 1981-82, 1982-83, 1983-84, 1985-86, 1987-88, 1989-90; *Runners-up* 1898-99, 1909-10, 1968-69, 1973-74, 1974-75, 1977-78, 1984-85, 1986-87, 1988-89, 1990-91; *Division 2 Champions* 1893-94, 1895-96, 1904-05, 1961-62. *FA Cup: Winners* 1964-65, 1973-74, 1985-86, 1988-89, 1991-92; *Runners-up* 1913-14, 1949-50, 1970-71, 1976-77, 1987-88, 1995-96. *Football League Cup: Winners* 1980-81, 1981-82, 1982-83, 1983-84, 1994-95; *Runners-up* 1977-78, 1986-87, 1995-96 *League Super Cup: Winners* 1985-86. *Champions' Cup: Winners* 1976-77, 1977-78, 1980-81; 1983-84; *Runners-up* 1984-85. *Cup-Winners' Cup: Runners-up* 1965-66.

UEFA Cup: Winners 1972-73, 1975-76. *European Super Cup: Winners* 1977; *Runners-up* 1984. *World Club Championship: Runners-up* 1981, 1984.

European Record: CC (12): 64-65 (SF), 66-67 (2), 73-74 (2), 76-77 (W), 77-78 (W), 78-79 (1), 79-80 (1), 80-81 (W), 81-82 (QF), 82-83 (QF), 83-84 (W), 84-85 (F); **CWC** (5): 65-66 (F), 71-72 (2), 74-75 (2), 92-93 (2), 96-97 (SF); **UEFA** (9) 67-68 (3), 68-69 (1), 69-70 (2), 70-71 (SF), 72-73 (W), 75-76 (W), 91-92 (QF), 94-95 (2), 97-98 (2).

Managers: W.E. Barclay 1892-96; Tom Watson 1896-1915; David Ashworth 1920-22; Matt McQueen 1923-28; George Patterson 1928-36 (continued as secretary); George Kay 1936-51; Don Welsh 1951-56; Phil Taylor 1956-59; Bill Shankly 1959-74; Bob Paisley 1974-83; Joe Fagan 1983-85; Kenny Dalglish 1985-91; *(FAPL)* Graeme Souness 1991-94; Roy Evans Jan 1994-.

Season 1997-98

Biggest Home Win:	5-0 v West Ham United
Biggest Home Defeat:	1-3 v Manchester United
Biggest Away Win:	3-0 v Crystal Palace
Biggest Away Defeat:	1-4 v Cheslea
Biggest Home Att:	44,432 v Bolton Wanderers
Smallest Home Att:	34,705 v Sheffield Wednesday
Average Attendance:	40,628
Leading Scorer:	Michael Owen – 18

All-Time Records

Record FAPL Win:	6-0 v Manchester City, 28/10/95
Record FAPL Defeat:	1-5 v Coventry City, 19/12/92
Record FL Win:	10-1 v Rotherham Town, Division 2, 18/2/1896 and 9-0 v Crystal Palace, Division 1, 12/9/89
Record FL Defeat:	1-9 v Birmingham City, Division 2, 11/12/54
Record Cup Win:	11-0 v Stromsgodset Drammen, CWC 1R1L, 17/9/74
Record Fee Received:	£7m from Aston Villa for Stan Collymore, 5/97
Record Fee Paid:	£8.5m to N. Forest for Stan Collymore, 6/95
Most FL Apps:	Ian Callaghan, 640, 1960-78
Most FAPL Apps:	212 – Steve McManaman, 1992-98
Most FAPL Goals:	92 – Robbie Fowler, 1993-98
Highest Scorer in FAPL Season:	Robbie Fowler, 28, 1995-96
Record Attendance (all-time):	61,905 v Wolves, FA Cup R4, 2/2/52
Record Attendance (FAPL):	44,619 v Everton, 20/3/93
Most FAPL Goals in Season:	68, 1997-98 – 38 games
Most FAPL Points in Season:	74, 1994-95 – 42 games

Player	Tot	St	Sb	Snu	PS	Gls	Y	R	Fa	La	Fg	Lg
BABB … … … … …	19	18	1	8	1	0	5	0	0	2	0	0
BARNES … … … …	0	0	0	1	0	0	0	0	0	0	0	0
BERGER … … … …	22	6	16	9	2	3	0	0	1	3	0	1
BJORNEBYE … …	25	24	1	3	4	0	4	0	0	3	0	0
CARRAGHER … …	20	17	3	10	2	0	2	0	0	2	0	0
FOWLER… … … …	20	19	1	0	4	9	1	1	1	4	0	3
FRIEDEL … … …	11	11	0	7	0	0	0	0	0	0	0	0
GUDNASON … … …	0	0	0	3	0	0	0	0	0	0	0	0
HARKNESS … … …	25	24	1	8	3	0	6	0	1	4	0	0
INCE … … … …	31	31	0	1	1	8	8	0	1	4	0	0
JAMES … … … …	27	27	0	11	0	0	0	0	1	5	0	0
JONES, Rob … … …	21	20	1	3	6	0	1	0	0	2	0	0
KENNEDY … … …	1	0	1	1	0	0	0	0	0	0	0	0
KVARME … … … …	23	22	1	8	3	0	2	0	1	2	0	0
LEONHARDSEN …	28	27	1	0	7	6	2	0	1	5	0	0
MATTEO … … … …	25	24	1	0	0	0	1	0	1	4	0	0
McATEER … … …	21	15	6	3	2	2	3	0	1	3	0	0
McMANAMAN …	36	36	0	1	2	11	0	0	1	5	0	0
MURPHY … … …	16	6	10	10	4	0	1	0	1	0	0	0
NIELSON … … … …	0	0	0	12	0	0	0	0	0	0	0	0
OWEN … … … …	36	34	2	1	4	18	4	1	0	4	0	4
REDKNAPP… … …	20	20	0	0	2	3	3	0	1	3	1	1
RIEDLE … … … …	25	18	7	5	9	6	1	0	1	5	0	0
RIZZO … … … …	0	0	0	4	0	0	0	0	0	0	0	0
ROBERTS … … …	0	0	0	3	0	0	0	0	0	0	0	0
RUDDOCK … … …	3	2	1	2	1	0	0	0	0	1	0	0
THOMAS … … …	11	10	1	2	2	1	3	0	0	1	0	0
THOMPSON … … …	5	1	4	5	0	1	1	0	0	0	0	0
WARNER … … …	0	0	0	7	0	0	0	0	0	0	0	0
WILLIAMS … … …	0	0	0	1	0	0	0	0	0	0	0	0
WRIGHT … … … …	6	6	0	2	0	0	0	0	0	0	0	0

5-Year Record

49/2

	Div.	P	W	D	L	F	A	Pts	Pos	FAC	FLC
93-94	PL	42	17	9	16	59	55	60	8	3	4
94-95	PL	42	21	11	10	65	37	74	4	QF	W
95-96	PL	38	20	11	7	70	34	71	3	F	4
96-97	PL	38	19	11	8	62	37	68	4	4	QF
97-98	PL	38	18	11	9	68	42	65	3	3	SF

Consistent – But…

During four years as manager of Liverpool, Roy Evans has taken the club to two Wembley cup finals and not finished lower than fourth in the Premiership. Maybe given Liverpool's glorious record over the past three decades, it is a record of underachieving and not for the first time the 1997/98 season heard calls for his head. It is a record which most clubs would happily settle for.

Some impressive signings were made during the close season with England star Paul Ince returning to this country from Italy for £4.2m. Oyvind Leonhardsen joined for £3.5m, Karl-heinz Riedle moved to Anfield for £1.6m and an eventual £3m will be invested in the exciting talent of Crewe's 20 year old midfielder Danny Murphy. With the transfer of Anfield misfit Stan Collymore to Aston Villa, £7m was quickly recouped while John Barnes left on a free. The biggest success for Liverpool was the amazing emergence of Michael Owen in his first full season but even that could not compensate for the cruel injury which ruled Robbie Fowler out of the second-half of the season and the World Cup.

Liverpool began slowly with two away draws and a home defeat by Leicester. Already 17-year-old Owen had scored twice to demonstrate the talent which, towards the end of the season, was to make him the youngest player this century to play and score for his country. Steve McManaman put behind him rumours of a £12m move to Barcelona to open the scoring at Leeds on 26 August and Liverpool's first win of the season was made safe with Riedle's first goal. Ince scored his first goal in the next match, a 2-1 win over Sheffield Wednesday, as Liverpool embarked on a run of scoring 17 times in five consecutive home wins. Away from home Liverpool were experiencing problems until winning at Arsenal at the end of November but it was followed by a comprehensive 3-1 home defeat by Manchester United. Again they bounced back strongly with five successive wins. But the leaders were still nine points away and hopes of maintaining a title challenge faltered when just one of the next seven games were won. Third place was ultimately secured by emphatic 5-0 and 4-0 wins over West Ham and a depleted Arsenal but the final game was lost 1-0 at Derby.

The draw for the UEFA Cup was tough as Liverpool squared up to Celtic in the 1st Round. An outstanding last-minute McManaman equaliser clinched a 2-2 draw at Parkhead which, courtesy of a goalless draw at Anfield, took the Reds through to the 2nd Round. A dire 1st Leg performance ended with a 3-0 defeat in Strasbourg, and a 2-0 victory back home could not prevent the French side from progressing.

The FA Cup was a massive disappointment for Evans as he watched his side crash out in the 3rd Round for the third time in six years, this time at home to Coventry. Coming in at the 3rd Round of the Coca-Cola Cup, Liverpool won with ease at West Brom and at home to Grimsby before extending their good run against Newcastle with an extra-time success at St James's Park. Facing relegated Middlesbrough in the semi-final, Liverpool won the 1st Leg at Anfield 2-1 but were put out by two goals within the first four minutes of the return at the Riverside. ■

Results 1997-98

FA Carling Premiership

Date	Opponents	Ven	Res	Pos	Atten	Scorers
08-Aug	Wimbledon	A	1-1		26,106	Owen (72 pen)
12-Aug	Leicester C.	H	1-2		35,007	Ince (84)
22-Aug	Blackburn R.	A	1-1		29,076	Owen (53)
25-Aug	Leeds U.	A	2-0		39,775	McManaman (23); Riedle (75)
12-Sep	Sheffield W.	H	2-1		34,705	Ince (55); Thomas (68)
19-Sep	Southampton	A	1-1		15,252	Riedle (27)
21-Sep	Aston Villa	H	3-0		34,843	Fowler (56 pen); McManaman (79); Riedle (90)
26-Sep	West Ham U.	A	1-2		25,908	Fowler (52)
04-Oct	Chelsea	H	4-2		36,647	Berger (20, 35, 57); Fowler (64)
17-Oct	Everton	A	0-2		40,112	
24-Oct	Derby Co.	H	4-0		38,017	Fowler (27, 84); Leonhardsen (65); McManaman (88)
31-Oct	Bolton W.	A	1-1		25,000	Fowler (1)
07-Nov	Tottenham H.	H	4-0		38,005	McManaman (48); Owen (80); Leonhardsen (50); Redknapp (65)
21-Nov	Barnsley	H	0-1		41,001	
29-Nov	Arsenal	A	1-0		38,094	McManaman (56)
05-Dec	Manchester U.	H	1-3		41,027	Fowler (60 pen)
12-Dec	C. Palace	A	3-0		25,790	McManaman (39); Owen (55); Leonhardsen (61)
19-Dec	Coventry C.	H	1-0		39,707	Owen (14)
25-Dec	Leeds U.	H	3-1		43,854	Owen (46); Fowler (79, 83)
27-Dec	Newcastle U.	A	2-1		36,718	McManaman (31, 43)
09-Jan	Wimbledon	H	2-0		38,011	Redknapp (72, 84)
16-Jan	Leicester C.	A	0-0		21,633	
19-Jan	Newcastle U.	H	1-0		42,791	Owen (17)
30-Jan	Blackburn	A	0-0		43,890	
06-Feb	Southampton	H	2-3		43,550	Owen (24, 90)
13-Feb	Sheffield W.	A	3-3		35,405	Owen (27, 73, 78)
22-Feb	Everton	H	1-1		44,501	Ince (66)
27-Feb	Aston Villa	A	1-2		39,377	Owen (5 pen)
04-Mar	Bolton W.	H	2-1		44,532	Ince (58); Owen (65)
13-Mar	Tottenham H.	A	3-3		30,245	McManaman (20, 88); Ince (63)
27-Mar	Barnsley	A	3-2		18,684	Riedle (44, 59); McManaman (90)
09-Apr	Manchester U.	A	1-1		55,171	Owen (36)
12-Apr	C. Palace	H	2-1		43,007	Leonhardsen (29); Thompson (85)
17-Apr	Coventry C.	A	1-1		22,721	Owen (33)

24-Apr	Chelsea	A	1-4	34,639	Riedle (45)
01-May	West Ham U.	H	5-0	44,414	Owen (4); McAteer (21, 25);
					Leonhardsen (45); Ince (61)
05-May	Arsenal	H	4-0	44,417	Ince (28, 30); Owen (40);
					Leonhardsen (86)
09-May	Derby Co.	A	0-1	30,492	

FA Challenge Cup

Date	Opponents	Vn	Rnd	Res	Atten	Scorers
03-Jan	Coventry C.	H	3R	1-3	33,888	Redknapp (7)

Coca-Cola League Cup

Date	Opponents	Vn	Rnd	Res	Atten	Scorers
15-Oct	WBA	A	3R	2-0	21,986	Berger (52); Fowler (89)
18-Nov	Grimsby T.	A	4R	3-0	28,515	Owen (27, 45 pen, 57)
07-Jan	Newcastle Utd	A	QF	2-0	33,207	Owen (95); Fowler (103)
	aet					
27-Jan	Middlesbrough	H	SF1L	2-1	33,438	Redknapp (31); Fowler (82)
18-Feb	Middlesbrough	A	SF2L	0-2	29,828	
	Middlesbrough win 3-2 on aggregate.					

UEFA Cup

Date	Opponents	Vn	Rnd	Res	Atten	Scorers
16-Sep	Celtic	A	1R1L	2-2	50,000	Owen (6); McManaman (89)
30-Sep	Celtic	H	1R2L	0-0	38,205	
	2-2 on aggregate. Liverpool win on away goals rule.					
21-Oct	Strasbourg	A	2R1L	0-3	18,813	
04-Nov	Strasbourg	H	2R2L	2-0	32,426	Fowler (63 pen); Riedle (84)
	Strasbourg win 3-2 on aggregate.					

Manchester United

Came into being in 1902 upon the bankruptcy of Newton Heath. Predecessors appear to have been formed in 1878 as Newton Heath (LYR) when workers at the Carriage and Wagon Department at the Lancashire and Yorkshire Railway formed a club. This soon outgrew railway competition.

Turned professional in 1885 and founder members of Football Alliance in 1889. In 1892 Alliance runners-up Newton Heath were elected to an enlarged Division One of the Football League. In 1902 the club became Manchester United and, in February 1910, moved from Bank Street, Clayton, to Old Trafford. Premier League founder members 1992. Four times Premiership champions and the only side to have completed the Double twice.

Ground:	Old Trafford, Manchester, M16 0RA		
Phone:	0161-872 1661	**Box Office:**	0161-872 0199
Info:	0891 12 11 61		
Capacity:	44,622	**Pitch:**	116 yds x 76 yds
Colours:	Red, White, Black	**Nickname:**	Red Devils
Radio:	Manchester United Radio 1413AM		
Internet:	http://www.sky.co.uk/sports/manu/index.htm		

Chairman/CEO: Martin Edwards **Secretary:** Kenneth Merrett
Manager: Alex Ferguson **Assistant:** Brian Kidd

League History: 1892 Newton Heath elected to Division 1; 1894-1906 Division 2; 1906-22 Division 1; 1922-25 Division 2; 1925-31 Division 1; 1931-36 Division 2; 1936-37 Division 1; 1937-38 Division 2; 1938-74 Division 1; 1974-75 Division 2; 1975-92 Division 1; 1992- FA Premier League.

Honours: *FA Premier League: Champions* 1992-93, 1993-94, 1995-96, 1996-97; *Runners-up* 1994-95, 1997-98. *Football League: Division 1 Champions* 1907-8, 1910-11, 1951-52, 1955-56, 1956-57, 1964-65, 1966-67; *Runners-up* 1946-47, 1947-48, 1948-49, 1950-51, 1958-59, 1963-64, 1967-68, 1979-80, 1987-88, 1991-92; *Division 2 Champions* 1935-36, 1974-75; *Runners-up* 1896-97, 1905-06, 1924-25, 1937-38. *FA Cup: Winners* 1908-09, 1947-48, 1962-63, 1976-77, 1982-83, 1984-85, 1989-90, 1993-94, 1995-96; *Runners-up* 1957, 1958, 1976, 1979, 1995. *Football League Cup: Winners* 1991-92; *Runners-up* 1982-83, 1990-91, 1993-94. *Champions' Cup: Winners* 1967-68. *Cup-Winners' Cup: Winners* 1990-91. *League/Cup Double Performed:* 1993-94, 1995-96.

European Record: CC (9): 56-57 (SF), 57-58 (SF), 65-66 (SF), 67-68 (W), 68-69 (SF), 93-94 (SF), 94-95 (CL), 96-97 (SF), 97-98 (QF): CWC (5): 63-64 (QF), 77-78 (2), 83-84 (SF), 90-91 (W), 91-92 (2). UEFA (7): 64-65 (SF), 76-77 (2), 80-81 (1), 82-83 (1), 84-85 (QF), 92-93 (1), 95-96 (1).

Managers: Ernest Magnall 1900-12; John Robson 1914-21; John Chapman 1921-26; Clarence Hildrith 1926-27; Herbert Bamlett 1927-31; Walter Crickmer 1931-32; Scott Duncan 1932-37; Jimmy Porter 1938-44; Walter Crickmer 1944-45; Matt Busby 1945-69 (continued as GM then Director); Wilf McGuinness 1969-70; Frank O'Farrell 1971-72; Tommy Docherty 1972-77; Dave Sexton 1977-81; Ron Atkinson 1981-86; *(FAPL)* Alex Ferguson Nov 1986-.

Season 1997-98

Biggest Home Win:	7-0 v Barnsley
Biggest Home Defeat:	0-1 v Arsenal
Biggest Away Win:	5-2 v Wimbledon
Biggest Away Defeat:	0-2 v Sheffield Wednesday
Biggest Home Att:	55,281 v Tottenham Hotspur
Smallest Home Att:	55,008 v Southampton
Average Attendance:	55,164
Leading Scorer:	Andy Cole – 16

All-Time Records

Record FAPL Win:	9-0 v Ipswich Town, 4/3/95
Record FAPL Defeat:	3-6 v Southampton, 26/10/96
Record FL Win:	10-1 v Wolverhampton W., Division 2, 15/10/1892
Record FL Defeat:	0-7 v Blackburn R., Div. 1, 10/4/26; Aston Villa, Div. 1, 27/12/30; Wolves, Div. 2, 26/12/31
Record Cup Win:	10-0 v RSC Anderlecht, Champions' Cup, Pr2L, 26/9/56
Record Fee Received:	£7m from Internazionale (Italy) for Paul Ince 6/95
Record Fee Paid:	£7m to Newcastle United for Andy Cole 1/95 (inc. part exchange of Keith Gillespie – £1m)
Most FL Apps:	Bobby Charlton, 606, 1956-73
Most FAPL Apps:	219 – Peter Schmeichel, 1992-98
Most FAPL Goals:	70 – Eric Cantona, 1992-97

Highest Scorer in FAPL Season: Cantona, 18, 93-94 and Solskjaer, 18, 96-97
Record Attendance (all-time): 70,504 v Aston Villa, Division 1, 27/12/20
Record Attendance (FAPL): 55,314 v Wimbledon, 29/1/97
Most FAPL Goals in Season: 80, 1993-94 – 42 games
Most FAPL Points in Season: 92, 1993-94 – 42 games

Summary 1997-98

Player	Tot	St	Sb	Snu	PS	Gls	Y	R	Fa	La	Fg	Lg
BECKHAM	37	34	3	0	2	9	6	0	4	0	2	0
BERG	27	23	4	8	2	2	2	0	2	0	0	0
BROWN	2	1	1	0	0	0	0	0	0	0	0	0
BUTT	33	31	2	1	6	2	7	0	1	0	0	0
CASPER	0	0	0	3	0	0	0	0	0	0	0	0
CLEGG	3	1	2	6	1	0	0	0	3	0	0	0
COLE	33	31	2	0	6	16	6	0	3	1	5	0
CRUYFF	5	3	2	1	1	0	1	0	1	1	0	0
CULKIN	0	0	0	2	0	0	0	0	0	0	0	0
CURTIS	8	3	5	5	1	0	0	0	0	1	0	0
GIGGS	29	28	1	1	4	8	1	0	2	0	0	0
GREENING	0	0	0	1	0	0	0	0	0	0	0	0
HIGGINBOTTOM	1	0	1	0	0	0	0	0	0	0	0	0
IRWIN	25	23	2	1	4	2	4	0	4	1	0	0
JOHNSEN	22	18	4	1	7	2	2	0	3	1	1	0
KEANE	9	9	0	0	0	2	3	0	0	0	0	0
MAY	9	7	2	3	1	0	3	0	1	1	0	0
McCLAIR	13	2	11	17	2	0	0	0	3	1	0	0
MULRYNE	1	1	0	5	0	0	0	0	1	1	0	0
NEVILLE, G	34	34	0	2	5	0	2	0	3	0	0	0
NEVILLE, P	30	24	6	3	6	1	7	0	3	1	0	0
NEVLAND	1	0	1	1	0	0	0	0	3	1	0	0
NOTEMAN	0	0	0	1	0	0	0	0	0	0	0	0
PALLISTER	33	33	0	0	5	0	4	1	2	0	0	0
PILKINGTON	2	2	0	6	0	0	0	0	1	0	0	0
POBORSKY	10	3	7	6	3	2	1	0	0	1	0	0
SCHMEICHEL	32	32	0	0	0	1	0	0	4	0	0	0
SCHOLES	31	28	3	0	10	8	7	0	2	1	0	0
SHERINGHAM	31	28	3	3	5	9	2	0	3	0	5	0
SOLSKJAER	22	15	7	4	4	6	0	1	2	0	0	0
THORNLEY	5	0	5	5	0	0	0	0	2	1	0	0
TWISS	0	0	0	2	0	0	0	0	1	0	0	0
VAN DER GOUW	5	4	1	26	0	0	0	0	0	1	0	0
WALLWORK	1	0	1	0	0	0	0	0	0	0	0	0
Own Goals						4						

5-Year Record

58/2

	Div.	P	W	D	L	F	A	Pts	Pos	FAC	FLC
93-94	PL	42	27	11	4	80	38	92	1	W	F
94-95	PL	42	26	10	6	77	28	88	2	F	3
95-96	PL	38	25	7	6	73	35	82	1	W	2
96-97	PL	38	21	12	5	76	44	75	1	4	4
97-98	PL	38	23	8	7	73	26	77	2	5	3

170

Unprecedented Fizzle

Up until Christmas Manchester United appeared well on course for an unprecedented third league and cup double and, following excellent form in the Champions' Cup group matches, where there was a belief they could lift the European Cup for the first time in 30 years. Prior to Christmas, United lost just one Premiership match and won five of their six Champions' League fixtures as Alex Ferguson contemplated a clean sweep of the major honours. Possibly with one eye on Europe, United's league form dipped dramatically and, following defeat at Coventry on 28 December, Ferguson went on to suffer more defeats than in any of the previous five years of the Premiership. The Reds also failed to win any more games in Europe.

Following the signing of Henning Berg for £5m and Teddy Sheringham for £3.5m, United looked ominously good early on. Five of the first six league games were won and Peter Schmeichel waited 464 minutes before conceding his first Premiership goal. Chelsea were the first visiting side to take a point from Old Trafford while Leeds handed United their first defeat after eight unbeaten matches. But even that impressive start paled by comparison to a run of eight wins in nine games which included several thrashings; Barnsley 7-0, Sheffield Wednesday 6-1, Wimbledon 5-2 and Blackburn 4-0. Maybe most impressively of all, Liverpool was swept away 3-1 at Anfield. By Boxing Day United had scored 47 times in 20 games and led the table by six points. United were now hot favourites, with Andy Cole reigning supreme after notching 11 goals in ten Premiership matches.

United went into the new year on the back of a 2-0 win over Spurs and despite taking only one point from games with Southampton, Leicester and Bolton, by the end of February United held a seemingly impregnable 11-point lead. Defeat at Sheffield Wednesday slowed the charge and on 14 March Arsenal grabbed a vital victory at Old Trafford which cut United's lead to six points and the Gunners had three games in hand. Wins over Wimbledon and Blackburn kept United on top but draws at home to Liverpool and Newcastle could not repel Arsenal's ten-match winning run as the Reds' title hat-trick aspirations evaporated.

In the Champions' League United demonstrated they had learnt well from previous experiences and breezed through the group stage. Slovakian side Kosice were defeated 3-0 home and away, Feyenoord went down 2-1 at Old Trafford and 3-1 in Holland where Cole scored a hat-trick. United's greatest night, though, came at home where Juventus were beaten 3-2, despite taking the lead inside 30 seconds. A good result for United in the return would probably have put the Italians out but a late goal ensured Juventus's continued participation in the competition. A low-key quarter-final meeting in Monaco went satisfactorily as United returned home level at 0-0 only to fall behind early on in the 2nd leg and bow out on the away goals rule following an Ole Gunnar Solskjaer equaliser.

Holders Chelsea were imperiously cast aside 5-3 at Stamford Bridge in the 3rd Round of the FA Cup and Walsall went the same way with Cole netting two in both games. Barnsley held out for a draw in Round Five before causing a sensation by winning the replay 3-2 at Oakwell. United's interest in the Coca-Cola Cup was minimal with an under-strength side beaten 2-0 at Ipswich in the 3rd Round. ∎

Results 1997-98

FA Carling Premiership

Date	Opponents	Ven	Res	Atten	Scorers
09-Aug	Tottenham H.	A	2-0	26,359	Butt (82); OG (83, Vega)
12-Aug	Southampton	H	1-0	55,008	Beckham (78)
22-Aug	Leicester C.	A	0-0	21,221	
26-Aug	Everton	A	2-0	40,079	Beckham (29); Sheringham (51)
29-Aug	Coventry C.	H	3-0	55,074	Cole (1); Keane (72); Poborsky (89)
12-Sep	West Ham U.	H	2-1	55,068	Keane (21); Scholes (76)
19-Sep	Bolton W.	H	0-0	25,000	
23-Sep	Chelsea	H	2-2	55,163	Scholes (35); Solskjaer (86)
26-Sep	Leeds U.	A	0-1	39,952	
03-Oct	C. Palace	H	2-0	55,143	Sheringham (77); OG (29, Hreidarsson)
17-Oct	Derby Co.	A	2-2	30,014	Sheringham (51); Cole (83)
24-Oct	Barnsley	H	7-0	55,142	Cole (7, 18, 44); Giggs (42, 56); Scholes (58); Poborsky (79)
31-Oct	Sheffield W.	H	6-1	55,259	Cole (19, 38); Sheringham (13, 62); Solskjaer (40, 74)
08-Nov	Arsenal	A	2-3	38,302	Sheringham (32, 41)
21-Nov	Wimbledon	A	5-2	26,903	Butt (47); Beckham (66, 74); Scholes (80); Cole (85)
29-Nov	Blackburn R.	H	4-0	55,175	Solskjaer (17, 53); OG (59, Henchoz); OG (85 Kenna)
05-Dec	Liverpool	A	3-1	41,027	Cole (51,74); Beckham (70)
14-Dec	Aston Villa	H	1-0	55,151	Giggs (51)
20-Dec	Newcastle U.	A	1-0	36,767	Cole (67)
25-Dec	Everton	H	2-0	55,167	Berg (14); Cole (34)
27-Dec	Coventry C.	A	2-3	23,054	Solskjaer (30); Sheringham (47)
09-Jan	Tottenham H.	H	2-0	55,281	Giggs (44, 67)
18-Jan	Southampton	A	0-1	15,241	
30-Jan	Leicester C.	H	0-1	55,156	
6-Feb	Bolton W.	H	1-1	55,156	Cole (85)
17-Feb	Aston Villa	A	2-0	39,372	Beckham (82); Giggs (89)
20-Feb	Derby Co.	H	2-0	55,170	Giggs (19); Irwin (71 pen)
27-Feb	Chelsea	A	1-0	34,511	P.Neville (31)
06-Mar	Sheffield W.	A	0-2	39,427	
10-Mar	West Ham U.	A	1-1	25,892	Scholes (65)
13-Mar	Arsenal	H	0-1	55,174	
27-Mar	Wimbledon	H	2-0	55,306	Johnsen (83); Scholes (90)

05-Apr	Blackburn R.	A	3-1	30,547	Cole (56); Scholes (73); Beckham (90)
09-Apr	Liverpool	H	1-1	55,171	Johnsen (12)
17-Apr	Newcastle U.	H	1-1	55,194	Beckham (37)
26-Apr	C. Palace	A	3-0	26,180	Scholes (6); Butt (21); Cole (84)
03-May	Leeds U.	H	3-0	55,167	Giggs (6); Irwin (31 pen); Beckham (59)
09-May	Barnsley	A	2-0	18,694	Cole (5); Sheringham (67)

FA Challenge Cup

Date	Opponents	Vn	Rnd	Res	Atten	Scorers
04-Jan	Chelsea	A	3R	5-3	34,792	Beckham (23, 28); Cole (45, 65); Sheringham (74)
24-Jan	Walsall	H	4R	5-1	54,669	Cole (10, 65); Solskjaer (39, 68); Johnsen (74)
15-Feb	Barnsley	H	5R	1-1	54,700	Sheringham (42)
25-Feb	Barnsley	A	5RR	2-3	18,655	Sheringham (56); Cole (81)

Coca-Cola League Cup

Date	Opponents	Vn	Rnd	Res	Atten	Scorers
14-Oct	Ipswich T.	A	3R	0-2	22,173	

UEFA Champions' League

Date	Opponents	Vn	Rnd	Res	Atten	Scorers
17-Sep	Kosice	A	B	3-0	9,950	Irwin (31); Berg (61); Cole (88)
01-Oct	Juventus	H	B	3-2	53,118	Sheringham (28); Scholes (69); Giggs (90)
22-Oct	Feyenoord	H	B	2-1	53,118	Scholes (31); Irwin (72 pen)
05-Nov	Feyenoord	A	B	3-1	45,000	Cole (31, 44, 74)
27-Nov	Kosice	H	B	3-0	53,535	Cole (39); OG (85); Sheringham (90)
10-Dec	Juventus	A	B	0-1	47,786	
04-Mar	Monaco	A	QF1L	0-0	15,000	
18-Mar	Monaco	H	QF2L	1-1	53,683	Solskjaer (53)

1-1 on aggregate. Monaco win on away goals rule.

Middlesbrough

Formed in 1876 and played first game in 1877. Turned professional in 1889, but reverted to amateur status shortly afterwards, being early winners of the FA Amateur Cup. League football was first played in Middlesbrough by the Ironpolis side for one season, 1893-94. Middlesbrough turned professional again, were elected to Division Two in 1899, and moved to Ayresome Park in 1903. They were founder members of the Premier League in 1993 but were relegated in their first season. Moved to purpose-built stadium in 1995 coinciding with return to Premiership. Reached and lost both Cup Finals in 1997 in addition to being relegated to Division 1.

Ground: The Cellnet Riverside Stadium, Middlesbrough, TS3 6RS
Phone: 01642-877700   **Fax:** 0164-877840
Box Office: 01642-877745
Info: 0891 42 42 00   **Club Shop:** 01642-877720
Colours: Red with Black, White with Black, Red with Black
Capacity: 31,000 (rising to 35,000 during 1998-99)
Nickname: The Boro
Radio: 100.7FM Century Radio
Internet: –

Chairman: Steve Gibson   **CEO:** Keith Lamb
Secretary: Karen Nelson
Manager: Bryan Robson   **Assistant:** Viv Anderson
First Team Coach: John Pickering   **Physios:** Bob Ward, Tommy Johnson

League History: 1899 Elected to Division 2; 1902-24 Division 1; 1924-27 Division 2; 1927-28 Division 1; 1928-29 Division 2; 1929-54 Division 1; 1954-66 Division 2; 1966-67 Division 3; 1967-74 Division 2; 1974-82 Division 1; 1982-86 Division 2; 1986-87 Division 3; 1988-89 Division 1; 1989-92 Division 2; 1992-93 FAPL; 1993-95 Division 1; 1995-97 FAPL; 1997- Division 1

Honours: *Football League: Division 1 (new) Champions* 1994-95; *Runners-up* 1997-98; *Division 2 Champions* 1926-27, 1928-29, 1973-74; *Runners-up* 1901-02, 1991-92; *Division 3 Runners up* 1966-67, 1986-87. *FA Cup: Runners-up* 1996-97. *League Cup: Runners-up* 1996-97, 1997-98. *FA Amateur Cup: Winners* 1895, 1898. *Anglo-Scottish Cup: Winners* 1975-76.

European Record: Never qualified

Managers: John Robson 1899-05; Alex Massie 1905-06; Andy Atkin 1906-09; J. Gunter 1908-10; Andy Walker 1910-11; Tom McIntosh 1911-19; James Howie 1920-23; Herbert Bamlett 1923-26; Peter McWilliam 1927-34; Wilf Gillow 1933-44; David Jack 1944-52; Walter Rowley 1952-54; Bob Dennison 1954-63; Raich Carter 1963-66; Stan Anderson 1966-73; Jack Charlton 1973-77; John Neal 1977-81; Bobby Murdoch 1981-82; Malcolm Allison 1982-84; Willie Maddren 1984-86; Bruce Rioch 1986-90; Colin Todd 1990-91; Lennie Lawrence 1991-94; *(FAPL)* Bryan Robson May 1994-.

Season 1997-98

Biggest Home Win:	6-0 v Swindon Town
Biggest Home Defeat:	1-2 v Sheffield United
Biggest Away Win:	4-1 v Oxford United
Biggest Away Defeat:	0-5 v QPR
Biggest Home Att:	30,128 v Bury
Smallest Home Att:	29,414 v Charlton Athletic
Leading Scorer:	Mikkel Beck – 14

All-Time Records

Record FAPL Win:	4-1 v Leeds United, 22/8/92 and
	4-1 v Manchester City, 9/12/95
Record FAPL Defeat:	0-5 v Chelsea, 04/2/96 and
	1-5 v Aston Villa, 17/1/93
Record FL Win:	9-0 v Brighton & HA, D2 23/8/58
Record FL Defeat:	0-9 v Blackburn Rovers, D2 6/11/54
Record Cup Win:	9-3 v Goole Town, FAC1, 9/1/15
Record Fee Received:	£5.75m from Everton for Nicky Barmby, 10/96
Record Fee Paid:	£7m to Juventus for Fabrizio Ravanelli, 7/96
Record Attendance (all-time):	53,596 v Newcastle Utd, D1 27/12/49
	at Ayresome Park
Record Attendance (FAPL):	30,215 v Tottenham Hotspur, 19/10/96
	at Cellnet Stadium – also record
Most FL Apps:	Tim Williamson, 563, 1902-23
Most FAPL Apps:	81 – Derek Whyte, 1992-97
Most FAPL Goals:	27 – Chris Morris, 1992-97
Highest Scorer in FAPL Season:	Fabrizio Ravanelli, 16, 1996-97
Most FAPL Goals in Season:	54, 1992-93 – 42 games
Most FAPL Points in Season:	44, 1992-93 – 42 games

Summary 1997-98

Player	Tot	St	Sb	Snu	PS	Gls	Fa	La	Fg	Lg
ARMSTRONG	11	7	4	0	2	7	0	0	0	0
BAKER	3	2	1	0	2	0	1	4	0	0
BECK	38	32	6	4	8	14	2	7	0	1
BERESFORD, M	3	3	0	0	0	0	0	0	0	0
BLACKMORE	2	1	1	2	1	0	0	0	0	0
BRANCA	11	11	0	1	3	9	0	2	0	1
CAMPBELL	8	4	4	7	2	0	2	5	1	1
DIBBLE	2	2	0	1	0	0	0	0	0	0
EMERSON	21	21	0	0	3	4	0	4	0	0
FABIO	0	0	0	0	0	0	0	0	0	0
FESTA	38	36	2	0	1	2	2	7	0	0
FLEMING	37	35	2	2	0	1	0	2	0	0
FREESTONE	4	2	2	5	0	0	0	2	0	1
GASCOIGNE	7	7	0	0	3	0	0	1	0	0
HARRISON	14	11	3	1	1	0	2	4	0	0
HIGNETT	33	27	6	2	7	7	2	5	1	3
KINDER	34	33	1	3	3	2	1	5	0	0
LIDDLE	7	2	5	6	0	0	0	2	0	0
MADDISON	16	10	6	1	3	4	3	4	0	0
MERSON	45	45	0	0	4	12	3	7	1	3
MOORE	4	3	1	1	0	0	0	1	0	0
MORENO	9	6	3	6	1	0	2	0	0	0
MUSTOE	34	33	1	0	3	3	3	7	2	0
ORMEROD	17	10	7	3	3	3	2	2	0	0
PEARSON	19	19	0	0	4	2	1	4	0	0
RAVANELLI	2	2	0	0	0	1	0	0	0	0
RICARD	9	3	6	0	1	2	0	1	0	0
ROBERTS	9	9	0	2	0	0	0	1	0	0
SCHWARZER	32	32	0	0	0	0	3	7	0	0
STAMP	10	8	2	8	2	0	1	1	0	0
STOCKDALE	1	1	0	0	0	0	1	0	0	0
SUMMERBELL	6	4	2	2	3	0	0	1	0	1
THOMAS	11	11	0	0	2	0	0	0	0	0
TOWNSEND	38	36	2	0	5	2	3	6	0	0
TREVOR	0	0	0	0	0	0	0	0	0	0
VICKERS	35	32	3	2	2	0	3	6	0	0
WHYTE	8	5	3	4	0	0	0	1	0	0
Own Goals						2				

Sweet and Sour

Whilst the failure of Barnsley and Bolton to survive in the Premiership was hardly earth-shattering news, the dramatic fall from grace of Middlesbrough during 1996/97 also proved that money does not always buy success. What it does do though is help finance a new squad and following the departure of brilliant Brazilian Juninho to Atletico Madrid, Boro manager Bryan Robson had £12m to play with. One month into the season the previous season's top scorer, Ravanelli, went to Marseille for £5.3m and in the new year the last of Boro's South American imports, Emerson, moved to Tenerife for a further £4.2m. In came reformed Arsenal winger Paul Merson for £5m and the experienced Andy Townsend for just £500,000 and as deadline day approached Robson invested almost £8.5m on five players including Paul Gascoigne from Rangers. Merson certainly played his part to the full as the England player finished the season as Boro's leading scorer.

Given such figures Boro were clearly on a different playing field to the rest of the Nationwide League but they did not have things all their own way. Their season got off to a good start with a 2-1 victory over Charlton but Boro lost to both Stoke and Sheffield United within their first four home games. The latter defeat left Boro down in eighth place some eight points adrift of Forest but with two games in hand. Just one of the next 14 games was lost and despite slipping to a shock 2-0 defeat at Manchester City and a 3-0 reversal at Charlton, Boro ended the year in pole position.

With a run of seven games undefeated and only four goals conceded, Boro had a chance to open up a six-point lead with a trip to Forest on 1 March but came away beaten 4-0 and followed it up four days later with a 5-0 drubbing at Queens Park Rangers. The response was perfect with Branca, Neil Maddison and Armstrong each scoring twice in a 6-0 thrashing of Swindon. Indeed, from conceding nine goals in two games Boro let in just five more in their remaining 11 games and scored 22 in the process, including a 4-1 home win over Oxford City on the final day of the season to clinch the second automatic promotion place at the expense of neighbouring Sunderland.

Boro's FA Cup campaign kicked off with a replay victory over QPR but hopes of reaching the final for a second successive year were ended at the Riverside by Arsenal, despite Merson grabbing a consolation goal against his former club.

For the second year running Boro enjoyed great success in the Coca-Cola Cup. After beating Barnet 1-0 in the 2nd Round, Middlesbrough beat Sunderland for the first of three times with a 2-0 victory at the Riverside. Extra time was required to remove Bolton and a last-minute Craig Hignett goal took Boro past Reading. In the semi-final 1st Leg, Boro surrendered a 2-1 advantage to Liverpool at Anfield but with Merson and Branca scoring inside the first four minutes of the return, a magnificent aggregate victory was assured. Boro, excluding keeper Mark Schwarzer, were below par in the final, and for the second time in a year lost to Chelsea at Wembley on a day when Gascoigne was booked on his return to English football. ∎

Results 1997-98

Nationwide League Division 1

Date	Opponents	Ven	Res	Atten	Scorers
09-Aug	Charlton A.	H	2-1	22,414	Festa (80); Ravenelli (90)
23-Aug	Stoke C.	H	0-1	30,122	
30-Aug	Tranmere R.	A	2-0	12,095	Mustoe (25); Beck (54)
02-Sep	Stockport Co.	A	1-1	8,257	Merson (6)
13-Sep	Bradford C.	A	2-2	17,767	Kinder (42); Ormerod (77)
20-Sep	Birmingham C.	H	3-1	30,125	Kinder (22); Emerson (43); Beck (40)
28-Sep	Sunderland	A	2-1	34,819	Emerson (67); Mustoe (78)
05-Oct	Sheffield U.	H	1-2	30,000	Beck (19)
18-Oct	Crewe Alex.	A	1-1	5,759	Townsend (48)
21-Oct	Oxford U.	A	4-1	8,306	Emerson (36); Merson (90); Fleming (81); Mustoe (79)
25-Oct	Port Vale	H	2-1	30,096	Merson (10, 68 pen)
28-Oct	Huddersfield T.	H	3-0	29,965	Merson (13); Beck (18, 57)
01-Nov	Wolverh'n W.	A	0-1	26,895	
05-Nov	Portsmouth	H	1-1	29,724	Townsend (65)
08-Nov	QPR	H	3-0	30,706	Beck (22); Merson (37); Ormerod (90)
15-Nov	Norwich C.	A	3-1	16,110	Beck (39); Merson (52); Ormerod (55)
22-Nov	Swindon T.	A	2-1	15,228	Merson (22); Emerson (75)
26-Nov	N. Forest	H	0-0	30,143	
29-Nov	WBA	H	1-0	30,164	Beck (34)
02-Dec	Ipswich	A	1-1	13,619	Merson (33)
06-Dec	Bury	A	1-0	8,016	Beck (59)
13-Dec	Reading	H	4-0	29,876	Hignett (77, 90); Beck (79, 85)
20-Dec	Manchester C.	A	0-2	28,097	
26-Dec	Huddersfield T.	A	1-0	18,820	OG (Gray, 75)
28-Dec	Stockport Co.	H	3-1	30,166	Hignett (10); Beck (65, 88)
10-Jan	Charlton A.	A	0-3	15,742	
17-Jan	Ipswich	H	1-1	30,081	Pearson (63)
04-Feb	Tranmere R.	H	3-0	29,540	Hignett (31); Merson (38, 65)
07-Feb	Birmingham C.	A	1-1	20,634	Festa (38)
14-Feb	Bradford C.	H	1-0	30,165	Hignett (49)
21-Feb	Sunderland	H	3-1	30,227	Branca (31, 68); Armstrong (87); Maddison (80)
25-Feb	Crewe Alex.	H	1-0	29,936	
01-Mar	N. Forest	A	0-4	25,286	
04-Mar	QPR	A	0-5	11,580	

11-Mar	Swindon T.	H	6-0	29,581	Branca (16, 88); Maddison (22, 55); Armstrong (50, 73)
14-Mar	Portsmouth	A	0-0	17,003	
22-Mar	Norwich C.	H	3-0	30,040	Maddison (22); Armstrong (71); Beck (90)
04-Apr	WBA	A	1-2	20,620	Branca (76)
06-Apr	Sheffield U.	A	0-1	18,421	
11-Apr	Bury	H	4-0	30,218	Ricard (29); Branca (63, 73, 83)
13-Apr	Reading	A	1-0	14,501	Branca (8)
17-Apr	Manchester C.	H	1-0	30,182	Armstrong (44)
24-Apr	Port Vale	A	1-0	12,096	Merson (2)
29-Apr	Wolverh'n W.	H	1-1	29,878	Ricard (12)
03-May	Oxford Utd	H	4-1	30,228	Armstrong (47, 48); Hignett (57, 63)

FA Challenge Cup

Date	Opponents	Vn	Rnd	Res	Atten	Scorers
03-Jan	QPR	A	3R	2-2	13,379	Hignett (33); Mustoe (63)
13-Jan	QPR	H	3RR	2-0	21,817	Campbell (54); Mustoe (59)
24-Jan	Arsenal	H	4R	1-2	28,264	Merson (62)

Coca-Cola League Cup

Date	Opponents	Vn	Rnd	Res	Atten	Scorers
16-Sep	Barnet	H	2R1L	1-0	9,611	Freestone (56)
23-Sep	Barnet	A	2R2L	2-0	3,968	Beck (45); Merson (67 pen)
	Middlesbrough win 3-0 on aggregate					
15-Oct	Sunderland	H	3R	2-0	26,451	Campbell (58); Hignett (90)
18-Nov	Bolton W.	H	4R	2-1	22,801	Summerbell (39); Hignett (115)
	aet					
06-Jan	Reading	A	QF	1-0	13,072	Hignett (89)
27-Jan	Liverpool	A	SF1L	1-2	33,438	Merson (29)
18-Feb	Liverpool	H	SF2L	2-0	29,828	Merson (2 pen); Branca (4)
	Middlesbrough win 3-2 on aggregate					
29-Mar	Chelsea	A	F	0-2	77,698	*aet. Played at Wembley*

4-Year Record

	Div.	P	W	D	L	F	A	Pts	Pos	FAC	FLC
93-94	1	46	18	13	15	66	54	67	9	3	3
94-95	1	46	23	13	10	67	40	82	1	3	3
95-96	PL	38	11	10	17	35	50	43	12	4	4
96-97	PL	38	10	12	16	51	60	39	19	F	F

Newcastle United

Formed 1882 as Newcastle East End on the amalgamation of Stanley and Rosewood. Founder members, as a professional club, of the Northern League in 1889. Moved from Chillington Road, Heaton, in 1892 to take over the home of the defunct Newcastle West End, with several of those associated with the West End side joining the newcomers.

Applied for Football League Division One membership in 1892, failed and decided against a place in the new Second Division, staying in the Northern League. Later in 1892 changed name to Newcastle United. Elected to an expanded Football League Division Two in 1893.

Ground: St James's Park, Newcastle-upon-Tyne, NE1 4ST
Phone: 0191-201 8400   **Fax:** 0191-201 8600
Box Office: 0191-261 1571   **CC Bookings:** 0191-261 1571
Info: 0891 12 11 90   **Clubshop:** 0191-201 8426
Colours: Black/White, Black, Black   **Nickname:** Magpies
Capacity: 36,401   **Pitch:** 115 yds x 75 yds
Radio: 97.1FM Metro Radio
Internet: http://www.newcastle-utd.co.uk/nufc

President: Bob Young   **Chairman:** tba
CEO: tba   **D.O. Football Admin:** Russell Cushing
Manager: Kenny Dalglish
Assistants: Terry McDermott, Kenny Burns
Coaches: Chris McMenemy, Arthur Cox
Physio: Derek Wright

League History: 1893 Elected to Division 2; 1898-1934 Division 1; 1934-48 Division 2; 1948-61 Division 1; 1961-65 Division 2; 1965-78 Division 1; 1978-84 Division 2; 1984-89 Division 1; 1989-92 Division 2; 1992-1993 Division 1; 1993- FA Premier League.

Honours: *FA Premier League: Runners-up* 1995-96, 1996-97. *Football League: Division 1 Champions* 1904-05, 1906-07, 1908-09, 1926-27, 1992-93; *Division 2 Champions* 1964-65; *Runners-up* 1897-98, 1947-48. *FA Cup: Winners* 1909-10, 1923-24, 1931-32, 1950-51, 1951-52, 1954-55; *Runners-up* 1904-05, 1905-06, 1907-08, 1910-11, 1973-74, 1997-98. *Football League Cup: Runners-up* 1975-76. *Texaco Cup: Winners* 1973-74, 1974-75. *UEFA Cup: Winners* 1968-69.

European Record: CC (1) 97-98 (CL) : –; CWC (0): – ; UEFA (6): 68-69 (W), 69-70 (QF), 70-71 (2), 77-78 (2), 94-95 (2), 96-97 (QF).

Managers: Frank Watt 1895-1932 (secretary until 1932); Andy Cunningham 1930-35; Tom Mather 1935-39; Stan Seymour 1939-47 (hon. manager); George Martin 1947-50; Stan Seymour 1950-54 (hon. manager); Duggie Livingstone; 1954-56, Stan Seymour (hon. manager) 1956-58; Charlie Mitten 1958-61; Norman Smith 1961-62; Joe Harvey 1962-75; Gordon Lee 1975-77; Richard Dinnis 1977; Bill McGarry 1977-80; Arthur Cox 1980-84; Jack Charlton 1984; Willie McFaul 1985-88; Jim Smith 1988-91; Ossie Ardiles 1991-92; *(FAPL)* Kevin Keegan Feb 1992-Jan 1997; Kenny Dalglish Jan 1997-.

Season 1997-98

Biggest Home Win:	3-1 v Chelsea
Biggest Home Defeat:	1-3 v Wimbledon
Biggest Away Win:	2-1 v Crystal Palace
Biggest Away Defeat:	1-4 v Leeds United
Biggest Home Att:	36,783 v Aston Villa
Smallest Home Att:	36,256 v Wimbledon
Average Attendance:	36,695
Leading Scorer:	John Barnes – 6

All-Time Records

Record FAPL Win:	7-1 v Swindon Town, 12/3/94
	7-1 v Tottenham Hotspur, 28/12/96
Record FAPL Defeat:	0-3 v Queens Park Rangers, 4/2/95
Record FL Win:	13-0 v Newport County, Division 2, 5/10/46
Record FL Defeat:	0-9 v Burton Wanderers, Division 2, 15/4/1895
Record Cup Win:	9-0 v Southport (at Hillsborough),
	FA Cup R4, 1/2/32
Record Fee Received:	£7m from Manchester United for Andy Cole, 1/95 (inc. part exchange)
Record Fee Paid:	£15m to Blackburn R. for Alan Shearer, 7/97
Most FL Apps:	Jim Lawrence, 432, 1904-22
Most FAPL Apps:	173 – Robert Lee, 1993-98
Most FAPL Goals:	55 – Andy Cole, 1993-95

Highest Scorer in FAPL Season: Andy Cole, 34, 1993-94
Record Attendance (all-time): 68,386 v Chelsea, Division 1, 3/9/30
Record Attendance (FAPL): 36,589 v Tottenham Hotspur, 5/5/96
Most FAPL Goals in Season: 82, 1993-94 – 42 games
Most FAPL Points in Season: 78, 1995-96 – 38 games

Summary 1997-98

Player	Tot	St	Sb	Snu	PS	Gls	Y	R	Fa	La	Fg	Lg
ALBERT	23	21	2	7	3	0	8	0	4	3	0	0
ANDERSSON	12	10	2	2	5	2	0	0	3	0	0	0
ASPRILLA	10	8	2	0	3	2	0	0	1	0	0	0
BARNES	26	22	4	8	8	6	0	0	5	3	0	0
BARTON	23	17	6	1	3	3	7	0	5	2	0	0
BATTY	32	32	0	0	1	1	9	3	6	2	0	0
BEARDSLEY	0	0	0	1	0	0	0	0	0	0	0	0
BERESFORD	18	17	1	0	3	2	3	0	3	3	0	0
BRAYSON	0	0	0	1	0	0	0	0	0	1	0	0
CRAWFORD	0	0	0	4	0	0	0	0	0	0	0	0
DABIZAS	11	10	1	0	0	1	2	0	2	0	0	0
ELLIOT	0	0	0	3	0	0	0	0	0	0	0	0
GILLESPIE	29	25	4	2	8	4	2	0	5	2	0	0
GIVEN	24	24	0	11	0	0	1	0	4	0	0	0
GRIFFIN	4	4	0	2	2	0	0	0	0	0	0	0
HAMILTON	12	7	5	9	4	0	0	0	1	2	0	1
HISLOP	13	13	0	18	0	0	0	0	3	3	0	0
HOWEY	14	11	3	5	4	0	0	0	5	1	0	0
HUGHES	4	4	0	11	1	0	0	0	1	1	0	0
KEIDEL	0	0	0	1	0	0	0	0	0	0	0	0
KETSBAIA	31	16	15	4	4	3	3	0	5	2	0	0
LEE	28	26	2	0	3	4	3	0	6	2	0	0
PEACOCK	20	19	1	3	1	0	4	0	1	3	0	0
PEARCE	25	25	0	2	1	0	4	0	7	0	0	0
PINAS	0	0	0	2	0	0	0	0	0	0	0	0
PISTONE	28	28	0	0	0	0	6	0	5	1	0	0
RUSH	10	6	4	8	2	0	1	0	1	2	0	1
SHEARER	17	15	2	0	0	2	2	0	6	0	0	0
SPEED	13	13	0	0	0	1	1	0	4	0	0	0
SRNICEK	1	1	0	9	0	0	0	0	0	0	0	0
TERRIER	0	0	0	1	0	0	0	0	0	0	0	0
TOMASSON	23	17	6	11	6	3	1	0	2	3	0	1
WATSON	29	27	2	2	0	1	3	0	4	3	0	0

60 3

Under Fire

Looking forward to his first full season as manager of Newcastle United, Kenny Dalglish had the added challenge of a Champions' League programme with which to contend and boosted his squad accordingly with eight new faces. Most expensive was Italian defender Allesandro Pistone at £4.3m while the most experienced were former England stars Stuart Pearce and John Barnes. Other signings included goalkeeper Shay Given, versatile Dane Jon-Dahl Tomasson and colourful Georgian Temuri Ketsbaia and after the turn of the year Dalglish spent around £13m to make several signings including Andreas Andersson and Gary Speed. Dalglish released veteran Peter Beardsley and, more controversially, the enigmatic Asprilla in January for over £6m. Crucially, Newcastle lost Alan Shearer for much of the season through injury but when he did return a defensive approach seemed a waste of the most prolific goalscoring talent in Premiership history.

Two goals by Asprilla, against Sheffield Wednesday, got Newcastle's season off to a flying start which was continued with another three wins in the next four games. Despite having 12 points from five games, Newcastle were six points shy of the leaders who had already played an extra three matches. Defeat at Chelsea appeared no more than a minor irritation as a last-minute Warren Barton goal beat Tottenham but the Magpies then embarked on a 14-match run which produced just two victories. Goals were proving hard to come by and but for two goals in five minutes by Keith Gillespie against Barnsley, Newcastle would have gone six consecutive matches without scoring. Two wins in three games looked to have dispelled relegation chatter only for the side to plummet the depths again with one lone success from a dozen outings. Shearer grabbed a vital late winner against Barnsley while safety was finally confirmed in the penultimate league match of the season which saw both Nikolaos Dabizas and Speed score their first Premiership goals in a 3-1 win over Chelsea.

In the Champions' League a goal in the last-minute of extra-time by Ketsbaia carried United past Croatia Zagreb for an aggregate 4-3 victory in the qualifying round before a stunning hat-trick of headed goals by Asprilla gave Newcastle an unforgettable 3-2 win over Barcelona. After gaining a fortuitous draw away to Dynamo Kiev, Newcastle lost to PSV Eindhoven, home and away, and at Barcelona which put them out of the competition. A 2-0 win over Kiev in the return was academic as the Russians had already won the group.

Newcastle's FA Cup campaign was certainly eventful. A creditable start was made with victory at Everton before unflattering comments by Dalglish inflamed a 4th Round meeting with non-leaguers Stevenage. At the second attempt and thanks to a fit again Shearer, Newcastle progressed but clearly lost the public relations battle. Shearer also took care of Tranmere before a 3-1 win over Barnsley set up a semi-final meeting with Sheffield United. Once again Shearer was Newcastle's hero as he took them through to the final for the first time in 24 years. But on the day they were a comfortable second to Arsenal.

Newcastle's Coca-Cola Cup exploits began in Round Three with a home win over Hull before United became the first visiting side to win at Derby's Pride Park. For the second time in three years the quarter-final was the end of the road with Liverpool, after extra-time, winning on Tyneside. ∎

Results 1997-98

FA Carling Premiership

Date	Opponents	Ven	Res	Atten	Scorers
08-Aug	Sheffield W.	H	2-1	36,771	Asprilla (2, 71)
22-Aug	Aston Villa	H	1-0	36,783	Beresford (12)
12-Sep	Wimbledon	H	1-3	36,256	Barton (31)
19-Sep	West Ham U.	A	1-0	25,884	Barnes (43)
23-Sep	Everton	A	1-0	36,705	Lee (87)
26-Sep	Chelsea	A	0-1	31,563	
03-Oct	Tottenham H.	H	1-0	36,709	Barton (89)
17-Oct	Leeds U.	A	1-4	39,834	Gillespie (62)
24-Oct	Blackburn R.	H	1-1	36,716	Gillespie (27)
31-Oct	Leicester C.	H	3-3	36,574	Barnes (4 pen); Tomasson (45); Beresford (90)
07-Nov	Coventry C.	A	2-2	22,679	Barnes (31); Lee (87)
21-Nov	Southampton	H	2-1	37,759	Barnes (54, 75)
28-Nov	C. Palace	A	2-1	28,065	Ketsbaia (45); Tomasson (64)
30-Nov	Bolton W.	A	0-1	24,494	
05-Dec	Arsenal	H	0-1	36,571	
12-Dec	Barnsley	A	2-2	18,687	Gillespie (44, 49)
16-Dec	Derby Co.	H	0-0	36,289	
20-Dec	Manchester U.	A	0-1	36,767	
25-Dec	Derby Co.	A	0-1	30,232	
27-Dec	Liverpool	H	1-2	36,718	Watson (16)
09-Jan	Sheffield W.	A	1-2	29,446	Tomasson (20)
16-Jan	Bolton W.	H	2-1	36,767	Barnes (6); Ketsbaia (90)
19-Jan	Liverpool	A	0-1	42,791	
31-Jan	Aston Villa	A	1-0	38,266	Batty (58)
06-Feb	West Ham U.	A	0-1	36,736	
21-Feb	Leeds U.	H	1-1	36,511	Ketsbaia (85)
27-Feb	Everton	A	0-0	37,972	
13-Mar	Coventry C.	H	0-0	36,767	
17-Mar	C. Palace	H	1-2	36,565	Shearer (77)
27-Mar	Southampton	A	1-2	15,251	Lee (46)
30-Mar	Wimbledon	A	0-0	15,478	
10-Apr	Arsenal	A	1-3	38,102	Barton (79)
12-Apr	Barnsley	H	2-1	36,534	Andersson (40); Shearer (86)
17-Apr	Manchester U.	A	1-1	55,194	Andersson (11)
24-Apr	Tottenham H.	A	0-2	35,847	
28-Apr	Leicester C.	A	0-0	21,699	
01-May	Chelsea	H	3-1	36,710	Dabizas (38); Lee (42); Speed (58)
09-May	Blackburn R.	A	0-1	29,300	

FA Challenge Cup

Date	Opponents	Vn	Rnd	Res	Atten	Scorers
04-Jan	Everton	A	3R	1-0	20,885	Rush (67)
25-Jan	Stevenage B.	A	4R	1-1	8,040	Shearer (3)
04-Feb	Stevenage B.	H	4RR	2-1	36,705	Shearer (16, 65)
14-Feb	Tranmere R.	H	5R	1-0	36,675	Shearer (22)
08-Mar	Barnsley	H	6R	3-1	36,695	Ketsbaia (16); Speed (27); Batty (90)
	Sheffield U.	Hil	SF	1-0		Shearer
16-May	Arsenal	W	F	0-2		

Coca-Cola League Cup

Date	Opponents	Vn	Rnd	Res	Atten	Scorers
15-Oct	Hull C.	H	3R	2-0	35,856	Hamilton (47); Rush (83)
18-Nov	Derby Co.	A	4R	1-0	27,364	Tomasson (72)
07-Jan	Liverpool	H	QF	0-2	33,207	*aet*

UEFA Champions' League

Date	Opponents	Vn	Rnd	Res	Atten	Scorers
13-Aug	C. Zagreb	H	Q1L	2-1	34,465	Beresford (21,71)
27-Aug	C. Zagreb	A	Q2L	2-2	34,000	Asprilla (44 pen); Ketsbaia (114)

aet. Newcastle qualify for league stage 4-3 on aggregate.

Date	Opponents	Vn	Rnd	Res	Atten	Scorers
17-Sep	Barcelona	H	C	3-2	35,274	Asprilla (21 pen, 30, 49)
01-Oct	Dynamo Kiev	A	C	2-2	100,000	Beresford (78); OG (84)
22-Oct	PSV	A	C	0-1	29,200	
05-Nov	PSV	H	C	0-2	35,214	
27-Nov	Barcelona	A	C	0-1		
10-Dec	Dynamo Kiev	H	C	2-0	33,694	Barnes (10); Pearce (21)

Newcastle United do not qualify for knock-out phase.

5-Year Record

	Div.	P	W	D	L	F	A	Pts	Pos	FAC	FLC
93-94	PL	42	23	8	11	82	41	77	3	4	3
94-95	PL	42	20	12	10	67	47	72	6	QF	4
95-96	PL	38	24	6	8	66	37	78	2	3	QF
96-97	PL	38	19	11	8	73	40	68	2	4	4
97-98	PL	38	11	11	16	35	44	44	13	F	QF

Nottingham Forest

Founded in 1865 by players of a hockey-like game, shinney, who played at the Forest Recreation Ground. They played their first game in 1866. Had several early homes, including a former Notts County ground, The Meadows, and Trent Bridge Cricket Ground.

Founder members of the Football Alliance in 1889 and champions in 1892 when elected to an extended Football League top division. In 1898 moved from the Town Ground to the City Ground at West Bridgford. Run by a committee until 1982, the last league club to become a limited company. Premier League founder members 1992. Relegated after one season, but promoted back at the first attempt, only to be relegated once again in 1997.

Ground:	City Ground, Nottingham NG2 5FJ		
Phone:	0115-952 6000	**Fax:**	0115-952 600
Box Office:	0115-952 6002	**CC Bookings:**	0115-971 8181
Info:	0115-952 6016 (24 hrs)		
News:	0891 12 11 74	**Clubshop:**	0115-952 6026
Capacity:	30,539	**Pitch:**	116 yds x 77 yds
Colours:	Red, White, Red	**Nickname:**	Reds
Radio:	945AM/999AM GEM AM		
Internet:	http//:www.nottinghamforest.co.uk		

CEO Phillip Soar		**Secretary:** Paul White	
Manager: Dave Bassett			
Coaches: Liam O'Kane and Steve Beaglehole			
Physio: John Haselden			

League History: 1892 elected to Division 1; 1906-07 Division 2; 1907-11 Division 1; 1911-22 Division 2; 1922-25 Division 1; 1925-49 Division 2; 1949-51 Division 3 (S); 1951-57 Division 2; 1957-72 Division 1; 1972-77 Division 2; 1977-92 Division 1; 1992-93 FA Premier League; 1993-94 Division 1; 1994- FA Premier League.

Honours: *Football League: Division 1 Champions* 1977-78; *Runners-up* 1966-67, 1978-79; *Division 2 Champions* 1906-07, 1921-22; *Runners-up* 1956-57; *Division 3 (S) Champions* 1950-51. *FA Cup: Winners* 1898, 1959; *Runners-up* 1991. *Anglo-Scottish Cup: Winners* 1976-77. *Football League Cup: Winners* 1977-78, 1978-79, 1988-89, 1989-90; *Runners-up* 1979-80, 1991-92. *Simod Cup: Winners* 1989. *Zenith Data Systems Cup: Winners* 1991-92. *Champions' Cup: Winners* 1978-79, 1979-80 *European Super Cup :*

Winners 1979-80; *Runners-up* 1980-81. *World Club Championship: Runners-up* 1980-81.

European Record: CC (3): 78-79 (W), 79-80 (W), 80-81 (1); CWC (0): –; UEFA (5): 61-62 (1), 67-68 (2), 83-84 (3), 84-85 (1), 95-96 (QF).

Managers: Harry Radford 1889-97; Harry Haslam 1897-09; Fred Earp 1909-12; Bob Masters 1912-25; Jack Baynes 1925-29; Stan Hardy 1930-31; Noel Watson 1931-36; Harold Wightman 1936-39; Billy Walker 1939-60; Andy Beattie 1960-63; John Carey 1963-68; Matt Gillies 1969-72; Dave Mackay 1972-73; Allan Brown 1973-75; *(FAPL)* Brian Clough 1975-93; Frank Clark June 93-Dec 96; Stuart Pearce Dec 96-Jun 97; Dave Bassett Jun 97-.

Season 1997-98

Biggest Home Win:	5-2 v Charlton Athletic
Biggest Home Defeat:	0-3 v Sunderland
Biggest Away Win:	4-1 v Crewe Alexandra
Biggest Away Defeat:	2-4 v Charlton Athletic, 0-3 v Bradford City
Biggest Home Att:	29, 302 v Reading
Smallest Home Att:	16,524 v Norwich City
Leading Scorer:	Pierre van Hooijdonk – 29

All-Time Records

Record FAPL Win:	7-1 v Sheffield Wednesday, 1/4/95
Record FAPL Defeat:	0-7 v Blackburn Rovers (away), 18/11/95
Record FL Win:	12-0 v Leicester Fosse, Division 1, 12/4/09
Record FL Defeat:	1-9 v Blackburn R, Division 2, 10/4/37
Record Cup Win:	14-0 v Clapton (away), FA Cup R1, 17/1/1891
Record Fee Received:	£8.5m from Liverpool for Stan Collymore, 6/95
Record Fee Paid:	£3.5m > 4.5m to Celtic for Pierre van Hooijdonk, 3/97
Most FL Apps:	Bob McKinlay, 614, 1951-70
Most FAPL Apps:	150 – Mark Crossley, 1992-97
Most FAPL Goals:	24 – Bryan Roy, 1994-9
Record Attendance (all-time):	49,945 v Manchester Utd, Div 1, 28/10/67
Record Attendance (FAPL):	29,263 v Manchester United, 27/11/95
Highest Scorer in FAPL Season:	Stan Collymore, 23, 1994-95
Most FAPL Goals in Season:	72, 1994-95 – 42 games
Most FAPL Points in Season:	77, 1994-95 – 42 games

Summary 1997-98

Player	Tot	St	Sb	Snu	PS	Gls	Fa	La	Fg	Lg
ALLEN	2	1	1	0	1	0	0	2	0	1
ARMSTRONG	17	4	13	17	1	0	1	4	0	1
BART-WILLIAMS	33	30	3	0	2	4	0	3	0	0
BEASANT	39	39	0	0	0	0	1	2	0	0
BONALAIR	30	23	7	3	5	2	1	1	0	0
CAMPBELL	41	41	0	0	4	23	1	2	0	0
CHETTLE	43	43	0	0	4	1	1	3	0	0
COOPER	32	32	0	0	1	5	1	1	0	0
FETTIS	0	0	0	0	0	0	0	1	0	0
GEMMILL	43	42	1	0	7	2	1	3	0	0
GUINAN	2	1	1	11	1	0	0	1	0	1
HAREWOOD	1	1	0	0	0	0	0	0	0	0
HJELDE	28	23	5	4	3	1	1	2	0	2
HOOIJDONK	41	40	1	0	1	29	1	4	1	4
HOWE	0	0	0	0	0	0	0	1	0	0
JOHNSON, A	32	23	9	5	6	4	0	3	0	0
JOHNSON, D	6	5	1	0	3	0	0	0	0	0
LYTTLE	34	34	0	0	6	0	1	4	0	0
McGREGOR	0	0	0	2	0	0	0	0	0	0
MOORE	9	2	7	4	0	1	1	2	0	0
PASCALO	6	6	0	9	0	0	0	1	0	0
PHILLIPS	0	0	0	0	0	0	0	2	0	0
ROGERS	45	45	0	0	7	1	1	4	0	0
SAUNDERS	8	6	2	1	2	2	0	3	0	2
SMITH	0	0	0	0	0	1	0	0	0	0
STONE	30	28	2	1	5	2	0	0	0	0
THOM	0	0	0	0	0	0	0	1	0	0
THOMAS	19	13	6	3	2	3	0	1	0	1
WARNER	0	0	0	0	0	0	0	1	0	0
WOAN	20	10	10	7	6	1	0	1	0	0

5-Year Record

	Div.	P	W	D	L	F	A	Pts	Pos	FAC	FLC
93-94	1	46	23	14	9	74	49	83	2	3	5
94-95	PL	42	22	11	9	72	43	77	3	4	4
95-96	PL	38	15	13	10	50	54	58	9	QF	2
96-97	PL	38	6	16	16	31	59	34	20	5	3
97-98	1	46	28	10	8	82	42	94	1	3	2

Bassett Aims to Replant Forest

If there is one club which adds substance to the theory that there is a growing gulf between the Premiership and the Nationwide League then it has to be Nottingham Forest. By virtue of winning the Division One Championship for a second time in five years, Forest are the first club to have twice fallen from the Premiership then won the Football League title at the first time of asking.

That said, Forest invested well. Manager Dave Bassett collected over £3m from the departure of Alf-Inge Haaland and Bryan Roy. He brought in Andy Johnson and Alan Rogers from Norwich and Tranmere for over £4m and overseas players Marco Pascalo and Jon Olav Hjelde for £1.35m. Bassett also acquired Geoff Thomas and Thierry Bonalair on free transfers but the signing which turned Forest into champions and the second highest scorers in the division was one which took place towards the end of their unsuccessful battle against relegation the previous season – Pierre van Hooijdonk.

The Dutchman formed a formidable partnership with Kevin Campbell who answered his critics superbly as the duo scored in excess of 50 league goals between them, with van Hooijdonk alone scoring 29 times.

Forest set a cracking pace from the off with four consecutive wins, including 4-1 and 4-0 thumpings of Norwich and QPR, the latter including van Hooijdonk's first hat-trick for the club, but were surprisingly brought down to earth when former Forest boss Frank Clark took his Manchester City side to the City Ground and won 3-1. A draw at Swindon, who made a good start, and defeat at Sheffield United sent Forest down to fifth but victory over Portsmouth returned Bassett's side to the top of the table after eight games. With one defeat from 14 games – two in the first 21 games – Forest were well on the path to promotion and proved their credentials against other top sides. Draws were collected at Sunderland and Middlesbrough while Charlton were thrashed 5-2 with van Hooijdonk being the destroyer with another hat-trick.

The return match with Middlesbrough was crucial to Forest's title aspirations. Two successive draws had allowed Boro to open up a three-point lead but with van Hooijdonk scoring twice Forest pulled off an amazing 4-0 victory. But Forest failed to capitalise fully on that success and were immediately pegged back by Sunderland who dished out a 3-0 defeat at the City Ground. Unabashed Forest duly put the record straight with a Campbell hat-trick setting up a 4-1 win at Crewe. Forest were now three points clear and, with seven wins in eight games, carried themselves into an unassailable position. Results elsewhere during the final week handed Forest the title and they celebrated with van Hooijdonk's 34th goal of the season in a 1-1 draw at West Brom.

Forest's FA Cup venture ended in the 3rd Round for the third successive year as Charlton dished out a 4-1 trouncing at the Valley. Just three months after dropping out of the Premiership, Forest found themselves playing in the 1st Round of the Coca-Cola Cup and duly crushed Doncaster 8-0 at Belle Vue before a more sedate 2-1 success at the City Ground. But Walsall ensured that the goal feast was over with a 1-0 1st Leg victory in Nottingham before putting Forest out 3-2 on aggregate at Bescot Stadium. ■

Results 1997-98

Date	Opponents	Ven	Res	Atten	Scorers
09-Aug	Port Vale	A	1-0	23,681	Campbell (39)
13-Aug	Norwich C.	H	4-1	16,524	Van Hooijdonk (22); Thomas (57,61); Campbell (59)
23-Aug	Oxford U.	A	1-0	9,486	Bart Williams (71)
30-Aug	QPR	A	4-0	18,804	Van Hooijdonk (44, 48, 87); Saunders (80)
03-Sep	Manchester C.	H	1-3	23,681	Campbell (81)
07-Sep	Swindon T.	A	0-0	13,051	
13-Sep	Sheffield U.	A	0-1	24,536	
20-Sep	Portsmouth	H	1-0	17,292	Van Hooijdonk (34)
27-Sep	Stoke C.	A	1-0	19,018	Campbell (67)
03-Oct	Huddersfield	A	2-0	11,258	Cooper (67); Saunders (73)
18-Oct	Tranmere R.	H	2-2	17,009	Van Hooijdonk (18); Gemmill (42)
21-Oct	WBA	H	1-0	19,243	Campbell (75)
24-Oct	Reading	A	3-3	12,610	Van Hooijdonk (3, 48 pen); Campbell (64)
01-Nov	Crewe Alex.	H	3-1	18,862	Van Hooijdonk (54, 86); Campbell (9)
04-Nov	Bury	A	0-2	6,731	
08-Nov	Sunderland	A	1-1	33,610	Hjelde (24)
15-Nov	Birmingham C.	H	1-0	19,610	Campbell (17)
22-Nov	Charlton A.	H	5-2	18,532	Van Hooijdonk (21, 50, 56); Woan (76); Campbell (83)
26-Nov	Middlesbrough	A	0-0	30,143	
29-Nov	Ipswich T.	A	1-0	17,580	Campbell (65)
06-Dec	Bradford C.	H	2-2	17,943	Cooper (13); Bonalair (63)
14-Dec	Wolvh'n W.	A	1-2	24,635	Johnson (84)
20-Dec	Stockport Co.	H	2-1	16,701	Van Hooijdonk (81 pen); Stone (85)
26-Dec	Swindon T.	H	3-0	26,500	Campbell (10, 22); Johnson (29)
28-Dec	Manchester C.	A	3-2	31,839	Van Hooijdonk (31 pen, 53 pen); Campbell (50)
10-Jan	Port Vale	H	2-1	17,639	Van Hooijdonk (27, 83)
17-Jan	Norwich C.	A	0-1	17,059	
24-Jan	QPR	A	1-0	13,220	Cooper (85)
31-Jan	Oxford U.	H	1-3	18,392	Van Hooijdonk (27 pen)
07-Feb	Portsmouth	A	1-0	15,033	
17-Feb	Huddersfield T.	H	3-0	18,231	Van Hooijdonk (30, 80); Bonalair (67)

21-Feb	Stoke C.	A	1-1	16,899	Moore (87)
24-Feb	Tranmere R.	A	0-0	7,377	
01-Mar	Middlesbrough	H	4-0	25,286	Van Hooijdonk (53, 85 pen); Campbell (55); Cooper (75)
04-Mar	Sunderland	H	0-3	29,009	
07-Mar	Crewe Alex.	A	4-1	5,759	Bart-Williams (10); Campbell (15, 25, 30)
14-Mar	Bury	H	3-0	19,846	OG (Lucketti 63); Van Hooijdonk (69); Rogers (82)
21-Mar	Birmingham C.	A	2-1	24,663	Van Hooijdonk (84, 88)
28-Mar	Charlton A.	A	2-4	15,815	Campbell (16, 90)
01-Apr	Sheffield U.	H	3-0	21,512	Thomas (21); Campbell (28, 83)
05-Apr	Ipswich T.	H	2-1	22,292	Cooper (53); Van Hooijdonk (58)
11-Apr	Bradford C.	A	0-3	17,248	Campbell (38); Gemmill (62); Bart-Williams (82)
13-Apr	Wolvh'n W.	H	3-0	22,863	A.Johnson (33); Van Hooijdonk (40); Campbell (90)
18-Apr	Stockport Co.	A	2-2	9,892	Van Hooijdonk (26); A.Johnson (67)
26-Apr	Reading	H	1-0	29,302	Bart-Williams (88)
03-May	WBA	A	1-1	23,013	Stone (18)

FA Challenge Cup

Date	Opponents	Vn	Rnd	Res	Atten	Scorers
03-Jan	Charlton A.	A	3R	1-4	13,827	Van Hooijdonk (56)

Coca-Cola League Cup

Date	Opponents	Vn	Rnd	Res	Atten	Scorers
11-Aug	Doncaster R.	A	1R1L	8-0	4,547	Thomas (11); Saunders (15, 78); Hjelde (30, 55); Van Hooijdonk (47, 83); Allen (86)
27-Aug	Doncaster R.	H	1R2L	2-1	9,908	Guinan (5); Hooijdonk (57)
	N. Forest win 10-1 on aggregate					
17-Sep	Walsall	H	2R1L	0-1	7,841	
24-Sep	Walsall	A	2R2L	2-2	6,037	Van Hooijdonk (48); Armstrong (91)

aet Walsall win 3-2 on aggregate

Sheffield Wednesday

Founded in 1867 by members of the Wednesday Cricket Club and played at Highfield before moving to Myrtle Road. Were first holders of the Sheffield FA Cup. The club played at Sheaf House then Endcliff and became professionals in 1886. In 1887 moved to Olive Grove.

Refused admission to the Football League, the club was founder member, and first champions, of the Football Alliance in 1889. In 1892 most Alliance clubs became founder members of Football League Division Two, but Wednesday were elected to an enlarged top division. The club moved to Hillsborough in 1899. Founder members of the Premier League 1992.

Ground:	Hillsborough, Sheffield, S6 1SW		
Phone:	0114-221 2121	**News:** 0891 12 11 86	
Box Office:	0114-221 2400	**Fax:** 0114-221 2401	
Info:	0891 12 11 86		
Capacity:	36,020	**Pitch:** 115 yds x 77 yds	
Colours:	Blue/White, Blue, Blue	**Nickname:** The Owls	
Radio:	BBC Radio Sheffield 88.6 and 104.1FM		
Internet:	http://www.swfc.co.uk		

Chairman: D.G. Richards		**Vice-Chairman:** K.T. Addy
Secretary: Graham Mackrell FCCA		
Manager: Danny Wilson		**Coach:**
Physio: David Galley		

League History: 1892 Elected to Division 1; 1899-1900 Division 2; 1900-20 Division 1; 1920-26 Division 2; 1926-37 Division 1; 1937-50 Division 2; 1950-51 Division 1; 1951-52 Division 2; 1952-55 Division 1; 1955-56 Division 2; 1956-58 Division 1; 1958-59 Division 2; 1959-70 Division 1; 1970-75 Division 2; 1975-80 Division 3; 1980-84 Division 2; 1984-90 Division 1; 1990-91 Division 2; 1991-92 Division 1; 1992- FA Premier League.

Honours: *Football League: Division 1 Champions* 1902-03, 1903-04, 1928-29, 1929-30; *Runners-up* 1960-61; *Division 2 Champions* 1899-1900, 1925-26, 1951-52, 1955-56, 1958-59; *Runners-up* 1949-50, 1983-84. *FA Cup: Winners* 1895-96, 1906-07, 1934-35; *Runners-up* 1889-90, 1965-66, 1992-93; *Football League Cup: Winners* 1990-91; *Runners-up* 1992-93.

European Record: CC (0): –; CWC (0): – ; UEFA (3): 61-62 (QF), 63-64 (2), 92-93 (2).

Managers: Arthur Dickinson 1891-1920; Robert Brown 1920-33; Billy Walker 1933-37; Jimmy McMullan 1937-42; Eric Taylor 1942-58 (continued as GM to 1974); Harry Catterick 1958-61; Vic Buckingham 1961-64; Alan Brown 1964-68; Jack Marshall 1968-69; Danny Williams 1969-71; Derek Dooley 1971-73; Steve Burtenshaw 1974-75; Len Ashurst 1975-77; Jackie Charlton 1977-83; Howard Wilkinson 1983-88; Peter Eustace 1988-89; Ron Atkinson 1989-91; *(FAPL)* Trevor Francis June 1991-May 1995; David Pleat July 1995-Nov 97; Ron Atkinson Nov 1997-Jun 98; Danny Wilson Aug-98–.

Season 1997-98

Biggest Home Win:	5-0 v Bolton Wanderers
Biggest Home Defeat:	1-4 v Chelsea
Biggest Away Win:	3-1 v Everton
Biggest Away Defeat:	2-7 v Blackburn Rovers, 1-6 v Manchester United
Biggest Home Att:	39,427 v Manchester United
Smallest Home Att:	21,087 v Coventry City
Average Attendance:	28,709
Leading Scorer:	Paolo Di Canio – 12

All-Time Records

Record FAPL Win:	6-2 v Leeds United, 16/12/95
Record FAPL Defeat:	1-7 v Nottingham Forest, 1/4/95
Record FL Win:	9-1 v Birmingham, Division 1, 13/12/30
Record FL Defeat:	0-10 v Aston Villa, Division 1, 5/10/12
Record Cup Win:	12-0 v Halliwell, FA Cup R1, 17/1/1891
Record Fee Received:	£2.7m from Blackburn R. for Paul Warhurst, 9/93
Record Fee Paid:	£3m to Internazionale for Benito Carbone, 10/96
	£3m to Celtic for Paolo Di Canio, 8/97
Most FL Apps:	Andy Wilson, 502, 1900-20
Most FAPL Apps:	219 – Peter Atherton, 1992-98
Most FAPL Goals:	48 – Mark Bright, 1992-97

Highest Scorer in FAPL Season: Bright, 19, 1993-94

Record Attendance (all-time): 72,841 v Man City, FA Cup R5, 17/2/34

Record Attendance (FAPL): 39,427 v Manchester United, 97-98

Most FAPL Goals in Season: 76, 1993-94 – 42 games

Most FAPL Points in Season: 64, 1993-94 – 42 games

Player	Tot	St	Sb	Snu	PS	Gls	Y	R	Fa	La	Fg	Lg
AGOGO	1	0	1	0	0	0	0	0	0	0	0	0
ALEXANDERSSON	6	5	1	1	2	0	0	0	2	0	1	0
ATHERTON	27	27	0	0	2	3	7	0	3	1	0	0
BARRETT	10	10	0	0	2	0	1	1	0	0	0	0
BLONDEAU	6	5	1	3	0	0	4	0	0	0	0	0
BOOTH	23	21	2	1	4	7	1	1	2	0	0	0
BRISCOE	7	3	4	3	2	0	0	0	0	2	0	0
CARBONE	33	28	5	0	7	9	8	1	2	1	0	0
CLARKE	3	2	1	32	0	0	0	0	0	2	0	0
CLOUGH	1	1	0	3	1	0	0	0	0	1	0	0
COLLINS	19	8	11	1	4	5	2	0	0	2	0	0
DI CANIO	35	34	1	0	8	12	10	0	3	2	0	2
DONALDSON	5	1	4	0	1	0	0	0	0	0	0	0
GROBBELAAR	0	0	0	5	0	0	0	0	0	0	0	0
HINCHCLIFFE	15	15	0	0	0	1	0	0	0	0	0	0
HIRST	6	3	3	0	0	0	0	0	0	0	0	0
HUMPHREYS	7	2	5	10	2	0	1	0	3	1	0	0
HYDE	21	14	7	4	10	1	7	0	1	0	0	0
MAGILTON	20	13	7	7	4	1	1	0	1	2	0	0
MAYRLEB	3	0	3	3	0	0	0	0	0	0	0	0
NEWSOME	25	25	0	0	2	2	2	0	3	1	0	0
NICOL	7	4	3	6	2	0	1	0	0	0	0	0
NOLAN	27	27	0	0	2	0	1	0	3	2	0	0
OAKES	4	0	4	10	0	0	0	0	2	0	0	0
PEMBRIDGE	34	31	3	0	15	4	4	0	3	2	0	0
PORIC	3	0	3	2	0	0	0	0	0	1	0	0
PRESSMAN	36	36	0	0	1	0	0	0	3	2	0	0
QUINN	1	0	1	0	0	0	1	0	0	0	0	0
RUDI	22	19	3	0	5	0	2	0	3	0	0	0
SANETTI	2	1	1	0	0	0	0	0	0	0	0	0
SEDLOSKI	4	3	1	0	1	0	0	0	0	0	0	0
STEFANOVIC	20	19	1	3	2	2	8	1	0	1	0	0
THOME	6	6	0	2	1	0	1	0	0	0	0	0
WALKER	38	38	0	0	1	0	0	0	3	2	0	0
WHITTINGHAM	28	17	11	7	6	4	1	0	1	2	0	0
Own Goals						0						1

62/4

The Waiting Game

One year on from making their best ever start to a season, Sheffield Wednesday found themselves on the rocks early in 1997/98 with just one victory in nine Premiership matches. Along the way Wednesday were slaughtered 7-2 at Blackburn and crushed 5-2 home by Derby. Not that the dire results unsettled Italian Benito Carbone who had seven goals in the bag after just ten games.

Such a poor start to the season may not have come as a complete surprise to outsiders given that Wednesday won just two of the final nine games of the previous campaign. Manager David Pleat, however, had more faith in his players and by the start of the season had added only Paulo Di Canio from Celtic for £3m and Patrick Blondeau from Monaco for £1.8m to his existing squad. Waving farewell to Hillsborough were Regi Blinker, Orlando Trustfull and three other squad members. In September Jim Magilton joined from Southampton for £1.6m and a month later David Hirst went in the opposite direction for £2m.

After that poor start Pleat was walking a thin line and when four points from two games was followed by defeat at one of his previous clubs, Tottenham, a home reversal by Crystal Palace and a 6-1 mauling at Manchester United, Wednesday decided that Pleat's time was up. Pleat's number two Peter Shreeves took charge of the side for the visit of Bolton and wondered what all the fuss was about as Andy Booth, making his first appearance of the season after injury, scored a hat-trick in Wednesday's 5-0 stroll, all the goals coming before half time.

By the time of their next Premiership match a fortnight later Wednesday had appointed Ron Atkinson as manager for his second stint at Hillsborough. Big Ron's first test was a triumph, with Booth scoring again as Arsenal went down to only their second defeat of the season. Mid table Southampton and struggling Barnsley also became victims of the Owls recovery which saw the talented Di Canio score three times in that four match winning run. A trip to West Ham in December terminated the run and the point that Atkinson still had plenty of work to do was emphasised by a 4-1 home defeat against Chelsea. Wednesday's form for the rest of the season was erratic to say the least, with never more than two consecutive games being won or lost. Indeed it still needed a 3-1 win at Everton, with Mark Pembridge scoring twice and top scorer Di Canio the other, towards the end of the campaign to maintain Wednesday's ever present record in the Premiership. The season closed with successive defeats by Aston Villa and Crystal Palace.

Hopes of matching or improving the previous seasons run to the last eight of the FA Cup were not high following a 3rd Round clash with Watford. After a disappointing penalty shoot-out replay victory at Hillsborough, Wednesday departed the competition after a crushing home defeat by Blackburn. Wednesday's poor early season form continued in the Coca-Cola cup where Division Two side Grimsby, after a 2-0 win at Blundell Park, went down only 3-2 at Hillsborough to pull off a shock 4-3 aggregate victory.

Atkinson paid the price for failing to continue the early upturn in results when he was informed shortly after the close of the season that he was not being retained. As the World Cup Finals entered their final phase the Hillsborough side were still seeking a name to fill the hot-seat. ∎

Results 1997-98

Date	Opponents	Ven	Res	Atten	Scorers
08-Aug	Newcastle U.	A	1-2	36,771	Carbone (7)
12-Aug	Leeds U.	H	1-3	31,520	Hyde (70)
22-Aug	Wimbledon	A	1-1	11,503	Di Canio (74)
24-Aug	Blackburn R.	A	2-7	19,618	Carbone (7, 46)
29-Aug	Leicester C.	H	1-0	24,851	Carbone (55)
12-Sep	Liverpool	A	1-2	34,705	Collins (81)
19-Sep	Coventry C.	H	0-0	21,087	
23-Sep	Derby Co.	H	2-5	22,391	Di Canio (5); Carbone (13 pen)
26-Sep	Aston Villa	A	2-2	32,044	Collins (25); Whittingham (42)
03-Oct	Everton	H	3-1	24,486	Carbone (78, 82 pen); Di Canio (89)
18-Oct	Tottenham H.	A	2-3	25,097	Collins (71); Di Canio (84)
24-Oct	C. Palace	H	1-3	22,072	Collins (57)
31-Oct	Manchester U.	A	1-6	55,259	Whittingham (66)
07-Nov	Bolton W.	H	5-0	25,067	Booth (28, 33, 48); Di Canio (20); Whittingham (26)
21-Nov	Arsenal	H	2-0	34,373	Booth (42); Whittingham (86)
28-Nov	Southampton	A	3-2	15,244	Atherton (27); Collins (68); Di Canio (84)
07-Dec	Barnsley	H	2-1	29,086	Stefanovic (19); Di Canio (88)
12-Dec	West Ham U.	A	0-1	24,344	
19-Dec	Chelsea	H	1-4	28,334	Pembridge (81)
25-Dec	Blackburn R.	H	0-0	33,502	
27-Dec	Leicester C.	A	1-1	20,800	Booth (85)
09-Jan	Newcastle U.	H	2-1	29,446	Di Canio (1); Newsome (51)
16-Jan	Leeds U.	A	2-1	33,166	Newsome (51); Booth (83)
30-Jan	Wimbledon	H	1-1	22,655	Pembridge (14)
06-Feb	Coventry C.	A	0-1	18,375	
13-Feb	Liverpool	H	3-3	35,405	Carbone (7); Di Canio (63); Hinchcliffe (69)
20-Feb	Tottenham H.	H	1-0	29,871	Di Canio (33)
27-Feb	Derby Co.	A	0-3	30,203	
06-Mar	Manchester U.	H	2-0	39,427	Atherton (26); Di Canio (88)
13-Mar	Bolton W.	A	2-3	24,847	Booth(28); Atherton (58)
27-Mar	Arsenal	A	0-1	38,087	
03-Apr	Southampton	H	1-0	29,677	Carbone (79)
10-Apr	Barnsley	A	1-2	18,692	Sefanovic (86)
12-Apr	West Ham U.	H	1-1	28,036	Magilton (59)
17-Apr	Chelsea	A	0-1	29,075	

24-Apr	Everton	A	3-1	35,497	Pembridge (5, 38); Di Canio (90)
01-May	Aston Villa	H	1 3	34,177	Sanetti (88)
09-May	C. Palace	A	0-1	16,876	

FA Challenge Cup

Date	Opponents	Vn	Rnd	Res	Atten	Scorers
03-Jan	Watford	A	3R	1-1	18,306	Alexandersson (64)
14-Jan	Watford	H	3RR	0-0	18,707	
	aet. Sheffield W. won 5-3 on penalties.					
26-Jan	Blackburn R.	H	4R	0-3	15,940	

Coca-Cola League Cup

Date	Opponents	Vn	Rnd	Res	Atten	Scorers
17-Sep	Grimsby T.	A	2R1L	0-2	6,429	
01-Oct	Grimsby T.	H	2R2L	3-2	11,120	OG (16 Davison); Di Canio (64, 88)

Grimsby T. won 4-3 on aggregate.

5-Year Record

	Div.	P	W	D	L	F	A	Pts	Pos	FAC	FLC
93-94	PL	42	16	16	10	76	54	64	7	4	SF
94-95	PL	42	13	12	17	49	57	51	13	4	4
95-96	PL	38	10	10	18	48	61	40	15	3	4
96-97	PL	38	14	15	9	50	51	57	7	6	2
97-98	PL	38	12	8	18	52	67	44	16	4	2

Southampton

Formed 1885 by members of the St Mary's Young Men's Association, St Mary's FC. The church link was dropped, though the name retained, in 1893. In 1895 applied for a Southern League place, but were refused, only to be invited to fill a subsequent vacancy. 'St Mary's' was dropped after two seasons. Moved from the County Cricket Ground to the Dell in 1898.

Six times Southern League champions, Southampton were founder members of Football League Division Three in 1920 (this becoming Division Three (South) the following season), of Division Three at the end of regionalisation in 1958, and of the Premier League, 1992.

Ground: The Dell, Milton Road, Southampton, SO9 4XX

Phone: 01703-220505   **News:** 0891 12 15 93

Box Office: 01703-228575

Capacity: 15,288

Pitch: 110 yds x 72 yds

Colours: Red/White, Black, Black   **Nickname:** The Saints

Radio: Radio Solent 96.1FM

Internet: http://www.soton.ac.uk

President: Ted Bates   **Chairman:** RJG Lowe

Secretary: Brian Truscott

Manager: David Jones

Assistants: John Sainty, John Mortimore, Terry Cooper

Physio: Don Taylor

League History: 1920 Original Member of Division 3; 1921 Division 3 (S); 1922-53 Division 2; 1953-58 Division 3 (S); 1958-60 Division 3; 1960-66 Division 2; 1966-74 Division 1; 1974-78 Division 2; 1978-92 Division 1; 1992- FA Premier League.

Honours: *Football League: Division 1 Runners-up 1983-84; Division 2 Runners-up 1965-66, 1977-78; Division 3 (S) Champions 1921-22; Runners-up 1920-21; Division 3 Champions 1959-60. FA Cup: Winners 1975-76; Runners-up 1900, 1902. Football League Cup: Runners-up 1978-79. Zenith Data Systems Cup: Runners-up 1991-92.*

European Record: CWC (1): 76-77 (QF). UEFA (5): 69-70 (3), 71-72 (1), 81-82 (2), 82-83 (1), 84-85 (1).

Managers: Cecil Knight 1894-95; Charles Robson 1895-97; E. Arnfield 1897-1911 (continued as secretary); George Swift 1911-12; E. Arnfield 1912-19; Jimmy McIntyre 1919-24; Arthur Chadwick 1925-31; George Kay 1931-

36; George Cross 1936-37; Tom Parker 1937-43; (J.R. Sarjantson stepped down from the board to act as secretary-manager 1943-47 with the next two listed being team managers during this period); Arthur Dominy 1943-46; Bill Dodgin Snr 1946-49; Sid Cann 1949-51; George Roughton 1952-55; Ted Bates 1955-73; Lawrie McMenemy 1973-85; Chris Nicholl 1985-91; *(FAPL)* Ian Branfoot 1991-94; Alan Ball Jan 1994-July 1995; Dave Merrington July 1995-June 1996; Graeme Souness July 1996-May 1997; David Jones July 1997-.

Season 1997-98

Biggest Home Win:	4-1 v Barnsley
Biggest Home Defeat:	1-3 v Arsenal
Biggest Away Win:	3-2 v Liverpool, 2-0 v Everton
Biggest Away Defeat:	0-4 v Derby County
Biggest Home Att:	15,251 v Newcastle United
Smallest Home Att:	14,815 v Wimbledon
Average Attendance:	15,168
Leading Scorer:	Matt Le Tissier – 11

All-Time Records

Record FAPL Win:	6-3 v Manchester United, 20/10/96
Record FAPL Defeat:	1-7 v Everton, 16/11/96
Record FL Win:	9-3 v Wolverhampton W., Division 2, 18/9/65
Record FL Defeat:	0-8 v Tottenham Hotspur, Division 2, 28/3/36; Everton, Division 1, 20/11/71
Record Cup Win:	7-1 v Ipswich Town, FA Cup R3, 7/1/61
Record Fee Received:	£7.5m from Blackburn R. for Kevin Davies, 7/97
Record Fee Paid:	£2.0m to Sheffield W. for David Hirst, 10/97
Most FL Apps:	Terry Payne, 713, 1956-74
Most FAPL Apps:	203 – Matt Le Tissier, 1992-98
Most FAPL Goals:	91 – Matt Le Tissier, 1992-98

Highest Scorer in FAPL Season: Matt Le Tissier, 25, 1993-94
Record Attendance (all-time): 31,044 v Man United, Division 1, 8/10/69
Record Attendance (FAPL): 19,654 v Tottenham Hotspur, 15/8/92
Most FAPL Goals in Season: 61, 1994-95 – 42 games
Most FAPL Points in Season: 54, 1994-95 – 42 games

Player	Tot	St	Sb	Snu	PS	Gls	Y	R	Fa	La	Fg	Lg
BASHAM	9	0	9	1	0	0	0	0	0	0	0	0
BENALI	33	32	1	1	2	1	2	2	1	3	0	0
BERESFORD	10	10	0	0	1	0	0	0	0	0	0	0
BOWEN	3	1	2	0	2	0	0	0	0	0	0	0
CHARLTON	3	2	1	1	2	0	0	0	0	2	0	0
DAVIES	25	20	5	1	4	9	5	0	1	4	0	3
DODD	36	36	0	0	2	1	2	0	1	3	0	0
DRYDEN	13	11	2	6	1	0	2	0	0	1	0	0
EVANS	10	6	4	0	2	0	0	0	0	3	0	1
FLAHAVAN	0	0	0	4	0	0	0	0	0	0	0	0
GIBBENS	2	2	0	4	1	0	0	0	0	0	0	0
HIRST	28	28	0	0	12	9	3	0	1	1	0	0
HUGHES	13	6	7	5	1	0	1	0	1	0	0	0
JOHANSEN	6	3	3	10	3	0	1	0	0	2	0	0
JONES	38	38	0	0	0	0	0	0	1	4	0	0
Le TISSIER	26	25	1	2	15	11	6	0	1	3	0	3
LUNDEKVAM	31	31	0	0	3	0	7	0	0	4	0	0
MADDISON	6	5	1	3	2	1	0	0	0	0	0	0
MAGILTON	5	5	0	0	0	0	1	0	0	0	0	0
MONKOU	32	30	2	1	1	1	5	1	1	3	0	1
MOSS	0	0	0	20	0	0	0	0	0	0	0	0
NEILSON	8	3	5	1	0	0	2	0	0	2	0	0
OAKLEY	33	32	1	0	10	1	3	0	1	4	0	0
OSTENSTAD	29	21	8	0	4	11	4	0	1	1	0	0
PALMER	26	26	0	0	0	3	6	1	1	3	0	0
RICHARDSON	28	25	3	5	9	0	1	0	1	4	0	0
ROBINSON	1	0	1	3	0	0	0	0	0	0	0	0
SLATER	11	3	8	3	3	0	1	0	0	1	0	0
SPEDDING	7	4	3	2	3	0	0	0	0	1	0	0
TAYLOR	0	0	0	14	0	0	0	0	0	0	0	0
TODD	10	9	1	7	1	0	1	0	0	1	0	0
VAN GOBBEL	2	1	1	0	1	0	0	0	0	0	0	0
WARNER	1	0	1	2	0	0	0	0	0	0	0	0
WILLIAMS	20	3	17	7	2	0	2	0	1	3	0	0
Own Goals						2						

Jones the Success

The appointment of Dave Jones as manager of Southampton was a bold move by the Saints and flies in the face of present day appointments in the Premiership which tend to veer towards either overseas coaches or top line foreign players being given their head for the first time. Jones had done an outstanding job in two years as manager of Stockport and brought with him two players from his former club – goalkeeper Paul Jones and defender Lee Todd. Paul Jones was a great success as was striker Kevin Davies who joined the Saints at a cost of £700,000 from Chesterfield and left a year later to join Blackburn in a £7.5m deal. Davies scored 12 times in his one season at the Dell despite being hampered by injury. Jones further increased his squad during the season and opted for more Premiership experience when spending £4.5m on bringing in Carlton Palmer, David Hirst and John Beresford. The books were balanced with Jones releasing ten players before the season was out.

Being amongst the favourites to struggle, Southampton gave the bookies plenty to smile about when kicking off the season with three defeats although two of them were against Manchester United and Arsenal. Neil Maddison celebrated his tenth season with the Saints by scoring their only goal of the season but by then they were on the path to the Arsenal defeat. Davies' first goal clinched victory over Crystal Palace but by the time Derby won 4-0 at Pride Park, Southampton had played nine games and collected just four points. Not surprisingly they were at the foot of the table. The return of Matt Le Tissier after breaking his arm during pre-season was instrumental in the Saints edging above Barnsley a week later with a 3-0 win over West Ham. A defeat at Blackburn was followed by Hirst scoring twice on his home debut during a 3-2 win over Tottenham. Further wins over Everton and Barnsley lifted the Saints to 13th.

A run of three more defeats sent Southampton slipping back into trouble before three wins and three draws carried them to the safe sanctuary of mid table. Two of those wins were high points in Southampton's season with Davies getting the winner at home to both Chelsea and Manchester United. In the other success, against Leicester, Francis Benali finally scored his first goal for the club after 11 years on their books. Arsenal cut short the celebrations with a 3-0 win to put the brakes on the climb but immediately the Saints hit back with two late Hirst goals pulling off a magnificent 3-2 win at Liverpool. A home defeat by Coventry ensued but another three successes raised the possibility of qualifying for Europe before the season ended on the back of two wins in nine games. During the final ten games Le Tissier confirmed his return to form with seven goals.

Derby County relished the visit of Southampton in the 3rd Round of the FA Cup and duly beat the Saints for the third time during the season, all without conceding a goal. The Saints fared better in the Coca-Cola Cup, kicking off with victory in both legs of a 2nd Round clash with Brentford. Davies' late strike took them past Barnsley but Chelsea was a Stamford Bridge too far in the 4th Round as the Saints went down 2-1 in extra-time. ■

Results 1997-98

Date	Opponents	Ven	Res	Atten	Scorers
08-Aug	Bolton W.	H	0-1	15,206	
12-Aug	Manchester U.	A	0-1	55,008	
22-Aug	Arsenal	H	1-3	15,246	Maddison (25)
26-Aug	C. Palace	H	1-0	15,032	Davies (57)
29-Aug	Chelsea	A	2-4	30,008	Davies (25); Monkou (59)
12-Sep	Coventry C.	A	0-1	18,659	
19-Sep	Liverpool	H	1-1	15,252	Davies (48)
23-Sep	Leeds U.	H	0-2	15,102	
26-Sep	Derby Co.	A	0-4	25,625	
03-Oct	West Ham U.	H	3-0	15,212	Ostenstad (64); Davies (65); Dodd (69)
17-Oct	Blackburn R.	A	0-1	24,130	
24-Oct	Tottenham H.	H	3-2	15,225	OG (54, Vega); Hirst (67, 79)
01-Nov	Everton	A	2-0	29,565	Le Tissier (24); Davies (54)
07-Nov	Barnsley	H	4-1	15,018	Le Tissier (2); Palmer (5); Davies (35); Hirst (53)
21-Nov	Newcastle U.	A	1-2	36,759	Davies (6)
28-Nov	Sheffield W.	H	2-3	15,442	Hirst (47); Palmer (55)
06-Dec	Wimbledon	A	0-1	12,009	
12-Dec	Leicester C.	H	2-1	15,121	Le Tissier (11); Benali (53)
19-Dec	Aston Villa	A	1-1	29,343	Ostenstad (22)
25-Dec	C. Palace	A	1-1	22,853	Oakley (39)
28-Dec	Chelsea	H	1-0	15,231	Davies (16)
09-Jan	Bolton W.	A	0-0	23,333	
18-Jan	Manchester U.	H	1-0	15,241	Davies (3)
30-Jan	Arsenal	A	0-3	38,056	
06-Feb	Liverpool	A	3-2	43,550	Hirst (8 pen, 90); Ostenstad (85)
17-Feb	Coventry C.	H	1-2	15,091	Le Tissier (79 pen)
20-Feb	Blackburn R.	H	3-0	15,162	Ostenstad (19, 88); Hirst (75)
27-Feb	Leeds U.	A	1-0	28,791	Hirst (54)
06-Mar	Everton	H	2-1	15,102	Le Tissier (69); Ostenstad (86)
13-Mar	Barnsley	A	3-4	18,368	Ostenstad (25); Le Tissier (41, 71)
27-Mar	Newcastle U.	H	2-1	15,251	OG (68, Pearce); Le Tissier (85 pen)
03-Apr	Sheffield W.	A	0-1	29,677	
10-Apr	Wimbledon	H	0-1	14,815	
13-Apr	Leicester C.	A	3-3	20,708	Ostenstad (17, 27); Hirst (49)
17-Apr	Aston Villa	H	1-2	15,238	Le Tissier (19)
24-Apr	West Ham U.	A	4-2	25,878	Le Tissier (39); Ostenstad (63, 85); Palmer (79)

| 01-May | Derby Co. | H | 0-2 | 15,202 | |
| 09-May | Tottenham H. | A | 1-1 | 35,995 | Le Tissier |

FA Challenge Cup

Date	*Opponents*	*Vn*	*Rnd*	*Res*	*Atten*	*Scorers*
03-Jan	Derby Co.	A	3R	0-2	27,992	

Coca-Cola League Cup

Date	*Opponents*	*Vn*	*Rnd*	*Res*	*Atten*	*Scorers*
17-Sep	Brentford	H	2R1L	3-1	8,004	Monkou (37); Davies (60); Evans (69)
30-Sep	Brentford	A	2R2L	2-0	3,957	Le Tissier (31, 44)
	Southampton win 5-1 on aggregate.					
14-Oct	Barnsley	A	3R	2-1	9,019	Le Tissier (15); Davies (88)
19-Nov	Chelsea	A	4R	1-2	20,968	Davies (52)
	aet					

5-Year Record

	Div.	*P*	*W*	*D*	*L*	*F*	*A*	*Pts*	*Pos*	*FAC*	*FLC*
93-94	PL	42	12	7	23	49	66	43	18	3	2
94-95	PL	42	12	18	12	61	63	54	10	5	3
95-96	PL	38	9	11	18	34	52	38	17	QF	4
96-97	PL	38	10	11	17	50	56	41	16	3	QF
97-98	PL	38	14	6	18	50	55	48	12	3	4

Tottenham Hotspur

Formed in 1882 by members of the schoolboys' Hotspur CC as Hotspur FC and had early church connections. Added 'Tottenham' in 1884 to distinguish club from London Hotspur FC. Turned professional in 1895 and elected to the Southern League in 1896 having been rebuffed by the Football League.

Played at two grounds (Tottenham Marshes and Northumberland Park) before moving to the site which became known as White Hart Lane in 1899. Joined the Football League Second Division in 1908. Having failed to gain a place in the re-election voting, they secured a vacancy caused by a late resignation. Premier League founder members 1992.

Ground:	748 High Road, Tottenham, London, N17 0AP		
Phone:	0181-365 5000	**News:** 0891 33 55 55	
Box Office:	0181-365 5050	**Tickets:** 0891 33 55 66	
Capacity:	36,000	**Pitch:** 110 yds x 73 yds	
Colours:	White, Navy Blue, White	**Nickname:** Spurs	
Radio:	1548AM Capital Gold		
Internet:	http://www.spurs.co.uk		

Chairman:	Alan Sugar	**President:** W.E. Nicholson OBE
CEO:	Claude Littner	**Secretary:** Peter Barnes
Manager:	Christian Gross	**Physio:** Tony Lenaghan

League History: 1908 Elected to Division 2; 1909-15 Division 1; 1919-20 Division 2; 1920-28 Division 1; 1928-33 Division 2; 1933-35 Division 1; 1935-50 Division 2; 1950-77 Division 1; 1977-78 Division 2; 1978-92 Division 1; 1992- FA Premier League.

Honours: *Football League: Division 1 Champions* 1950-51, 1960-61; *Runners-up* 1921-22, 1951-52, 1956-57, 1962-63; *Division 2 Champions* 1919-20, 1949-50; *Runners-up* 1908-09, 1932-33. *FA Cup: Winners* 1900-01, 1920-21, 1960-61, 1961-62, 1966-67, 1980-81, 1981-82, 1990-91; *Runners-up* 1986-87. *Football League Cup: Winners* 1970-71, 1972-73; *Runners-up* 1981-82; *Cup-Winners' Cup: Winners* 1962-63; *Runners-up:* 1981-82. *UEFA Cup: Winners* 1971-72, 1983-84; *Runners-up:* 1973-74.

European Record: CC (1): 61-62 (SF); CWC (6): 62-63 (W), 63-64 (2), 67-68 (2), 81-82 (SF), 82-83 (2), 91-92 (QF). UEFA (5): 71-72 (W), 72-73 (SF), 73-74 (F), 83-84 (W), 84-85 (QF).

Managers: Frank Brettell 1898-99; John Cameron 1899-1907; Fred Kirkham 1907-08; Peter McWilliam 1912-27; Billy Minter 1927-29; Percy Smith 1930-35; Jack Tresadern 1935-38; Peter McWilliam 1938-42; Arthur Turner 1942-46; Joe Hulme 1946-49; Arthur Rowe 1949-55; Jimmy Anderson 1955-58; Bill Nicholson 1958-74; Terry Neill 1974-76; Keith Burkinshaw 1976-84; Peter Shreeves 1984-86; David Pleat 1986-87; Terry Venables 1987-91; Peter Shreeves 1991-92; *(FAPL)* Doug Livermore 1992-June 93; Ossie Ardiles June 1993-Nov 94; Gerry Francis Nov 94-Nov 97; Christian Gross Nov 97-.

Season 1997-98

Biggest Home Win:	3-0 v Barnsley
Biggest Home Defeat:	1-6 v Chelsea
Biggest Away Win:	6-2 v Wimbledon
Biggest Away Defeat:	0-4 v Coventry C. and Liverpool
Biggest Home Att:	35,847 v Newcastle United
Smallest Home Att:	25,097 v Sheffield Wednesday
Average Attendance:	29,144
Leading Scorer:	Jurgen Klinsmann – 9

All-Time Records

Record FAPL Win:	6-2 v Wimbledon, 2/5/98
	5-0 v Oldham Athletic, 18/9/93
Record FAPL Defeat:	1-7 v Newcastle United, 28/12/96
Record FL Win:	9-0 v Bristol Rovers, Division 2, 22/10/77
Record FL Defeat:	0-7 v Liverpool, Division 1, 2/9/1978
Record Cup Win:	13-2 v Crewe Alex., FA Cup, R4 replay, 3/2/60
Record Fee Received:	£5.5m from Lazio for Paul Gascoigne, 5/92
Record Fee Paid:	£6.0m to Newcastle Utd for Les Ferdinand, 7/97
Most FL Apps:	Steve Perryman, 655, 1969-86
Most FAPL Apps:	172 – Ian Walker, 1992-98
Most FAPL Goals:	76 – Teddy Sheringham, 1992-97
Highest Scorer in FAPL Season:	Jurgen Klinsmann, 24, 1994-95
Record Attendance (all-time):	75,038 v Sunderland, FA Cup R6, 5/3/38
Record Attendance (FAPL):	33,709 v Arsenal, 12/12/92
Most FAPL Goals in Season:	66, 1994-95 – 42 games
Most FAPL Points in Season:	62, 1994-95 – 42 games

Summary 1997-98

Player	Tot	St	Sb	Snu	PS	Gls	Y	R	Fa	La	Fg	Lg
ALLEN	4	1	3	2	1	0	0	0	0	0	0	0
ANDERTON	15	7	8	1	5	0	0	0	0	0	0	0
ARBER	0	0	0	2	0	0	0	0	0	0	0	0
ARMSTRONG	19	13	6	2	5	5	2	0	1	2	0	1
AUSTIN	0	0	0	0	0	0	0	0	0	0	0	0
BAARDSEN	9	9	0	26	0	0	0	0	3	0	0	0
BERTI	17	17	0	0	5	3	5	0	2	0	0	0
BRADY	9	0	9	0	0	0	0	0	0	0	0	0
BROWN	0	0	0	2	0	0	0	0	0	0	0	0
CALDERWOOD	26	21	5	10	5	4	3	0	2	2	1	0
CAMPBELL	34	34	0	0	2	0	5	0	3	3	1	0
CARR	38	37	1	0	3	0	2	0	3	2	0	0
CLAPHAM	0	0	0	1	0	0	0	0	0	0	0	0
CLEMENCE	17	12	5	5	3	0	1	0	2	2	1	0
DOMINGUEZ	18	8	10	3	2	2	4	0	1	3	0	0
EDINBURGH	16	13	3	0	5	0	4	1	0	2	0	0
FENN	4	0	4	2	1	0	0	0	0	1	0	1
FERDINAND	21	19	2	0	7	5	2	0	2	1	0	0
FOX	32	32	0	3	9	3	3	0	2	3	0	1
GAIN	0	0	0	1	0	0	0	0	0	0	0	0
GINOLA	34	34	0	0	7	6	7	0	3	3	1	2
GRODAS	0	0	0	10	0	0	0	0	0	0	0	0
HOWELLS	20	14	6	0	2	0	3	0	1	1	0	0
IVERSEN	13	8	5	0	2	0	1	0	0	0	0	0
KLINSMANN	15	15	0	0	2	9	1	0	3	0	0	0
MABBUTT	11	8	3	11	0	0	1	0	0	1	0	0
MAHORN	2	2	0	1	2	0	0	0	1	1	0	1
McVEIGH	0	0	0	0	0	0	0	0	0	0	0	0
NIELSEN	25	21	4	6	4	3	2	0	0	1	0	0
SAIB	9	3	6	0	1	1	0	0	0	0	0	0
SCALES	10	9	1	9	1	0	1	0	0	2	0	0
SINTON	19	14	5	2	6	0	1	0	1	1	0	0
VEGA	25	22	3	0	0	3	4	1	3	2	0	0
WALKER	29	29	0	0	0	0	0	0	0	1	3	0
WILSON	16	16	0	1	7	0	1	0	3	0	0	0
Own Goals						0					1	0

Only four subs named in away game at Newcastle United.

Ginola the Saviour

After a disappointing campaign in 1996/97, Tottenham supporters were stunned to learn of the departure of Teddy Sheringham to Manchester United for just £3.5m and that Spurs paid almost double for his replacement, Les Ferdinand, caused further consternation. Also moving south from Tyneside was David Ginola, whose genius shone in an otherwise dire season. Ferdinand began the season promisingly with three goals in four games but when he joined long-term injury victim Chris Armstrong on the sick list, Spurs struggled for goals.

Opening the season against Manchester United was probably not quite what Spurs wanted and they duly went down 2-0 at White Hart Lane despite Sheringham missing a penalty. Another defeat at West Ham followed before successive home wins over Derby and Villa eased the early tension. But that was as good as it got and the pressure on Francis grew quickly. With just one success from their next 11 Premiership games, Spurs were heading down the table at pace and the end came for Francis when he resigned on 19 November following three successive defeats, the last being a 4-0 thrashing at Liverpool.

New manager Christian Gross was given as rough a baptism as any with Tottenham, against Crystal Palace, going down to the second of three successive home defeats. Gross looked to be getting the ship back on an even keel with victory at fellow strugglers Everton only for Chelsea, after being stretched at times in the first half, to hand the club its heaviest home defeat since 1935 with a 6-1 thrashing. Again Spurs performed reasonably well in their next game but still suffered a 4-0 drubbing at Coventry. Gross looked abroad for salvation and found it in the form of fans' favourite Jurgen Klinsmann, who was having a none too happy time in Italy.

But only one more win was achieved before the end of the year, with Barnsley being despatched 3-0 at White Hart Lane, and that was just one of two successes in 11 Premiership games as Spurs slipped into the relegation zone. Gross, according to the press, was living on borrowed time almost from day one and the glowing reviews heaped on neighbours Arsenal did little to appease the Spurs faithful. Klinsmann struggled early on but the news did get better as Armstrong, Ferdinand and even Darren Anderton returned from injury. With Ginola finding his touch, Spurs went on a run of one defeat in five games before another four-match winless run in April plunged them back into trouble. D-Day for Tottenham came at Barnsley on 18 April. Defeat would almost certainly have precipitated relegation but, despite having Ramon Vega dismissed, Gross's side gained a draw through a Colin Calderwood goal and suddenly the pressure seemed to ease. One week later a fine performance secured a vital 2-0 win over Newcastle before safety was secured on the back of four Klinsmann goals during a 6-2 slaughter of Wimbledon at Selhurst Park.

Tottenham's cup form was equally unimpressive. After struggling to put out Carlisle United in the Coca-Cola Cup, a home defeat was suffered against Derby County. Some bizarre goalkeeping by Fulham's Maik Taylor contributed to Tottenham surviving one round of the FA Cup before being put out in a storming replay at Barnsley. The close season saw the departure of the long-serving Gary Mabbutt and David Howells. ∎

Results 1997-98

Date	Opponents	Ven	Res	Atten	Scorers
09-Aug	Manchester U.	H	0-2	26,359	
12-Aug	West Ham U.	A	1-2	25,354	Ferdinand (81)
22-Aug	Derby Co.	H	1-0	25,886	Calderwood (45)
26-Aug	Aston Villa	H	3-2	26,317	Ferdinand (15, 66); Fox (77)
29-Aug	Arsenal	A	0-0	38,102	
12-Sep	Leicester C.	A	0-3	20,683	
19-Sep	Blackburn R.	H	0-0	26,573	
22-Sep	Bolton W.	A	1-1	23,433	Armstrong (71)
26-Sep	Newcastle U.	A	0-1	36,609	
03-Oct	Wimbledon	H	0-0	26,261	
17-Oct	Sheffield W.	H	3-2	25,097	Ginola (45); Dominguez (6); Armstrong (39)
24-Oct	Southampton	A	2-3	15,255	Dominguez (41); Ginola (54)
31-Oct	Leeds U.	A	0-1	26,441	
07-Nov	Liverpool	A	0-4	38,006	
23-Nov	C. Palace	H	0-1	25,634	
28-Nov	Everton	A	2-0	36,670	Vega (71); Ginola (75)
05-Dec	Chelsea	H	1-6	28,476	Vega (43)
12-Dec	Coventry C.	A	0-4	19,499	
19-Dec	Barnsley	H	3-0	28,232	Nielson (5); Ginola (11, 17)
25-Dec	Aston Villa	A	1-4	38,644	Calderwood (59)
27-Dec	Arsenal	H	1-1	29,610	Nielson (28)
09-Jan	Manchester U.	A	0-2	55,281	
16-Jan	West Ham U.	H	1-0	30,284	Klinsmann (7)
30-Jan	Derby Co.	A	1-2	30,187	Fox (46)
06-Feb	Blackburn R.	A	3-0	30,388	Berti (37); Armstrong (89); Fox (90)
13-Feb	Leicester C.	H	1-1	28,355	Calderwood (51)
20-Feb	Sheffield W.	A	0-1	29,871	
28-Feb	Bolton W.	H	1-0	29,032	Nielsen (45)
03-Mar	Leeds U.	A	0-1	31,394	
13-Mar	Liverpool	H	3-3	30,245	Klinsmann (12); Ginola (48); Vega (80)
27-Mar	C. Palace	A	3-1	26,116	Berti (55); Armstrong (72); Klinsmann (77)
03-Apr	Everton	H	1-1	35,624	Armstrong (73)
10-Apr	Chelsea	A	0-2	34,149	
12-Apr	Coventry C.	H	1-1	33,463	Berti (68)
17-Apr	Barnsley	A	1-1	18,692	Calderwood (47)
24-Apr	Newcastle U.	H	2-0	35,847	Klinsmann (31); Ferdinand (72)

| 01-May | Wimbledon | A | 6-2 | 25,820 | Ferdinand (17); Klinsmann (41, 54, 58, 60); Saib (79) |
| 09-May | Southampton | H | 1-1 | 35,995 | Klinsmann (27) |

FA Challenge Cup

Date	Opponents	Vn	Rnd	Res	Atten	Scorers
05-Jan	Fulham	H	3R	3-1	27,909	Clemence (20); Calderwood (28); OG (62 Taylor)
24-Jan	Barnsley	H	4R	1-1	28,722	Campbell (30)
04-Feb	Barnsley	A	4RR	1-3	18,220	Ginola (72)

Coca-Cola League Cup

Date	Opponents	Vn	Rnd	Res	Atten	Scorers
17-Sep	Carlisle Utd	H	2R1L	3-2	19,255	Fenn (1); Fox (73); Mahorn (78)
30-Sep	Carlisle Utd	A	2R2L	2-0	13,571	Ginola (43 pen); Armstrong (51)
	Tottenham H. win 5-2 on aggregate					
15-Oct	Derby Co.	H	3R	1-2	20,390	Ginola (22)

5-Year Record

	Div.	P	W	D	L	F	A	Pts	Pos	FAC	FLC
93-94	PL	42	11	12	19	54	59	45	15	4	5
94-95	PL	42	16	14	12	66	58	62	7	SF	3
95-96	PL	38	16	13	9	50	38	61	8	5	3
96-97	PL	38	13	7	18	44	51	46	10	3	4
97-98	PL	38	11	11	16	44	56	44	14	4	3

West Ham United

Thames Ironworks founded 1895, to give recreation for the shipyard workers. Several different grounds were used as the club entered the London League (1896) and won the championship (1898). In 1899, having become professional, won the Southern League Second Division (London) and moved into Division One.

On becoming a limited liability company the name was changed to West Ham United. Moved from the Memorial Ground to a pitch in the Upton Park area, known originally as 'The Castle', in 1904. Elected to an expanded Football League Division Two for the 1919-20 season and never subsequently out of the top two divisions.

Ground: Boleyn Ground, Green Street, Upton Park, London E13 9AZ
Phone: 0181-548 2748   **News:** 0891 12 11 65
Box Office: 0181-548 2700
Capacity: 25,985   **Pitch:** 112 yds x 72 yds
Colours: Claret, White, White   **Nickname:** The Hammers
Radio: 1548AM Capital Gold
Internet: http://westhamunited.co.uk

Chairman: Terence Brown   **Vice-Chairman:** Martin Cearns
CEO/DOF: Peter Storrie
Manager: Harry Redknapp   **Assistant:** Frank Lampard
First Team Coaches: Paul Hilton, Tony Carr
Physios: John Green and Josh Collins

League History: 1919 Elected to Division 2; 1923-32 Division 1; 1932-58 Division 2; 1958-78 Division 1; 1978-81 Division 2; 1981-89 Division 1; 1989-91 Division 2; 1991-1993 Division 2; 1993- FA Premier League.

Honours: *Football League: Division 1 Runners-up* 1992-93; *Division 2 Champions* 1957-58, 1980-81; *Runners-up* 1922-23, 1990-91. *FA Cup: Winners* 1964, 1975, 1980; *Runners-up* 1922-23. *Football League Cup: Runners-up* 1966, 1981. *Cup-Winners' Cup: Winners* 1964-65; *Runners-up* 1975-76.

European Record: CC (0): –; CWC (4): 64-65 (W), 65-66 (SF), 75-76 (F), 80-81 (QF); UEFA (0): –.

Managers: Syd King 1902-32; Charlie Paynter 1932-50; Ted Fenton 1950-61; Ron Greenwood 1961-74 (continued as GM to 1977); John Lyall 1974-

89; Lou Macari 1989-90; *(FAPL)* Billy Bonds Feb 1990-Aug 1994; Harry Redknapp Aug 1994-.

Season 1997-98

Biggest Home Win:	6-0 v Barnsley
Biggest Home Defeat:	0-1 v Newcastle United
Biggest Away Win:	2-1 v Barnsley and Wimbledon
Biggest Away Defeat:	0-5 v Liverpool
Biggest Home Att:	25,908 v Liverpool and Southampton
Smallest Home Att:	22,477 v Coventry City
Average Attendance:	24,969
Leading Scorer:	John Hartson – 15

All-Time Records

Record FAPL Win:	6-0 v Barnsley, 10/1/98
Record FAPL Defeat:	0-5 v Sheffield Wednesday, 18/12/93
Record FL Win:	8-0 v Rotherham United, Division 2, 8/3/58
	Sunderland, Division 1, 19/10/68
Record FL Defeat:	2-8 v Blackburn Rovers, Division 1, 26/12/63
Record Cup Win:	10-0 v Bury, League Cup, R2 2nd leg, 25/10/83
Record Fee Received:	£4.5m from Everton for Slaven Bilic, 5/97
Record Fee Paid:	£3.2m > £5m to Arsenal for John Hartson, 3/97
Most Apps:	Billy Bonds, 663, 1967-88
Most FAPL Apps:	169 – Ludek Miklosko, 1992-98
Most FAPL Goals:	51 – Tony Cottee, 1992-97

Highest Scorer in FAPL Season: John Hartson, 15, 1997-98
Record Attendance (all-time): 42,322 v Tottenham H., Div 1, 17/10/70
Record Attendance (FAPL): 28,832 v Manchester United, 26/2/94
Most FAPL Goals in Season: 56, 1997-98 – 38 games
Most FAPL Points in Season: 56, 1997-98 – 38 games

Player	Tot	St	Sb	Snu	PS	Gls	Y	R	Fa	La	Fg	Lg
ABOU	19	12	7	4	6	5	1	1	5	2	0	1
ALEXANDER	0	0	0	1	0	0	0	0	0	0	0	0
ALVES	4	0	4	4	0	0	0	0	0	0	0	0
BERKOVIC	35	34	1	1	12	7	2	0	6	5	2	0
BERTHE	0	0	0	5	0	0	0	0	0	0	0	0
BISHOP	3	3	0	12	0	0	0	0	0	1	0	0
BREACKER	19	18	1	1	5	0	3	0	3	4	0	0
COYNE	0	0	0	7	0	0	0	0	0	0	0	0
DOWIE	12	7	5	6	1	0	2	0	1	3	0	0
FERDINAND	35	35	0	0	1	0	3	0	6	5	0	0
FINN	0	0	0	1	0	0	0	0	0	0	0	0
FORREST	13	13	0	21	0	0	0	0	4	3	0	0
HARTSON	32	32	0	0	1	15	4	2	5	5	3	6
HODGES	2	0	2	11	0	0	0	0	3	0	0	0
HUGHES	5	2	3	2	0	0	1	0	0	1	0	0
IMPEY	19	19	0	1	5	0	0	0	3	3	0	0
KEITH	0	0	0	1	0	0	0	0	0	0	0	0
KITSON	13	12	1	1	7	4	1	0	2	2	1	0
LAMA	12	12	0	6	0	0	1	0	2	0	0	0
LAMPARD	31	27	4	2	0	4	5	0	6	5	1	4
LAZARIDIS	28	27	1	0	3	2	2	0	6	1	0	0
LOMAS	33	33	0	0	0	2	6	1	5	4	1	0
MEAN	3	0	3	11	0	0	0	0	0	0	0	0
MIKLOSKO	13	13	0	0	0	0	0	0	0	2	0	0
MONCUR	20	17	3	1	5	1	7	0	3	1	0	0
MOORE	1	0	1	2	0	0	0	0	0	0	0	0
OMOYIMNI	5	1	4	2	0	2	0	0	0	0	0	0
PEARCE	30	30	0	1	1	1	1	0	6	3	1	0
POTTS	23	14	9	12	2	0	2	0	5	4	0	0
RIEPER	5	5	0	0	1	0	1	0	0	0	0	0
ROWLAND	7	6	1	11	0	0	0	0	0	2	0	0
SEALEY	0	0	0	10	0	0	0	0	0	0	0	0
SINCLAIR	14	14	0	0	1	7	5	0	6	5	0	0
TERRIER	1	0	1	2	0	0	0	0	0	0	0	0
UNSWORTH	32	32	0	0	1	2	8	1	4	5	0	0
Own Goals						3						

54·5

Hammers' Promise Shows

West Ham United's most successful season of the five years the club has spent in the Premiership was based upon something which the Hammers have not been graced with for many years – a formidable home record. Only Arsenal won more home games but at the end of the season it was poor away form which cost the Hammers the chance of playing in Europe after a 17-year absence.

Manager Harry Redknapp brought in Eyal Berkovic, Andy Impey and Craig Forrest at a cost of almost £3.5m and added David Unsworth three days into the season for a further £1m. In October Ian Pearce was snapped up for £1.6m and after the turn of the year more attacking flair was brought to the side with the £2.3m signing of Trevor Sinclair. With the sale of Slaven Bilic, all Redknapp's summer outgoings were covered in one transfer.

Redknapp had been criticised for seemingly paying over the odds during the previous season for John Hartson, but the Welsh international scored in wins over Barnsley and Tottenham as West Ham won their opening two games for the first time in 11 years. Hartson ended the season as second only to Andy Cole in the league and cup goalscoring stakes. But for disciplinary problems, he could well have reached the 30 mark.

Hopes of building on their promising start were undone to some degree by their away record which saw them lose on nine of the next ten trips away from Upton Park. But at home West Ham were almost unstoppable, with defeat by Newcastle being the only blemish in the first ten home games. Most impressive victories were over Liverpool 2-1, Crystal Palace 4-1 and Barnsley 6-0 during which French youngster Samassi Abou scored his first two goals for the club. A run of eight consecutive away defeats was halted two days after Christmas when the double was completed over Wimbledon and after a defeat at Tottenham the Hammers won their third and last away match with revenge over Newcastle. UEFA Cup qualification was a genuine possibility even up until the last day of the season but a run of one win in seven games during April and May dented their prospects. A 4-2 home defeat by Southampton made qualification unlikely but the season had an amazing finale with Hammers supporters seeing 24 goals in just four games.

In the FA Cup West Ham had an almighty struggle in putting out non-league side Emley before winning 2-1 at Manchester City from a goal down. In the 5th Round Blackburn gained a draw at Upton Park and, despite being on the rack for most of the replay, West Ham took the game into extra-time before winning a penalty shoot-out. Such good fortune was not on their side in the 6th Round as, at the end of two 1-1 draws with Arsenal, it was the Gunners who won the dreaded shoot-out.

After a 2nd Round 1st Leg defeat at Huddersfield in the Coca-Cola Cup, a Hartson hat-trick put the record straight and Hartson added a brace during an impressive 3-0 3rd Round victory over Aston Villa. Frank Lampard joined in the goal rush with a treble in a 4-1 win over Walsall, but as with the FA Cup it was Arsenal, at Upton Park, who terminated the Hammers' Wembley bid with a 2-1 win. ∎

Results 1997-98

FA Carling Premiership

Date	Opponents	Ven	Res	Atten	Scorers
08-Aug	Barnsley	A	2-1	18,667	Hartson (56); Lampard (77)
12-Aug	Tottenham H.	H	2-1	25,354	Hartson (3); Berkovic (70)
22-Aug	Everton	A	1-2	34,356	OG (23, Watson)
26-Aug	Coventry C.	A	1-1	18,289	Kitson (64)
29-Aug	Wimbledon	H	3-1	24,516	Hartson (47); Rieper (54); Berkovic (55)
12-Sep	Manchester U.	A	1-2	55,068	Hartson (14)
19-Sep	Newcastle U.	H	0-1	25,884	
23-Sep	Arsenal	A	0-4	38,012	
26-Sep	Liverpool	H	2-1	25,908	Hartson (14); Berkovic (64)
03-Oct	Southampton	A	0-3	15,212	
17-Oct	Bolton W.	H	3-0	24,867	Berkovic (69); Hartson (78, 89)
26-Oct	Leicester C.	A	1-2	20,201	Berkovic (58)
08-Nov	Chelsea	A	1-2	34,382	Hartson (84 pen)
22-Nov	Leeds U.	A	1-3	30,031	Lampard (65)
28-Nov	Aston Villa	H	2-1	24,976	Hartson (18, 47)
02-Dec	C. Palace	H	4-1	23,335	Hartson (30); Berkovic (45); Unsworth (47); Lomas (71)
05-Dec	Derby Co.	A	0-2	29,300	
12-Dec	Sheffield W.	H	1-0	24,344	Kitson (69)
19-Dec	Blackburn R.	A	0-3	21,653	
25-Dec	Coventry C.	H	1-0	22,477	Kitson (17)
27-Dec	Wimbledon	A	2-1	22,087	OG (30, Kimble); Kitson (54)
09-Jan	Barnsley	H	6-0	23,714	Lampard (5); Abou (28, 52); Moncur (57); Hartson (45); Lazaridis (89)
16-Jan	Tottenham H.	A	0-1	30,284	
30-Jan	Everton	H	2-2	25,905	Sinclair (9, 47)
06-Feb	Newcastle U.	A	1-0	36,736	Lazaridis (16)
20-Feb	Bolton W.	H	1-1	25,000	Sinclair (66)
01-Mar	Arsenal	H	0-0	25,717	
10-Mar	Manchester U.	H	1-1	25,892	Sinclair (6)
13-Mar	Chelsea	H	2-1	25,829	Sinclair (67); Unsworth (73)
29-Mar	Leeds U.	H	3-0	24,107	Hartson (7); Abou (22); Pearce (68)
03-Apr	Aston Villa	A	0-2	39,372	
10-Apr	Derby	H	0-0	25,155	
12-Apr	Sheffield W.	A	1-1	28,036	Berkovic (7)
17-Apr	Blackburn R.	H	2-1	24,733	Hartson (6, 26)
24-Apr	Southampton	H	2-4	25,878	Sinclair (41); Lomas (82)
01-May	Liverpool	A	0-5	44,414	

| 04-May | C. Palace | A | 3-3 | 19,129 | OG (4, Curcic); Omoyimni (68, 89) |
| 09-May | Leicester C. | H | 4-3 | 25,781 | Lampard (15); Abou (31, 74); Sinclair (65) |

FA Challenge Cup

Date	Opponents	Vn	Rnd	Res	Atten	Scorers
03-Jan	Emley	H	3R	2-1	18,629	Lampard (4); Hartson (82)
25-Jan	Man. City	A	4R	2-1	26,495	Berkovic (28); Lomas (76)
14-Feb	Blackburn R.	H	5R	2-2	25,729	Kitson (26); Berkovic (44)
25-Feb	Blackburn R.	A	5RR	1-1	21,972	Hartson (103)
	aet. West Ham win 5-4 on penalties					
08-Mar	Arsenal	A	6R	1-1	38,077	Pearce (12)
17-Mar	Arsenal	H	6RR	1-1	25,859	Hartson (84)
	aet. Arsenal win 4-3 on penalties					

Coca-Cola League Cup

Date	Opponents	Vn	Rnd	Res	Atten	Scorers
16-Sep	Huddersfield	A	2R1L	0-1	8,525	
	Huddersfield	H	2R2L	3-0	16,137	Hartson (31, 45, 77)
	West Ham Utd win 3-1 on aggregate					
15-Oct	Aston Villa	H	3R	3-0	20,360	Hartson (9, 81), Lampard (17)
19-Nov	Walsall	H	4R	4-1	17,463	Lampard (15, 73, 74); Hartson (15)
06-Jan	Arsenal	H	QF	1-2	24,770	Abou (75)

5-Year Record

	Div.	P	W	D	L	F	A	Pts	Pos	FAC	FLC
93-94	PL	42	13	13	16	47	58	52	13	6	3
94-95	PL	42	13	11	18	44	48	50	14	4	4
95-96	PL	38	14	9	15	43	52	51	10	4	3
96-97	PL	38	10	12	16	39	48	42	14	3	4
97-98	PL	38	16	8	14	56	57	56	8	6	QF

Wimbledon

Founded 1889 as Wimbledon Old Centrals, an old boys' side of the Central School playing on Wimbledon Common. Member of the Southern Suburban League, the name was changed to Wimbledon in 1905. Moved to Plough Lane in 1912. Athenian League member for two seasons before joining the Isthmian League in 1921.

FA Amateur Cup winners 1963 and seven times Isthmian League champions. Turned professional in 1965, joining the Southern League, of which they were champions three times before being elected to Football League Division Four in 1977. Started ground sharing at Selhurst Park in 1991 and founder member of the Premier League 1992.

Ground: Selhurst Park, South Norwood, London SE25 6PY
Phone: 0181-771 2233   **News:** 0891 12 11 75
Box Office: 0181-771 8841
Colours: All Blue with Yellow trim   **Nickname:** The Dons
Capacity: 26,995   **Pitch:** 110 yds x 74 yds
Radio: 1548AM Capital Gold
Internet: –

Chairman: S. G. Reed   **Vice-Chairman:** J. Lelliott
Owner: Sam Hamman   **CEO:** David Barnard
Secretary: Steve Rooke
Manager: Joe Kinnear   **Tech Director:** Terry Burton
Coaches: Terry Lawrie Sanchez, David Kemp, Mick Harford
Physio: Steve Allen

League History: 1977 Elected to Division 4; 1979-80 Division 3; 1980-81 Division 4; 1981-82 Division 3; 1982-83 Division 4; 1983-84 Division 3; 1984-86 Division 2; 1986-92 Division 1; 1992- FA Premier League.

Honours: *Football League: Division 3 Runners-up 1983-84; Division 4 Champions 1982-83. FA Cup: Winners 1987-88. FA Amateur Cup: Winners* 1963.

European Record: Never qualified. InterToto Cup (1995).

Managers: Les Henley 1955-71; Mike Everitt 1971-73; Dick Graham 1973-74; Allen Batsford 1974-78; Dario Gradi 1978-81; Dave Bassett 1981-87; Bobby Gould 1987-90; Ray Harford 1990-91; Peter Withe 1991; *(FAPL)* Joe Kinnear January 1992-.

Season 1997-98

Biggest Home Win:	4-1 v Barnsley
Biggest Home Defeat:	2-6 v Tottenham Hotspur
Biggest Away Win:	3-0 v Crystal Palace
Biggest Away Defeat:	0-5 v Wimbledon
Biggest Home Att:	26,309 v Manchester United
Smallest Home Att:	7,976 v Barnsley
Average Attendance:	16,683
Leading Scorer:	Cort, Ekoku, Euell, M.Hughes, Leaburn – 4 each

All-Time Records

Record FAPL Win:	4-0 v Crystal Palace, 9/4/93
	4-0 v Everton, 7/9/96
Record FAPL Defeat:	1-7 v Aston Villa, 11/2/95
Record FL Win:	6-0 v Newport County, Division 3, 3/9/83
Record FL Defeat:	0-8 v Everton, League Cup R2, 29/8/78
Record Cup Win:	7-2 v Windsor & Eton, FA Cup R1, 22/11/80
Record Fee Received:	£4.5m from Newcastle for Warren Barton, 6/95
Record Fee Paid:	£2m to Millwall for Ben Thatcher, 7/96
Most FL Apps:	430 – Alan Cork, 1977-92
Most FAPL Apps:	184 – Robbie Earle, 1992-98
Most FAPL Goals:	58 – Dean Holdsworth, 1992-97

Record Scorer in FAPL Season: Dean Holdsworth, 19, 1992-93

Record Attendance (all-time): 30,115 v Manchester United, 8/5/93

Record Attendance (FAPL): 30,115 v Manchester United, 8/5/93

Most FAPL Goals in Season: 56, 1992-93 and 56, 1993-94 – 42 games

Most FAPL Points in Season: 65, 1993-94 – 42 games

Summary 1997-98

Player	Tot	St	Sb	Snu	PS	Gls	Y	R	Fa	La	Fg	Lg
ARDLEY	34	31	3	0	6	2	1	0	5	0	1	0
BLACKWELL	35	35	0	0	2	0	4	0	4	0	0	0
CASTLEDINE	6	3	3	4	1	0	1	0	3	3	0	2
CLARKE	14	1	13	13	0	0	0	0	4	3	0	1
CORT	22	16	6	3	5	4	0	0	5	2	0	2
CUNNINGHAM	32	32	0	0	1	0	2	0	3	3	0	0
EARLE	22	20	2	2	2	3	0	0	3	1	0	0
EKOKU	16	11	5	1	4	4	0	0	1	2	0	0
EUELL	19	14	5	2	10	4	1	0	2	3	1	3
FEAR	8	5	3	2	0	2	2	0	2	1	0	0
FRANCIS	2	0	2	5	0	0	0	0	0	0	0	0
GAYLE	30	21	9	6	13	2	1	0	4	3	1	1
HEALD	0	0	0	38	0	0	0	0	0	2	0	0
HOLDSWORTH	5	4	1	2	4	0	1	0	0	1	0	0
HUGHES, Ceri	17	13	4	8	5	1	1	0	2	2	0	0
HUGHES, M.	29	29	0	1	2	4	7	0	4	0	2	0
JONES	24	22	2	0	5	0	2	0	4	2	1	0
JUPP	3	3	0	5	1	0	1	0	2	1	0	0
KENNEDY	4	4	0	0	2	0	0	0	0	0	0	0
KIMBLE	25	23	2	4	0	0	7	0	3	1	0	0
LEABURN	16	15	1	0	3	4	0	0	0	0	0	0
McALLISTER	7	4	3	7	1	0	0	0	0	3	0	0
PERRY	35	35	0	0	0	1	7	0	5	3	0	0
REEVES	0	0	0	9	0	0	0	0	0	1	0	0
ROBERTS	12	12	0	0	0	1	3	0	0	0	0	0
SOLBAKKEN	6	4	2	5	0	1	1	0	2	0	0	0
SULLIVAN	38	38	0	0	0	0	0	0	5	1	0	0
THATCHER	26	23	3	4	2	0	2	2	3	3	0	0
Own Goals						1						

5-Year Record

	Div.	P	W	D	L	F	A	Pts	Pos	FAC	FLC
93-94	PL	42	18	11	13	56	53	65	6	5	5
94-95	PL	42	15	11	16	48	65	56	9	5	3
95-96	PL	38	10	11	17	55	70	41	14	QF	2
96-97	PL	38	15	11	12	49	46	56	8	SF	SF
97-98	PL	38	10	14	14	34	46	44	15	5	3

Dons Double Heartbreak

Wimbledon started and finished the 1997/98 season poorly but in between did just enough to take their remarkable run in the top flight of English football into a 13th year. Yet again manager Joe Kinnear will not have been in the running for the Manager of the Year Award but the achievements of a club still searching for its own permanent home are a tribute to the former Eire international. Time and again the Dons have been written off but it does look as though Kinnear will need to modify his squad during the close season after ending the campaign with one win in ten games and only scoring in three of those matches.

The Dons made just one summer signing with Ceri Hughes joining from Luton at an eventual cost of £1.15m while £3.5m was collected from Oyvind Leonhardsen's move to Liverpool. Close on that figure was also made from Dean Holdsworth's move to Bolton and in March the notorious Vinnie Jones moved across the capital to QPR for £500,000. Early in the season Kinnear brought in Michael Hughes for £800,000 and as the transfer deadline moved closer he also signed Andy Roberts, Mark Kennedy and Carl Leaburn for a little over £3m.

Wimbledon began the season with three successive home matches. Marcus Gayle and Jason Euell scored in draws with Liverpool and Sheffield Wednesday before Chelsea won 2-0 at Selhurst Park. Defeat at West Ham handed the Dons an early visit to the foot of the table but a fine 3-1 win at Newcastle and, two matches later, a 4-1 home win over Barnsley, gave them breathing space. A draw at Tottenham suggested that Wimbledon were on the way up only for Blackburn to win the next match at Selhurst Park. Indeed the Dons had to wait until February until they won two consecutive matches with a 3-0 win over Crystal Palace and a 2-1 success against Aston Villa. Leaburn scored three times in those two games, having joined the club a month earlier from Charlton where he earned a reputation for being a striker who couldn't score goals. On the flipside, Wimbledon's longest losing run was also just two games while their total of 14 draws was the second highest in the Premiership.

The Dons' run over the last ten games is particularly alarming as they failed to score in seven of the games, drew five of those matches 0-0 and were hammered 5-0 and 6-2 by Arsenal and Spurs. Peter Fear scored two excellent goals against Tottenham, which were his first Premiership goals for the club since December 1994.

Success for Wimbledon is always most likely to come in the cups but, one year after reaching the semi-final of both domestic competitions, the Dons experienced a disappointing time. In the FA Cup Wimbledon came from behind to deservedly win a 3rd Round replay at Wrexham and followed it up with victory at Huddersfield through a Neil Ardley goal. But a third Nationwide League side, Wolves, claimed a Premiership scalp in the 5th Round with a 2-1 replay victory at Molineux. Euell scored three times as Wimbledon hammered Millwall 9-2 on aggregate in the 2nd Round of the Coca-Cola Cup but the party ended there with the Dons going down 2-0 in extra-time at Bolton in the 3rd Round. ■

Results 1997-98

FA Carling Premiership

Date	Opponents	Ven	Res	Atten	Scorers
08-Aug	Liverpool	H	1-1	26,106	Gayle (56)
22-Aug	Sheffield W.	H	1-1	11,503	Euell (17)
25-Aug	Chelsea	H	0-2	22,237	
29-Aug	West Ham U.	A	1-3	24,516	Ekoku (80)
12-Sep	Newcastle U.	A	3-1	36,526	Cort (1); Perry (58); Ekoku (75)
19-Sep	C. Palace	H	0-1	16,747	
22-Sep	Barnsley	H	4-1	7,976	Cort (49); Earle (64); C.Hughes (67); Ekoku (83)
26-Sep	Tottenham H.	A	0-0	26,261	
03-Oct	Blackburn R.	A	0-1	15,600	
17-Oct	Aston Villa	A	2-1	32,087	Earle (39); Cort (62)
21-Oct	Derby Co.	A	1-1	28,595	OG (70, Rowett)
24-Oct	Leeds U.	H	1-0	15,718	Ardley (28)
31-Oct	Coventry C.	H	1-2	11,210	Cort (27)
09-Nov	Leicester C.	A	1-0	18,533	Gayle (50)
21-Nov	Manchester U.	H	2-5	26,309	Ardley (67); M.Hughes (70)
28-Nov	Bolton W.	A	0-1	22,703	
06-Dec	Southampton	H	1-0	12,009	Earle (17)
12-Dec	Everton	A	0-0	28,533	
25-Dec	Chelsea	A	1-1	34,100	M.Hughes (28)
27-Dec	West Ham U.	H	1-2	22,087	Solbakken (89)
09-Jan	Liverpool	A	0-2	38,011	
16-Jan	Derby Co.	H	0-0	13,031	
30-Jan	Sheffield W.	A	1-1	22,655	M.Hughes (21)
08-Feb	C. Palace	A	3-0	14,410	Leaburn (47,51); Euell (57)
20-Feb	Aston Villa	H	2-1	13,131	Euell (10); Leaburn (38)
27-Feb	Barnsley	A	1-2	17,102	Euell (72)
10-Mar	Arsenal	H	0-1	22,291	
13-Mar	Leicester C.	H	2-1	13,229	Roberts (14); M.Hughes (61)
27-Mar	Manchester U.	A	0-2	55,306	
30-Mar	Newcastle U.	H	0-0	15,478	
03-Apr	Bolton W.	H	0-0	11,356	
10-Apr	Southampton	A	1-0	14,815	Leaburn (38)
12-Apr	Everton	H	0-0	15,131	
17-Apr	Arsenal	A	0-5	38,024	
24-Apr	Blackburn R.	A	0-0	24,848	
28-Apr	Coventry C.	A	0-0	17,968	
01-May	Tottenham H.	H	2-6	25,820	Fear (21, 29)
09-May	Leeds U.	A	1-1	38,172	Ekoku (88)

FA Challenge Cup

Date	Opponents	Vn	Rnd	Res	Atten	Scorers
04-Jan	Wrexham	H	3R	0-0	6,349	
13-Jan	Wrexham	A	3RR	3-2	9,539	Hughes (17, 26); Gayle (35)
24-Jan	Huddersfield	A	4R	1-0	14,533	Ardley (62)
14-Feb	Wolverh'n W.	H	5R	1-1	15,322	Euell (14)
25-Feb	Wolverh'n W.	A	5RR	1-2	25,112	Jones (48)

Coca-Cola League Cup

Date	Opponents	Vn	Rnd	Res	Atten	Scorers
16-Sep	Millwall	H	2R1L	5-1	6,949	Cort (23 pen, 79); Clarke (44); Euell (56); Castledine (86)
01-Oct	Millwall	A	2R2L	4-1	3,591	Euell (22, 43), Castledine (47), Gayle (50)
	Wimbledon win 9-2 on aggregate					
14-Oct	Bolton W.	A	3R	0-2	9,875	
	aet					

D1: Barnsley

Formed in 1887 by the Rev. Preedy as Barnsley St Peter, a reflection of the church connection. St Peter was dropped ten years later, a year before Barnsley were elected to the Second Division of the Football League. The early years were unremarkable save the fact that the FA Cup was won in 1912, two years after they had been beaten finalists.

The club remained in the lower reaches of the League, dropping down to the old Fourth Division for three seasons from 1965-68. Division One status was achieved in 1992 and the club completed a remarkable rise into the Premiership at the end of 1997. Relegation followed immediately, however.

Ground:	Oakwell Ground, Barnsley, South Yorkshire, S71 1ET		
Phone:	01226-211211	**Box Office:**	01226-211211
Info:	0891-12 11 52		
Capacity:	19,101	**Pitch:**	110 yds x 75 yds
Colours:	Red, White, Red	**Nickname:**	The Tykes or Reds

President:	A. Raynor JP	**Chairman:**	J. A. Dennis
Secretary:	Michael Spinks (General Manager)		
Manager:	Danny Wilson	**Coach:**	Eric Winstanley
Physio:	Michael Tarmley, Paul Smith		
Internet:	http://www.yorkshire-web.co.uk/bfc/BFC.HTML		

League History: 1898 Elected to Division 2; 1932-34 Division 3N; 1934-38 Division 2; 1938-39 Division 3N; 1946-53 Division 2; 1953-55 Division 3N; 1955-59 Division 2; 1959-65 Division 3; 1965-68 Division 4; 1968-72 Division 3; 1972-79 Division 4; 1979-81 Division 3; 1981-92 Division 2; 1992-1997 Division 1; 1997-98 FAPL; 1998- Division 1.

Honours: Football League: *Division 1 Runners-up 1996-97; Division 3N Champions 1933-34, 1938-39, 1954-55; Runners-up 1953-54; Division 3 Runners-up 1980-81; Division 4 Runners-up 1967-68; Promoted 1978-79. FA Cup: Winners 1911-12; Runners-up 1909-10.*

European Record: Never qualified.

Managers: Arthur Fairclough 1898-1901; John McCartney 1901-04; Arthur Fairclough 1904-12; John Hastie 1912-14; Percy Lewis 1914-19; Peter Sant 1919-33; John Commins 1926-29; Arthur Fairclough 1929-30; Brough Fletcher 1930-37; Angus Seed 1937-53; Tim Ward 1953-60; Johnny Steele 1960-71; John McSeveney 1971-72; Johnny Steele 1972-73; Jim Iley 1973-

78; Allan Clarke 1978-80; Norman Hunter 1980-84; Bobby Collins 1984-85; Allan Clarke 1985-89; Mel Machin 1989-93; Viv Anderson 1993-94; Danny Wilson June 1994-.

Season 1997-98

Biggest Home Win:	4-3 v Southampton
Biggest Home Defeat:	0-6 v Chelsea
Biggest Away Win:	1-0 v Aston Villa, C. Palace, and Liverpool
Biggest Away Defeat:	0-7 v Manchester United
Biggest Home Att:	18,694 v Manchester United
Smallest Home Att:	17,102 v Wimbledon
Average Attendance:	18,443
Leading Scorer:	Neil Redfearn – 10

All-Time Records

Record FAPL Win:	4-3 v Southampton, 14/5/98
Record FAPL Defeat:	0-7 v Manchester United, 25/10/98
Record FL Win:	9-0 v Loughborough Town, Division 2, 28/1/1889
	9-0 v Accrington St, Division 3N, 3/2/34
Record FL Defeat:	0-9 v Notts County, Division 2, 19/11/27
Record Cup Win:	6-0 v Blackpool, FA Cup 1RR, 20/1/10
	6-0 v Peterborough Utd, Lg Cup, 1R2L, 15/9/81
Record Fee Received:	£1.5m from N. Forest for Carl Tiler, 5/91
Record Fee Paid:	£1.5m to Partizan Belgrade for Gjorgi Hristov, 6/97
Most FL Apps:	514, Barry Murphy, 1962-78
Most FAPL Apps:	37 – Neil Redfearn, 1997-98
Most FAPL Goals:	10 – Neil Redfearn, 1997-98

Highest Scorer in FAPL Season: Neil Redfearn, 10, 1997-98
Record Attendance (all-time): 40,255 v Stoke City, FA Cup 5R, 15/2/36
Record Attendance (FAPL): 18,694 v Manchester United, 1997-98
Most FAPL Goals in Season: 37, 1997-98 – 38 games
Most FAPL Points in Season: 35, 1997-98 – 38 games

Player	Tot	St	Sb	Snu	PS	Gls	Y	R	Fa	La	Fg	Lg
APPLEBY	15	13	2	7	5	0	2	0	2	3	0	0
BARNARD	35	33	2	0	2	2	7	1	5	3	2	0
BOSANCIC	17	13	4	7	3	2	8	1	4	0	0	0
BULLOCK, M	33	23	10	4	9	0	3	0	5	2	0	0
BULLOCK, T	0	0	0	2	0	0	0	0	0	0	0	0
DE ZEEUW	26	26	0	1	0	0	6	0	5	2	0	0
EADEN	35	32	3	0	0	0	4	0	5	2	0	0
FJORTOFT	15	12	3	0	9	6	0	0	0	0	0	0
HENDRIE	20	7	13	3	3	1	0	0	4	0	2	0
HRISTOV	23	11	12	10	9	4	3	1	6	3	0	1
JONES, S.	12	12	0	0	5	1	0	0	1	0	2	0
KRIZAN	12	12	0	4	5	0	2	0	1	3	0	0
LEESE	9	8	1	23	0	0	0	0	0	0	0	0
LIDDELL	26	13	13	5	11	1	1	0	5	2	1	2
MARCELLE	20	9	11	11	7	0	0	0	4	2	0	0
MARKSTEDT	7	6	1	2	2	0	2	0	1	0	0	0
McCLARE	0	0	0	1	0	0	0	0	0	0	0	0
MORGAN	11	10	1	1	0	0	3	1	3	0	0	0
MOSES	35	32	3	0	1	0	7	0	6	2	0	0
REDFEARN	37	37	0	0	0	10	2	0	6	3	2	2
SHERIDAN	26	20	6	5	5	0	5	1	4	3	0	1
SHIRTLIFF	4	4	0	0	2	0	1	0	0	1	0	0
TEN HEUVEL	2	0	2	1	0	0	0	0	0	1	0	0
THOMPSON	2	2	0	1	1	0	0	0	0	1	0	0
TINKLER	25	21	4	2	7	2	3	0	2	2	0	0
WARD	29	28	1	0	3	8	5	0	6	3	1	1
WATSON	30	30	0	6	1	0	0	0	6	1	0	0
WILKINSON	5	4	1	1	2	0	0	0	0	0	0	0

5-Year Record

	Div.	P	W	D	L	F	A	Pts	Pos	FAC	FLC
93-94	1	46	16	7	23	55	67	55	18	5	2
94-95	1	46	20	12	14	63	52	72	6	3	2
95-96	1	46	14	18	14	60	66	60	10	3	3
96-97	1	46	22	14	10	76	55	80	2	4	2
97-98	PL	38	10	5	23	37	82	35	19	6	3

Tyketanic Sinks with All Fans

Starting their first ever season in the top flight of English football as just about the hottest favourites ever for relegation, Barnsley were considered as little more than cannon fodder for the big guns. Indeed, defeats of 5-0, 6-0 and 7-0 were suffered, but Barnsley gained the nation's affection for their endearing spirit and the magnificent support of their fans.

Not having the presumed advantage of the large budget of many of the sides in whose company they now mingled, manager Danny Wilson's purchases were modest. During the close season he smashed the club record transfer fee when signing Georgi Hristov for £1.5m and later in the campaign added strikers Ashley Ward and Jan Aage Fjortoft for a little over £2m.

Club captain Neil Redfearn got the Tykes off to a dream start by putting them ahead against West Ham at Oakwell on the first day of the season but the game ended in defeat. Three days later Redfearn clinched Barnsley's first ever points in the Premiership with victory over a Crystal Palace side which had also won promotion the previous season. The writing was very much on the wall following their next match as Vialli scored four times for Chelsea in a 6-0 home defeat but again Barnsley fought back to beat the other promoted side, Bolton. But with just two wins from the next 16 games, Barnsley were anchored to the foot of the table. That run included eight games when three or more goals were conceded with Manchester United and Arsenal helping themselves to seven and six respectively. Amazingly, one of the two wins was at Anfield where Ward's goal ensured the biggest shock league result of the season.

The year closed with a home win over Derby but the first league game of the new year was disastrous as the Tykes went down 6-0 at West Ham. On the final day of February, Barnsley beat Wimbledon 3-1. It was their fifth successive home match without defeat and sparked a run of three straight wins which lifted them to 18th and level on points with Spurs, who sat one place outside the relegation zone. But with a home defeat by Liverpool, which saw Barnsley reduced to just eight men, and reversals against Blackburn and Leeds, their main hope of avoiding the drop was to beat Tottenham on 18 April. Redfearn put Barnsley ahead and Spurs had Vega sent off but that is where Barnsley's season ended. Spurs equalised and the Yorkshire club failed to score in their final three games as the bookies were ultimately proved right. Barnsley's demise was generally greeted with great disappointment as the majority of Premiership fans took them to their heart.

The cup draws, particularly the FA Cup, could have been kinder to a struggling club. In the 3rd Round Bolton lost at Oakwell for a second time while in the 4th Round Barnsley drew at Tottenham before winning a thrilling replay. But it was in the next round they covered themselves in glory with a home replay victory over Manchester United after having a potential match-winning penalty controversially rejected late in the first meeting. Again they were drawn against Premiership opposition in the 6th Round and it was to be one top flight side too many as they bowed out with a 1-0 defeat. After disposing of Chesterfield in the Coca-Cola Cup, Barnsley lost to Premiership opposition in the form of Southampton. ■

Results 1997-98

FA Carling Premiership

Date	Opponents	Ven	Res	Atten	Scorers
08-Aug	West Ham U.	H	1-2	18,667	Redfearn (9)
11-Aug	C. Palace	A	1-0	21,547	Redfearn (56)
23-Aug	Chelsea	H	0-6	18,170	
26-Aug	Bolton W.	H	2-1	18,661	Tinkler (12); Hristov (47)
29-Aug	Derby Co.	A	0-1	27,232	
12-Sep	Aston Villa	H	0-3	18,649	
19-Sep	Everton	A	2-4	32,659	Redfearn (32); Barnard (78)
22-Sep	Wimbledon	A	1-4	7,688	Tinkler (41)
26-Sep	Leicester C.	H	0-2	18,660	
03-Oct	Arsenal	A	0-5	38,049	
19-Oct	Coventry C.	H	2-0	17,463	Ward (11); Redfearn (66 pen)
24-Oct	Manchester U.	A	0-7	55,142	
31-Oct	Blackburn R.	H	1-1	18,665	Bosanacic (79)
07-Nov	Southampton	A	1-4	15,081	Bosanacic (37 pen)
21-Nov	Liverpool	H	1-0	41,011	Ward (35)
28-Nov	Leeds U.	H	2-3	18,690	Liddell (8); Ward (28)
07-Dec	Sheff W.	A	1-2	29,086	Redfearn (29)
12-Dec	Newcastle U.	H	2-2	18,687	Redfearn (9); Hendrie (75)
19-Dec	Tottenham H.	A	0-3	28,232	
25-Dec	Bolton W.	A	1-1	25,000	Hristov (20)
27-Dec	Derby Co.	H	1-0	18,686	Ward (67)
09-Jan	West Ham U.	A	0-6	23,714	
16-Jan	C. Palace	H	1-0	17,819	Ward (26)
30-Jan	Chelsea	A	0-2	34,442	
06-Feb	Everton	H	2-2	18,672	Fjortoft (24); Barnard (63)
20-Feb	Coventry C.	A	0-1	20,265	
27-Feb	Wimbledon	H	2-1	17,102	Fjortoft (25, 63)
10-Mar	Aston Villa	A	1-0	29,519	Ward (17)
13-Mar	Southampton	H	4-3	18,368	Ward (17); S. Jones (32); Fjortoft (42); Redfearn (57 pen)
27-Mar	Liverpool	H	2-3	18,684	Redfearn (37, 85 pen)
30-Mar	Blackburn R.	A	1-2	24,179	Hristov (68)
03-Apr	Leeds U.	A	1-2	37,749	Hristov (44)
10-Apr	Sheffield W.	H	2-1	18,692	Ward (65); Fjortoft (71)
12-Apr	Newcastle U.	A	1-2	36,534	Fjortoft (50)
17-Apr	Tottenham H.	H	1-1	18,692	Redfearn (19)
24-Apr	Arsenal	H	0-2	18,691	
01-May	Leicester C.	A	0-1	21,293	
09-May	Man Utd	H	0-2	18,694	

FA Challenge Cup

Sponsored by Littlewoods Pools

Date	Opponents	Vn	Rnd	Res	Atten	Scorers
03-Jan	Bolton W.	H	3R	1-0	15,042	Barnard (26)
24-Jan	Tottenham H.	A	4R	1-1	28,722	Redfearn (59 pen)
04-Feb	Tottenham H.	H	4RR	3-1	18,220	Ward (50); Redfearn (58); Barnard (88)
15-Feb	Man. Utd	A	5R	1-1	54,700	Hendrie (38)
25-Feb	Man. Utd	H	5RR	3-2	18,655	Hendrie (9); Jones (45, 65)
08-Mar	Newcastle Utd	A	6R	1-3	36,695	Liddell (57)

Coca-Cola League Cup

Date	Opponents	Vn	Rnd	Res	Atten	Scorers
16-Sep	Chesterfield	A	2R1L	2-1	6,318	Redfearn (87 pen); Ward (90)
30-Sep	Chesterfield	H	2R2L	4-1	8,417	Liddell (37); Redfearn (44); Sheridan (55); Hristov (84)
	Barnsley won 6-2 on aggregate					
14-Oct	Southampton	H	3R	1-2	9,019	Liddell (26)

D1: Bolton Wanderers

Formed in 1874 as a Sunday School side, Christ Church. This connection ended in 1877 when they adopted their present name. Turned professional in 1895 and were Football League founder members. Moved from Pikes Lane to present ground in 1895. Members of the reorganised Division One on formation of the Premier League, they were promoted to the Premier League for the 1995-96 season and, after being relegated straight back, bounced back into the top flight at the first attempt as Division One Champions.

Ground: The Reebok Stadium, Mansell Way, Horwich, Bolton
Phone: 01204-698800   **Box Office:** 01204-389200
Info: 0891-12 11 64
Capacity: 25,000   **Pitch:** tba
Colours: White, Navy Blue, Navy Blue   **Nickname:** The Trotters

President: Nat Lofthouse OBE   **Chairman:** G. Hargreaves
Secretary: Des McBain
Manager: Colin Todd   **Coach:** Ian Porterfield
Physio: E. Simpson
Internet: http://www.boltonwfc.co.uk

League History: 1892 Founder members of League; 1899-00 Division 2; 1900-03 Division 1; 1903-05 Division 2; 1905-08 Division 1; 1900-09 Division 2; 1909-10 Division 1; 1910-11 Division 2; 1911-33 Division 1; 1933-35 Division 2; 1935-64 Division 1; 1964-71 Division 2; 1971-73 Division 1; 1973-78 Division 2; 1978-80 Division 1; Division 2; 1983-87 Division 3; 1987-88 Division 4; 1988-92 Division 3; 1992-93 Division 2; 1993-94 Division 1; 1994-96 FAPL; 1996-1997 Division ; 1997-98 FAPL.

Honours: *Football League: Division One Champions* 1996-97. *Division Two Champions* 1908-09, 1977-78; *Division Three Champions* 1972-73. *FA Cup: Winners* 1922-23, 1925-26, 1928-29, 1957-58; *Runners-up* 1883-84, 1903-04, 1952-53. *League Cup: Runners-up* 1994-95; *FA Charity Shield: Winners* 1958. *Sherpa Van Trophy: Winners* 1988-89. *Freight Rover Trophy: Runners-up* 1985-86.

European Record: Never qualified.

Managers: Tom Rawthorne 1874-85; J. J. Bentley 1885-86; W. G. Struthers 1886-87; Fitzroy Norris 1887; J. J. Bentley 1887-95; Harry Downs 1895-96; Frank Brettell 1896-98; John Somerville 1889-1910; Will Settle 1910-15; Tom Mather 1915-19; Charles Foweraker 1991-44; Walter Rowley 1944-50;

Bill Ridding 1951-68; Nat Lofthouse 1968-70; Jimmy McIlroy 1971; Jimmy Meadows 1971; Nat Lofthouse 1971; Jimmy Armfield 1971-74; Ian Greaves 1974-80; Stan Anderson 1980-81; George Mulhall 1981-82; John McGovern 1982-85; Charlie Wright 1985; Phil Neal 1985-92; Bruce Rioch 1992-1995; *(FAPL)* Roy McFarland/Colin Todd June 1995-Jan 1996; Colin Todd Jan 1996-

Season 1997-98

Biggest Home Win: 5-2 v Crystal Palace
Biggest Home Defeat: 1-2 v Coventry City
Biggest Away Win: 3-1 v Sheffield Wednesday
Biggest Away Defeat: 2-6 v Chelsea
Biggest Home Att: 25,000 (numerous occasions)
Smallest Home Att: 22,703 v Wimbledon
Average Attendance: 24,353
Leading Scorer: Nathan Blake – 12

All-Time Records

Record FAPL Win: 5-2 v Crystal Palace (H), 1997-98
Record FAPL Defeat: 0-6 v Manchester United (H), 25/2/96
Record FL Win: 8-0 v Barnsley, Division 2, 6/10/34
Record FL Defeat: 0-7 v Burnley 1/3/1890, Sheffield Wednesday, 1/3/15 and Manchester City, 21/3/36 all Division 1 away.
Record Cup Win: 13-0 v Sheffield Utd, FA Cup 2Rd, 1/2/1890
Record Fee Received: £4.5m from Liverpool for Jason McAteer, 9/95
Record Fee Paid: £1.5m to Barnsley for Gerry Taggart 8/95 and £1.5m to Partizan Belgrade for Sasa Curcic
Most FL Apps: Eddie Hopkinson, 519, 1956-70
Most FAPL Apps: 65 – Keith Branagan, 1995-96, 1997-98
Most FAPL Goals: 13 – Nathan Blake , 1995-96, 1997-98
Highest Scorer in FAPL Season: Nathan Blake, 12, 1997-98
Record Attendance (all-time): 69,912 v Man City, FA Cup R5, 18/2/33
at Burnden Park
Record Attendance (FAPL): 25,000 (numerous occasions)
Most FAPL Goals in Season: 41, 1997-98 – 38 games
Most FAPL Points in Season: 41, 1997-98 – 38 games

Summary 1997-98

Player	Tot	St	Sb	Snu	PS	Gls	Y	R	Fa	La	Fg	Lg
AIJOFREE	2	2	0	5	0	0	0	0	0	0	0	0
BEARDSLEY	17	14	3	6	7	2	1	0	1	3	0	1
BERGSSON	35	34	1	0	1	2	9	1	1	3	0	0
BLAKE	35	35	0	0	2	12	5	1	1	3	0	2
BRANAGAN	34	34	0	0	2	0	0	0	0	3	0	0
CARR	5	0	5	4	0	0	0	0	0	0	0	0
COLEMAN	0	0	0	1	0	0	0	0	0	0	0	0
COX	21	20	1	2	1	1	4	0	1	0	0	0
ELLIOTT	4	4	0	0	2	0	0	0	0	0	0	0
FAIRCLOUGH	11	10	1	3	3	0	2	0	0	0	0	0
FISH	22	22	0	3	4	2	0	0	1	1	0	0
FRANDSEN	38	38	0	0	5	2	7	0	1	4	0	1
GIALLANZA	3	0	3	3	0	0	0	0	0	0	0	0
GUNNLAUGSSON	15	2	13	9	1	0	0	0	1	3	0	1
HOLDSWORTH	20	17	3	0	4	3	6	0	0	0	0	0
JAASKELAINEN	0	0	0	8	0	0	0	0	0	0	0	0
JOHANSEN	17	5	12	16	3	1	2	0	0	3	0	0
MCANESPIE	2	1	1	6	1	0	0	0	0	2	0	0
McGINLAY	8	5	3	0	2	0	1	0	0	3	0	2
PHILLIPS	22	21	1	11	3	1	5	0	0	2	0	0
POLLOCK	26	25	1	1	5	1	2	0	1	4	0	1
SALAKO	7	0	7	2	1	0	0	0	0	0	0	0
SELLARS	22	22	0	0	3	2	6	0	1	3	0	0
SHERIDAN	12	12	0	3	3	0	0	0	0	0	0	0
STRONG	0	0	0	2	0	0	0	0	0	2	0	0
TAGGART	15	14	1	2	1	0	5	1	0	1	0	0
TAYLOR	12	10	2	4	5	3	0	0	0	0	0	0
THOMPSON	33	33	0	0	2	9	6	1	1	4	0	1
TODD	25	23	2	7	1	0	4	1	1	4	0	1
WARD	6	4	2	28	0	0	0	0	1	1	0	0
WHITLOW	11	11	0	1	0	0	0	0	1	3	0	0

5-Year Record

	Div.	P	W	D	L	F	A	Pts	Pos	FAC	FLC
93-94	1	46	16	7	23	63	64	59	14	6	2
94-95	1	42	20	12	14	67	45	77	3	3	F
95-96	PL	38	8	5	25	39	71	29	20	4	4
96-97	1	46	28	14	4	100	53	98	1	4	4
97-98	PL	38	9	13	16	41	61	40	18	3	4

Reality Too Strong Again

Promotion to the Premiership, a move to the new Reebok Stadium, victory at Southampton on the opening day of the season. Everything seemed to be going Bolton Wanderers' way late in the summer of 1997 but it was not long before the harsh reality of Bolton's previous visit to the Premiership returned to haunt them. On that occasion the club was relegated at the first attempt and, with the Southampton result being the only one in their first ten games in favour of Colin Todd's side, it was clear that another season of struggle lay ahead.

Todd spent over £6m to bolster his promoted side, much of it on Robbie Elliott and Mark Fish. Neil Cox joined from relegated Middlesbrough while a gamble was taken on the experience of the gifted but ageing Peter Beardsley. With goals hard to come by, Todd signed Dean Holdsworth from Wimbledon for £3.5m in October but his return of three Premiership goals hardly justified the fee and it was Nathan Blake who ended the season as top scorer. Former goalscoring hero John McGinlay left the club in November.

Bolton had to wait until 1 September before the inaugural match at the Reebok Stadium, which was a goalless draw with Derby and, although Bolton lost just one of their first 11 home games, only three ended with all the points going their way. Chelsea were Bolton's biggest scalp, but on opposition soil Wanderers were experiencing all manner of problems with a 5-0 drubbing at Sheffield Wednesday being meted out before their second away success at the end of April. Crucially, Todd's side failed to take maximum points at home to the other struggling clubs. Barnsley, Everton and Tottenham all achieved draws at the Reebok before Wanderers were shattered on 31 January by a 5-1 defeat after visitors Coventry had fallen a goal behind. That game came during a 12-match winless run and by the time of Sheffield Wednesday's visit on 14 March the safety zone of 17th place was some six points away.

A 3-2 win for Bolton was ample revenge for the earlier thrashing and it was followed by a brace of Alan Thompson goals which saw off Leicester and took Bolton to within three points of fast sinking Everton. Arsenal slowed the momentum and, with just one win in five games, again Bolton looked doomed. Fortunately for Bolton they had the bonus of a home match with Crystal Palace on the 2 May which, coming on the back of an outstanding 3-1 win at Aston Villa, could yet prove to be their get out of jail card. Palace were thumped 5-2 in a game of several stunning goals, but when a point on the final day of the season would have seen them to safety, Bolton could not raise themselves sufficiently and returned to the Nationwide League following a 2-0 defeat at Stamford Bridge.

For the fourth consecutive year Bolton made little headway in the FA Cup, bowing out of the competition at the first hurdle following a trip to Barnsley. Their Coca-Cola Cup venture was slightly more successful with a fluctuating 7-5 aggregate victory over Leyton Orient in the 2nd Round being followed by a 2-0 extra-time success over Wimbledon. But the run was ended by one of the sides replacing them in the Premiership, Middlesbrough. ∎

FA Carling Premiership

Date	Opponents	Ven	Res	Atten	Scorers
08-Aug	Southampton	A	1-0	15,206	Blake (42)
22-Aug	Coventry C.	A	2-2	16,633	Blake (69, 76)
25-Aug	Barnsley	A	1-2	18,661	Beardsley (31)
31-Aug	Everton	H	0-0	23,131	
12-Sep	Arsenal	A	1-4	38,138	Thompson (13)
19-Sep	Man Utd	H	0-0	25,000	
22-Sep	Tottenham H.	H	1-1	23,433	Thompson (20 pen)
26-Sep	C. Palace	A	2-2	17,134	Beardsley (36); Johansen (66)
03-Oct	Aston Villa	A	0-1	24,196	
17-Oct	West Ham U.	A	0-3	24,864	
25-Oct	Chelsea	H	1-0	24,080	Holdsworth (72)
31-Oct	Liverpool	H	1-1	25,000	Blake (84)
07-Nov	Sheffield W.	A	0-5	25,027	
21-Nov	Leicester C.	A	0-0	20,644	
28-Nov	Wimbledon	H	1-0	22,703	Blake (90)
30-Nov	Newcastle U.	H	1-0	24,494	Blake (22)
05-Dec	Blackburn R.	A	1-3	25,003	Frandsen (83)
13-Dec	Derby Co.	H	3-3	23,037	Thompson (50); Blake (72); Pollock (77)
19-Dec	Leeds Utd	A	0-2	31,163	
25-Dec	Barnsley	H	1-1	25,000	Bergsson (38)
27-Dec	Everton	A	2-3	37,149	Bergsson (42): Sellars (43)
09-Jan	Southampton	H	0-0	23,333	
16-Jan	Newcastle U.	A	1-2	36,767	Blake (72)
30-Jan	Coventry C.	H	1-5	25,000	Sellars (22)
06-Feb	Man Utd	A	1-1	55,156	Taylor (60)
20-Feb	West Ham U.	H	1-1	25,000	Blake (86)
28-Feb	Tottenham H.	A	0-1	29,032	
06-Mar	Liverpool	A	1-2	44,532	Thompson (7)
13-Mar	Sheffield W.	H	3-2	24,847	Frandsen (31); Blake (53); Thompson (68 pen)
27-Mar	Leicester C.	H	2-0	25,000	Thompson (62, 90)
30-Mar	Arsenal	H	0-1	25,000	
03-Apr	Wimbledon	A	0-0	11,356	
10-Apr	Blackburn R.	H	2-1	25,000	Holdsworth (20); Taylor (67)
12-Apr	Derby Co.	A	0-4	29,126	
17-Apr	Leeds Utd	H	2-3	25,000	Thompson (57); Fish (90)
24-Apr	Aston Villa	A	3-1	38,392	Cox (18); Taylor (41); Blake (83)

| 01-May | C. Palace | H | 5-2 | 24,449 | Blake (6); Fish (20);
Phillips (30); Thompson (74);
Holdsworth (79) |
| 09-May | Chelsea | A | 0-2 | 34,845 | |

FA Challenge Cup

Sponsored by Littlewoods Pools

Date	Opponents	Vn	Rnd	Res	Atten	Scorers
03-Jan	Barnsley	A	3R	0-1	15,042	

Coca-Cola League Cup

Date	Opponents	Vn	Rnd	Res	Atten	Scorers
16-Sep	Leyton O.	A	2R1L	3-1	4,128	Todd (13); Frandsen (20); McGinlay (79)
30-Sep	Leyton O.	H	2R2L	4-4	6,444	Blake (8, 35); McGinlay (65 pen); Gunnlaugsson (66)

Bolton Wanderers win 7-5 on aggregate

14-Oct	Wimbledon	H	3R	2-0	9,875	Pollock (91), Beardsley (94)
	aet					
18-Nov	Middlesbrough	A	4R	1-2	22,801	Thompson (33)
	aet					

D1: Crystal Palace

Founded in 1905 to play at the Crystal Palace Ground where, earlier, a Crystal Palace staff team had successfully played. Joined the Southern League for 1905-06 when they were Champions of Division Two. Soon moved to Herne Hill, then to The Nest, Selhurst. Founder members and first champions of the Football League Third Division 1920-21. Moved to Selhurst Park in 1924.

Founder members of the old Fourth Division in 1958, they reached the First Division for the first time as Second Division runners-up in 1969. Premier League founder members 1992. Relegated after one season, but promoted back at the first attempt, only to be relegated in 1994-95, winning their place back through the play-offs at the end of the 1996-97 season.

Ground:	Selhurst Park, South Norwood, London SE25 6PU		
Phone:	0181-768 6000	**Box Office:**	0181-771 8841
News:	0891 400 333		
Capacity:	26,995	**Pitch:**	110 yds x 74 yds
Colours:	Red/Blue, Red, Red	**Nickname:**	The Eagles
Radio:	1548AM Capital Gold		
Internet:	–		

Chairman:	M. Goldberg	**Club Secretary:**	Mike Hurst
Manager:	Terry Venables	**Coach:**	Ray Lewington
Physio:	Gary Sadler		

League History: 1920 Original Members of Division 3; 1921-25 Division 2; 1925-58 Division 3(S); 1958-61 Division 4; 1961-64 Division 3, 1964-69 Division 2; 1969-73 Division 1; 1973-74 Division 2; 1974-77 Division 3; 1977-79 Division 2; 1979-81 Division 1; 1981-89 Division 2; 1989-92 Division 1; 1992-93 FA Premier League; 1993-94 Division 1; 1994-95 FA Premier League; 1995-97 Division 1; 1997-98 FA Premier League.

Honours: *Football League: Division 1 Champions* 1993-94; *Division 2 Champions* 1978-79; *Runners-up* 1968-69; *Play-off Winners* 1996-97; *Division 3 Runners-up* 1963-64; *Division 3(S) Champions* 1920-21; *Runners-up* 1928-29, 1930-31, 1938-39; *Division 4 Runners-up* 1960-61. *FA Cup: Runners-up* 1989-90. *Zenith Data System Cup: Winners* 1991.

European Record: Never qualified.

Managers: John T. Robson 1905-07; Edmund Goodman 1907-25 (had been secretary since 1905 and afterwards continued in this position to 1933); Alec Maley 1925-27; Fred Maven 1927-30, Jack Tresadern 1930-35, Tom Bromilow 1935-36, R.S. Moyes 1936; Tom Bromilow 1936-39; George Irwin 1939-47; Jack Butler 1947-49; Ronnie Rooke 1949-50; Charlie Slade and Fred Dawes (joint managers) 1950-51; Laurie Scott 1951-54; Cyril Spiers 1954-58; George Smith 1958-60; Authur Rowe 1960-62; Dick Graham 1962-66; Bert Head 1966-72; Malcolm Allison 1973-76; Terry Venables 1976-80; Ernie Walley 1980; Malcolm Allison 1980-81; Dario Gradi 1981; Steve Kember 1981-82; Alan Mullery 1982-84; Steve Coppell 1984-93; Alan Smith June 1993-95; Steve Coppell (TD) 1995-96; Dave Bassett Feb 1996-97; Steve Coppell 1997-Mar 98; Atillio Lombardo (PM) Mar 98-Apr 98; Ray Lewington (C) Apr 98-Jun 98; Terry Venables June 1998-.

Season 1997-98

Biggest Home Win:	3-1 v Derby County
Biggest Home Defeat:	0-3 (six occasions)
Biggest Away Win:	3-1 v Sheffield Wednesday
Biggest Away Defeat:	2-6 v Chelsea
Biggest Home Att:	26,186 v Chelsea
Smallest Home Att:	14,410 v Wimbldeon
Average Attendance:	21,983
Leading Scorer:	Neil Shipperley – 7

All-Time Records

Record FAPL Win:	4-1 v Middlesbrough 12/4/93 and v Coventry City 2/11/95
Record FAPL Defeat:	1-6 v Liverpool 20/8/95
Record FL Win:	9-0 v Barrow, Division 4, 10/10/1959
Record FL Defeat:	0-9 v Burnley, FA Cup R2 replay, 10/2/1909 and 0-9 v Liverpool, Division 1, 12/9/90
Record Cup Win:	8-0 v Southend U, League Cup, R2 L2, 25/9/90
Record Fee Received:	£2.5m from Arsenal for Ian Wright, 9/91
Record Fee Paid:	£2.25m to Millwall for Andy Roberts, 6/95
Most FAPL Apps:	79 – Nigel Martyn, 1992-95
Most FAPL Goals:	23 – Chris Armstrong, 1992-95
Most FL Apps:	Jim Cannon, 571, 1973-88
Record Attendance (all-time):	41,482 v Burnley, Division 2, 11/5/79
Record Attendance (FAPL):	30,115 v Manchester United, 21/4/93

Highest Scorer in FAPL Season: Chris Armstrong, 15, 1992-93
Most FAPL Goals in Season: 48, 1992-93 – 42 games
Most FAPL Points in Season: 49, 1992-93 – 42 games

Player	Tot	St	Sb	Snu	PS	Gls	Y	R	Fa	La	Fg	Lg
BENT	16	10	6	1	3	5	2	0	0	0	0	0
BILLIO	3	1	2	0	1	0	1	0	0	0	0	0
BONETTI	2	0	2	0	0	0	0	0	0	0	0	0
BOXALL	1	0	1	3	0	0	0	0	0	1	0	0
BROLIN	13	13	0	0	4	0	2	0	3	0	0	0
BURTON	2	1	1	1	0	0	0	0	1	0	0	0
CURCIC	8	6	2	0	3	1	0	0	0	0	0	0
DAVIES	1	0	1	2	0	0	0	0	0	0	0	0
DYER	24	21	3	3	11	4	4	0	4	1	4	0
EDWORTHY	34	33	1	0	0	0	6	1	4	1	0	0
EMBLEN	13	8	5	5	5	0	2	0	2	0	2	0
FOLAN	1	0	1	1	0	0	0	0	0	0	0	0
FREEDMAN	8	2	6	0	2	0	0	0	0	2	0	0
FULLERTON	25	19	6	2	2	1	11	0	3	2	0	0
GINTY	5	2	3	4	0	0	0	0	1	0	0	0
GORDON	37	36	1	0	0	2	3	0	4	2	0	0
HREIDARSSON	30	26	4	7	0	2	8	0	4	2	0	0
ISMAEL	13	13	0	1	2	0	4	1	0	0	0	0
JANSEN	8	5	3	0	1	3	0	0	0	0	0	0
LINIGHAN	26	26	0	5	3	0	4	0	3	2	0	0
LOMBARDO	24	21	3	0	9	5	3	0	0	0	0	0
McKENZIE	3	0	3	1	0	0	0	0	1	0	0	0
MILLER	38	38	0	0	0	0	0	0	4	2	0	0
MORRISON	1	0	1	0	0	1	0	0	0	0	0	0
MUSCATT	9	9	0	1	4	0	3	0	0	1	0	0
NASH	0	0	0	35	0	0	0	0	0	0	0	1
NDAH	3	2	1	1	1	0	0	0	0	1	0	0
ORMSHAW	0	0	0	3	0	0	0	0	0	0	0	0
PADAVANO	10	8	2	1	8	1	1	0	0	0	0	0
PITCHER	0	0	0	1	0	0	0	0	0	0	0	0
QUINN	1	0	1	12	0	0	0	0	0	0	0	0
ROBERTS	25	25	0	0	1	0	5	0	4	1	0	0
RODGER	29	27	2	1	4	2	2	0	3	1	0	0
SHIPPERLEY	25	17	8	2	3	7	1	0	1	2	0	0
SMITH	18	16	2	1	2	0	1	1	3	0	0	0
THOMPSON	0	0	0	2	0	0	0	0	0	0	0	0
TUTTLE	9	8	1	0	3	0	5	0	0	1	0	0
VEART	6	1	5	4	0	0	1	0	0	2	0	1
WARHURST	22	22	0	1	8	3	3	0	1	1	0	0
ZOHAR	6	2	4	8	1	0	0	0	0	2	0	0

Eagles Long Way Off Nest

With both of their two previous ventures in the Premiership having lasted for the duration of one season, Crystal Palace manager Steve Coppell sought to build on their return to the top flight with the purchase of some experienced players. Close on £8m was spent prior to the start of the season with Neil Emblen, Attilio Lombardo, Paul Warhurst, Itzhak Zohar and goalkeeper Kevin Miller all moving to Selhurst Park. Part of the funding for the new arrivals came from the £3.25m sale of David Hopkin to Leeds. The success of those signings is debatable as Emblem and Zohar were later moved on at a loss of almost £2m. Undeterred, Palace still tried to stave off relegation with more expensive signings during the season, including Michele Padavano £1.75m, Valerien Ismael £2.75m, Matt Jansen £1m and Bolton misfit Sasa Curcic for £1m.

One of the most remarkable features of the Eagles' season was that when top scorer Neil Shipperley scored the winning goal at Tottenham on 24 November, it took Palace into the top ten and they had still yet to win a home match. All five successes up to that point had been away from home starting with victory at Everton on the opening day of the season, Leeds a fortnight later, Wimbledon and Sheffield Wednesday. The win against Wimbledon was, ironically, their only league success at Selhurst Park before mid-April. The 'home' match with Wimbledon was lost 3-0. With their total of home victories on course to be the lowest in the Premiership's six-year history, it was vital that Palace kept picking up points away from home but the win at Spurs precipitated a 15-match winless run which just about sealed their fate. The Palace faithful had their long wait for a home league success ended on 18 April when Derby were beaten 3-1. On the final day of the season a last-minute goal from the debut-making Clinton Morrison secured a second home success as the double was completed over Sheffield Wednesday.

Coppell stepped down to be replaced by Lombardo, whose lack of command of the English language did little to help Palace's cause. When relegation was confirmed, the Italian wasted no time in declaring that management was not for him. Ray Lewington replaced him briefly and rumours were confirmed when Terry Venables was appointed to look after team affairs for the start of the 1998-99 season.

Palace had problems at both ends of the pitch throughout the season. On 13 occasions they conceded three or more goals in the league while no player could muster more than a single goal in a Premiership game. That said, Shipperley did score in five consecutive Premiership matches running from October through to December.

Having gone out of the FA Cup in the 3rd Round for the two previous seasons, Palace did enjoy some success this time round. Scunthorpe had the rare honour of losing at Selhurst Park and somewhat more surprisingly Leicester went the same way in the 4th Round as Bruce Dyer scored all the goals in a 3-0 win for the Eagles. But after gaining a creditable draw at Highbury in the 5th Round it was business as usual at Selhurst Park as Arsenal won the replay 2-1.

The Coca-Cola Cup brought nothing but humiliation when Hartlepool won the 1st Leg of their 2nd Round tie 1-0 in Cleveland and then held out for a 2-1 defeat in the return to grab a sensational away goals triumph. ∎

Results 1997-98

Date	Opponents	Ven	Res	Atten	Scorers
08-Aug	Everton	A	2-1	35,716	Lombardo (34); Dyer (62 pen)
11-Aug	Barnsley	H	0-1	21,547	
22-Aug	Leeds U.	A	2-0	29,076	Warhurst (22); Lombardo (51)
26-Aug	Southampton	A	0-1	15,032	
29-Aug	Blackburn R.	H	1-2	20,849	Dyer (51)
12-Sep	Chelsea	H	0-3	26,186	
19-Sep	Wimbledon	A	1-0	16,747	Lombardo (79)
23-Sep	Coventry C.	A	1-1	15,900	Fullerton (9)
26-Sep	Bolton W.	H	2-2	17,134	Warhurst (9); Gordon (19)
03-Oct	Man Utd	A	0-2	55,143	
17-Oct	Arsenal	H	0-0	26,180	
24-Oct	Sheffield W.	A	3-1	22,072	Hreidarsson (27); Rodger (52); Shipperley (60)
07-Nov	Aston Villa	H	1-1	21,097	Shipperley (42)
23-Nov	Tottenham H.	A	1-0	25,634	Shipperley (57)
28-Nov	Newcastle U.	H	1-2	26,085	Shipperley (66)
02-Dec	West Ham U.	A	1-4	23,335	Shipperley (41)
05-Dec	Leicester C.	A	1-1	19,991	Padovano (43)
12-Dec	Liverpool	H	0-3	25,790	
19-Dec	Derby Co.	A	0-0	26,590	
25-Dec	Southampton	H	1-1	22,853	Shipperley (61)
27-Dec	Blackburn R.	A	2-2	23,872	Dyer (11); Warhurst (48)
09-Jan	Everton	H	1-3	23,311	Dyer (16 pen)
16-Jan	Barnsley	A	0-1	17,819	
30-Jan	Leeds U.	H	0-2	25,248	
08-Feb	Wimbledon	H	0-3	14,410	
20-Feb	Arsenal	A	0-1	38,094	
27-Feb	Coventry C.	H	0-3	21,810	
10-Mar	Chelsea	A	2-6	31,917	Hreidarsson (7); Bent (87)
13-Mar	Aston Villa	A	1-3	33,781	Jansen (62)
17-Mar	Newcastle U.	H	2-1	36,565	Lombardo (14); Jansen (23)
27-Mar	Tottenham H.	H	1-3	26,116	Shipperley (82)
10-Apr	Leicester C.	H	0-3	18,771	
12-Apr	Liverpool	A	1-2	43,007	Bent (72)
17-Apr	Derby Co.	H	3-1	18,101	Jansen (73); Curcic (80); Bent (90)
26-Apr	Man Utd	H	0-3	26,180	
01-May	Bolton W.	A	2-5	24,449	Gordon (8); Bent (16)

| 04-May | West Ham U. | H | 3-3 | 19,129 | Bent (44); Rodger (48); Lombardo (63) |
| 09-May | Sheffield W. | H | 1-0 | 16,876 | Morrison (90) |

FA Challenge Cup

Sponsored by Littlewoods Pools

Date	Opponents	Vn	Rnd	Res	Atten	Scorers
03-Jan	Scunthorpe Utd	H	3R	2-0	11,624	Emblen (45, 87)
24-Jan	Leicester C.	H	4R	3-0	15,489	Dyer (33, 62, 66)
15-Feb	Arsenal	A	5R	0-0	37,164	
25-Feb	Arsenal	H	5RR	1-2	15,674	Dyer (35)

Coca-Cola League Cup

Date	Opponents	Vn	Rnd	Res	Atten	Scorers
16-Sep	Hull C.	A	2R1L	0-1	9,323	
30-Sep	Hull C.	H	2R2L	2-1	6,407	Veart (56); Ndah (77)

aet. 2-2 on aggregate. Hull C. win on away goals rule.

5-Year Record

	Div.	P	W	D	L	F	A	Pts	Pos	FAC	FLC
93-94	1	46	27	9	10	73	46	90	1	3	3
94-95	PL	42	11	12	19	34	49	45	19	SF	SF
95-96	1	46	20	15	11	67	48	75	3	3	3
96-97	1	46	19	14	13	78	48	71	6	3	3
97-98	PL	38	8	9	21	37	71	33	20	5	2

Appearance Totals

Team	Tot	St	Sb	Snu	PS	Gls	Y	R	Fa	La	Fg	Lg
Arsenal	504	418	86	104	86	68	71	3	118	63	10	9
Aston Villa	472	418	55	135	55	49	46	2	50	14	7	0
Barnsley	511	418	93	97	93	37	64	5	81	41	10	7
Blackburn R.	492	418	74	116	74	57	52	5	52	38	11	7
Bolton W.	480	418	62	128	62	41	65	5	13	52	0	10
Chelsea	500	418	82	108	82	71	65	3	13	81	3	11
Coventry C.	473	418	55	135	55	46	69	5	64	50	8	7
Crystal Palace ...	499	418	81	109	81	37	72	3	46	27	6	2
Derby County	507	418	89	101	89	52	78	2	27	52	2	8
Everton	503	418	85	105	85	41	74	5	12	38	0	7
Leeds United	473	418	55	135	55	57	67	5	49	51	9	9
Leicester C.	497	418	79	111	79	51	45	2	27	13	4	1
Liverpool	477	418	59	131	59	68	49	2	13	62	1	9
Manchester U.	494	418	76	114	76	73	58	2	54	14	13	0
Newcastle U.	480	418	62	128	62	35	60	3	89	39	0	3
Sheffield W.	505	418	87	103	87	52	62	4	38	27	1	3
Southampton	505	418	87	103	87	50	55	4	13	53	0	8
Tottenham H.	507	418	89	100	89	44	53	2	39	36	5	6
West Ham U.	469	418	51	139	51	56	54	5	75	61	9	11
Wimbledon	487	418	69	121	69	34	44	2	66	41	6	9

KEY TO CLUB DIRECTORY ABBREVIATIONS
Stats relating to FA Carling Premiership Season

Tot	Total appearances in season – this is St + Sb.
St	Total number of times player was in starting line-up.
Sb	Total number of times player came on as sub.
Snu	Total number of times player was sub but not used (Sub not used).
PS	Total number of times player was substituted (Player Subbed).
Gls	Total number of goals scored.
Y	Total number of Yellow cards received.
R	Total number of Red cards received. (Note: A red card issued due to a second yellow card is recorded as 1Y and 1R.)
Fa/La	Total number of appearances in FA Cup and League Cup.
Fg/Lg	Total number of goals scored in FA Cup and League Cup.
†	Player no longer with club at time of going to press.

Stats File

The Stats File supplies the most complete summary of every club's existence, not to be found anywhere else. First comes a complete PWDLFA for every division the club has competed in and then for each of the major cup competitions. The league summaries are given for combined divisions. Thus 'Division 1n/2' relates to the new Division 1 which was also the old Division 2. The values of Yr, B, W are the number of Years (seasons) in that division, and the Best and Worst positions achieved in the division.

This is followed by a list of sequences relating to the Football League. Dates for the start and end of the sequence are given:

Winning Run	The highest number of successive wins
Without Defeat	The highest number of games gone without a defeat
Without Win	The highest number of games gone without a win
Drawn Games	The highest number of successive drawn games
Without Draw	The highest number of games gone without a draw
Losing Run	The highest number of successive defeats
Clean Sheets	The highest games gone without conceding a goal
Goals Scored	The highest number of successive games in which a goal has been scored
No Goals For	The highest number of games gone in which a goal has not been scored by the team
SOS Undefeated	SOS = Start of Season. This is the number of games at the start of a season before a defeat (thus games were either won or drawn)
SOS No Wins	Number of games at the start of the season without a win

There may be several instances of a particular sequence. In such cases the number of times the sequence occurred is listed in brackets and the last two occasions it happened are detailed. Thus:

Clean Sheets (5)

would indicate that the specified number of clean sheets have been maintained on five different occasions.

Arsenal

Division	P	W	D	L	F	A	Pts	Yr	B	W
Premier/1:	3336	1426	869	1041	5344	4389	4038	81	1	20
Division 1n/2:	428	216	73	139	824	550	505	13	2	10

Cup Records	P	W	D	L	F	A
FA Cup:	343	171	83	89	561	376
League Cup:	161	90	39	32	285	144

Sequence	Games	Start		End
Winning Run:	10	12-Sep-87	to	14-Nov-87
	10	11-Mar-98	to	03-May-98
Without Defeat:	26	28-Apr-90	to	19-Jan-91
Without Win:	23	28-Sep-12	to	01-Mar-13
Drawn Games:	6	04-Mar-61	to	01-Apr-61
Without Draw:	28	04-Apr-83	to	26-Dec-83
Losing Run:	7	12-Feb-77	to	12-Mar-77
Clean Sheets:	8	10-Apr-03	to	03-Oct-03
	8	31-Jan-98	to	31-Mar-98
Goals Scored:	31	03-May-30	to	28-Feb-31
No Goals For:	6	25-Feb-87	to	28-Mar-87
SOS Undefeated:	23	1990-91		
SOS No Wins (3):	8	1927-28		
	8	1912-13		

Aston Villa

Division	P	W	D	L	F	A	Pts	Yr	B	W
Premier/1:	3386	1426	756	1204	5793	5154	3849	87	1	22
Division 1n/2:	422	179	111	132	617	487	491	10	1	21
Division 2n/3:	92	51	21	20	139	78	123	2	1	4

Cup Records	P	W	D	L	F	A
FA Cup:	370	194	75	101	770	467
League Cup:	180	102	42	36	346	206
A/F Members Cup:	12	6	0	6	21	17

Sequence	Games	Start		End
Winning Run:	9	15-Oct-10	to	10-Dec-10
Without Defeat (3):	15	18-Dec-09	to	26-Mar-10
	15	12-Mar-49	to	27-Aug-49
Without Win:	12	10-Nov-73	to	2-Feb-74
	12	27-Dec-86	to	25-Mar-87
Drawn Games:	6	12-Sep-81	to	10-Oct-81
Without Draw:	51	01-Jan-1891	to	17-Dec-1892
Losing Run:	11	23-Mar-63	to	4-May-63
Clean Sheets:	7	27-Oct-23	to	8-Dec-23

Goals Scored:	35	10/11/1894	to	12/12/1895
No Goals For (4):	5	11-Jan-92	to	8-Feb-92
	5	29-Feb-92	to	21-Mar-92
SOS Undefeated:	11	1932-33		
SOS No Wins (3):	9	1958-59		
	9	1966-67		

Blackburn Rovers

Division	P	W	D	L	F	A	Pts	Yr	B	W
Premier/1:	2264	870	527	867	3750	3704	2382	60	1	22
Division 1n/2:	1446	583	364	499	2134	1981	1723	34	1	22
Division 2n/3:	230	104	59	67	299	249	267	5	1	13

Cup Records	P	W	D	L	F	A
FA Cup:	340	166	72	102	655	405
League Cup:	119	50	28	41	187	161
A/F Members Cup:	13	8	0	5	21	16

Sequence	Games	Start		End
Winning Run:	8	01-Mar-80	to	07-Apr-80
Without Defeat:	23	30-Sep-87	to	27-Feb-88
Without Win:	16	11-Nov-78	to	24-Mar-79
Drawn Games:	5	06-Apr-74	to	16-Apr-74
	5	11-Oct-75	to	01-Nov-75
Without Draw:	30	13-Nov-65	to	27-Aug-66
Losing Run:	7	12-Mar-66	to	16-Apr-66
Clean Sheets:	6	11-Apr-81	to	02-May-81
Goals Scored:	32	24-Apr-54	to	26-Feb-55
No Goals For (12):	4	19-Oct-85	to	09-Nov-85
	4	19-Oct-92	to	07-Nov-92
SOS Undefeated:	10	1989-90		
	10	1913-14		
SOS No Wins:	11	1996-97		

Charlton Athletic

Division	P	W	D	L	F	A	Pts	Yr	B	W
Premier/1:	746	262	171	313	1082	1209	732	18	2	22
Division 1n/2:	1628	576	425	627	2395	2583	1795	38	2	22
Division 2n/3:	184	83	39	62	274	245	205	4	3	14

Cup Records	P	W	D	L	F	A
FA Cup:	176	66	41	69	252	254
League Cup:	105	39	21	45	165	172
A/F Members Cup:	14	4	3	7	17	24

Sequence	Games	Start		End
Winning Run:	8	21-Mar-98	to	25-Apr-98
Without Defeat:	15	04-Oct-80	to	20-Dec-80
Without Win:	16	26-Feb-55	to	22-Aug-55
Drawn Games:	6	13-Dec-92	to	16-Jan-93
Without Draw:	22	03-Nov-56	to	30-Mar-57
Losing Run:	10	11-Apr-90	to	15-Sep-90
Clean Sheets:	7	22-Dec-23	to	09-Feb-24
	7	04-Apr-98	to	03-May-98
Goals Scored:	25	26-Dec-35	to	07-Sep-36
No Goals For:	5	06-Sep-22	to	30-Sep-22
SOS Undefeated:	12	1927-28		
SOS No Wins:	9	1970-71		

Chelsea

Division	P	W	D	L	F	A	Pts	Yr	B	W
Premier/1:	2600	916	688	996	3764	4058	2710	63	1	22
Division 1n/2:	786	383	202	201	1323	887	1048	19	1	18

Cup Records	P	W	D	L	F	A
FA Cup:	293	135	77	81	483	333
League Cup:	132	58	34	40	224	170
A/F Members Cup:	27	18	3	6	55	41

Sequence	Games	Start		End
Winning Run:	8	06-Oct-27	to	19-Nov-27
	8	15-Mar-89	to	08-Apr-89
Without Defeat:	27	29-Oct-88	to	08-Apr-89
Without Win:	21	3-Nov-87	to	02-Apr-88
Drawn Games:	6	20-Aug-69	to	13-Sep-69
Without Draw:	24	10-Sep-32	to	11-Feb-33
Losing Run:	7	01-Nov-52	to	20-Dec-52
Clean Sheets:	9	04-Nov-05	to	25-Dec-05
Goals Scored:	27	31-Aug-85	to	22-Mar-86
	27	29-Oct-88	to	08-Apr-89
No Goals For:	9	14-Mar-81	to	02-May-81
SOS Undefeated:	14	1925-26		
SOS No Wins:	6	1914-15		
	6	1988-89		

Coventry City

Division	P	W	D	L	F	A	Pts	Yr	B	W
Premier/1:	1276	399	369	508	1482	1786	1380	31	6	20
Division 1n/2:	756	279	186	291	1050	1099	744	18	1	22
Division 2n/3:	230	93	66	71	403	347	252	5	1	15
Division 3n/4:	46	24	12	10	84	47	60	1	2	2

Cup Records	P	W	D	L	F	A
FA Cup:	183	72	39	72	284	274
League Cup:	124	61	21	42	210	183
A/F Members Cup:	10	2	2	6	8	15

Sequence	Games	Start		End
Winning Run:	6	20-Apr-54	to	28-Aug-54
	6	25-Apr-64	to	05-Sep-64
Without Defeat:	25	26-Nov-66	to	13-May-67
Without Win:	19	30-Aug-19	to	20-Dec-19
Drawn Games:	6	28-Sep-96	to	16-Nov-96
Without Draw:	25	06-Sep-26	to	12-Feb-27
Losing Run:	9	30-Aug-19	to	11-Oct-19
Clean Sheets:	6	28-Apr-34	to	03-Sep-34
Goals Scored:	25	10-Sep-66	to	25-Feb-67
No Goals For:	11	11-Oct-19	to	20-Dec-19
SOS Undefeated:	15	1937-38		
SOS No Wins:	19	1919-20		

Derby County

Division	P	W	D	L	F	A	Pts	Yr	B	W
Premier/1:	2278	865	535	878	3590	3597	2337	60	1	22
Division 1n/2:	1466	598	357	511	2293	2062	1712	35	1	22
Division 2n/3:	92	42	28	22	145	95	154	2	3	7

Cup Records	P	W	D	L	F	A
FA Cup:	295	138	54	103	554	451
League Cup:	130	51	32	47	206	168
A/F Members Cup:	16	7	2	7	24	24

Sequence	Games	Start		End
Winning Run:	9	15-Mar-69	to	19-Apr-69
Without Defeat:	22	08-Mar-69	to	20-Sep-69
Without Win:	20	15-Dec-90	to	23-Apr-91
Drawn Games:	6	26-Mar-27	to	18-Apr-27
Without Draw:	28	25-Sep-26	to	19-Mar-27
Losing Run (3):	8	17-Apr-65	to	01-Sep-65
	8	12-Dec-87	to	10-Feb-88
Clean Sheets:	6	08-Apr-12	to	22-Apr-12

Goals Scored:	29	03-Dec-60	to	06-Sep-61
No Goals For:	8	30-Oct-20	to	18-Dec-20
SOS Undefeated:	16	1948-49		
SOS No Wins:	9	1990-91		

Everton

Division	P	W	D	L	F	A	Pts	Yr	B	W
Premier/1:	3720	1534	907	1279	5958	5270	4256	95	1	22
Division 1n/2:	168	77	45	46	348	257	199	4	1	16

Cup Records	P	W	D	L	F	A
FA Cup:	359	194	71	94	665	400
League Cup:	127	62	30	35	235	137
A/F Members Cup:	15	9	2	4	36	25

Sequence	Games	Start		End
Winning Run:	12	24-Mar-1894	to	13-Oct-1894
Without Defeat:	20	29-Apr-78	to	16-Dec-78
Without Win:	14	06-Mar-37	to	04-Sep-37
Drawn Games (3):	5	05-Oct-74	to	26-Oct-74
	5	04-May-77	to	16-May-77
Without Draw:	26	22-Feb-58	to	18-Oct-58
Losing Run (7):	6	04-Nov-72	to	09-Dec-72
	6	26-Dec-96	to	29-Jan-97
Clean Sheets:	7	01-Nov-94	to	17-Dec-94
Goals Scored:	40	15-Mar-30	to	07-Mar-31
No Goals For:	6	03-Mar-51	to	31-Mar-51
	6	08-Dec-93	to	01-Jan-94
SOS Undefeated:	19	1978-79		
SOS No Wins:	12	1994-95		

Leeds United

Division	P	W	D	L	F	A	Pts	Yr	B	W
Premier/1:	1832	747	470	615	2744	2491	2105	44	1	22
Division 1n/2:	1144	483	309	352	1731	1451	1417	27	1	19
Division 1n/2:*	380	140	77	163	575	616	357	10	4	19

* as Leeds City

Cup Records	P	W	D	L	F	A
FA Cup:	207	87	50	70	329	275
League Cup:	131	60	23	48	216	177
A/F Members Cup:	17	7	3	7	24	29

Sequence	Games	Start		End
Winning Run:	9	26-Sep-31	to	21-Nov-31
Without Defeat:	34	26-Oct-68	to	26-Aug-69

Without Win:	17	01-Feb-47	to	26-May-47
Drawn Games:	5	09-Apr-62	to	24-Apr-62
	5	19-Apr-97	to	09-Aug-97
Without Draw:	24	12-Sep-36	to	13-Feb-37
Losing Run:	6	26-Apr-47	to	26-May-47
	6	06-Apr-96	to	02-May-96
Clean Sheets:	9	03-Mar-28	to	14-Apr-28
Goals Scored:	30	27-Aug-27	to	25-Feb-28
No Goals For:	6	30-Jan-82	to	10-Mar-82
SOS Undefeated:	29	1973-74		
SOS No Wins:	6	1951-52		
	6	1935-36		

Leicester City

Division	P	W	D	L	F	A	Pts	Yr	B	W
Premier/1:	1710	550	446	714	2584	2966	1626	41	2	22
Division 1n/2:	2074	854	514	706	3212	2933	2401	52	1	22

Cup Records	P	W	D	L	F	A
FA Cup:	240	101	52	87	359	339
League Cup:	117	51	24	42	181	152
A/F Members Cup:	12	6	2	4	17	14

Sequence	Games	Start		End
Winning Run:	7	15-Feb-08	to	28-Mar-08
	7	24-Jan-25	to	17-Mar-25
Without Defeat:	19	06-Feb-71	to	18-Aug-71
Without Win:	18	12-Apr-75	to	01-Nov-75
Drawn Games:	6	21-Apr-73	to	01-Sep-73
	6	21-Aug-76	to	18-Sep-76
Without Draw:	44	30-Jan-09	to	26-Mar-10
Losing Run:	7	28-Nov-31	to	16-Jan-32
	7	28-Aug-90	to	29-Sep-90
Clean Sheets:	7	14-Feb-20	to	27-Mar-20
Goals Scored:	31	12-Nov-32	to	28-Aug-33
No Goals For:	7	21-Nov-87	to	01-Jan-88
SOS Undefeated:	11	1899-00		
SOS No Wins:	15	1975-76		

Liverpool

Division	P	W	D	L	F	A	Pts	Yr	B	W
Premier/1:	3336	1518	833	985	5480	4216	4233	83	1	22
Division 1n/2:	428	243	82	103	977	571	568	11	1	11

Cup Records	P	W	D	L	F	A
FA Cup:	363	188	85	90	584	342
League Cup:	167	96	43	28	328	140

Sequence	Games	Start		End
Winning Run:	12	21-Apr-90	to	06-Oct-90
Without Defeat:	31	4-May-87	to	16-Mar-88
Without Win:	14	12-Dec-53	to	20-Mar-54
Drawn Games:	6	19-Feb-75	to	19-Mar-75
Without Draw:	23	28-Nov-81	to	01-May-82
Losing Run:	9	29-Apr-1899	to	14-Oct-1899
Clean Sheets:	8	30-Dec-22	to	03-Mar-23
Goals Scored:	29	27-Apr-57	to	11-Jan-58
No Goals For (4):	5	18-Dec-71	to	22-Jan-72
	5	01-Sep-93	to	02-Oct-93
SOS Undefeated:	29	1987-88		
SOS No Wins:	9	1894-95		

Manchester United

Division	P	W	D	L	F	A	Pts	Yr	B	W
Premier/1:	2980	1308	764	908	4969	4077	3730	73	1	22
Division 1n/2:	816	406	168	242	1433	966	980	22	1	20

Cup Records	P	W	D	L	F	A
FA Cup:	345	181	80	84	620	414
League Cup:	129	70	25	34	222	141

Sequence	Games	Start		End
Winning Run:	14	15-Oct-04	to	03-Jan-05
Without Defeat:	26	04-Feb-56	to	13-Oct-56
Without Win:	16	03-Nov-28	to	09-Feb-29
	16	19-Apr-30	to	25-Oct-30
Drawn Games:	6	30-Oct-88	to	27-Nov-88
Without Draw:	26	23-Nov-1895	to	26-Sep-1896
Losing Run:	14	26-Apr-30	to	25-Oct-30
Clean Sheets (3):	7	20-Sep-24	to	01-Nov-24
	7	08-May-97	to	30-Aug-97
Goals Scored:	27	11-Oct-58	to	04-Apr-59
No Goals For (3):	5	26-Jan-24	to	23-Feb-24
	5	07-Feb-81	to	07-Mar-81
SOS Undefeated:	15	1985-86		
SOS No Wins:	12	1930-31		

Middlesbrough

Division	P	W	D	L	F	A	Pts	Yr	B	W
Premier/1:	1982	685	478	819	2918	3157	1894	49	3	22
Division 1n/2:	1556	651	377	528	2466	2094	1870	37	1	21
Division 2n/3:	92	51	19	22	154	94	149	2	2	2

Cup Records	P	W	D	L	F	A
FA Cup:	270	100	73	97	420	374
League Cup:	125	51	31	43	185	147
A/F Members Cup:	22	13	1	8	35	23

Sequence	Games	Start		End
Winning Run:	9	16-Feb-74	to	06-Apr-74
Without Defeat:	24	08-Sep-73	to	19 Jan 74
Without Win:	19	03-Oct-81	to	06-Mar-82
Drawn Games:	8	03-Apr-71	to	01-May-71
Without Draw:	33	02-May-25	to	27-Feb-26
Losing Run:	8	25-Aug-54	to	18-Sep-54
	8	26-Dec-95	to	17-Feb-96
Clean Sheets:	7	07-Nov-87	to	19-Dec-87
Goals Scored:	26	21-Sep-46	to	08-Mar-47
No Goals For (10):	4	05-Dec-81	to	06-Feb-82
	4	02-Nov-93	to	04-Dec-93
SOS Undefeated:	10	1910-11		
SOS No Wins:	9	1954-55		
	9	1982-83		

Newcastle United

Division	P	W	D	L	F	A	Pts	Yr	B	W
Premier/1:	2742	1088	654	1000	4278	3983	2990	68	1	21
Division 1n/2:	1046	481	218	347	1798	1438	1318	26	1	20

Cup Records	P	W	D	L	F	A
FA Cup:	312	147	77	88	551	387
League Cup:	97	41	15	41	150	130
A/F Members Cup:	9	3	1	5	18	21

Sequence	Games	Start		End
Winning Run:	13	25-Apr-92	to	18-Oct-92
Without Defeat:	14	22-Apr-50	to	30-Sep-50
Without Win:	21	14-Jan-78	to	23-Aug-78
Drawn Games (14):	4	21-Dec-85	to	11-Jan-86
	4	20-Jan-90	to	24-Feb-90
Without Draw:	34	16-Nov-1895	to	5-Dec-1896
Losing Run:	10	23-Aug-77	to	15-Oct-77
Clean Sheets:	6	06-Mar-82	to	03-Apr-82

Goals Scored:	25	15-Apr-39	to	26-Dec-46
No Goals For:	6	31-Dec-38	to	15-Feb-39
	6	29-Oct-88	to	03-Dec-88
SOS Undefeated (3):	11	1950-51		
	11	1994-95		
SOS No Wins:	10	1898-99		

Nottingham Forest

Division	P	W	D	L	F	A	Pts	Yr	B	W
Premier/1:	2140	793	540	807	3034	3102	2374	55	1	22
Division 1n/2:	1584	599	394	591	2414	2353	1643	38	1	21

Cup Records	P	W	D	L	F	A
FA Cup:	342	146	88	108	566	445
League Cup:	148	81	35	32	294	162
A/F Members Cup:	15	11	1	3	35	19

Sequence	Games	Start		End
Winning Run (4):	7	29-Aug-21	to	01-Oct-21
	7	09-May-79	to	01-Sep-79
Without Defeat:	42	26-Nov-77	to	25-Nov-78
Without Win:	16	21-Mar-13	to	11-Oct-13
	16	21-Aug-96	to	17-Dec-96
Drawn Games:	7	29-Apr-78	to	02-Sep-78
Without Draw:	21	23-Mar-1895	to	14-Dec-1895
Losing Run:	14	21-Mar-13	to	27-Sep-13
Clean Sheets:	6	26-Nov-21	to	26-Dec-21
	6	19-Apr-80	to	09-May-80
Goals Scored:	22	28-Mar-31	to	07-Nov-31
No Goals For:	6	02-Sep-70	to	03-Oct-70
SOS Undefeated:	16	1978-79		
SOS No Wins:	10	1929-30		

Sheffield Wednesday

Division	P	W	D	L	F	A	Pts	Yr	B	W
Premier/1:	2506	959	598	949	3897	3908	2704	64	1	22
Division 1n/2:	1088	460	281	347	1693	1401	1285	26	1	22
Division 2n/3:	230	83	76	71	297	266	242	5	3	20

Cup Records	P	W	D	L	F	A
FA Cup:	354	167	84	103	633	441
League Cup:	125	60	30	35	208	151
A/F Members Cup:	9	3	1	5	12	15

Sequence	Games	Start		End
Winning Run:	9	23-Apr-04	to	15-Oct-04
Without Defeat:	19	10-Dec-60	to	08-Apr-61
Without Win:	20	23-Oct-54	to	12-Mar-55
	20	11-Jan-75	to	30-Aug-75
Drawn Games (3):	5	01-Dec-90	to	26-Dec-90
	5	24-Oct-92	to	28-Nov-92
Without Draw:	22	30-Nov-07	to	18-Apr-08
Losing Run:	7	07-Jan-1893	to	18-Mar-1893
Clean Sheets (4):	5	21-Feb-61	to	18-Mar-61
	5	04-Apr-92	to	20-Apr-92
Goals Scored:	40	14-Nov-59	to	29-Oct-60
No Goals For:	8	08-Mar-75	to	12-Apr-75
SOS Undefeated:	15	1983-84		
SOS No Wins:	17	1974-75		

Southampton

Division	P	W	D	L	F	A	Pts	Yr	B	W
Premier/1:	1150	384	318	448	1568	1695	1320	28	2	20
Division 1n/2:	1428	559	353	516	2221	2140	1471	34	2	21
Division 2n/3:	92	43	20	29	194	155	106	2	1	14

Cup Records	P	W	D	L	F	A
FA Cup:	282	113	75	94	432	364
League Cup:	143	62	42	39	236	171
A/F Members Cup:	13	8	0	5	24	14

Sequence	Games	Start		End
Winning Run:	6	03-Mar-92	to	04-Apr-92
Without Defeat:	19	05-Sep-21	to	31-Dec-21
Without Win:	20	30-Aug-69	to	27-Dec-69
Drawn Games:	7	28-Dec-94	to	11-Feb-95
Without Draw:	27	24-Jan-31	to	10-Oct-31
Losing Run (9):	5	29-Nov-93	to	18-Dec-93
	5	16-Nov-96	to	07-Dec-96
Clean Sheets:	8	17-Apr-22	to	26-Aug-22
Goals Scored:	24	05-Sep-66	to	11-Feb-67
No Goals For:	5	26-Aug-22	to	09-Sep-22
	5	01-Sep-37	to	15-Sep-37
SOS Undefeated:	7	1950-51		
SOS No Wins (3):	7	1976-77		
	7	1937-38		

Tottenham Hotspur

Division	P	W	D	L	F	A	Pts	Yr	B	W
Premier/1:	2596	1047	631	918	4130	3769	3000	63	1	22
Division 1n/2:	668	311	172	185	1253	851	794	16	1	12

Cup Records	P	W	D	L	F	A
FA Cup:	339	171	86	82	652	403
League Cup:	141	80	25	36	258	151

Sequence	Games	Start		End
Winning Run:	13	23-Apr-60	to	01-Oct-60
Without Defeat:	22	31-Aug-49	to	31-Dec-49
Without Win:	16	29-Dec-34	to	13-Apr-35
Drawn Games:	5	01-Feb-69	to	18-Mar-69
	5	20-Sep-75	to	18-Oct-75
Without Draw:	19	15-Feb-30	to	13-Sep-30
Losing Run:	7	01-Jan-94	to	27-Feb-94
Clean Sheets (4):	5	17-Dec-94	to	02-Jan-95
	5	21-Nov-95	to	16-Dec-95
Goals Scored:	32	09-Apr-49	to	31-Dec-49
	32	24-Feb-62	to	24-Nov-62
No Goals For:	6	28-Dec-85	to	08-Feb-86
SOS Undefeated:	16	1960-61		
SOS No Wins:	12	1912-13		

West Ham United

Division	P	W	D	L	F	A	Pts	Yr	B	W
Premier/1:	1788	615	441	732	2656	2877	1869	43	3	22
Division 1n/2:	1230	537	300	393	1958	1622	1444	29	1	20

Cup Records	P	W	D	L	F	A
FA Cup:	268	113	75	80	414	355
League Cup:	163	83	36	44	315	198
A/F Members Cup:	10	4	1	5	22	21

Sequence	Games	Start		End
Winning Run:	9	19-Oct-85	to	14-Dec-85
Without Defeat:	27	27-Dec-80	to	10-Oct-81
Without Win:	17	31-Jan-76	to	21-Aug-76
Drawn Games:	5	07-Sep-68	to	05-Oct-68
Without Draw:	29	14-Dec-29	to	13-Sep-30
Losing Run:	9	28-Mar-32	to	29-Aug-32
Clean Sheets (5):	5	23-Nov-85	to	21-Dec-85
	5	26-Dec-90	to	19-Jan-91
Goals Scored:	27	22-Jan-27	to	15-Oct-27
	27	05-Oct-57	to	04-Apr-58

252

No Goals For:	5	01-May-71	to	23-Aug-71
SOS Undefeated:	21	1990-91		
SOS No Wins:	11	1973-74		

Wimbledon

Division	P	W	D	L	F	A	Pts	Yr	B	W
Premier/1:	478	169	147	162	616	617	654	12	6	15
Division 1n/2:	84	37	23	24	129	112	134	2	3	12
Division 2n/3:	138	50	34	54	210	232	174	3	2	24
Division 3n/4:	184	91	47	46	304	204	258	4	1	13

Cup Records	P	W	D	L	F	A
FA Cup:	113	47	29	37	144	143
League Cup:	78	31	21	26	113	100
A/F Members Cup:	10	2	1	7	11	18

Sequence	Games	Start		End
Winning Run:	7	09-Apr-83	to	07-May-83
Without Defeat:	22	15-Jan-83	to	14-May-83
Without Win:	14	23-Feb-80	to	15-Apr-80
	14	16-Sep-95	to	23-Dec-95
Drawn Games (5):	4	29-Apr-95	to	13-May-95
	4	26-Oct-96	to	23-Nov-96
Without Draw:	20	15-Oct-83	to	15-Feb-84
Losing Run:	7	16-Sep-95	to	06-Nov-95
Clean Sheets (6):	4	30-Jan-93	to	20-Feb-93
	4	31-Mar-98	to	13-Apr-98
Goals Scored:	23	18-Feb-84	to	22-Sep-84
No Goals For:	5	13-Apr-95	to	04-May-95
	5	27-Apr-96	to	27-Aug-96
SOS Undefeated:	13	1978-79		
SOS No Wins:	9	1981-82		

FA PREMIER LEAGUE CLUB TRANSFERS 1997-98

Player	From	To	Fee
Graeme Le Saux	Blackburn R.	Chelsea	£5.0m
Henning Berg	Blackburn R.	Manchester U.	£5.0m
Paolo Di Canio	Celtic	Sheffield W.	£3.0m
Neil Emblen	Wolverhampton W.	C. Palace	£2.0m
Jose Dominguez	Sporting Lisbon	Tottenham H.	£1.5m
Regi Blinker	Sheffield W.	Celtic	£1.5m
Danny Williamson	West Ham U.	Everton	Swap + £1.0m
David Unsworth	Everton	West Ham U.	Swap
Itzak Zohar	Royal Antwerp	C. Palace	£1.2m
Graham Fenton	Blackburn R.	Leicester C.	£1.1m
Deon Burton	Portsmouth	Derby Co.	£1.0m
Orlando Trustfull	Sheffield W.	Vitesse Arnhem	£800,000
Darren Barnard	Bristol C.	Barnsley	£750,000
Stig Johansen	Bodo-Glimt	Southampton	£600,000
Tony Cottee	Selangor (Malaysia)	Leicester C.	£500,000
Peter Beardsley	Newcastle U.	Bolton W.	£450,000
Tony Scully	C. Palace	Manchester C.	£300,000
Sean Flynn	Derby Co.	WBA	£260,000
Mixu Paatelainen	Bolton Wa.	Wolverhampton W.	£200,000
Kevin Cooper	Derby Co.	Stockport Co.	£150,000
Christopher Wreh	Monaco	Arsenal	Free
Pegguy Arphexad	Racing Club (Paris)	Leicester C.	Free
Tony Dorigo	Leeds U.	Torino	Free
John Barnes	Liverpool	Newcastle U.	Free
Ronny Rosenthal	Tottenham H.	Watford	Free
Ian Rush	Leeds U.	Newcastle U.	Free

Player	From	To	Fee
Ian Pearce	Blackburn R.	West Ham U.	£1.6m > £2.3m
Mark Fish	Lazio	Bolton W.	£2.0m
Jim Magilton	Southampton	Sheffield W.	£1.6m
Marc Rieper	West Ham U.	Celtic	£1.4m
Andy Impey	QPR	West Ham U.	£1.3m

Ashley Ward	Derby Co.	Barnsley	£1.3m
Carlton Palmer	Leeds U.	Southampton	£1.0m
Tony Yeboah	Leeds U.	Hamburg	£1.0m
Michael Hughes	West Ham U.	Wimbledon	£800,000 > £1.6m
Mike Whitlow	Leicester C.	Bolton W.	£700,000
Tore Pedersen	St Pauli	Blackburn R.	£500,000
Alan Fettis	N. Forest	Blackburn R.	£300,000
Paul Shaw	Arsenal	Millwall	£250,000
Paul Wilkinson	Barnsley	Millwall	£150,000
Kevin Richardson	Coventry C.	Southampton	£150,000
Leon Townley	Tottenham H.	Brentford	£50,000
Jason Harris	C. Palace	L. Orient	£25,000
Bruce Grobbelaar	Oxford U.	Sheffield W.	Nominal
Stuart Brock	Aston Villa	Kidderminster H.	Free
Matthew George	Aston Villa	Sheffield U.	Free
Andrew Tretton	Derby Co.	Gresley R.	Free

October 1997

Player	From	To	Fee
Dean Holdsworth	Wimbledon	Bolton W.	£3.5m
David Hirst	Sheffield W.	Southampton	£2.0m
Brad Friedel	Columbus Crew	Liverpool	£1.0m
Petter Rudi	Molde	Sheffield W.	£800,000
Mike Evans	Southampton	WBA	£750,000
Ian Selley	Arsenal	Fulham	£500,000
Samassi Abou	Cannes	West Ham U.	£300,000
Stalle Solbakken	Lillestrom	Wimbledon	£250,000
Neil Maddison	Southampton	Middlesbrough	£250,000
Christer Warren	Southampton	Bournemouth	£50,000
Glenn Helder	Arsenal	NAC Breda	Undisclosed
James Smith	Wolverhampton W.	C. Palace	Swap
Kevin Muscat	C. Palace	Wolverhampton W.	Swap
Doughie Freedman	C. Palace	Wolverhampton W.	Swap
Ivano Bonetti	C. Palace	Genoa	Free
Tomas Brolin	Leeds U.	Released	Free
Franz Carr	Reggiana	Bolton W.	Free
George Donnis	Blackburn R.	Released	Free
Daniel Potter	Chelsea	Colchester U.	Free
Wayne Sutton	Derby Co.	Woking	Free
Jason Dozzell	Tottenham H.	Ipswich T.	Non-contract
David Regis	Barnsley	L. Orient	Non-contract
Jonathan Scargil	Sheffield W.	Chesterfield	Non-contract
Ivano Bonetti	Bologna	C. Palace	Monthly

November 1997

Player	From	To	Fee
Michele Padovano	Juventus	C. Palace	£1.7m
Thomas Myhre	Viking Stavanger	Everton	£800,000
Maik Taylor	Southampton	Fulham	£700,000
John McGinlay	Bolton W.	Bradford C.	£625,000
Paul Trollope	Derby Co.	Fulham	£600,000
George Ndah	C. Palace	Swindon T.	£500,000
Graham Stuart	Everton	Sheffield U.	£500,000
Peter Markstedt	Vasteras SK	Barnsley	£250,000
Alan Neilson	Southampton	Fulham	£250,000
Bjorn Johansen	Tromso	Southampton	£200,000
Jussi Jaaskelainen	VPS (Finland)	Bolton W.	£100,000
Steve McAnespie	Bolton W.	Fulham	£100,000
Paul Simpson	Derby Co.	Wolverhampton W.	£75,000
David Curtolo	Vastras	Aston Villa	Nominal
Carlos Gonzales	Sydney Olympic	Newcastle U.	Undisclosed
Ralf Keidel	FC Schweinfurt	Newcastle U.	Undisclosed
Carl Tiler	Sheffield U.	Everton	Swap
Mitch Ward	Sheffield U.	Everton	Swap
Dave Beasant	Southampton	N. Forest	Free
Brian Borrows	Coventry C.	Swindon T.	Free
Paul Dalglish	Liverpool	Newcastle U.	Free
Andrew Tretton	Derby Co.	Chesterfield	Non-contract
Steve Lenagh	Sheffield W.	Chesterfield	Monthly

December 1997

Player	From	To	Fee
Viorel Moldovan	Grasshopper	Coventry C.	£3.25m
Karel Poborsky	Manchester U.	Benfica	£3.0m
Chris Coleman	Blackburn R.	Fulham	£2.1m
N. Alexandersson	Gothenburg	Sheffield W.	£750,000
George Boateng	Feyenoord	Coventry C.	£250,000
Jurgen Klinsmann	Sampdoria	Tottenham H.	£175,000
Gareth Davies	C. Palace	Reading	£175,000
Haukua Gudnason	Keflavik	Liverpool	£150,000
Scott Murray	Aston Villa	Bristol C.	£150,000
Carl Veart	C. Palace	Millwall	£50,000
Jason Jones	Liverpool	Swansea	Free
Mickael Madar	Dep La Coruna	Everton	Free

January 1998

Player	From	To	Fee
Faustino Asprilla	Newcastle U.	Parma	£6.1m
Andreas Andersson	AC Milan	Newcastle U.	£3.6m
Andy Hinchcliffe	Everton	Sheffield W.	£3.0m
Valerien Ismael	Strasbourg	C. Palace	£2.75m
Trevor Sinclair	QPR	West Ham U.	£2.3m
Includes swap of Dowie and Rowland valued at £500,000			
Andrew Griffin	Stoke C.	Newcastle U.	£1.5m > £2.25m
Patrick Blondeau	Sheffield W.	Bordeaux	£1.2m
Matt Carbone	Derby Co.	WBA	£800,000
Jan Aage Fjortoft	Sheffield U	Barnsley	£800,000
Pierre Laurent	Leeds U.	Bastia	£500,000
Wayne Collins	Sheffield W.	Fulham	£400,000 > £550,000
Aljosa Asanovic	Derby Co.	Napoli	£350,000
Carl Leaburn	Charlton A.	Wimbledon	£300,000
Simon Charlton	Southampton	Birmingham C.	£250,000
Frode Grodas	Chelsea	Tottenham H.	£250,000
John O'Kane	Manchester U.	Everton	£250,000 > £450,000
Christian Mayrleb	FC Tirol	Sheffield W.	£200,000
Marcus Bent	Brentford	C. Palace	£150,000 > £300,000
Mark Robins	Leicester C.	Dep. Orense	Nominal
Neil Mustoe	Manchester U.	Wigan A.	Unknown
Iain Dowie	West Ham U.	QPR	Swap
Keith Rowland	West Ham U.	QPR	Swap
Nicola Berti	Internazionale	Tottenham H.	Free
Tomas Brolin	Leeds U.	C. Palace	Free
Kevin Mather	Tottenham H.	Southend U.	Free
David Terrier	West Ham U.	Newcastle U.	Free
Itzak Zohar	C. Palace	M. Haifa	Free

February 1998

Player	From	To	Fee
Gary Speed	Everton	Newcastle U.	£5.5m
Moussa Saib	Valencia	Tottenham H.	£2.3m
Callum Davidson	St Johnstone	Blackburn R.	£1.75m
John Beresford	Newcastle U.	Southampton	£1.5m
Martin Hiden	Rapid Vienna	Leeds U.	£1.3m
Don Hutchison	Sheffield U.	Everton	£1.0m
Matt Jansen	Carlisle U.	C. Palace	£1.0m > £2.0m
Sasa Curcic	Aston Villa	C. Palace	£1.0m
Goce Sedloski	Hajduk Split	Sheffield W.	£750,000 > £1.25m
Theo Zagorakis	PAOK Salonika	Leicester C.	£750,000

Rory Delap	Carlisle U.	Derby Co.	£500,000 > £1.0m
Kyle Lightbourne	Coventry C.	Stoke C.	£500,000
Stephen Bywater	Rochdale	West Ham U.	£300,000 > £2.3m
John Hills	Everton	Blackpool	£75,000
Matthew Robinson	Southampton	Portsmouth	£50,000
Nick Wright	Derby Co.	Carlisle U.	£35,000
	Payable only if Carlisle avoided relegation		
Valur Gislason	Arsenal	Stromsgodset	Undisclosed
Jon O'Connor	Everton	Sheffield U.	Swap
Earl Barrett	Everton	Sheffield W.	Free
Simon Coleman	Bolton W.	Southend U.	Free
Jehad Muntasser	Arsenal	Bristol C.	Free
Andrew Catley	Southampton	Exeter C.	Non-contract
Mark Quayle	Everton	Southport	Non-contract
Franz Carr	Bolton W.	WBA	Monthly
Adem Poric	Sheffield W.	Rotherham	Monthly
Russell Watkinson	Southampton	Bristol C.	Monthly

March 1998

Player	From	To	Fee
Nikolaos Dabizas	Olympiakos	Newcastle U.	£2m
Mark Kennedy	Liverpool	Wimbledon	£1.75m
Lars Bohinen	Blackburn R.	Derby Co.	£1.45m
Andy Roberts	C. Palace	Wimbledon	£1.2m > £1.6m
Jamie Pollock	Bolton W.	Manchester C.	£1.0m
Jonathan Greening	York C.	Manchester U.	£1.0m
Neil Emblen	C. Palace	Wolverhampton W.	£900,000
Phillippe Clement	Racing Genk	Coventry C.	£625,000
Matt McKay	Chester C.	Everton	£500,000 > £750,000
Vinnie Jones	Wimbledon	QPR	£500,000
Javier Margas	Universidad	West Ham U.	£500,000
Steve Claridge	Leicester C.	Wolverhampton W.	£350,000
Jamie Clapham	Tottenham H.	Ipswich T.	£300,000
James Coppinger	Darlington	Newcastle U.	* £250,000
Paul Robinson	Darlington	Newcastle U.	* £250,000
	* Could rise to combined fee of £1.8m		
Paul Brayson	Newcastle U.	Reading	£100,000
Robbie Slater	Southampton	Wolverhampton W.	£75,000
Steve Davies	Barnsley	Oxford U.	£75,000
Jimmy Crawford	Newcastle U.	Reading	£50,000
Stuart Jones	Weston-S-Mare	Sheffield W.	£20,000 > £100,000
Bryan Small	Bolton W.	Bury	Undisclosed
Vince Bartram	Arsenal	Gillingham	Free
Ian Bishop	West Ham U.	Manchester C.	Free
O'Neill Donaldson	Sheffield W.	Stoke C.	Free

Sean Hessey	Leeds U.	Huddersfield T.	Free
Richard Jobson	Leeds U.	Manchester C.	Free
Neville Southall	Everton	Stoke C.	Free
Emerson Thome	Benfica	Sheffield W.	Free
Mohamed Berthe	Gaz Ajaccio	West Ham U.	Free
Steven Blaney	West Ham U.	Brentford	Free
Stuart Nethercott	Tottenham H.	Millwall	Free
John Salako	Coventry C.	Bolton W.	Free
Russell Watkinson	Southampton	Millwall	Free
Paul Mahorn	Tottenham H.	Port Vale	Non-contract

May 1998

Jaap Stam	PSV Eindhoven	Manchester United	£10.75m
Pierluigi Casiraghi	Lazio	Chelsea	£5.4m
Horacio Carbonari	Rosario Central	Derby County	£2.7m
Clyde Wijnhard	Willem II	Leeds United	£1.5m
Jimmy Corbett	Gillingham	Blackburn Rovers	£525,000
Ben Thornley	Manchester United	Huddersfield T.	tbc

June 1998

Kevin Davies	Southampton	Blackburn Rovers	£7.25m
Marcel Desailly	AC Milan	Chelsea	£4.6m
Alan Thompson	Bolton Wanderers	Aston Villa	£4.5m
Stephane Guivarc'h	Auxerre	Newcastle United	£3.5m
Jon Dahl Tomasson	Newcastle United	Feyenoord	£2.5m
Albert Ferrer	Barcelona	Chelsea	£2.2m
Sean Dundee	Karlsruhe	Liverpool	£2.0m
Danny Granville	Chelsea	Leeds United	£1.6m
Neil Redfearn	Bolton Wanderers	Charlton Athletic	£1.0m
Chris Powell	Derby County	Charlton Athletic	£825,000
Jean-Guy Wallemme	Lens	Coventry City	£700,000
David Grodin	Saint Etienne	Arsenal	£500,000
Grant Brebner	Manchester United	Reading	£300,000
Ian Brightwell	Manchester City	Coventry City	Free
Alan Reeves	Wimbledon	Swindon Town	Free
Darren Peacock	Newcastle United	Blackburn Rovers	Free
Brian Laudrup	Rangers	Chelsea	Free

Note: Where two figures are given, ie, £500,000 > £1.2m, this indicates that the transfer fee was an initial down-payment of £500,000 and could rise to £1.2m. Normally the additional payment is staged and will depend on the number of appearances made by the player (for example, an additional £250,000 might be payable when the player has made 50 appearances for his new club) and other factors, such as if the player goes on to win international recognition etc.

PLAYER LOANS 1997-98

August 1997

Player	From	To
Dave Beasant	Southampton	N. Forest
Mark Stein	Chelsea	Ipswich T.
Craig Smith	Derby Co.	Rochdale
John Hills	Everton	Swansea C.
Jason Harris	C. Palace	Lincoln C.
Paul Crichton	WBA	Aston Villa
David Regis	Barnsley	Scunthorpe U.
Neil Moss	Southampton	Gillingham
Michael Watt	Aberdeen	Blackburn R.

September 1997

Brian Borrows	Coventry C.	Swindon T.
Jason Bowell	Birmingham C.	Southampton
Chris Casper	Manchester U.	Swindon T.
Nigel Clough	Manchester C.	Sheffield W.
Simon Coleman	Bolton W.	Wolverhampton W.
Steve Davis	Barnsley	York C.
Ian Moore	N. Forest	West Ham U.
Isiah Rankin	Arsenal	Colchester U.
Bryan Small	Bolton W.	Luton T.

October 1997

Vince Bartram	Arsenal	Huddersfield T.
Michael Black	Arsenal	Millwall
Brian Borrows	Coventry C.	Swindon T.
Nicky Colgan	Chelsea	Brentford
Paul Gibson	Manchester U.	Mansfield
Valur Gislason	Arsenal	Brighton & HA
Scott Jones	Barnsley	Notts Co.
Chris Kiwomya	Arsenal	Selangor
Leon McKenzie	C. Palace	Fulham
John O'Kane	Manchester U.	Bradford C.
Per Pedersen	Blackburn R.	B. Moenchengladbach
David Rocastle	Chelsea	Hull C.
Paul Simpson	Derby Co.	Wolverhampton W.

November 1997

Paulo Alves	Sporting Lisbon	West Ham U.
Daniel Boxall	C. Palace	Oldham A.
Tony Cottee	Leicester C.	Birmingham C.

Paul Dalglish	Newcastle U.	Bury
Lee Hodges	West Ham U.	Plymouth Ar.
Lee Hodges	West Ham U.	Plymouth Ar.
Greg Strong	Bolton W.	Blackpool
David Thompson	Liverpool	Swindon T.
Tony Warner	Liverpool	Swindon T.
Nicky Wright	Derby Co.	Carlisle U.

December 1997

Simon Brown	Tottenham H.	Lincoln C.
Simon Charlton	Southampton	Birmingham C.
Martin Foster	Leeds U.	Bury
Andy Gray	Leeds U.	Bury
Steve Harper	Newcastle U.	Huddersfield T.
Bernard Lama	PSG	West Ham U.
David Lee	Chelsea	Sheffield U.
Adam Reed	Blackburn R.	Rochdale
Neville Southall	Everton	Southend U.
Bryan Small	Bolton W.	Bradford C.
Paul Teather	Manchester U.	AFC Bournemouth
Scott Taylor	Bolton W.	Rotherham
Neil Thompson	Barnsley	Oldham A.
Ronnie Wallwork	Manchester U.	Carlisle U.

January 1998

Earl Barrett	Everton	Sheffield U.
Grant Brebner	Manchester U.	Cambridge U.
Laurent Charvert	Cannes	Chelsea
James Clapham	Tottenham H.	Ipswich T.
Steve Claridge	Leicester C.	Portsmouth
O'Neill Donaldson	Sheffield W.	Oxford U.
Neale Fenn	Tottenham H.	L. Orient
John Hills	Everton	Blackpool
Scott Howie	Motherwell	Coventry C.
Richard Jobson	Leeds U.	Southend U.
Damien Johnson	Blackburn R.	N. Forest
Mark Kennedy	Liverpool	QPR
Kyle Lightbourne	Coventry C.	Fulham
Stuart Nethercott	Tottenham H.	Millwall
Darren Pitcher	C. Palace	L. Orient
Michael O'Neill	Coventry C.	Aberdeen
Bryan Small	Bolton W.	Bury
Bob Taylor	WBA	Bolton W.

February 1998

Steve Basham	Southampton	Wrexham
Peter Beardsley	Bolton W.	Manchester C.
Danny Boxall	C. Palace	Oldham A.

Guy Branston	Leicester C.	Colchester U.
Grant Brebner	Manchester U.	Hibernian
Nick Colgan	Chelsea	Reading
James Crawford	Newcastle U.	Dundee U.
Steve Davis	Barnsley	Oxford U.
Stuart Elliot	Newcastle U.	Swindon T.
Laurens Ten Heuvel	Barnsley	Northampton T.
Danny Hill	Tottenham H.	Cardiff C.
Stig Johansen	Southampton	Bristol C.
John O'Connor	Everton	Sheffield U.
Emanuelle Omoyinmi	West Ham U.	Dundee U.
Graham Paxton	Newcastle U.	Millwall
Ian Rush	Newcastle U.	Sheffield U.
Craig Smith	Derby Co.	Rushden & D.
Neville Southall	Everton	Stoke C.
Michael Thomas	Liverpool	Middlesbrough
Julian Watts	Leicester C.	Huddersfield T.
Tony Williams	Blackburn R.	QPR
Mark Wilson	Manchester U.	Wrexham

March 1998

Rory Allen	Tottenham H.	Luton T.
Peter Beardsley	Bolton W.	Fulham
David Brown	Manchester U.	Hull C.
Neale Fenn	Tottenham H.	Norwich C.
Paddy Kelly	Newcastle U.	Reading
Neil Ruddock	Liverpool	QPR
Les Sealey	West Ham U.	Bury
Bob Taylor	WBA	Bolton W.
Scott Taylor	Bolton W.	Blackpool
Graeme Tomlinson	Manchester U.	Millwall
Neil Finn	West Ham U.	Dorchester T.
Gaetano Giallana	Nantes	Bolton W.
Robert Hughes	Aston Villa	Carlisle U.
Robin Hulbert	Swindon T.	Newcastle U.
Michael O'Neill	Coventry C.	Reading
Cosimo Sarli	Torino	Southampton
Mark Stein	Chelsea	AFC Bournemouth
John Spencer	QPR	Everton
Neil Thompson	Barnsley	York C.
Ronald Wallwork	Manchester U.	Stockport Co.

A-Z
FA Premier League Players 1998-99

Notes: The players are listed in alphabetical order and are those who are likely to feature in the Premiership action during the 1998-99 season. As a rule, fringe players who played at least one game in 1997-98 are included. There are exceptions though – for instance, players making a large number of appearances on the bench without actually getting on the pitch. This is true for reserve goalkeepers. *Previous Club Details* includes all Premiership games played to date. Specific appearance details for 1997-98 can be found in the *Club Directory* section. A club with * next to it in the *Previous Club Details* list indicates that the figures do not include those for the 1997-98 season. Under Fee, an 'm' indicates million, thus £3.5m should be read as £3,500,000 or £3.5 million; 'k' indicates thousand (kilo) thus £350k should be read as £350,000.

NL=Non-League; Train=Trainee; App=Apprentice; sby=Schoolboy. When figures are given for a non-English club they refer to the relevant country's league and cup competitions.

ABOU Samassi   25   West Ham United

Full Name: Samassi Abou
DOB: 04/04/73 Gabona, Ivory Coast

Previous Club Details

Club	Signed	Fee	Tot	Start	Sub	FA	FL	Lge	FA	FL
					Apps				*Goals*	
Martiques, Lyon, Cannes										
West Ham U.	Oct-97	£400k	19	12	7	5	2	5	0	1

FAPL Summary by Club

West Ham U.	1997-98		19	12	7	5	2	5	0	1
Totals			*19*	*12*	*7*	*5*	*2*	*5*	*0*	*1*

ADAMS Tony   31   Arsenal

Full Name: Anthony Alexander Adams
DOB: 10/10/66   Romford, Essex

Previous Club Details

Club	Signed	Fee	Tot	Start	Sub	FA	FL	Lge	FA	FL
					Apps				*Goals*	
Arsenal	Jan-84	NL	421	417	4	41	59	30	8	5

FAPL Summary by Club

Arsenal	92-93 to 97-98		172	169	3	23	25	10	7	3
Totals			*172*	*169*	*3*	*23*	*25*	*10*	*7*	*3*

ALBERT Philippe *31* Newcastle United

Full Name: Philippe Albert
DOB: 10/08/67 Bouillon, Belgium

Previous Club Details

Club	Signed	Fee	Tot	Start	Sub	FA	FL	Lge	FA	FL
					Apps				*Goals*	
Anderlecht										
Newcastle U.	Aug-94	£2.65m	90	84	6	8	12	8	1	2

FAPL Summary by Club

Club			Tot	Start	Sub	FA	FL	Lge	FA	FL
Newcastle U.	94/5 to 97/8		90	84	6	8	12	8	1	2
Totals			*90*	*84*	*6*	*8*	*12*	*8*	*1*	*2*

ALEXANDERSSON Niclas Sheffield Wednesday

Full Name: Niclas Alexandersson
DOB: 29/12/71, Vessigebro, Sweden

Previous Club Details

Club	Signed	Fee	Tot	Start	Sub	FA	FL	Lge	FA	FL
					Apps				*Goals*	
Vessigebro, Halmstads, IFK Gothenburg										
Sheffield W.	Dec-97	£750k	6	5	1	2	0	0	1	0

FAPL Summary by Club

Club			Tot	Start	Sub	FA	FL	Lge	FA	FL
Sheffield W.	1997-98		6	5	1	2	0	0	1	0
Totals			*6*	*5*	*1*	*2*	*0*	*0*	*1*	*0*

ALLEN Graham Everton

Full Name: Graham Allen
DOB: 08/04/77, Franworth

Previous Club Details

Club	Signed	Fee	Tot	Start	Sub	FA	FL	Lge	FA	FL
					Apps				*Goals*	
Everton	12/94	Train	6	2	4	0	0	0	0	0

FAPL Summary by Club

Club			Tot	Start	Sub	FA	FL	Lge	FA	FL
Everton	96/7 to 97/8		6	2	4	0	0	0	0	0
Totals			*6*	*2*	*4*	*0*	*0*	*0*	*0*	*0*

ALLEN Rory Tottenham Hotspur

ALLEN Rory *20*

Full Name: Rory Allen
DOB: 17/10/77, Beckenham

Previous Club Details

Club	Signed	Fee	Tot	Start	Sub	FA	FL	Lge	FA	FL
					Apps				*Goals*	
Tottenham	3/96	Train	16	10	6	1	3	2	0	2

FAPL Summary by Club

Club			Tot	Start	Sub	FA	FL	Lge	FA	FL
Tottenham	96/7 to 97/8		25	22	3	1	3	2	0	2
Totals			*25*	*22*	*3*	*1*	*3*	*2*	*0*	*2*

ANDERSSON Anders Blackburn Rovers

Full Name: Anders Andersson
DOB: 15/03/74, Tomellia, Sweden

Previous Club Details

Club	Signed	Fee	Tot	Start	Sub	FA	FL	Lge	FA	FL
					Apps				*Goals*	
Malmo FF										
Blackburn R.	Jul-97		4	1	3			0	0	1

FAPL Summary by Club

Club			Tot	Start	Sub	FA	FL	Lge	FA	FL
Blackburn R.	1997-98		4	1	3			0	0	1
Totals			*4*	*1*	*3*			*0*	*0*	*1*

ANDERSSON Andreas *14* Newcastle United

Full Name: Andreas Andersson
DOB: 10/4/74, Stockholm, Sweden

Previous Club Details

Club	Signed	Fee	Tot	Start	Sub	FA	FL	Lge	FA	FL
					Apps				*Goals*	
Tidaholms, Degerfors, IFK, Milan										
Newcastle U.	Jan-98	£3.6m	12	10	2	3	0	2	0	0

FAPL Summary by Club

Club			Tot	Start	Sub	FA	FL	Lge	FA	FL
Newcastle U.	1997-98		12	10	2	3	0	2	0	0
Totals			*12*	*10*	*2*	*3*	*0*	*2*	*0*	*0*

ANDERTON Darren *26* Tottenham Hotspur

Full Name: Darren Robert Anderton
DOB: 03/03/72, Southampton
Previous Club Details

Club	Signed	Fee	Tot	Start	Sub	FA	FL	Lge	FA	FL
Portsmouth	Feb-90	Train	62	53	9	8	5	7	5	1
Tottenham H.	Jun-92	£1.75m	147	131	16	14	12	22	2	4
FAPL Summary by Club										
Tottenham H.	92/3 to 97/8		147	131	16	14	12	22	2	4
Totals			147	131	16	14	12	22	2	4

Full Name: Steven Craig Armstrong
DOB: 23/05/75, South Shields
Previous Club Details

Club	Signed	Fee	Tot	Start	Sub	FA	FL	Lge	FA	FL
N. Forest	Jun-92	Trainee	17	13	4	1	4	0	0	0
Burnley	Dec-94	Loan	4	4	0	0	0	0	0	0
Bristol R.	Jan-96	Loan	0	4				0	0	0
Notts Co.	Aug-96	Loan	10	9	1			0	0	0
Gillingham	Oct-96	Loan	10	10		2		0	0	0
Watford	Nov-97	Loan	α(2)15	15						

ANELKA Nicolas — Arsenal

Full Name: Nicolas Anelka
DOB: 14/03/79, Versailles
Previous Club Details

Club	Signed	Fee	Tot	Start	Sub	FA	FL	Lge	FA	FL
Paris St Germain	—	Train	2	2	0	0	0	0	0	0
Arsenal	Jan-97	£500k	30	16	14	9	4	6	1	0
FAPL Summary by Club										
Arsenal	96/7 to 97/8		30	16	14	9	4	6	1	0
Totals			30	16	14	9	4	6	1	0

ARMSTRONG Chris — Tottenham Hotspur

Full Name: Christopher Peter Armstrong
DOB: 19/06/71, Newcastle
Previous Club Details

Club	Signed	Fee	Tot	Start	Sub	FA	FL	Lge	FA	FL
Wrexham	Mar-89	Free	60	40	20	1	3	13	0	4
Millwall	Aug-91	£50k	28	11	17	1	4	5	0	2
C. Palace	Sep-92	£1m	118	118	0	8	8	46	5	6
Tottenham H.	Jul-94	£4.5m	67	61	6	7	8	25	4	5
FAPL Summary by Club										
C. Palace	92/3 to 94/5		75	75	0	6	5	23	5	5
Tottenham H.	95/6 to 97/8		67	61	6	7	8	25	4	5
Totals			142	136	6	13	13	48	9	10

ARDLEY Neal — Wimbledon

Full Name: Neal Christopher Ardley
DOB: 01/09/72, Epsom
Previous Club Details

Club	Signed	Fee	Tot	Start	Sub	FA	FL	Lge	FA	FL
Wimbledon	Jul-91		139	123	16	20	16	10	1	2
FAPL Summary by Club										
Wimbledon	92/3 to 97/8		130	115	15	20	16	10	1	2
Totals			130	115	15	20	16	10	1	2

ARPHEXAD Pegguy — Leicester City

Full Name: Pegguy Arphexad
DOB:
Previous Club Details
Racing Club Paris

Club	Signed	Fee	Tot	Start	Sub	FA	FL	Lge	FA	FL
Leicester C.	Aug-97	Free	5	5	0	0	0	0	0	0
FAPL Summary by Club										
Leicester C.	1997-98		5	5	0	0	0	0	0	0
Totals			5	5	0	0	0	0	0	0

ARMSTRONG Craig — Nottingham Forest

ATHERTON Peter — Sheffield Wednesday

Full Name: Peter Atherton
DOB: 06/04/70, Orrell

Previous Club Details

Club	Signed	Fee	Apps Tot	Start	Sub	FA	FL	Goals Lge	FA	FL
Wigan A.	Feb-88		149	145	4	7	8	1	1	0
Coventry C.	Aug-91	£300k	114	113	1	2	8	4	0	0
Sheffield W.	Jun-94	£800k	140	140	0	8	10	6	0	0

FAPL Summary by Club

Coventry C.	92/3 to 93/4		79	78	1	2	4	2	0	0
Sheffield W.	94/5 to 97/8		140	140	0	11	11	6	0	0
Totals			219	218	1	13	15	8	0	0

BAARDSEN Espen — Tottenham Hotspur

Full Name: Espen Baardsen
DOB: 7/12/77, San Rafael, Ca.

Previous Club Details

Club	Signed	Fee	Apps Tot	Start	Sub	FA	FL	Goals Lge	FA	FL
San Francisco All Blacks										
Tottenham H.	Jul-96	Free	11	10	1	3	0	0	0	0

FAPL Summary by Club

Tottenham H.	96/7 to 97/8		11	10	1	3	0	0	0	0
Totals			11	10	1	3	0	0	0	0

BABAYARO Celestine — Chelsea

Full Name: Celestine Babayaro
DOB: 29/08/78, Nigeria

Previous Club Details

Club	Signed	Fee	Apps Tot	Start	Sub	FA	FL	Goals Lge	FA	FL
Anderlecht										
Chelsea	Apr-97	£2.25m	8	8	0	0	2	0	0	0

FAPL Summary by Club

Chelsea	1997-98		8	8	0	0	2	0	0	0
Totals			8	8	0	0	2	0	0	0

BABB Phil — Liverpool

Full Name: Phillip Andrew Babb
DOB: 30/11/70, London

Previous Club Details

Club	Signed	Fee	Apps Tot	Start	Sub	FA	FL	Goals Lge	FA	FL
Bradford C.	Aug-90	Free	80	73	7	3	6	14	0	1
Coventry C.	Jul-92	£500k	77	70	7	2	5	3	0	1
Liverpool	Sep-94	£3.6m	103	100	3	11	16	1	0	0

FAPL Summary by Club

Coventry C.	92/3 to 94/5		77	70	7	2	5	3	0	1
Liverpool	94/5 to 97/8		103	100	3	11	16	1	0	0
Totals			180	170	10	13	21	4	0	1

BAIANO Francesco — Derby County

Full Name: Francesco Baiano
DOB: 24/2/68, Napoli

Previous Club Details

Club	Signed	Fee	Apps Tot	Start	Sub	FA	FL	Goals Lge	FA	FL
Fiorentina										
Derby Co.	Jul-97	£650k	33	30	3	0	1	12	1	0

FAPL Summary by Club

Derby Co.	1997-98		33	30	3	0	1	12	1	0
Totals			33	30	3	0	1	12	1	0

BALL Michael — Everton

Full Name: Michael Ball
DOB: 02/10/77, Liverpool

Previous Club Details

Club	Signed	Fee	Apps Tot	Start	Sub	FA	FL	Goals Lge	FA	FL
Everton	10/96	Train	30	23	7	1	2	1	0	0

FAPL Summary by Club

Everton	96/7 to 97/8		30	23	7	1	2	1	0	0
Totals			30	23	7	1	2	1	0	0

BARMBY Nicky — Everton

Full Name: Nicholas Jonathan Barmby
DOB: 11/02/74, Hull

(handwritten: 27)

Previous Club Details

Club	Signed	Fee	Apps Tot	Start	Sub	FA	FL	Goals Lge	FA	FL
Tottenham	Apr-91	Train	87	81	6	13	8	20	5	1
Middlesbro'	Aug-95	£5.25m	50	43	7	3	4	8	1	1
Everton	Oct-96	£5.75m	55	48	7	3	2	6	1	2

FAPL Summary by Club

Club			Tot	Start	Sub	FA	FL	Lge	FA	FL
Tottenham	92/3 to 94/5		87	81	6	13	8	20	5	1
Middlesbro'	1995-96		32	32	0	3	0	6	1	0
Middlesbro'	1996-97		10	10	0	0	1	0	1	0
Everton	96/7 to 97/8		55	48	7	3	2	7	7	4
Totals			184	171	13	19	14	34	7	4

BARNES John — Newcastle United

Full Name: John Charles Bryan Barnes
DOB: 07/11/63, Jamaica, West Indies

(handwritten: 34)

Previous Club Details

Club	Signed	Fee	Apps Tot	Start	Sub	FA	FL	Goals Lge	FA	FL
Watford	Jul-81		233	232	1	31	21	65	11	7
Liverpool	Jun-87	£900k	314	310	4	51	26	84	16	3
Newcastle	Aug-97	Free	26	22	4	5	3	0	0	0

FAPL Summary by Club

Club			Tot	Start	Sub	FA	FL	Lge	FA	FL
Liverpool	92/3 to 96/7		162	158	4	19	16	22	6	0
Newcastle U.	1997-98		26	22	4	5	3	6	0	0
Totals			188	180	8	24	19	28	6	0

BARNESS Tony — Charlton Athletic

Full Name: Anthony Barness
DOB: 25/03/73, Lewisham, London

Previous Club Details

Club	Signed	Fee	Apps Tot	Start	Sub	FA	FL	Goals Lge	FA	FL
Charlton A.	Mar-91		27	21	6	3	2	1	0	0
Chelsea	Sep-92	£350k	14	12	2	2	0	2	0	0
Middlesbro'	Aug-93	Loan	1	1	0	0	0	0	0	0
Southend U.	Feb-96	Loan	5	5	0	9	1	5	3	0
Charlton A.	Aug-96	£165k	75	66	9	1	5	3	0	0

FAPL Summary by Club

Club			Tot	Start	Sub	FA	FL	Lge	FA	FL
Chelsea	92/3 to 95/6		14	12	2	2	0	2	0	0
Totals			14	12	2	2	0	2	0	0

BARRETT Earl — Sheffield Wednesday

(handwritten: 31)

Full Name: Earl Delisser Barrett
DOB: 28/04/67, Rochdale

Previous Club Details

Club	Signed	Fee	Apps Tot	Start	Sub	FA	FL	Goals Lge	FA	FL
Manchester C.	Apr-85	Train	3	2	1	0	1	0	0	0
Oldham Ath.	Mar-86	Loan	12	12	0	2	14	20	7	1
Chester C.	Nov-87	£35k	183	181	2	14	20	7	1	1
Aston Villa	Feb-92	£1.7m	119	118	1	9	15	1	1	0
Everton	Jan-95	£1.7m	74	73	1	2	4	0	0	0
Sheffield W.	Feb-98	Free	10	10	0	0	0	0	0	0

BARRY Gareth — Aston Villa

Full Name: Gareth Barry

Previous Club Details

Club	Signed	Fee	Apps Tot	Start	Sub	FA	FL	Goals Lge	FA	FL
Aston Villa	Signed		2	1	1	0	0	0	0	0

FAPL Summary by Club

Club			Tot	Start	Sub	FA	FL	Lge	FA	FL
Aston Villa	1997-98		2	1	1	0	0	0	0	0
Totals			2	1	1	0	0	0	0	0

BART-WILLIAMS Chris — Nottingham Forest *(24)*

Full Name: Christopher Gerald Bart-Williams
DOB: 16/06/74, Sierra Leone

Previous Club Details

Apps: Tot, Start, Sub, FA, FL — Goals: Lge, FA, FL

Club	Signed	Fee	Tot	Start	Sub	FA	FL	Lge	FA	FL
L. Orient	Jul-91	—	36	34	2	0	4	2	2	4
Sheffield W.	Nov-91	£275k	124	95	29	12	16	16	2	4
N. Forest	Jul-95	£2.5m	82	79	3	9	9	4	0	0

FAPL Summary by Club

Club			Tot	Start	Sub	FA	FL	Lge	FA	FL
Sheffield W.	92/3 to 94/5		109	83	26	11	16	17	1	3
N. Forest	95/6 to 96/7		49	49	0	9	5	1	0	0
Totals			158	132	26	20	21	18	1	3

BARTON Warren — Newcastle United *(30)*

Full Name: Warren Dean Barton
DOB: 19/03/69, Stoke Newington

Previous Club Details

Apps: Tot, Start, Sub, FA, FL — Goals: Lge, FA, FL

Club	Signed	Fee	Tot	Start	Sub	FA	FL	Lge	FA	FL
Maidstone U.	Jul-87	£10k	42	41	1	3	2	1	0	0
Wimbledon	Jun-90	£300k	180	178	2	11	16	10	0	1
Newcastle U.	Jun-95	£4m+	76	65	11	8	3	0	0	0

FAPL Summary by Club

Club			Tot	Start	Sub	FA	FL	Lge	FA	FL
Wimbledon	92/3 to 94/5		101	99	2	6	12	6	0	1
Newcastle U.	95/6 to 97/8		72	61	11	9	8	0	0	2
Totals			173	160	13	15	20	6	0	3

BASHAM Steve — Southampton

Full Name: Steve Basham
DOB: 02/12/77, Southampton

Previous Club Details

Apps: Tot, Start, Sub, FA, FL — Goals: Lge, FA, FL

Club	Signed	Fee	Tot	Start	Sub	FA	FL	Lge	FA	FL
Southampton			15	1	14	0	0	0	0	0

FAPL Summary by Club

Club			Tot	Start	Sub	FA	FL	Lge	FA	FL
Southampton	96/7 to 97/8		15	1	14	0	0	0	0	0
Totals			15	1	14	0	0	0	0	0

BATTY David — Newcastle United *(29)*

Full Name: David Batty
DOB: 02/12/68, Leeds

Previous Club Details

Apps: Tot, Start, Sub, FA, FL — Goals: Lge, FA, FL

Club	Signed	Fee	Tot	Start	Sub	FA	FL	Lge	FA	FL
Leeds U.	Jul-87	Train	211	201	10	12	17	4	0	0
Blackburn R.	Oct-93	£2.75m	54	53	1	5	6	1	0	0
Newcastle U.	Feb-96	£3.75m	75	75	0	9	4	3	0	0

FAPL Summary by Club

Club			Tot	Start	Sub	FA	FL	Lge	FA	FL
Leeds U.	92/3 to 93/4		39	38	1	3	2	1	0	0
Blackburn R.	93/4 to 95/6		54	53	1	5	6	1	0	0
Newcastle U.	95/6 to 97/8		75	75	0	9	4	3	0	0
Totals			168	166	2	17	12	5	0	0

BEAGRIE Peter — Everton *(32)*

Full Name: Peter Sydney Beagrie
DOB: 28/11/65, Middlesbrough

Previous Club Details

Apps: Tot, Start, Sub, FA, FL — Goals: Lge, FA, FL

Club	Signed	Fee	Tot	Start	Sub	FA	FL	Lge	FA	FL
Middlesbrough	Sep-83	—	32	24	8	0	1	2	0	0
Sheffield W.	Aug-86	£35k	84	81	3	5	4	11	0	0
Stoke C.	Jun-88	£210k	54	54	0	3	4	7	1	1
Everton	Nov-89	£750k	149	88	61	11	11	9	0	3
Sunderland	Sep-91	Loan	5	5	0	2	0	0	0	0
Man. C.	Mar-94	£1.1m	6	4	2	0	0	0	0	0

FAPL Summary by Club

Club			Tot	Start	Sub	FA	FL	Lge	FA	FL
Everton	92/3 to 93/4		51	40	11	2	7	7	0	0
Man. C.	93/4 to 95/6		51	46	5	4	8	3	1	0

(continued from previous page)

FAPL Summary by Club

Club	Season	Tot	Start	Sub	FA	FL	Lge	FA	FL
Everton	1997-98	6	4	2	0	0	0	0	0
Totals		*108*	*90*	*18*	*6*	*15*	*10*	*1*	*0*

(handwritten: 25)

BEASANT Dave — Nottingham Forest

(handwritten: 39)

Full Name: David John Beasant
DOB: 20/03/59, Willesden

Previous Club Details

Club	Signed	Fee	Tot	Start	Sub	FA	FL	Lge	FA	FL
Wimbledon	Aug-79	£1k	340	340	0	27	21	0	1	0
Newcastle U.	Jun-88	£800k	20	20	0	2	2	0	0	0
Chelsea	Jan-89	£725k	133	133	0	5	11	0	0	0
Grimsby T.	Oct-92	Loan	6	6	0	0	1	0	0	0
Wolver'n W.	Jan-93	Loan	4	4	0	0	0	0	0	0
Southampton	Nov-93	£300k	88	86	2	9	8	0	1	0
N. Forest	Nov-97	Free	39	39	0	1	2	0	2	0

FAPL Summary by Club

Club	Season	Tot	Start	Sub	FA	FL	Lge	FA	FL
Chelsea	1992-93	17	17	0	0	0	0	0	0
Southampton	93/4 to 96/7	88	86	2	9	8	0	1	0
Totals		*105*	*103*	*2*	*9*	*8*	*0*	*1*	*0*

BEATTIE James — Blackburn Rovers

Full Name: James Beattie
DOB: 27/02/78, Lancaster

Previous Club Details

Club	Signed	Fee	Tot	Start	Sub	FA	FL	Lge	FA	FL
Blackburn R.		Train	3	0	3	1	1	1	0	0

FAPL Summary by Club

Club	Season	Tot	Start	Sub	FA	FL	Lge	FA	FL
Blackburn R.	1997-98	3	0	3	1	1	1	0	0
Totals		*3*	*0*	*3*	*1*	*1*	*1*	*0*	*0*

BECK Mikkel — Middlesbrough

Full Name: Mikkel Beck
DOB: 12/05/73, Denmark

Previous Club Details

Club	Signed	Fee	Tot	Start	Sub	FA	FL	Lge	FA	FL
Fortuna Köln										
Middlesbro'	Aug-96	Free	63	54	9	8	14	19	2	5

FAPL Summary by Club

Club	Season	Tot	Start	Sub	FA	FL	Lge	FA	FL
Middlesbro'	1996-97	25	22	3	6	7	5	2	4
Totals		*25*	*22*	*3*	*6*	*7*	*5*	*2*	*4*

BECKHAM David — Manchester United

(handwritten: 23)

Full Name: David Beckham
DOB: 02/05/75, Leytonstone

Previous Club Details

Club	Signed	Fee	Tot	Start	Sub	FA	FL	Lge	FA	FL
Manchester U.	Jan-93	Trai	110	95	15	11	5	23	4	0
Preston NE	Feb-95	Loan	5	4	1	0	0	2	0	0

FAPL Summary by Club

Club	Season	Tot	Start	Sub	FA	FL	Lge	FA	FL
Manchester U.	94/5 to 97/8	110	95	15	11	5	23	4	0
Totals		*110*	*95*	*15*	*11*	*5*	*23*	*4*	*0*

BEENEY Mark — Leeds United

(handwritten: 30)

Full Name: Mark Raymond Beeney
DOB: 30/12/67, Tunbridge Wells

Previous Club Details

Club	Signed	Fee	Tot	Start	Sub	FA	FL	Lge	FA	FL
Gillingham	Aug-85		2	2	0	0	3	0	0	0
Maidstone U.	Feb-87		50	50	0	0	11	0	0	0
Aldershot	Mar-90	Loan	7	7	0	0	0	0	0	0
Brighton	Mar-91	£30k	69	68	1	7	6	0	0	0
Leeds U.	Apr-93	£350k	46	45	1	5	4	0	0	0

FAPL Summary by Club

Club	Season	Tot	Start	Sub	FA	FL	Lge	FA	FL
Leeds U.	92/3 to 97/8	35	35	0	5	4	0	0	0
Totals		*35*	*35*	*0*	*5*	*4*	*0*	*0*	*0*

BENALI Francis — **Southampton** *(29)*

Full Name: Francis Vincent Benali
DOB: 30/12/68, Southampton

Previous Club Details

Club	Signed	Fee	Tot	Start	Sub	FA	FL	Lge	FA	FL
			Apps					*Goals*		
Southampton	Jan-87		253	225	28	20	26	1	0	0

FAPL Summary by Club

Club			Tot	Start	Sub	FA	FL	Lge	FA	FL
Southampton	92/3 to 97/8		186	172	14	9	15	1	0	0
Totals			186	172	14	9	15	1	0	0

BERESFORD John — **Southampton** *(32)*

Full Name: John Beresford
DOB: 04/09/66, Sheffield

Previous Club Details

Club	Signed	Fee	Tot	Start	Sub	FA	FL	Lge	FA	FL
			Apps					*Goals*		
Manchester C.	Sep-83	App	0	0	0	0	0	0	0	0
Barnsley	Aug-86	Free	88	79	9	5	7	5	1	2
Portsmouth	Mar-89	£300k	107	102	5	11	12	8	0	2
Newcastle U.	Jul-92	£650k	179	176	3	18	17	3	1	0
Southampton	Feb-98	£1.5m	10	10	0	0	0	0	0	0

FAPL Summary by Club

Club			Tot	Start	Sub	FA	FL	Lge	FA	FL
Newcastle U.	93/4 to 97/8		137	134	3	14	12	2	1	0
Southampton	1997-98		10	10	0	0	0	0	0	0
Totals			147	144	3	14	12	2	1	0

BERG Henning — **Manchester United** *(28)*

Full Name: Henning Berg
DOB: 01/09/69, Eidsvell

Previous Club Details

Club	Signed	Fee	Tot	Start	Sub	FA	FL	Lge	FA	FL
			Apps					*Goals*		
Lillestrom										
Blackburn R.	Jan-93	£400k	159	154	5	10	16	4	0	0
Man. U.	Aug-97	£5.0m	27	23	4	2	0	2	0	0

FAPL Summary by Club

Club			Tot	Start	Sub	FA	FL	Lge	FA	FL
Blackburn R.	92/3 to 96/7		159	154	5	10	16	4	0	0
Man.U.	1997-98		27	23	4	2	0	2	0	0
Totals			186	177	9	12	16	6	0	0

BERGER Patrik — **Liverpool** *(24)*

Full Name: Patrik Berger
DOB: 10/11/73, Prague

Previous Club Details

Club	Signed	Fee	Tot	Start	Sub	FA	FL	Lge	FA	FL
			Apps					*Goals*		
Slavia Prague	1991		89	83	6			24		
B.Dortmund	Jun-95		25	13	12			4		
Liverpool	Aug-96	£3.25m	45	19	26	3	6	9	0	1

FAPL Summary by Club

Club			Tot	Start	Sub	FA	FL	Lge	FA	FL
Liverpool	96/7 to 97/8		45	19	26	3	6	9	0	1
Totals			45	19	26	3	6	9	0	1

BERGKAMP Dennis — **Arsenal** *(29)*

Full Name: Dennis Nicolaas Bergkamp
DOB: 18/05/69, Amsterdam, Netherlands

Previous Club Details

Club	Signed	Fee	Tot	Start	Sub	FA	FL	Lge	FA	FL
			Apps					*Goals*		
Ajax	Jul-86		185	185	0			103		
Inter Milan	Jul-93	£12m	52	50	2			11		
Arsenal	Jul-95	£7.5m	90	89	1	10	13	39	4	8

FAPL Summary by Club

Club			Tot	Start	Sub	FA	FL	Lge	FA	FL
Arsenal	95/6 to 97/8		90	89	1	10	13	39	4	8
Totals			90	89	1	10	13	39	4	8

BERKOVIC Eyal — West Ham United *(handwritten: 26)*

Full Name: Eyal Berkovic
DOB: 02/04/72, Haifa

Previous Club Details

			Apps					Goals		
Club	Signed	Fee	Tot	Start	Sub	FA	FL	Lge	FA	FL
Maccabi Haifa			128	126	2			25		
Southampton	Sep-96	£1m	28	26	2	1	6	4	0	2
West Ham U.	Jun-97	£1.75m	35	34	1	6	5	7	2	0

FAPL Summary by Club

		Apps					Goals		
		Tot	Start	Sub	FA	FL	Lge	FA	FL
Southampton	1996-97	28	26	2	1	6	4	0	2
West Ham U.	1997-98	35	34	1	6	5	7	2	0
Totals		*63*	*60*	*3*	*7*	*11*	*11*	*2*	*2*

BERTI Nicola — Tottenham Hotspur *(handwritten: 31)*

Full Name: Nicola Berti
DOB: 14/4/67, Salsomaggiore

Previous Club Details

			Apps					Goals		
Club	Signed	Fee	Tot	Start	Sub	FA	FL	Lge	FA	FL
Internazionale										
Tottenham H.	Jan-98	Free	17	17	0	2	0	3	0	0

FAPL Summary by Club

		Apps					Goals		
		Tot	Start	Sub	FA	FL	Lge	FA	FL
Tottenham H.	1997-98	17	17	0	2	0	3	0	0
Totals		*17*	*17*	*0*	*2*	*0*	*3*	*0*	*0*

BILIC Slaven — Everton *(handwritten: 30)*

Full Name: Slaven Bilic
DOB: 11/09/68, Croatia

Previous Club Details

			Apps					Goals		
Club	Signed	Fee	Tot	Start	Sub	FA	FL	Lge	FA	FL
Karlsruhe										
West Ham U.	Dec-95	£1.3m	48	48	0	1	5	2	0	1
Everton	May-97	£4.5m	24	22	2	2	3	0	0	0

FAPL Summary by Club

		Apps					Goals		
		Tot	Start	Sub	FA	FL	Lge	FA	FL
West Ham U.	95/6 to 96/7	48	48	0	1	5	2	0	1
Everton	1997-98	24	22	2	2	3	0	0	0
Totals		*72*	*72*	*2*	*3*	*8*	*2*	*0*	*1*

BJORNEBYE Stig Inge — Liverpool *(handwritten: 29)*

Full Name: Stig Inge Bjornebye
DOB: 11/12/69, Norway

Previous Club Details

			Apps					Goals		
Club	Signed	Fee	Tot	Start	Sub	FA	FL	Lge	FA	FL
Rosenborg (Nor)										
Liverpool	Dec-92	£600k	116	112	4	11	14	2	1	0

FAPL Summary by Club

		Apps					Goals		
		Tot	Start	Sub	FA	FL	Lge	FA	FL
Liverpool	92/3 to 97/8	116	112	4	10	15	2	0	0
Totals		*116*	*112*	*4*	*10*	*15*	*2*	*0*	*0*

BLACKWELL Dean — Wimbledon *(handwritten: 29)*

Full Name: Dean Robert Blackwell
DOB: 05/12/69, Camden

Previous Club Details

			Apps					Goals		
Club	Signed	Fee	Tot	Start	Sub	FA	FL	Lge	FA	FL
Wimbledon	Jul-88	Train	154	132	22	21	11	1	0	0
Plymouth Ar.	Mar-90	Loan	7	5	2	0	0	0	0	0

FAPL Summary by Club

		Apps					Goals		
		Tot	Start	Sub	FA	FL	Lge	FA	FL
Wimbledon	92/3 to 97/8	112	100	12	17	9	0	0	0
Totals		*112*	*100*	*12*	*17*	*9*	*0*	*0*	*0*

BOA MORTE Luis — Arsenal *(handwritten: 20)*

Full Name: Luis Boa Morte Pereira
DOB: 04/08/78, Lisbon

Previous Club Details

			Apps					Goals		
Club	Signed	Fee	Tot	Start	Sub	FA	FL	Lge	FA	FL
Sporting Lisbon										
Arsenal	Jul-97	£1.75m	15	4	11	4	1	0	0	2

FAPL Summary by Club

		Tot	Start	Sub	FA	FL	Lge	FA	FL
Arsenal	1997-98	15	4	11	4	1	0	0	2
Totals		15	4	11	4	1	0	0	2

BOATENG George — Coventry City

Full Name: George Boateng
DOB: 05/09/75, Accra (Ghana)

Apps **23** (handwritten)

Previous Club Details

			Apps					Goals		
Club	Signed	Fee	Tot	Start	Sub	FA	FL	Lge	FA	FL
Feyenoord										
Coventry C.	Dec-97	£250k	14	14	0	5	0	1	0	0

FAPL Summary by Club

		Tot	Start	Sub	FA	FL	Lge	FA	FL
Coventry C.	1997-98	14	14	0	5	0	1	0	0
Totals		14	14	0	5	0	1	0	0

BOHINEN Lars — Derby County

Full Name: Lars Bohinen
DOB: 08/09/69, Vadso, Norway

Apps **19** (handwritten)

Previous Club Details

			Apps					Goals		
Club	Signed	Fee	Tot	Start	Sub	FA	FL	Lge	FA	FL
Young Boys Berne										
N. Forest	Nov-93	£450k	64	59	5	2	8	6	1	2
Blackburn R.	Oct-95	£700k	59	41	18	3	5	7	0	1
Derby Co.	Mar-98	£1.45m	9	9	0	2	0	· 1	0	0

FAPL Summary by Club

		Tot	Start	Sub	FA	FL	Lge	FA	FL
N. Forest	94/5 to 95/6	41	37	4	1	5	6	0	2
Blackburn R.	95/6 to 97/8	59	41	18	3	5	7	1	0
Derby Co.	1997-98	9	9	0	2	0	1	0	0
Totals		109	87	22	6	10	14	1	3

BOLAND Willie — Coventry City

Full Name: Willie Boland
DOB: 06/08/75, Republic of Ireland

Apps **23** (handwritten)

Previous Club Details

			Apps					Goals		
Club	Signed	Fee	Tot	Start	Sub	FA	FL	Lge	FA	FL
Coventry C.	Nov-92	Inrs	63	43	20	1	6	0	0	0

FAPL Summary by Club

		Tot	Start	Sub	FA	FL	Lge	FA	FL
Coventry C.	92/3 to 97/8	63	43	20	1	6	0	0	0
Totals		63	43	20	1	6	0	0	0

BONALAIR Thierry — Nottingham Forest

Full Name: Thierry Bonalair
DOB: 14/06/66, Paris

Apps **3½** (handwritten)

Previous Club Details

			Apps					Goals		
Club	Signed	Fee	Tot	Start	Sub	FA	FL	Lge	FA	FL
Neuchatel Xamax										
N. Forest	Jun-97	Free	30	23	7	1	1	2	0	0

BOOTH Andy — Sheffield Wednesday

Full Name: Andrew David Booth
DOB: 06/12/73, Huddersfield

Previous Club Details

			Apps					Goals		
Club	Signed	Fee	Tot	Start	Sub	FA	FL	Lge	FA	FL
Huddersfield	Jul-92	Train	123	109	14	6	7	54	3	3
Sheffield W.	Jul-96	£2.7m	58	53	5	6	2	17	3	3

FAPL Summary by Club

		Tot	Start	Sub	FA	FL	Lge	FA	FL
Sheffield W.	96/7 to 97/8	58	53	5	6	2	17	3	3
Totals		58	53	5	6	2	17	3	3

BOSNICH Mark — Aston Villa

Full Name: Mark John Bosnich
DOB: 13/01/72, Sydney, Australia

Apps **26** (handwritten)

Previous Club Details

			Apps					Goals		
Club	Signed	Fee	Tot	Start	Sub	FA	FL	Lge	FA	FL
Manchester U.	Jun-89									
Croatia Sydney	Aug-91									
Aston Villa	Feb-92	Free	164	164	0	17	21	0	0	0

FAPL Summary by Club

Club	Signed	Fee	Tot	Start	Sub	FA	FL	Lge	FA	FL
Aston Villa	92/3 to 97/8		163	163	0	17	21	0	0	0
Totals			163	163	0	17	21	0	0	0

BOULD Steve

Full Name: Stephen Andrew Bould
DOB: 16/11/62, Stoke

Previous Club Details

				Apps				Goals		
Club	Signed	Fee	Tot	Start	Sub	FA	FL	Lge	FA	FL
Stoke C.	Nov-80		183	179	4	13	6	0	0	1
Torquay U.	Oct-82	Loan	9	9	0	2	0	0	0	0
Arsenal	Jun-89	£390k	268	257	11	25	34	5	0	1

FAPL Summary by Club

Club	Signed	Fee	Tot	Start	Sub	FA	FL	Lge	FA	FL
Arsenal	92/3 to 97/8		156	150	6	13	24	1	0	1
Totals			156	150	6	13	24	1	0	1

BOWEN Mark

Full Name: Mark Rosslyn Bowen
DOB: 07/12/63, Neath

Previous Club Details

				Apps				Goals		
Club	Signed	Fee	Tot	Start	Sub	FA	FL	Lge	FA	FL
Tottenham H.	Dec-81	App	17	14	3	3	0	2	0	
Norwich C.	Jul-87	£97k	320	315	5	30	34	24	1	
West Ham U.	Jul-96	Free	17	15	2	0	3	1	0	
Shimizu (J)	Mar-97	Free								
Charlton A.	Sep-97	Free	37	35	2	3	0	0	0	

FAPL Summary by Club

Club	Signed	Fee	Tot	Start	Sub	FA	FL	Lge	FA	FL
Norwich C.	92/3 to 94/5		119	117	2	7	12	8	0	0
West Ham U.	1996-97		17	15	2	0	3	1	0	0
Totals			136	132	4	7	15	9	0	0

Arsenal

Leeds United

BOWYER Lee

Full Name: Lee David Bowyer
DOB: 03/01/77, London

Previous Club Details

				Apps				Goals		
Club	Signed	Fee	Tot	Start	Sub	FA	FL	Lge	FA	FL
Charlton A.	Apr-94	Train	46	46		3	7	8	5	1
Leeds U.	Jul-96	£3m	61	53	8	7	3	7	2	1

FAPL Summary by Club

Club	Signed	Fee	Tot	Start	Sub	FA	FL	Lge	FA	FL
Leeds U.	96/7 to 97/8		57	53	4	7	3	7	2	1
Totals			57	53	4	7	3	7	2	1

Tottenham Hotspur

BRADY Garry

Full Name: Garry Brady
DOB: 07/09/76, Glasgow

Previous Club Details

				Apps				Goals		
Club	Signed	Fee	Tot	Start	Sub	FA	FL	Lge	FA	FL
Tottenham H.		Train	9	0	9	0	0	0	0	0

FAPL Summary by Club

Club	Signed	Fee	Tot	Start	Sub	FA	FL	Lge	FA	FL
Tottenham H.	1997-98		9	0	9	0	0	0	0	0
Totals			9	0	9	0	0	0	0	0

Everton

BRANCH Michael

Full Name: Michael Paul Branch
DOB: 18/10/72, Liverpool

Previous Club Details

				Apps				Goals		
Club	Signed	Fee	Tot	Start	Sub	FA	FL	Lge	FA	FL
Everton	Oct-95	Train	34	15	19	1	1	3	0	0

FAPL Summary by Club

Club	Signed	Fee	Tot	Start	Sub	FA	FL	Lge	FA	FL
Everton	95/6 to 97/8		34	15	19	1	1	3	0	0
Totals			34	15	19	1	1	3	0	0

BREACKER Tim — West Ham United *(33)*

Full Name: Timothy Sean Breacker
DOB: 02/07/65, Bicester

Previous Club Details

Club	Signed	Fee	Apps					Goals		
			Tot	Start	Sub	FA	FL	Lge	FA	FL
Luton T.	May-83		210	204	6	13	24	4	3	0
West Ham U.	Oct-90	£600k	237	227	10	27	20	8	0	0

FAPL Summary by Club

| West Ham U. | 93/4 to 97/8 | | 140 | 132 | 8 | 13 | 14 | 3 | 0 | 0 |
| Totals | | | 140 | 132 | 8 | 13 | 14 | 3 | 0 | 0 |

BREEN Gary — Coventry City *(24)*

Full Name: Gary Patrick Breen
DOB: 12/12/73, Hendon

Previous Club Details

Club	Signed	Fee	Apps					Goals		
			Tot	Start	Sub	FA	FL	Lge	FA	FL
Maidstone U.	Mar-91	Free	19	19	0	0	0	0	0	0
Gillingham	Jul-92	Free	51	45	6	5	6	1	0	0
Peterborough	Aug-94	£70k	69	68	1	6	6	4	0	1
Bir'ham C.	Feb-96	£400k	40	37	3	1	4	2	0	0
Coventry C.	Jan-97	£2.5m	39	38	1	5	4	1	0	0

FAPL Summary by Club

| Coventry C. | 96/7 to 97/8 | | 39 | 38 | 1 | 5 | 4 | 1 | 0 | 0 |
| Totals | | | 39 | 38 | 1 | 5 | 4 | 1 | 0 | 0 |

BRIGHT Mark — Charlton Athletic *(35)*

Full Name: Mark Abraham Bright
DOB: 06/06/62, Stoke

Previous Club Details

Club	Signed	Fee	Apps					Goals		
			Tot	Start	Sub	FA	FL	Lge	FA	FL
Port Vale	Oct-81		29	18	11	1	2	10	1	0
Leicester C.	Jul-84	£33k	42	26	16	1	4	6	0	0
C. Palace	Nov-86	£75k	227	224	3	14	22	90	2	11
Sheffield W.	Sep-92	£375k	133	112	21	13	21	50	7	11
Millwall	Dec-96	Loan	3	3	0	0	0	1	0	0
Charlton A.	Apr-97	Free	23	18	5	2	0	9	0	0

FAPL Summary by Club

C. Palace	1992-93		5	5	0					
Sheffield W.	92-93 to 96-97		133	112	21	13	21	48	7	11
Totals			138	117	21	13	21	48	7	11

BRISCOE Lee — Sheffield Wednesday *(22)*

Full Name: Lee Stephen Briscoe
DOB: 30/09/75, Pontefract

Previous Club Details

Club	Signed	Fee	Apps					Goals		
			Tot	Start	Sub	FA	FL	Lge	FA	FL
Sheffield W.	May-94		46	36	10	0	3	0	0	0

FAPL Summary by Club

| Sheffield W. | 93/4 to 97/8 | | 45 | 36 | 9 | 0 | 3 | 0 | 0 | 0 |
| Totals | | | 45 | 36 | 9 | 0 | 3 | 0 | 0 | 0 |

BROOMES Marlon — Blackburn Rovers *(20)*

Full Name: Marlon Charles Broomes
DOB: 28/11/77, Birmingham

Previous Club Details

Club	Signed	Fee	Apps					Goals		
			Tot	Start	Sub	FA	FL	Lge	FA	FL
Blackburn R.	11/94	Train	4	2	2	0	0	0	0	0
Swindon T.	1/97	Loan	12	12	0	0	0	0	0	0

FAPL Summary by Club

| Blackburn R. | 1997-98 | | 4 | 2 | 2 | 0 | 1 | 0 | 0 | 0 |
| Totals | | | 4 | 2 | 2 | 0 | 1 | 0 | 0 | 0 |

BURROWS David — Coventry City *(29)*

Full Name: David Burrows
DOB: 25/10/68, Dudley

Previous Club Details

Club	Signed	Fee	Apps					Goals		
			Tot	Start	Sub	FA	FL	Lge	FA	FL
West Brom	Oct-86		46	37	9	2	4	1	0	0

(Continuation of previous entry)

Aston Villa

Club	Signed	Fee	Tot	Start	Sub	FA	FL	Lge	FA	FL
Liverpool	Oct-88	£550k	146	135	11	17	16	3	0	0
West Ham U.	Sep-93	Swap	29	29	0	3	3	1	0	1
Everton	Sep-94	Swap +	19	19	0	2	2	0	0	0
Coventry C.	Mar-95	£1.1m	72	71	1	6	6	2	0	0
FAPL Summary by Club										
Liverpool	1992-93		30	29	1	0	5	3	0	0
West Ham U.	93/4 to 94/5		29	29	0	3	3	1	0	1
Everton	1994-95		19	19	0	2	2	0	0	0
Coventry C.	94/5 to 97/8		74	73	1	2	7	16	3	0
Totals			*152*	*150*		*7*	*16*	*3*	*0*	*1*

BURTON Deon
Full Name: Deon John Burton
DOB: 25/10/76, Ashford
Previous Club Details

Derby County

Club	Signed	Fee	Tot	Start	Sub	FA	FL	Lge	FA	FL
Portsmouth	Feb-94	Train	62	42	20	1	5	10	1	2
Cardiff C.	Dec-96	Loan	5	5	0	0	0	2	0	0
Derby Co.	Aug-97	£1.0m	29	12	17	2	1	3	0	0
FAPL Summary by Club										
Derby Co.	1997-98		29	12	17	2	1	3	0	0
Totals			*29*	*12*	*17*	*2*	*1*	*3*	*0*	*0*

BUTT Nicky
Full Name: Nicholas Butt
DOB: 21/01/75, Manchester
Previous Club Details

Manchester United

Club	Signed	Fee	Tot	Start	Sub	FA	FL	Lge	FA	FL
Manchester U.	Jan-93	Train	115	97	18	13	13	3	10	1
FAPL Summary by Club										
Manchester U.	92/3 to 97/8		115	97	18	13	13	3	10	1
Totals			*115*	*97*	*18*	*13*	*13*	*3*	*10*	*1*

BYFIELD Darren
Full Name: Darren Byfield
DOB: 29/09/76, Birmingham
Previous Club Details

Aston Villa

Club	Signed	Fee	Tot	Start	Sub	FA	FL	Lge	FA	FL
Aston Villa		Train	7	1	6	1		0	0	0
FAPL Summary by Club										
Aston Villa	1997-98		7	1	6	1		0	0	1
Totals			*7*	*1*	*6*	*1*		*0*	*0*	*1*

CADAMARTERI Danny
Full Name: Daniel Cadamarteri
DOB: 12/10/79, Bradford
Previous Club Details

Everton

18

Club	Signed	Fee	Tot	Start	Sub	FA	FL	Lge	FA	FL
Everton	Oct-96	Train	27	15	12	1	3	4	0	1
FAPL Summary by Club										
Everton	96/7 to 97/8		27	15	12	1	3	4	0	1
Totals			*27*	*15*	*12*	*1*	*3*	*4*	*0*	*1*

CALDERWOOD Colin
Full Name: Colin Calderwood
DOB: 20/01/65, Stranraer
Previous Club Details

Tottenham Hotspur

33

Club	Signed	Fee	Tot	Start	Sub	FA	FL	Lge	FA	FL
Mansfield T.	Mar-82		100	97	3	6	4	1	1	0
Swindon T.	Jul-85	£30k	330	328	2	17	35	20	1	1
Tottenham	Jul-93	£1.25m	151	141	10	16	15	7	1	0
FAPL Summary by Club										
Tottenham	93/4 to 97/8		151	141	10	16	15	7	1	0
Totals			*151*	*141*	*10*	*16*	*15*	*7*	*1*	*0*

CAMPBELL Sol

Tottenham Hotspur

Full Name: Sulzeer Jeremiah Campbell
DOB: 18/09/74, Newham, London   *23*

Previous Club Details

Club	Signed	Fee	Apps Tot	Start	Sub	FA	FL	Goals Lge	FA	FL
Tottenham	Sep-92	Train	168	159	9	16	16	2	1	2

FAPL Summary by Club

Club			Apps Tot	Start	Sub	FA	FL	Goals Lge	FA	FL
Tottenham 92/3 to 97/8										
Totals			*168*	*159*	*9*	*16*	*16*	*2*	*1*	*2*

CAMPBELL Kevin   Nottingham Forest   *28*

Full Name: Kevin Joseph Campbell
DOB: 04/02/70, Lambeth

Previous Club Details

Club	Signed	Fee	Apps Tot	Start	Sub	FA	FL	Goals Lge	FA	FL
Arsenal	Feb-88	Train	166	124	42	19	24	46	2	6
L. Orient	Jan-89	Loan	16	16	0	0	0	9	0	0
Leicester C.	Nov-89	Loan	11	11	0	1	0	5	0	0
N. Forest	Jun-95	£2.5m	78	77	1	11	2	32	3	0

FAPL Summary by Club

Club			Apps Tot	Start	Sub	FA	FL	Goals Lge	FA	FL
Arsenal 92/3 to 94/5			97	79	18	12	18	22	1	6
N. Forest 95/6 to 96/7			38	37	1	10	0	9	3	0
Totals			*135*	*116*	*19*	*22*	*18*	*31*	*4*	*6*

CAMPBELL Stuart   Leicester City   *20*

Full Name: Stuart Pearson Campbell
DOB: 09/12/77, Corby

Previous Club Details

Club	Signed	Fee	Apps Tot	Start	Sub	FA	FL	Goals Lge	FA	FL
Leicester C.	Jul-96	Train	21	10	11	2	3	0	0	0

FAPL Summary by Club

Club			Apps Tot	Start	Sub	FA	FL	Goals Lge	FA	FL
Leicester C. 1996-97			21	10	11	2	3	0	0	0
Totals			*21*	*10*	*11*	*2*	*3*	*0*	*0*	*0*

CARBONE Benito   Sheffield Wednesday

Full Name: Benito Carbone   *27*
DOB: 14/08/71, Bagnara Calabra, Italy

Previous Club Details

Club	Signed	Fee	Apps Tot	Start	Sub	FA	FL	Goals Lge	FA	FL
Torino	1988		8					5		
Reggina	1990		31					4		
Casertana	1991		31					6		
Ascoli	1992		28					6		
Torino	1993		28	25	3			6		
Napoli	1994		29	27	2			4		
Inter Milan	1995		31	25	6			2		
Sheffield W.	Oct-96	£3m	58	52	6	4	1	15	0	0

FAPL Summary by Club

Club			Apps Tot	Start	Sub	FA	FL	Goals Lge	FA	FL
Sheffield W. 96/7 to 97/8										
Totals			*58*	*52*	*6*	*4*	*1*	*15*	*0*	*0*

CARR Stephen   Tottenham Hotspur   *22*

Full Name: Stephen Carr
DOB: 29/08/76, Dublin

Previous Club Details

Club	Signed	Fee	Apps Tot	Start	Sub	FA	FL	Goals Lge	FA	FL
Tottenham	Aug-93		65	62	3	4	6	0	0	0

FAPL Summary by Club

Club			Apps Tot	Start	Sub	FA	FL	Goals Lge	FA	FL
Tottenham 93-94 to 97-98			65	62	3	4	6	0	0	0
Totals			*65*	*62*	*3*	*4*	*6*	*0*	*0*	*0*

CARRAGHER Jamie   Liverpool   *20*

Full Name: James Carragher
DOB: 28/01/78, Bootle

Previous Club Details

Club	Signed	Fee	Apps Tot	Start	Sub	FA	FL	Goals Lge	FA	FL
Liverpool		Train	22	18	4	0	3	0	0	0

FAPL Summary by Club

Liverpool 96/7 to 97/8 and Totals (continued from previous entry):

Club	Signed/Season	Fee	Tot	Start	Sub	FA	FL	Lge	FA	FL
Liverpool	96/7 to 97/8		22	18	4	0	3	1	0	0
Totals			22	18	4	0	3	1	0	0

CARSLEY Lee — Derby County *24*

Full Name: Lee Kevin Carsley
DOB: 28/04/74, Birmingham

Previous Club Details

Club	Signed	Fee	Tot	Start	Sub	FA	FL	Lge	FA	FL
Derby Co.	Jul-92	Train	116	102	14	5	10	4	0	0

FAPL Summary by Club

Club	Season		Tot	Start	Sub	FA	FL	Lge	FA	FL
Derby Co.	96/7 to 97/8		58	49	9	4	4	1	0	0
Totals			58	49	9	4	4	1	0	0

CASTLEDINE Stewart — Wimbledon *25*

Full Name: Stewart Mark Castledine
DOB: 22/01/73, Wandsworth

Previous Club Details

Club	Signed	Fee	Tot	Start	Sub	FA	FL	Lge	FA	FL
Wimbledon	Jul-91		27	17	10	0	5	4	0	3
Wycombe W.	Aug-95	Loan	7	7	0	0	0	3	0	0

FAPL Summary by Club

Club	Season		Tot	Start	Sub	FA	FL	Lge	FA	FL
Wimbledon	93/4 to 97/8		25	17	8	5	4	4	0	3
Totals			25	17	8	5	4	4	0	3

CHAPPLE Phil — Charlton Athletic *31*

Full Name: Phillip Richard Chapple
DOB: 26/11/66, Norwich

Previous Club Details

Club	Signed	Fee	Tot	Start	Sub	FA	FL	Lge	FA	FL
Norwich	Jul-85	App								
Cambridge U.	Mar-88		187	183	4	23	11	19	1	2
Charlton A.	Aug-93	£100k	142	128	14	9	11	15	0	0

CHARLES Gary — Aston Villa *28*

Full Name: Gary Andrew Charles
DOB: 13/04/70, Newham

Previous Club Details

Club	Signed	Fee	Tot	Start	Sub	FA	FL	Lge	FA	FL
N. Forest	Nov-87		56	54	2	10	9	1	1	0
Leicester C.	Mar-89	Loan	8	5	3	0	1	0	0	0
Derby Co.	Jul-93	£750k	61	61	0	1	3	3	0	0
Aston Villa	Jan-95	£2.9m	68	62	6	6	9	2	0	0

FAPL Summary by Club

Club	Season		Tot	Start	Sub	FA	FL	Lge	FA	FL
N. Forest	1992-93		14	14	0	0	0	0	0	0
Aston Villa	94/5 to 97/8		68	62	6	6	9	2	0	0
Totals			82	76	6	6	9	2	0	0

CHETTLE Steve — Nottingham Forest *29*

Full Name: Stephen Chettle
DOB: 27/09/68, Nottingham

Previous Club Details

Club	Signed	Fee	Tot	Start	Sub	FA	FL	Lge	FA	FL
N. Forest	Aug-86	App	368	354	14	36	45	8	0	1

FAPL Summary by Club

Club	Season		Tot	Start	Sub	FA	FL	Lge	FA	FL
N. Forest	92/3 to 96/7		140	139	1	16	11	0	0	0
Totals			140	139	1	16	11	0	0	0

CLARKE Adrian — Arsenal *23*

Full Name: Adrian James Clarke
DOB: 28/10/74, Cambridge

Previous Club Details

Club	Signed	Fee	Tot	Start	Sub	FA	FL	Lge	FA	FL
Arsenal	Jul-93	Train	7	4	3	0	0	0	0	0
Rotherham U.	Dec-96	Loan								
Southampton	Mar-97	Loan								

CLARKE Steve — Chelsea

Full Name: Stephen Clarke
DOB: 29/08/63, Saltcoats

FAPL Summary by Club

Club			Tot	Start	Sub	FA	FL	Lge	FA	FL
Arsenal 94-95 to 95-96			7	4	3	2	0	0	0	0
Totals			7	4	3	2	0	0	0	0

Previous Club Details

Club	Signed	Fee	Tot	Start	Sub	FA	FL	Lge	FA	FL
						Apps			Goals	
St Mirren										
Chelsea	Jan-87	£422k	330	321	9	36	26	7	1	1

35

FAPL Summary by Club

Club			Tot	Start	Sub	FA	FL	Lge	FA	FL
Chelsea 92/3 to 97/8			167	160	7	28	16	1	0	0
Totals			167	160	7	28	16	1	0	0

CLARKE Andy — Wimbledon

Full Name: Andrew Weston Clarke
DOB: 22/07/67, Islington

Previous Club Details

Club	Signed	Fee	Tot	Start	Sub	FA	FL	Lge	FA	FL
						Apps			Goals	
Barnet	NL									
Wimbledon	Feb-91	£250k	170	74	96	17	25	17	2	4

30

FAPL Summary by Club

Club			Tot	Start	Sub	FA	FL	Lge	FA	FL
Wimbledon 92/3 to 97/8			124	54	70	12	14	11	2	2
Totals			124	54	70	12	14	11	2	2

CLARKE Matt — Sheffield Wednesday

Full Name: Mathew John Clarke
DOB: 03/11/73, Sheffield

Previous Club Details

Club	Signed	Fee	Tot	Start	Sub	FA	FL	Lge	FA	FL
						Apps			Goals	
Rotherham	Jul-92	Train	124	123	1	3	6	0	0	0
Sheffield W.	Jul-96	£325k	4	2	2	0	0	0	0	0

24

FAPL Summary by Club

Club			Tot	Start	Sub	FA	FL	Lge	FA	FL
Sheffield W. 96/7 to 97/8			4	2	2	0	0	0	0	0
Totals			4	2	2	0	0	0	0	0

CLEGG Michael — Manchester United

Full Name: Michael Clegg
DOB: 03/07/77, Tameside

Previous Club Details

Club	Signed	Fee	Tot	Start	Sub	FA	FL	Lge	FA	FL
						Apps			Goals	
Manchester U.	Jul-95	Train	7	4	3	4	1	0	0	0

21

FAPL Summary by Club

Club			Tot	Start	Sub	FA	FL	Lge	FA	FL
Manchester U. 96/7 to 97/8			7	4	3	4	1	0	0	0
Totals			7	4	3	4	1	0	0	0

CLEMENCE Stephen — Tottenham Hotspur

Full Name: Stephen Clemence
DOB: 31/03/78, Liverpool

Previous Club Details

Club	Signed	Fee	Tot	Start	Sub	FA	FL	Lge	FA	FL
						Apps			Goals	
Tottenham H.		Train	17	12	5	2	2	0	1	0

19

FAPL Summary by Club

Club			Tot	Start	Sub	FA	FL	Lge	FA	FL
Tottenham H. 1997-98			17	12	5	2	2	0	1	0
Totals			17	12	5	2	2	0	1	0

COLE Andy — Manchester United

Full Name: Andrew Alexander Cole
DOB: 15/10/71, Nottingham

Previous Club Details

Club	Signed	Fee	Tot	Start	Sub	FA	FL	Lge	FA	FL
						Apps			Goals	
Arsenal	Oct-89	Train	1	0	1	0	0	0	0	0
Fulham	Sep-91	Loan	13	13	0	0	0	3	0	0
Bristol C.	Mar-92	£500k	41	41	0	7	3	20	4	4
Newcastle U.	Mar-93	£1.75m	70	69	1	4	7	55	1	8
Manchester U.	Jan-95	£7m+	105	90	15	13	24	45	7	7

26

FAPL Summary by Club

Club			Tot	Start	Sub	FA	FL	Lge	FA	FL
				Apps					*Goals*	
Newcastle U. 9/4 to 94/5			58	58	0	4	7	43	1	8
Manchester U. 94/5 to 97/8			105	90	15	13	2	45	7	0
Totals			*163*	*148*	*15*	*17*	*9*	*88*	*8*	*8*

COLLYMORE Stan — Aston Villa

Full Name: Stanley Victor Collymore
DOB: 22/01/71, Stone

Previous Club Details

Club	Signed	Fee	Tot	Start	Sub	FA	FL	Lge	FA	FL
				Apps					*Goals*	
C. Palace	Jan-91	£100k	20	4	16	0	5	1	0	1
Southend U.	Nov-92	£100k	30	30	0	3	0	15	3	0
N. Forest	Jul-93	£2.0m	65	64	1	2	9	41	1	2
Liverpool	Jul-95	£8.5m	59	54	5	5	9	26	7	0
Aston Villa	May-97	£7m	25	23	2	4	1	6	1	0

FAPL Summary by Club

Club			Tot	Start	Sub	FA	FL	Lge	FA	FL
C. Palace 1992-93			2	0	2	0	2	0	0	0
Liverpool 94/5 to 96/7			97	91	6	11	8	49	8	2
Aston Villa 1997-98			25	23	2	4	1	6	1	0
Totals			*124*	*114*	*10*	*15*	*11*	*55*	*9*	*2*

COOPER Colin — Nottingham Forest

Full Name: Colin Terence Cooper
DOB: 28/02/67, Durham

Previous Club Details

Club	Signed	Fee	Tot	Start	Sub	FA	FL	Lge	FA	FL
				Apps					*Goals*	
Middlesbrough	Jul-84		188	183	5	13	18	6	6	0
Millwall	Jul-91	£300k	77	77	0	1	6	6	0	0
N. Forest	Jun-93	£1.7m	177	176	1	12	14	20	1	2

FAPL Summary by Club

Club			Tot	Start	Sub	FA	FL	Lge	FA	FL
N. Forest 94/5 to 96/7			108	108	0	9	9	8	0	1
Totals			*108*	*108*	*0*	*9*	*9*	*8*	*0*	*1*

CORT Carl — Wimbledon

Full Name: Carl Edward Richard Cort
DOB: 01/11/77, London

Previous Club Details

Club	Signed	Fee	Tot	Start	Sub	FA	FL	Lge	FA	FL
				Apps					*Goals*	
Wimbledon	Jun-96	Train	23	16	7	5	2	4	0	2
Lincoln C.	Feb-97	Loan	6	5	1	0	1	0	0	0

FAPL Summary by Club

Club			Tot	Start	Sub	FA	FL	Lge	FA	FL
Wimbledon 96/7 to 97/8			23	16	7	5	2	4	0	2
Totals			*23*	*16*	*7*	*5*	*2*	*4*	*0*	*2*

COTTEE Tony — Leicester City

Full Name: Anthony Richard Cottee
DOB: 11/07/65, West Ham

Previous Club Details

Club	Signed	Fee	Tot	Start	Sub	FA	FL	Lge	FA	FL
				Apps					*Goals*	
West Ham U.	Sep-82		212	203	9	24	19	92	11	14
Everton	Aug-88	£2.3m	184	161	23	21	23	72	11	4
West Ham U.	Sep-94	£300k	67	63	4	5	8	23	1	4
Selangor	Oct-96	£750k								
Leicester C.	Aug-97	£500k	19	7	12	2	1	4	1	0

FAPL Summary by Club

Club			Tot	Start	Sub	FA	FL	Lge	FA	FL
Everton 92/3 to 94/5			68	64	4	4	8	28	3	0
West Ham U. 94/5 to 96/7			67	63	4	5	2	23	1	4
Leicester C. 1997-98			19	7	12	2	1	4	1	0
Totals			*154*	*134*	*20*	*9*	*17*	*55*	*5*	*4*

CRITTENDEN Nicky — Chelsea

Full Name: Nicolas Crittenden
DOB: 11/11/78, Bracknell

Previous Club Details

Club	Signed	Fee	Tot	Start	Sub	FA	FL	Lge	FA	FL
				Apps					*Goals*	
Chelsea		Jnrs	2	0	2	0	1	0	0	0

FAPL Summary by Club

Club			Tot	Start	Sub	FA	FL	Lge	FA	FL
Chelsea 1997-98			2	0	2	0	1	0	0	0
Totals			*2*	*0*	*2*	*0*	*1*	*0*	*0*	*0*

CROFT Gary — Blackburn Rovers

Full Name: Gary Croft
DOB: 17/02/74, Burton on Trent

Previous Club Details

Club	Signed	Fee	Apps Tot	Start	Sub	FA	FL	Goals Lge	FA	FL
Grimsby T.	Jul-92	Train	149	139	10	10	7	3	1	0
Blackburn R.	Mar-96	£1.7m	28	23	5	5	2	5	1	0

FAPL Summary by Club

Club			Tot	Start	Sub	FA	FL	Lge	FA	FL
Blackburn R. 96/7 to 97/8			28	23	5	5	2	5	1	0
Totals			*28*	*23*	*5*	*5*	*2*	*5*	*1*	*0*

CROSSLEY Mark — Nottingham Forest

Full Name: Mark Geoffrey Crossley
DOB: 16/06/69, Barnsley

Previous Club Details

Club	Signed	Fee	Apps Tot	Start	Sub	FA	FL	Goals Lge	FA	FL
N. Forest	Jul-87		271	270	1	32	34	0	0	0

FAPL Summary by Club

Club			Tot	Start	Sub	FA	FL	Lge	FA	FL
N. Forest 92/3 to 96/7			150	150	0	12	9	0	0	0
Totals			*150*	*150*	*0*	*12*	*9*	*0*	*0*	*0*

CRUYFF Jordi — Manchester United

Full Name: Johan Jordi Cruyff
DOB: 09/02/74, Amsterdam

Previous Club Details

Club	Signed	Fee	Apps Tot	Start	Sub	FA	FL	Goals Lge	FA	FL
Barcelona	1994		41	32	9			11		
Manchester U.	Aug-96	£1.4m	21	14	7	1	2	3	0	0

FAPL Summary by Club

Club			Tot	Start	Sub	FA	FL	Lge	FA	FL
Manchester U. 96/7 to 97/8			21	14	7	1	2	3	0	0
Totals			*21*	*14*	*7*	*1*	*2*	*3*	*0*	*0*

CUNNINGHAM Kenny — Wimbledon

Full Name: Kenneth Edward Cunningham
DOB: 28/06/71, Dublin

Previous Club Details

Club	Signed	Fee	Apps Tot	Start	Sub	FA	FL	Goals Lge	FA	FL
Millwall	Sep-89		136	132	4	11	10	1	0	0
Wimbledon	Nov-94	£1.3m	129	128	1	22	12	0	0	0

FAPL Summary by Club

Club			Tot	Start	Sub	FA	FL	Lge	FA	FL
Wimbledon 94/5 to 97/8			129	128	1	21	12	0	0	0
Totals			*129*	*128*	*1*	*21*	*12*	*0*	*0*	*0*

CURTIS John — Manchester United

Full Name: John Curtis
DOB: 03/09/78, Nuneaton

Previous Club Details

Club	Signed	Fee	Apps Tot	Start	Sub	FA	FL	Goals Lge	FA	FL
Man. U.	Train		8	3	5	0	1	0	0	0

FAPL Summary by Club

Club			Tot	Start	Sub	FA	FL	Lge	FA	FL
Man. U. 1997-98			8	3	5	0	1	0	0	0
Totals			*8*	*3*	*5*	*0*	*1*	*0*	*0*	*0*

DABIZAS Nikolaos — Newcastle United

Full Name: Nikolaos Dabizas
DOB: 3/8/73, Amypeo

Previous Club Details

Club	Signed	Fee	Apps Tot	Start	Sub	FA	FL	Goals Lge	FA	FL
Olympiakos										
Newcastle U.	Mar-98	£2.0m	11	10	1	2	0	1	0	0

FAPL Summary by Club

Club			Tot	Start	Sub	FA	FL	Lge	FA	FL
Newcastle U. 1997-98			11	10	1	2	0	1	0	0
Totals			*11*	*10*	*1*	*2*	*0*	*1*	*0*	*0*

DAHLIN Martin — Blackburn Rovers

Full Name: Martin Dahlin
DOB: 16/04/68, Lund (Sweden)

Previous Club Details			Apps					Goals		
Club	Signed	Fee	Tot	Start	Sub	FA	FL	Lge	FA	FL
Malmo	1992		41	33	8			18		
B.Monchengladbach			94	87	7			48		
AS Roma			3	3	0			0		
B.Monchengladbach	Jul-97	Loan	19	19	0			10		
Blackburn R.	Jul-97	£2.0m	21	11	10	1	2	4	0	2

FAPL Summary by Club		Apps					Goals		
Blackburn R.	1997-98	21	11	10	1	2	4	0	2
Totals		*21*	*11*	*10*	*1*	*2*	*4*	*0*	*2*

DAILLY Christian — Derby County

Full Name: Christian Dailly
DOB: 23/10/73, Dundee

Previous Club Details			Apps					Goals		
Club	Signed	Fee	Tot	Start	Sub	FA	FL	Lge	FA	FL
Dundee U.	1990	Inrs	140	108	32	16	7	10		
Derby Co.	Aug-96	£1m	66	61	5	7	5	10	4	0

FAPL Summary by Club		Apps					Goals		
Derby Co.	96/7 to 97/8	66	61	5	7	5	10	4	0
Totals		*66*	*61*	*5*	*7*	*5*	*10*	*4*	*0*

DAVIDSON Callum — Blackburn Rovers

Full Name: Callum Davidson
DOB: 25/06/76, Stirling

Previous Club Details			Apps					Goals		
Club	Signed	Fee	Tot	Start	Sub	FA	FL	Lge	FA	FL
St Johnstone	Sby		29							
Blackburn R.	Feb-98	£1.75m	1	1	0	0	0	0	0	0

FAPL Summary by Club		Apps					Goals		
Blackburn R.	1997-98	1	1				0	0	0
Totals		*1*	*1*				*0*	*0*	*0*

DAVIES Kevin — Blackburn Rovers

Full Name: Kevin Cyril Davies
DOB: 26/03/77, Sheffield

Previous Club Details			Apps					Goals		
Club	Signed	Fee	Tot	Start	Sub	FA	FL	Lge	FA	FL
Chesterfield	Apr-94	Train	129	113	16	10	9	22	6	1
Southampton	May-97	£750k	25	20	5	1	4	9	0	3

FAPL Summary by Club		Apps					Goals		
Southampton	1997-98	25	20	5	1	4	9	0	3
Totals		*25*	*20*	*5*	*1*	*4*	*9*	*0*	*3*

DE GOEY Ed — Chelsea

Full Name: Edward De Goey
DOB: 20/12/66, Gouda, Holland

Previous Club Details			Apps					Goals		
Club	Signed	Fee	Tot	Start	Sub	FA	FL	Lge	FA	FL
Sparta Rotterdam										
Feyenoord										
Chelsea	Jul-97	£2.5m	28	28	0	1	4	0	0	0

FAPL Summary by Club		Apps					Goals		
Chelsea	1997-98	28	28	0	1	4	0	0	0
Totals		*28*	*28*	*0*	*1*	*4*	*0*	*0*	*0*

DELAP Rory — Derby County

Full Name: Rory John Delap
DOB: 06/07/76, Sutton Codlfield

Previous Club Details			Apps					Goals		
Club	Signed	Fee	Tot	Start	Sub	FA	FL	Lge	FA	FL
Carlisle U.	Jul-94	Train	56	32	24	3	4	7	0	0

Club	Signed	Fee	Apps					Goals		
			Tot	Start	Sub	FA	FL	Lge	FA	FL
Derby Co.	Feb-98	£500k	13	10	3	0	0	0	0	0
FAPL Summary by Club										
Derby Co.	1997-98		13	10	3	0	0	0	0	0
Totals			*13*	*10*	*3*			*0*	*0*	*0*

Sheffield Wednesday

DI CANIO Paulo

Full Name: Paulo Di Canio
DOB: 9/7/68, Rome

Previous Club Details

Club	Signed	Fee	Apps					Goals		
			Tot	Start	Sub	FA	FL	Lge	FA	FL
Milan, Celtic										
Sheffield W.	Jul-97	£3m	35	34	1	3	2	12	0	2
FAPL Summary by Club										
Sheffield W.	1997-98		35	34	1	3	2	12	0	2
Totals			*35*	*34*	*1*	*3*	*2*	*12*	*0*	*2*

Chelsea

DI MATTEO Roberto

Full Name: Roberto Di Matteo
DOB: 29/05/70, Schaffhausen, Switzerland

Previous Club Details

Club	Signed	Fee	Apps					Goals		
			Tot	Start	Sub	FA	FL	Lge	FA	FL
Schaffhausen	1988		50					2		
Zurich (Swi)	1991		34					6		
Aarau (Swi)	1992		31					1		
Lazio (Ita)	1993		88					7		
Chelsea	Jul-96	£4.9m	64	61	3	8	7	10	2	3
FAPL Summary by Club										
Chelsea	96/7 to 97/8		64	61	3	8	7	10	2	3
Totals			*64*	*61*	*3*	*8*	*7*	*10*	*2*	*3*

West Ham United

DICKS Julian

Full Name: Julian Andrew Dicks
DOB: 08/08/68, Bristol

Previous Club Details

Club	Signed	Fee

Club	Signed	Fee	Apps					Goals		
			Tot	Start	Sub	FA	FL	Lge	FA	FL
Birmingham C.	Apr-86	£300k	89	83	6	5	6	1	0	0
West Ham U.	Mar-88	£1.5m	159	159	0	14	19	29	2	5
West Ham U.	Oct-94	£500k	94	94	0	3	3	21	0	3
FAPL Summary by Club										
West Ham U.	1993-94		7	7	0	0	0	1	0	0
West Ham U.	94/5 to 96/7		94	94	0	7	10	21	3	3
Totals			*125*	*125*	*0*	*8*	*13*	*25*	*0*	*3*

Arsenal

DIXON Lee

Full Name: Lee Michael Dixon
DOB: 17/03/64, Manchester

Previous Club Details

Club	Signed	Fee	Apps					Goals		
			Tot	Start	Sub	FA	FL	Lge	FA	FL
Burnley	Jul-82	Inns	4	4	0	1	0	0	0	0
Chester C.	Feb-84	Free	57	56	1	0	8	1	0	0
Bury	Jul-85	Free	45	45	0	4	5	5	1	0
Stoke C.	Jul-86	£40k	71	71	0	7	6	5	0	0
Arsenal	Jan-88	£400k	352	346	6	36	45	20	1	0
FAPL Summary by Club										
Arsenal	92/3 to 97/8		199	195	4	23	29	5	0	0
Totals			*199*	*195*	*4*	*23*	*29*	*5*	*0*	*0*

Southampton

DODD Jason

Full Name: Jason Robert Dodd
DOB: 02/11/70, Bath

Previous Club Details

Club	Signed	Fee	Apps					Goals		
			Tot	Start	Sub	FA	FL	Lge	FA	FL
Southampton	Mar-89	£50k	231	215	16	22	29	7	1	0
FAPL Summary by Club										
Southampton	92/3 to 97/8		161	151	10	12	14	7	1	0
Totals			*161*	*151*	*10*	*12*	*14*	*7*	*1*	*0*

DOMINGUEZ Jose — Tottenham Hotspur

Full Name: Jose Dominguez

Previous Club Details

Club	Signed	Fee	Apps					Goals		
			Tot	Start	Sub	FA	FL	Lge	FA	FL
Tottenham H.			18	8	10	1	3	2	0	0

FAPL Summary by Club

Tottenham H.	1997-98		18	8	10	1	3	2	0	0
Totals			*18*	*8*	*10*	*1*	*3*	*2*	*0*	*0*

DRAPER Mark — Aston Villa

Full Name: Mark Draper
DOB: 11/11/70, Long Eaton

Previous Club Details

Club	Signed	Fee	Apps					Goals		
			Tot	Start	Sub	FA	FL	Lge	FA	FL
Notts Co.	Dec-88	Train	222	206	16	10	15	40	2	2
Leicester C.	Jul-94	£1.25m	39	39	0	2	9	4	0	0
Aston Villa	Jul-95	£3.25m	96	95	1	9	11	5	2	1

FAPL Summary by Club

Leicester C.	1994-95		39	39	0	2	9	5	0	0
Aston Villa	95/6 to 97/8		96	95	1	9	11	5	2	1
Totals			*135*	*134*	*1*	*11*	*13*	*10*	*2*	*1*

DRYDEN Richard — Southampton

Full Name: Richard Andrew Dryden
DOB: 14/06/69, Stroud

Previous Club Details

Club	Signed	Fee	Apps					Goals		
			Tot	Start	Sub	FA	FL	Lge	FA	FL
Bristol R.	Jul-87	Train	13	12	1	2	3	0	0	0
Exeter C.	Sep-88	Loan	6	6	0	2	0	0	0	0
Exeter C.	Mar-89		86	86	0	2	7	13	0	0
Notts Co.	Aug-91	£250k	31	30	1	0	2	0	0	0
Plymouth A.	Nov-92	Loan	5	5	0	1	0	0	0	0
Birmingham C.	Mar-93	£165k	48	48	0	5	5	0	0	0
Bristol C.	Dec-94	£140k	37	32	5	2	4	2	0	0
Southampton	Aug-96	£150k	42	39	3	3	0	7	1	0

FAPL Summary by Club

Southampton	96/7 to 97/8		42	39	3	3	0	7	1	0
Totals			*42*	*39*	*3*	*3*	*0*	*7*	*1*	*0*

DUBERRY Michael — Chelsea

Full Name: Michael Wayne Duberry
DOB: 14/10/75, London

Previous Club Details

Club	Signed	Fee	Apps					Goals		
			Tot	Start	Sub	FA	FL	Lge	FA	FL
Chelsea	Jun-93	Train	61	59	2	10	5	1	2	0
Bournemouth	Sep-95	Loan	7	7						

FAPL Summary by Club

Chelsea	93-94 to 97-98		61	59	2	10	5	1	2	0
Totals			*61*	*59*	*2*	*10*	*5*	*1*	*2*	*0*

DUBLIN Dion — Coventry City

Full Name: Dion Dublin
DOB: 22/04/69, Leicester

Previous Club Details

Club	Signed	Fee	Apps					Goals		
			Tot	Start	Sub	FA	FL	Lge	FA	FL
Norwich C.	Mar-88	Train	0	0	0					
Cambridge U.	Aug-88	Free	156	133	23	21	10	52	11	5
Manchester U.	Aug-92	£1m	12	4	8	2	2	0	2	1
Coventry C.	Sep-94	£2m	135	134	1	13	11	59	7	3

FAPL Summary by Club

Manchester U.	92/3 to 93/4		12	4	8	2	2	0	2	1
Coventry C.	94/5 to 97/8		135	134	1	13	11	59	7	4
Totals			*147*	*138*	*9*	*15*	*13*	*61*	*7*	*4*

DUCROS Andrew — Coventry City

Full Name: Andrew Ducros
DOB: 16/09/77, Evesham

Previous Club Details

Club	Signed	Fee	Apps					Goals		
			Tot	Start	Sub	FA	FL	Lge	FA	FL
Coventry C.	9/94	Train	8	2	6	0		1	0	0

FAPL Summary by Club

Club			Apps					Goals		
Coventry C.	96/7 to 97/8									
Totals			*8*	*2*	*6*	*0*		*1*	*0*	*0*

DUFF Damien — Blackburn Rovers

Full Name: Damien Anthony Duff
DOB: 02/03/79, Ballboden

Previous Club Details

Club	Signed	Fee	Apps					Goals		
			Tot	Start	Sub	FA	FL	Lge	FA	FL
Blackburn R.	3/96	Train	27	18	9	0	3	4	1	0

FAPL Summary by Club

Club			Apps					Goals		
Blackburn R.	96/7 to 97/8		27	18	9	0	3	4	1	0
Totals			*27*	*18*	*9*	*0*	*3*	*4*	*1*	*0*

DUNNE Richard — Everton

Full Name: Richard Patrick Dunne
DOB: 21/09/79, Dublin

Club	Signed	Fee	Apps					Goals		
			Tot	Start	Sub	FA	FL	Lge	FA	FL
Everton	10/96	Train	10	8	2	2	2	0	0	0

FAPL Summary by Club

Club			Apps					Goals		
Everton	96/7 to 97/8		10	8	2	2	2	0	0	0
Totals			*10*	*8*	*2*	*2*	*2*	*0*	*0*	*0*

EARLE Robbie — Wimbledon

Full Name: Robert Gerald Earle
DOB: 27/01/65, Newcastle-under-Lyme

Previous Club Details

Club	Signed	Fee	Apps					Goals		
			Tot	Start	Sub	FA	FL	Lge	FA	FL
Port Vale	Jul-82	Jnrs	294	284	10	21	23	77	4	4
Wimbledon	Jul-91	£775k	224	222	2	31	21	51	7	5

FAPL Summary by Club

Club			Apps					Goals		
Wimbledon	92/3 to 97/8		184	182	2	29	19	37	7	5
Totals			*184*	*182*	*2*	*29*	*19*	*37*	*7*	*5*

EDINBURGH Justin — Tottenham Hotspur

Full Name: Justin Charles Edinburgh
DOB: 18/12/69, Brentwood

Previous Club Details

Club	Signed	Fee	Apps					Goals		
			Tot	Start	Sub	FA	FL	Lge	FA	FL
Southend U.	Jul-88	Train	37	36	1	2	3	0	0	0
Tottenham H.	Jul-90	£150k	190	170	20	22	23	1	0	0

FAPL Summary by Club

Club			Apps					Goals		
Tottenham H.	92/3 to 97/8		151	134	17	17	15	0	0	0
Totals			*151*	*134*	*17*	*17*	*15*	*0*	*0*	*0*

EHIOGU Ugo — Aston Villa

Full Name: Ugochuku Ehiogu
DOB: 03/11/72, Hackney

Previous Club Details

Club	Signed	Fee	Apps					Goals		
			Tot	Start	Sub	FA	FL	Lge	FA	FL
WBA	Jul-89		2	0	2	0	0	0	0	0
Aston Villa	Jul-91	£40k	179	168	11	16	9	16	1	1

FAPL Summary by Club

Club			Apps					Goals		
Aston Villa	92/3 to 97/8		171	164	7	15	16	6	1	1
Totals			*171*	*164*	*7*	*15*	*16*	*6*	*1*	*1*

EKOKU Efan — Wimbledon

Full Name: Efangwu Goziem Ekoku
DOB: 08/06/67, Manchester

Previous Club Details

Club	Signed	Fee	Apps					Goals		
			Tot	Start	Sub	FA	FL	Lge	FA	FL
Bournemouth	May-90	£100k	62	43	19	7	2	21	2	0
Norwich C.	Mar-93	£500k	37	26	11	2	3	15	0	1
Wimbledon	Oct-94	£900k	101	91	10	17	8	31	3	1

FAPL Summary by Club

Club	Tot	Start	Sub	FA	FL	Lge	FA	FL
Norwich C. 92/3 to 94/5	37	26	11	1	3	15	0	2
Wimbledon 94/5 to 97/8	101	91	10	17	8	31	3	3
Totals	*138*	*117*	*21*	*18*	*11*	*46*	*3*	*5*

ELLIOTT Matt

Full Name: Matthew Stephen Elliott
DOB: 01/11/68, Wandsworth

Previous Club Details

			Apps					Goals		
Club	Signed	Fee	Tot	Start	Sub	FA	FL	Lge	FA	FL
Charlton A.	Sep-88	£5k NL	0	0				0		
Torquay U.	Mar-89	£10k	124	123	1	9	9	15	2	2
Scunthorpe	Mar-92	£50k	61	61	0	2	6	8	0	0
Oxford U.	Nov-93	£150k	148	148	0	11	16	21	1	0
Leicester C.	Jan-97	£1.6m	53	53	0	4	1	11	0	0

FAPL Summary by Club

Club	Tot	Start	Sub	FA	FL	Lge	FA	FL
Leicester C. 9/67 to 97/8	53	53		4	1	11	0	0
Totals	*53*	*53*		*4*	*1*	*11*	*0*	*0*

ELLIOTT Steve

Full Name: Steven Elliott
DOB: 29/10/78, Derby

Previous Club Details

			Apps					Goals		
Club	Signed	Fee	Tot	Start	Sub	FA	FL	Lge	FA	FL
Derby Co.		Train	3	3	0	1	2	0	0	0

FAPL Summary by Club

Club	Tot	Start	Sub	FA	FL	Lge	FA	FL
Derby Co. 1997-98	3	3		1	2	0	0	0
Totals	*3*	*3*		*1*	*2*	*0*	*0*	*0*

ERANIO Stefano

Full Name: Stefano Eranio
DOB: 29/12/66, Genova

Previous Club Details

			Apps					Goals		
Club	Signed	Fee	Tot	Start	Sub	FA	FL	Lge	FA	FL
Genoa	1985		213					13		
Milan	1990		98					6		
Derby Co.	May-97	Free	23	23	0	1	1	5	0	0

FAPL Summary by Club

Club	Tot	Start	Sub	FA	FL	Lge	FA	FL
Derby Co. 1997-98	23	23	0	1	1	5	0	0
Totals	*23*	*23*	*0*	*1*	*1*	*5*	*0*	*0*

Wimbledon

EUELL Jason

Full Name: Jason Euell
DOB: 06/02/77, South London

Previous Club Details

			Apps					Goals		
Club	Signed	Fee	Tot	Start	Sub	FA	FL	Lge	FA	FL
Wimbledon	Jun-95	Train	35	22	13	8	4	8	1	3

FAPL Summary by Club

Club	Tot	Start	Sub	FA	FL	Lge	FA	FL
Wimbledon 95/6 to 97/8	35	22	13	8	4	8	1	3
Totals	*35*	*22*	*13*	*8*	*4*	*8*	*1*	*3*

Southampton

EVANS Micky

Full Name: Michael James Evans
DOB: 01/01/73, Plymouth

Previous Club Details

			Apps					Goals		
Club	Signed	Fee	Tot	Start	Sub	FA	FL	Lge	FA	FL
Plymouth Ar.	Mar-91		166	133	33	12	9	38	3	0
Southampton	Mar-97	£500k	22	14	8	3	4	4	0	1
WBA	Oct-97	£750k								

FAPL Summary by Club

Club	Tot	Start	Sub	FA	FL	Lge	FA	FL
Southampton 96/7 to 97/8	22	14	8	3	4	4	0	1
Totals	*22*	*14*	*8*	*3*	*4*	*4*	*0*	*1*

Everton

FARRELLY Gareth

Full Name: Gareth Farrelly
DOB: 28/08/75, Dublin

Previous Club Details

			Apps					Goals		
Club	Signed	Fee	Tot	Start	Sub	FA	FL	Lge	FA	FL
Aston Villa	Jan-92	Train	8	2	6	0	1	0	0	0
Rotherham U.	Mar-95	Loan	10	9	1	0	0	2	0	0

Everton | Jul-97 | £700k | 0 | | | 0 | | | 0 | 0

FAPL Summary by Club

Club	Season	Tot	Start	Sub	FA	FL	Lge	FA	FL
Aston Villa	95/6 to 96/7	7	2	5	0	1		0	0
Everton	1997-98	26	18	8	1	1	1	0	1
Totals		*33*	*20*	*13*	*1*	*2*	*1*	*0*	*1*

FEAR Peter — Wimbledon

Full Name: Peter Stanley Fear
DOB: 10/09/1973, Sutton

Previous Club Details

			Apps					Goals		
Club	Signed	Fee	Tot	Start	Sub	FA	FL	Lge	FA	FL
Wimbledon	Jul-92		71	51	20	5	10	4	0	1

FAPL Summary by Club

Club	Season	Tot	Start	Sub	FA	FL	Lge	FA	FL
Wimbledon	92/3 to 97/8	71	51	20	5	10	4	0	1
Totals		*71*	*51*	*20*	*5*	*10*	*4*	*0*	*1*

FENN Neale — Tottenham Hotspur

Full Name: Neale Fenn
DOB: 18/01/77, Tottenham

Previous Club Details

			Apps					Goals		
Club	Signed	Fee	Tot	Start	Sub	FA	FL	Lge	FA	FL
Tottenham H.	Jul-95	Train	8	0	8	1	1	0	0	1

FAPL Summary by Club

Club	Season	Tot	Start	Sub	FA	FL	Lge	FA	FL
Tottenham H.	96/7 to 97/8	8	0	8	1	1	0	0	1
Totals		*8*	*0*	*8*	*1*	*1*	*0*	*0*	*1*

FENTON Graham — Leicester City

Full Name: Graham Anthony Fenton
DOB: 22/05/74, Wallsend

Previous Club Details

			Apps					Goals		
Club	Signed	Fee	Tot	Start	Sub	FA	FL	Lge	FA	FL
Aston Villa	Feb-92		32	16	16	0	7	3	0	5
WBA	Jan-94	Loan	7	7	0	0	0	3	0	0
Blackburn R.	Dec-95	£1.5m	27	9	18	1	2	7	0	0
Leicester C.	Aug-97	£1.1m	23	9	14	1	1	3	0	0

FAPL Summary by Club

Club	Season	Tot	Start	Sub	FA	FL	Lge	FA	FL
Aston Villa	93/4 to 95/6	32	16	16	0	7	3	0	0
Blackburn R.	95/6 to 96/7	27	9	18	1	2	7	0	0
Leicester C.	1997-98	23	9	14	1	1	3	0	0
Totals		*82*	*34*	*48*	*2*	*10*	*13*	*0*	*0*

FERDINAND Les — Tottenham Hotspur

Full Name: Leslie Ferdinand
DOB: 18/12/66, Acton

Previous Club Details

			Apps					Goals		
Club	Signed	Fee	Tot	Start	Sub	FA	FL	Lge	FA	FL
QPR	Apr-87	£15k	163	152	11	8	13	80	3	7
Brentford	Mar-88	Loan	3	3	0	0	0	0	0	0
Besiktas	Jun-88	Loan								
Newcastle U.	Jun-95	£6m	68	67	1	5	6	41	2	3
Tottenham H.	Jul-97	£6m	21	19	2	1	5	5	0	0

FAPL Summary by Club

Club	Season	Tot	Start	Sub	FA	FL	Lge	FA	FL
QPR	92/3 to 94/5	110	109	1	8	4	60	3	5
Newcastle U.	95/6 to 96/7	68	67	1	5	6	41	2	3
Tottenham H.	1997-98	21	19	2	1	5	5	0	0
Totals		*199*	*195*	*4*	*14*	*15*	*106*	*5*	*8*

FERDINAND Rio — West Ham United

Full Name: Rio Gavin Ferdinand
DOB: 07/11/78, London

Previous Club Details

			Apps					Goals		
Club	Signed	Fee	Tot	Start	Sub	FA	FL	Lge	FA	FL
West Ham U.	Nov-95	Train	51	46	5	7	6	2	0	0
Bournemouth	Nov-96	Loan	10	10	0	0	0	0	0	0

FAPL Summary by Club

Club	Season	Tot	Start	Sub	FA	FL	Lge	FA	FL
West Ham U.	95/6 to 97/8	51	46	5	7	6	2	0	0
Totals		*51*	*46*	*5*	*7*	*6*	*2*	*0*	*0*

FERGUSON Duncan — Everton

Full Name: Duncan Ferguson
DOB: 27/12/71, Stirling

Previous Club Details

Club	Signed	Fee	Apps Tot	Start	Sub	FA	FL	Goals Lge	FA	FL
Dundee	Feb-90	Free nl	79	75	4	9	6	27	4	2
Rangers	Jul-93	£4m	14	8	6	3	4	2	0	3
Everton	Oct-94	£4m	103	97	6	9	4	33	4	0

FAPL Summary by Club

Everton	94/5 to 97/8		103	97	6	9	4	33	4	0
Totals			103	97	6	9	4	33	4	0

FESTA Gianluca — Middlesbrough

Full Name: Gianluca Festa
DOB: 12/03/69, Cagliari, Italy

Previous Club Details

Club	Signed	Fee	Apps Tot	Start	Sub	FA	FL	Goals Lge	FA	FL
Cagliari	1986		3					0		
Fersulcis (Int)	1987		26					0		
Cagliari	1988		153					2		
Roma	1993		21	20	1			0		
Inter Milan	1993		66	63	3			3		
Middlesbro'	Jan-97	£2.2m	51	49	2	7	11	3	1	0

FAPL Summary by Club

Middlesbro'	1996-97		13	13	0	5	4	1	1	0
Totals			13	13	0	5	4	1	1	0

FETTIS Alan — Blackburn Rovers

Full Name: Alan William Fettis
DOB: 01/02/71, Belfast

Previous Club Details

Club	Signed	Fee	Apps Tot	Start	Sub	FA	FL	Goals Lge	FA	FL
Ards										
Hull C.	Aug-91	£50k	134	131	4	5	8	2	0	0
WBA	Nov-95	Loan	3	3				0	0	0
N. Forest	Jan-96	£250k	4	4		0	1	0	1	0
Blackburn R.	Sep-97	£300k	8	7	1	1	3	0	0	0

FAPL Summary by Club

N. Forest	1996-97		4	4	0	1	0	0	0	0
Blackburn R.	1997-98		8	7	1	3	1	0	0	0
Totals			12	11	1	4	1	0	0	0

FILAN John — Blackburn Rovers

Full Name: John Richard Filan
DOB: 08/02/70, Sydney, Australia

Previous Club Details

Club	Signed	Fee	Apps Tot	Start	Sub	FA	FL	Goals Lge	FA	FL
Sydney, Budapest										
Cambridge U.	Mar-93	£40k	68	68	0	3	6	0	0	0
N. Forest	Dec-94	Loan	0	0	0	0	0	0	0	0
Coventry C.	Mar-95	£300k	16	15	1	0	1	0	0	0
Blackburn R.			7	7	0	1	0	0	0	0

FAPL Summary by Club

Coventry C.	94/5 to 96/7		16	15	1	0	2	0	0	0
Blackburn R.	1997-98		7	7	0	1	0	0	0	0
Totals			23	22	1	1	2	0	0	0

FLEMING Curtis — Middlesbrough

Full Name: Curtis Fleming
DOB: 08/10/68, Manchester

Previous Club Details

Club	Signed	Fee	Apps Tot	Start	Sub	FA	FL	Goals Lge	FA	FL
Middlesbro'	Aug-91	£50k	193	179	14	13	19	2	0	1

FAPL Summary by Club

Middlesbro'	92/3 to 96/7		68	66	2	7	8	1	0	1
Totals			68	66	2	7	8	1	0	1

FLITCROFT Garry — Blackburn Rovers

Full Name: Garry William Flitcroft
DOB: 06/11/72, Bolton

Previous Club Details

Club	Signed	Fee	Apps Tot	Start	Sub	FA	FL	Goals Lge	FA	FL
Man. C.	Jul-91	Train	115	109	6	14	12	13	2	0
Bury	Mar-92	Loan	12	12	0	0	0	4	0	1
Blackburn R.	Mar-96	£3.2m	64	58	6	4	4	3	0	1

FAPL Summary by Club

		Apps Tot	Start	Sub	FA	FL	Goals Lge	FA	FL
Manchester C.	92/3 to 95/6	115	109	6	14	12	13	2	0
Blackburn R.	95/6 to 97/8	64	58	6	4	4	3	0	1
Totals		179	167	12	18	16	16	2	2

FLO Tore Andre — Chelsea

Full Name: Tore Andre Flo
DOB: 15/06/73, Norway

Previous Club Details

Club	Signed	Fee	Apps Tot	Start	Sub	FA	FL	Goals Lge	FA	FL
Tromso	1995		26					18		
SK Brann	1996		24					19		
Chelsea	Jun-97		34	16	18	1	4	11	0	2

FAPL Summary by Club

		Apps Tot	Start	Sub	FA	FL	Goals Lge	FA	FL
Chelsea	1997-98	34	16	18	1	4	11	0	2
Totals		34	16	18	1	4	11	0	2

FLOWERS Tim — Blackburn Rovers

Full Name: Timothy David Flowers
DOB: 03/02/67, Kenilworth

Previous Club Details

Club	Signed	Fee	Apps Tot	Start	Sub	FA	FL	Goals Lge	FA	FL
Wolves	Aug-84		63	63	0	2	5	0	0	0
Southampton	Jun-86	£70k	192	192	0	16	26	0	0	0
Swindon T.	Mar-87	Loan	2	2	0	0	0	0	0	0
Swindon T.	Nov-87	Loan	5	5	0	0	0	0	0	0
Blackburn R.	Nov-93	£2.4m	166	165	1	13	13	0	0	0

FAPL Summary by Club

		Apps Tot	Start	Sub	FA	FL	Goals Lge	FA	FL
Southampton	92/3 to 93/4	54	54	0	1	5	0	0	0
Blackburn R.	93/4 to 97/8	166	165	1	9	17	0	0	0
Totals		220	219	1	10	22	0	0	0

FORREST Craig — West Ham United

Full Name: Craig Lorne Forrest
DOB: 20/09/67, Vancouver, Canada

Previous Club Details

Club	Signed	Fee	Apps Tot	Start	Sub	FA	FL	Goals Lge	FA	FL
Ipswich T.	Aug-85		200	200	0	10	11	0	0	0
Colchester U.	Mar-88	Loan	11	11	0	2	1	0	0	0
Chelsea	Mar-97	Loan	3	3	0	1	0	0	0	0
West Ham U.	Jul-97		13	13	0	0	3	0	0	0

FAPL Summary by Club

		Apps Tot	Start	Sub	FA	FL	Goals Lge	FA	FL
Ipswich T.	92/3 to 94/5	74	74	0	5	5	0	0	0
West Ham U.	1997-98	13	13	0	4	3	0	0	0
Totals		87	87	0	9	8	0	0	0

FOWLER Robbie — Liverpool

Full Name: Robert Bernard Fowler
DOB: 09/04/75, Liverpool

Previous Club Details

Club	Signed	Fee	Apps Tot	Start	Sub	FA	FL	Goals Lge	FA	FL
Liverpool	Apr-92	Train	160	156	4	17	25	92	9	20

FAPL Summary by Club

		Apps Tot	Start	Sub	FA	FL	Goals Lge	FA	FL
Liverpool	93/4 to 97/8	160	156	4	17	25	92	7	19
Totals		160	156	4	17	25	92	7	19

FOX Ruel — Tottenham Hotspur

Full Name: Ruel Adrian Fox
DOB: 14/01/68, Ipswich

Previous Club Details

Club	Signed	Fee	Apps Tot	Start	Sub	FA	FL	Goals Lge	FA	FL
Norwich C.	Jan-86	App.	172	148	24	15	16	22	1	3
Newcastle U.	Feb-94	£2.25m	58	56	2	5	3	12	0	1
Tottenham H.	Oct-95	£4.2m	83	77	6	8	7	10	0	1

FAPL Summary by Club

Club			Tot	Start	Sub	FA	FL	Lge	FA	FL
Norwich C.	92/3 to 93/4		59	57	2	4	5	11	0	2
Newcastle U.	93/4 to 95/6		58	56	2	5	3	12	0	1
Tottenham H.	95/6 to 97/8		83	77	6	8	7	10	0	1
Totals			*200*	*190*	*10*	*17*	*15*	*33*	*0*	*4*

Liverpool

FRIEDEL Brad

Full Name: Brad Friedel
DOB: 18/5/71, Lakewood, Ohio

Previous Club Details

Club	Signed	Fee	Apps Tot	Start	Sub	FA	FL	Goals Lge	FA	FL
Galatasaray, Columbus Crew										
Liverpool	Dec-97	£1.0m	11	11	0	0	0	0	0	0

FAPL Summary by Club

Club			Tot	Start	Sub	FA	FL	Lge	FA	FL
Liverpool	1997-98		11	11		0	0	0	0	0
Totals			*11*	*11*		*0*	*0*	*0*	*0*	*0*

Blackburn Rovers

GALLACHER Kevin

Full Name: Kevin William Gallacher
DOB: 23/11/66, Clydebank

Previous Club Details

Club	Signed	Fee	Apps Tot	Start	Sub	FA	FL	Goals Lge	FA	FL
Coventry C.	Jan-90	£900k	100	99	1	4	11	28	0	7
Blackburn R.	Mar-93	£1.5m	123	116	7	12	8	41	4	2

FAPL Summary by Club

Club			Tot	Start	Sub	FA	FL	Lge	FA	FL
Coventry C.	1992-93		20	19	1	1	2	6	0	0
Blackburn R.	92/3 to 97/8		123	116	7	12	8	41	4	2
Totals			*143*	*135*	*8*	*13*	*10*	*47*	*4*	*2*

Arsenal

GARDE Remi

Full Name: Remi Garde
DOB: 03/04/66, L' Arbresle

Previous Club Details

Club	Signed	Fee	Apps Tot	Start	Sub	FA	FL	Goals Lge	FA	FL
O. Lyonnais	1990		81	81	0			13		
Strasbourg	1995		68	64	4			3		
Arsenal	Aug-96	Free	21	13	8	1	0	0	0	0

FAPL Summary by Club

Club			Tot	Start	Sub	FA	FL	Lge	FA	FL
Arsenal	96/7 to 97/8		21	13	8	1	0	0	0	0
Totals			*21*	*13*	*8*	*1*	*0*	*0*	*0*	*0*

Middlesbrough

GASCOIGNE Paul

Full Name: Paul Gascoigne
DOB: 27/05/67, Gateshead

Previous Club Details

Club	Signed	Fee	Apps Tot	Start	Sub	FA	FL	Goals Lge	FA	FL
Newcastle U.	1984	Train	92	92				21		
Tottenham H.	Jul-88		92	92				19		
Lazio	Jul-92		41	41				6		
Rangers	Jul-95		54	54				27		
Middlesbrough			7	7	0	0	1	0	0	0

Wimbledon

GAYLE Marcus

Full Name: Marcus Anthny Gayle
DOB: 27/09/70, Hammersmith

Previous Club Details

Club	Signed	Fee	Apps Tot	Start	Sub	FA	FL	Goals Lge	FA	FL
Brentford	Jul-89		156	118	38	8	9	22	2	0
Wimbledon	Mar-94	£250k	133	108	25	18	14	17	3	5

FAPL Summary by Club

Club			Tot	Start	Sub	FA	FL	Lge	FA	FL
Wimbledon	93/4 to 97/8		133	108	25	18	14	17	3	5
Totals			*133*	*108*	*25*	*18*	*14*	*17*	*3*	*5*

GEMMILL Scot — Nottingham Forest

Full Name: Scot Gemmill
DOB: 02/01/71, Paisley

Previous Club Details

Club	Signed	Fee	Tot	Start	Sub	FA	FL	Lge	FA	FL
			Apps					*Goals*		
N. Forest	Jan-90		224	209	15	20	29	21	3	1

FAPL Summary by Club

Club			Tot	Start	Sub	FA	FL	Lge	FA	FL
N. Forest	92/3 to 96/7		107	96	11	15	10	3	1	0
Totals			107	96	11	15	10	3	1	0

GERRARD Paul — Everton

Full Name: Paul William Gerrard
DOB: 22/01/73, Heywood

Previous Club Details

Club	Signed	Fee	Tot	Start	Sub	FA	FL	Lge	FA	FL
			Apps					*Goals*		
Oldham A.	Nov-91		119	118	1	7	7	0	0	0
Everton	Aug-96	£1m	9	8	1	2	0	0	0	0

FAPL Summary by Club

Club			Tot	Start	Sub	FA	FL	Lge	FA	FL
Oldham A.	92/3 to 93/4		41	40	1	2	2	0	0	0
Everton	96/7 to 97/8		9	8	1	2	0	0	0	0
Totals			50	48	2	4	2	0	0	0

GIGGS Ryan — Manchester United

Full Name: Ryan Joseph Giggs
DOB: 29/11/73, Cardiff

Previous Club Details

Club	Signed	Fee	Tot	Start	Sub	FA	FL	Lge	FA	FL
			Apps					*Goals*		
Manchester U.	Dec-90		236	217	19	31	28	50	12	5

FAPL Summary by Club

Club			Tot	Start	Sub	FA	FL	Lge	FA	FL
Manchester U.	92/3 to 97/8		196	184	12	28	12	45	5	3
Totals			196	184	12	28	12	45	5	3

GILLESPIE Keith — Newcastle United

Full Name: Keith Robert Gillespie
DOB: 18/02/75, Bangor

Previous Club Details

Club	Signed	Fee	Tot	Start	Sub	FA	FL	Lge	FA	FL
			Apps					*Goals*		
Manchester U.	Feb-93	Train	9	6	3	0	0	1	0	0
Wigan A.	Sep-93	Loan	8	8	0	3	0	4	0	1
Newcastle U.	Jan-95	£1m	106	89	17	11	7	11	2	1

FAPL Summary by Club

Club			Tot	Start	Sub	FA	FL	Lge	FA	FL
Manchester U.	1994-95		9	3	6	1	0	1	1	0
Newcastle U.	94/5 to 97/8		106	89	17	11	7	11	2	1
Totals			115	92	23	12	7	12	3	1

GINOLA David — Tottenham Hotspur

Full Name: David Ginola
DOB: 25/01/67, Gassin, nr St Tropez, France

Previous Club Details

Club	Signed	Fee	Tot	Start	Sub	FA	FL	Lge	FA	FL
			Apps					*Goals*		
PSG (France)										
Newcastle U.	Jul-95	£2.5m	58	54	4	4	6	6	0	0
Tottenham H.	Jun-97		34	34	0	3	3	6	1	2

FAPL Summary by Club

Club			Tot	Start	Sub	FA	FL	Lge	FA	FL
Newcastle U.	95/6 to 96/7		58	54	4	4	6	6	0	0
Tottenham H.	1997-98		34	34	0	3	3	6	1	2
Totals			92	88	4	7	9	12	1	2

GIVEN Shay — Newcastle United

Full Name: Seamus John Given
DOB: 20/04/76, Lifford

Previous Club Details

Club	Signed	Fee	Tot	Start	Sub	FA	FL	Lge	FA	FL
			Apps					*Goals*		
Celtic										
Blackburn R.	Aug-94		2	2	0	0	0	0	0	0
Swindon	Aug-95	Loan	5	5	0	0	0	0	0	0
Sunderland	Jan-96	Loan	17	17	0	0	1	0	0	0

(continued)

Club	Signed	Fee	Tot	Start	Sub	FA	FL	Lge	FA	FL
Newcastle U.	Jun-97		24	24	0	4	0	0	0	0
FAPL Summary by Club										
Blackburn R.	1996-97		2	2	0	0	0	0	0	0
Newcastle U.	1997-98		24	24	0	4	0	0	0	0
Totals			*26*	*26*	*0*	*4*	*0*	*1*	*0*	*0*

GRANT Tony — Everton

Full Name: Anthony James Grant
DOB: 14/11/74, Liverpool

Previous Club Details

Club	Signed	Fee	Tot	Start	Sub	FA	FL	Lge	FA	FL
Everton	Jul-93	Train	43	30	13	4	4	4	0	0
Swindon T.	Jan-96	Loan	3	3	0	0	1	0	0	0
FAPL Summary by Club										
Everton	94/5 to 97/8		43	30	13	4	4	2	0	0
Totals			*43*	*30*	*13*	*4*	*4*	*2*	*0*	*0*

GRANVILLE Danny — Leeds United

Full Name: Daniel Patrick Granville
DOB: 19/01/75, Islington

Previous Club Details

Club	Signed	Fee	Tot	Start	Sub	FA	FL	Lge	FA	FL
Cambridge U.	19/5/93	Train	99	89	10	4	5	7	0	0
Chelsea	Mar-97	£300k	18	12	6	3	3	0	0	0
Leeds U.	Jun-98	£1.6m								
FAPL Summary by Club										
Chelsea	96/7 to 97/8		18	12	6	3	3	0	0	0
Totals			*18*	*12*	*6*	*3*	*3*	*0*	*0*	*0*

GRAYSON Simon — Aston Villa

Full Name: Simon Nicholas Grayson
DOB: 16/12/69, Ripon

Previous Club Details

Club	Signed	Fee	Tot	Start	Sub	FA	FL	Lge	FA	FL
Leeds U.	Jun-88	Train	2	2	0	0	0	0	0	0
Leicester C.	Mar-92	£50k	188	175	13	9	18	4	0	2
Aston Villa			33	28	5	4	1	0	2	0
FAPL Summary by Club										
Leicester C.	94-95 to 96-97		70	70	0	6	9	0	0	2
Aston Villa	1997-98		33	28	5	4	1	0	2	2
Totals			*103*	*98*	*5*	*10*	*10*	*0*	*2*	*2*

GRIFFIN Andy — Newcastle United

Full Name: Andrew Griffin
DOB: 07/03/79, Billinge

Previous Club Details

Club	Signed	Fee	Tot	Start	Sub	FA	FL	Lge	FA	FL
Stoke C.	Sep-96	Train	34	29	5	1	1	0	0	0
Newcastle U.	Jan-98	£1.5m	4	4	0	0	0	0	0	0
FAPL Summary by Club										
Newcastle U.	1997-98		4	4	0	0	0	0	0	0
Totals			*4*	*4*	*0*	*0*	*0*	*0*	*0*	*0*

GRIMANDI Gilles — Arsenal

Full Name: Gilles Grimandi
DOB: 11/11/70, Gap, France

Previous Club Details

Club	Signed	Fee	Tot	Start	Sub	FA	FL	Lge	FA	FL
AS Monaco			90	60	30			3		
Arsenal	Jun-97	£1.5m	22	16	6	5	3	1	0	0
FAPL Summary by Club										
Arsenal	1997-98		22	16	6	5	3	1	0	0
Totals			*22*	*16*	*6*	*5*	*3*	*1*	*0*	*0*

GRODAS Frode — Tottenham Hotspur

Full Name: Frode Grodas
DOB: 24/10/69, Norway

Previous Club Details

			Apps					Goals		
Club	Signed	Fee	Tot	Start	Sub	FA	FL	Lge	FA	FL
Lillestrom	1990		117	117						
Chelsea	Nov-96	Free	21	20	1	5	1	0	0	0
Tottenham H.	Jan-98	£250k	0	0				0	0	0

FAPL Summary by Club

			Apps					Goals		
Chelsea	1996-97		21	20	1	5	1	0	0	0
Totals			*21*	*20*	*1*	*5*	*1*	*0*	*0*	*0*

GUPPY Steve — Leicester City

Full Name: Stephen Guppy
DOB: 29/03/69, Winchester

Previous Club Details

			Apps					Goals		
Club	Signed	Fee	Tot	Start	Sub	FA	FL	Lge	FA	FL
Wycombe W.	1989		41	41	0	8	4	8	2	0
Newcastle U.	Aug-94	£150k	0	0				0	0	0
Port Vale	Nov-94	£225k	105	102	3	8	7	12	1	2
Leicester C.	Feb-97	£850k	50	49	1	2	1	2	0	0

FAPL Summary by Club

			Apps					Goals		
Leicester C.	96/7 to 97/8		50	49	1	2	1	2	0	0
Totals			*50*	*49*	*1*	*2*	*1*	*2*	*0*	*0*

HAALAND Alf Inge — Leeds United

Full Name: Alf Inge Rasdal Haaland
DOB: 23/11/72, Stavanger, Norway

Previous Club Details

			Apps					Goals		
Club	Signed	Fee	Tot	Start	Sub	FA	FL	Lge	FA	FL
Young Boys										
N. Forest	Jan-94		75	66	9	6	7	7	0	0
Leeds U.	Jun-97	£1.6m	32	26	6	2	3	7	0	0

FAPL Summary by Club

			Apps					Goals		
N. Forest	94-95 to 96-97		71	63	8	6	4	7	0	0
Leeds U.	1997-98		32	26	6	2	3	7	0	1
Totals			*103*	*89*	*14*	*8*	*7*	*14*	*0*	*1*

HALL Marcus — Coventry City

Full Name: Marcus Thomas Hall
DOB: 24/03/76, Coventry

Previous Club Details

			Apps					Goals		
Club	Signed	Fee	Tot	Start	Sub	FA	FL	Lge	FA	FL
Coventry C.	7/94	Train	68	56	12	9	10	1	0	1

FAPL Summary by Club

			Apps					Goals		
Coventry C.	94/5 to 97/8		68	56	12	9	10	1	0	1
Totals			*68*	*56*	*12*	*9*	*10*	*1*	*0*	*1*

HALL Richard — West Ham United

Full Name: Richard Anthony Hall
DOB: 14/03/72, Ipswich

Previous Club Details

			Apps					Goals		
Club	Signed	Fee	Tot	Start	Sub	FA	FL	Lge	FA	FL
Scunthorpe U.	Mar-90		22	22	0	3	2	3	1	0
Southampton	Feb-91	£200k	126	119	7	15	12	12	3	1
West Ham U.	Jul-96	£1.9m	7	7	0	0	0	0	0	0

FAPL Summary by Club

			Apps					Goals		
Southampton	92/3 to 95/6		99	98	1	7	9	9	1	1
West Ham U.	1996-97		7	7	0	0	0	0	0	0
Totals			*106*	*105*	*1*	*7*	*9*	*9*	*1*	*1*

HALLE Gunnar — Leeds United

Full Name: Gunnar Halle
DOB: 11/08/65, Oslo, Norway

Previous Club Details

			Apps					Goals		
Club	Signed	Fee	Tot	Start	Sub	FA	FL	Lge	FA	FL
Lillestrom										

(continued from previous page)

Club	Signed	Fee	Tot	Start	Sub	FA	FL	Lge	FA	FL
Oldham A.	Feb-91	£280k	188	185	3	8	16	17	2	2
Leeds U.	Dec-96	£400k	53	51	2	6	3	2	0	0
FAPL Summary by Club										
Oldham A.	92/3 to 93/4		63	62	1	3	4	6	0	1
Leeds U.	96/7 to 97/8		53	51	2	6	9	7	0	0
Totals			116	113	3	9	13	13	0	1

HAMILTON Des

Newcastle United

Full Name: Derrick Vivian Hamilton
DOB: 15/08/76, Bradford

Previous Club Details

			Apps					*Goals*		
Club	Signed	Fee	Tot	Start	Sub	FA	FL	Lge	FA	FL
Bradford C.	Jun-94	Train	88	67	21	5	1	6	0	0
Newcastle U.	Mar-97	£1.6m	12	7	5	1	2	0	0	1
FAPL Summary by Club										
Newcastle U.	1997-98		12	7	5	1	2	0	0	1
Totals			12	7	5	1	2	0	0	1

HARKNESS Steve

Liverpool

Full Name: Steven Harkness
DOB: 27/08/71, Carlisle

Previous Club Details

			Apps					*Goals*		
Club	Signed	Fee	Tot	Start	Sub	FA	FL	Lge	FA	FL
Carlisle U.	Mar-89		13	12	1	0	0	1	0	0
Liverpool	Jul-89	£75k	96	86	10	5	14	3	0	1
Huddersfield	Sep-93	Loan	5	5	0	0	0	0	0	0
Southend U.	Feb-95	Loan	6	6	0	0	0	0	0	0
FAPL Summary by Club										
Liverpool	92/3 to 97/8		85	79	6	3	11	3	0	1
Totals			85	79	6	3	11	3	0	1

HARLEY Jon

Chelsea

Full Name: Jon Harley
DOB: 26/09/79, Maidstone

Previous Club Details

			Apps					*Goals*		
Club	Signed	Fee	Tot	Start	Sub	FA	FL	Lge	FA	FL
Chelsea	Train		3	3	0	0	0	0	0	0
FAPL Summary by Club										
Chelsea	1997-98		3	3	0	0	0	0	0	0
Totals			3	3	0	0	0	0	0	0

HARTE Ian

Leeds United

Full Name: Ian Harte
DOB: 31/08/77, Drogheda

Previous Club Details

			Apps					*Goals*		
Club	Signed	Fee	Tot	Start	Sub	FA	FL	Lge	FA	FL
Leeds Utd	Dec-95	Train	30	24	6	4	4	2	0	1
FAPL Summary by Club										
Leeds U.	95/6 to 97/8		30	24	6	4	4	2	0	1
Totals			30	24	6	4	4	2	0	1

HARTSON John

West Ham United

Full Name: John Hartson
DOB: 05/04/75, Swansea

Previous Club Details

			Apps					*Goals*		
Club	Signed	Fee	Tot	Start	Sub	FA	FL	Lge	FA	FL
Luton Town	Dec-92	Tra n								
Arsenal	Jan-95	£2.5m								
West Ham U.	Feb-97	£3.2m								
FAPL Summary by Club										
Arsenal	94-95 to 96-97		53	44	9	3	6	14	1	1
West Ham U.	96/7 to 97/8		43	43	0	5	5	20	3	6
Totals			96	87	9	8	11	34	4	7

HASSELBAINK Jimmy — Leeds United

Full Name: Jimmy Floyd Hasselbaink
DOB: 27/3/72, Surinam
Previous Club Details
Telstar, Campomairoense, Boavista

| | | | | Apps | | | | Goals | | |
Club	Signed	Fee	Tot	Start	Sub	FA	FL	Lge	FA	FL
Leeds U.	Jun-97	£2m	33	30	3	4	3	16	4	2
FAPL Summary by Club										
Leeds U.	1997-98		33	30	3	4	3	16	4	2
Totals			*33*	*30*	*3*	*4*	*3*	*16*	*4*	*2*

HEALD Paul — Wimbledon

Full Name: Paul Andrew Heald
DOB: 20/09/68, Wath-on-Dearne
Previous Club Details

| | | | | Apps | | | | Goals | | |
Club	Signed	Fee	Tot	Start	Sub	FA	FL	Lge	FA	FL
Sheffield U.	Jun-87	Train	0	0	0	0	0	0	0	0
L. Orient	Dec-88	Unk.	176	176	0	9	13	0	0	0
Coventry T.	Mar-92	Loan	2	1	1	0	0	0	0	0
Swindon T.	Mar-94	Loan	2	2	0	0	0	0	0	0
Wimbledon	Aug-95	£125k	20	20	0	5	0	0	0	0
FAPL Summary by Club										
Swindon T.	1993-94		3	2	1	0	1	0	0	0
Wimbledon	95/6 to 9/78		20	20	0	5	0	0	0	0
Totals			*23*	*22*	*1*	*5*	*1*	*0*	*0*	*0*

HEDMAN Magnus — Coventry City

Full Name: Magnus Hedman
DOB: 19/03/77, Sweden
Previous Club Details
AIK Stockholm

| | | | | Apps | | | | Goals | | |
Club	Signed	Fee	Tot	Start	Sub	FA	FL	Lge	FA	FL
Coventry C.	Jul-97	£500k	14	14	0	3	0	0	0	0
FAPL Summary by Club										
Coventry C.	1997-98		14	14	0	3	0	0	0	0
Totals			*14*	*14*	*0*	*3*	*0*	*0*	*0*	*0*

HENDRIE Lee — Aston Villa

Full Name: Lee Hendrie
DOB: 18/05/77, Birmingham
Previous Club Details

| | | | | Apps | | | | Goals | | |
Club	Signed	Fee	Tot	Start	Sub	FA	FL	Lge	FA	FL
Aston Villa		Train	24	15	9	7	0	3	0	0
FAPL Summary by Club										
Aston Villa	95/6 to 9/78		24	15	9	7	0	3	0	0
Totals			*24*	*15*	*9*	*7*	*0*	*3*	*0*	*0*

HENDRY Colin — Blackburn Rovers

Full Name: Edward Colin James Hendry
DOB: 07/12/65, Keith
Previous Club Details

| | | | | Apps | | | | Goals | | |
Club	Signed	Fee	Tot	Start	Sub	FA	FL	Lge	FA	FL
Blackburn R.	Mar-87	£30k	102	99	3	4	22	5	0	0
Manchester C.	Nov-89	£700k	63	57	6	5	5	2	0	1
Blackburn R.	Nov-91	£700k	234	229	5	18	23	12	0	0
FAPL Summary by Club										
Blackburn R.	92/3 to 9/78		204	203	1	17	23	8	0	0
Totals			*204*	*203*	*1*	*17*	*23*	*8*	*0*	*0*

HESKEY Emile — Leicester City

Full Name: Emile Heskey
DOB: 11/01/78, Leicester
Previous Club Details

| | | | | Apps | | | | Goals | | |
Club	Signed	Fee	Tot	Start	Sub	FA	FL	Lge	FA	FL
Leicester C.	Oct-95	Train	101	91	10	5	11	27	5	2
FAPL Summary by Club										
Leicester C.	94/5 to 9/78		71	71	0	5	9	20	0	2
Totals			*71*	*71*	*0*	*5*	*9*	*20*	*0*	*2*

HIDEN Martin — Leeds United

Full Name: Martin Hiden
DOB: 11/3/73

Previous Club Details
Strum Graz, Rapid Vienna

Club	Signed	Fee	Tot	Start	Sub	FA	FL	Lge	FA	FL
Leeds U.	Feb-98	£1.3m	11	11	0	1	0	0	0	0

FAPL Summary by Club

		Tot	Start	Sub	FA	FL	Lge	FA	FL
Leeds U.	1997-98	11	11	0	1	0	0	0	0
Totals		11	11	0	1	0	0	0	0

HIGNETT Craig — Middlesbrough

Full Name: Craig Hignett
DOB: 12/01/70, Prescot

Previous Club Details

Club	Signed	Fee	Tot	Start	Sub	FA	FL	Lge	FA	FL
Liverpool	May-88	Train								
Crewe Al.		Free	121	108	13	12	10	42	8	4
Middlesbro'	Nov-92	£500k	153	125	28	12	23	33	3	12

FAPL Summary by Club

		Tot	Start	Sub	FA	FL	Lge	FA	FL
Middlesbro'	92/3 to 96-97	65	54	11	7	13	13	2	3
Totals		65	54	11	7	13	13	2	3

HINCHCLIFFE Andy — Sheffield Wednesday

Full Name: Andrew George Hinchcliffe
DOB: 05/02/69, Manchester

Previous Club Details

Club	Signed	Fee	Tot	Start	Sub	FA	FL	Lge	FA	FL
Manchester C.	Feb-86		112	107	5	12	11	8	1	1
Everton	Jul-90	£800k	182	170	12	14	23	6	1	0
Sheffield W.	Jan-98	£3.0m	15	15	0	1	0	0	0	0

FAPL Summary by Club

		Tot	Start	Sub	FA	FL	Lge	FA	FL
Everton	92/3 to 97/8	143	134	9	9	18	6	1	1
Sheffield W.	1997-98	15	15	0	0	0	0	1	0
Totals		158	149	9	9	18	7	1	1

HIRST David — Southampton

Full Name: David Eric Hirst
DOB: 07/12/67, Cudworth

Previous Club Details

Club	Signed	Fee	Tot	Start	Sub	FA	FL	Lge	FA	FL
Barnsley	Nov-85		28	26	2	0	1	9	0	0
Sheffield W.	Aug-86	£200k	294	261	33	19	35	106	6	11
Southampton	Oct-97	£2.0m	28	28	0	1	1	9	0	0

FAPL Summary by Club

		Tot	Start	Sub	FA	FL	Lge	FA	FL
Sheffield W.	92/3 to 97/8	105	93	12	9	13	34	1	4
Southampton	1997-98	28	28	0	1	1	9	0	0
Totals		133	121	12	10	13	43	1	4

HISLOP Shaka — Newcastle United

Full Name: Neil Hislop
DOB: 22/02/69, London

Previous Club Details

Club	Signed	Fee	Tot	Start	Sub	FA	FL	Lge	FA	FL
Reading	Sep-92		104	104	0	3	10	0	0	0
Newcastle U.	Aug-95	£1.58m	53	53	0	6	8	0	0	0

FAPL Summary by Club

		Tot	Start	Sub	FA	FL	Lge	FA	FL
Newcastle U.	95/6 to 97/8	53	53	0	6	8	0	0	0
Totals		53	53	0	6	8	0	0	0

HITCHCOCK Kevin — Chelsea

Full Name: Kevin Joseph Hitchcock
DOB: 05/10/62, Canning Town

Previous Club Details

Club	Signed	Fee	Tot	Start	Sub	FA	FL	Lge	FA	FL
N. Forest	Aug-83	£15k	0	0	0	0	0	0	0	0
Mansfield T.	Feb-84	Loan	14	14	0	0	0	0	0	0

Club	Signed	Fee	Tot	Start	Sub	FA	FL	Lge	FA	FL
Mansfield T.	Jun-84	£140k	168	168	0	10	12	0	0	0
Chelsea	Mar-88	£250k	93	90	3	14	10	0	0	0
Northampton	Dec-90	Loan	17	17	0	0	0	0	0	0
FAPL Summary by Club										
Chelsea	92/3 to 97/8		58	55	3	10	10	0	0	0
Totals			58	55	3	10	10	0	0	0

HJELDE Jon Olav — Nottingham Forest

Full Name: Jon Olav Hjelde
DOB: 20/07/72, Levanger, Norway

Previous Club Details

				Apps				Goals		
Club	Signed	Fee	Tot	Start	Sub	FA	FL	Lge	FA	FL
Rosenborg										
N. Forest	Aug-97	£600k	28	23	5	1	2	1	0	2

HODGES Lee — West Ham United

Full Name: Lee Leslie Hodges
DOB: 02/03/78, Plaistow

Previous Club Details

				Apps				Goals		
Club	Signed	Fee	Tot	Start	Sub	FA	FL	Lge	FA	FL
West Ham U.	Mar-95	Train	2	2	0	0	0	0	0	0
Exeter C.	Dec-96	Loan	17	16	1	0	0	0	0	0
L. Orient	Feb-97	Loan	3	3	0	0	0	0	0	0
FAPL Summary by Club										
West Ham U.	1997-98		2	2	0	0	0	0	0	0
Totals			2	2	0	0	0	0	0	0

HOLMES Matty — Charlton Athletic

Full Name: Matthew Jason Holmes
DOB: 01/08/69, Luton

Previous Club Details

				Apps				Goals		
Club	Signed	Fee	Tot	Start	Sub	FA	FL	Lge	FA	FL
Bournemouth	Aug-88	Train	114	105	9	10	7	8	0	0
Cardiff C.	Mar-89	Loan	1	1	0	0	1	0	0	0
West Ham U.	Aug-92	£40k	76	63	13	6	4	5	0	0
Blackburn R.	Aug-95	£1.2m	8	8	0	1	0	1	0	0
Charlton A.	Aug-97	£250k	16	10	6	1	0	1	0	0
FAPL Summary by Club										
West Ham U.	93-94 to 94-95		58	57	1	5	4	4	0	0
Blackburn R.	1995-96		8	7	1	0	0	1	0	0
Totals			66	64	2	5	4	5	0	0

HOPKIN David — Leeds United

Full Name: David Hopkin
DOB: 21/08/70, Greenock

Previous Club Details

				Apps				Goals		
Club	Signed	Fee	Tot	Start	Sub	FA	FL	Lge	FA	FL
Morton	1989	nl	48	33	15	2	2	4	1	2
Chelsea	Sep-92	£300k	40	21	19	5	1	1	0	1
C. Palace	Jul-95	£850k	83	79	4	3	6	21	0	6
Leeds U.	Jul-97	£3.25m	25	22	3	1	4	1	1	0
FAPL Summary by Club										
Chelsea	92/3 to 94/5		40	21	19	5	1	1	0	1
Leeds U.	1997-98		25	22	3	6	5	2	0	0
Totals			65	43	22					

HOULT Russell — Derby County

Full Name: Russell Hoult
DOB: 28/03/91, Leicester

Previous Club Details

				Apps				Goals		
Club	Signed	Fee	Tot	Start	Sub	FA	FL	Lge	FA	FL
Leicester C.	Mar-91		10	10	0	3	0	0	0	0
Lincoln C.	Aug-91	Loan	2	2	0	1	0	0	0	0
Bolton W.	Nov-93	Loan	4	3	1	0	0	0	0	0
Lincoln C.	Aug-94	Loan	16	15	1	2	1	0	0	0
Derby Co.	Feb-95	£300k	90	88	2	1	3	0	0	0

FAPL Summary by Club

		Apps				Goals	
Club	Tot	Start	Sub	FA	FL	Lge	FA	FL
Derby Co. 96/7 to 97/8	34	33	1	0	1	0	0	0
Totals	34	33	1	0	1	0	0	0

HOWELLS David — Tottenham Hotspur

Full Name: David Howells
DOB: 15/12/67, Guildford

Previous Club Details

			Apps					Goals		
Club	Signed	Fee	Tot	Start	Sub	FA	FL	Lge	FA	FL
Tottenham H.	Jan-85	App	277	238	39	22	31	22	0	4

FAPL Summary by Club

Club	Tot	Start	Sub	FA	FL	Lge	FA	FL
Tottenham H. 92/3 to 97/8	143	132	11	13	12	8	0	2
Totals	143	132	11	13	12	8	0	2

HOWEY Steve — Newcastle United

Full Name: Stephen Norman Howey
DOB: 26/10/71, Sunderland

Previous Club Details

			Apps					Goals		
Club	Signed	Fee	Tot	Start	Sub	FA	FL	Lge	FA	FL
Newcastle U.	Dec-89	Train	168	146	22	18	16	6	0	1

FAPL Summary by Club

Club	Tot	Start	Sub	FA	FL	Lge	FA	FL
Newcastle U. 93/4 to 97/8	94	89	5	10	10	3	0	0
Totals	94	89	5	10	10	3	0	0

HUCKERBY Darren — Coventry City

Full Name: Darren Carl Huckerby
DOB: 27/04/76, Nottingham

Previous Club Details

			Apps					Goals		
Club	Signed	Fee	Tot	Start	Sub	FA	FL	Lge	FA	FL
Lincoln C.	Jul-93	Train	30	20	10	1	2	0	0	0
Newcastle U.	Nov-95	£400k	1	0	1			0	0	0
Millwall	Sep-96	Loan	6	6		1	0	3	0	0
Coventry C.	Nov-96	£1m	59	53	6	7	10	19	3	0

FAPL Summary by Club

		Apps				Goals	
Club	Tot	Start	Sub	FA	FL	Lge	FA	FL
Newcastle U. 1995-96	1	0	1			0	0	0
Coventry C. 96/7 to 97/8	59	53	6	7	10	19	3	0
Totals	60	53	7	7	10	19	3	0

HUGHES Aaron — Newcastle United

Full Name: Aaron Hughes
DOB: 08/11/79, Magherafelt

Previous Club Details

			Apps					Goals		
Club	Signed	Fee	Tot	Start	Sub	FA	FL	Lge	FA	FL
Newcastle U.		Train	4	4		0	1	0	0	0

FAPL Summary by Club

Club	Tot	Start	Sub	FA	FL	Lge	FA	FL
Newcastle U. 1997-98	4	4		0	1	0	0	0
Totals	4	4		0	1	0	0	0

HUGHES Ceri — Wimbledon

Full Name: Ceri Morgan Hughes
DOB: 26/02/71, Pontypridd

Previous Club Details

			Apps					Goals		
Club	Signed	Fee	Tot	Start	Sub	FA	FL	Lge	FA	FL
Luton Town	Jul-89	Train	175	157	18	13	17	24	1	2
Wimbledon	Jul-97	£400k	17	13	4	2	2	1	0	0

FAPL Summary by Club

Club	Tot	Start	Sub	FA	FL	Lge	FA	FL
Wimbledon 1997-98	17	13	4	2	2	1	0	0
Totals	17	13	4	2	2	1	0	0

HUGHES David — Southampton

Full Name: David Robert Hughes
DOB: 30/12/72, St Albans

Previous Club Details

			Apps					Goals		
Club	Signed	Fee	Tot	Start	Sub	FA	FL	Lge	FA	FL
Southampton	Jul-91	Jnr	44	15	29	6	4	3	1	0

FAPL Summary by Club

Club	Tot	Start	Sub	FA	FL	Lge	FA	FL
Southampton 93/4 to 97/8	44	15	29	6	4	3	1	0
Totals	44	15	29	6	4	3	1	0

HUGHES Mark — Chelsea

Full Name: Leslie Mark Hughes
DOB: 01/11/63, Wrexham

Previous Club Details

			Apps					Goals		
Club	Signed	Fee	Tot	Start	Sub	FA	FL	Lge	FA	FL
Manchester U.	Nov-80	App	89	85	4	10	6	37	4	4
Barcelona	Jul-86	£2.5m	0	0	0	0	0	0	0	0
B. Munich	Oct-87	Loan	0	0	0	0	0	0	0	0
Manchester U.	Jul-88	£1.5m	256	251	5	35	32	82	13	12
Chelsea	Jul-95	£1.5m	95	88	7	14	10	25	9	3

FAPL Summary by Club

			Apps					Goals		
Club			Tot	Start	Sub	FA	FL	Lge	FA	FL
Manchester U.	92/3 to 94/5		111	110	1	15	11	35	6	6
Chelsea	95/6 to 97/8		95	88	7	14	10	25	9	3
Totals			206	198	8	29	21	60	15	9

HUGHES Michael — Wimbledon

Full Name: Michael Eamonn Hughes
DOB: 02/08/71, Larne

Previous Club Details

			Apps					Goals		
Club	Signed	Fee	Tot	Start	Sub	FA	FL	Lge	FA	FL
Manchester C.	Aug-88	Train	26	25	1	1	0	0	1	0
Strasbourg	Jul-92	£450k	78	73	5	7	7	7	5	1
West Ham U.	Nov-94	Free	83	76	7	7	7	7	1	0
Wimbledon	Sep-97	£800k	29	29	0	4	0	2	2	0

FAPL Summary by Club

			Apps					Goals		
Club			Tot	Start	Sub	FA	FL	Lge	FA	FL
West Ham U.			83	76	7	7	7	7	1	0
Wimbledon	1997/8		29	29	0	4	0	2	2	0
Totals			112	105	7	11	7	9	3	0

HUGHES Paul — Chelsea

Full Name: Paul Hughes
DOB: 19/04/76, Hammersmith

Previous Club Details

			Apps					Goals		
Club	Signed	Fee	Tot	Start	Sub	FA	FL	Lge	FA	FL
Chelsea	Jul-94	Train	21	13	8	1	0	2	0	0

FAPL Summary by Club

			Apps					Goals		
Club			Tot	Start	Sub	FA	FL	Lge	FA	FL
Chelsea	96/7 to 97/8		21	13	8	1	0	2	0	0
Totals			21	13	8	1	0	2	0	0

HUGHES Steve — Arsenal

Full Name: Stephen John Hughes
DOB: 18/09/76, Reading

Previous Club Details

			Apps					Goals		
Club	Signed	Fee	Tot	Start	Sub	FA	FL	Lge	FA	FL
Arsenal	Jul-95	Train	33	17	16	8	5	3	1	1

FAPL Summary by Club

			Apps					Goals		
Club			Tot	Start	Sub	FA	FL	Lge	FA	FL
Arsenal	94/5 to 97/8		33	17	16	8	5	3	1	1
Totals			33	17	16	8	5	3	1	1

HUMPHREYS Richie — Sheffield Wednesday

Full Name: Richard John Humphreys
DOB: 30/11/77, Sheffield

Previous Club Details

			Apps					Goals		
Club	Signed	Fee	Tot	Start	Sub	FA	FL	Lge	FA	FL
Sheffield W.	Feb-96	Train	41	17	24	7	2	3	2	0

FAPL Summary by Club

			Apps					Goals		
Club			Tot	Start	Sub	FA	FL	Lge	FA	FL
Sheffield W.	95/6 to 97/8		41	17	24	7	2	3	2	0
Totals			41	17	24	7	2	3	2	0

HUNT Jon — Derby County

Full Name: Jonathan Richard Hunt
DOB: 02/11/71, Camden

Previous Club Details

			Apps					Goals		
Club	Signed	Fee	Tot	Start	Sub	FA	FL	Lge	FA	FL
Barnet	1989	Jnrs	33	12	21	1	1	0	0	0
Southend U.	Jul-93	Free	49	41	8	1	4	6	0	0

Club	Signed	Fee	Tot	Start	Sub	FA	FL	Lge	FA	FL
Birmingham C.	Sep-94	£50k	77	67	10	4	15	18	1	2
Derby Co.	Jul-97	£500k								

FAPL Summary by Club

Club	Signed	Tot	Start	Sub	FA	FL	Lge	FA	FL
Derby Co.	1997-98	19	19			12		0	0
Totals		*19*	*19*			*12*	*12*	*0*	*0*

Everton

HUTCHISON Don

Full Name: Donald Hutchison
DOB: 09/05/71, Gateshead

Previous Club Details

Club	Signed	Fee	Apps Tot	Start	Sub	FA	FL	Goals Lge	FA	FL
Hartlepool U.	Mar-90		24	19	5	2	2	3	0	0
Liverpool	Nov-90	£175k	45	33	12	3	8	7	1	0
West Ham U.	Aug-94	£1.5m	35	30	5	1	3	11	0	0
Sheffield U.*	Jan-96	£1.2m	60	56	4	4	5	4	0	0
Everton	Feb-98	£1.0m	11	11	0	0	1	0	1	0

FAPL Summary by Club

Club	Signed	Tot	Start	Sub	FA	FL	Lge	FA	FL
Liverpool	92/3 to 93/4	42	33	9	3	8	7	0	2
West Ham U.	94/5 to 95/6	28	23	5	1	0	9	0	0
Everton	1997-98	11	11	0	0	1	0	0	0
Totals		*81*	*67*	*14*	*4*	*11*	*17*	*0*	*4*

Sheffield Wednesday

HYDE Graham

Full Name: Graham Hyde
DOB: 10/11/70, Doncaster

Previous Club Details

Club	Signed	Fee	Apps Tot	Start	Sub	FA	FL	Goals Lge	FA	FL
Sheffield W.	May-88	Train	170	126	44	18	20	11	2	2

FAPL Summary by Club

Club	Signed	Tot	Start	Sub	FA	FL	Lge	FA	FL
Sheffield W.	92/3 to 97/8	138	102	36	12	18	9	1	2
Totals		*138*	*102*	*36*	*12*	*18*	*9*	*1*	*2*

Charlton Athletic

ILIC Sasa

Full Name: Sasa Ilic
DOB: Australia

Previous Club Details

Club	Signed	Fee	Apps Tot	Start	Sub	FA	FL	Goals Lge	FA	FL
Charlton A.	1997		15	15	0	0	0	0	0	0

West Ham United

IMPEY Andy

Full Name: Andrew Rodney Impey
DOB: 30/09/71, Hammersmith

Previous Club Details

Club	Signed	Fee	Apps Tot	Start	Sub	FA	FL	Goals Lge	FA	FL
QPR *	Jun-90	£35k	187	177	10	10	16	13	1	3
West Ham U.	Sep-97	£1.3m	19	19	0	1	0	0	0	0

FAPL Summary by Club

Club	Signed	Tot	Start	Sub	FA	FL	Lge	FA	FL
West Ham U.	92/3 to 97/8	161	157	4	10	16	11	1	2
Totals		*161*	*157*	*4*	*10*	*16*	*11*	*1*	*2*

Liverpool

INCE Paul

Full Name: Paul Emerson Carlyle Ince
DOB: 21/10/67, Ilford

Previous Club Details

Club	Signed	Fee	Apps Tot	Start	Sub	FA	FL	Goals Lge	FA	FL
West Ham U.	Jul-85		72	66	6	10	9	7	1	3
Manchester U.	Aug-89	£125k	170	167	3	21	24	20	1	2
Internazionale	Jun-95	£7.5m								
Liverpool	Jul-97		31	31	0	1	4	8	0	0

FAPL Summary by Club

Club	Signed	Tot	Start	Sub	FA	FL	Lge	FA	FL
Manchester U.	92/3 to 94/5	116	116	0	15	19	4	1	0
Liverpool	1997-98	31	31	0	1	4	8	0	0
Totals		*147*	*147*	*0*	*16*	*27*	*12*	*1*	*0*

Manchester United

IRWIN Denis

Full Name: Joseph Denis Irwin
DOB: 31/10/65, Cork
Previous Club Details

Club	Signed	Fee	Apps Tot	Start	Sub	FA	FL	Goals Lge	FA	FL
Leeds U.	Nov-83	App	72	72	0	3	5	1	0	0
Oldham A.	May-86		167	166	1	13	19	4	0	3
Manchester U.	Jun-90	£625k	281	275	6	36	31	17	6	0
FAPL Summary by Club										
Manchester U.	92/3 to 97/8		209	205	4	30	16	13	6	0
Totals			209	205	4	30	16	13	6	0

IVERSEN Steffen — Tottenham Hotspur
Full Name: Steffen Iversen
DOB: 10/11/76, Oslo, Norway
Previous Club Details

Club	Signed	Fee	Apps Tot	Start	Sub	FA	FL	Goals Lge	FA	FL
Rosenborg	1995		25	8	17			8		
Tottenham H.	Nov-96	£2.7m	29	24	5	5	6	6	0	0
FAPL Summary by Club										
Tottenham H.	96/7 to 97/8		29	24	5	5	6	6	0	0
Totals			29	24	5	5	6	6	0	0

IZZET Muzzy — Leicester City
Full Name: Mustafa Izzet
DOB: 31/10/74, Mile End, London
Previous Club Details

Club	Signed	Fee	Apps Tot	Start	Sub	FA	FL	Goals Lge	FA	FL
Chelsea	May-93	Train								
Leicester C.	Mar-96	£800k	80	78	2	5	8	8	0	1
FAPL Summary by Club										
Leicester C.	96/7 to 97/8		71	70	1	5	8	7	0	1
Totals			71	70	1	5	8	7	0	1

JACKSON Mark — Leeds United
Full Name: Mark Graham Jackson
DOB: 30/09/77, Leeds
Previous Club Details

Club	Signed	Fee	Apps Tot	Start	Sub	FA	FL	Goals Lge	FA	FL
Leeds U.	Jul-95	Train	19	11	8		4	0	0	0
FAPL Summary by Club										
Leeds U.	95/6 to 97/8		19	11	8		4	0	0	0
Totals			19	11	8		4	0	0	0

JAMES David — Liverpool
Full Name: David Benjamin James
DOB: 01/08/70, Welwyn Garden City
Previous Club Details

Club	Signed	Fee	Apps Tot	Start	Sub	FA	FL	Goals Lge	FA	FL
Watford	Jul-88	Train	89	89	0	2	6	0	0	0
Liverpool	Jul-92	£1m	188	187	1	18	22	0	0	0
FAPL Summary by Club										
Liverpool	92/3 to 97/8		188	187	1	18	21	0	0	0
Totals			188	187	1	18	21	0	0	0

JOACHIM Julian — Aston Villa
Full Name: Julian Kevin Joachim
DOB: 12/09/74, Peterborough
Previous Club Details

Club	Signed	Fee	Apps Tot	Start	Sub	FA	FL	Goals Lge	FA	FL
Leicester C.	Sep-92	Train	99	77	22	5	9	25	1	3
Aston Villa	Feb-96	£1.5m	52	23	29	3	1	12	0	0
FAPL Summary by Club										
Leicester C.	1994-95		15	11	4	0	2	3	0	0
Aston Villa	95/6 to 97/8		52	23	29	3	1	12	0	0
Totals			67	34	33	3	3	15	0	0

JOHANSEN Martin — Coventry City

Southampton

Full Name: Martin Johansen
DOB: 22/07/72, Golstrup, Denmark
Previous Club Details

Club	Signed	Fee	Apps			FA	FL	Goals		
			Tot	Start	Sub			Lge	FA	FL
FC Copenhagen										
Coventry C.	Jul-97	Free	2	0	2	0	1	0	0	0
FAPL Summary by Club										
Coventry C.	*1997-98*		*2*	*0*	*2*	*0*	*1*	*0*	*0*	*0*
Totals			2	0	2	0	1	0	0	0

JOHANSEN Stig

Southampton

Full Name: Stig Johansen
DOB: 13/6/72, Norway
Previous Club Details

Club	Signed	Fee	Apps			FA	FL	Goals		
			Tot	Start	Sub			Lge	FA	FL
Bodo-Glimt										
Southampton	Aug-97	£600k	6	3	3	0	2	0	0	0
FAPL Summary by Club										
Southampton	*1997-98*		*6*	*3*	*3*	*0*	*2*	*0*	*0*	*0*
Totals			6	3	3	0	2	0	0	0

JOHNSEN Ronnie

Manchester United

Full Name: Ronald Johnsen
DOB: 10/06/69
Previous Club Details

Club	Signed	Fee	Apps			FA	FL	Goals		
			Tot	Start	Sub			Lge	FA	FL
Lillestrom	1995									
Besiktas	1996									
Manchester U.	Jul-96	£1.2m	53	44	9	5	1	2	1	0
FAPL Summary by Club										
Manchester U.	*96/7 to 97/8*		*53*	*44*	*9*	*5*	*1*	*2*	*1*	*0*
Totals			53	44	9	5	1	2	1	0

JONES Keith

Charlton Athletic

Full Name: Keith Aubrey Jones
DOB: 14/10/65, Dulwich
Previous Club Details

Club	Signed	Fee	Apps			FA	FL	Goals		
			Tot	Start	Sub			Lge	FA	FL
Chelsea	Aug-83	App	52	43	9	1	11	7	0	3
Brentford	Sep-87	£40k	169	167	2	13	15	13	4	2
Southend U.	Oct-91	£175k	90	88	2	5	4	4	0	0
Charlton A.	Sep-94	£150k	120	114	6	5	5	4	1	0

JONES Paul

Southampton

Full Name: Paul Steven Jones
DOB: 18/4/67, Chick
Previous Club Details

Club	Signed	Fee	Apps			FA	FL	Goals		
			Tot	Start	Sub			Lge	FA	FL
Wolver'n W.	Jul-91	£40k nl	33	33		5	2	0	0	0
Stockport Co.		£60k	46	46	0	4	11	0	0	0
Southampton	Jul-96		38	38		1	4	0	0	0
FAPL Summary by Club										
Southampton	*1997-98*		*38*	*38*	*0*	*1*	*4*	*0*	*0*	*0*
Totals			38	38	0	1	4	0	0	0

JONES Rob

Liverpool

Full Name: Robert Marc Jones
DOB: 05/11/71, Wrexham
Previous Club Details

Club	Signed	Fee	Apps			FA	FL	Goals		
			Tot	Start	Sub			Lge	FA	FL
Crewe Alex.	Dec-88		75	59	16	3	9	2	0	0
Liverpool	Oct-91	£300k	183	182	1	27	22	0	0	0
FAPL Summary by Club										
Liverpool	*92/3 to 97/8*		*155*	*154*	*1*	*18*	*22*	*0*	*0*	*0*
Totals			155	154	1	18	22	0	0	0

JONES Steve

Charlton Athletic

JONES Stephen Gary

Full Name: Stephen Gary Jones
DOB: 17/03/70, Cambridge

Previous Club Details

			Apps					Goals		
Club	Signed	Fee	Tot	Start	Sub	FA	FL	Lge	FA	FL
West Ham U.	Nov-92	£22.5k	10	4	6			4	1	0
Bournemouth	Oct-94	150k	74	71	3	3	4	24	1	3
West Ham U.	May-96		8	5	3		1	2		
Charlton A.	Feb-97	£400k	26	20	6	1	2	7	0	0

FAPL Summary by Club

West Ham U.	93/4 to 96/7		18	9	9	6	1	2	1	0
Totals			*18*	*9*	*9*	*6*	*1*	*2*	*1*	*0*

Wimbledon

JUPP Duncan

Full Name: Duncan Jupp
DOB: 25/01/75, Guildford

Previous Club Details

			Apps					Goals		
Club	Signed	Fee	Tot	Start	Sub	FA	FL	Lge	FA	FL
Fulham	Dec-93	Train	105	101	4	10	12	1	2	2
Wimbledon	6/96	£125k	9	9	0	4	3	0	0	0

FAPL Summary by Club

Wimbledon	96/7 to 97/8		9	9	0	4	2	0	0	0
Totals			*9*	*9*	*0*	*4*	*2*	*0*	*0*	*0*

Leicester City

KAAMARK Pontus

Full Name: Pontus Sven Kaamark
DOB: 05/04/69, Vasteras, Sweden

Previous Club Details

			Apps					Goals		
Club	Signed	Fee	Tot	Start	Sub	FA	FL	Lge	FA	FL
IFK Gothenburg	1990									
Leicester C.	Nov-95	£840k	46	45	1	4	3	0	0	0

FAPL Summary by Club

Leicester C.	96/7 to 97/8		45	44	1	4	3	0	0	0
Totals			*45*	*44*	*1*	*4*	*3*	*0*	*0*	*0*

Manchester United

KEANE Roy

Full Name: Roy Maurice Keane
DOB: 10/08/71, Cork

Previous Club Details

			Apps					Goals		
Club	Signed	Fee	Tot	Start	Sub	FA	FL	Lge	FA	FL
Cobh Ramblers										
N. Forest	Jun-90	£10k	114	114	0	18	17	22	3	6
Manchester U.	Jul-93	£3.75m	121	116	5	23	11	17	1	0

FAPL Summary by Club

N. Forest	1992-93		40	40	0	4	5	6	1	0
Manchester U.	93/4 to 97/8		121	116	5	23	11	17	1	0
Totals			*161*	*156*	*5*	*27*	*16*	*23*	*2*	*1*

Leicester City

KELLER Kasey

Full Name: Kasey Keller
DOB: 27/11/69, Washington USA

Previous Club Details

			Apps					Goals		
Club	Signed	Fee	Tot	Start	Sub	FA	FL	Lge	FA	FL
Millwall	Feb-92	Free	176	176	0	8	14	0	0	0
Leicester C.	Aug-96	£900k	64	64	0	6	9	0	0	0

FAPL Summary by Club

Leicester C.	96/7 to 97/8		64	64	0	6	9	0	0	0
Totals			*64*	*64*	*0*	*6*	*9*	*0*	*0*	*0*

Leeds United

KELLY Gary

Full Name: Gary Kelly
DOB: 09/07/74, Drogheda

Previous Club Details

			Apps					Goals		
Club	Signed	Fee	Tot	Start	Sub	FA	FL	Lge	FA	FL
Leeds U.	Sep-91		192	188	4	20	19	2	0	0

FAPL Summary by Club

Leeds U.	93/4 to 97/8		188	186	2	20	18	2	2	0
Totals			*188*	*186*	*2*	*20*	*18*	*2*	*2*	*0*

KENNA Jeff — Blackburn Rovers

Full Name: Jeffrey Jude Kenna
DOB: 27/08/70, Dublin

Previous Club Details

Club	Signed	Fee	Tot	Start	Sub	FA	FL	Lge	FA	FL
Southampton	Apr-89	Train	114	110	4	4	4	0	0	0
Blackburn R.	Mar-95	£1.5m	115	115	0	7	8	1	0	0

FAPL Summary by Club

Club			Tot	Start	Sub	FA	FL	Lge	FA	FL
Southampton	92/3 to 94/5		98	95	3	7	7	4	0	0
Blackburn R.	94/5 to 97/8		115	115	0	7	8	1	0	0
Totals			213	210	3	14	12	5	0	0

KENNEDY Mark — Wimbledon

Full Name: Mark Kennedy
DOB: 15/05/76, Dublin

Previous Club Details

Club	Signed	Fee	Tot	Start	Sub	FA	FL	Lge	FA	FL
Millwall	May-92	Train	43	37	6	4	7	9	1	2
Liverpool	Mar-95	£1.5m	16	5	11	1	2	0	0	0
Wimbledon	Mar-98	£1.75m	4	4	0	0	0	0	0	0

FAPL Summary by Club

Club			Tot	Start	Sub	FA	FL	Lge	FA	FL
Liverpool	94/5 to 97/8		16	5	11	1	2	0	0	0
Wimbledon	1997-98		4	4	0	0	0	0	0	0
Totals			20	9	11	1	2	0	0	0

KEOWN Martin — Arsenal

Full Name: Martin Raymond Keown
DOB: 24/07/66, Oxford

Previous Club Details

Club	Signed	Fee	Tot	Start	Sub	FA	FL	Lge	FA	FL
Arsenal	Jan-84	App	22	22	0	5	6	0	0	0
Brighton &HA	Feb-85	Loan	23	21	2	2	0	2	1	0
Aston Villa	Jun-86	£200k	112	109	3	6	13	3	0	1
Everton	Aug-89	£750k	96	92	4	13	11	0	0	0
Arsenal	Feb-93	£2m	165	147	18	17	18	1	0	1

FAPL Summary by Club

Club			Tot	Start	Sub	FA	FL	Lge	FA	FL
Everton	1992-93		13	13	0	2	4	0	0	0
Arsenal	92/3 to 97/8		165	147	18	17	22	2	0	1
Totals			178	160	18	19	22	3	0	1

KETSBAIA Temuri — Newcastle United

Full Name: Temuri Ketsbaia
DOB: 18/3/68, Gale, Georgia

Previous Club Details

D.Sukhumi, D.Tbilisi, Anorthosis Famagusta, AEK Athens

Club	Signed	Fee	Tot	Start	Sub	FA	FL	Lge	FA	FL
Newcastle U.	Jul-97	Free	31	16	15	5	2	3	0	0

FAPL Summary by Club

Club			Tot	Start	Sub	FA	FL	Lge	FA	FL
Newcastle U.	1997-98		31	16	15	5	2	3	0	0
Totals			31	16	15	5	2	3	0	0

KEWELL Harry — Leeds United

Full Name: Harold Kewell
DOB: 22/09/78, Australia

Previous Club Details

NSW Academy

Club	Signed	Fee	Tot	Start	Sub	FA	FL	Lge	FA	FL
Leeds U.	1295		32	28	4	4	2	5	2	1

FAPL Summary by Club

Club			Tot	Start	Sub	FA	FL	Lge	FA	FL
Leeds U.	95/6 to 97/8		32	28	4	4	2	5	2	1
Totals			32	28	4	4	2	5	2	1

KHARINE Dimitri — Chelsea

Full Name: Dimitri Kharine
DOB: 16/08/68, Moscow

Previous Club Details

Club	Signed	Fee	Apps					Goals		
			Tot	Start	Sub	FA	FL	Lge	FA	FL
CSKA Moscow										
Chelsea	Dec-92	£200k	117	117	0	12	8	0	0	0
FAPL Summary by Club										
Chelsea	92/3 to 97/8		117	117	0	12	8	0	0	0
Totals			*117*	*117*	*0*	*12*	*8*	*0*	*0*	*0*

KIMBLE Alan — Wimbledon

Full Name: Alan Frank Kimble
DOB: 06/08/66, Dagenham

Previous Club Details

Club	Signed	Fee	Apps					Goals		
			Tot	Start	Sub	FA	FL	Lge	FA	FL
Charlton A.	Aug-84		6	6	0	0	0	1	0	0
Exeter C.	Aug-85	Loan	1	1	0	0	1	0	0	0
Cambridge U.	Aug-86	Free	299	295	4	29	24	24	1	0
Wimbledon	Jul-93	£175k	127	122	5	20	15	0	0	0
FAPL Summary by Club										
Wimbledon	93/4 to 97/8		127	122	5	20	15	0	0	0
Totals			*127*	*122*	*5*	*20*	*15*	*0*	*0*	*0*

KINDER Vladimir — Middlesbrough

Full Name: Vladimir Kinder
DOB: 04/03/69, Bratislava

Previous Club Details

Club	Signed	Fee	Apps					Goals		
			Tot	Start	Sub	FA	FL	Lge	FA	FL
Slovan Bratislava	1990		148	140	8	4	0	19	6	3
Middlesbrough	Jan-97	£1m	40	37	3	3	4	6	3	0
FAPL Summary by Club										
Middlesbrough	1996-97		6	4	2	3	1	0	0	0
Totals			*6*	*4*	*2*	*3*	*1*	*0*	*0*	*0*

KINSELLA Mark — Charlton Athletic

Full Name: Mark Anthony Kinsella
DOB: 12/08/72, Dublin

Previous Club Details

Club	Signed	Fee	Apps					Goals		
			Tot	Start	Sub	FA	FL	Lge	FA	FL
Colchester U.	Aug-89	Free	180	174	6	11	11	17	3	3
Charlton A.	Sep-96	£150k	83	83	0	4	3	11	1	0

KITSON Paul — West Ham United

Full Name: Paul Kitson
DOB: 09/01/71, Peterlee

Previous Club Details

Club	Signed	Fee	Apps					Goals		
			Tot	Start	Sub	FA	FL	Lge	FA	FL
Leicester C.	Dec-88		50	39	11	5	6	5	1	3
Derby Co.	Mar-92	£1.3m	105	105	0	5	7	36	1	3
Newcastle U.	Sep-94	£2.25m	36	26	10	9	5	10	3	1
West Ham U.	Feb-97	£2.3m	27	26	1	2	2	12	1	0
FAPL Summary by Club										
Newcastle U.	94/5 to 96/7		36	26	10	9	5	10	3	1
West Ham U.	96/7 to 97/8		27	26	1	2	2	12	1	0
Totals			*63*	*52*	*11*	*11*	*7*	*22*	*4*	*1*

KVARME Bjorn Tore — Liverpool

Full Name: Bjorn Tore Kvarme
DOB: 17/07/72, Trondheim

Previous Club Details

Club	Signed	Fee	Apps					Goals		
			Tot	Start	Sub	FA	FL	Lge	FA	FL
Rosenborg	1990		67	59	8			1		
Liverpool	Jan-97	Free	38	37	1	2	2	0	0	0
FAPL Summary by Club										
Liverpool	96/7 to 97/8		38	37	1	2	2	0	0	0
Totals			*38*	*37*	*1*	*2*	*2*	*0*	*0*	*0*

LAMBOURDE Bernard — Chelsea

Full Name: Bernard Lambourde
DOB: 11/05/71, Guadeloupe

Previous Club Details

			Apps					Goals		
Club	Signed	Fee	Tot	Start	Sub	FA	FL	Lge	FA	FL
Cannes, Bordeaux										
Chelsea	Jun-97	£1.5m	7	5	2	0	3	0	0	0
FAPL Summary by Club										
Chelsea	1997-98		7	5	2	0	3	0	0	0
Totals			7	5	2	0	3	0	0	0

LAMPARD Frank — West Ham United

Full Name: Frank Lampard Jnr
DOB: 21/06/78, Romford

Previous Club Details

			Apps					Goals		
Club	Signed	Fee	Tot	Start	Sub	FA	FL	Lge	FA	FL
West Ham U.	Jul-95	Train	46	30	16	7	7	4	1	4
Swansea C.	Oct-95	Loan	9	8	1	0	1	0	0	0
FAPL Summary by Club										
West Ham U.	95/6 to 97/8		46	30	16	7	7	4	1	4
Totals			46	30	16	7	7	4	1	4

LAURSEN Jacob — Derby County

Full Name: Jacob Laursen
DOB: 06/10/71, Denmark

Previous Club Details

			Apps					Goals		
Club	Signed	Fee	Tot	Start	Sub	FA	FL	Lge	FA	FL
Silkeborg			128					8		
Derby Co.	Jul-96	£500k	64	62	2	3	4	3	2	0
FAPL Summary by Club										
Derby Co.	96/7 to 97/8		64	62	2	3	4	2	2	0
Totals			64	62	2	3	4	2	2	0

LAZARIDIS Stan — West Ham United

Full Name: Stanley Lazaridis
DOB: 16/08/72, Perth, W. Australia

Previous Club Details

			Apps					Goals		
Club	Signed	Fee	Tot	Start	Sub	FA	FL	Lge	FA	FL
West Adelaide (Aus)										
West Ham U.	Aug-95	£300k	54	42	12	8	6	3	0	0
FAPL Summary by Club										
West Ham U.	95/6 to 97/8		54	42	12	8	6	3	0	0
Totals			54	42	12	8	6	3	0	0

LE SAUX Graeme — Chelsea

Full Name: Graeme Pierre Le Saux
DOB: 17/10/68, Jersey

Previous Club Details

			Apps					Goals		
Club	Signed	Fee	Tot	Start	Sub	FA	FL	Lge	FA	FL
Chelsea	Dec-87	Free NL	90	77	13	8	13	8	0	1
Blackburn R.	Mar-93	Swap	130	128	2	8	10	7	0	1
Chelsea	Aug-97	£5.0m	26	26	0	1	4	1	1	1
FAPL Summary by Club										
Chelsea	1992-93		14	10	4	1	4	0	0	0
Blackburn R.	92/3 to 96/7		130	128	2	8	10	7	0	1
Chelsea	1997-98		26	26	0	1	4	1	1	1
Totals			170	164	6	10	18	8	1	1

LE TISSIER Matt — Southampton

Full Name: Matthew Paul Le Tissier
DOB: 14/10/68, Guernsey

Previous Club Details

			Apps					Goals		
Club	Signed	Fee	Tot	Start	Sub	FA	FL	Lge	FA	FL
Southampton	Oct-86	App	383	346	37	31	45	151	12	26

FAPL Summary by Club

Club	Signed	Fee	Apps					Goals		
			Tot	Start	Sub	FA	FL	Lge	FA	FL
Southampton 92/3 to 97/8			210	203	7	15	19	91	7	15
Totals			*210*	*203*	*7*	*15*	*19*	*91*	*7*	*15*

LEABURN Carl   Wimbledon

Full Name: Carl Winston Leaburn
DOB: 30/03/69, Lewisham

Previous Club Details

Club	Signed	Fee	Apps					Goals		
			Tot	Start	Sub	FA	FL	Lge	FA	FL
Charlton A.	Apr-87	App	322	276	46	21	19	53	4	5
Wimbledon	Jan-98	£300k	16	15	1	0	0	4	0	0

FAPL Summary by Club

Club			Tot	Start	Sub	FA	FL	Lge	FA	FL
Wimbledon 1997-98			16	15	1	0	0	4	0	0
Totals			*16*	*15*	*1*	*0*	*0*	*4*	*0*	*0*

LEBOEUF Franck   Chelsea

Full Name: Franck Leboeuf
DOB: 22/01/68, Marseille

Previous Club Details

Club	Signed	Fee	Apps					Goals		
			Tot	Start	Sub	FA	FL	Lge	FA	FL
Hyeres	1986		14					1		
Meaux	1987		39					3		
Laval	1988		69					10		
Strasbourg	1991		189					49		
Chelsea	Jul-96	£2.5m	58	58	0	8	6	11	1	0

FAPL Summary by Club

Club			Tot	Start	Sub	FA	FL	Lge	FA	FL
Chelsea 96/7 to 97/8			58	58	0	8	6	11	1	0
Totals			*58*	*58*	*0*	*8*	*6*	*11*	*1*	*0*

LEE David   Chelsea

Full Name: David John Lee
DOB: 26/11/69, Kingswood

Previous Club Details

Club	Signed	Fee	Apps					Goals		
			Tot	Start	Sub	FA	FL	Lge	FA	FL
Chelsea	Jul-88		151	119	32	14	20	10	0	1
Reading	Jan-92	Loan	5	5	0	0	0			
Plymouth Ar.	Mar-92	Loan	9	9	0	0	0			
Portsmouth	Aug-94	Loan	5	4	1	0	0	1		

FAPL Summary by Club

Club			Tot	Start	Sub	FA	FL	Lge	FA	FL
Chelsea 92/3 to 97/8			79	66	13	9	13	4	0	0
Totals			*79*	*66*	*13*	*9*	*13*	*4*	*0*	*0*

LEE Robert   Newcastle United

Full Name: Robert Martin Lee
DOB: 01/02/66, West Ham

Previous Club Details

Club	Signed	Fee	Apps					Goals		
			Tot	Start	Sub	FA	FL	Lge	FA	FL
Charlton A.	Jul-83		298	274	24	14	19	59	2	1
Newcastle U.	Sep-92	£700k	209	206	3	20	15	43	4	3

FAPL Summary by Club

Club			Tot	Start	Sub	FA	FL	Lge	FA	FL
Newcastle U. 93/4 to 97/8			173	170	3	16	12	33	2	2
Totals			*173*	*170*	*3*	*16*	*12*	*33*	*2*	*2*

LENNON Neil   Leicester City

Full Name: Neil Francis Lennon
DOB: 25/06/71, Lurgan

Previous Club Details

Club	Signed	Fee	Apps					Goals		
			Tot	Start	Sub	FA	FL	Lge	FA	FL
Manchester C.	Aug-89	Train	1	0				0	0	0
Crewe Al.	Sep-90	Free	147	142	5	12	9	15	1	1
Leicester C.	Feb-96	£750k	87	86	1	4	8	4	0	1

FAPL Summary by Club

Club			Tot	Start	Sub	FA	FL	Lge	FA	FL
Leicester C. 96/7 to 97/8			72	72	0	4	8	3	0	1
Totals			*72*	*72*	*0*	*4*	*8*	*3*	*0*	*1*

LEONHARDSEN Oyvind
Liverpool

Full Name: Oyvind Leonhardsen
DOB: 17/08/70, Norway

Previous Club Details

			Apps					Goals		
Club	Signed	Fee	Tot	Start	Sub	FA	FL	Lge	FA	FL
Rosenborg	1992		63	63	0			20		
Wimbledon	Jan-95	£660k	76	73	3	17	9	13	2	1
Liverpool	Jun-97	£3.5m	28	27	1	1	5	6	0	0

FAPL Summary by Club

			Apps					Goals		
			Tot	Start	Sub	FA	FL	Lge	FA	FL
Wimbledon	94/5 to 96/7		76	73	3	17	9	13	2	1
Liverpool	1997-98		28	27	1	1	5	6	0	0
Totals			*104*	*100*	*4*	*18*	*14*	*19*	*2*	*1*

LIDDELL Andy
Barnsley

Full Name: Andrew Mark Liddell
DOB: 28/06/73, Leeds

Previous Club Details

			Apps					Goals		
Club	Signed	Fee	Tot	Start	Sub	FA	FL	Lge	FA	FL
Barnsley	Jul-91	Train	190	139	51	12	11	34	1	3

FAPL Summary by Club

			Apps					Goals		
			Tot	Start	Sub	FA	FL	Lge	FA	FL
Barnsley	1997-98		26	13	13	5	2	1	1	2
Totals			*26*	*13*	*13*	*5*	*2*	*1*	*1*	*2*

LILLEY Derek
Leeds United

Full Name: Derek Lilley
DOB: 09/02/74, Paisley

Previous Club Details

			Apps					Goals		
Club	Signed	Fee	Tot	Start	Sub	FA	FL	Lge	FA	FL
Greenock M.	Aug-91		180					57		
Leeds U.	Mar-97	£500k+	18	4	14	1	3	1	0	0

FAPL Summary by Club

			Apps					Goals		
			Tot	Start	Sub	FA	FL	Lge	FA	FL
Leeds U.	96/7 to 97/8		18	4	14	1	3	1	0	0
Totals			*18*	*4*	*14*	*1*	*3*	*1*	*0*	*0*

LOMAS Stephen
West Ham United

Full Name: Stephen Martin Lomas
DOB: 18/01/74, Hanover

Previous Club Details

			Apps					Goals		
Club	Signed	Fee	Tot	Start	Sub	FA	FL	Lge	FA	FL
Manchester C.	Jan-91	Train	111	102	9	11	15	8	1	2
West Ham U.	Mar-97	£1.6m	40	40	0	5	4	2	1	0

FAPL Summary by Club

			Apps					Goals		
			Tot	Start	Sub	FA	FL	Lge	FA	FL
Manchester C.	93/4 to 95/6		76	67	9	8	13	5	1	2
West Ham U.	96/7 to 97/8		40	40	0	5	4	2	1	0
Totals			*116*	*107*	*9*	*13*	*17*	*7*	*2*	*2*

LUNDEKVAM Claus
Southampton

Full Name: Claus Lundekvam
DOB: 22/02/73, Norway

Previous Club Details

			Apps					Goals		
Club	Signed	Fee	Tot	Start	Sub	FA	FL	Lge	FA	FL
SK Brann	1993		37	33	4					
Southampton	1996		60	59	1	1	12	0	0	0

FAPL Summary by Club

			Apps					Goals		
			Tot	Start	Sub	FA	FL	Lge	FA	FL
Southampton	96/7 to 97/8		60	59	1	1	12	0	0	0
Totals			*60*	*59*	*1*	*1*	*12*	*0*	*0*	*0*

LYTTLE Des
Nottingham Forest

Full Name: Desmond Lyttle
DOB: 24/09/71, Wolverhampton

Previous Club Details

			Apps					Goals		
Club	Signed	Fee	Tot	Start	Sub	FA	FL	Lge	FA	FL
Swansea C.	Jul-92	£12.5k	46	46	0	5	2	1	1	0
N. Forest	Jul-93	£375k	174	171	3	15	19	3	0	0

FAPL Summary by Club

			Apps					Goals		
			Tot	Start	Sub	FA	FL	Lge	FA	FL
N. Forest	94/5 to 96/7		103	100	3	12	8	2	0	0
Totals			*103*	*100*	*3*	*12*	*8*	*2*	*0*	*0*

Everton

MADAR Michael

Full Name: Michael Madar
DOB: 08/05/68, Paris

Previous Club Details

Cannes, Monaco, Deportivo La Coruna

Club	Signed	Fee	Tot	Start	Sub	FA	FL	Lge	FA	FL
Everton	Dec-97	Free	17	15	2			0	6	0	0

FAPL Summary by Club

Everton	1997-98		17	15	2			0	6	0	0
Totals			*17*	*15*	*2*			*0*	*6*	*0*	*0*

(Apps: Tot, Start, Sub, FA, FL — Goals: Lge, FA, FL)

Arsenal

MANNINGER Alex

Full Name: Alex Manninger
DOB: Salzburg, Austria

Previous Club Details

Club	Signed	Fee	Tot	Start	Sub	FA	FL	Lge	FA	FL
Vorwarts Seyr	1995		5	5	0			0	0		
C. Salzburg	1995		0	1	0						
Grazer AK	1996		23					0			
Arsenal	Mar-97	£500k	7	7	0	5	5	0	0	0	0

FAPL Summary by Club

Arsenal	1997-98		7	7	0	5	5	0	0	0
Totals			*7*	*7*	*0*	*5*	*5*	*0*	*0*	*0*

Middlesbrough

MADDISON Neil

Full Name: Neil Stanley Maddison
DOB: 02/10/69, Darlington

Previous Club Details

Club	Signed	Fee	Tot	Start	Sub	FA	FL	Lge	FA	FL
Southampton	Apr-88	Train	168	149	19	13	14	12	0	0
Middlesbrough	Oct-97	£250k	16	10	6	3	4	4	0	0

FAPL Summary by Club

Southampton	92/3 to 97/8		151	141	10	10	12	17	0	0
Totals			*151*	*141*	*10*	*10*	*12*	*17*	*0*	*0*

Leicester City

MARSHALL Ian

Full Name: Ian Paul Marshall
DOB: 20/03/66, Liverpool

Previous Club Details

Club	Signed	Fee	Tot	Start	Sub	FA	FL	Lge	FA	FL
Everton	Mar-84	App	15	9	6	0	2	1	0	1
Oldham A.	Mar-88	£100k	170	165	5	14	17	36	3	6
Ipswich Town	Aug-93	£750k	82	77	5	9	6	13	3	2
Leicester C.	Aug-96	£800k	52	41	11	6	1	15	3	1

FAPL Summary by Club

Oldham A.	1992-93		27	26	1	1	3	2	0	0
Ipswich T.	93/4 to 94/5		47	42	5	5	5	13	0	2
Leicester C.	96/7 to 97/8		52	41	11	6	1	15	3	1
Totals			*126*	*109*	*17*	*12*	*7*	*30*	*6*	*3*

Sheffield Wednesday

MAGILTON Jim

Full Name: James Magilton
DOB: 06/05/69, Belfast

Previous Club Details

Club	Signed	Fee	Tot	Start	Sub	FA	FL	Lge	FA	FL
Liverpool	May-86	App	0	0		0	0	0		
Oxford U.	Oct-90	£100k	150	150	0	8	9	34	4	1
Southampton	Feb-94	£600k	130	124	6	12	14	13	3	2
Sheffield W.	Sep-97	£1.6m	20	13	7	1	2	1	0	0

FAPL Summary by Club

Southampton	93/4 to 97/8		130	124	6	12	14	13	3	3
Sheffield W.	1997-98		20	13	7	1	2	1	0	0
Totals			*150*	*137*	*13*	*13*	*16*	*14*	*3*	*2*

Leeds United

MARTYN Nigel

Full Name: Nigel Anthony Martyn
DOB: 11/08/66, St Austell

Previous Club Details

Club	Signed	Fee	Tot	Start	Sub	FA	FL	Lge	FA	FL
Bristol R.	Aug-87	NL	101	101	0	6	6	0	0	0
C. Palace	Nov-89	£1m	189	189	0	13	25	0	0	0

				Apps				Goals		
Club	Signed	Fee	Tot	Start	Sub	FA	FL	Lge	FA	FL
Leeds U.	Jul-96	£2.25m	74	74	0	8	7	0	0	0

FAPL Summary by Club

				Apps				Goals		
C. Palace	92/3 to 94/5		79	79	0	8	15	0	0	0
Leeds U.	96/7 to 97/8		74	74	0	8	7	0	0	0
Totals			*153*	*153*	*0*	*16*	*22*	*0*	*0*	*0*

MASKELL Craig

Full Name: Craig Dell Maskell
DOB: 10/04/68, Aldershot

Southampton

Previous Club Details

				Apps				Goals		
Club	Signed	Fee	Tot	Start	Sub	FA	FL	Lge	FA	FL
Southampton	Apr-86	App	6	2	4	1	0	0	0	0
Huddersfield	May-88	£20k	87	86	1	8	6	43	3	4
Reading	Aug-90	£250k	72	60	12	7	3	26	0	1
Swindon T.	Jul-92	£225k	47	40	7	3	4	21	0	0
Southampton	Feb-94	£250k	17	8	9	2	1	0	0	0
Bristol C.	Dec-95	Loan	5	5						
Brighton	Mar-96	£40k	19	15	4					

FAPL Summary by Club

				Apps				Goals		
Swindon T.	1993-94		14	8	6	2	2	3	0	0
Southampton	93/4 to 95/6		17	8	9	2	2	0	0	0
Totals			*31*	*16*	*15*	*4*	*4*	*3*	*0*	*0*

MATTEO Dominic

Full Name: Dominic Matteo
DOB: 28/04/74, Dumfries

Liverpool

Previous Club Details

				Apps				Goals		
Club	Signed	Fee	Tot	Start	Sub	FA	FL	Lge	FA	FL
Liverpool	May-92	Train	74	64	10	5	9	0	0	0
Sunderland	Mar-95	Loan	1	1	0	0	0	0	0	0

FAPL Summary by Club

				Apps				Goals		
Liverpool	93/4 to 97/8		74	53	21	4	9	0	0	0
Totals			*74*	*53*	*21*	*4*	*9*	*0*	*0*	*0*

MAY David

Full Name: David May
DOB: 24/06/70, Oldham

Manchester United

Previous Club Details

				Apps				Goals		
Club	Signed	Fee	Tot	Start	Sub	FA	FL	Lge	FA	FL
Blackburn R.	Jun-88	Train	123	123	0	10	13	5	2	1
Manchester U.	Jul-94	£1.4m	73	61	12	5	5	6	0	1

FAPL Summary by Club

				Apps				Goals		
Blackburn R.	92/3 to 93/4		74	74	0	7	10	2	1	2
Manchester U.	94/5 to 97/8		73	61	12	5	5	6	0	1
Totals			*147*	*135*	*12*	*12*	*15*	*8*	*1*	*3*

MAYBURY Alan

Full Name: Alan Maybury
DOB: 08/08/78, Dublin

Leeds United

Previous Club Details

				Apps				Goals		
Club	Signed	Fee	Tot	Start	Sub	FA	FL	Lge	FA	FL
Leeds U.	Aug-95		13	10	3	1	0	0	0	0

FAPL Summary by Club

				Apps				Goals		
Leeds U.	95/6 to 97/8		13	10	3	1	0	0	0	0
Totals			*13*	*10*	*3*	*1*	*0*	*0*	*0*	*0*

MAYRLEB Christian

Full Name: Christian Mayrleb

Sheffield Wednesday

Previous Club Details

				Apps				Goals		
Club	Signed	Fee	Tot	Start	Sub	FA	FL	Lge	FA	FL
FC Tirol										
Sheffield W.	Jan-98	£20k	3	0	3	0	0	0	0	0

FAPL Summary by Club

				Apps				Goals		
Sheffield W.	1997-98		3	0	3	0	0	0	0	0
Totals			*3*	*0*	*3*	*0*	*0*	*0*	*0*	*0*

McALLISTER Brian

Full Name: Brian McAllister

Wimbledon

Full Name: Brian McAllister
DOB: 30/11/70, Glasgow

Previous Club Details

Club	Signed	Fee	Apps					Goals		
			Tot	Start	Sub	FA	FL	Lge	FA	FL
Wimbledon	Feb-89	Train	85	74	11	8	9	0	0	0
Plymouth Ar.	Dec-90	Loan	8	7	1	0	0	0	0	0
Crewe Al.	Mar-96	Loan	13	13	0	0	0	0	1	0

FAPL Summary by Club

Club			Tot	Start	Sub	FA	FL	Lge	FA	FL
Wimbledon	92/3 to 97/8		72	64	8	8	9	0	0	0
Totals			72	64	8	8	9	0	0	0

Coventry City

McALLISTER Gary

Full Name: Gary McAllister
DOB: 25/12/64, Motherwell

Previous Club Details

Club	Signed	Fee	Apps					Goals		
			Tot	Start	Sub	FA	FL	Lge	FA	FL
Leicester C.	Aug-85	£125k	201	199	2	5	15	46	2	3
Leeds U.	Jun-90	£1m	231	230	1	24	26	32	6	4
Coventry C.	Jun-96	£3m	52	52	0	4	8	6	0	3

FAPL Summary by Club

Club			Tot	Start	Sub	FA	FL	Lge	FA	FL
Leeds U.	92/3 to 95/6		151	151	0	17	15	25	5	2
Coventry C.	96/7 to 97/8		52	52	0	4	8	6	0	3
Totals			203	203	0	21	23	31	5	5

Liverpool

McATEER Jason

Full Name: Jason McAteer
DOB: 18/06/71, Birkenhead

Previous Club Details

Club	Signed	Fee	Apps					Goals		
			Tot	Start	Sub	FA	FL	Lge	FA	FL
Bolton W.	Jan-92	NL	113	108	5	11	11	8	3	2
Liverpool	Sep-95	£4.5m	87	78	9	10	11	3	3	0

FAPL Summary by Club

Club			Tot	Start	Sub	FA	FL	Lge	FA	FL
Bolton W.	1995-96		4	4	0	0	0	0	0	0
Liverpool	95/6 to 97/8		87	78	9	10	11	3	3	0
Totals			91	82	9	10	11	3	3	0

Everton

McCANN Gavin

Full Name: Gavin McCann
DOB: 10/01/78, Blackpool

Previous Club Details

Club	Signed	Fee	Apps					Goals		
			Tot	Start	Sub	FA	FL	Lge	FA	FL
Everton		Train	11	5	6	0	0	0	0	0

FAPL Summary by Club

Club			Tot	Start	Sub	FA	FL	Lge	FA	FL
Everton	1997-98		11	5	6	0	0	0	0	0
Totals			11	5	6	0	0	0	0	0

Blackburn Rovers

McKINLAY Billy

Full Name: William McKinlay
DOB: 22/04/69, Glasgow

Previous Club Details

Club	Signed	Fee	Apps					Goals		
			Tot	Start	Sub	FA	FL	Lge	FA	FL
Dundee U.			220	210	10	26	21	23	4	3
Blackburn R.	Oct-95	£1.75m	74	62	12	8	4	3	0	1

FAPL Summary by Club

Club			Tot	Start	Sub	FA	FL	Lge	FA	FL
Blackburn R.	95/6 to 97/8		74	62	12	8	4	3	0	1
Totals			74	62	12	8	4	3	0	1

Leicester City

McMAHON Sam

Full Name: Samuel Keiron McMahon
DOB: 09/02/76, Newark

Previous Club Details

Club	Signed	Fee	Apps					Goals		
			Tot	Start	Sub	FA	FL	Lge	FA	FL
Leicester C.	Jul-94	Train	5	0	5	0	2	1	0	0

FAPL Summary by Club

Club			Tot	Start	Sub	FA	FL	Lge	FA	FL
Leicester C.	94/5 to 97/8		2	0	2	0	1	0	0	0
Totals			2	0	2	0	1	0	0	0

McMANAMAN Steve — Liverpool

Full Name: Steven McManaman
DOB: 11/02/72, Bootle

Previous Club Details

Club	Signed	Fee	Apps			FA	FL	Goals		
			Tot	Start	Sub			Lge	FA	FL
Liverpool	Feb-90	Train	244	233	11	29	33	42	5	10

FAPL Summary by Club

Liverpool	92/3 to 97/8		212	207	5	20	28	37	2	7
Totals			212	207	5	20	28	37	2	7

McPHAIL Steve — Leeds United

Full Name: Stephen McPhail
DOB: 09/12/79, Dublin

Previous Club Details

Club	Signed	Fee	Apps			FA	FL	Goals		
			Tot	Start	Sub			Lge	FA	FL
Leeds U.		Train	4	0	4	2	0	0	0	0

FAPL Summary by Club

Leeds U.	1997-98		4	0	4	2	0	0	0	0
Totals			4	0	4	2	0	0	0	0

MEAN Scott — West Ham United

Full Name: Scott Mean
DOB: 12/12/73, Crawley

Previous Club Details

Club	Signed	Fee	Apps			FA	FL	Goals		
			Tot	Start	Sub			Lge	FA	FL
Bournemouth	Aug-92	Train	74	52	22	3	8	8	0	0
West Ham U.	Nov-96		3	0	3	0	0	0	0	0

FAPL Summary by Club

West Ham U.	1997-98		3	0	3	0	0	0	0	0
Totals			3	0	3	0	0	0	0	0

MENDEZ Alberto — Arsenal

Full Name: Alberto Mendez Rodriguez
DOB: 24/10/74, Nurnberg, Germany

Previous Club Details

Club	Signed	Fee	Apps			FA	FL	Goals		
			Tot	Start	Sub			Lge	FA	FL
FC Feucht										
Arsenal	Jul-97	£250k	3	1	2	0	2	0	0	1

FAPL Summary by Club

Arsenal	1997-98		3	1	2	0	2	0	0	1
Totals			3	1	2	0	2	0	0	1

MENDONCA Clive — Charlton Athletic

Full Name: Clive Paul Mendonca
DOB: 09/09/68, Tullington

Previous Club Details

Club	Signed	Fee	Apps			FA	FL	Goals		
			Tot	Start	Sub			Lge	FA	FL
Sheffield U.	Sep-86	App	13	8	5	0	4	0	0	0
Doncaster R.	Feb-88	Loan	2	2	0	0	0	1	0	0
Rotherham U.	Mar-88	£35k	84	71	13	5	7	27	2	1
Sheffield U.	Aug-91	£110k	10	4	6	0	2	1	0	0
Grimsby T.	Jan-92	Loan	10	10	0	0	3	3	0	0
Grimsby T.	Aug-92	£85k	156	151	5	8	11	57	2	3
Charlton A.	May-97	£700k	41	41	0	2	2	23	1	1

MIKLOSKO Ludek — West Ham United

Full Name: Ludek Miklosko
DOB: 09/12/61, Protesov, Czechoslovakia

Previous Club Details

Club	Signed	Fee	Apps			FA	FL	Goals		
			Tot	Start	Sub			Lge	FA	FL
Banik Ostrava										
West Ham U.	Feb-90	£300k	315	315	0	25	25	0	0	0

FAPL Summary by Club

West Ham U.	93/4 to 97/8		169	169	0	13	15	0	0	0
Totals			169	169	0	13	15	0	0	0

MILOSEVIC Savo — Aston Villa

Full Name: Savo Milosevic
DOB: 02/09/73, Bijeljina, Yugoslavia

Previous Club Details

Club	Signed	Fee	Apps Tot	Start	Sub	FA	FL	Goals Lge	FA	FL
Partizan Belgrade										
Aston Villa	Jul-95	£3.5m	90	84	6	10	9	29	2	1
FAPL Summary by Club										
Aston Villa	95/6 to 97/8		90	84	6	10	9	29	2	1
Totals			*90*	*84*	*6*	*10*	*9*	*29*	*2*	*1*

MOLDOVAN Viorel — Coventry City

Full Name: Viorel Moldovan
DOB: 8/7/72, Romania

Previous Club Details

Club	Signed	Fee	Apps Tot	Start	Sub	FA	FL	Goals Lge	FA	FL
Grasshopper										
Coventry C.	Dec-97	£3.25m	10	5	5	4	0	1	1	0
FAPL Summary by Club										
Coventry C.	1997-98		10	5	5	4	0	1	1	0
Totals			*10*	*5*	*5*	*4*	*0*	*1*	*1*	*0*

MOLENAAR Robert — Leeds United

Full Name: Robert Molenaar
DOB: 27/02/69, Zaandam, Holland

Previous Club Details

Club	Signed	Fee	Apps Tot	Start	Sub	FA	FL	Goals Lge	FA	FL
FC Volendam	1992		107	107	0			3		
Leeds U.	Jan-97	£1m	34	30	4	5	3	3	1	0
FAPL Summary by Club										
Leeds U.	96/7 to 97/8		34	30	4	5	3	3	1	0
Totals			*34*	*30*	*4*	*5*	*3*	*3*	*1*	*0*

MONCUR John — West Ham United

Full Name: John Frederick Moncur
DOB: 22/09/66, Stepney

Previous Club Details

Club	Signed	Fee	Apps Tot	Start	Sub	FA	FL	Goals Lge	FA	FL
Tottenham H.	Aug-84	App	21	10	11	0	3	1	0	0
Doncaster R.	Sep-86	Loan	4	4	0	0	0	0	0	0
Cambridge U.	Mar-87	Loan	4	3	1	0	0	0	0	0
Portsmouth	Mar-89	Loan	7	5	2	0	1	0	0	0
Brentford	Oct-89	Loan	5	5	0	0	0	1	0	0
Ipswich T.	Oct-91	Loan	6	5	1	0	0	0	0	0
N. Forest	Feb-92	Loan	5	0	5	0	4	0	1	0
Swindon T.	Mar-92	£80k	58	53	5	7	11	5	1	2
West Ham U.	Jun-94	£900k	97	92	5	5	11	5	1	2
FAPL Summary by Club										
Swindon Town	1993-94		41	41	0	1	3	4	0	0
West Ham U.	94/5 to 97/8		97	92	5	7	11	5	1	2
Totals			*138*	*133*	*5*	*8*	*14*	*9*	*1*	*2*

MONKOU Ken — Southampton

Full Name: Kenneth John Monkou
DOB: 29/11/64, Necare, Surinam

Previous Club Details

Club	Signed	Fee	Apps Tot	Start	Sub	FA	FL	Goals Lge	FA	FL
Chelsea	Mar-89	£100k	94	92	2	3	12	2	0	0
Southampton	Aug-92	£750k	176	168	8	14	19	9	0	2
FAPL Summary by Club										
Southampton	92/3 to 97/8		176	168	8	14	19	9	0	2
Totals			*176*	*168*	*8*	*14*	*19*	*9*	*0*	*2*

MOORE Ian — Nottingham Forest

Full Name: Ian Ronald Moore
DOB: 26/08/76, Birkenhead

Previous Club Details			Apps					Goals		
Club	Signed	Fee	Tot	Start	Sub	FA	FL	Lge	FA	FL
Tranmere R.	Jul-94	Train	58	41	17	2	5	12	1	0
N. Forest	Mar-97	£1m	14	3	11	3	1	1	0	0
Bradford C.	Mar-96	Loan	6	6	0					
FAPL Summary by Club										
N. Forest	1996-97		5	1	4			0	0	0
Totals			*5*	*1*	*4*			*0*	*0*	*0*

MORRIS Jody

Chelsea

Full Name: Jody Morris
DOB: 22/12/78, London

Previous Club Details			Apps					Goals		
Club	Signed	Fee	Tot	Start	Sub	FA	FL	Lge	FA	FL
Chelsea	Jan-96	Train	25	15	10	0	3	1	0	2
FAPL Summary by Club										
Chelsea	95/6 to 97/8		25	15	10	0	3	1	0	2
Totals			*25*	*15*	*10*	*0*	*3*	*1*	*0*	*2*

MURPHY Danny

Liverpool

Full Name: Daniel Benjamin Murphy
DOB: 18/03/77, Chester

Previous Club Details			Apps					Goals		
Club	Signed	Fee	Tot	Start	Sub	FA	FL	Lge	FA	FL
Crewe Alex.	Mar-94	Train	134	110	24	7	7	27	4	0
Liverpool	Jul-97		16	6	10	1	0	0	0	0
FAPL Summary by Club										
Liverpool	1997-98		16	6	10	1	0	0	0	0
Totals			*16*	*6*	*10*	*1*	*0*	*0*	*0*	*0*

MYERS Andy

Chelsea

Full Name: Andrew John Myers
DOB: 03/11/73, Hounslow

Previous Club Details			Apps					Goals		
Club	Signed	Fee	Tot	Start	Sub	FA	FL	Lge	FA	FL
Chelsea	Jun-91	Train	83	73	10	8	10	3	2	1
FAPL Summary by Club										
Chelsea	92/3 to 97/8		69	64	5	8	8	2	1	0
Totals			*69*	*64*	*5*	*8*	*8*	*2*	*1*	*0*

Everton

MYHRE Thomas

Full Name: Thomas Myhre
DOB: 16/10/73, Norway

Previous Club Details			Apps					Goals		
Club	Signed	Fee	Tot	Start	Sub	FA	FL	Lge	FA	FL
Viking Stavanger										
Everton	Nov-97		22	22	0	1	0	0	0	0
FAPL Summary by Club										
Everton	1997-98		22	22	0	1	0	0	0	0
Totals			*22*	*22*	*0*	*1*	*0*	*0*	*0*	*0*

Aston Villa

NELSON Fernando

Full Name: Fernando Nelson
DOB: 05/11/71, Lisbon

Previous Club Details			Apps					Goals		
Club	Signed	Fee	Tot	Start	Sub	FA	FL	Lge	FA	FL
Sporting Lisbon	1991		115	113	2			3		
Aston Villa	Jul-96	£1.75m	59	54	5	2	3	0	0	0
FAPL Summary by Club										
Aston Villa	96/7 to 97/8		59	54	5	2	3	0	0	0
Totals			*59*	*54*	*5*	*2*	*3*	*0*	*0*	*0*

Manchester United

NEVILLE Phil

Full Name: Philip John Neville

DOB: 21/01/77, Bury

Previous Club Details

			Apps					Goals		
Club	Signed	Fee	Tot	Start	Sub	FA	FL	Lge	FA	FL
Manchester U.	Jun-94	Train	74	61	13	11	4	1	0	0

FAPL Summary by Club

			Apps					Goals		
Manchester U.	94/5 to 97/8		74	61	13	11	4	1	0	0
Totals			*74*	*61*	*13*	*11*	*4*	*1*	*0*	*0*

NEVILLE Gary — Manchester United

Full Name: Gary Alexander Neville

DOB: 18/02/75, Bury

Previous Club Details

			Apps					Goals		
Club	Signed	Fee	Tot	Start	Sub	FA	FL	Lge	FA	FL
Manchester U.	Jan-93	Train	115	111	4	16	5	1	0	0

FAPL Summary by Club

Manchester U.	94/5 to 97/8		114	110	4	16	5	1	0	0
Totals			*114*	*110*	*4*	*16*	*5*	*1*	*0*	*0*

NEWSOME Jon — Sheffield Wednesday

Full Name: Jonathan Newsome

DOB: 06/09/70, Sheffield

Previous Club Details

			Apps					Goals		
Club	Signed	Fee	Tot	Start	Sub	FA	FL	Lge	FA	FL
Sheffield Wed.	Jul-89	Train	7	6	1			0	0	0
Leeds U.	Jun-91	£150k	76	62	14	4	5	3	3	1
Norwich C.	Jun-94	£1m	62	61	1	6	2	7	1	0
Sheffield W.	Mar-96	£1.6m	43	43	0	6	2	4	4	0

FAPL Summary by Club

Leeds U.	92/3 to 93/4		66	55	11	4	4	3	1	0
Norwich C.	1994-95		35	35	0	4	0	2	4	0
Sheffield W.	95/6 to 97/8		43	43	0	6	2	4	9	8
Totals			*144*	*133*	*11*	*14*	*9*	*8*	*0*	*0*

NEWTON Eddie — Chelsea

Full Name: Edward John Ikem Newton

DOB: 13/12/71, Hammersmith

Previous Club Details

			Apps					Goals		
Club	Signed	Fee	Tot	Start	Sub	FA	FL	Lge	FA	FL
Chelsea	May-90	Train	158	138	20	18	17	8	1	1
Cardiff C.	Jan-92	Loan	18	18	0	0	0	4	0	0

FAPL Summary by Club

Chelsea	92/3 to 97/8		157	138	19	18	17	7	1	0
Totals			*157*	*138*	*19*	*18*	*17*	*7*	*1*	*0*

NEWTON Shaun — Charlton Athletic

Full Name: Shaun O'Neill Newton

DOB: 20/08/75, Camberwell

Previous Club Details

			Apps					Goals		
Club	Signed	Fee	Tot	Start	Sub	FA	FL	Lge	FA	FL
Charlton A.	Jul-93	Train	173	135	38	9	15	15	0	2

NICHOLLS Mark — Chelsea

Full Name: Mark Nicholls

DOB: 30/05/77, Hillingdon

Previous Club Details

			Apps					Goals		
Club	Signed	Fee	Tot	Start	Sub	FA	FL	Lge	FA	FL
Chelsea		Train	27	11	16	1	2	3	0	0

FAPL Summary by Club

Chelsea	96/7 to 97/8		27	11	16	1	2	3	0	0
Totals			*27*	*11*	*16*	*1*	*2*	*3*	*0*	*0*

NICOL Steve — Sheffield Wednesday

Full Name: Stephen Nicol

DOB: 01/12/61, Irvine

Previous Club Details

			Apps					Goals		
Club	Signed	Fee	Tot	Start	Sub	FA	FL	Lge	FA	FL
Liverpool	Oct-81	£300k	342	328	15	50	42	36	3	4
Notts Co.	Jan-95	Free	32	32	0	1	1	2	0	0

Sheffield Wednesday (continued)

Club	Signed	Fee	Tot	Start	Sub	FA	FL	Lge	FA	FL
Sheffield W.	Nov-95	Free	49	41	8	3	0	0	0	0

FAPL Summary by Club

Club	Signed	Fee	Tot	Start	Sub	FA	FL	Lge	FA	FL
Liverpool	92/3 to 94/5		67	63	4	3	7	1	0	0
Sheffield W.	95/6 to 97/8		49	41	8	3	0	0	0	0
Totals			116	104	12	6	7	1	0	0

NIELSEN Allan — Tottenham Hotspur

Full Name: Allan Nielsen
DOB: 13/03/71

Previous Club Details

Club	Signed	Fee	Tot	Start	Sub	FA	FL	Lge	FA	FL
Bayern Munich										
Esbjerg			3							
OB Odense	1992		55	53	2	1		9		
FC Copenhagen	1995		25	25	1			3		
Brondby	1996	£100k	38	38	0			9		
Tottenham H.			54	49	5	1	4	9		

FAPL Summary by Club

Club	Signed	Fee	Tot	Start	Sub	FA	FL	Lge	FA	FL
Tottenham H.	96/7 to 97/8		54	49	5	1	4	9	0	0
Totals			54	49	5	1	4	9	0	0

NILSSON Roland — Coventry City

Full Name: Nils Lennart Roland Nilsson
DOB: 27/11/63, Helsingborg, Sweden

Previous Club Details

Club	Signed	Fee	Tot	Start	Sub	FA	FL	Lge	FA	FL
Sheffield W.	Nov-89	£375k	15	15	0	15	16	2	0	1
Helsingborg		Loan								
Coventry C.			32	32	0	4	3	1	0	1

FAPL Summary by Club

Club	Signed	Fee	Tot	Start	Sub	FA	FL	Lge	FA	FL
Sheffield W.	92/3 to 93/4		70	70	0	11	11	1	0	0
Coventry C.	1997-98		32	32	0	4	3	0	0	1
Totals			102	102	0	15	14	1	0	1

NOLAN Ian — Sheffield Wednesday

Full Name: Ian Robert Nolan
DOB: 09/01/70, Liverpool

Previous Club Details

Club	Signed	Fee	Tot	Start	Sub	FA	FL	Lge	FA	FL
Preston		Train								
Tranmere R.	Aug-91	£10k	88	87	1	7	10	1	1	0
Sheffield W.	Aug-94	£1.5m	136	136	0	11	12	4	0	0

FAPL Summary by Club

Club	Signed	Fee	Tot	Start	Sub	FA	FL	Lge	FA	FL
Sheffield W.	94/5 to 97/8		136	136	0	11	12	4	0	0
Totals			136	136	0	11	12	4	0	0

O'KANE John — Everton

Full Name: John Andrew O'Kane
DOB: 15/11/74, Nottingham

Previous Club Details

Club	Signed	Fee	Tot	Start	Sub	FA	FL	Lge	FA	FL
Manchester U.	Jan-93	Train	2	1	1	0	2	0	0	0
Bury	Oct-96	Loan _x2)	13	11	2	0	0	0	0	0
Everton	Jan-98	£250k	12	12	0	0	0	0	0	0

FAPL Summary by Club

Club	Signed	Fee	Tot	Start	Sub	FA	FL	Lge	FA	FL
Manchester U.	95/6 to 96/7		2	1	1	0	2	0	0	0
Everton	1997-98		12	12	0	0	0	0	0	0
Totals			14	13	1	0	2	0	0	0

O'NEILL Michael — Coventry City

Full Name: Michael O'Neill

Previous Club Details

Club	Signed	Fee	Tot	Start	Sub	FA	FL	Lge	FA	FL
Coventry C.			5	3	2	1	0	0	0	0

FAPL Summary by Club

Club	Signed	Fee	Tot	Start	Sub	FA	FL	Lge	FA	FL
Coventry C.	96/7 to 97/8		5	3	2	1	0	0	0	0
Totals			5	3	2	1	0	0	0	0

OAKES Michael

Aston Villa

Full Name: Michael Oakes
DOB: 30/10/73, Northwich

Previous Club Details

			Apps				Goals		
Club	Signed	Fee	Tot	Start	Sub	FA	FL	Lge	FA	FL
Aston Villa	Jul-91		28	26	2	0	1	0	0	0
Scarborough	Nov-93	Loan	1	1	0	0	0	0	0	0

FAPL Summary by Club

Aston Villa	96/7 to 97/8		28	26	2	0	1	0	0	0
Totals			28	26	2	0	1	0	0	0

OAKES Scott

Sheffield Wednesday

Full Name: Scott John Oakes
DOB: 05/08/72, Leicester

Previous Club Details

			Apps				Goals		
Club	Signed	Fee	Tot	Start	Sub	FA	FL	Lge	FA	FL
Leicester C.	May-90	Train	3	1	2	0	0	0	0	0
Luton Town	Oct-91		173	136	37	14	6	27	5	1
Sheffield W.	Aug-96	£450k	23	7	16	2	0	1	0	0

FAPL Summary by Club

Sheffield W.	96/7 to 97/8		23	7	16	2	0	1	0	0
Totals			23	7	16	2	0	1	0	0

OAKLEY Matthew

Southampton

Full Name: Matthew Oakley
DOB: 17/08/77, Peterborough

Previous Club Details

			Apps				Goals		
Club	Signed	Fee	Tot	Start	Sub	FA	FL	Lge	FA	FL
Southampton	Jul-95		72	60	12	5	11	4	1	0

FAPL Summary by Club

Southampton	94/5 to 97/8		72	60	12	5	11	4	1	0
Totals			72	60	12	5	11	4	1	0

OGRIZOVIC Steve

Coventry City

Full Name: Steven Ogrizovic
DOB: 12/09/57, Mansfield

Previous Club Details

			Apps				Goals		
Club	Signed	Fee	Tot	Start	Sub	FA	FL	Lge	FA	FL
Chesterfield	Jul-77		16	16	0	0	0	0	0	0
Liverpool	Nov-77	£70k	4	4	0	0	5	0	0	0
Shrewsbury Tn	Aug-82	£70k	84	84	0	0	7	0	0	0
Coventry C.	Jun-84	£72k	502	502	0	34	49	0	1	0

FAPL Summary by Club

Coventry C.	92/3 to 97/8		186	186	0	15	17	0	0	0
Totals			186	186	0	15	17	0	0	0

OMOYIMNI Emmanuel

West Ham United

Full Name: Emmanuel Omoyimni
DOB: 28/12/77, Nigeria

Previous Club Details

			Apps				Goals		
Club	Signed	Fee	Tot	Start	Sub	FA	FL	Lge	FA	FL
West Ham U.	May-95	Train	6	1	5	0	0	0	0	0
Bournemouth	Sep-96	Loan	7	5	2	0	0	0	0	0

FAPL Summary by Club

West Ham U.	96/7 to 97/8		6	1	5	0	0	2	0	0
Totals			6	1	5	0	0	2	0	0

OSTENSTAD Egil

Southampton

Full Name: Egil Ostenstad
DOB: 02/01/72, Haugesund, Norway

Previous Club Details

			Apps				Goals		
Club	Signed	Fee	Tot	Start	Sub	FA	FL	Lge	FA	FL
Viking FK	1990		104	81	23			31		
Southampton	Oct-96	£800k	59	50	9	2	7	21	1	3

FAPL Summary by Club

Southampton	96/7 to 97/8		59	50	9	2	7	21	1	3
Totals			59	50	9	2	7	21	1	3

OSTER John
Everton

Full Name: John Morgan Oster
DOB: 08/12/78, Boston

Previous Club Details

Club	Signed	Fee	Apps					Goals		
			Tot	Start	Sub	FA	FL	Lge	FA	FL
Grimsby Town	Jul-96	Train	24	21	3	1		0	1	0
Everton	Jul-97	£1.5m	31	16	15	1	3	1	0	2

FAPL Summary by Club

			Tot	Start	Sub	FA	FL	Lge	FA	FL
Everton	1997-98		31	16	15	1	3	1	0	2
Totals			31	16	15	1	3	1	0	2

OVERMARS Marc
Arsenal

Full Name: Marc Overmars
DOB: 29/03/73, Emst, Holland

Previous Club Details

Club	Signed	Fee	Apps					Goals		
			Tot	Start	Sub	FA	FL	Lge	FA	FL
Willem II			31	31				1		
Ajax	Jul-92		135	130	5			36		
Arsenal	Jul-97	£7.0m	32	32	0	9	3	12	2	2

FAPL Summary by Club

			Tot	Start	Sub	FA	FL	Lge	FA	FL
Arsenal	1997-98		32	32	0	9	3	12	2	2
Totals			32	32	0	9	3	12	2	2

OWEN Michael
Liverpool

Full Name: Michael Owen
DOB: 14/12/79, Chester

Previous Club Details

Club	Signed	Fee	Apps					Goals		
			Tot	Start	Sub	FA	FL	Lge	FA	FL
Liverpool	Dec-96	Jnrs	38	35	3	3	0	19	0	4

FAPL Summary by Club

			Tot	Start	Sub	FA	FL	Lge	FA	FL
Liverpool	96/7 to 97/8		38	35	3	3	0	19	0	4
Totals			38	35	3	3	0	19	0	4

PALLISTER Gary
Manchester United

Full Name: Gary Andrew Pallister
DOB: 30/06/65, Ramsgate

Previous Club Details

Club	Signed	Fee	Apps					Goals		
			Tot	Start	Sub	FA	FL	Lge	FA	FL
Middlesbrough	Nov-84	NL	156	156	0	10	10	0	0	0
Darlington	Oct-85	Loan	7	7	0			0	0	0
Manchester U.	Aug-89	£2.3m	317	314	3	37	36	12	8	2

FAPL Summary by Club

			Tot	Start	Sub	FA	FL	Lge	FA	FL
Manchester U.	92/3 to 97/8		206	206	0	23	16	8	2	2
Totals			206	206	0	23	16	8	2	2

PALMER Carlton
Southampton

Full Name: Carlton Lloyd Palmer
DOB: 05/12/65, Rowley Regis

Previous Club Details

Club	Signed	Fee	Apps					Goals		
			Tot	Start	Sub	FA	FL	Lge	FA	FL
WBA	Dec-84		121	114	7	4	8	4	0	1
Sheffield W.	Feb-89	£750k	205	204	1	18	31	14	2	1
Leeds U.	Jun-94	£2.6m	102	100	2	12	12	5	1	0
Southampton	Sep-97	£1.0m	26	26	0	1	3	3	0	0

FAPL Summary by Club

			Tot	Start	Sub	FA	FL	Lge	FA	FL
Sheffield W.	92/3 to 93/4		71	70	1	11	16	6	2	1
Leeds U.	94/5 to 96/7		102	100	2	12	12	5	1	0
Southampton	1997-98		26	26	0	1	3	3	0	0
Totals			199	196	3	24	31	14	3	1

PARKER Garry
Leicester City

Full Name: Garry Stuart Parker
DOB: 07/09/65, Oxford

Previous Club Details

Club	Signed	Fee	Apps					Goals		
			Tot	Start	Sub	FA	FL	Lge	FA	FL
Luton Town	May-83	App	42	31	11	8	4	5	3	0
Hull C.	Feb-86	£72k	84	82	2	4	5	8	0	0

PARLOUR Ray — Arsenal

Full Name: Raymond Parlour
DOB: 07/03/73, Romford

Previous Club Details

			Apps					Goals		
Club	Signed	Fee	Tot	Start	Sub	FA	FL	Lge	FA	FL
Arsenal	Mar-91	Train	170	135	35	19	20	11	2	0

FAPL Summary by Club

Arsenal	92/3 to 97/8		164	133	31	19	20	10	2	0
Totals			*164*	*133*	*31*	*19*	*20*	*10*	*2*	*0*

(continued from preceding entry)

			Apps					Goals		
N. Forest	Mar-88	£260k	103	99	4	16	23	17	5	4
Aston Villa	Nov-91	£650k	95	91	4	13	14	0	1	0
Leicester C.	Feb-95	£300k	107	87	20	9	13	10	2	1

FAPL Summary by Club

Aston Villa	92/3 to 94/5		70	66	4	5	12	11	0	0
Leicester C.	94/5 to 97/8		67	51	16	7	9	7	2	1
Totals			*137*	*117*	*20*	*12*	*21*	*18*	*2*	*1*

PEACOCK Darren — Blackburn Rovers

Full Name: Darren Peacock
DOB: 03/02/68, Bristol

Previous Club Details

			Apps					Goals		
Club	Signed	Fee	Tot	Start	Sub	FA	FL	Lge	FA	FL
Newport Co.	Feb-86	App	28	24	4	1	2	1	0	0
Hereford U.	Mar-89		59	56	3	6	4	0	1	0
QPR	Dec-90	£200k	126	123	3	12	6	6	0	0
Newcastle U.	Mar-94	£2.7m	133	131	2	10	14	2	0	2
Blackburn R.	Jun-98									

FAPL Summary by Club

QPR	92/3 to 93/4		68	65	3	8	5	0	0	1
Newcastle U.	93/4 to 97/8		133	131	2	10	14	2	0	3
Totals			*201*	*196*	*5*	*12*	*22*	*7*	*0*	*3*

PEARCE Stuart — Newcastle United

Full Name: Stuart Pearce
DOB: 24/04/62, Shepherds Bush

Previous Club Details

			Apps					Goals		
Club	Signed	Fee	Tot	Start	Sub	FA	FL	Lge	FA	FL
Coventry C.	Oct-83	£25k	52	52	0	0	4	0	0	0
N. Forest	Jun-85	£200k	401	401	0	37	60	63	9	10
Newcastle U.	Jul-97	Free	25	25	0	0	7	0	0	0

FAPL Summary by Club

N. Forest	92/3 to 96/7		123	123	0	10	11	18	2	3
Newcastle U.	1997-98		25	25	0	0	7	0	0	0
Totals			*148*	*148*	*0*	*10*	*18*	*18*	*2*	*3*

PEARCE Ian — West Ham United

Full Name: Ian Anthony Pearce
DOB: 07/05/74, Bury St Edmunds

Previous Club Details

			Apps					Goals		
Club	Signed	Fee	Tot	Start	Sub	FA	FL	Lge	FA	FL
Chelsea	Aug-91	Jnrs	4	0	4	0	0	0	0	0
Blackburn R.	Oct-93	£300k	62	43	19	8	3	3	1	1
West Ham U.	Sep-97	£1.6m	30	30	0	3	6	3	1	0

FAPL Summary by Club

Chelsea	1992-93		1	0	1	0	0	0	0	0
Blackburn R.	93/4 to 97/8		62	43	19	8	3	3	1	1
West Ham U.	1997-98		30	30	0	3	6	3	1	0
Totals			*93*	*73*	*20*	*9*	*11*	*6*	*2*	*1*

PEARSON Nigel — Middlesbrough

Full Name: Nigel Graham Pearson
DOB: 21/08/63, Nottingham

Previous Club Details

			Apps					Goals		
Club	Signed	Fee	Tot	Start	Sub	FA	FL	Lge	FA	FL
Shrewsbury T.	Nov-81	£5k	153	153	0	6	19	5	0	0
Sheffield W.	Oct-87	£250k	180	176	4	15	19	14	1	5

Middlesbrough Jul-94 £500k — continuation of previous entry

Club	Signed	Fee	Tot	Start	Sub	FA	FL	Lge	FA	FL
			Apps					*Goals*		
Middlesbrough	Jul-94	£500k	106	102	4	9	14	3	0	0
FAPL Summary by Club										
Sheffield W.	92/3 to 93/4		21	17	4	2	5	1	0	0
Middlesbrough	95/6 to 96/7		54	53	1	6	10	0	0	0
Totals			*75*	*70*	*5*	*8*	*15*	*1*	*0*	*0*

PEDERSEN Tore — Blackburn Rovers

Full Name: Tore Pedersen
DOB: 29/09/62, Fredrikstad, Norway
Previous Club Details

Club	Signed	Fee	Tot	Start	Sub	FA	FL	Lge	FA	FL
			Apps					*Goals*		
St Pauli										
Blackburn R.	Sep-97	£500k	5	3	2	0	3	0	0	0
FAPL Summary by Club										
Blackburn R.	1997-98		5	3	2	0	3	0	0	0
Totals			*5*	*3*	*2*	*0*	*3*	*0*	*0*	*0*

PEMBRIDGE Mark — Sheffield Wednesday

Full Name: Mark Anthony Pembridge
DOB: 29/11/70, Merthyr Tydfil
Previous Club Details

Club	Signed	Fee	Tot	Start	Sub	FA	FL	Lge	FA	FL
			Apps					*Goals*		
Luton Town	Jul-89	Train	60	60		4	2	6	0	0
Derby Co.	Jun-92	£1.25m	110	108	2	6	9	28	3	1
Sheffield W.	Jul-95	£900k	93	88	5	7	6	12	1	1
FAPL Summary by Club										
Sheffield W.	95/6 to 97/8		93	88	5	7	6	12	1	1
Totals			*93*	*88*	*5*	*7*	*6*	*12*	*1*	*1*

PERRY Chris — Wimbledon

Full Name: Christopher John Perry
DOB: 26/04/73, Surrey
Previous Club Details

Club	Signed	Fee	Tot	Start	Sub	FA	FL	Lge	FA	FL
			Apps					*Goals*		
Wimbledon	Jul-91		133	125	8	22	14	2	0	1
FAPL Summary by Club										
Wimbledon	93/4 to 97/8		133	125	8	22	13	2	1	0
Totals			*133*	*125*	*8*	*22*	*13*	*2*	*1*	*0*

PETIT Manu — Arsenal

Full Name: Emmanuel Petit
DOB: 22/09/70, Dieppe
Previous Club Details

Club	Signed	Fee	Tot	Start	Sub	FA	FL	Lge	FA	FL
			Apps					*Goals*		
ES Argues										
AS Monaco			185	184	1			4		
Arsenal	Jun-97	£3.5m	32	32	0	7	3	2	0	0
FAPL Summary by Club										
Arsenal	1997-98		32	32	0	7	3	2	0	0
Totals			*32*	*32*	*0*	*7*	*3*	*2*	*0*	*0*

PETRESCU Dan — Chelsea

Full Name: Dan Vasile Petrescu
DOB: 22/12/67, Bucharest
Previous Club Details

Club	Signed	Fee	Tot	Start	Sub	FA	FL	Lge	FA	FL
			Apps					*Goals*		
CSA Steaua	Jun-86		2	2				0		
Olt Scornicesti	Jul-86		24	24				0		
CSA Steaua	Jul-87		93	93				27		
Foggia (Italy)	Jul-91		55	55				6		
Genoa (Italy)	Jul-93		24	24				1		
Sheffield W.	Aug-94	£1.25m	37	28	9	2	2	3	0	0
Chelsea	Nov-95	£2.3m	89	87	2	14	5	10	1	2
FAPL Summary by Club										
Sheffield W.	94/5 to 95/6		37	28	9	2	2	3	0	0
Chelsea	95/6 to 97/8		89	87	2	14	5	10	1	2
Totals			*126*	*115*	*11*	*16*	*7*	*13*	*1*	*2*

PHELAN Terry — Everton

Full Name: Terence Michael Phelan
DOB: 16/03/67, Manchester

Previous Club Details

			Apps					Goals		
Club	Signed	Fee	Tot	Start	Sub	FA	FL	Lge	FA	FL
Leeds U.	Aug-84	Free	14	12	2	0	3	0		
Swansea C.	Jul-86	Free	45	45	0	4	16	0		
Wimbledon	Jul-87	£100k	159	155	4	16	15	1	0	
Manchester C.	Aug-92	£2.5m	103	102	1	8	11	0		
Chelsea	Nov-95	£900k	16	15	1	1	1	0		
Everton	Dec-96	£850k	24	23	1	1	0	0		

FAPL Summary by Club

Club			Tot	Start	Sub	FA	FL	Lge	FA	FL
Manchester C. 92/3 to 95/6			103	102	1	8	11	0		
Chelsea 95/6 to 96/7			16	15	1	1	1	0		
Everton 96/7 to 97/8			24	23	1	1	0	0		
Totals			143	140	3	17	13	0		

PILKINGTON Kevin — Manchester United

Full Name: Kevin William Pilkington
DOB: 08/03/74, Hitchin

Previous Club Details

			Apps					Goals		
Club	Signed	Fee	Tot	Start	Sub	FA	FL	Lge	FA	FL
Manchester U.	Jul-92	Trainee	6	4	2	2	1	0	0	0
Rochdale	Feb-96	Loan	6	6	0	0	0	0	0	0
Rotherham U.	Jan-97	Loan	17	17	0	0	0	0	0	0

FAPL Summary by Club

Club			Tot	Start	Sub	FA	FL	Lge	FA	FL
Manchester U. 94/5 to 97/8			6	4	2	2	1	0	0	0
Totals			6	4	2	2	1	0	0	0

PISTONE Alessandro — Newcastle United

Full Name: Alessandro Pistone
DOB: 27/7/75, Milan

Previous Club Details

			Apps					Goals		
Club	Signed	Fee	Tot	Start	Sub	FA	FL	Lge	FA	FL
Vicenza, Crevalcore, Internazionale										
Newcastle U.	Jul-97	£4.3m	28	28	0	5	1	0	0	0

FAPL Summary by Club

Club			Tot	Start	Sub	FA	FL	Lge	FA	FL
Newcastle U. 1997-98			28	28	0	5	1	0	0	0
Totals			28	28	0	5	1	0	0	0

PLATT David — Arsenal

Full Name: David Andrew Platt
DOB: 10/06/66, Oldham

Previous Club Details

			Apps					Goals		
Club	Signed	Fee	Tot	Start	Sub	FA	FL	Lge	FA	FL
Crewe Alex.	Jan-85		134	134	0	3	6	55	1	0
Aston Villa	Feb-88	£200k	121	121	0	4	14	50	2	10
Bari	Jul-91	£5.5m	29	29	0	0	0	11	0	0
Juventus			16	16	0	0	0	3	0	0
Sampdoria			29	29	0	0	0	9	0	0
Arsenal	Jul-95	£4.75m	88	65	23	6	10	13	0	2

FAPL Summary by Club

Club			Tot	Start	Sub	FA	FL	Lge	FA	FL
Arsenal 95/6 to 97/8			88	65	23	6	10	13	0	2
Totals			88	65	23	6	10	13	0	2

POOM Mart — Derby County

Full Name: Mart Poom
DOB: 03/02/72, Tallinn

Previous Club Details

			Apps					Goals		
Club	Signed	Fee	Tot	Start	Sub	FA	FL	Lge	FA	FL
FC Will										
Flora Tallinn										
Portsmouth	Aug-94	£200k	4	4	0	0	4	0	0	0
Flora Tallinn			7	7	0	0	0	0	0	0

Derby Co. Mar-97 £500k ... (continued)

Club	Signed	Fee	Tot	Start	Sub	FA	FL	Lge	FA	FL
Derby Co.	Mar-97	£500k	40	40	0	2	3	0	0	0
FAPL Summary by Club										
Derby Co.	96/7 to 97/8		40	40	0	2	3	0	0	0
Totals			*40*	*40*	*0*	*2*	*3*	*0*	*0*	*0*

POTTS Steve — West Ham United

Full Name: Steven John Potts
DOB: 07/05/67, Hartford, USA

Previous Club Details

			Apps					Goals		
Club	Signed	Fee	Tot	Start	Sub	FA	FL	Lge	FA	FL
West Ham U.	Jul-83		360	333	27	40	36	1	0	0
FAPL Summary by Club										
West Ham U.	93/4 to 97/8		160	148	12	17	15	0	0	0
Totals			*160*	*148*	*12*	*17*	*15*	*0*	*0*	*0*

POWELL Darryl — Derby County

Full Name: Darryl Anthony Powell
DOB: 15/11/71, Lambeth

Previous Club Details

			Apps					Goals		
Club	Signed	Fee	Tot	Start	Sub	FA	FL	Lge	FA	FL
Portsmouth	Dec-88		132	83	49	10	14	16	0	3
Derby Co.	Jul-95	£750k	94	77	17	9	10	6	0	0
FAPL Summary by Club										
Derby Co.	96/7 to 97/8		57	40	17	9	8	1	0	0
Totals			*57*	*40*	*17*	*9*	*8*	*1*	*0*	*0*

POWELL Chris — Charlton Athletic

Full Name: Christopher George Robin Powell
DOB: 08/09/69, Lambeth

Previous Club Details

Club	Signed	Fee	Tot	Start	Sub	FA	FL	Lge	FA	FL
C. Palace	Dec-87	Train	3	2	1	0	1	0	0	0
Aldershot	Jan-90	Loan	11	11	0	0	2	0	0	0
Southend U.	Aug-90	Free	248	246	2	8	13	3	0	0

Club	Signed	Fee	Tot	Start	Sub	FA	FL	Lge	FA	FL
Derby Co.	Jan-96	£750k	91	88	3	5	5	1	1	0
FAPL Summary by Club										
Derby Co.	96/7 to 97/8		71	69	2	6	8	1	1	0
Totals			*71*	*69*	*2*	*6*	*8*	*1*	*1*	*0*

POYET Gustavo — Chelsea

Full Name: Gustavo Poyet
DOB: 15/11/67, Montevideo

Previous Club Details

			Apps					Goals		
Club	Signed	Fee	Tot	Start	Sub	FA	FL	Lge	FA	FL
River Plate, Grenoble, Bellavista										
Real Zaragoza			240					60		
Chelsea	Jul-97		14	11	3	0	0	4	0	0
FAPL Summary by Club										
Chelsea	1997-98		14	11	3	0	0	4	0	0
Totals			*14*	*11*	*3*	*0*	*0*	*4*	*0*	*0*

PRESSMAN Kevin — Sheffield Wednesday

Full Name: Kevin Paul Pressman
DOB: 06/11/67, Fareham

Previous Club Details

			Apps					Goals		
Club	Signed	Fee	Tot	Start	Sub	FA	FL	Lge	FA	FL
Sheffield W.	Nov-85		232	232	0	15	29	0	0	0
Stoke C.	Mar-92	Loan	4	4	0	0	0	0	0	0
FAPL Summary by Club										
Sheffield W.	92/3 to 97/8		173	173	0	15	20	0	0	0
Totals			*173*	*173*	*0*	*15*	*20*	*0*	*0*	*0*

PRIOR Spencer — Leicester City

Full Name: Spencer Justin Prior
DOB: 22/04/71, Hockley

Previous Club Details

			Apps					Goals		
Club	Signed	Fee	Tot	Start	Sub	FA	FL	Lge	FA	FL
Southend U.	May-89		135	135	0	5	9	3	0	0

Previous Club Details

Club	Signed	Fee	Tot	Start	Sub	FA	FL	Lge	FA	FL
Norwich C.	Jun-93	£200k	73	67	6	2	11	1	0	1
Leicester C.	Aug-96	£600k	64	61	3	5	7	0	0	0

FAPL Summary by Club

Club	Signed	Fee	Tot	Start	Sub	FA	FL	Lge	FA	FL
Norwich C.	93/4 to 94/5		30	25	5	1	4	0	0	0
Leicester C.	96/7 to 97/8		64	61	3	5	7	0	0	0
Totals			*94*	*86*	*8*	*6*	*11*	*0*	*0*	*1*

RADEBE Lucas   Leeds United

Full Name: Lucas Radebe
DOB: 12/04/69, Johannesburg

Previous Club Details

Club	Signed	Fee	Tot	Start	Sub	FA	FL	Lge	FA	FL
Kaiser Chiefs										
Leeds U.	Sep-94	£250k	84	73	11	11	9	0	1	0

FAPL Summary by Club

Club	Signed	Fee	Tot	Start	Sub	FA	FL	Lge	FA	FL
Leeds U.	94/5 to 97/8		84	73	11	11	9	0	1	0
Totals			*84*	*73*	*11*	*11*	*9*	*0*	*1*	*0*

REDKNAPP Jamie   Liverpool

Full Name: Jamie Frank Redknapp
DOB: 25/06/73, Barton on Sea

Previous Club Details

Club	Signed	Fee	Tot	Start	Sub	FA	FL	Lge	FA	FL
Bournemouth	Jun-90	Train	13	6	7					
Liverpool	Jan-91	£350k	177	154	23	16	25	19	2	5

FAPL Summary by Club

Club	Signed	Fee	Tot	Start	Sub	FA	FL	Lge	FA	FL
Liverpool	92/3 to 97/8		170	149	21	13	25	18	1	6
Totals			*170*	*149*	*21*	*13*	*25*	*18*	*1*	*6*

RIBEIRO Bruino   Leeds United

Full Name: Bruino Ribeiro
DOB: 22/10/75, Setubal

Previous Club Details

Club	Signed	Fee	Tot	Start	Sub	FA	FL	Lge	FA	FL
Vitoria Setubal										

Southampton

Club	Signed	Fee	Tot	Start	Sub	FA	FL	Lge	FA	FL
Leeds U.	Jun-97	£500k	29	28	1	3	3	3	0	1

FAPL Summary by Club

Club	Signed	Fee	Tot	Start	Sub	FA	FL	Lge	FA	FL
Leeds U.	1997-98		29	28		3	3	3	0	1
Totals			*29*	*28*		*3*	*3*	*3*	*0*	*1*

RICHARDSON Kevin

Full Name: Kevin Richardson
DOB: 04/12/62, Newcastle

Previous Club Details

Club	Signed	Fee	Tot	Start	Sub	FA	FL	Lge	FA	FL
Everton	Dec-80	App	109	95	14	13	13	16	1	3
Watford	Sep-86	£225k	39	39		3	2	5	1	2
Arsenal	Aug-87	£200k	96	88	8	9	16	5	1	2
Real Sociedad	Jun-90	£750k								
Aston Villa	Aug-91	£450k	143	142	1	12	15	13	0	3
Coventry C.	Feb-95	£300k	78	75	3	7	8	7	1	0
Southampton	Sep-97	£150k	28	25	3	1	4	0	0	0

FAPL Summary by Club

Club	Signed	Fee	Tot	Start	Sub	FA	FL	Lge	FA	FL
Aston Villa	92/3 to 94/5		101	100	1	7	13	8	0	3
Coventry C.	94/5 to 97/8		78	75	3	7	8	8	0	1
Southampton	1997-98		28	25	3	1	4	0	0	0
Totals			*207*	*200*	*7*	*15*	*25*	*8*	*0*	*4*

RIEDLE Karl Heinz   Liverpool

Full Name: Karl Heinz Riedle
DOB: 16/9/65, Germany

Previous Club Details

Club	Signed	Fee	Tot	Start	Sub	FA	FL	Lge	FA	FL
B. Dortmund										
Liverpool	Jul-97	£1.8m	25	18	7	1	5	6	0	0

FAPL Summary by Club

Club	Signed	Fee	Tot	Start	Sub	FA	FL	Lge	FA	FL
Liverpool	1997-98		25	18	7	1	5	6	0	0
Totals			*25*	*18*	*7*	*1*	*5*	*6*	*0*	*0*

RIPLEY Stuart — Blackburn Rovers

Full Name: Stuart Edward Ripley
DOB: 20/11/67, Middlesbrough

Previous Club Details

			Apps					Goals		
Club	Signed	Fee	Tot	Start	Sub	FA	FL	Lge	FA	FL
Middlesbrough	Nov-85	App	249	210	39	18	23	26	4	1
Bolton W.	Feb-86	Loan	5	5	0	1	0	0	1	0
Blackburn R.	Jul-92	£1.3m	187	172	15	14	18	13	3	0

FAPL Summary by Club

			Apps					Goals		
			Tot	Start	Sub	FA	FL	Lge	FA	FL
Blackburn R.	92/3 to 97/8		187	172	15	14	18	13	3	0
Totals			187	172	15	14	18	13	3	0

ROBERTS Andy — Wimbledon

Full Name: Andrew James Roberts
DOB: 20/03/74, Dartford

Previous Club Details

			Apps					Goals		
Club	Signed	Fee	Tot	Start	Sub	FA	FL	Lge	FA	FL
Millwall	Oct-91	Train	138	132	6	7	12	5	0	2
C. Palace	Jul-95	£2.52m	108	106	2	8	8	2	0	0
Wimbledon	Mar-98	£1.2m>	12	12	0	0	0	1	0	0

FAPL Summary by Club

			Apps					Goals		
			Tot	Start	Sub	FA	FL	Lge	FA	FL
C. Palace	1997-98		25	25	0	4	1	0	0	0
Wimbledon	1997-98		12	12	0	0	0	1	0	0
Totals			37	37	0	4	1	1	0	0

ROBERTSON David — Leeds United

Full Name: David Robertson
DOB: 17/10/68, Aberdeen

Previous Club Details

			Apps					Goals		
Club	Signed	Fee	Tot	Start	Sub	FA	FL	Lge	FA	FL
Aberdeen	1986		135					3		
Rangers	1991		161					10		
Leeds U.	May-97	£500k	26	24	2	1	4	0	0	0

FAPL Summary by Club

			Apps					Goals		
			Tot	Start	Sub	FA	FL	Lge	FA	FL
Leeds U.	1997-98		26	24	2	1	4	0	0	0
Totals			26	24	2	1	4	0	0	0

ROBINSON John — Charlton Athletic

Full Name: John Robert Campbell Robinson
DOB: 29/08/71, Bulawayo, Zimbabwe

Previous Club Details

			Apps					Goals		
Club	Signed	Fee	Tot	Start	Sub	FA	FL	Lge	FA	FL
Brighton &HA	Apr-89	Train	57	52	5	3	5	6	0	1
Charlton A.	Sep-92	£75k	185	179	8	12	13	23	2	4

ROGERS Alan — Nottingham Forest

Full Name: Alan Rogers
DOB: 03/01/77, Liverpool

Previous Club Details

			Apps					Goals		
Club	Signed	Fee	Tot	Start	Sub	FA	FL	Lge	FA	FL
Tranmere R.	Jul-95	Train	57	53	4	1	2	7	0	1
N. Forest	Jul-97	£2m	45	45	0	4	1	1	0	0

ROWETT Gary — Derby County

Full Name: Gary Rowett
DOB: 06/03/74, Bromsgrove

Previous Club Details

			Apps					Goals		
Club	Signed	Fee	Tot	Start	Sub	FA	FL	Lge	FA	FL
Cambridge U.	Sep-91		63	51	12	7	7	9	0	1
Everton	May-94	£20k	4	2	2	0	0	0	0	0
Blackpool	Jan-95	Loan	17	17	0	0	0	0	0	0
Derby Co.	Jul-95	£300k	105	101	4	10	12	3	0	2

FAPL Summary by Club

			Apps					Goals		
			Tot	Start	Sub	FA	FL	Lge	FA	FL
Everton	93/4 to 94/5		4	2	2	0	0	0	0	0
Derby Co.	96/7 to 97/8		69	67	2	8	10	3	0	3
Totals			73	69	4	8	10	3	0	3

RUDDOCK Neil — Liverpool

Full Name: Neil Ruddock
DOB: 09/05/68, Wandsworth
Previous Club Details

Club	Signed	Fee	Apps			FA	FL	Goals		
			Tot	Start	Sub			Lge	FA	FL
Millwall	Mar-86	App	4	2	2	2	0	0	0	0
Tottenham H.	Apr-86	£50k	9	7	2	2	0	1	0	0
Millwall	Jun-88	£300k	2	0	2	0	2	1	0	3
Southampton	Feb-89	£250k	107	100	7	10	15	9	3	1
Tottenham H.	Jul-92	£750k	38	38	0	5	4	3	0	0
Liverpool	Jul-93	£2.5m	116	111	5	11	20	11	0	1
FAPL Summary by Club										
Tottenham H.	1992-93		38	38	0	5	4	3	0	0
Liverpool	93/4 to 97/8		116	111	5	11	20	11	0	1
Totals			154	149	5	16	24	14	0	1

RUDI Petter — Sheffield Wednesday

Full Name: Petter Rudi
DOB: 17/9/73, Norway
Previous Club Details

Club	Signed	Fee	Apps			FA	FL	Goals		
			Tot	Start	Sub			Lge	FA	FL
Perugia, Molde										
Sheffield W.	Oct-97	£800k	22	19	3	3	0	0	0	0
FAPL Summary by Club										
Sheffield W.	1997-98		22	19	3	3	0	0	0	0
Totals			22	19	3	3	0	0	0	0

RUFUS Richard — Charlton Athletic

Full Name: Richard Raymond Rufus
DOB: 12/01/75, Lewisham
Previous Club Details

Club	Signed	Fee	Apps			FA	FL	Goals		
			Tot	Start	Sub			Lge	FA	FL
Charlton A.	Jul-93	Train	146	143	3	7	8	0	0	0

SAIB Moussa — Tottenham Hotspur

Full Name: Moussa Saib
DOB: 6/3/69, Theniet, Algeria
Previous Club Details

Club	Signed	Fee	Apps			FA	FL	Goals		
			Tot	Start	Sub			Lge	FA	FL
Valencia										
Tottenham H.	Feb-98	£2.3m	9	3	6	0	0	1	0	0
FAPL Summary by Club										
Tottenham H.	1997-98		8	2	6	0	0	1	0	0
Totals			8	2	6	0	0	1	0	0

SAVAGE Rob — Leicester City

Full Name: Robert William Savage
DOB: 18/10/74, Wrexham
Previous Club Details

Club	Signed	Fee	Apps			FA	FL	Goals		
			Tot	Start	Sub			Lge	FA	FL
Manchester U.	Jul-93	Train	0	0	0	0	0	0	0	0
Crewe Al.	Jul-94	Free	77	74	3	5	10	5	1	0
Leicester C.			35	28	7	2	1	2	1	1
FAPL Summary by Club										
Leicester C.	1997-98		35	28	7	2	1	2	1	1
Totals			35	28	7	2	1	2	1	1

SCALES John — Tottenham Hotspur

Full Name: John Robert Scales
DOB: 04/07/66, Harrogate
Previous Club Details

Club	Signed	Fee	Apps			FA	FL	Goals		
			Tot	Start	Sub			Lge	FA	FL
Bristol R.	Jul-85		72	68	4	6	3	2	1	0
Wimbledon	Jul-87	£70k	240	235	5	21	19	11	1	1
Liverpool	Sep-94	£3.5m	65	65	0	14	10	2	0	2
Tottenham H.	Dec-96	£2.6m	22	19	3	0	2	0	0	0

(continued)

FAPL Summary by Club

Club			Apps					Goals		
			Tot	Start	Sub	FA	FL	Lge	FA	FL
Wimbledon 92/3 to 94/5			72	72	0	8	7	1	1	0
Liverpool 94/5 to 96/7			65	65	0	14	10	2	0	2
Tottenham H. 96/7 to 97/8			22	19	3	3	2	0	1	2
Totals			159	156	3	22	19	3	1	2

SCHMEICHEL Peter — Manchester United

Full Name: Peter Boleslaw Schmeichel
DOB: 18/11/68, Gladsone, Denmark

Previous Club Details

Club	Signed	Fee	Tot	Start	Sub	FA	FL	Lge	FA	FL
Manchester U.	Aug-91	£550k	259	259	0	33	17	0	0	0

FAPL Summary by Club

Club			Tot	Start	Sub	FA	FL	Lge	FA	FL
Manchester U. 92/3 to 97/8			219	219	0	30	11	0	0	0
Totals			219	219	0	30	11	0	0	0

SCHOLES Paul — Manchester United

Full Name: Paul Scholes
DOB: 16/11/74, Salford

Previous Club Details

Club	Signed	Fee	Tot	Start	Sub	FA	FL	Lge	FA	FL
Manchester U.	Jan-93	Train	88	56	32	8	7	26	3	5

FAPL Summary by Club

Club			Tot	Start	Sub	FA	FL	Lge	FA	FL
Manchester U. 94/5 to 97/8			98	66	32	9	7	26	3	5
Totals			98	66	32	9	7	26	3	5

SCHWARZER Mark — Middlesbrough

Full Name: Mark Schwarzer
DOB: 06/10/72, Australia

Previous Club Details

Club	Signed	Fee	Tot	Start	Sub	FA	FL	Lge	FA	FL
FC Kaiserslautern			4	4	0	0	0	0	0	0
Bradford C.	Nov-96	£350k	13	13	0	3	0	0	0	0
Middlesbrough	Feb-97	£1.5m	39	39	0	3	10	0	0	0

FAPL Summary by Club

Club			Tot	Start	Sub	FA	FL	Lge	FA	FL
Middlesbrough 1996-97			7	7	0	3	0	0	0	0
Totals			7	7	0	3	0	0	0	0

SCIMECA Ricky — Aston Villa

Full Name: Riccardo Scimeca
DOB: 13/08/75, Leamington

Previous Club Details

Club	Signed	Fee	Tot	Start	Sub	FA	FL	Lge	FA	FL
Aston Villa	Jul-93		55	34	21	8	6	0	0	0

FAPL Summary by Club

Club			Tot	Start	Sub	FA	FL	Lge	FA	FL
Aston Villa 95/6 to 97/8			55	34	21	8	6	0	0	0
Totals			55	34	21	8	6	0	0	0

SEAMAN David — Arsenal

Full Name: David Andrew Seaman
DOB: 19/09/63, Rotherham

Previous Club Details

Club	Signed	Fee	Tot	Start	Sub	FA	FL	Lge	FA	FL
Leeds U.	Sep-81	App						0	0	0
Peterborough	Aug-82	£4k	91	91	0	5	10	0	0	0
Birmingham C.	Oct-84	£100k	75	75	0	5	4	0	0	0
QPR	Aug-86	£225k	141	141	0	17	13	0	0	0
Arsenal	May-90	£1.3m	280	280	0	36	31	0	0	0

FAPL Summary by Club

Club			Tot	Start	Sub	FA	FL	Lge	FA	FL
Arsenal 92/3 to 97/8			200	200	0	21	30	0	0	0
Totals			200	200	0	21	30	0	0	0

SEDLOSKI Goce — Sheffield Wednesday

Full Name: Goce Sedloski
DOB: 10/4/74, Macedonia

Previous Club Details

Club	Signed	Fee	Tot	Start	Sub	FA	FL	Lge	FA	FL
Hajduk Split										

Newcastle United

Club	Signed	Fee	Tot	Start	Sub	FA	FL	Lge	FA	FL
Sheffield W.	Feb-98	£750k	4	3	1	0	0	0	0	
FAPL Summary by Club										
Sheffield W.	*1997-98*		*4*	*3*		*1*	*0*	*0*	*0*	*0*
Totals			*4*	*3*		*1*	*0*	*0*	*0*	*0*

Leeds United

SHARPE Lee

Full Name: Lee Stuart Sharpe
DOB: 27/05/71, Halesowen
Previous Club Details

				Apps				Goals		
Club	Signed	Fee	Tot	Start	Sub	FA	FL	Lge	FA	FL
Torquay U.	May-88		14	9	5	0	0	3	0	0
Manchester U.	May-88	£185k	193	160	33	29	23	21	1	3
Leeds U.	Jul-96	£4.5m	26	26	0	1	3	5	0	1
FAPL Summary by Club										
Manchester U.	*92/3 to 95/6*		*116*	*100*	*16*	*19*	*8*	*17*	*3*	*2*
Leeds U.	*1996-97*		*26*	*26*	*0*	*1*	*3*	*5*	*0*	*1*
Totals			*142*	*126*	*16*	*20*	*11*	*22*	*3*	*3*

SHAW Richard

Full Name: Richard Edward Shaw
DOB: 11/09/68, Brentford
Previous Club Details

Coventry City

				Apps				Goals		
Club	Signed	Fee	Tot	Start	Sub	FA	FL	Lge	FA	FL
C. Palace	Sep-86	App	207	193	14	18	30	3	0	0
Hull C.	Dec-89	Loan	4	4	0	0	0	0	0	0
Coventry C.	Nov-95	£1m	89	89	0	10	7	0	0	0
FAPL Summary by Club										
C. Palace	*92/3 to 94/5*		*74*	*73*	*1*	*9*	*11*	*0*	*0*	*0*
Coventry C.	*95/6 to 97/8*		*89*	*89*	*0*	*10*	*7*	*0*	*0*	*0*
Totals			*163*	*162*	*1*	*19*	*18*	*0*	*0*	*0*

Newcastle United

SHEARER Alan

Full Name: Alan Shearer
DOB: 13/08/70, Newcastle
Previous Club Details

				Apps				Goals		
Club	Signed	Fee	Tot	Start	Sub	FA	FL	Lge	FA	FL
Southampton	Apr-88		118	105	13	14	18	23	4	11
Blackburn R.	Jul-92	£3.6m	138	132	6	8	16	112	2	14
Newcastle U.	Jul-96	£15m	48	46	2	9	1	27	1	1
FAPL Summary by Club										
Blackburn R.	*92/3 to 95/6*		*138*	*132*	*6*	*8*	*16*	*112*	*2*	*12*
Newcastle U.	*96/7 to 97/8*		*48*	*46*	*2*	*9*	*1*	*27*	*1*	*1*
Totals			*186*	*178*	*8*	*17*	*17*	*139*	*3*	*13*

SHEPHERD Paul

Full Name: Paul Shepherd
DOB: 17/11/77, Leeds
Previous Club Details

Leeds United

				Apps				Goals		
Club	Signed	Fee	Tot	Start	Sub	FA	FL	Lge	FA	FL
Leeds U.			1	1	0	0	0	0	0	0
FAPL Summary by Club										
Leeds U.	*1996-97*		*1*	*1*	*0*	*0*	*0*	*0*	*0*	*0*
Totals			*1*	*1*	*0*	*0*	*0*	*0*	*0*	*0*

SHERINGHAM Teddy

Manchester United

Full Name: Edward Paul Sheringham
DOB: 02/04/66, Walthamstow
Previous Club Details

				Apps				Goals		
Club	Signed	Fee	Tot	Start	Sub	FA	FL	Lge	FA	FL
Millwall	Jan-84	App	220	205	15	12	17	93	5	8
Aldershot	Feb-85	Loan	5	4	1	0	4	0	0	0
N. Forest	Jul-91	£2m	42	42	0	4	10	14	2	5
Tottenham H.	Aug-92	£2.1m	166	163	3	17	14	76	13	7
Manchester U.	Jun-97	£3.5m	30	27	3	3	3	9	5	0

(SHERINGHAM — continued)

FAPL Summary by Club

Club	Period	Tot	Start	Sub	FA	FL	Lge	FA	FL
N. Forest	1992-93	3	3	0	0	0	1	0	0
Tottenham H.	92/3 to 96/7	166	163	3	22	18	75	17	12
Manchester U.	1997-98	30	27	3	3	0	5	0	0
Totals		*199*	*193*	*6*	*25*	*18*	*85*	*22*	*12*

SHERWOOD Tim — Blackburn Rovers

Full Name: Timothy Alan Sherwood
DOB: 06/02/69, St Albans

Previous Club Details

Club	Signed	Fee	Tot	Start	Sub	FA	FL	Lge	FA	FL
Watford	Feb-87	Train	32	23	9	9	5	2		
Norwich C.	Jul-89	£175k	71	66	5	5	4	7	1	0
Blackburn R.	Feb-92	£500k	227	220	7	17	24	22	4	1

FAPL Summary by Club

Club	Period	Tot	Start	Sub	FA	FL	Lge	FA	FL
Blackburn R.	92/3 to 97/8	217	214	3	17	23	22	4	1
Totals		*217*	*214*	*3*	*17*	*23*	*22*	*4*	*1*

SHILTON Sam — Coventry City

Full Name: Sam Shilton
DOB: 21/07/78, Nottingham

Previous Club Details

Club	Signed	Fee	Tot	Start	Sub	FA	FL	Lge	FA	FL
Plymouth Ar.	Sby		2	2	0	0	0	0	0	0
Coventry C.										

FAPL Summary by Club

Club	Period	Tot	Start	Sub	FA	FL	Lge	FA	FL
Coventry C.	1997-98	2	2	0	0	0	0	0	0
Totals		*2*	*2*	*0*	*0*	*0*	*0*	*0*	*0*

SHORT Craig — Everton

Full Name: Craig Jonathan Short
DOB: 25/06/68, Bridlington

Previous Club Details

Club	Signed	Fee	Tot	Start	Sub	FA	FL	Lge	FA	FL
Scarborough	Oct-87	NL	63	61	2	2	6	0	1	0
Notts Co	Jul-89	£100k	128	128	0	8	6	8	1	1
Derby Co.	Sep-92	£2.5m	118	118	0	7	11	9	4	0
Everton	Jul-95	£2.7m	77	68	9	4	5	4	0	0

FAPL Summary by Club

Club	Period	Tot	Start	Sub	FA	FL	Lge	FA	FL
Everton	95/6 to 97/8	77	68	9	4	5	4	0	0
Totals		*77*	*68*	*9*	*4*	*5*	*4*	*0*	*0*

SINCLAIR Trevor — West Ham United

Full Name: Trevor Sinclair
DOB: 02/03/73, Dulwich

Previous Club Details

Club	Signed	Fee	Tot	Start	Sub	FA	FL	Lge	FA	FL
Blackpool	Aug-90	Train	112	84	28	7	8	15	1	3
QPR *	Aug-93		102	99	3	4	9	7	0	0
West Ham U.	Jan-98	£2.3m	14	14	0	0	0	0	0	0

FAPL Summary by Club

Club	Period	Tot	Start	Sub	FA	FL	Lge	FA	FL
QPR	93/4 to 95/6	102	99	3	4	9	6	0	0
West Ham U.	1997-98	14	14	0	0	0	0	0	0
Totals		*116*	*113*	*3*	*4*	*9*	*6*	*0*	*0*

SINCLAIR Frank — Chelsea

Full Name: Frank Mohammed Sinclair
DOB: 03/12/71, Lambeth

Previous Club Details

Club	Signed	Fee	Tot	Start	Sub	FA	FL	Lge	FA	FL
Chelsea	May-90	Train	169	163	6	18	17	7	1	2
WBA	Dec-91	Lcan	6	6	0	0	1	0	0	0

FAPL Summary by Club

Club			Apps					Goals		
			Tot	Start	Sub	FA	FL	Lge	FA	FL
Chelsea	92/3 to 97/8		157	151	6	17	18	6	1	2
Totals			*157*	*151*	*6*	*17*	*18*	*6*	*1*	*2*

SINTON Andy — Tottenham Hotspur

Full Name: Andrew Sinton
DOB: 19/03/66, Newcastle

Previous Club Details

Club	Signed	Fee	Apps					Goals		
			Tot	Start	Sub	FA	FL	Lge	FA	FL
Cambridge U.	Apr-83	App	93	90	3	11	6	13	6	1
Brentford	Dec-85	£25k	149	149	0	13	14	28	2	3
QPR	Mar-89	£350k	160	160	0	13	5	23	6	0
Sheffield W.	Aug-93	£2.75m	60	54	6	2	3	6	0	0
Tottenham H.	Jan-96	£1.5m	61	54	7	4	10	3	0	0

FAPL Summary by Club

Club			Apps					Goals		
			Tot	Start	Sub	FA	FL	Lge	FA	FL
QPR	1992-93		36	36	0	2	4	7	0	0
Sheffield W.	93/4 to 95/6		60	54	6	2	3	6	0	0
Tottenham H.	95/6 to 97/8		61	54	7	4	10	3	0	0
Totals			*157*	*144*	*13*	*8*	*17*	*16*	*0*	*0*

SOLIS Mauricio — Derby County

Full Name: Mauricio Mora Solis
DOB: 13/12/72, Costa Rica

Previous Club Details

Club	Signed	Fee	Apps					Goals		
			Tot	Start	Sub	FA	FL	Lge	FA	FL
CS Heridiano										
Derby Co.	Mar-97	£600k	11	3	8	0	0	0	0	0

FAPL Summary by Club

Club			Apps					Goals		
			Tot	Start	Sub	FA	FL	Lge	FA	FL
Derby Co.	96/7 to 97/8		11	3	8	0	0	0	0	0
Totals			*11*	*3*	*8*	*0*	*0*	*0*	*0*	*0*

SOLSKJAER Ole Gunnar — Manchester United

Full Name: Ole Gunnar Solskjaer
DOB: 26/02/73, Kristiansund

Previous Club Details

Club	Signed	Fee	Apps					Goals		
			Tot	Start	Sub	FA	FL	Lge	FA	FL
Molde	1995		26	26	0	0	0	20	0	0
Manchester U.	Jul-96	£1.5m	55	40	15	5	5	24	0	0

FAPL Summary by Club

Club			Apps					Goals		
			Tot	Start	Sub	FA	FL	Lge	FA	FL
Manchester U.	96/7 to 97/8		55	40	15	5	5	24	0	0
Totals			*55*	*40*	*15*	*5*	*5*	*24*	*0*	*0*

SOLTVEDT Trond — Coventry City

Full Name: Trond Egil Soltvedt
DOB: 15/02/67, Norway

Previous Club Details

Club	Signed	Fee	Apps					Goals		
			Tot	Start	Sub	FA	FL	Lge	FA	FL
Rosenborg										
Coventry C.	Jun-97	£500k	30	26	4	4	2	1	0	0

FAPL Summary by Club

Club			Apps					Goals		
			Tot	Start	Sub	FA	FL	Lge	FA	FL
Coventry C.	1997-98		30	26	4	4	2	1	0	0
Totals			*30*	*26*	*4*	*4*	*2*	*1*	*0*	*0*

SOUTHGATE Gareth — Aston Villa

Full Name: Gareth Southgate
DOB: 03/09/70, Watford

Previous Club Details

Club	Signed	Fee	Apps					Goals		
			Tot	Start	Sub	FA	FL	Lge	FA	FL
C. Palace	Jan-89	Train	152	148	4	9	24	15	0	1
Aston Villa	Jul-95	£2.5m	91	91	0	10	10	2	0	1

FAPL Summary by Club

Club			Apps					Goals		
			Tot	Start	Sub	FA	FL	Lge	FA	FL
C. Palace	92/3 to 94/5		75	75	0	8	13	4	0	4
Aston Villa	95/6 to 97/8		91	91	0	10	10	2	0	1
Totals			*166*	*166*	*0*	*18*	*23*	*6*	*0*	*5*

SPEED Gary — Newcastle United

Full Name: Gary Andrew Speed
DOB: 08/09/69, Hawarden

Previous Club Details				*Apps*					*Goals*	
Club	Signed	Fee	Tot	Start	Sub	FA	FL	Lge	FA	FL
Leeds U.	Jun-88	Train	248	231	17	21	26	39	5	11
Everton	Jul-96	£3.5m	58	58	0	2	5	16	1	1
Newcastle U.	Feb-98	£5.5m	13	13	0	4	0	1	0	0
FAPL Summary by Club										
Leeds U.	92/3 to 95/6		143	142	1	11	14	22	5	5
Everton	96/7 to 97/8		58	58	0	2	5	16	1	1
Newcastle U.	1997-98		13	13	0	4	0	1	0	0
Totals			*214*	*213*	*1*	*17*	*19*	*39*	*6*	*6*

SPENCER John — Everton

Full Name: John Spencer
DOB: 11/09/70, Glasgow

Previous Club Details				*Apps*					*Goals*	
Club	Signed	Fee	Tot	Start	Sub	FA	FL	Lge	FA	FL
Rangers	1989	Jnrs	13	7	6	0	2	2	0	0
Morton	Mar-89	Loan	4	4	0	0	0	1	0	0
Chelsea	Aug-92	£450k	103	75	28	20	9	26	4	2
QPR *	Nov-96	£2.5m								
Everton			6	3	3	0	0	0	0	0
FAPL Summary by Club										
Chelsea	92-93 to 96-97		103	75	28	20	9	36	4	2
Everton	1997-98		6	3	3	0	0	0	0	0
Totals			*109*	*78*	*31*	*20*	*9*	*36*	*4*	*2*

SRNICEK Pavel — Newcastle United

Full Name: Pavel Srnicek
DOB: 10/03/68, Ostrava, Czechoslovakia

Previous Club Details				*Apps*					*Goals*	
Club	Signed	Fee	Tot	Start	Sub	FA	FL	Lge	FA	FL
Banik Ostrava										
Newcastle U.	Feb-91	£350k	149	148	1	11	11	0	0	0
FAPL Summary by Club										
Newcastle U.	93/4 to 97/8		97	96	1	7	9	0	0	0
Totals			*97*	*96*	*1*	*7*	*9*	*0*	*0*	*0*

STAUNTON Steve — Aston Villa

Full Name: Stephen Staunton
DOB: 19/01/69, Drogheda

Previous Club Details				*Apps*					*Goals*	
Club	Signed	Fee	Tot	Start	Sub	FA	FL	Lge	FA	FL
Liverpool	Sep-86	£20k	65	55	10	16	8	0	1	4
Bradford C.	Nov-87	Loan	8	7	1	0	2	0	0	0
Aston Villa	Aug-91	£1.1m	208	205	3	20	19	16	1	1
FAPL Summary by Club										
Aston Villa	92/3 to 97/8		171	168	3	16	17	13	1	1
Totals			*171*	*168*	*3*	*16*	*17*	*13*	*1*	*1*

STEFANOVIC Dejan — Sheffield Wednesday

Full Name: Dejan Stefanovic
DOB: 28/10/74, Yugoslavia

Previous Club Details				*Apps*					*Goals*	
Club	Signed	Fee	Tot	Start	Sub	FA	FL	Lge	FA	FL
Red Star Belgrade										
Sheffield W.	Dec-95	£2m	55	51	4	2	2	4	0	0
FAPL Summary by Club										
Sheffield W.	95/6 to 97/8		55	51	4	2	2	4	0	0
Totals			*55*	*51*	*4*	*2*	*2*	*4*	*0*	*0*

STIMAC Igor — Derby County

Full Name: Igor Stimac
DOB: 06/09/67

Previous Club Details

Club	Signed	Fee
Hajduk Split, Cadiz, Hajduk Split		
Derby Co.	Oct-95	£1.5m

Club		Apps		FA	FL		Goals	
	Tot	Start	Sub			Lge	FA	FL
	70	70	0	12	9	3	0	0

FAPL Summary by Club

Club		Apps		FA	FL		Goals	
	Tot	Start	Sub			Lge	FA	FL
Derby Co. 96/7 to 97/8	43	43	0	11	9	2	0	0
Totals	*43*	*43*	*0*	*11*	*9*	*2*	*0*	*0*

STONE Steve — Nottingham Forest

Full Name: Steven Brian Stone
DOB: 20/08/71, Gateshead

Previous Club Details

Club	Signed	Fee
N. Forest	May-89	Train

Club		Apps		FA	FL		Goals	
	Tot	Start	Sub			Lge	FA	FL
N. Forest	166	164	2	10	14	18	8	0

FAPL Summary by Club

Club		Apps		FA	FL		Goals	
	Tot	Start	Sub			Lge	FA	FL
N. Forest 92/3 to 96/7	92	91	1	8	7	13	0	0
Totals	*92*	*91*	*1*	*8*	*7*	*13*	*0*	*0*

STRACHAN Gavin — Coventry City

Full Name: Gavin Strachan
DOB: 23/12/78, Aberdeen

Previous Club Details

Club	Signed	Fee
Coventry C.	Train	

Club		Apps		FA	FL		Goals	
	Tot	Start	Sub			Lge	FA	FL
Coventry C.	9	2	7	4	0	0	0	0

FAPL Summary by Club

Club		Apps		FA	FL		Goals	
	Tot	Start	Sub			Lge	FA	FL
Coventry C. 1997-98	9	2	7	4	0	0	0	0
Totals	*9*	*2*	*7*	*4*	*0*	*0*	*0*	*0*

STURRIDGE Dean — Derby County

Full Name: Dean Constantine Sturridge
DOB: 27/07/73, Birmingham

Previous Club Details

Club	Signed	Fee
Derby Co.	Jul-91	Train
Torquay U.	Dec-94	Loan

Club		Apps		FA	FL		Goals	
	Tot	Start	Sub			Lge	FA	FL
Derby Co.	122	102	20	9	13	41	2	2
Torquay U.	10	10	0					

FAPL Summary by Club

Club		Apps		FA	FL		Goals	
	Tot	Start	Sub			Lge	FA	FL
Derby Co. 96/7 to 97/8	60	53	7	9	13	20	2	2
Totals	*60*	*53*	*7*	*9*	*13*	*20*	*2*	*2*

SULLIVAN Neil — Wimbledon

Full Name: Neil Sullivan
DOB: 24/02/70, Sutton

Previous Club Details

Club	Signed	Fee
Wimbledon	Jul-88	Train
C. Palace	May-92	Loan

Club		Apps		FA	FL		Goals	
	Tot	Start	Sub			Lge	FA	FL
Wimbledon	106	105	1	20	8	0	0	0
C. Palace	1	1	0	0	0	0	0	0

FAPL Summary by Club

Club		Apps		FA	FL		Goals	
	Tot	Start	Sub			Lge	FA	FL
Wimbledon 92/3 to 97/8	104	103	1	20	8	0	0	0
Totals	*104*	*103*	*1*	*20*	*8*	*0*	*0*	*0*

SUTTON Chris — Blackburn Rovers

Full Name: Christopher Roy Sutton
DOB: 10/03/73, Nottingham

Previous Club Details

Club	Signed	Fee
Norwich C.	Jul-91	Train
Blackburn R.	Jul-94	£5m

Club		Apps		FA	FL		Goals	
	Tot	Start	Sub			Lge	FA	FL
Norwich C.	102	89	13	10	9	35	5	3
Blackburn R.	113	108	5	8	11	44	4	5

FAPL Summary by Club

Club		Apps		FA	FL		Goals	
	Tot	Start	Sub			Lge	FA	FL
Norwich C. 92/3 to 93/4	79	73	6	4	7	33	2	3
Blackburn R. 94/5 to 97/8	113	108	5	8	11	44	4	6
Totals	*192*	*181*	*11*	*12*	*18*	*77*	*6*	*6*

TAYLOR Ian — Aston Villa

Full Name: Ian Kenneth Taylor
DOB: 04/06/68, Birmingham

Previous Club Details

			Apps					Goals		
Club	Signed	Fee	Tot	Start	Sub	FA	FL	Lge	FA	FL
Port Vale	Jul-92	£15k NL	83	83		6	4	28	1	2
Sheffield W.	Jul-94	£1m	14	9	5	0	4	1	0	1
Aston Villa	Dec-94	£1m	113	105	8	8	9	12	1	1

FAPL Summary by Club

Club			Tot	Start	Sub	FA	FL	Lge	FA	FL
Sheffield W.	1994-95		14	9	5	0	4	1	0	1
Aston Villa	94/5 to 97/8		113	105	8	8	9	12	1	1
Totals			127	114	13	8	13	13	1	2

TELFER Paul — Coventry City

Full Name: Paul Norman Telfer
DOB: 21/10/71, Edinburgh

Previous Club Details

			Apps					Goals		
Club	Signed	Fee	Tot	Start	Sub	FA	FL	Lge	FA	FL
Luton Town	Nov-88	Train	144	136	8	14	5	19	2	0
Coventry C.	Jul-95	£1.5m	98	95	3	11	10	4	3	2

FAPL Summary by Club

Club			Tot	Start	Sub	FA	FL	Lge	FA	FL
Coventry C.	95/6 to 97/8		98	95	3	11	10	4	3	2
Totals			98	95	3	11	10	4	3	2

THATCHER Ben — Wimbledon

Full Name: Benjamin David Thatcher
DOB: 30/11/75, Swindon

Previous Club Details

			Apps					Goals		
Club	Signed	Fee	Tot	Start	Sub	FA	FL	Lge	FA	FL
Millwall	Jun-96	Train	90	87	3	7	6	1	0	0
Wimbledon	Jul-96	£1.8m	35	32	3	3	3	0	0	0

FAPL Summary by Club

Club			Tot	Start	Sub	FA	FL	Lge	FA	FL
Wimbledon	96/7 to 97/8		35	32	3	3	3	0	0	0
Totals			35	32	3	3	3	0	0	0

THOMAS Tony — Everton

Full Name: Anthony Thomas
DOB: 12/07/71, Liverpool

Previous Club Details

			Apps					Goals		
Club	Signed	Fee	Tot	Start	Sub	FA	FL	Lge	FA	FL
Tranmere R.	Feb-89	Train	257	254	3	7	24	12	0	1
Everton			7	6	1	1	1	0	0	0

FAPL Summary by Club

Club			Tot	Start	Sub	FA	FL	Lge	FA	FL
Everton	1997-98		7	6	1	1	1	0	0	0
Totals			7	6	1	1	1	0	0	0

THOMAS Geoff — Nottingham Forest

Full Name: Geoffrey Thomas
DOB: 05/08/64, Manchester

Previous Club Details

			Apps					Goals		
Club	Signed	Fee	Tot	Start	Sub	FA	FL	Lge	FA	FL
Rochdale	Aug-82	Free NL	11	10	1			1		
Crewe Alex.	Mar-84	Free	125	120	5	2	8	20	0	3
C. Palace	Jun-87	£50k	195	192	3	14	26	26	2	3
Wolver'n W.	Jun-93	£800k	46	36	10	1	8	0	1	0
Nottingham F.			19	13	6		3	0	1	

FAPL Summary by Club

Club			Tot	Start	Sub	FA	FL	Lge	FA	FL
C. Palace	1992-93		29	28	1			2	0	0
Totals			29	28	1			2	0	0

THOMAS Michael — Liverpool

Full Name: Michael Lauriston Thomas
DOB: 24/08/67, Lambeth

Previous Club Details

			Apps					Goals		
Club	Signed	Fee	Tot	Start	Sub	FA	FL	Lge	FA	FL
Arsenal	Dec-84	App	163	149	14	17	23	24	1	5
Portsmouth	Dec-86	Loan	3	3	0			0	0	0
Liverpool	Dec-91	£1.5m	123	95	28	17	10	10	2	1

FAPL Summary by Club

Club	Tot	Start	Sub	FA	FL	Lge	FA	FL
Liverpool 92/3 to 97/8	106	79	27	13	10	6	0	1
Totals	*106*	*79*	*27*	*13*	*10*	*6*	*0*	*1*

THOME Emerson — Sheffield Wednesday

Full Name: Emerson Thome
DOB: Brazil

Previous Club Details

Club	Signed	Fee	Tot	Start	Sub	FA	FL	Lge	FA	FL
Benfica										
Sheffield W.	Mar-98	Free	6	6	0			0	0	0

FAPL Summary by Club

Club	Tot	Start	Sub	FA	FL	Lge	FA	FL
Sheffield W. 1997-98	6	6	0			0	0	0
Totals	*6*	*6*	*0*			*0*	*0*	*0*

THOMPSON David — Liverpool

Full Name: David Thompson
DOB: 12/09/77, Birkenhead

Previous Club Details

Club	Signed	Fee	Tot	Start	Sub	FA	FL	Lge	FA	FL
Liverpool		Train	8	2	6	0	1	0	0	0

FAPL Summary by Club

Club	Tot	Start	Sub	FA	FL	Lge	FA	FL
Liverpool 96/7 to 97/8	8	2	6	0	1	0	0	0
Totals	*8*	*2*	*6*	*0*	*1*	*0*	*0*	*0*

THOMPSON Alan — Aston Villa

Full Name: Alan Thompson
DOB: 22/12/73, Newcastle

Previous Club Details

Club	Signed	Fee	Tot	Start	Sub	FA	FL	Lge	FA	FL
Newcastle U.	Mar-91	Train	16	13	3	1		1	0	0
Bolton W.	Jul-93	£250k	157	143	14	8	25	34	2	5
Aston Villa	Jul-98	£4.5m								

FAPL Summary by Club

Club	Tot	Start	Sub	FA	FL	Lge	FA	FL
Bolton W. 95/6 to 97/8	59	56	3	2	9	10	0	2
Totals	*59*	*56*	*3*	*2*	*9*	*10*	*0*	*2*

THOMSEN Claus — Everton

Full Name: Claus Thomsen
DOB: 31/05/70, Aarhus, Denmark

Previous Club Details

Club	Signed	Fee	Tot	Start	Sub	FA	FL	Lge	FA	FL
AGF Aarhus	1990		96	95	1			13		
Ipswich Town	Jun-94	£250k	81	77	4	5	8	7	1	0
Everton	Jan-97	£900k	24	17	7	1	1	0	0	0

FAPL Summary by Club

Club	Tot	Start	Sub	FA	FL	Lge	FA	FL
Ipswich Town 1994-95	33	31	2	1	2	5	0	0
Everton 96/7 to 97/8	24	17	7	1	4	5	0	0
Totals	*57*	*48*	*9*	*2*	*6*	*10*	*0*	*0*

THORN Andy — Wimbledon

Full Name: Andrew Charles Thorn
DOB: 12/11/66, Carshalton

Previous Club Details

Club	Signed	Fee	Tot	Start	Sub	FA	FL	Lge	FA	FL
Wimbledon	Nov-84	App	107	106	1	9	7	4	2	0
Newcastle U.	Aug-88	£850k	36	36	0	2	4	0	1	0
C. Palace	Dec-89	£650k	128	128	0	10	19	3	0	4
Wimbledon	Oct-94	Free	37	33	4	3	2	1	0	0

FAPL Summary by Club

Club	Tot	Start	Sub	FA	FL	Lge	FA	FL
C. Palace 1992-93	34	34	0			0	1	0
Wimbledon 94/5 to 95/6	37	33	4	3	8	1	0	0
Totals	*71*	*67*	*4*	*3*	*8*	*1*	*1*	*0*

THORNLEY Ben — Manchester United

Full Name: Benjamin Lindsay Thornley
DOB: 21/04/75, Bury

[continued entry]

Everton

Previous Club Details

Club	Signed	Fee	Tot	Start	Sub	FA	FL	Lge	FA	FL
Manchester U.	Jan-93	Train	9	1	8	2	3	0	0	0
Stockport Co.	Nov-95	Loan	10	8	2	0	1	2	0	0
Huddersfield	Feb-96	Loan	12	12	0	2	0	1	0	0

FAPL Summary by Club

Club			Tot	Start	Sub	FA	FL	Lge	FA	FL
Manchester U. 93/4 to 97/98			9	1	8	2	3	0	0	0
Totals			*9*	*1*	*8*	*2*	*3*	*0*	*0*	*0*

TILER Carl

Full Name: Carl Tiler
DOB: 11/01/70, Sheffield

Everton

Previous Club Details

Club	Signed	Fee	Tot	Start	Sub	FA	FL	Lge	FA	FL
Barnsley	Aug-88	Train	71	67	4	5	4	3	0	0
N. Forest	May-91	£1.4m	69	67	2	6	11	1	0	0
Swindon Town	Nov-94	Loan	2	2	0	0	0	0	0	0
Aston Villa	Oct-95	£750k	14	12	2	2	1	1	0	0
Sheffield U.	Mar-97	£650k	10	10	0	0	0	0	0	0
Everton	Nov-97	Swap	19	19	0	1	0	0	0	0

FAPL Summary by Club

Club			Tot	Start	Sub	FA	FL	Lge	FA	FL
N. Forest 92/3 to 94/5			40	40	0	5	5	1	0	0
Aston Villa 95/6 to 96/7			12	10	2	2	1	1	0	0
Everton 1997-98			19	19	0	1	0	0	0	0
Totals			*71*	*69*	*2*	*8*	*6*	*2*	*0*	*0*

TISDALE Paul

Full Name: Paul Tisdale
DOB: 14/01/73, Malta

Southampton

Previous Club Details

Club	Signed	Fee	Tot	Start	Sub	FA	FL	Lge	FA	FL
Southampton	Jun-91	Jnr	16	5	11	5	2	1	0	0
Northampton	Mar-92	Loan	5	5	0	0	0	0	0	0
Huddersfield	Nov-96	Loan								

[continued entry]

Southampton

Club	Signed	Fee	Tot	Start	Sub	FA	FL	Lge	FA	FL
Ipswich T.	Jan-97	Loan								

FAPL Summary by Club

Club			Tot	Start	Sub	FA	FL	Lge	FA	FL
Southampton 94/5 to 95/6			15	5	10	1	1	1	0	0
Totals			*15*	*5*	*10*	*1*	*1*	*1*	*0*	*0*

TODD Lee

Full Name: Lee Todd
DOB: 07/03/72, Hartlepool

Southampton

Previous Club Details

Club	Signed	Fee	Tot	Start	Sub	FA	FL	Lge	FA	FL
Stockport Co.	Jul-90	Free	225	214	11	17	26	1	1	0
Southampton			10	9	1	0	1	0	0	0

FAPL Summary by Club

Club			Tot	Start	Sub	FA	FL	Lge	FA	FL
Southampton 1997-98			10	9	1	0	1	0	0	0
Totals			*10*	*9*	*1*	*0*	*1*	*0*	*0*	*0*

TOWNSEND Andy

Full Name: Andrew David Townsend
DOB: 23/07/63, Maidstone

Middlesbrough

Previous Club Details

Club	Signed	Fee	Tot	Start	Sub	FA	FL	Lge	FA	FL
Southampton	Jan-85	£35k	83	77	6	5	8	6	4	0
Norwich C.	Aug-88	£300k	71	66	5	10	4	8	2	0
Chelsea	Jul-90	£1.2m	110	110	0	7	17	12	0	7
Aston Villa	Jul-93	£2.1m	131	130	1	12	20	8	3	2
Middlesbro'	Jul-97		38	36	2	3	6	2	0	0

FAPL Summary by Club

Club			Tot	Start	Sub	FA	FL	Lge	FA	FL
Chelsea 1992-93			41	41	0	1	6	4	0	3
Aston Villa 93/4 to 97/8			132	131	1	12	20	8	0	2
Totals			*173*	*172*	*1*	*13*	*26*	*12*	*0*	*5*

ULLATHORNE Robert — Leicester City

Full Name: Robert Ullathorne
DOB: 11/10/71, Wakefield

Previous Club Details

Club	Signed	Fee	Apps					Goals		
			Tot	Start	Sub	FA	FL	Lge	FA	FL
Norwich C.	Jul-90	Train	94	86	8	8	12	7	1	0
Osasuna										
Leicester C.	Feb-97	£600k	6	3	3	0	1	1	0	0

FAPL Summary by Club

Leicester C.	93/4 to 97/8		49	41	8	5	5	3	5	0
Totals			49	41	8	5	5	3	5	0

VAN DER GOUW Rai — Manchester United

Full Name: Raimond Van der Gouw
DOB: 24/03/63, Oldenzaal, Holland

Previous Club Details

Club	Signed	Fee	Apps					Goals		
			Tot	Start	Sub	FA	FL	Lge	FA	FL
Vitesse Arnhem	1990		188	188						
Manchester U.	Jul-96		7	6	1	0	3	0	0	0

FAPL Summary by Club

Manchester U.	96/7 to 97/8		7	6	1	0	3	0	0	0
Totals			7	6	1	0	3	0	0	0

UNSWORTH David — West Ham United

Full Name: David Gerald Unsworth
DOB: 16/10/73, Chorley

Previous Club Details

Club	Signed	Fee	Apps					Goals		
			Tot	Start	Sub	FA	FL	Lge	FA	FL
Everton	Jun-92	Train	116	108	8	7	7	11	0	0
West Ham U.	Aug-97	Swap	32	32	0	4	5	2	0	0

FAPL Summary by Club

Everton	92/3 to 96/7		114	107	7	7	7	10	0	0
West Ham U.	1997-98		32	32	0	4	5	2	0	0
Totals			146	139	7	11	12	12	0	0

VAN DER LAAN Robin — Derby County

Full Name: Robertus Petrus Van Der Laan
DOB: 05/09/68, Schiedam, Holland

Previous Club Details

Club	Signed	Fee	Apps					Goals		
			Tot	Start	Sub	FA	FL	Lge	FA	FL
Wageningen										
Port Vale	Feb-91	£80k	176	154	22	10	12	24	1	1
Derby Co.	Aug-95	£475k	65	51	4	2	7	8	3	0
Wolverh'n W.	Oct-96	Loan	7	7	0	0	0	0	0	0

FAPL Summary by Club

Derby Co.	96/7 to 97/8		26	22	4	1	4	2	3	0
Totals			26	22	4	1	4	2	3	0

UPSON Mathew — Arsenal

Full Name: Mathew James Upson
DOB: 18/04/79, Hartismere

Previous Club Details

Club	Signed	Fee	Apps					Goals		
			Tot	Start	Sub	FA	FL	Lge	FA	FL
Luton Town	Apr-96	Train	1	0	1	0	0	0	0	0
Arsenal	May-97	£1m	5	5	0	1	2	0	0	0

FAPL Summary by Club

Arsenal	1997-98		5	5	0	1	2	0	0	0
Totals			5	5	0	1	2	0	0	0

VAN HOOIJDONK Pierre — Nottingham Forest

Full Name: Peirre van Hooijdonk
DOB: 29/11/69, Steenbergen, Holland

Previous Club Details

Club	Signed	Fee	Apps					Goals		
			Tot	Start	Sub	FA	FL	Lge	FA	FL
RBC Roosendaal	1993		47	47				35		
NAC Breda										
Celtic	Jan-95	£1.5m	62	61	1	10	4	40	9	3
N. Forest	Mar-97	£3.5m	49	48	1	1	4	30	1	4
Totals			49	48	1	1	4	30	1	4

FAPL Summary by Club (continued)

			Apps					Goals		
Club	Signed	Fee	Tot	Start	Sub	FA	FL	Lge	FA	FL
N. Forest 1996-97			8	8		0	0	1	0	
Totals			*8*	*8*		*0*	*0*	*1*	*0*	

VEGA Ramon — Tottenham Hotspur

Full Name: Ramon Vega
DOB: 14/06/71, Switzerland

Previous Club Details

			Apps					Goals		
Club	Signed	Fee	Tot	Start	Sub	FA	FL	Lge	FA	FL
Grasshopper	1990		156	154	2			13		
Cagliari	Aug-96									
Tottenham H.	Jan-97	£3.75m	33	30	3	3	2	4	0	0

FAPL Summary by Club

	Apps					Goals		
	Tot	Start	Sub	FA	FL	Lge	FA	FL
Tottenham H. 96/7 to 97/8	33	30	3	3	2	4	0	0
Totals	*33*	*30*	*3*	*3*	*2*	*4*	*0*	*0*

VIALLI Gianluca — Chelsea

Full Name: Gianluca Vialli
DOB: 09/07/64, Cremona

Previous Club Details

			Apps					Goals		
Club	Signed	Fee	Tot	Start	Sub	FA	FL	Lge	FA	FL
Cremonese	1980		105					23		
Sampdoria	1984		223					82		
Juventus	Jun-05		102					38		
Chelsea	Jun-96	Free	49	37	12	6	4	20	4	0

FAPL Summary by Club

	Apps					Goals		
	Tot	Start	Sub	FA	FL	Lge	FA	FL
Chelsea 96/7 to 97/8	49	37	12	6	4	20	4	0
Totals	*49*	*37*	*12*	*6*	*4*	*20*	*4*	*0*

VICKERS Steve — Middlesbrough

Full Name: Stephen Vickers
DOB: 13/10/67, Bishop Auckland

Previous Club Details

			Apps					Goals		
Club	Signed	Fee	Tot	Start	Sub	FA	FL	Lge	FA	FL
Tranmere R.	Sep-85		311	310	1	19	21	11	3	5
Middlesbrough	Dec-93	£700k	166	159	7	16	21	7	0	2

FAPL Summary by Club

	Apps					Goals		
	Tot	Start	Sub	FA	FL	Lge	FA	FL
Middlesbrough 95/6 to 96/7	61	58	3	9	12	1	0	2
Totals	*61*	*58*	*3*	*9*	*12*	*1*	*0*	*2*

VIEIRA Patrick — Arsenal

Full Name: Patrick Vieira
DOB: 23/06/76, Dakar, Senegal

Previous Club Details

			Apps					Goals		
Club	Signed	Fee	Tot	Start	Sub	FA	FL	Lge	FA	FL
AS Cannes	1993		36	32	4			2		
Milan	1995		2	1				0		
Arsenal	Aug-96	£3.5m	64	61	3	12	5	4	0	0

FAPL Summary by Club

	Apps					Goals		
	Tot	Start	Sub	FA	FL	Lge	FA	FL
Arsenal 96/7 to 97/8	64	61	3	12	5	4	0	0
Totals	*64*	*61*	*3*	*12*	*5*	*4*	*0*	*0*

WALKER Ian — Tottenham Hotspur

Full Name: Ian Michael Walker
DOB: 31/10/71, Watford

Previous Club Details

			Apps					Goals		
Club	Signed	Fee	Tot	Start	Sub	FA	FL	Lge	FA	FL
Tottenham H.	Dec-89	Train	191	190	1	16	16	0	0	0
Oxford U.	Aug-90	Loan	2	2	0			0	0	0

FAPL Summary by Club

	Apps					Goals		
	Tot	Start	Sub	FA	FL	Lge	FA	FL
Tottenham H. 92/3 to 97/8	172	171	1	16	15	0	0	0
Totals	*172*	*171*	*1*	*16*	*15*	*0*	*0*	*0*

WALKER Des — Sheffield Wednesday

Full Name: Desmond Sinclair Walker
DOB: 26/11/65, Hackney

Previous Club Details

			Apps					Goals		
Club	Signed	Fee	Tot	Start	Sub	FA	FL	Lge	FA	FL
N. Forest	Nov-83		264	259	5	27	40	1	0	0
Sampdoria	Aug-92	£1.5m								

Club	Signed	Fee	Tot	Start	Sub	FA	FL	Lge	FA	FL
Sheffield W.	Jul-93	£2.70m	190	190	0	15	17	0	0	0

FAPL Summary by Club

		Tot	Start	Sub	FA	FL	Lge	FA	FL
Sheffield W.	93/4 to 97/8	190	190		15	17	0	0	0
Totals		190	190		15	17	0	0	0

WALLACE Rod — Leeds United

Full Name: Rodney Seymour Wallace
DOB: 02/10/69, Greenwich

Previous Club Details

				Apps					Goals	
Club	Signed	Fee	Tot	Start	Sub	FA	FL	Lge	FA	FL
Southampton	Apr-88	Train	128	111	17	10	19	45	3	6
Leeds U.	Jun-91	£1.6m	212	187	25	21	19	53	4	8

FAPL Summary by Club

		Tot	Start	Sub	FA	FL	Lge	FA	FL
Leeds U.	92/3 to 97/8	178	153	25	20	16	42	4	6
Totals		178	153	25	20	16	42	4	6

WALSH Steve — Leicester City

Full Name: Steven Walsh
DOB: 03/11/64, Preston

Previous Club Details

				Apps					Goals	
Club	Signed	Fee	Tot	Start	Sub	FA	FL	Lge	FA	FL
Wigan A.	Sep-82	Jnrs	125	123	2	2	6	7	4	0
Leicester C.	Jun-86	£100k	335	330	5	12	32	50	1	3

FAPL Summary by Club

		Tot	Start	Sub	FA	FL	Lge	FA	FL
Leicester C.	94/5 to 97/8	53	50	3	3	9	5	1	0
Totals		53	50	3	3	9	5	1	0

WANCHOPE Paulo — Derby County

Full Name: Paulo Cesar Wanchope
DOB: 31/07/76, Costa Rica

Previous Club Details

				Apps					Goals	
Club	Signed	Fee	Tot	Start	Sub	FA	FL	Lge	FA	FL
CS Heridiano	Mar-97	£600k								
Derby Co.			37	32	5	2	4	14	0	4

FAPL Summary by Club

		Tot	Start	Sub	FA	FL	Lge	FA	FL
Derby Co.	96/7 to 97/8	37	32	5	2	4	14	0	4
Totals		37	32	5	2	4	14	0	4

WARD Mitch — Everton

Full Name: Mitchum David Ward
DOB: 19/06/71, Sheffield

Previous Club Details

				Apps					Goals	
Club	Signed	Fee	Tot	Start	Sub	FA	FL	Lge	FA	FL
Sheffield U.*	Jul-89		148	132	16	9	11	10	2	2
Crewe Alex.	Nov-90	Loan	4	4				0		
Everton	Nov-97	Swap	8	8				0		

FAPL Summary by Club

		Tot	Start	Sub	FA	FL	Lge	FA	FL
Sheffield U.	92/3 to 93/4	48	42	6	5	3	1	2	1
Everton	1997-98	8	8	0	0	1	0		
Totals		56	50	6	5	3	1	2	1

WARNER Vance — Nottingham Forest

Full Name: Vance Warner
DOB: 03/09/74, Leeds

Previous Club Details

				Apps					Goals	
Club	Signed	Fee	Tot	Start	Sub	FA	FL	Lge	FA	FL
N. Forest			5	4	1	0	1	0	0	0
Grimsby T.	Feb-96	Loan	3	3	0	0	0	0	0	0

FAPL Summary by Club

		Tot	Start	Sub	FA	FL	Lge	FA	FL
N. Forest	94/5 to 96/7	4	3	1	0	0	0	0	0
Totals		4	3	1	0	0	0	0	0

WATSON Steve — Newcastle United

Full Name: Stephen Craig Watson
DOB: 01/04/74, North Shields

Previous Club Details

				Apps					Goals	
Club	Signed	Fee	Tot	Start	Sub	FA	FL	Lge	FA	FL
Newcastle U.	Apr-91	Train	201	172	29	17	16	12	0	1

FAPL Summary by Club

			Tot	Start	Sub	FA	FL	Lge	FA	FL
Newcastle U.	93/4 to 97/8		147	126	21	10	16	11	0	0
Totals			*147*	*126*	*21*	*10*	*16*	*11*	*0*	*1*

WATSON David

Barnsley

Full Name: David Neil Watson
DOB: 10/11/73, Barnsley

Previous Club Details

				Apps				*Goals*		
Club	Signed	Fee	Tot	Start	Sub	FA	FL	Lge	FA	FL
Barnsley	Jul-92	Train	172	172	0	11	14	0	0	0

FAPL Summary by Club

			Tot	Start	Sub	FA	FL	Lge	FA	FL
Barnsley	1997-98		30	30	0	6	1	0	0	0
Totals			*30*	*30*	*0*	*6*	*1*	*0*	*0*	*0*

WATSON Dave

Everton

Full Name: David Watson
DOB: 20/11/61, Liverpool

Previous Club Details

				Apps				*Goals*		
Club	Signed	Fee	Tot	Start	Sub	FA	FL	Lge	FA	FL
Liverpool	May-79	Jnrs	0	0	0	0	0	0	0	0
Norwich C.	Nov-80	£100k	212	212	0	18	21	11	1	0
Everton	Aug-86	£900k	395	392	3	46	38	23	5	6

FAPL Summary by Club

			Tot	Start	Sub	FA	FL	Lge	FA	FL
Everton	92/3 to 97/8		195	193	2	14	15	6	2	1
Totals			*195*	*193*	*2*	*14*	*15*	*6*	*2*	*1*

WATTS Julian

Leicester City

Full Name: Julian Watts
DOB: 17/03/71, Sheffield

Previous Club Details

				Apps				*Goals*		
Club	Signed	Fee	Tot	Start	Sub	FA	FL	Lge	FA	FL
Rotherham U.	Jul-90	Train	20	17	3	4	1	1	0	0
Sheffield W.	Mar-92	£80k	15	12	3	0	0	0	0	0
Shrewsbury T.	Dec-92	Loan	9	9	0	0	0	0	0	0
Leicester C.	Mar-96	£210k	37	31	6	3	7	1	0	0

FAPL Summary by Club

			Tot	Start	Sub	FA	FL	Lge	FA	FL
Sheffield W.	92/3 to 95/6		15	12	3	0	1	1	0	0
Leicester C.	96/7 to 97/8		28	22	6	3	7	0	0	0
Totals			*43*	*34*	*9*	*3*	*8*	*2*	*0*	*0*

WETHERALL David

Leeds United

Full Name: David Wetherall
DOB: 14/03/71, Sheffield

Previous Club Details

				Apps				*Goals*		
Club	Signed	Fee	Tot	Start	Sub	FA	FL	Lge	FA	FL
Sheffield W.	Jul-89	Train	0	0	0	0	0	0	0	0
Leeds U.	Jul-91	£125k	181	174	7	20	20	12	3	2

FAPL Summary by Club

			Tot	Start	Sub	FA	FL	Lge	FA	FL
Leeds U.	92/3 to 97/8		180	174	6	20	20	12	3	2
Totals			*180*	*174*	*6*	*20*	*20*	*12*	*3*	*2*

WHELAN Noel

Coventry City

Full Name: Noel Whelan
DOB: 30/12/74, Leeds

Previous Club Details

				Apps				*Goals*		
Club	Signed	Fee	Tot	Start	Sub	FA	FL	Lge	FA	FL
Leeds U.	Mar-93	Train	48	28	20	2	5	7	0	1
Coventry C.	Dec-95	£2m	77	76	1	11	4	20	3	0

FAPL Summary by Club

			Tot	Start	Sub	FA	FL	Lge	FA	FL
Leeds U.	92/3 to 95/6		48	28	20	2	5	7	0	1
Coventry C.	95/6 to 97/8		77	76	1	11	4	20	3	0
Totals			*125*	*104*	*21*	*13*	*9*	*27*	*3*	*1*

WHITTINGHAM Guy — Sheffield Wednesday

Full Name: Guy Whittingham
DOB: 10/11/64, Evesham

Previous Club Details

			Apps					Goals		
Club	Signed	Fee	Tot	Start	Sub	FA	FL	Lge	FA	FL
Portsmouth	Jun-89	NL	160	149	11	10	8	88	10	3
Aston Villa	Jul-93	£1.2m	25	17	8	0	5	5	0	0
Wolver'n W.	Feb-94	Loan	13	13	0	1	0	8	0	0
Sheffield W.	Dec-94	£700k	111	89	22	8	8	22	1	2

FAPL Summary by Club

Aston Villa	93/4 to 94/5		25	17	8	8	5	5	0	1
Sheffield W.	94/5 to 97/8		111	89	22	8	8	22	1	2
Totals			136	106	30	8	13	27	1	3

WILCOX Jason — Blackburn Rovers

Full Name: Jason Malcolm Wilcox
DOB: 15/03/71, Farnworth

Previous Club Details

			Apps					Goals		
Club	Signed	Fee	Tot	Start	Sub	FA	FL	Lge	FA	FL
Blackburn R.	Jun-89	Train	219	198	21	17	17	27	1	0

FAPL Summary by Club

Blackburn R.	92/3 to 97/8		162	149	13	17	15	23	1	0
Totals			162	149	13	17	15	23	1	0

WILLEMS Ron — Derby County

Full Name: Ron Willems
DOB: 20/09/66, Epe, Holland

Previous Club Details

			Apps					Goals		
Club	Signed	Fee	Tot	Start	Sub	FA	FL	Lge	FA	FL
PEC Zwolle			43					7		
FC Twente			85					16		
Ajax			47					15		
Grasshopper			56					18		
Derby Co.	Jul-95	£300k	59	41	18	3	2	13	2	1

FAPL Summary by Club

Derby Co.	96/7 to 97/8		26	10	16	2	0	2	2	0
Totals			26	10	16	2	0	2	2	0

Southampton

WILLIAMS Andy — Southampton

Full Name: Andrew Williams
DOB: 06/10/77, Bristol

Previous Club Details

			Apps					Goals		
Club	Signed	Fee	Tot	Start	Sub	FA	FL	Lge	FA	FL
Southampton	Jul-94	Train	20	3	17	2	0	1	3	0

FAPL Summary by Club

Southampton	1997-98		20	3	17	1	3	0	0	0
Totals			20	3	17	1	3	0	0	0

WILLIAMS Mike — Sheffield Wednesday

Full Name: Michael Anthony Williams
DOB: 21/11/69, Bradford

Previous Club Details

			Apps					Goals		
Club	Signed	Fee	Tot	Start	Sub	FA	FL	Lge	FA	FL
Sheffield W.	Feb-91	NL	23	16	7	0	5	1	0	0
Halifax Town	Dec-92	Loan	9	9	0	0	0	0	0	0

FAPL Summary by Club

Sheffield W.	92/3 to 96/7		23	16	7	0	5	1	0	0
Totals			23	16	7	0	5	1	0	0

WILLIAMS Paul — Coventry City

Full Name: Paul Darren Williams
DOB: 26/03/71, Burton

Previous Club Details

			Apps					Goals		
Club	Signed	Fee	Tot	Start	Sub	FA	FL	Lge	FA	FL
Derby Co.	Jul-89	Train	160	153	7	8	12	25	3	2
Lincoln C.	Nov-89	Loan	3	3	0	0	2	0	0	0
Coventry C.	Aug-95	£750k	84	76	8	6	10	4	0	1

Everton

(continued from previous entry)

			Apps					Goals		
	Signed	Fee	Tot	Start	Sub	FA	FL	Lge	FA	FL
FAPL Summary by Club										
Coventry C.	95/6 to 97/8		84	76	8	6	10	4	0	1
Totals			84	76	8	6	10	4	0	1

WILLIAMSON Danny

Full Name: Daniel Alan Williamson
DOB: 05/12/73, Newham

Previous Club Details

			Apps					Goals		
Club	Signed	Fee	Tot	Start	Sub	FA	FL	Lge	FA	FL
West Ham U.	Jul-92	Train	51	47	4	5	3	5	0	0
Doncaster R.	Oct-93	Loan	13	10	3	2	0	1	2	0
Everton	Aug-97	£1.0m+	15	15	0	3	1	2	0	0
FAPL Summary by Club										
West Ham U.	93/4 to 96/7		51	47	4	5	3	5	0	0
Everton	1997-98		15	15	0	5	5	5	0	0
Totals			66	62	4					

Leicester City

WILSON Stuart

Full Name: Stuart Wilson
DOB: 16/9/77, Leicester

Previous Club Details

			Apps					Goals		
Club	Signed	Fee	Tot	Start	Sub	FA	FL	Lge	FA	FL
Leicester C.	Jul-96	Train	13	0	13	3	1	3	0	0
FAPL Summary by Club										
Leicester C.	96/7 to 97/8		13	0	13	3	1	3	0	0
Totals			13	0	13	3	1	3	0	0

Tottenham Hotspur

WILSON Clive

Full Name: Clive Euclid Aklana Wilson
DOB: 13/11/61, Manchester

Previous Club Details

			Apps					Goals		
Club	Signed	Fee	Tot	Start	Sub	FA	FL	Lge	FA	FL
Manchester C.	Dec-79	Jnrs	109	107	2	10	9	2	0	2
Chester C.	Sep-82	Loan	21	21	0	2	0	2	0	0
Chelsea	Mar-87	£250k	81	68	13	4	6	5	0	0
QPR	Jul-90	£450k	172	170	2	8	16	12	1	1
Tottenham H.	Jun-95	Free	70	67	3	8	7	1	1	0
FAPL Summary by Club										
QPR	92/3 to 94/5		119	119	0	6	10	6	1	1
Tottenham H.	95/6 to 97/8		70	67	3	8	7	2	1	1
Totals			189	186	3	14	16	7	2	1

Arsenal

WINTERBURN Nigel

Full Name: Nigel Winterburn
DOB: 11/12/63, Nuneaton

Previous Club Details

			Apps					Goals		
Club	Signed	Fee	Tot	Start	Sub	FA	FL	Lge	FA	FL
Wimbledon	Sep-83	Free	165	164	1	12	13	8	0	3
Arsenal	May-87	£407k	382	381	1	41	48	8	8	3
FAPL Summary by Club										
Arsenal	92/3 to 97/8		212	211	1	24	29	4	0	1
Totals			212	211	1	24	29	4	0	1

Chelsea

WISE Dennis

Full Name: Dennis Frank Wise
DOB: 15/12/66, Kensington

Previous Club Details

			Apps					Goals		
Club	Signed	Fee	Tot	Start	Sub	FA	FL	Lge	FA	FL
Wimbledon	Mar-85	Free	135	127	8	11	14	27	4	6
Chelsea	Jul-90	£1.6m	244	237	7	25	47	27	6	6
FAPL Summary by Club										
Chelsea	92/3 to 97/8		173	167	6	20	18	27	4	3
Totals			173	167	6	20	18	27	4	3

WOAN Ian — Nottingham Forest

Full Name: Ian Simon Woan
DOB: 14/12/67, Heswall

Previous Club Details

			Apps					Goals		
Club	Signed	Fee	Tot	Start	Sub	FA	FL	Lge	FA	FL
N. Forest	Mar-90	£80k	207	186	21	15	18	31	5	1
FAPL Summary by Club										
N. Forest	92/3 to 96/7		130	124	6	15	9	17	4	0
Totals			*130*	*124*	*6*	*15*	*9*	*17*	*4*	*0*

WRIGHT Ian — Arsenal

Full Name: Ian Edward Wright
DOB: 03/11/63, Woolwich

Previous Club Details

			Apps					Goals		
Club	Signed	Fee	Tot	Start	Sub	FA	FL	Lge	FA	FL
C. Palace	Aug-85	Free	225	206	19	11	19	89	3	9
Arsenal	Sep-91	£2.5m	221	212	9	16	29	128	12	29
FAPL Summary by Club										
Arsenal	92/3 to 97/8		191	182	9	16	26	104	12	27
Totals			*191*	*182*	*9*	*16*	*26*	*104*	*12*	*27*

WREH Chris — Arsenal

Full Name: Christopher Wreh
DOB: 14/05/75, Monrovia

Previous Club Details

			Apps					Goals		
Club	Signed	Fee	Tot	Start	Sub	FA	FL	Lge	FA	FL
Guingamp, Monaco										
Arsenal	Aug-97		16	7	9	6	3	3	1	0
FAPL Summary by Club										
Arsenal	1997-98		16	7	9	6	3	3	1	0
Totals			*16*	*7*	*9*	*6*	*3*	*3*	*1*	*0*

WRIGHT Mark — Liverpool

Full Name: Mark Wright
DOB: 01/08/63, Dorchester on Thames

Previous Club Details

			Apps					Goals		
Club	Signed	Fee	Tot	Start	Sub	FA	FL	Lge	FA	FL
Oxford U.	Aug-80		10	8	2	1	0	0	0	0
Southampton	Mar-82	£80k	170	170	0	17	25	7	1	2
Derby Co.	Aug-87	£760k	144	144	0	5	15	10	0	3
Liverpool	Jul-91	£2.2m	158	156	2	18	16	5	0	1
FAPL Summary by Club										
Liverpool	92/3 to 97/8		137	135	2	9	15	5	0	2
Totals			*137*	*135*	*2*	*9*	*15*	*5*	*0*	*2*

WRIGHT Alan — Aston Villa

Full Name: Alan Geoffrey Wright
DOB: 28/09/71, Ashton-under-Lyme

Previous Club Details

			Apps					Goals		
Club	Signed	Fee	Tot	Start	Sub	FA	FL	Lge	FA	FL
Blackpool	Apr-89	Jnrs	98	91	7	8	12	0	0	0
Blackburn R.	Oct-91	£400k	74	67	7	5	8	1	0	0
Aston Villa	Mar-95	£1m	121	119	2	12	11	3	0	0
FAPL Summary by Club										
Blackburn R.	92/3 to 94/5		41	35	6	4	8	0	0	0
Aston Villa	94/5 to 97/8		121	119	2	12	11	3	0	0
Totals			*162*	*154*	*8*	*16*	*19*	*3*	*0*	*0*

YATES Dean — Derby County

Full Name: Dean Richard Yates
DOB: 26/10/67, Leicester

Previous Club Details

			Apps					Goals		
Club	Signed	Fee	Tot	Start	Sub	FA	FL	Lge	FA	FL
Notts Co.	Jun-85	App	312			20	24	33	3	3
Derby Co.	Jan-95	£350k	68	65	3	3	3	3	0	0

FAPL Summary by Club

Club					*Apps*				*Goals*	
Derby Co.	96/7 to 97/8		19	16	3	2	0	0	0	0
Totals			*19*	*16*	*3*	*2*	*0*	*0*	*0*	*0*

YORKE Dwight

Aston Villa

Full Name: Dwight Yorke
DOB: 03/11/71, Tobago, West Indies

Previous Club Details

Club	Signed	Fee	Tot	Start	Sub	FA	FL	Lge	FA	FL
					Apps				*Goals*	
Aston Villa	Dec-89	£120k	230	194	36	24	22	73	13	8

FAPL Summary by Club

Club			Tot	Start	Sub	FA	FL	Lge	FA	FL
Aston Villa	92/3 to 97/8		178	159	19	17	19	60	9	8
Totals			*178*	*159*	*19*	*17*	*19*	*60*	*9*	*8*

ZAGORAKIS Theo

Leicester City

Full Name: Theo Zagorakis

Previous Club Details

Club	Signed	Fee	Tot	Start	Sub	FA	FL	Lge	FA	FL
					Apps				*Goals*	
PAOK Salonika										
Leicester C.	Feb-98	£750k	14	12	2	2	0	0	1	0

FAPL Summary by Club

Club			Tot	Start	Sub	FA	FL	Lge	FA	FL
Leicester C.	1997-98		14	12	2	2	0	0	1	0
Totals			*14*	*12*	*2*	*2*	*0*	*0*	*1*	*0*

FAPL Summary by Club

Club					*Apps*				*Goals*	
Chelsea	96/7 to 97/8		50	45	5	8	4	16	4	0
Totals			*50*	*45*	*5*	*8*	*4*	*16*	*4*	*0*

ZOLA Gianfranco

Chelsea

Full Name: Gianfranco Zola
DOB: 05/07/66, Oliena (Sardinia)

Previous Club Details

Club	Signed	Fee	Tot	Start	Sub	FA	FL	Lge	FA	FL
					Apps				*Goals*	
Nuorse (C2)	1984		31					10		
Torres (C1)	1986		88					21		
Napoli	1989		105	102	3			32		
Parma	1993		94	93				47		
Chelsea	Nov-96	£4.5m	50	45	5	8	4	16	4	0

A-Z PREMIER LEAGUE MANAGERS

Surname	Forename	Club	St	Start	End	P	W	D	L	F	A	PTS	PPG
ARDILES	Ossie	Tottenham H.	F	Jun-93	Oct-94	54	16	14	24	75	83	62	1.15
ATKINSON	Ron	Aston Villa	F	Jun-91	Nov-94	98	38	27	33	118	114	141	1.44
ATKINSON	Ron	Coventry C.	F	Feb-95	Oct-96	62	17	17	28	56	81	68	1.1.0
ATKINSON	Ron	Sheffield W.	F	Nov-97	Jun-98	24	9	5	10	29	32	32	1.33
BALL	Alan	Southampton	F	Jan-94	Jul-95	60	19	22	19	87	93	79	1.32
BALL	Alan	Manchester C.	F	Jul-95	1996	38	9	11	18	33	58	38	1.00
BARRON	Jim	Aston Villa	C	Nov-94	1996	1	1	0	0	4	3	3	3.00
BASSETT	Dave	Sheffield U.	F	Jan-88	Dec-95	84	22	28	34	96	113	94	1.12
BONDS	Billy	West Ham U.	F	Apr-90	Aug-94	42	13	13	16	47	58	52	1.24
BRANFOOT	Ian	Southampton	F	Jun-91	Jan-94	66	18	14	34	77	97	68	1.03
BURLEY	George	Ipswich T.	F	Dec-94		22	4	2	16	16	53	14	0.64
CLARK	Frank	Nottingham F.	F	May-93	Dec-96	97	38	31	28	136	126	145	1.49
CLOUGH	Brian	Nottingham F.	F	Jan-75	May-93	42	10	10	22	41	62	40	0.95
COPPELL	Steve	Crystal Palace	F	1984	May-93	42	11	5	15	48	61	49	1.17
COPPELL	Steve	Crystal Palace	F	May-97	Mar-98	27	5	8	14	21	41	24	0.89
DALGLISH	Kenny	Blackburn R.	F	Oct-91	May-95	126	72	28	26	211	121	244	1.94
DALGLISH	Kenny	Newcastle U.	F	Jan-97		54	19	17	18	68	60	74	1.37
DEEHAN	John	Norwich C.	F	Jan-94	Jun-09	61	12	23	26	66	89	59	0.97
EVANS	Allan	Leicester C.	C	Nov-94	Dec-94	4	1	1	2	5	7	4	1.00
EVANS	Roy	Liverpool	F	Jan-94		172	83	46	43	280	173	295	1.72
FERGUSON	Alex	Manchester U.	F	Nov-86		240	146	60	34	446	202	498	2.08
FRANCIS	Gerry	QPR	F	Jun-91	Nov-94	56	24	14	18	88	76	86	1.54
FRANCIS	Gerry	Tottenham H.	F	Nov-94	Nov-97	119	43	36	40	156	151	165	1.39
FRANCIS	Trevor	Sheffield W.	F	Jun-91	May-95	126	44	42	40	180	162	174	1.38
GODDARD	Paul	Ipswich T.	C	Dec-94	Dec-94	3	0	1	2	4	7	2	0.67
GORMAN	John	Swindon T.	F	Jun-93	Nov-94	42	5	15	22	47	100	30	0.71

Surname	Forename	Club	St	Start	End	P	W	D	L	F	A	PTS	PPG
GOULD	Bobby	Coventry C.	F	Jun-92	Oct-93	54	16	19	19	66	73	67	1.24
GRAHAM	George	Arsenal	F	May-86	Feb-95	112	41	38	33	132	98	161	1.44
GRAHAM	George	Leeds U.	F	Sep-96		71	26	20	25	80	75	98	1.38
GREGORY	John	Aston Villa	F	Feb-98		11	9	0	2	11	10	27	2.45
GROSS	Christian	Tottenham H.	F	Nov-97		23	8	7	8	27	25	31	1.35
GULLITT	Ruud	Chelsea	PM	Jun-96	Feb-98	64	30	14	20	110	82	104	1.63
HARFORD	Ray	Blackburn R.	F	Jun-95	Oct-96	58	16	21	21	79	89	69	1.19
HARVEY	Colin	Everton	C	Dec-93	Jan-94	7	0	1	6	2	12	1	0.14
HODDLE	Glenn	Chelsea	F	Jun-93	May-96	122	38	41	43	145	152	155	1.27
HODGSON	Ray	Blackburn R.	F	Jun-97		38	16	10	12	57	52	58	1.53
HORTON	Brian	Manchester C.	F	Aug-93	May-95	80	21	30	29	90	108	93	1.16
HOUGHTON	Chris	Tottenham H.	C	Nov-97	Nov-97	1	0	0	1	0	1	0	0.00
HOUSTON	Stuart	Arsenal	C	Feb-95	Jun-95	14	5	2	7	13	17	17	1.21
HOUSTON	Stuart	Arsenal	C	Aug-96	Sep-96	5	2	2	1	9	7	8	1.60
JONES	Dave	Southampton	F	Jul-97		38	14	6	18	50	55	48	1.26
KEEGAN	Kevin	Newcastle U.	F	Feb-92	Jan-97	143	78	30	35	253	147	264	1.85
KENDALL	Howard	Everton	F	Nov-90	Dec-93	60	22	11	27	73	78	77	1.28
KENDALL	Howard	Everton	F	Jul-97	Jul-98	38	9	13	16	41	56	40	1.05
KINNEAR	Joe	Wimbledon	F	Jan-92		240	82	70	88	298	335	316	1.32
LAWRENCE	Lennie	Middlesbrough	F	Jul-91	May-94	42	11	11	20	54	75	44	1.05
LEWINGTON	Ray	Crystal Palace	C	Apr-98	May-98	4	1	1	2	6	11	4	1.00
LITTLE	Brian	Leicester C.	F	May-91	Nov-94	14	2	3	9	14	26	9	0.64
LITTLE	Brian	Aston Villa	F	Nov-94	Feb-98	130	51	36	43	159	136	189	1.45
LIVERMORE/CLEMENCE	Doug/Ray	Tottenham H.	F	May-92	Jun-93	42	16	11	15	60	66	59	1.40
LOMBARDO	Atillio	Crystal Palace	PM	Mar-98	Apr-98	7	2	0	5	10	19	6	0.86
LYALL	John	Ipswich T.	F	May-90	Dec-94	101	24	34	43	101	146	106	1.05
McDERMOTT	Terry	Newcastle U.	C	Jan-97	Jan-97	1	0	1	0	0	2	1	1.00
McFARLAND	Roy	Bolton W.	F	Jun-95	Jan-96	22	2	4	16	21	44	10	0.45
McGHEE	Mark	Leicester C.	F	Dec-94	Dec-95	24	3	7	14	26	47	16	0.67

Surname	Forename	Club	St	Start	End	P	W	D	L	F	A	PTS	PPG
MERRINGTON	Dave	Southampton	F	Jul-95	Jul-96	38	9	11	18	34	52	38	1.00
MORTIMORE	John	Southampton	C	Jan-94	Jan-94	1	1	0	0	1	0	3	3.00
NEAL	Phil	Coventry C.	F	Oct-93	Feb-95	58	18	18	22	54	69	72	1.24
O'NEILL	Martin	Leicester C.	C	Dec-95	May-97	76	25	25	26	97	105	100	1.32
PARKES	Tony	Blackburn R.	C	Oct-96	May-97	28	9	5	14	36	29	38	1.36
PEARCE	Stuart	Nottingham F.	PM	Dec-96	May-97	21	5	9	7	17	30	24	1.14
PERRYMAN	Steve	Tottenham H.	C	Nov-94	Nov-94	1	0	0	1	0	2	0	0.00
PLEAT	David	Sheffield W.	F	Jun-95	Nov-97	89	26	23	35	116	147	106	1.19
PORTERFIELD	Ian	Chelsea	F	Jun-91	Feb-93	29	9	13	10	32	36	37	1.28
REDKNAPP	Harry	West Ham U.	F	Aug-94		156	53	43	63	182	205	199	1.28
REID	Peter	Manchester C.	F	Jun-91	Aug-93	46	15	13	18	57	56	58	1.26
REID	Peter	Sunderland	F	Mar-95		38	10	13	10	35	53	40	1.05
RICE	Pat	Arsenal	C	Sep-96	Sep-96	3	3	0	0	8	1	9	3.00
RIOCH	Bruce	Arsenal	F	Jun-95	Aug-96	38	17	12	9	49	32	63	1.66
ROBSON	Bryan	Middlesbrough	F	May-94		76	21	22	33	86	110	82	1.08
ROYLE	Joe	Oldham A.	F	Jul-82	Nov-94	84	22	23	39	105	142	89	1.06
ROYLE	Joe	Everton	F	Nov-94	Mar-97	97	36	21	30	136	116	139	1.43
SHREEVES	Peter	Sheffield W.	C	Nov-97		1	1	0	0	5	3	3	3.00
SMITH	Alan	Crystal Palace	F	Jun-93	May-95	42	11	12	19	34	49	45	1.07
SMITH	Jim	Derby Co.	F	Jun-95		76	27	20	29	97	107	101	1.33
SOUNESS	Graeme	Liverpool	F	Apr-91	Jan-94	68	28	18	22	106	87	102	1.5
SOUNESS	Graeme	Southampton	F	Jul-96		38	10	11	17	50	56	41	1.08
STRACHAN	Gordon	Coventry C.	F	Oct-96		66	20	19	27	80	84	87	1.32
TODD	Colin	Bolton W.	F	Jan-96		54	15	14	25	59	88	59	1.09
VIALLI	Gianluca	Chelsea	PM	Feb-98		13	6	0	7	19	16	18	1.38
WALKER	Mike	Norwich C.	F	Jun-92	Jan-94	65	31	16	18	97	91	109	1.68
WALKER	Mike	Everton	F	Jan-94	Nov-94	31	6	9	16	29	52	27	0.87
WATSON	Dave	Everton	C	Apr-97	May-97	7	1	3	3	7	12	6	0.86
WEBB	David	Chelsea	F	Feb-93	May-93	13	5	4	4	19	18	19	1.46

Surname	Forename	Club	St	Start	End	P	W	D	L	F	A	PTS	PPG
WENGER	Arsène	Arsenal	F	Oct-96		68	37	18	13	113	57	129	1.90
WILKINS	Ray	QPR	F	Nov-94	1996	108	35	25	48	136	156	130	1.20
WILKINSON	Howard	Leeds U.	F	Oct-88	Sep-96	174	66	53	55	231	214	250	1.44
WILSON	Danny	Barnsley	F	Jun-94		38	10	5	23	37	82	35	0.92

St=Status: F=Full-time, C=Caretaker, PM=Player-Manager

FA Premier League
Stadium Guide

Notes: The following pages contain brief directions to each of the Premiership grounds for the forthcoming season. These are supplemented by maps which provide a generalised picture of the area and roads surrounding the stadium. They do not provide a complete picture of all roads and are not to scale. Use them in conjunction with the directions and they will help you to find your way to the stadium in question.

Stadiums are represented by the football on each map. Local train stations are also shown. Clubs' telephone numbers and those relating to ticket purchase are also provided – note some of these numbers are charged at premium rate. Contact the clubs for further details.

Club	Number	Ticket Details
Arsenal	0171 704 4000	0171 704 4242
Aston Villa	0121 327 2299	0891 121848
Blackburn Rovers	01254 698888	0891 121179
Charlton Athletic	0181 333 4000	0181 333 4010
Chelsea	0171 385 5545	0891 121011
Coventry City	01203 234000	01203 23020
Derby County	01332 340105	01332 672226
Everton	0151 521 2020	0891 121599
Leeds United	0113 271 6037	0891 121180
Leicester City	0115 255 5000	0116 291 5232
Liverpool	0151 263 2361	0151 260 9999
Manchester United	0161 872 1661	0161 872 0199
Middlesbrough	01642 877700	01642 877745
Newcastle United	0191 232 8361	0891 121190
Nottingham Forest	0115 982 4444	0115 982 4445
Sheffield Wednesday	0114 243 3122	0114 233 7233
Southampton	01703 220505	01703 228575
Tottenham Hotspur	0181 365 5000	0181 365 5050
West Ham United	0181 548 2748	0181 548 2700
Wimbledon	0181 771 2233	0181 771 8841

ARSENAL

Arsenal Stadium, Highbury, London, N5 1BU

Highbury is a mixture of old and new. The East and West Stands reek tradition and invite images of the famous marble halls. In truth though they are antiquated and the views from the back of the lower section of these stands is awful. They can also be very stuffy and hot. In contrast, the two-tier North (Bank) Stand is immaculate inside and offers modern facilities – it is, however, designated for home supporters. The South (Clock End) Stand entertains away supporters and also executive boxes – there is talk of rebuilding this to increase the ground's capacity.

Directions

From North: M1, J2 follow sign for the City. After Holloway Road station (c 6 miles) take third left into Drayton Park. Then right into Aubert Park after ³/₄ mile and 2nd left into Avenell Road. *From South:* Signs for Bank of England then Angel from London Bridge. Right at traffic lights towards Highbury roundabout. Follow Holloway Road then third right into Drayton Park, thereafter as above. *From West:* A40 (M) to A501 ring road. Left at Angel to Highbury roundabout, then as above. *Parking:* It's worth considering parking away from the ground and then taking the Tube. Otherwise get there early and leave late.

Rail: Finsbury Park or Drayton Park.   *Tube:* Arsenal – Piccadilly Line.

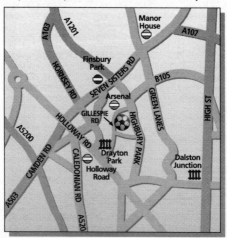

ASTON VILLA

Villa Park, Trinity Road, Birmingham, B6 6HE

Villa Park is easy to find but often difficult to get to due to snarl-ups on the motorway. Always allow plenty of time and think about spending the morning in Brum. Villa Park's stature as a home for many an FA Cup semi-final speaks volumes for the ground which is well placed and has an enjoyable atmosphere. The Trinity Road Stand is one of the most distinctive in the country with its towers and red brick frontage. The North Stand and Doug Ellis Stand are fairly typical of the new stands in England with away seating for both in adjacent corners. Facilities do leave a little to be desired. The Hoult Stand was built on what was one of the biggest kop areas in England and offers an excellent view.

Directions

M6 J6, follow signs for Birmingham NE. Third exit at roundabout then right into Ashton Hall Rd after ¹/₂ mile.

Parking: Another ground where if you are coming by car you need to arrive early to find somewhere to park within an acceptable walking distance of the ground. It's not easy but possible – just make a note of where you parked!

Rail: Witton.

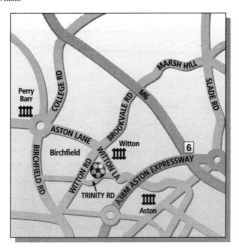

BLACKBURN ROVERS

Ewood Park, Blackburn, BB2 4JF

Ewood Park could be described as the House that Jack built – but that would be rather unkind, not least because the visiting supporters' facilities are amongst the best in the Premiership. Jack Walker's steely millions helped rebuild a decaying ground and it is ironic that the three new stands make the stand first rebuilt in 1987 – the Walkersteel Stand – look rather dated. On the opposite side the Jack Walker Stand contains the executive boxes whilst home support is located mainly in the Blackburn Stand itself. The Darwen End is where visiting supporters are housed. The Darwen River runs alongside the ground and this is a good landmark to use.

Directions

From North, South & West: M6 J31, follow signs for Blackburn then Bolton Road. Turn left after 1½ miles into Kidder Street.
From East: A677 or A679 following signs for Bolton Road, then as above.
Parking: Reasonable all around and it's a case of what you can get when you arrive, either in the streets, the local industrial estates or the schools.
Rail: Blackburn Central.

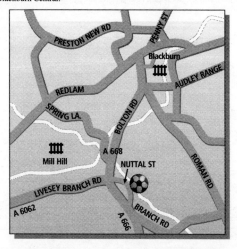

CHARLTON ATHLETIC

The Valley, Floyd Road, Charlton, SE7 8BL

The Valley is almost the ancestral home of Charlton. On the verge of bankruptcy the club had to move away from the ground for a number of years but returned there for a fixture on 5th December 1992. They returned to a brand new stadium and one that has undergone further expansion during the close season to take its capacity to 21,500. Despite this 25% increase it remains one of the smallest stadiums in the Premiership. Although it provides a good atmosphere it is not overly exciting but this can be offset by the fact that it is very easy to locate via car or public transport. Well served by stations, it also has ample off-street parking especially if you are prepared to park up a 15-minute walk or so from the stadium.

Directions

From North & West: The Blackwall Tunnel (A102M) runs just to the west of the ground and this is accessed through the centre of London from the M1 (A405 East) or M11 (see South directions as well). Once through the Tunnel take the second exit which is signposted for the Woolwich ferry. Continue following signs to the Ferry along A206 until traffic lights with Charlton Church Road on right. Turn here and then take second left into Floyd Road. Ground is on right.

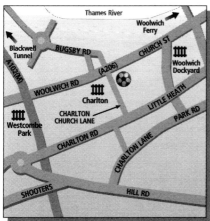

From East: M25 J2. Head towards London on A2. Exit A2 towards Woolwich Ferry (about 11 miles) onto A206. Continue on to Woolwich Road towards Blackwall Tunnel and look out for Charlton Church Road on left at lights. Then as above. *From South:* M25, J3. A20 towards London. Join A2 towards London/Blackwall Tunnel. Then as above.

CHELSEA

Stamford Bridge, London, SW6 1HS

Stamford Bridge had a complete overhaul during the close season with West Stand and old Shed End (South Stand) undergoing a rebuild to completely enclose the stadium and bring it in line with the main East Stand and Matthew Harding Stand. All-in-all this should make it one of the most atmospheric grounds in the Premiership. The South Stand forms part of the Chelsea Village complex and also houses a line of executive boxes. It, like the Matthew Harding Stand, includes a large video screen. In recent seasons the lower parts of the East Stand have been used to house visiting supporters.

Directions
From North & East: A1 or M1 to central London and Hyde Park corner. Follow signs for Guildford (A3) and then Knightsbridge (A4). After a mile, turn left into Fulham Road. *From South:* A219 Putney Bridge then follow signs for West End joining A308 and then into Fulham Road. *From West:* M4 then A4 to central London. Follow A3220 to Westminster; after ¾ mile right at crossroads into Fulham Road. *Parking:* Forget it. If travelling from the north leave your car at Stanmore and travel in on the tube.
Rail/Tube: Fulham Broadway (District line).

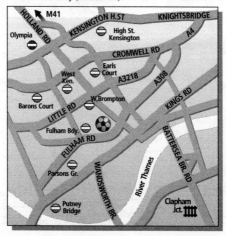

352

COVENTRY CITY

Highfield Road, King Richard St, Coventry, CV2 4FW

Highfield Road was famous as being the first all-seater stadium in England, years before the 'concept' was ever mooted. The ground though is rather nondescript but does provide a good atmosphere to make for an enjoyable event. Visiting supporters are normally located at the west end of the Sky Blue Stand and the view in general is excellent. Not all Sky Blue fans can say the same though; in recent years the corners of the ground have been closed in and the view from seats here is wanting to say the least.

Directions

From North & West: M6 J3, after 3¹/₂ miles turn left into Eagle Street and straight on to Swan Lane. *From South & East:* M1 to M45 then A45 to Ryton-on-Dunsmore where third exit at roundabout is A423. After one mile turn right into B4110. Left at T-junction then right into Swan Lane.

Parking: There is plenty of street parking. In fact, you can get within a few minutes walk of the ground even close to kick-off times, but you need to know your way around the side streets to achieve this.

Rail: Coventry.

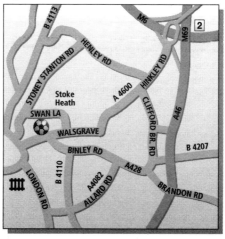

DERBY COUNTY

Pride Park Stadium, Derby

Pride Park Stadium is the brand new home for the Rams, after its official opening by the Queen in July 1997. The 30,000 capacity stadium is one of the modern 'horseshoe' designs with upper and lower decks. There are positions for disabled people in the north-east corner. The South Stand has been allocated to away supporters and the accommodation in this stand will be adjusted to suit the number of visitors. The concourse behind the horseshoe contains good facilities, including food outlets and adequate toilets for men and women. There are also TV screens so that you don't miss any action. The 'Baseball Ground' pub is sited in the north-east corner by the ticket office, club shop and administration . The main West Stand contains executive boxes, players' facilities and a restaurant. There are additional boxes and a business club in the north-west corner stand.

Directions

From North & West: Follow signs for A52 and Nottingham, left off A52 after Derby city centre. *From South & East:* M1 J25, on to A52. Follow yellow signs for football stadium. First slip road off dual carriageway into Pride Park. You can see the stadium and car parks ahead, beyond retail park.

Parking: 2,200 capacity next to the stadium. There are buses from Derby city centre. *Rail:* Derby Station, 10 minutes walk.

EVERTON

Goodison Park, Liverpool, L4 4EL

Goodison Park was always at the forefront of development – it was the first ground to have a two-tier stand and then the first to go one better with a three-tier stand. Visiting supporters occupy the open end of the Bullens Road Stand which itself swings around into the Gwladys Street Stand. Sandwiched in between here and the Main Stand is, uniquely, a church – St Luke the Evangelist has probably seen a lot of Evertonians praying for wins down the years! The Park End Stand is the most recent development, being completed in 1994, and this now tends to house the main Evertonian support.

Directions

From North: M6 J8, take A58 to A580 and follow into Walton Hall Avenue.
From South & East: M6 J21A to M62, turn right into Queen's Drive then, after 4 miles, left into Walton Hall Avenue.
From West: M53 through Wallasey Tunnel, follow signs for Preston on A580. Walton Hall Avenue is signposted.
Parking: The Stanley Park car park has 100 spaces for a couple of quid. This is actually located at the Anfield end of the park.
Rail: Liverpool Lime Street.

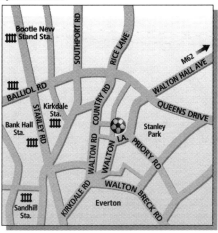

LEEDS UNITED

Elland Road, Leeds, LS11 0ES

Elland Road towers out of the southern end of Leeds and is actually best viewed from a northbound train, out to the right were the massive East Stand dominates the ground. With a capacity of 17,000, this makes the rest of the ground look rather small in contrast. Facilities here are very good with its open plan nature. Visiting supporters are allocated in the corner between the East and South Stands and the facilities here leave a little to be desired. That said, the view is good if you don't mind watching the game from this point.

Directions
From North & East: A58, A61, A63 or A64 into city centre and then on to M621. Leave motorway after 1½ miles on to A643 and Elland Road.
From West: Take M62 to M621 then as above.
From South: M1 then M621 then as above.
Parking: Plenty of space. Car parks near the ground fill up early.
Rail: Leeds City – about 30 minute walk (1.5 miles).

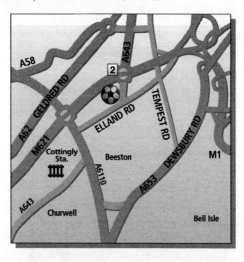

LEICESTER CITY

City Stadium, Filbert Street, Leicester, LE2 7FL

Filbert Street is one of my favourite grounds, with a mixture of old and new. The new Carling Stand dominates the stadium and sitting in the upper tier of this you can easily look over the tops of the other stands. Opposite, the low East Stand is used to house visiting supporters and its compact nature helps to add to the atmosphere for those inside it. The Filbert Street end contains the famous executive boxes which extend over seated areas.

Directions

From South: M1 J21. Follow A5460 towards Leicester (avoid Ring Road). Continue for close on two miles until dual carriageway ends and you go under a railway bridge. At next set of lights turn right into Upperton Road. Go over bridge and Leicester City ground is located in the street running parallel to Upperton Road. This is a one-way system and access is only available to official cars for the LCFC club car park. *From North:* Leave M1 J22, or take A46, A607 to town centre. Towards Rugby via Almond Road, Aylestone Road, and then left into Walnut Street and Filbert Street for the ground.

From West: M69 and A50 to Aylestone Road, and then as North.

Parking: Try one of the roads running off to the left at the point around the railway bridge mentioned in the directions above. There is a maze of roads here. Avoid going further down Upperton Road.

Rail: Leicester.

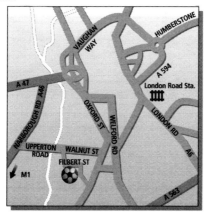

LIVERPOOL

Anfield Road, Liverpool, L4 0TH

Anfield minus the standing Kop really isn't the same. The Kop Stand is an excellent facility and blends in perfectly with the rest of the ground, but... At the opposite end of the ground the Anfield Road Stand is where the visitors' accommodation is located. The Main Stand includes a paddock at the front with a two-tier Centenary Stand completing the ground.

Directions

From North: M6 J8, follow A58 to Walton Hall Avenue and pass Stanley Park, turning left into Anfield Road. *From South/East:* To end of M62 and right into Queens Drive (A5058). After three miles turn left into Utting Avenue and right after one mile into Anfield Road. *From West:* M53 through Wallasey Tunnel, follow signs for Preston then turn into Walton Hall Avenue and right into Anfield Road before Stanley Park.

Parking: Very, very difficult. The Stanley Park Car Park is utilised mainly by the club on match days and unless you arrive very early there is little chance of getting a space. *Rail:* Liverpool Lime Street (main). Sandhill (local).

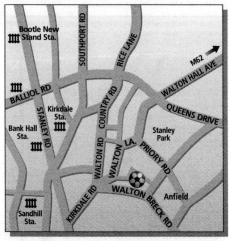

MANCHESTER UNITED

Old Trafford, Manchester, M16 0RA

Old Trafford has the biggest capacity of any football ground in England except Wembley. The North Stand had a third tier added prior to Euro '96 to bring the total accommodation possibility to over 55,000. The view from the top of here though leaves a bit to be desired, especially when the ball is on the far touchline. That apart, Old Trafford is arguably the best football stadium in England and is one that has been able to retain its own atmosphere despite going all-seater. Facilities are excellent and visiting supporters are generally located at the East Stand end.

Directions

From North: From the M63 Junction 4 follow the signs for Manchester (A5081). Turn right after 2½ miles into Warwick Road. *From South:* From the M6 Junction 19. Follow the A556 then the A56 (Altrincham). From Altrincham follow the signs for Manchester, turning left into Warwick Road after six miles. *From East:* From the M62 Junction 17 take the A56 to Manchester. Follow the signs South and then to Chester. Turn right into Warwick Road after two miles.

Parking: Pretty good – a case of finding a location you like in one of the many 'Match-day' car parks. Getting away is murder. *Rail:* Old Trafford (Metrolink).

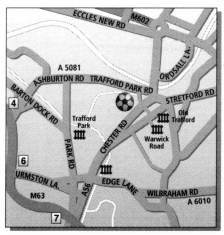

MIDDLESBROUGH

The Cellnet Riverside Stadium, Middlesbrough, TS3 6RS

The Riverside was built at a cost of £13 million which seems remarkably cheap at today's prices. Indeed, when Boro staged their first game there against Chelsea on 26th August 1995 they had spent more on big-name stars in the close season prior to their return to the Premiership. By the start of the following season the stars had gone but the stadium remained and current plans call for the two open corners to be closed in to further increase the capacity. Premiership fans returning this season will also find that the link roads are fully in place (at a cost of another £6 million!) Equally, Middlesbrough station is only a short walk away and this is well worth contemplating if your journey is long.

Directions

From South: A1(M), exit at Thirsk A186/A19 Teesside. Continue on to A19 dual carriageway towards Middlesbrough for just over 30 miles. Exit onto A66 and follow signs towards Middlesbrough. Follow this dual carriageway for just over two miles and look to see stadium on right. At roundabout, turn right and follow directions to stadium.

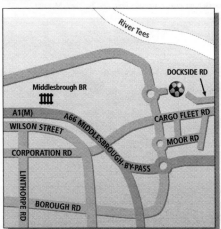

From North: Take A19 towards Middlesbrough and exit on to A66 after crossing River Tees. Continue on by-pass until main roundabout after Middlesbrough station. Turn left at roundabout for ground.

From West: A1(M) J57. Follow signs to Teesside A66. Join A66 and continue for about 15 miles as it passes the A19. Then as above.

NEWCASTLE UNITED

St James's Park, Newcastle-Upon-Tyne, NE1 4ST

St James's Park remains one of the noisiest grounds in England but there has still been a loss of atmosphere here since it was redeveloped by Sir John Hall, who has the Leazes End stand named in his honour. Visiting fans are located in the corner here. The Gallowgate End is the first stand you come to when walking up from the town centre. The main Milburn Stand includes an exclusive seated area which will set you back £3000 a seat for the season. No wonder it's called the **Platinum Club**. I'll take three…

Directions

From South: Follow A1, A68 then A6127 to cross the Tyne. At roundabout, first exit into Moseley Street. Left into Neville Street, right at end for Clayton Street and then Newgate Street. Left for Leazes Park Road. *From West:* A69 towards city centre. Left into Clayton Street for Newgate Street, left again for Leazes Park Road. *From North:* A1 then follow signs for Hexham until Percy Street. Right into Leazes Park Road.

Parking: There are some designated areas but it is so close to the town centre that using one of the city centre multi-storeys and taking the short walk is easy.

Rail: Newcastle Central (¹/₂ mile).

NOTTINGHAM FOREST

The City Ground, Nottingham, NG2 5FJ

The City Ground backs on to the famous River Trent. In days gone by visiting supporters might have occasionally found themselves going for an unscheduled swim. Thankfully this is not the case anymore! The approach and areas immediately around the ground are very interesting and the local pubs make for an entertaining stop. The ground itself was refurbished for Euro '96 and the Trent Stand is particularly impressive. The one thing about the ground, despite what you might read elsewhere, is that parking is terrible. I have never managed to get close and now always resort to parking at the Racecourse (signposted as a Park and Ride site) and then take a leisurely 30 minute walk in. You can catch the bus but you have to bully the driver to stop before he goes into the city. Some people refer to parking across the river at Notts County's ground but I have never managed this myself. Getting to the ground by car is time consuming because it is a long way from the motorway and Saturday traffic adds to the delays. Allow plenty of time.

Directions

From North: M1 J26. Follow A610 towards Nottingham. Join the Ring Road A6514 (signposted A52, Derby). Follow this, keeping towards A52, Derby. Keep left when road splits on A52. At roundabout turn left towards crematorium.

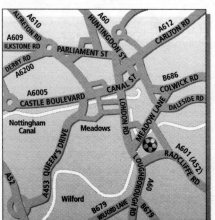

Continue straight (Nottingham A60) and turn right when road divides (Grantham A52). Ground on right. *From South:* M2 J24. Follow A453 Nottingham South. Continue towards Nottingham and after about seven miles exit before flyover towards Grantham A52, Newark A46. Follow signs Grantham, Melton and then signs to Nottingham Forest FC.

SHEFFIELD WEDNESDAY

Hillsborough, Sheffield, S6 1SW

Hillsborough has always had a reputation as being one of the best grounds in the country. From a visiting supporter's point of view this will probably be true as the away fans have generally been accommodated in the upper tier of the West Stand behind the goal. In general the ground is rather plain although the introduction of the Sheffield Wednesday Bank last season was an inspiration and certainly adds to the entertainment value.

Directions

From North: M1 J34 then A6109 to Sheffield. At roundabout after 1½ miles take third exit then turn left after three miles into Harries Road. *From South & East:* M1 J31 or 33 to A57. At roundabout take Prince of Wales Road exit. A further six miles then turn left into Harries Road South.

From West: A57 to A6101 then turn left after four miles at T junction into Penistone Road.

Parking: The streets off the A61 are good hunting grounds for a car parking space. Try and get close to the ground – this area is hilly!

Rail: Sheffield Midland.

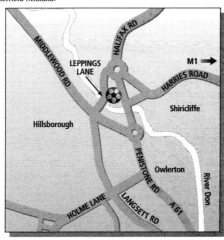

SOUTHAMPTON

The Dell, Milton Road, Southampton, SO9 4XX

After 31 applications, Southampton have finally got permission to build a new ground. It can't come soon enough. **The Dell** is very distinctive but also very cramped and even the addition of new stands behind each of the goals has done little to help matters. Visiting supporters are normally directed to the Archers Road end of the East Stand.

Directions

From North: A33 into The Avenue then right into Northlands Road. Right at the end into Archers Road. *From East:* M27 then A334 and signs for Southampton along A3024. Follow signs for the West into Commercial Road, right into Hill Lane then first right into Milton Road.

From West: Take A35 then A3024 towards city centre. Left into Hill Lane and first right into Milton Road.

Parking: The Dell is probably the worst place in the Premiership for parking. The best bet is to arrive early and find a school selling spaces in its playground, otherwise the city centre and a short walk.

Rail: Southampton Central.

TOTTENHAM HOTSPUR

White Hart Lane, High Road, London, N17 0AP

White Hart Lane is now pretty much complete and the majority of seats offer a good view of the pitch. For those unsighted moments you can glance at one of the two JumboTrons as games are normally fed live straight to them (no contentious replays though). The screens are located high at each end of the ground as is the octagonal-shaped ground control room which hangs from the South Stand. This stand also has a rather peculiar (I think) translucent roof. The redevelopment has virtually enclosed the ground into what some describe as a Sugar Bowl!

Directions:

A406 North Circular to Edmonton. At traffic lights follow signs for Tottenham along A1010 then Fore Street for ground.
Parking: Traffic along the High Street on match days (and shopping Saturdays) is a nightmare. Parking is equally as fraught. Arrive early, park, walk and expect to leave late.
Rail: White Hart Lane (adjacent). *Tube:* Seven Sisters and Tottenham Hale (Victoria Line) or Manor House (Piccadilly Line).

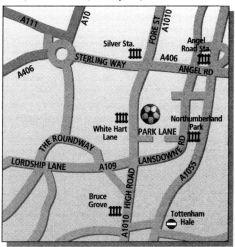

WEST HAM UNITED

Boleyn Ground, Green St, Upton Park, London, E13

Upton Park has its own unique atmosphere and an excellent range of facilities which includes Chinese and Mexican take-aways! The Bobby Moore Stand at the Castle Street end of the ground is the main focal point – two tiers and the executive suites. Visiting supporters generally find themselves at the other end in the North Stand where the facilities are not quite as good.

Directions:

From North & West: North Circular to East Ham then Barking Rd for 1½ miles until traffic lights. Turn right into Green Street.

From South: Blackwall Tunnel then A13 to Canning Town. Then A124 to East Ham, Green Street on left after two miles.

From East: A13 then A117 and A124. Green Street on right after ¾ miles.

Parking: Plenty of off-street parking available but beware that the traffic can become quite congested.

Tube: Upton Park (¼ mile).

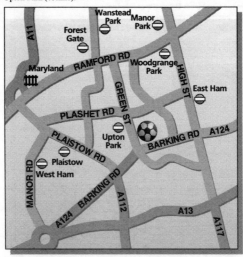

WIMBLEDON

Selhurst Park, South Norwood, London, SE25

Selhurst Park is the home from home for the Dons who share the ground with Crystal Palace. It is located in the suburbs of south-east London and is one of those places where you always underestimate the amount of time you need to get there. Always allow extra time and then some, no matter how you plan to travel.

Directions

From North: M1/A1 to North Circular A406 and Chiswick. Follow South Circular A205 to Wandsworth then A3 and A214 towards Streatham and A23. Then left on to B273 for one mile and turn left at end into High Street and Whitehorse Lane. *From South:* On A23 follow signs for Crystal Palace along B266 going through Thornton Heath into Whitehorse Lane. *From East:* A232 Croydon Road to Shirley joining A215, Norwood Road. Turn left after 2½ miles into Whitehorse Lane. *From West:* M4 to Chiswick then as above.

Parking: If early you can use Sainsbury's at the Whitehorse Lane End or in local streets. *Rail:* Selhurst, Norwood Junction or Thornton Heath.

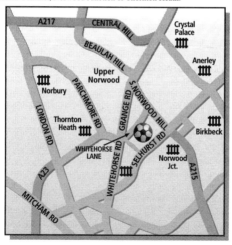

Form 'n' Encounter Guide

Our unique *Form 'n' Encounter Guide* will allow you to plan your season's FA Carling Premiership schedule by providing you with a form guide which helps you to predict what are likely to be the most exciting games to attend on a day-by-day basis. The next few pages provide the home records for each of this season's Premiership sides in a simple PWDLFA format. From page 374 you will find the individual results from the previous five years' Premiership encounters for the corresponding fixtures. Please do check that the game you are looking to attend is on before you set out. Match dates and kick-off times are all subject to change to cope with TV schedules and the like.

Cup matches and European Championship 2000 qualifiers for the home countries are shown in *italic*.

Dates given for the UEFA European club competitions are for the three days of events. UEFA Cup games are played on Tuesdays, Champions' League games on Wednesdays and Cup-Winners' Cup games on Thursdays.

Matches listed in **bold** have been selected for live transmission on Sky Sports at the time of going to press.

Opponents	*P*	*W*	*D*	*L*	*F*	*A*	*Pt*
Arsenal v							
Aston Villa	6	1	3	2	5	5	6
Blackburn R.	6	1	3	2	3	5	6
Charlton A.	0	0	0	0	0	0	0
Chelsea	6	4	2	0	12	6	14
Coventry C.	6	3	2	1	8	5	11
Derby Co.	2	1	1	0	3	2	4
Everton	6	4	1	1	13	4	13
Leeds U.	6	4	1	1	10	6	13
Leicester C.	3	2	1	0	5	2	7
Liverpool	6	1	1	4	2	5	4
Manchester U.	6	2	2	2	7	7	8
Middlesbrough	3	1	2	0	4	2	5
Newcastle U.	5	3	0	2	9	6	9
N. Forest	4	2	2	0	5	2	8
Sheffield W.	6	5	1	0	12	4	16
Southampton	6	5	0	1	16	7	16
Tottenham H.	6	1	4	1	6	6	7
West Ham U.	5	3	0	2	7	3	9
Wimbledon	6	1	2	3	7	6	5

Opponents	*P*	*W*	*D*	*L*	*F*	*A*	*Pt*
Aston Villa v							
Arsenal	6	2	2	2	6	9	8
Blackburn R.	6	2	1	3	3	6	7
Charlton A.	0	0	0	0	0	0	0
Chelsea	6	2	0	4	5	8	6
Coventry C.	6	3	3	0	9	2	12
Derby	2	2	0	0	4	1	6
Everton	6	4	2	0	8	3	14
Leeds U.	6	4	2	0	8	1	14
Leicester C.	3	0	2	1	6	8	2
Liverpool	6	5	0	1	11	6	15
Manchester U.	6	2	1	3	6	7	7
Middlesbrough	3	2	1	0	6	1	7
Newcastle U.	5	0	2	3	3	8	2
N. Forest	4	2	1	1	5	4	7
Sheffield W.	6	2	3	1	10	8	9
Southampton	6	2	3	1	7	5	9
Tottenham H.	6	4	2	0	9	3	14
West Ham U.	5	2	2	1	6	4	8
Wimbledon	6	4	0	2	16	4	12

Opponents	P	W	D	L	F	A	Pt

Blackburn Rovers v

Opponents	P	W	D	L	F	A	Pt
Arsenal … … …	6	2	2	2	7	9	8
Aston Villa	6	4	1	1	13	4	13
Charlton A.	0	0	0	0	0	0	0
Chelsea … … …	6	5	1	0	11	2	16
Coventry C.	6	4	1	1	17	7	13
Derby County	2	1	0	1	2	2	3
Everton … … …	6	3	1	2	11	9	10
Leeds U.	6	3	1	2	10	8	10
Leicester C.	3	2	0	1	10	7	6
Liverpool … …	6	4	1	1	15	7	13
Manchester U.	6	1	1	4	8	12	4
Middlesbrough	3	1	2	0	2	1	5
Newcastle U.	5	5	0	0	6	1	15
N. Forest	4	3	1	0	15	2	10
Sheffield W.	6	5	1	0	19	5	16
Southampton	6	5	1	0	10	4	16
Tottenham H.	6	3	0	3	5	8	9
West Ham U.	5	4	0	1	13	7	12
Wimbledon	6	4	2	0	11	4	14

Charlton Athletic v

Charlton have not played any games in the Premiership prior to 1998-99.

Chelsea v

Opponents	P	W	D	L	F	A	Pt
Arsenal … … …	6	3	0	3	6	9	9
Aston Villa	6	1	2	3	4	6	5
Blackburn R.	6	0	2	4	5	9	2
Charlton A.	0	0	0	0	0	0	0
Coventry C.	6	3	2	1	12	8	11
Derby County	2	2	0	0	7	1	6
Everton … … …	6	3	2	1	10	6	11
Leeds U.	6	2	3	1	6	5	9
Leicester C.	3	3	0	0	7	1	9
Liverpool	6	3	3	0	8	3	12
Manchester U.	6	1	2	3	6	10	5
Middlesbrough	3	3	0	0	10	0	9
Newcastle U.	5	3	2	0	5	2	11
N. Forest	4	1	2	1	2	3	5
Sheffield W.	6	1	4	1	5	6	7
Southampton	6	4	1	1	11	5	13
Tottenham H.	6	3	3	0	11	6	12
West Ham U.	5	3	0	2	9	6	9
Wimbledon	6	2	2	2	11	10	8

Coventry City v

Opponents	P	W	D	L	F	A	Pt
Arsenal … … …	6	1	3	2	4	6	6
Aston Villa	6	1	0	5	5	9	3
Blackburn R.	6	3	2	1	10	4	11
Charlton A.	0	0	0	0	0	0	0
Chelsea … … …	6	3	2	1	11	8	11
Derby County	2	1	0	1	2	2	3
Everton … … …	6	2	3	1	4	3	9
Leeds U.	6	2	3	1	7	7	9
Leicester C.	3	1	1	1	4	4	4
Liverpool … …	6	3	2	1	9	4	11
Manchester U.	6	1	0	5	5	13	3
Middlesbrough	3	2	1	0	5	1	7
Newcastle U.	5	2	2	1	6	5	8
N. Forest	4	0	2	2	1	5	2
Sheffield W.	6	3	2	1	5	2	11
Southampton	6	2	3	1	7	6	9
Tottenham H.	6	3	0	3	9	9	9
West Ham U.	5	1	3	1	7	7	6
Wimbledon	6	0	4	2	6	9	4

Derby County v

Opponents	P	W	D	L	F	A	Pt
Arsenal … … …	2	1	0	1	4	3	3
Aston Villa	2	1	0	1	2	2	3
Blackburn R.	2	1	1	0	3	1	4
Charlton A.	0	0	0	0	0	0	0
Chelsea … … …	2	1	0	1	3	3	3
Coventry C.	2	2	0	0	5	2	6
Crystal Palace	1	0	1	0	0	0	1
Everton … … …	2	1	0	1	3	2	3
Leeds U.	2	0	1	1	3	8	1
Leicester C.	2	1	0	1	2	4	3
Liverpool	2	1	0	1	1	1	3
Manchester U.	2	0	2	0	3	3	2
Middlesbrough	1	1	0	0	2	1	3
Newcastle U.	2	1	0	1	1	1	3
N. Forest	1	0	1	0	0	0	1
Sheffield W.	2	1	1	0	5	2	4
Southampton	2	1	1	0	5	1	4
Tottenham H.	2	2	0	0	6	3	6
West Ham U.	2	2	0	0	3	0	6
Wimbledon	2	0	1	1	1	3	1

Everton v

Opponents	P	W	D	L	F	A	Pt
Arsenal … … …	6	0	4	2	4	8	4
Aston Villa	6	2	1	3	5	8	7

Opponents	P	W	D	L	F	A	Pt
Blackburn R. ...	6	3	0	3	5	8	9
Charlton A. ...	0	0	0	0	0	0	0
Chelsea	6	2	2	2	12	10	8
Coventry C. ...	6	0	5	1	5	7	5
Derby County ...	2	1	0	1	2	2	3
Leeds U. ...	6	4	2	0	10	1	14
Leicester C. ...	3	0	3	0	3	3	3
Liverpool	6	4	2	0	10	3	14
Manchester U. ...	6	1	0	5	3	10	3
Middlesbrough	3	1	1	1	7	4	4
Newcastle U. ...	5	2	1	2	5	5	7
N. Forest	4	3	0	1	9	2	9
Sheffield W. ...	6	1	2	3	7	12	5
Southampton ...	6	4	1	1	12	4	13
Tottenham H. ...	6	1	2	3	3	6	5
West Ham U. ...	5	4	0	1	8	3	12
Wimbledon ...	6	1	3	2	6	9	6

Leeds United v

	P	W	D	L	F	A	Pt
Arsenal	6	3	2	1	7	5	11
Aston Villa ...	6	3	3	0	7	2	12
Blackburn R. ...	6	2	4	0	13	6	10
Charlton A. ...	0	0	0	0	0	0	0
Chelsea	6	4	1	1	13	6	13
Coventry C. ...	6	3	2	1	13	9	11
Derby County ...	2	1	1	0	4	3	4
Everton	6	4	2	0	9	2	14
Leicester C. ...	3	2	0	1	5	2	6
Liverpool ...	6	2	1	3	5	8	7
Manchester U. ...	6	3	1	2	6	8	10
Middlesbrough	3	1	1	1	4	2	4
Newcastle U. ...	5	1	2	2	5	4	5
N. Forest ...	4	2	0	2	5	7	6
Sheffield W. ...	6	2	1	3	8	8	7
Southampton ...	6	2	3	1	3	2	9
Tottenham H. ...	6	3	2	1	10	4	11
West Ham U. ...	5	4	1	0	9	3	13
Wimbledon ...	6	4	2	0	12	4	14

Leicester City v

	P	W	D	L	F	A	Pt
Arsenal	3	1	1	1	5	6	4
Aston Villa ...	3	2	1	0	3	1	7
Blackburn R. ...	3	0	3	0	2	2	3
Charlton A. ...	0	0	0	0	0	0	0
Chelsea	3	1	1	1	4	4	4
Coventry C. ...	3	0	2	1	3	5	2

Opponents	P	W	D	L	F	A	Pt
Derby County ...	2	1	0	1	5	4	3
Everton	3	0	1	2	3	5	1
Leeds	3	2	0	1	3	3	6
Liverpool ...	3	0	1	2	1	5	1
Manchester U. ...	3	0	2	1	2	6	2
Middlesbrough	3	1	0	0	1	1	3
Newcastle U. ...	3	1	1	1	3	3	4
N. Forest ...	2	0	1	1	4	6	1
Sheffield W. ...	3	1	1	1	2	2	4
Southampton ...	3	2	1	0	9	7	7
Tottenham H. ...	3	2	1	0	7	2	7
West Ham U. ...	3	1	0	2	3	4	3
Wimbledon ...	3	1	0	2	4	5	3

Liverpool v

	P	W	D	L	F	A	Pt
Arsenal	6	4	1	1	12	3	13
Aston Villa ...	6	5	0	1	15	5	15
Blackburn R. ...	6	3	2	1	7	3	11
Charlton A. ...	0	0	0	0	0	0	0
Chelsea	6	6	0	0	18	6	18
Coventry C. ...	6	3	1	2	9	5	10
Derby County ...	2	2	0	0	6	1	6
Everton	6	2	3	1	6	5	9
Leeds U. ...	6	5	0	1	16	2	15
Leicester C. ...	3	1	1	1	4	3	4
Manchester U. ...	6	2	1	3	10	11	7
Middlesbrough	3	3	0	0	10	2	9
Newcastle U. ...	5	4	0	1	11	8	12
N. Forest ...	4	3	1	0	9	4	10
Sheffield W. ...	6	5	0	1	10	3	15
Southampton ...	6	3	2	1	13	9	11
Tottenham H. ...	6	3	2	1	14	6	11
West Ham U. ...	5	3	2	0	9	0	11
Wimbledon ...	6	2	3	1	11	7	9

Manchester United v

	P	W	D	L	F	A	Pt
Arsenal	6	4	1	1	6	1	13
Aston Villa ...	6	3	3	0	6	2	12
Blackburn R. ...	6	4	2	0	12	4	14
Charlton A. ...	0	0	0	0	0	0	0
Chelsea	6	1	3	2	7	6	6
Coventry C. ...	6	5	1	0	14	1	16
Crystal Palace ...	3	3	0	0	6	0	9
Derby County ...	2	1	0	1	4	3	3
Everton	6	4	1	1	9	5	13
Leeds U. ...	6	4	2	0	7	0	14

Opponents	P	W	D	L	F	A	Pt
Leicester C. ...	3	1	1	1	4	3	4
Liverpool ...	6	3	3	0	9	5	12
Middlesbrough	3	2	1	0	8	3	7
Newcastle U.	5	2	3	0	6	2	9
N. Forest ...	4	3	0	1	12	3	9
Sheffield W. ...	6	5	1	0	18	4	16
Southampton	6	6	0	0	13	4	18
Tottenham H. ...	6	5	1	0	11	2	16
West Ham U. ...	5	5	0	0	10	2	15
Wimbledon ...	6	5	0	1	13	4	15

Middlesbrough v

Opponents	P	W	D	L	F	A	Pt
Arsenal	3	1	0	2	3	5	3
Aston Villa ...	3	1	0	2	5	7	3
Blackburn R. ...	3	3	0	0	7	3	9
Charlton A. ...	0	0	0	0	0	0	0
Chelsea	3	2	1	0	3	0	7
Coventry C. ...	3	2	0	1	6	3	6
Derby County ...	1	1	0	0	6	1	3
Everton ...	3	1	0	2	5	6	3
Leeds U. ...	3	1	2	0	5	2	5
Leicester C. ...	1	0	0	1	0	2	0
Liverpool ...	3	1	1	1	6	6	4
Manchester U.	3	0	2	1	3	6	2
Newcastle U. ...	2	0	1	1	2	3	1
N. Forest ...	3	0	1	2	2	4	1
Sheffield W. ...	3	2	1	0	8	4	7
Southampton ...	3	1	1	1	2	2	4
Tottenham H. ...	3	1	0	2	3	4	3
West Ham U. ...	2	2	0	0	8	3	6
Wimbledon ...	3	1	1	1	3	2	4

Newcastle United v

Opponents	P	W	D	L	F	A	Pt
Arsenal	5	3	0	2	6	3	9
Aston Villa ...	5	5	0	0	14	5	15
Blackburn R. ...	5	2	3	0	6	4	9
Charlton A. ...	0	0	0	0	0	0	0
Chelsea	5	4	1	0	12	4	13
Coventry C. ...	5	4	1	0	15	0	13
Derby County ...	2	1	1	0	3	1	4
Everton ...	5	5	0	0	9	1	15
Leeds U. ...	5	2	2	1	8	5	8
Leicester C. ...	3	2	1	0	10	7	7
Liverpool ...	5	2	2	1	8	5	8
Manchester U.	5	1	2	2	7	4	5
Middlesbrough	2	2	0	0	4	1	6

Opponents	P	W	D	L	F	A	Pt
N. Forest ...	3	3	0	0	10	2	9
Sheffield W. ...	5	4	0	1	11	6	12
Southampton ...	5	3	0	2	9	5	9
Tottenham H. ...	5	2	2	1	12	6	8
West Ham U. ...	5	3	1	1	8	2	10
Wimbledon ...	5	4	0	1	15	5	12

Nottingham Forest v

Opponents	P	W	D	L	F	A	Pt
Arsenal	4	1	1	2	4	5	4
Aston Villa ...	4	0	2	2	2	4	2
Blackburn R. ...	4	0	1	3	4	12	1
Charlton A. ...	0	0	0	0	0	0	0
Chelsea	4	2	1	1	5	1	7
Coventry C. ...	4	1	2	1	3	2	5
Derby County ...	1	0	1	0	1	1	1
Everton ...	4	2	0	2	5	5	6
Leeds U. ...	4	2	2	0	7	3	8
Leicester C. ...	2	1	1	0	1	0	4
Liverpool ...	4	2	2	0	4	2	8
Manchester U.	4	0	2	2	2	8	2
Middlesbrough	3	2	1	0	3	1	7
Newcastle U. ...	3	0	3	0	1	1	3
Sheffield W. ...	4	2	0	2	6	6	6
Southampton ...	4	2	0	2	6	5	6
Tottenham H. ...	4	3	1	0	8	5	10
West Ham U. ...	3	0	2	1	2	4	2
Wimbledon ...	4	2	2	0	9	4	8

Sheffield Wednesday v

Opponents	P	W	D	L	F	A	Pt
Arsenal	6	4	1	1	7	2	13
Aston Villa ...	6	2	1	3	7	8	7
Blackburn R. ...	6	1	3	2	4	5	6
Charlton A. ...	0	0	0	0	0	0	0
Chelsea	6	1	3	2	8	11	6
Coventry C. ...	6	2	3	1	10	6	9
Derby	2	0	1	1	2	5	1
Everton ...	6	4	1	1	15	9	13
Leeds U. ...	6	1	4	1	14	12	7
Leicester C. ...	3	3	0	0	4	1	9
Liverpool ...	6	1	4	1	10	9	7
Manchester U.	6	2	3	1	9	7	9
Middlesbrough	3	1	0	2	5	5	3
Newcastle U. ...	5	1	2	2	3	5	5
N. Forest ...	4	2	0	2	6	10	6
Southampton ...	6	3	3	0	12	6	12
Tottenham H. ...	6	4	0	2	10	8	12

Opponents	P	W	D	L	F	A	Pt
West Ham U.	5	2	2	1	7	2	8
Wimbledon	6	2	3	1	9	7	9

Southampton v

Opponents	P	W	D	L	F	A	Pt
Arsenal	6	2	1	3	4	9	7
Aston Villa	6	3	0	3	9	6	9
Blackburn R.	6	4	2	0	11	3	14
Charlton A.	0	0	0	0	0	0	0
Chelsea	6	3	1	2	7	5	10
Coventry C.	6	2	3	1	7	6	9
Derby County	2	1	0	1	3	3	3
Everton	6	2	3	1	8	7	9
Leeds U.	6	0	2	4	3	11	2
Leicester C.	3	1	2	0	6	5	5
Liverpool	6	2	1	3	8	10	7
Manchester U.	6	3	1	2	13	10	10
Middlesbrough	3	3	0	0	8	2	9
Newcastle U.	5	4	1	0	10	5	13
N. Forest	4	0	2	2	7	9	2
Sheffield W.	6	0	2	4	6	10	2
Tottenham H.	6	3	2	1	8	6	11
West Ham U.	5	2	2	1	6	3	8
Wimbledon	6	1	3	2	5	6	6

Tottenham Hotspur v

Opponents	P	W	D	L	F	A	Pt
Arsenal	6	3	2	1	5	3	11
Aston Villa	6	2	2	2	8	8	8
Blackburn R.	6	2	1	3	8	9	7
Charlton A.	0	0	0	0	0	0	0
Chelsea	6	0	3	3	5	12	3
Coventry C.	6	1	1	4	7	11	4
Derby	2	1	1	0	2	1	4
Everton	6	3	3	0	8	5	12
Leeds U.	6	3	2	1	9	4	11
Leicester C.	3	1	1	1	3	3	4
Liverpool	6	1	3	2	9	11	6
Manchester U.	6	1	1	4	6	8	4
Middlesbrough	3	1	2	0	4	3	5
Newcastle U.	5	2	1	2	9	7	7
N. Forest	4	1	0	3	3	7	3
Sheffield W.	6	3	1	2	9	9	10
Southampton	6	4	1	1	13	6	13
West Ham U.	5	3	0	2	6	6	9
Wimbledon	6	2	3	1	7	5	9

West Ham United v

Opponents	P	W	D	L	F	A	Pt
Arsenal	5	0	2	3	1	5	2
Aston Villa	5	2	1	2	4	7	7
Blackburn R.	5	3	1	1	8	5	10
Charlton A.	0	0	0	0	0	0	0
Chelsea	5	3	0	2	8	8	9
Coventry C.	5	3	1	1	8	6	10
Derby County	2	0	2	0	1	1	2
Everton	5	1	3	1	8	8	6
Leeds U.	5	1	1	3	4	5	4
Leicester C.	3	3	0	0	6	3	9
Liverpool	5	2	1	2	7	5	7
Manchester U.	5	0	4	1	6	7	4
Middlesbrough	2	1	1	0	2	0	4
Newcastle U.	5	1	1	3	5	8	4
N. Forest	3	2	0	1	4	2	6
Sheffield W.	5	3	1	1	9	4	10
Southampton	5	4	1	0	11	6	13
Tottenham H.	5	2	1	2	9	10	7
Wimbledon	5	2	1	2	7	6	7

Wimbledon v

Opponents	P	W	D	L	F	A	Pt
Arsenal	6	1	1	4	6	14	4
Aston Villa	6	2	2	2	13	14	8
Blackburn R.	6	2	2	2	7	7	8
Charlton A.	0	0	0	0	0	0	0
Chelsea	6	0	4	2	3	6	4
Coventry C.	6	1	1	4	7	10	4
Derby County	2	0	2	0	1	1	2
Everton	6	2	2	2	10	8	8
Leeds U.	6	4	1	1	7	4	13
Leicester C.	3	2	0	1	5	5	6
Liverpool	6	3	3	0	7	3	12
Manchester U.	6	1	0	5	6	15	3
Middlesbrough	3	1	2	0	3	1	5
Newcastle U.	5	2	3	0	11	8	9
N. Forest	4	3	1	0	5	2	10
Sheffield W.	6	2	3	1	10	8	9
Southampton	6	3	0	3	7	7	9
Tottenham H.	6	2	1	3	7	11	7
West Ham U.	5	1	1	3	4	6	4

Date	Match /Event	93-94	94-95	95-96	96-97	97-98
09-Aug	**FA Charity Shield: Arsenal v Manchester U.**					
11-13 Aug	*UEFA Competitions – Qualifying/Preliminary Rounds 1st leg*					
15-Aug	Blackburn R. v Derby Co. ... ... –	–	–	–	1-2	1-0
15-Aug	Coventry C. v Chelsea 1-1	2-2	1-0	3-1	3-2	
15-Aug	Everton v Aston Villa... 0-1	2-2	1-0	0-1	1-4	
15-Aug	Manchester U. v Leicester C. ... ... –	1-1	–	3-1	0-1	
15-Aug	Middlesbrough v Leeds U. ... ... –	–	1-1	0-0	–	
15-Aug	Newcastle U. v Charlton A. ... ... –	–	–	–	–	
15-Aug	Sheffield W. v West Ham U. ... 5-0	1-0	0-1	0-0	1-1	
15-Aug	Wimbledon v Tottenham H.... ... 2-1	1-2	0-1	1-0	2-6	
16-Aug	Southampton v Liverpool ... 4-2	0-2	1-3	0-1	1-1	
17-Aug	**Arsenal v N. Forest** ... ... –	1-0	1-1	2-0	–	
22-Aug	Charlton A. v Southampton ... ... –	–	–	–	–	
22-Aug	Chelsea v Newcastle U. 1-0	1-1	1-0	1-1	1-0	
22-Aug	Derby County v Wimbledon ... ... –	–	–	0-2	1-1	
22-Aug	Leicester C. v Everton ... ... –	2-2	–	1-2	0-1	
22-Aug	Liverpool v Arsenal 0-0	3-0	3-1	2-0	4-0	
22-Aug	N. Forest v Coventry C... ... ... –	2-0	0-0	0-1	–	
22-Aug	Tottenham H. v Sheffield W. ... 1-3	3-1	1-0	1-1	3-2	
22-Aug	West Ham U. v Manchester U. ... 2-2	1-1	0-1	2-2	1-1	
23-Aug	**Aston Villa v Middlesbrough** ... –	–	0-0	1-0	–	
24-Aug	**Leeds U. v Blackburn R.** ... 3-3	1-1	0-0	0-0	4-0	
25-27 Aug	*UEFA Competitions – Qualifying/Preliminary Rounds 2nd leg*					
28-Aug	*UEFA Super Cup: Chelsea v Real Madrid, Monaco*					
29-Aug	Arsenal v Charlton A. ... ... –	–	–	–	–	
29-Aug	Blackburn R. v Leicester C. ... ... –	3-0	–	2-4	5-3	
29-Aug	Coventry C. v West Ham U. ... 1-1	2-0	2-2	1-3	1-1	
29-Aug	Everton v Tottenham H. 0-1	0-0	1-1	1-0	0-2	
29-Aug	Middlesbrough v Derby County ... –	–	–	6-1	–	
29-Aug	Sheffield W. v Aston Villa 0-0	1-2	2-0	2-1	1-3	
29-Aug	Southampton v N. Forest ... ... –	1-1	3-4	2-2	–	
29-Aug	Wimbledon v Leeds U. 1-0	0-0	2-4	2-0	1-0	
30-Aug	**Newcastle U. v Liverpool** ... 3-0	1-1	2-1	1-1	1-2	
05-Sep	*Sweden v England, European Championship Qualifying Group 5*					
08-Sep	Charlton A. v Manchester U. ... ... –	–	–	–	–	
08-Sep	Leeds U. v Southampton 0-0	0-0	1-0	0-0	0-1	
09-Sep	Aston Villa v Newcastle U. 0-2	0-2	1-1	2-2	0-1	
09-Sep	**Chelsea v Arsenal** 0-2	2-1	1-0	0-3	2-3	

Date	Match /Event	93-94	94-95	95-96	96-97	97-98
09-Sep	Derby County v Sheffield W. ... ... –		–	–	2-2	3-0
09-Sep	Leicester C. v Manchester U. ... ... –	0-4	–	2-2	0-0
09-Sep	Liverpool v Coventry C. 1-0	2-3	0-0	1-2	1-0
09-Sep	N. Forest v Everton ... ... –	2-1	3-2	0-1	–
09-Sep	Tottenham H. v Blackburn R. ... 0-2	3-1	2-3	2-1	0-0
09-Sep	West Ham U. v Wimbledon 0-2	3-0	1-1	0-2	3-1
12-Sep	Aston Villa v Wimbledon ... 0-1	7-1	2-0	5-0	1-2
12-Sep	Charlton A. v Derby County ... –	–	–	–	–
12-Sep	Chelsea v N. Forest ... ... –	0-2	1-0	1-1	–
12-Sep	Everton v Leeds U. 1-1	3-0	2-0	0-0	2-0
12-Sep	Leicester C. v Arsenal ... ... –	2-1	–	0-2	3-3
12-Sep	Manchester U. v Coventry C. ... 0-0	2-0	1-0	3-1	3-0
12-Sep	Newcastle U. v Southampton ... 1-2	5-1	1-0	0-1	2-1
12-Sep	Sheffield W. v Blackburn R. ... 1-2	0-1	2-1	1-1	0-0
12-Sep	West Ham U. v Liverpool ... 1-2	3-0	0-0	1-2	2-1
13-Sep	**Tottenham H. v Middlesbrough** –	–	1-1	1-0	–
15-17 Sep	*UEFA Competitions – 1st Round (1st leg) matches*					
19-Sep	Coventry C. v Newcastle U. 2-1	0-0	0-1	2-1	2-2
19-Sep	Derby County v Leicester C. ... –	–	–	2-0	0-4
19-Sep	Leeds U. v Aston Villa 2-0	1-0	2-0	0-0	1-1
19-Sep	Liverpool v Charlton A. ... ... –	–	–	–	–
19-Sep	Middlesbrough v Everton ... ... –	–	0-2	4-2	–
19-Sep	N. Forest v West Ham U. ... ... –	1-1	1-1	0-2	–
19-Sep	Southampton v Tottenham H. ... 1-0	4-3	0-0	0-1	3-2
19-Sep	Wimbledon v Sheffield W. ... 2-1	0-1	2-2	4-2	1-1
20-Sep	**Arsenal v Manchester U.** ... 2-2	0-0	1-0	1-2	3-2
21-Sep	**Blackburn R. v Chelsea** 2-0	2-1	3-0	1-1	1-0
23-Sep	Manchester U. v Chelsea... ... 0-1	0-0	1-1	1-2	2-2
26-Sep	Aston Villa v Derby ... ... –	–	–	2-0	2-1
26-Sep	Charlton A. v Coventry C. ... ... –	–	–	–	–
26-Sep	Chelsea v Middlesbrough ... –	–	5-0	1-0	–
26-Sep	Everton v Blackburn R. 0-3	1-2	1-0	0-2	1-0
26-Sep	**Manchester U. v Liverpool** ... 1-0	2-0	2-2	1-0	1-1
26-Sep	Newcastle U. v N. Forest ... ... –	2-1	3-1	5-0	–
26-Sep	Sheffield W. v Arsenal 0-1	3-1	1-0	0-0	2-0
26-Sep	Tottenham H. v Leeds U. ... 1-1	1-1	2-1	1-0	0-1
27-Sep	**Leicester C. v Wimbledon** ... ... –	3-4	–	1-0	0-1
28-Sep	**West Ham U. v Southampton**... 3-3	2-0	2-1	2-1	2-1
29-01 Oct	*UEFA Competitions – 1st Round (2nd leg) matches*					

Date	Match /Event 93-94	94-95	95-96	96-97	97-98
03-Oct	Arsenal v Newcastle U. 2-1	2-3	2-0	0-1	3-1
03-Oct	Blackburn R. v West Ham U. ... 0-2	4-2	4-2	2-1	3-0
03-Oct	Coventry C. v Aston Villa 0-1	0-1	0-3	1-2	1-2
03-Oct	Derby County v Tottenham H. ... –	–	–	4-2	2-1
03-Oct	Leeds U. v Leicester C. ... ... –	2-1	–	3-0	0-1
03-Oct	Middlesbrough v Sheffield W. ... –	–	3-1	4-2	–
03-Oct	N. Forest v Charlton A. ... ... –	–	–	–	–
03-Oct	Southampton v Manchester U. ... 1-3	2-2	3-1	6-3	1-0
03-Oct	Wimbledon v Everton 1-1	2-1	2-3	4-0	0-0
04-Oct	**Liverpool v Chelsea** 2-1	3-1	2-0	5-1	4-2
10-Oct	*England v Bulgaria, European Championship Qualifying Group 5*				
14-Oct	*Luxembourg v England, European Championship Qualifying Group 5*				
17-Oct	Arsenal v Southampton 1-0	1-1	4-2	3-1	3-0
17-Oct	Chelsea v Charlton A. ... ... –	–	–	–	–
17-Oct	Everton v Liverpool 2-0	2-0	1-1	1-1	2-0
17-Oct	Manchester U. v Wimbledon ... 3-1	3-0	3-1	2-1	2-0
17-Oct	Middlesbrough v Blackburn R. ... –	–	2-0	2-1	–
17-Oct	Newcastle U. v Derby County ... ... –	–	–	3-1	0-0
17-Oct	N. Forest v Leeds U. ... ... –	3-0	2-1	1-1	–
17-Oct	West Ham U. v Aston Villa 0-0	1-0	1-4	0-2	2-1
18-Oct	**Coventry C. v Sheffield W.** ... 1-1	2-0	0-1	0-0	1-0
19-Oct	**Leicester C. v Tottenham H.** ... ... –	3-1	–	1-1	3-0
20-22 Oct	*UEFA Competitions – 2nd Round (1st leg) matches*				
24-Oct	Aston Villa v Leicester C. ... ... –	4-4		1-3	1-1
24-Oct	Charlton A. v West Ham U. ... ... –	–	–	–	–
24-Oct	Derby County v Manchester U. ... –	–	–	1-1	2-2
24-Oct	Leeds U. v Chelsea 4-1	2-3	1-0	2-0	3-1
24-Oct	Liverpool v N. Forest ... ... –	1-0	4-2	4-2	–
24-Oct	Sheffield W. v Everton 5-1	0-0	2-5	2-1	3-1
24-Oct	Southampton v Coventry C. 1-0	0-0	1-0	2-2	1-2
24-Oct	Tottenham H. v Newcastle U. ... 1-2	4-2	1-1	1-2	2-0
24-Oct	Wimbledon v Middlesbrough ... –	–	0-0	1-1	–
25-Oct	**Blackburn R. v Arsenal** 1-1	3-1	1-1	0-2	1-4
31-Oct	Chelsea v Aston Villa 1-1	1-0	1-2	1-1	0-1
31-Oct	Coventry C. v Arsenal 1-0	0-1	0-0	1-1	2-2
31-Oct	Derby County v Leeds U. ... ... –	–	–	3-3	0-5
31-Oct	Everton v Manchester U. 0-1	1-0	2-3	0-2	0-2
31-Oct	Leicester C. v Leeds ... ... –	1-3	–	1-0	1-0
31-Oct	Newcastle U. v West Ham U. ... 2-0	2-0	3-0	1-1	0-1

Date	Match /Event	93-94	94-95	95-96	96-97	97-98
31-Oct	Sheffield W. v Southampton ... 2-0		1-1	2-2	1-1	1-0
31-Oct	Wimbledon v Blackburn R. ... 4-1		0-3	1-1	1-0	0-1
01-Nov	**Middlesbrough v N. Forest** ... –			1-1	0-1	
02-Nov	**Tottenham H. v Charlton A.** ... ... –		–	–	–	–
03-05 Nov	*UEFA Competitions – 2nd Round (2nd leg) matches*					
07-Nov	Arsenal v Everton 2-0		1-1	1-2	3-1	4-0
07-Nov	Aston Villa v Tottenham H. 1-0		1-0	2-1	1-1	4-1
07-Nov	Blackburn R. v Coventry C. 2-1		4-0	5-1	4-0	0-0
07-Nov	Charlton A. v Leicester C. ... ... –		–	–	–	–
07-Nov	Liverpool v Derby County ...		–	–	2-1	4-0
07-Nov	Manchester U. v Newcastle U. ... 1-1		2-0	2-0	0-0	1-1
07-Nov	Newcastle U. v Wimbledon 4-0		2-1	6-1	2-0	1-3
07-Nov	N. Forest v Wimbledon ... ... –		3-1	4-1	1-1	–
07-Nov	Southampton v Middlesbrough ... –		–	2-1	4-0	–
07-Nov	West Ham U. v Chelsea 1-0		1-2	1-3	3-2	2-1
08-Nov	**Leeds U. v Sheffield W.** 2-2		0-1	2-0	0-2	1-2
14-Nov	Arsenal v Tottenham H. 1-1		1-1	0-0	3-1	0-0
14-Nov	Charlton A. v Middlesbrough ... ... –		–	–	–	–
14-Nov	Chelsea v Wimbledon 2-0		1-1	1-2	2-4	1-1
14-Nov	Liverpool v Leeds U. 2-0		0-1	5-0	4-0	3-1
14-Nov	Manchester U. v Blackburn R. ... 1-1		1-0	1-0	2-2	4-0
14-Nov	Newcastle U. v Sheffield W. ... 4-2		2-1	2-0	1-2	2-1
14-Nov	Southampton v Aston Villa ... 4-1		2-1	0-1	0-1	1-2
14-Nov	West Ham U. v Leicester C. ... ... –		1-0	–	1-0	4-3
15-Nov	**Coventry C. v Everton** 2-1		0-0	2-1		0-0
16-Nov	**N. Forest v Derby County** ... –		–	–	1-1	–
21-Nov	Aston Villa v Liverpool 2-1		2-0	0-2	1-0	2-1
21-Nov	Blackburn R. v Southampton ... 2-0		3-2	2-1	2-1	1-0
21-Nov	Leeds U. v Charlton A. ... ... –		–	–	–	–
21-Nov	Leicester C. v Chelsea ... ... –		1-1	–	1-3	2-0
21-Nov	Middlesbrough v Coventry C. ... ... –		–	2-1	4-0	–
21-Nov	Sheffield W. v Manchester U. ... 2-3		1-0	0-0	1-1	2-0
21-Nov	Tottenham H. v N. Forest ... –		1-4	0-1	0-1	–
21-Nov	Wimbledon v Arsenal 0-3		1-3	0-3	2-2	0-1
22-Nov	**Derby County v West Ham U.** ... –		–	–	1-0	2-0
23-Nov	**Everton v Newcastle U.** 0-2		2-0	1-3	2-0	0-0
24-25 Nov	*UEFA Competitions – 3rd Round (1st leg) matches (not CWC)*					
28-Nov	Arsenal v Middlesbrough ... ... –		–	1-1	2-0	–

Date	Match /Event 93-94	94-95	95-96	96-97	97-98
28-Nov	Charlton A. v Everton ... ... –	–	–	–	–
28-Nov	Chelsea v Sheffield W. 1-1	1-1	0-0	2-2	1-0
28-Nov	Coventry C. v Leicester C. ... ... –	4-2	–	0-0	0-2
28-Nov	Manchester U. v Leeds U. 0-0	0-0	1-0	1-0	3-0
28-Nov	N. Forest v Aston Villa ... ... –	1-2	1-1	0-0	–
28-Nov	Southampton v Derby County ... ... –	–	–	3-1	0-2
28-Nov	West Ham U. v Tottenham H. ... 1-3	1-2	1-1	4-3	2-1
29-Nov	**Liverpool v Blackburn R.** 0-1	2-1	3-0	0-0	0-0
05-Dec	Aston Villa v Manchester U. ... 1-2	1-2	3-1	0-0	0-2
05-Dec	Blackburn R. v Charlton A. ... ... –	–	–	–	–
05-Dec	Derby County v Arsenal ... ... –	–	–	1-3	3-0
05-Dec	Everton v Chelsea 4-2	3-3	1-1	1-2	3-1
05-Dec	Leeds U. v West Ham U. 1-0	2-2	2-0	1-0	3-1
05-Dec	Leicester C. v Southampton ... ... –	4-3	–	2-1	3-3
05-Dec	Tottenham H. v Liverpool 3-3	0-0	1-3	0-2	3-3
05-Dec	Wimbledon v Coventry C. 1-2	2-0	0-2	2-2	1-2
06-Dec	**Middlesbrough v Newcastle U.** ... –	–	1-2	1-1	–
07-Dec	**Sheffield W. v N. Forest** ... ... –	1-7	1-3	2-0	–
08-09 Dec	*UEFA Competitions – 3rd Round (2nd leg) matches (not CWC)*				
12-Dec	Aston Villa v Arsenal 1-2	0-4	1-1	2-2	1-0
12-Dec	Blackburn R. v Newcastle U. ... 1-0	1-0	2-1	1-0	1-0
12-Dec	Derby County v Chelsea ... ... –	–	–	3-2	0-1
12-Dec	Everton v Southampton 1-0	0-0	2-0	7-1	0-2
12-Dec	Leeds U. v Coventry C. 1-0	3-0	3-1	1-3	3-3
12-Dec	Leicester C. v N. Forest ... ... –	2-4	–	2-2	–
12-Dec	Middlesbrough v West Ham U. ... –	–	4-2	4-1	–
12-Dec	Sheffield W. v Charlton A. ... ... –	–	–	–	–
12-Dec	Tottenham H. v Manchester U. ... 0-1	0-1	4-1	1-2	0-2
13-Dec	**Wimbledon v Liverpool** 1-1	0-0	1-0	2-1	1-1
19-Dec	Arsenal v Leeds U. 2-1	1-3	2-1	3-0	2-1
19-Dec	Charlton A. v Aston Villa ... ... –	–	–	–	–
19-Dec	Coventry C. v Derby County ... ... –	–	–	1-2	1-0
19-Dec	Liverpool v Sheffield W.... 2-0	4-1	1-0	0-1	2-1
19-Dec	Manchester U. v Middlesbrough ... –	–	2-0	3-3	–
19-Dec	Newcastle U. v Leicester C. ... ... –	3-1	–	4-3	3-3
19-Dec	N. Forest v Blackburn R. ... ... –	0-2	1-5	2-2	–
19-Dec	Southampton v Wimbledon 1-0	2-3	0-0	0-0	0-1
19-Dec	West Ham U. v Everton 0-1	2-2	2-1	2-2	2-2
26-Dec	Arsenal v West Ham U. 0-2	0-1	1-0	2-0	4-0
26-Dec	Blackburn R. v Aston Villa 1-0	3-1	1-1	0-2	5-0

Date	Match /Event 93-94	94-95	95-96	96-97	97-98
26-Dec	Coventry C. v Tottenham H. ... 1-0	0-4	2-3	1-2	4-0
26-Dec	Everton v Derby County –	–	–	1-0	1-2
26-Dec	Manchester U. v N. Forest ... ... –	1-2	5-0	4-1	–
26-Dec	Middlesbrough v Liverpool ... ... –	–	2-1	3-3	–
26-Dec	Newcastle U. v Leeds U.... 1-1	1-2	2-1	3-0	1-1
26-Dec	Sheffield W. v Leicester C. ... ... –	1-0	–	2-1	1-0
26-Dec	Southampton v Chelsea 3-1	0-1	2-3	0-0	1-0
26-Dec	Wimbledon v Charlton A. ... ... –	–	–	–	–
28-Dec	Aston Villa v Sheffield W. ... 2-2	1-1	3-2	0-1	2-2
28-Dec	Charlton A. v Arsenal ... ... –	–	–	–	–
28-Dec	Chelsea v Manchester U.... 1-0	2-3	1-4	1-1	0-1
28-Dec	Derby County v Middlesbrough ... –	–	–	2-1	–
28-Dec	Leeds U. v Wimbledon ... 4-0	3-1	1-1	1-0	1-1
28-Dec	Leicester C. v Blackburn R. ... ... –	0-0	–	1-1	1-1
28-Dec	Liverpool v Newcastle U. 0-2	2-0	4-3	4-3	1-0
28-Dec	N. Forest v Southampton ... –	3-0	1-0	1-3	–
28-Dec	Tottenham H. v Everton 3-2	2-1	0-0	0-0	1-1
28-Dec	West Ham U. v Coventry C. ... 3-2	0-1	3-2	1-1	1-0
02-Jan	*FA Cup 3rd Round*				
09-Jan	Arsenal v Liverpool 1-0	0-1	0-0	1-2	0-1
09-Jan	Blackburn R. v Leeds U.... 2-1	1-1	1-0	0-1	3-4
09-Jan	Coventry C. v N. Forest... ... ... –	0-0	1-1	0-3	–
09-Jan	Everton v Leicester C. ... ... –	1-1	–	1-1	1-1
09-Jan	Manchester U. v West Ham U. ... 3-0	1-0	2-1	2-0	2-1
09-Jan	Middlesbrough v Aston Villa ... ... –	–	0-2	3-2	–
09-Jan	Newcastle U. v Chelsea 0-0	4-2	2-0	3-1	3-1
09-Jan	Sheffield W. v Tottenham H. ... 1-0	3-4	1-3	2-1	1-0
09-Jan	Southampton v Charlton A. ... ... –	–	–	–	–
09-Jan	Wimbledon v Derby County ... ... –	–	–	1-1	0-0
13-Jan	*FA Cup 3rd Round Replays*				
16-Jan	Aston Villa v Everton 0-0	0-0	1-0	3-1	2-1
16-Jan	Charlton A. v Newcastle U. ... –	–	–	–	–
16-Jan	Chelsea v Coventry C. 1-2	2-2	2-2	2-0	3-1
16-Jan	Derby County v Blackburn R.... ... –	–	–	0-0	3-1
16-Jan	Leeds U. v Middlesbrough ... ... –	–	0-1	1-1	–
16-Jan	Leicester C. v Liverpool ... ... –	1-2	–	0-3	0-0
16-Jan	Liverpool v Southampton ... 4-2	3-1	1-1	2-1	2-3
16-Jan	N. Forest v Arsenal ... ... –	2-2	0-1	2-1	–
16-Jan	Tottenham H. v Wimbledon.... ... 1-1	1-2	3-1	1-0	0-0
16-Jan	West Ham U. v Sheffield W. ... 2-0	0-2	1-1	5-1	1-0
23-Jan	*FA Cup 4th Round*				

Date	Match /Event 93-94	94-95	95-96	96-97	97-98
30-Jan	Arsenal v Chelsea 1-0	3-1	1-1	3-3	2-0
30-Jan	Blackburn R. v Tottenham H. 1-0	2-0	2-1	0-2	0-3
30-Jan	Coventry C. v Liverpool 1-0	1-1	1-0	0-1	1-1
30-Jan	Everton v N. Forest ... ... –	1-2	3-0	2-0	–
30-Jan	Manchester U. v Charlton A. ... ... –	–	–	–	–
30-Jan	Middlesbrough v Leicester C. ... ... –	–	–	0-2	–
30-Jan	Newcastle U. v Aston Villa 5-1	3-1	1-0	4-3	1-0
30-Jan	Sheffield W. v Derby ... ... –	–	–	0-0	2-5
30-Jan	Southampton v Leeds U. 0-2	1-3	1-1	0-2	0-2
30-Jan	Wimbledon v West Ham U. 1-2	1-0	0-1	1-1	1-2
06-Feb	Aston Villa v Blackburn R. 0-1	0-1	2-0	1-0	0-4
06-Feb	Charlton A. v Wimbledon ... ... –	–	–	–	–
06-Feb	Chelsea v Southampton 2-0	0-2	3-0	1-0	4-2
06-Feb	Derby County v Everton ... ... –	–	–	0-1	3-1
06-Feb	Leeds U. v Newcastle U. 1-1	0-0	0-1	0-1	4-1
06-Feb	Leicester C. v Sheffield W. ... ... –	0-1	–	1-0	1-1
06-Feb	Liverpool v Middlesbrough ... ... –	–	1-0	5-1	–
06-Feb	N. Forest v Manchester U. ... ... –	1-1	1-1	0-4	–
06-Feb	Tottenham H. v Coventry C. 1-2	1-3	3-1	1-2	1-1
06-Feb	West Ham U. v Arsenal 0-0	0-2	0-1	1-2	0-0
13-Feb	*FA Cup 5th Round*				
13-Feb	Aston Villa v Leeds U. 1-0	0-0	3-0	2-0	1-0
13-Feb	Charlton A. v Liverpool ... ... –	–	–	–	–
13-Feb	Chelsea v Blackburn R. 1-2	1-2	2-3	1-1	0-1
13-Feb	Everton v Middlesbrough ... ... –	–	4-0	1-2	–
13-Feb	Leicester C. v Derby County ... ... –	–	–	4-2	1-2
13-Feb	Manchester U. v Arsenal 1-0	3-0	1-0	1-0	0-1
13-Feb	Newcastle U. v Coventry C. 4-0	4-0	3-0	4-0	0-0
13-Feb	Sheffield W. v Wimbledon 2-2	0-1	2-1	3-1	1-1
13-Feb	Tottenham H. v Southampton ... 3-0	1-2	1-0	3-1	1-1
13-Feb	West Ham U. v N. Forest 3-1	3-1	1-0	0-1	–
19-Feb	Chelsea v Tottenham H. 4-3	1-1	0-0	3-1	2-0
20-Feb	Arsenal v Leicester C. ... ... –	1-1	–	2-0	2-1
20-Feb	Blackburn R. v Sheffield W. 1-1	3-1	3-0	4-1	7-2
20-Feb	Coventry C. v Manchester U. ... 0-1	2-3	0-4	0-2	3-2
20-Feb	Derby County v Charlton A. ... ... –	–	–	–	–
20-Feb	Leeds U. v Everton 3-0	1-0	2-2	1-0	0-0
20-Feb	Liverpool v West Ham U. 2-0	0-0	2-0	0-0	5-0
20-Feb	Middlesbrough v Tottenham H. ... ... –	–	0-1	0-3	–
20-Feb	N. Forest v Chelsea ... ... –	0-1	0-0	2-0	–
20-Feb	Southampton v Newcastle U. ... 2-1	3-1	1-0	2-2	2-1
20-Feb	Wimbledon v Aston Villa 2-2	4-3	3-3	0-2	2-1

Date	Match /Event	93-94	94-95	95-96	96-97	97-98
27-Feb	Aston Villa v Coventry C.	0-0	0-0	4-1	2-1	3-0
27-Feb	Charlton A. v N. Forest	–	–	–	–	–
27-Feb	Chelsea v Liverpool	1-0	0-0	2-2	1-0	4-1
27-Feb	Everton v Wimbledon	3-2	0-0	2-4	1-3	0-0
27-Feb	Manchester U. v Southampton ...	2-0	2-1	4-1	2-1	1-0
27-Feb	Newcastle U. v Arsenal	2-0	1-0	2-0	1-2	0-1
27-Feb	Sheffield W. v Middlesbrough ...	–	–	0-1	3-1	–
27-Feb	Tottenham H. v Derby	–	–	–	1-1	1-0
27-Feb	West Ham U. v Blackburn R. ...	1-2	2-0	1-1	2-1	2-1

02-04 Mar *UEFA Competitions – Quarter-Final (1st leg) matches*

06 Mar *FA Cup 6th Round*

Date	Match /Event	93-94	94-95	95-96	96-97	97-98
06-Mar	Arsenal v Sheffield W.	1-0	0-0	4-2	4-1	1-0
06-Mar	Blackburn R. v Everton	2-0	3-0	0-3	1-1	3-2
06-Mar	Coventry C. v Charlton A.	–	–	–	–	–
06-Mar	Derby County v Aston Villa	–	–	–	2-1	0-1
06-Mar	Leeds U. v Tottenham H.	2-0	1-1	1-3	0-0	1-0
06-Mar	Liverpool v Manchester U.	3-3	2-0	2-0	1-3	1-3
06-Mar	Middlesbrough v Chelsea	–	–	2-0	1-0	–
06-Mar	N. Forest v Newcastle U.	–	0-0	1-1	0-0	–
06-Mar	Southampton v West Ham U. ...	0-2	1-1	0-0	2-0	3-0
06-Mar	Wimbledon v Leicester C.	–	2-1	–	1-3	2-1

Date	Match /Event	93-94	94-95	95-96	96-97	97-98
12-Mar	Chelsea v West Ham U.	2-0	1-2	1-2	3-1	2-1

Date	Match /Event	93-94	94-95	95-96	96-97	97-98
13-Mar	Coventry C. v Blackburn R.....	2-1	1-1	5-0	0-0	2-0
13-Mar	Derby County v Liverpool	–	–	–	0-1	1-0
13-Mar	Everton v Arsenal	1-1	1-1	0-2	0-2	2-2
13-Mar	Leicester C. v Charlton A. ...	–	–	–	–	–
13-Mar	Middlesbrough v Southampton ...	–		0-0	0-1	–
13-Mar	Newcastle U. v Manchester U. ...	1-1	1-1	0-1	5-0	0-1
13-Mar	Sheffield W. v Leeds U.	3-3	1-1	6-2	2-2	1-3
13-Mar	Tottenham H. v Aston Villa ...	1-1	3-4	0-1	1-0	3-2
13-Mar	Wimbledon v N. Forest	–	2-2	1-0	1-0	–

16-18 Mar *UEFA Competitions – Quarter-Final (2nd leg) matches*

Date	Match /Event	93-94	94-95	95-96	96-97	97-98
20-Mar	Arsenal v Coventry C.	0-3	2-1	1-1	0-0	2-0
20-Mar	Aston Villa v Chelsea...	1-0	3-0	0-1	0-2	0-2
20-Mar	Blackburn R. v Wimbledon ...	3-0	2-1	3-2	3-1	0-0
20-Mar	Charlton A. v Tottenham H.	–	–	–	–	–
20-Mar	Leeds U. v Derby County	–	–	–	0-0	4-3
20-Mar	Liverpool v Leicester C.	–	2-0	–	1-1	1-2
20-Mar	Manchester U. v Everton	1-0	2-0	2-0	2-2	2-0
20-Mar	N. Forest v Middlesbrough... ...	–	–	1-0	1-1	–

Date	Match /Event	93-94	94-95	95-96	96-97	97-98
20-Mar	Southampton v Sheffield W. ... 1-1	0-0	0-1	2-3	2-3
20-Mar	West Ham U. v Newcastle U. ... 2-4	1-3	2-0	0-0	0-1
27-Mar	*England v Poland, European Championship Qualifying Group 5*					
31-Mar	*England v tbc, European Championship Qualifying Group 5*					
03-Apr	Aston Villa v West Ham U. 3-1	0-2	1-1	0-0	2-0
03-Apr	Blackburn R. v Middlesbrough ... –	–	1-0	0-0	–
03-Apr	Charlton A. v Chelsea ... ... –	–	–	–	–
03-Apr	Derby County v Newcastle U.... ... –	–	–	0-1	1-0
03-Apr	Leeds U. v N. Forest... ... ... –	1-0	1-3	2-0	–
03-Apr	Liverpool v Everton 2-1	0-0	1-2	1-1	1-1
03-Apr	Sheffield W. v Coventry C. 0-0	5-1	4-3	0-0	0-0
03-Apr	Southampton v Arsenal 0-4	1-0	0-0	0-2	1-3
03-Apr	Tottenham H. v Leicester C. ... ... –	1-0	–	1-2	1-1
03-Apr	Wimbledon v Manchester U. ... 1-0	0-1	2-4	0-3	2-5
05-Apr	Arsenal v Blackburn R. 1-0	0-0	0-0	1-1	1-3
05-Apr	Chelsea v Leeds U. 1-1	0-3	4-1	0-0	0-0
05-Apr	Coventry C. v Southampton... ... 1-1	1-3	1-1	1-1	1-0
05-Apr	Everton v Sheffield W. 0-2	1-4	2-2	2-0	1-3
05-Apr	Leicester C. v Aston Villa ... ... –	1-1	–	1-0	1-0
05-Apr	Manchester U. v Derby County ... –	–	–	2-3	2-0
05-Apr	Middlesbrough v Wimbledon ... ... –	–	1-2	0-0	–
05-Apr	Newcastle U. v Tottenham H. ... 0-1	3-3	1-1	7-1	1-0
05-Apr	N. Forest v Liverpool ... ... –	1-1	1-0	1-1	–
05-Apr	West Ham U. v Charlton A. ... ... –	–	–	–	–
06-08 Apr	*UEFA Competitions – Semi-Final (1st leg) matches*					
10-Apr	Aston Villa v Southampton ... 0-2	1-1	3-0	1-0	1-1
10-Apr	Blackburn R. v Manchester U. ... 2-0	2-4	1-2	2-3	1-3
10-Apr	Derby County v N. Forest ... ... –	–	0-0		
10-Apr	Everton v Coventry C. 0-0	0-2	2-2	1-1	1-1
10-Apr	Leeds U. v Liverpool 2-0	0-2	1-0	0-2	0-2
10-Apr	Leicester C. v West Ham U. ... ... –	1-2	–	0-1	2-1
10-Apr	Middlesbrough v Charlton A. ... ... –	–	–	–	–
10-Apr	Sheffield W. v Newcastle U. ... 0-1	0-0	0-2	1-1	2-1
10-Apr	Tottenham H. v Arsenal 0-1	1-0	2-1	0-0	1-1
10-Apr	Wimbledon v Chelsea 1-1	1-1	1-1	0-1	0-2
11-Apr	*FA Cup Semi-Finals*					
14-Apr	*FA Cup Semi-Final Replays*					
17-Apr	Arsenal v Wimbledon 1-1	0-0	1-3	0-1	5-0
17-Apr	Charlton A. v Leeds U. ... ... –	–	–	–	–

Date	Match /Event	93-94	94-95	95-96	96-97	97-98
17-Apr	Chelsea v Leicester C. ...... –		4-0	–	2-1	1-0
17-Apr	Coventry C. v Middlesbrough ... ... –		–	0-0	3-0	–
17-Apr	Liverpool v Aston Villa ... ... –	2-1	3-2	3-0	3-0	3-0
17-Apr	Manchester U. v Sheffield W. ... 5-0	5-0	1-0	2-2	2-0	6-1
17-Apr	Newcastle U. v Everton ... 1-0	1-0	2-0	1-0	4-1	1-0
17-Apr	N. Forest v Tottenham H. ... ... –		2-2	2-1	2-1	–
17-Apr	Southampton v Blackburn R. ... 3-1	3-1	1-1	1-0	2-0	3-0
17-Apr	West Ham U. v Derby County ... ... –		–	–	1-1	0-0
20-22 Apr	*UEFA Competitions – Semi Final (2nd leg) matches*					
24-Apr	Aston Villa v N. Forest ... ... –		0-2	1-1	2-0	–
24-Apr	Blackburn R. v Liverpool ... 2-0	2-0	3-2	2-3	3-0	1-1
24-Apr	Derby County v Southampton ... ... –		–	–	1-1	4-0
24-Apr	Everton v Charlton A. ... ... –		–	–	1-0	–
24-Apr	Leeds U. v Manchester U. 0-2	0-2	2-1	3-1	0-4	1-0
24-Apr	Leicester C. v Coventry C. ... ... –		2-2	–	0-2	1-1
24-Apr	Middlesbrough v Arsenal ... ... –		–	2-3	0-2	–
24-Apr	Sheffield W. v Chelsea 3-1	3-1	1-1	0-0	0-2	1-4
24-Apr	Tottenham H. v West Ham U. ... 1-4	1-4	3-1	0-1	1-0	1-0
24-Apr	Wimbledon v Newcastle U. ... 4-2	4-2	3-2	3-3	1-1	0-0
01-May	Arsenal v Derby County ... ... –		–	–	2-2	1-0
01-May	Charlton A. v Blackburn R. ... ... –		–	–	–	–
01-May	Chelsea v Everton 4-2	4-2	0-1	0-0	2-2	2-0
01-May	Coventry C. v Wimbledon ... 1-2	1-2	1-1	3-3	1-1	0-0
01-May	Liverpool v Tottenham H. ... 1-2	1-2	1-1	0-0	2-1	4-0
01-May	Manchester U. v Aston Villa ... 3-1	3-1	1-0	0-0	0-0	1-0
01-May	Newcastle U. v Middlesbrough ... –		–	1-0	3-1	–
01-May	N. Forest v Sheffield W. ... –		4-1	1-0	0-3	–
01-May	Southampton v Leicester C. ... –		2-2	–	2-2	2-1
01-May	West Ham U. v Leeds U. 0-1	0-1	0-0	1-2	0-2	3-0
08-May	Aston Villa v Charlton A. ... ... –		–	–	–	–
08-May	Blackburn R. v N. Forest ... ... –		3-0	7-0	1-1	–
08-May	Derby County v Coventry C. ... ... –		–	–	2-1	3-1
08-May	Everton v West Ham U. 0-1	0-1	1-0	3-0	2-1	2-1
08-May	Leeds U. v Arsenal 2-1	2-1	1-0	0-3	0-0	1-1
08-May	Leicester C. v Middlesbrough ... ... –		–	–	1-3	
08-May	Leicester C. v Newcastle U. ... –		1-3	–	2-0	0-0
08-May	Middlesbrough v Manchester U. ... –		–	0-3	2-2	–
08-May	Sheffield W. v Liverpool 3-1	3-1	1-2	1-1	1-1	3-3
08-May	Tottenham H. v Chelsea 1-1	1-1	0-0	1-1	1-2	1-6
08-May	Wimbledon v Southampton ... 1-0	1-0	0-2	1-2	3-1	1-0
12-May	*UEFA Cup Final*					

16-May	Arsenal v Aston Villa... 1-2	0-0	2-0	2-2	0-0
16-May	Charlton A. v Sheffield W.... ... ... –	–	–	–	–
16-May	Chelsea v Derby County ... ... –	–	–	3-1	4-0
16-May	Coventry C. v Leeds U. 0-2	2-1	0-0	2-1	0-0
16-May	Liverpool v Wimbledon 1-1	3-0	2-2	1-1	2-0
16-May	Manchester U. v Tottenham H.... 2-1	0-0	1-0	2-0	2-0
16-May	Newcastle U. v Blackburn R. ... 1-1	1-1	1-0	2-1	1-1
16-May	N. Forest v Leicester C.... ... ... –	1-0	–	0-0	–
16-May	Southampton v Everton 0-2	2-0	2-2	2-2	2-1
16-May	West Ham U. v Middlesbrough ... –	–	2-0	0-0	
19-May	*Cup-Winners' Cup Final*				
22-May	*FA Cup Final*				
26-May	*UEFA Champions' League Final*				
27-May	*FA Cup Final Replay*				

FA Carling
PREMIERSHIP
1999-2000
Pocket Annual

The 7th edition of the Premiership
bible will be available in
August 1999.
Into the next millennium!